WEBSTER'S
NEW WRLD®

Pocket Spanish Dictionary

Houghton Mifflin Harcourt
Boston • New York

ISBN 978-0-544-98775-3

Manufactured in the United States of America

3 4 5 6 7 8 9 - DP - 21 20 19 18 17 16

4500635164

Contents

Free Audio Content

Go to www.wiley.com/go/wnwpocketspanish to access free audio downloads featuring pronunciation of twenty-five key Spanish verbs. You will hear three regular verbs given in their full conjugations in all tenses and the remaining twenty-two in their full conjugations in the most common tenses.

Preface

This new edition of our *Pocket Spanish Dictionary* is an accurate, reliable tool for learners of Spanish. It has more than 25,000 words and expressions and thus provides a wide-ranging selection of the most useful and up-to-date vocabulary of both Spanish (in its different regional varieties) and English. In this edition we have paid particular attention to keeping up-to-date with the changing terminology of electronic communication, whether on the Internet or cellphone, by e-mail or text-messaging.

The dictionary is designed to be easily read and used, with bold headwords and a compact, but clearly presented format.

Phrasal verbs are indicated by a bullet point and are listed after the verb on which they are based (e.g., see entry for **get**).

Numbers are used to divide grammatical categories of headwords, while a solid block • denotes different categories of meaning within longer entries (e.g., see entry for **do**).

A number code (1-65) against a Spanish verb means that the verb is irregular. Model verbs for these irregular forms are displayed on pages (5) to (12) of the central supplement.

An asterisk against an English verb denotes that it is irregular. Forms for these verbs are located on pages (13) to (17) of the supplement. A double asterisk against a Spanish noun, however, means that the feminine noun takes the masculine definite article **el** (e.g., **el agua**). The plural form is **las**.

The syllabification of all English headwords is clearly shown, providing the user with extra help.

Users should note that for the purposes of alphabetical ordering, and following current Spanish practice, **ch** and **ll** are not considered as separate letters of the alphabet, as they were formerly, but each is incorporated at its respective position under **c** and **l**.

Finally, the book contains helpful supplementary material to aid communication. In the central supplement, in addition to information on irregular verbs, the user will find a section on the names of countries, regions and nationalities. And in an exciting new feature, ten conversation panels have been added throughout the text, with useful phrases for situations like meeting people, expressing opinions and using the telephone.

Guide to the pronunciation of Spanish

Table of phonetic symbols

Letter	Phonetic symbol	Examples	Approximate English equivalent
Vowels:			
a	[a]	gato, amar, mesa	as in father, but shorter
e	[e]	estrella, vez, firme	as in labor
i	[i]	bicho, iris	as in see, but shorter
o	[o]	bolo, cómodo, oso	between lot and taught
u	[u]	turista, puro, tribu	as in food, but shorter, but u in -que- or -qui- and -gue- or -gui- is silent (unless -güe- or -güi-)
Diphthongs:			
ai, ay	[ai]	baile, hay	as in life, aisle
au	[au]	fauna	as in fowl, house
ei, ey	[ei]	peine, ley	as in hate, feign
eu	[eu]	feudo	pronounce each vowel separately
oi, oy	[oi]	boina, hoy	as in boy
Semi-consonants:			
u	[w]	buey, cuando, fuiste	as in wait
i	[j]	viernes, vicio, ciudad, fiarse	as in yes
Consonants:			
b	[b]	boda, burro, ambos	as in be
	[β]	haba, trabar	a very light b
c	[k]	cabeza, cucu, acoso, frac	as in car, keep
	[s]	cocer, cielo	as s in silly, but in parts of Spain as in thing
ch	[tʃ]	chepa, ocho	as in chamber

Guide to the pronunciation of Spanish

d	[d]	de**d**o, an**d**ar	as in *d*ay
	[ð]	de**d**o, aca**d**emia, aba**d**	as in *th*is (often omitted in spoken Spanish when at the end of a word)
f	[f]	**f**iesta, a**f**ición	as in *f*or
g	[g]	**g**as, ran**g**o, **g**ula	as in *g*et
	[ɣ]	a**g**ua, a**g**osto, la**g**arto	a very light g
g	[χ]	**g**enio, le**g**ión	similar to Scottish [χ] in lo*ch*
h		**h**ambre, a**h**ínco	Spanish h is silent
j	[χ]	**j**abón, a**j**o, relo**j**	similar to Scottish [χ] in lo*ch*
k	[k]	**k**ilo, **k**imono	as in *c*ar, *k*eep
l	[l]	**l**abio, hábi**l**, e**l**egante	as in *l*aw
ll	[j]	**ll**uvia, ca**ll**e	similar to the sound in *y*ellow
m	[m]	**m**ano, a**m**igo, ha**m**bre	as in *m*an
n	[n]	**n**ata, rató**n**, a**n**tes, e**n**emigo	as in *n*ight
ñ	[ŋ]	a**ñ**o, **ñ**o**ñ**o	similar to the sound in o*ni*on
p	[p]	**p**i**p**a, **p**elo	as in *p*oint
q	[k]	**q**uiosco, **q**uerer, tabi**q**ue	as in *c*ar
r(r)	[r]	pe**r**o, co**r**rer, pad**r**e	always pronounced, rolled as in Scots
	[rr]	**r**eír, hon**r**ado, pe**rr**o	rr is a lengthened r sound
s	[s]	**s**auna, a**s**ado, corté**s**	similar to the s in hi*ss*ing
t	[t]	**t**eja, es**t**én, a**t**raco	as in *t*ime
v	[b]	**v**erbena, **v**ena	as in *b*e
	[β]	a**v**e, vi**v**o	a very light b
x	[ks]	é**x**ito, e**x**amen	as in e*x*ercise
	[s]	e**x**tensión	as in e*s*tate
y	[j]	**y**erno, a**y**er, re**y**	as in *y*es
	[i]	**y**	as in s*ee*, but shorter
z	[s]	**z**orro, a**z**ul, ca**z**a, soe**z**	as in si*ll*y, but in parts of Spain as in *th*ing

Stress rules

If a word ends in a vowel, **-n** or **-s**, the stress falls on the second last syllable: m**a**no, ex**a**men, bocad**i**llos

If a word has any other ending, the stress falls on the last syllable: cultur**a**l, Madr**i**d, ay**e**r

Exceptions to these rules carry a written accent on the stressed syllable: c**ó**modo, leg**ió**n, h**á**bil

Abbreviations   Abreviaturas

abbreviation	*abbr, abr*	abreviatura
adjective	*adj*	adjetivo
adverb	*adv*	adverbio
somebody, someone	*algn*	alguien
Latin America	*Am*	Hispanoamérica
Argentina	*Arg*	Argentina
article	*art*	artículo
Bolivia	*Bol*	Bolivia
Central America	*CAm*	Centroamérica
Caribe	*Carib*	Caribe
Colombia	*Col*	Colombia
conjunction	*conj*	conjunción
Southern Cone region	*CSur*	Cono Sur
(Argentina, Uruguay,		(Argentina, Uruguay,
Paraguay, Chile)		Paraguay, Chile)
definite	*def*	definido
demonstrative	*dem*	demostrativo
Ecuador	*Ecuad*	Ecuador
Spain	*Esp*	España
feminine	*f*	femenino
familiar	*fam*	familiar
figurative use	*fig*	uso figurado
feminine plural	*fpl*	femenino plural
future	*fut*	futuro
impersonal	*impers*	impersonal
indefinite	*indef*	indefinido
indeterminate	*indet*	indeterminado
indicative	*indic*	indicativo
interjection	*interj*	interjección
interrogative	*interr*	interrogativo
invariable	*inv*	invariable
irregular	*irreg*	irregular
masculine	*m*	masculino
Mexico	*Méx*	México
masculine plural	*mpl*	masculino plural
noun	*n*	nombre
Panama	*Pan*	Panamá
personal	*pers*	personal
plural	*pl*	plural
possessive	*poss, pos*	posesivo
past participle	*pp*	participio pasado
preposition	*prep*	preposición
present	*pres*	presente
preterite	*pret*	pretérito
pronoun	*pron*	pronombre
past tense	*pt*	pretérito
relative	*rel*	relativo
somebody, someone	*sb*	alguien
singular	*sing*	singular
something	*sth*	algo
subjunctive	*subj*	subjuntivo

Abbreviations   ## Abreviaturas

auxiliary verb	*v aux*	verbo auxiliar
Venezuela	*Ven*	Venezuela
intransitive verb	*vi*	verbo intransitivo
impersonal verb	*v impers*	verbo impersonal
reflexive verb	*vr*	verbo reflexivo
transitive verb	*vt*	verbo transitivo
cultural equivalent	≃	equivalente cultural

A

a *prep (dirección)* to; **llegar a Valencia** to arrive in Valencia; **subir al tren** to get on the train. ▪ *(lugar)* at, on; **a la derecha** on the right; **a lo lejos** in the distance; **a mi lado** next to me; **al sol** in the sun. ▪ *(tiempo)* at; **a las doce** at twelve o'clock; **a los tres meses/la media hora** three months/half an hour later; **al final** in the end; **al principio** at first. ▪ *(distancia)* **a cien kilómetros de aquí** a hundred kilometers from here. ▪ *(manera)* **a mano** by hand. ▪ *(proporción)* **a 90 kilómetros por hora** at 90 kilometers an hour; **a 30 pesos el kilo** thirty pesos a kilo; **tres veces a la semana** three times a week. ▪ **ganar cuatro a dos** to win four (to) two. ▪ *(complemento)* to; *(procedencia)* from; **díselo a Javier** tell Javier; **te lo di a ti** I gave it to you; **comprarle algo a algn** to buy sth from sb; *(para algn)* to buy sth for sb; **saludé a tu tía** I said hello to your aunt. ▪ *fam* **ir a por algn/algo** to go and get sb/ sth. ▪ *(verbo + a + infinitivo)* to; **aprender a nadar** to learn (how) to swim. ▪ **a decir verdad** to tell (you) the truth; **a no ser que** unless; **a ver** let's see; **¡a comer!** food's ready!; **¡a dormir!** bedtime!; **¿a que no lo haces?** *(desafío)* I bet you don't do it!

abajeño, -a *mf Am* lowlander.

abajo 1 *adv (en una casa)* downstairs; *(dirección)* down; **el piso de a.** the apartment downstairs; **ahí/aquí a.** down there/here; **la parte de a.** the bottom (part); **más a.** further down; **hacia a.** down; **venirse a.** *(edificio)* to fall down. **2** *interj* **¡a. la censura!** down with censorship!

abalanzarse [40] *vr* **a. sobre/ contra** to rush towards.

abalear *vt Andes, CAm, Ven* to shoot at.

abandonar *vt (lugar)* to leave; *(persona, cosa)* to abandon; *(proyecto, plan)* to give up.

abanico *m* fan; *(gama)* range.

abarcar [44] *vt (incluir)* to cover.

abarrotado, -a *adj* crammed (**de** with).

abarrote *m Andes, CAm, Méx* grocer's shop, grocery store; **abarrotes** groceries; **tienda de abarrotes** grocer's (shop), grocery store.

abastecer [33] **1** *vt* to supply. **2 abastecerse** *vr* to stock up (**de** o **con** with).

abatible *adj* folding; **asiento a.** folding seat.

abatido, -a *adj* downcast.

abatir 1 *vt (derribar)* to knock down; *(desanimar)* to depress. **2 abatirse** *vr (desanimarse)* to become depressed.

abdicar [44] *vti* to abdicate.

abdominales *mpl* sit-ups.

abecedario *m* alphabet.

abedul *m* birch.

abeja *f* bee; **a. reina** queen bee.

abejorro *m* bumblebee.

abertura *f (hueco)* opening; *(grieta)* crack.

abeto *m* fir (tree).

abierto, -a *adj* open; *(grifo)* (turned) on; *(persona)* open-minded.

abismo *m* abyss.

ablandar 1 *vt* to soften. **2 ablandarse** *vr* to go soft; *fig (persona)* to mellow.

abnegado, -a *adj* selfless.

abogado, -a *mf* lawyer; *(en tribunal supremo)* attorney; **a. defensor** counsel for the defense.

abolir *vt defectivo* to abolish.

abollar *vt* to dent.

abonado, -a *mf* subscriber.

abonar 1 *vt (tierra)* to fertilize; *(pagar)* to pay (for); *(subscribir)* to subscribe. **2 abonarse** *vr* to subscribe (**a** to).

abono *m (producto)* fertilizer; *(estiércol)* manure; *(pago)* payment;

(billete) season ticket; *(a revista etc)* subscription.

abordar *vt (persona)* to approach; *(barco)* to board; **a. un asunto** to tackle a subject.

aborrecer [33] *vt* to detest.

abortar 1 *vi (involuntariamente)* to miscarry, to have a miscarriage; *(intencionadamente)* to abort, to have an abortion. **2** *vt* to abort.

aborto *m* miscarriage; *(provocado)* abortion.

abrasar 1 *vti* to scorch. **2 abrasarse** *vr* to burn.

abrazadera *f* clamp.

abrazar [40] **1** *vt* to embrace. **2 abrazarse** *vr* **abrazarse a algn** to embrace sb; **se abrazaron** they embraced each other.

abrazo *m* hug.

abrelatas *m inv* can opener.

abreviar [43] **1** *vt* to shorten; *(texto)* to abridge; *(palabra)* to abbreviate. **2** *vi* to be quick o brief; **para a.** to cut a long story short.

abreviatura *f* abbreviation.

abridor *m (de latas, botellas)* opener.

abrigado, -a *adj* wrapped up.

abrigar [42] **1** *vt* to keep warm; *(esperanza)* to cherish; *(duda)* to harbor. **2** *vi* **esta chaqueta abriga mucho** this cardigan is very warm.

abrigo *m (prenda)* coat; **ropa de a.** warm clothes *pl*.

abril *m* April.

abrir[1] *m* **en un a. y cerrar de ojos** in the twinkling of an eye.

abrir[2] *(pp* **abierto) 1** *vi* to open. **2** *vt* to open; *(cremallera)* to undo; *(gas, grifo)* to turn on. **3 abrirse** *vr* to open; **abrirse paso** to make one's way.

abrochar *vt*, **abrocharse** *vr (botones)* to do up; *(camisa)* to button (up); *(cinturón)* to fasten; *(zapatos)* to tie up; *(cremallera)* to do up.

abrumar *vt* to overwhelm.

abrupto, -a *adj (terreno)* steep.

absceso *m* abscess.

absolutamente *adv* absolutely.

absoluto, -a *adj* absolute; **en a.** not at all.

absolver [4] *(pp* **absuelto)** *vt* to acquit.

absorbente *adj (papel)* absorbent; *(fascinante)* engrossing.

absorber *vt* to absorb.

absorto, -a *adj* engrossed (**en**).

abstenerse [24] *vr* to abstain (**de** from); *(privarse)* to refrain (**de** from).

abstracto, -a *adj* abstract.

abstraído, -a *adj (ensimismado)* engrossed (**en** in).

absuelto, -a *adj pp de* **absolver.**

absurdo, -a *adj* absurd.

abuchear *vt* to boo.

abuela *f* grandmother; *fam* grandma, granny.

abuelo *m* grandfather; *fam* grandad, grandpa; **abuelos** grandparents.

abultado, -a *adj* bulky.

abundancia *f* abundance; **... en a.** plenty of ...

abundante *adj* abundant.

aburrido, -a *adj* **ser a.** to be boring; **estar a.** to be bored; *(harto)* to be tired (**de** of).

aburrimiento *m* boredom; **¡qué a.!** what a bore!

aburrir 1 *vt* to bore. **2 aburrirse** *vr* to get bored.

abusar *vi (propasarse)* to go too far; **a. de** *(situación, persona)* to take (unfair) advantage of; *(poder, amabilidad)* to abuse; **a. de la bebida/ del tabaco** to drink/smoke too much o to excess.

abuso *m* abuse.

a. C. *abr de* **antes de Cristo** before Christ, BC.

acá *adv (lugar)* over here; **más a.** nearer; **¡ven a.!** come here!

acabar 1 *vt* to finish (off); *(completar)* to complete. **2** *vi* to finish; **a. de ...** to have just ...; **acaba de entrar** he has just come in; **acabaron casándose** o **por casarse** they ended up getting married. **3 acabarse** *vr* to finish; **se nos acabó la gasolina** we ran out of gas.

acacia f acacia.

academia f academy; **a. de idiomas** language school.

académico, -a adj & mf academic.

acalorado, -a adj hot; (debate etc) heated.

acampar vi to camp.

acantilado m cliff.

acaparar vt (productos) to hoard; (mercado) to corner.

acápite m Am (párrafo) paragraph.

acariciar [43] vt to caress; (pelo, animal) to stroke.

acarrear vt (transportar) to transport; (conllevar) to entail.

acaso adv perhaps, maybe; **por si a.** just in case; **si a. viene ...** if he should come ....

acatar vt to comply with.

acatarrado, -a adj estar a. to have a cold.

acatarrarse vr to catch a cold.

acceder vi a. a (consentir) to consent to.

accesible adj accessible; (persona) approachable.

acceso m (entrada) access; (en carretera) approach; **a. a Internet** Internet access.

accesorio, -a 1 adj (terreno) uneven; (viaje, vida) eventful. **2** mf casualty.

accidental adj accidental; **un encuentro a.** a chance meeting.

accidente m accident; **a. laboral** industrial accident.

acción f action; (acto) act; (en la bolsa) share; **poner en a.** to put into action; **película de a.** adventure film.

accionar vt to drive.

accionista mf shareholder.

acechar vt to lie in wait for.

aceite m oil; **a. de girasol/maíz/oliva** sunflower/corn/olive oil.

aceituna f olive; **a. rellena** stuffed olive.

acelerador m accelerator.

acelerar vt to accelerate.

acento m accent; (énfasis) stress.

acentuar [30] **1** vt to stress. **2** acen-tuarse vr to become more pronounced.

aceptar vt to accept.

acequia f irrigation ditch o channel.

acera f sidewalk.

acerca adv **a. de** about.

acercar [44] **1** vt to bring (over). **2** acercarse vr to approach (a -); (ir) to go; (venir) to come.

acero m steel; **a. inoxidable** stainless steel.

acérrimo, -a adj (partidario) staunch; (enemigo) bitter.

acertado, -a adj (solución) correct; (decisión) wise.

acertar [1] **1** vt (pregunta) to get right; (adivinar) to guess correctly. **2** vi to be right.

acertijo m riddle.

achacar [44] vt (atribuir) to attribute.

achaque m ailment.

achicharrar vt to burn to a crisp.

acholado, -a adj Andes mixed.

achuchar vt (empujar) to shove.

aciago, -a adj ill-fated.

acicalarse vr to dress up.

acidez f (de sabor) sharpness; **a. de estómago** heartburn.

ácido, -a 1 adj (sabor) sharp. **2** m acid.

acierto m (buena decisión) good choice.

aclamar vt to acclaim.

aclaración f explanation.

aclarado m rinse.

aclarar 1 vt (explicar) to explain; (color) to make lighter; (enjuagar) to rinse. **2** v impers (tiempo) to clear (up). **3** aclararse vr aclararse la voz to clear one's throat.

aclimatarse vr a. algo to get used to sth.

acné m acne.

acobardarse vr to get frightened.

acogedor, -a adj (habitación) cozy.

acoger [53] **1** vt (recibir) to receive; (persona desvalida) to take in. **2** acogerse vr acogerse a to take refuge in; **acogerse a la ley** to have recourse to the law.

acogida f reception, welcome.

acometer vt (emprender) to undertake; (atacar) to attack.

acomodado, -a adj well-off.

acomodador, -a mf usher.

acomodar 1 vt (alojar) to accommodate; (en cine etc) to find a place for. **2 acomodarse** vr (instalarse) to make oneself comfortable; (adaptarse) to adapt.

acompañante 1 mf companion. **2** adj accompanying.

acompañar vt to accompany; ¿te acompaño a casa? can I walk you home?; (en funeral) le acompaño en el sentimiento my condolences.

acomplejado, -a adj estar a. to have a complex (por about).

acomplejar 1 vt to give a complex. **2 acomplejarse** vr acomplejarse por to develop a complex about.

acondicionado, -a adj aire a. air conditioning.

acondicionador m conditioner.

acondicionar vt to prepare, to set up; (mejorar) to improve; (cabello) to condition.

aconsejable adj advisable.

aconsejar vt to advise.

acontecimiento m event.

acopio m hacer a. de to store.

acordar [2] **1** vt to agree; (decidir) to decide. **2 acordarse** vr to remember.

acordeón m accordion.

acordonar vt (zona) to cordon off.

acorralar vt to corner.

acortar vt to shorten.

acosar vt to harass; fig a. a algn a preguntas to bombard sb with questions.

acoso m harassment; **a. laboral** (workplace) bullying; **a. sexual** sexual harassment.

acostar [2] **1** vt to put to bed. **2 acostarse** vr to go to bed.

acostumbrado, -a adj usual; es lo a. it is the custom; a. al frío/calor used to the cold/heat.

acostumbrar 1 vi a. (soler) to be in the habit of. **2** vt **a. a algn a algo** (habituar) to get sb used to sth. **3 acostumbrarse** vr to get used (a to).

acotamiento m Méx (de autopista) shoulder.

acre m (medida) acre.

acreditar vt to be a credit to; (probar) to prove.

acreedor, -a mf creditor.

acrílico, -a adj acrylic.

acriollarse vr Am to adopt native ways.

acrobacia f acrobatics sing.

acta f (de reunión) minutes pl; (certificado) certificate.

actitud f attitude.

activar vt to activate; (avivar) to liven up.

actividad f activity.

activo, -a adj active.

acto m act; (ceremonia) ceremony; (de teatro) act; **en el a.** at once; **a. seguido** immediately afterwards.

actor m actor.

actriz f actress.

actuación f performance; (intervención) intervention.

actual adj current, present.

actualidad f present time; (hechos) current affairs pl; **en la a.** at present.

actualizar [40] vt (software, hardware) to upgrade.

actualmente adv (hoy en día) nowadays.

actuar [30] vi to act.

acuarela f watercolor.

acuario m aquarium.

acuciante adj urgent.

acudir vi (ir) to go; (venir) to come.

acuerdo m agreement; ¡**de a.!** all right!, OK!; **de a. con** in accordance with; **ponerse de a.** to agree.

acumular vt, **acumularse** vr to accumulate.

acuñar vt (moneda) to mint; (frase) to coin.

acurrucarse [44] vr to curl up.

acusación f accusation; (en juicio) charge.

acusado, -a 1 *mf* accused. **2** *adj (marcado)* marked.

acusar 1 *vt* to accuse (**de** of); *(en juicio)* to charge (**de** with). **2 acusarse** *vr (acentuarse)* to become more pronounced.

acústica *f* acoustics *sing*.

acústico, -a *adj* acoustic.

adaptador *m* adapter.

adaptar 1 *vt* to adapt; *(ajustar)* to adjust. **2 adaptarse** *vr* to adapt (oneself) (**a** to).

adecuado, -a *adj* appropriate.

a. de J. C. *abr de* **antes de Jesucristo** before Christ, BC.

adelantado, -a *adj* advanced; *(desarrollado)* developed; *(reloj)* fast; **pagar por a.** to pay in advance.

adelantamiento *m* overtaking.

adelantar 1 *vt* to move forward; *(reloj)* to put forward; *(en carretera)* to overtake; *(fecha)* to move forward. **2** *vi* to advance; *(progresar)* to make progress; *(reloj)* to be fast. **3 adelantarse** *vr (ir delante)* to go ahead; *(reloj)* to be fast.

adelante 1 *adv* forward; **más a.** *(lugar)* further on; *(tiempo)* later. **2** *interj* ¡a.! *(pase)* come in!

adelanto *m* advance; *(progreso)* progress; **el reloj lleva diez minutos de a.** the watch is ten minutes fast.

adelgazar [40] *vi* to slim.

ademán *m* gesture.

además *adv* moreover, furthermore; **a. de él** besides him.

adentro 1 *adv (dentro)* inside; **mar a.** out to sea; **tierra a.** inland. **2** *mpl* **decir algo para sus adentros** to say sth to oneself.

adherir [5] 1 *vt* to stick on. **2 adherirse** *vr* **adherirse a** to adhere to.

adhesión *f* adhesion.

adhesivo, -a *adj & m* adhesive.

adicción *f* addiction.

adicto, -a 1 *mf* addict. **2** *adj* addicted (**a** to).

adiestrar *vt* to train.

adinerado, -a *adj* wealthy.

adiós *(pl* **adioses)** *interj* goodbye; *fam* bye-bye; *(al cruzarse)* hello.

aditivo, -a *adj & m* additive.

adivinanza *f* riddle.

adivinar *vt* to guess.

adjetivo *m* adjective.

adjudicar [44] 1 *vt (premio, contrato)* to award; *(en subasta)* to sell. **2 adjudicarse** *vr* to appropriate.

adjuntar *vt* to enclose.

adjunto, -a 1 *adj* enclosed, attached. **2** *mf (profesor)* assistant teacher.

administración *f (gobierno)* authorities *pl*; *(de empresa)* management; *(oficina)* (branch) office; **a. central** *(gobierno)* central government; **a. pública** civil service.

administrador, -a 1 *mf* administrator. **2** *adj* administrating.

administrar *vt* to administer; *(dirigir)* to run.

administrativo, -a 1 *adj* administrative. **2** *mf (funcionario)* official.

admiración *f* admiration; *(ortográfica)* exclamation mark.

admirar 1 *vt* to admire; *(sorprender)* to amaze. **2 admirarse** *vr* to be amazed.

admisión *f* admission.

admitir *vt* to let in; *(aceptar)* to accept; *(permitir)* to allow; *(reconocer)* to acknowledge.

ADN *m abr de* **ácido desoxirribonucleico** deoxyribonucleic acid, DNA.

adobe *m* adobe.

adobo *m* marinade.

adolescencia *f* adolescence.

adolescente *adj & mf* adolescent.

adónde *adv* where (to)?

adonde *adv* where.

adondequiera *adv* where.

adopción *f* adoption.

adoptar *vt* to adopt.

adoptivo, -a *adj (hijo)* adopted; *(padres)* adoptive.

adorar *vt* to worship.

adormecer [33] 1 *vt* to make sleepy. **2 adormecerse** *vr (dormirse)* to doze off; *(brazo etc)* to go numb.

adormilarse *vr* to doze, to drowse.

adornar *vt* to adorn.

adorno *m* decoration; **de a.** decorative.

adosado, -a *adj* adjacent; *(casa)* semidetached.

adquirir [31] *vt* to acquire; *(comprar)* to purchase.

adquisición *f* acquisition; *(compra)* purchase.

adrede *adv* deliberately, on purpose.

aduana *f* customs *pl*.

aduanero, -a *mf* customs officer.

aducir [10] *vt* to adduce.

adueñarse *vr* **a. de** to take over.

aduje *pt indef de* **aducir**.

adular *vt* to adulate.

adulterar *vt* to adulterate.

adulterio *m* adultery.

adulto, -a *adj & mf* adult.

aduzco *indic pres de* **aducir**.

adverbio *m* adverb.

adversario, -a 1 *mf* opponent. **2** *adj* opposing.

adversidad *f* adversity; *(revés)* setback.

adverso, -a *adj* adverse.

advertencia *f* warning.

advertir [5] *vt* to warn; *(informar)* to advise; *(notar)* to notice.

adviento *m* Advent.

adyacente *adj* adjacent.

aéreo, -a *adj* aerial; *(correo, transporte)* air; **por vía aerea** by air.

aerodinámico, -a *adj* aerodynamic; **de línea aerodinámica** streamlined.

aeromoza *f Am* flight attendant.

aeronáutico, -a *adj* **la industria aeronáutica** the aeronautics industry.

aeroplano *m* light airplane.

aeropuerto *m* airport.

aerosol *m* aerosol.

afable *adj* affable.

afán *m* (*pl* afanes) *(esfuerzo)* effort; *(celo)* zeal.

afanarse *vr* **a. por conseguir algo** to do one's best to achieve sth.

afección *f* disease.

afectar *vt* **a. a** to affect; **le afectó mucho** she was deeply affected.

afecto *m* affection; **tomarle a. a algn** to become fond of sb.

afectuoso, -a *adj* affectionate.

afeitar *vt*, **afeitarse** *vr* to shave.

afeminado, -a *adj* effeminate.

aferrarse *vr* to cling (**a** to).

afianzar [40] *vt* to strengthen.

afiche *m Am* poster.

afición *f* liking; **tiene a. por la música** he is fond of music; *(de deporte)* **la a.** the fans *pl*.

aficionado, -a 1 *mf* enthusiast; *(no profesional)* amateur. **2** *adj* keen; *(no profesional)* amateur; **ser a. a algo** to be fond of sth.

aficionarse *vr* to take a liking (**a** to).

afilado, -a *adj* sharp.

afiliarse [43] *vr* **a. a** to join, to become a member of.

afinar *vt (puntería)* to sharpen; *(instrumento)* to tune.

afinidad *f* affinity.

afirmación *f* statement.

afirmar *vt (aseverar)* to state; *(afianzar)* to strengthen.

afligir [57] **1** *vt* to afflict. **2 afligirse** *vr* to be distressed.

aflojar 1 *vt* to loosen. **2 aflojarse** *vr (rueda)* to work loose.

afluencia *f* influx; **gran a. de público** great numbers of people.

afluente *m* tributary.

afónico, -a *adj* **estar a.** to have lost one's voice.

afortunado, -a *adj* lucky, fortunate.

afrontar *vt* to confront; **a. las consecuencias** to face the consequences.

afuera 1 *adv* outside; **la parte de a.** the outside; **más a.** further out. **2 afueras** *fpl* outskirts.

agachar 1 *vt* to lower. **2 agacharse** *vr* to duck.

agarrado, -a *adj fam (tacaño)* stingy, tight; **baile a.** cheek-to-cheek dancing.

agarrar 1 *vt* to grasp; *Am (tomar)* to take; **agárralo fuerte** hold it tight; **a.**

un taxi to take a taxi. **2 agarrarse** *vr* to hold on.

agasajar *vt* to smother with attentions.

agazaparse *vr* to crouch (down).

agencia *f* agency; *(sucursal)* branch; **a. de viajes** travel agency; **a. de seguros** insurance agency; **a. inmobiliaria** estate agency.

agenda *f* diary.

agente *mf* agent; **a. de policía** *(hombre)* policeman; *(mujer)* policewoman; **a. de seguros** insurance broker.

ágil *adj* agile.

agilidad *f* agility.

agilizar [40] *vt (trámites)* to speed up.

agitación *f* agitation; *(inquietud)* restlessness.

agitado, -a *adj* agitated; *(persona)* anxious; *(mar)* rough.

agitar 1 *vt (botella)* to shake. **2 agitarse** *vr (persona)* to become agitated.

aglomeración *f (de gente)* crowd.

agobiado, -a *adj* **a. de problemas** snowed under with problems; **a. de trabajo** up to one's eyes in work.

agobiante *adj (trabajo)* overwhelming; *(lugar)* claustrophobic; *(calor)* oppressive; *(persona)* tiresome.

agobiar [43] **1** *vt* to overwhelm. **2 agobiarse** *vr (angustiarse)* to worry too much.

agobio *m (angustia)* anxiety; *(sofoco)* suffocation.

agolparse *vr* to crowd.

agonía *f* agony, last days.

agonizar [40] *vi* to be dying.

agosto *m* August.

agotado, -a *adj (cansado)* exhausted; *(existencias)* sold out; *(provisiones)* exhausted; *(libro)* out of print.

agotador, -a *adj* exhausting.

agotamiento *m* exhaustion.

agotar 1 *vt (cansar)* to exhaust; *(acabar)* to use up (completely). **2 agotarse** *vr (acabarse)* to run out; *(producto)* to be sold out; *(persona)* to become exhausted *o* tired out.

agradable *adj* pleasant.

agradar *vti* to please; **no me agrada** I don't like it.

agradecer [33] *vt (dar las gracias)* to thank for; *(estar agradecido)* to be grateful to; **te lo agradezco mucho** thank you very much.

agradecido, -a *adj* grateful; **le estoy muy a.** I am very grateful to you.

agradecimiento *m* gratitude.

agrado *m* pleasure; **no es de su a.** it isn't to his liking.

agrandar 1 *vt* to enlarge. **2 agrandarse** *vr* to become larger.

agrario, -a *adj* agrarian.

agravar 1 *vt* to aggravate. **2 agravarse** *vr* to get worse.

agredir *vt defectivo* to assault.

agregado, -a *adj* **profesor a.** *(de escuela)* secondary school teacher; *(de universidad)* teaching assistant.

agregar [42] *vt (añadir)* to add.

agresión *f* aggression.

agresivo, -a *adj* aggressive.

agrícola *adj* agricultural.

agricultor, -a *mf* farmer.

agricultura *f* agriculture.

agridulce *adj* bittersweet.

agrietar *vt* to crack; *(piel, labios)* to chap. **2 agrietarse** *vr* to crack; *(piel)* to get chapped.

agringarse [42] *vr Am* to behave like a gringo.

agrio, -a *adj* sour.

agropecuario, -a *adj* agricultural.

agrupación *f* association.

agua** *f* water; **a. potable** drinking water; **a. corriente/del grifo** running/tap water; **a. dulce/salada** fresh/salt water; **a. mineral sin/con gas** still/fizzy mineral water.

aguacate *m (fruto)* avocado (pear).

aguacero *m* downpour.

aguafiestas *mf inv* spoilsport, wet blanket.

aguafuerte *m* etching.

aguanieve *f* sleet.

aguantar 1 *vt (soportar)* to tolerate; *(sostener)* to support; **no lo aguanto**

más I can't stand it any longer; **aguanta la respiración** hold your breath. **2 aguantarse** *vr (contenerse)* to keep back; *(resignarse)* to resign oneself; **no pude aguantarme la risa** I couldn't help laughing.

aguardar 1 *vt* to await. **2** *vi* to wait.

aguardiente *m* brandy.

aguarrás *m* turpentine.

aguatero, -a *mf Am* water-carrier o seller.

agudizar [40] *vt,* **agudizarse** *vr* to intensify.

agudo, -a *adj (dolor)* acute; *(voz)* high-pitched; *(sonido)* high.

aguijón *m* sting.

águila** *f* eagle.

aguja *f* needle; *(de reloj)* hand; *(de tocadiscos)* stylus.

agujerear *vt* to make holes in.

agujero *m* hole; **a. negro** black hole.

agujetas *fpl* **tener a.** to be stiff.

aguzar [40] *vt* **a. el oído** to prick up one's ears; **a. la vista** to look attentively.

ahí *adv* there; **a. está** there he/she/it is; **por a.** *(en esa dirección)* that way; *(aproximadamente)* over there.

ahijado, -a *mf* godchild; *(niño)* godson; *(niña)* goddaughter; **ahijados** godchildren.

ahínco *m* **con a.** eagerly.

ahogado, -a 1 *adj (en líquido)* drowned; *(asfixiado)* suffocated; **morir a.** to drown. **2** *mf* drowned person.

ahogar [42] *vt,* **ahogarse** *vr (en líquido)* to drown; *(asfixiar)* to suffocate; *(motor)* to flood.

ahondar 1 *vt* to deepen. **2** *vi* to go deep; *fig* **a. en un problema** to go into a problem in depth.

ahora 1 *adv* now; **a. mismo** right now; **de a. en adelante** from now on; **por a.** for the time being; **a. voy** I'm coming; **hasta a.** *(hasta el momento)* until now, so far; *(hasta luego)* see you later. **2** *conj* **a. bien** *(sin embargo)* however.

ahorcar [44] **1** *vt* to hang. **2 ahorcarse** *vr* to hang oneself.

ahorita, ahoritica *adv Andes, CAm, Carib, Méx fam (en el presente)* (right) now; **a. voy** I'm just coming; *(pronto)* in a second; *(hace poco)* just now, a few minutes ago.

ahorrar *vt* to save.

ahorrativo, -a *adj* thrifty.

ahorros *mpl* savings; **caja de a.** savings bank.

ahuevado, -a *adj Andes, CAm fam* stupid.

ahumado, -a *adj* smoked; *(bacon)* smoky.

ahuyentar *vt* to scare away.

aindiado, -a *adj Am* Indian-like.

airado, -a *adj* angry.

aire *m* air; *(de automóvil)* choke; *(viento)* wind; *(aspecto)* appearance; **a. acondicionado** air conditioning; **al a.** *(al descubierto)* uncovered; **al a. libre** in the open air; **en el a.** *(pendiente)* in the air; **tomar el a.** to get some fresh air; **cambiar de aires** to change one's surroundings; **darse aires** to put on airs.

aislado, -a *adj* isolated; *(cable)* insulated.

aislante 1 *adj* **cinta a.** insulating tape. **2** *m* insulator.

aislar *vt* to isolate; *(cable)* to insulate.

ajedrez *m (juego)* chess; *(piezas y tablero)* chess set.

ajeno, -a *adj* belonging to other people; **por causas ajenas a nuestra voluntad** for reasons beyond our control.

ajetreado, -a *adj* hectic.

ajetreo *m* activity, hard work, bustle.

ajo *m* garlic; **cabeza/diente de a.** head/clove of garlic.

ajustado, -a *adj* tight.

ajustar *vt* to adjust; *(apretar)* to tighten.

ajuste *m* adjustment; *(de precio)* fixing; *(de cuenta)* settlement; **a. de cuentas** settling of scores.

ajusticiar [43] *vt* to execute.

al *(contracción de* **a** *&* **el***) ver* **a**; **(al +**

infinitivo) **al salir** on leaving.
ala f wing; *(de sombrero)* brim.
alabar vt to praise.
alabastro m alabaster.
alacena f *(food)* cupboard.
alambrada f, **alambrado** m barbed wire fence.
alambre m wire; **a. de púas** barbed wire.
alameda f poplar grove; *(paseo)* avenue, boulevard.
álamo m poplar.
alarde m *(ostentación)* bragging; **hacer a. de** to show off.
alardear vi to brag.
alargadera f *(cable)* extension.
alargado, -a adj elongated.
alargar [42] **1** vt to lengthen; *(estirar)* to stretch; *(prolongar)* to prolong; *(dar)* to pass. **2 alargarse** vr to get longer; *(prolongarse)* to go on.
alarido m shriek; **dar un a.** to howl.
alarma f alarm; **falsa a.** false alarm; **señal de a.** alarm (signal).
alarmante adj alarming.
alarmar 1 vt to alarm. **2 alarmarse** vr to be alarmed.
alba** f dawn.
albañil m bricklayer; *(obrero)* building worker.
albaricoque m *(fruta)* apricot; *(árbol)* apricot tree.
alberca f *(depósito)* water tank; *Méx (para nadar)* swimming pool.
albergar [42] **1** vt *(alojar)* to house. **2 albergarse** vr to stay.
albergue m *(lugar)* hostel; *(refugio)* refuge; **a. juvenil** youth hostel.
albino, -a adj & mf albino.
albóndiga f meatball.
albornoz m bathrobe.
alborotar 1 vt *(desordenar)* to turn upside down. **2** vi to make a racket. **3 alborotarse** vr to get excited; *(mar)* to get rough.
alboroto m *(jaleo)* din, racket; *(desorden)* disturbance, uproar.
albufera f lagoon.
álbum m album.

alcachofa f artichoke.
alcalde m mayor.
alcaldesa f mayoress.
alcaldía f *(cargo)* mayorship; *(oficina)* mayor's office.
alcance m reach; **dar a. a** to catch up with; **fuera del a. de los niños** out of the reach of children.
alcantarilla f sewer; *(boca)* drain.
alcanzar [40] **1** vt to reach; *(persona)* to catch up with; *(conseguir)* to achieve. **2** vi *(ser suficiente)* to be sufficient.
alcaparra f *(fruto)* caper.
alcayata f hook.
alcazaba f citadel.
alcázar m *(fortaleza)* fortress; *(castillo)* castle.
alcoba f bedroom.
alcohol m alcohol.
alcoholemia f **prueba de a.** breath test.
alcohólico, -a adj & mf alcoholic.
alcoholímetro m Breathalyzer®.
alcornoque m cork oak.
alcurnia f ancestry.
aldea f village.
aleccionador, -a adj *(ejemplar)* exemplary.
alegar [42] vt *(aducir)* to claim.
alegrar 1 vt *(complacer)* to make glad; **me alegra que se lo hayas dicho** I am glad you told her. **2 alegrarse** vr to be glad; **me alegro de verte** I am pleased to see you.
alegre adj *(contento)* glad; *(color)* bright; *(música)* lively.
alegría f happiness.
alejado, -a adj remote.
alejar 1 vt to move further away. **2 alejarse** vr to go away.
alemán, -ana 1 adj & mf German. **2** m *(idioma)* German.
alentar [1] vt to encourage.
alergia f allergy.
alérgico, -a adj allergic.
alerta f & adj alert.
aleta f *(de pez)* fin; *(de foca, de nadador)* flipper.

aletargar [42] **1** *vt* to make lethargic. **2 aletargarse** *vr* to become lethargic.

aletear *vi* to flutter o flap its wings.

alfabetización *f* campaña de a. literacy campaign.

alfabeto *m* alphabet.

alfalfa *f* alfalfa grass.

alfarería *f* pottery.

alféizar *m* windowsill.

alférez *m* second lieutenant.

alfil *m* (en ajedrez) bishop.

alfiler *m* pin; *Andes, RP, Ven* a. de **gancho** (imperdible) safety pin.

alfombra *f* rug; (moqueta) carpet.

alga *f* (marina) seaweed.

álgebra** *f* algebra.

álgido, -a *adj* el punto a. the climax.

algo 1 *pron indef* (afirmativo) something; (interrogativo) anything; (cantidad indeterminada) some; **a. así** something like that; **¿a. más?** anything else?; **¿queda a. de pastel?** is there any cake left? **2** *adv* (un poco) somewhat; **está a. mejor** she's feeling a bit better.

algodón *m* cotton.

alguacil *m* bailiff.

alguien *pron indef* (afirmativo) somebody, someone; (interrogativo) anybody, anyone.

algún *adj* (delante de nombres masculinos en singular) ver **alguno**.

alguno, -a 1 *adj* (delante de nombre) (afirmativo) some; (interrogativo) any; **alguna que otra vez** now and then; **¿le has visto alguna vez?** have you ever seen him?; **no vino persona alguna** nobody came. **2** *pron indef* (afirmativo) someone, somebody; (interrogativo) anyone, anybody; **algunos, -as** some (people).

alhaja *f* jewel.

alhelí *m* (pl alhelíes) wallflower.

aliado, -a *adj* allied.

alianza *f* (pacto) alliance; (anillo) wedding ring.

aliarse [29] *vr* to ally, to become allies.

alicates *mpl* pliers *pl*.

aliciente *m* (atractivo) charm; (incentivo) incentive.

aliento *m* breath; **sin a.** breathless.

aligerar 1 *vt* (carga) to lighten; (acelerar) to speed up; **a. el paso** to quicken one's pace. **2** *vi fam* **¡aligera!** hurry up!

alijo *m* haul; **un a. de drogas** a consignment of drugs.

alimaña *f* vermin.

alimentación *f* (comida) food; (acción) feeding.

alimentar 1 *vt* (dar alimento) to feed; (ser nutritivo para) to be nutritious for. **2 alimentarse** *vr* **alimentarse con** o **de** to live on.

alimenticio, -a *adj* nutritious; **valor a.** nutritional value.

alimento *m* food.

alinear 1 *vt* to align. **2 alinearse** *vr* to line up.

aliñar *vt* (ensalada) to dress.

aliño *m* (de ensalada) dressing.

alistar 1 *vt* (en el ejército) to enlist. **2 alistarse** *vr* (en el ejército) to enlist; *Am* (prepararse) to get ready.

aliviar [43] **1** *vt* (dolor) to relieve; (carga) to lighten. **2 aliviarse** *vr* (dolor) to diminish.

alivio *m* relief.

allá *adv* (lugar alejado) over there; **a. abajo/arriba** down/up there; **más a.** further on; **más a. de** beyond; **a. tú** that's your problem.

allí *adv* there; **a. abajo/arriba** down/up there; **por a.** (movimiento) that way; (posición) over there.

alma** *f* soul.

almacén *m* (local) warehouse; **grandes almacenes** department store.

almacenar *vt* to store.

almanaque *m* calendar.

almeja *f* clam.

almendra *f* almond.

almendro *m* almond tree.

almíbar *m* syrup.

almirante *m* admiral.

almizcle *m* musk.

almohada *f* pillow.

almohadilla *f* (small) cushion.

almohadón *m* large pillow.

almorrana *f fam* pile.

almorzar [2] **1** *vi* to have lunch. **2** *vt* to have for lunch.

almuerzo *m* lunch.

aló *interj Andes, Carib* (al teléfono) hello.

alojamiento *m* accommodations; **dar a.** to accommodate.

alojar 1 *vt* to accommodate. **2 alojarse** *vr* to stay.

alondra *f* lark.

alpargata *f* canvas sandal.

alpinismo *m* mountaineering.

alpinista *mf* mountaineer.

alquilar *vt* to hire; (pisos, casas) to rent; 'se alquila' 'to let', 'for rent'.

alquiler *m* (acción) hiring; (de pisos, casas) letting; (precio) rental; (de pisos, casas) rent; **a. de coches** car rental; **de a.** (pisos, casas) to let; (coche) for hire; **en una casa de a.** in a rented house.

alquitrán *m* tar.

alrededor 1 *adv* (lugar) round. **2** *prep* **a. de** round; **a. de quince** about fifteen. **3 alrededores** *mpl* surrounding area *sing*.

alta *f* **dar de** o **el a.** (a un enfermo) to discharge from hospital.

altamente *adv* extremely.

altanero, -a *adj* arrogant.

altar *m* altar.

altavoz *m* loudspeaker.

alteración *f* (cambio) alteration; (alboroto) quarrel; (excitación) agitation.

alterar 1 *vt* to alter. **2 alterarse** *vr* (inquietarse) to be upset.

altercado *m* argument.

alternar 1 *vt* to alternate. **2** *vi* (relacionarse) to socialize. **3 alternarse** *vr* to alternate.

alternativa *f* alternative.

alterno, -a *adj* alternate.

altibajos *mpl* ups and downs.

altiplano *m* high plateau.

altitud *f* altitude.

altivez *f* arrogance.

alto¹ *m* (interrupción) stop; **dar el a. a algn** to tell sb to stop; **un a. el fuego** a cease-fire.

alto, -a¹ 1 *adj* (persona, árbol, edificio) tall; (montaña, techo, presión) high; (sonido) loud; (precio, tecnología) high; (agudo) high; **en lo a.** at the top; **clase alta** upper class; **en voz alta** aloud; **a altas horas de la noche** late at night. **2** *adv* high; (fuerte) loud; **¡habla más a.!** speak up. **3** *m* (altura) height; **¿cuánto tiene de a.?** how tall/high is it?

altoparlante *m Am* loudspeaker.

altura *f* height; (nivel) level; **de diez metros de a.** ten meters high; **estar a la a. de las circunstancias** to meet the challenge; *fig* **a estas alturas** by now.

alubia *f* bean.

alucinar 1 *vt* to hallucinate; *fig* (encantar) to fascinate. **2** *vi fam* to be amazed.

alud *m* avalanche.

aludir *vi* to allude.

alumbrar *vt* (iluminar) to illuminate; (parir) to give birth to.

aluminio *m* aluminum.

alumno, -a *mf* (de colegio) pupil; (de Universidad) student.

alusión *f* allusion.

alverja, alverjana *f Am* pea.

alza** *f* rise; **en a.** rising.

alzamiento *m* (rebelión) uprising.

alzar [40] **1** *vt* to raise; **a. los ojos/la vista** to look up. **2 alzarse** *vr* (levantarse) to rise; (rebelarse) to rebel.

ama *f* (dueña) owner; **a. de casa** housewife.

amabilidad *f* kindness; **tenga la a. de esperar** would you be so kind as to wait.

amable *adj* kind, nice.

amaestrar *vt* (animal) to train; (domar) to tame.

amainar *vi* (viento etc) to die down.

amamantar *vt* to breast-feed; (entre animales) to suckle.

amanecer [33] **1** *v impers* **¿a qué**

hora amanece? when does it get light?; **amaneció lluvioso** it was rainy at daybreak. **2** *vi* **amanecimos en Finlandia** we were in Finland at daybreak; **amaneció muy enfermo** he woke up feeling very ill. **3** *m* dawn; **al a.** at dawn.

amanerado, -a *adj* affected.

amante *mf* lover.

amapola *f* poppy.

amar 1 *vt* to love. **2 amarse** *vr* to love each other.

amargar [42] **1** *vt* to make bitter; *(relación)* to embitter. **2 amargarse** *vr* to become embittered.

amargo, -a *adj* bitter.

amargor *m*, **amargura** *f* bitterness.

amarillento, -a *adj* yellowish.

amarillo, -a *adj & m* yellow.

amarilloso, -a *adj Ven* yellowish.

amarrar *vt (atar)* to tie (up).

amasar *vt* to knead.

amateur *adj & mf* amateur.

ámbar *m* amber.

ambición *f* ambition.

ambicionar *vt* to have as an ambition; **ambiciona ser presidente** his ambition is to become president.

ambicioso, -a 1 *adj* ambitious. **2** *mf* ambitious person.

ambientador *m* air freshener.

ambiental *adj* environmental.

ambiente 1 *m* environment; *Andes, RP (habitación)* room. **2** *adj* environmental; **temperatura a.** room temperature.

ambiguo, -a *adj* ambiguous.

ámbito *m* field.

ambos, -as *adj & pron pl* both.

ambulancia *f* ambulance.

ambulatorio *m* surgery.

amedrentar *vt* to frighten.

amenaza *f* threat.

amenazador, -a, **amenazante** *adj* threatening.

amenazar [40] *vt* to threaten.

ameno, -a *adj* entertaining.

americana *f (prenda)* jacket.

americano, -a *adj & mf* American.

ametralladora *f* machine gun.

amigable *adj* friendly.

amígdala *f* tonsil.

amigdalitis *f* tonsillitis.

amigo, -a *mf* friend; **hacerse amigos** to become friends; **son muy amigos** they are very good friends.

aminorar *vt* to reduce; **a. el paso** to slow down.

amistad *f* friendship; **amistades** friends.

amistoso, -a *adj* friendly.

amnistía *f* amnesty.

amo *m (dueño)* owner.

amodorrarse *vr* to become sleepy.

amoldar *vt*, **amoldarse** *vr* to adapt.

amonestación *f* reprimand.

amontonar 1 *vt* to pile up. **2 amontonarse** *vr* to pile up; *(gente)* to crowd together.

amor *m* love; **hacer el a.** to make love; **a. propio** self-esteem.

amoratado, -a *adj (frío)* blue with cold; *(de un golpe)* black and blue.

amordazar [40] *vt (a una persona)* to gag.

amoroso, -a *adj* loving.

amortiguador *m (de vehículo)* shock absorber.

amortiguar [45] *vt (golpe)* to cushion; *(ruido)* to muffle.

amortizar [40] *vt* to pay off.

amotinar 1 *vt* to incite to riot. **2 amotinarse** *vr* to rise up.

amparar 1 *vt* to protect. **2 ampararse** *vr* to seek refuge.

ampliación *f* enlargement; *(de plazo, casa)* extension.

ampliar [29] *vt* to enlarge; *(casa, plazo)* to extend.

amplificador *m* amplifier.

amplio, -a *adj* large; *(ancho)* broad.

ampolla *f (vejiga)* blister; *(de medicina)* ampule.

amputar *vt* to amputate.

amueblar *vt* to furnish.

amuleto *m* amulet.

anaconda *f* anaconda.

anacronismo *m* anachronism.

anales *mpl* annals.

analfabeto, -a *mf* illiterate.

analgésico, -a *adj & m* analgesic.

análisis *m inv* analysis; **a. de sangre** blood test.

analizar [40] *vt* to analyze.

analogía *f* analogy.

análogo, -a *adj* analogous.

ananá *m* (*pl* ananaes), **ananás** *m* (*pl* ananases) *Am* pineapple.

anarquista *adj & mf* anarchist.

anatomía *f* anatomy.

ancho, -a 1 *adj* wide, broad; **a lo a.** breadthwise; **te está muy a.** it's too big for you. **2** *m* (*anchura*) width, breadth; **dos metros de a.** two meters wide; **¿qué a. tiene?** how wide is it?

anchoa *f* anchovy.

anchura *f* width, breadth.

anciano, -a 1 *adj* very old. **2** *mf* old person.

ancla** *f* anchor.

ándale *interj CAm, Méx fam* come on!

andaluz, -a *adj & mf* Andalusian.

andamiaje *m* scaffolding.

andamio *m* scaffold.

andar¹ *m*, **andares** *mpl* gait *sing*.

andar² [8] **1** *vi* to walk; (*coche etc*) to move; (*funcionar*) to work; *fam* **anda por los cuarenta** he's about forty; **¿cómo andamos de tiempo?** how are we on time?; **tu bolso debe de a. por ahí** your bag must be over there somewhere. **2** *vt* (*recorrer*) to walk.

andariego, -a *adj* fond of walking.

andén *m* (*en estación*) platform; *Andes, CAm* (*acera*) sidewalk.

andinismo *m Am* mountaineering.

andino, -a *adj & mf* Andean.

andrajo *m* rag.

anécdota *f* anecdote.

anegar *vt*, **anegarse** *vr* to flood.

anejo, -a *adj* attached (**a** to).

anemia *f* anemia.

anestesia *f* anesthesia.

anexión *f* annexation.

anexionar *vt* to annex.

anexo, -a 1 *adj* attached (**a** to). **2** *m* appendix.

anfitrión, -ona *mf* (*hombre*) host; (*mujer*) hostess.

ángel *m* angel; *Am* (*micrófono*) hand microphone.

angina *f* **tener anginas** to have tonsillitis; **a. de pecho** angina pectoris.

anglosajón, -ona *adj & mf* Anglo-Saxon.

angosto, -a *adj* narrow.

anguila *f* eel.

angula *f* elver.

ángulo *m* angle.

angustia *f* anguish.

anhelar *vt* to long for, to yearn for.

anhídrido *m* **a. carbónico** carbon dioxide.

anilla *f* ring.

anillo *m* ring.

animado, -a *adj* (*fiesta etc*) lively.

animadversión *f* animosity.

animal 1 *m* animal; *fig* (*basto*) brute. **2** *adj* animal.

animar 1 *vt* (*alentar*) to encourage; (*alegrar*) (*persona*) to cheer up; (*fiesta, bar*) to liven up. **2 animarse** *vr* (*persona*) to cheer up; (*fiesta, reunión*) to brighten up.

ánimo *m* (*valor, coraje*) courage; **estado de á.** state of mind; **con á. de** with the intention of; **¡á.!** cheer up!

aniñado, -a *adj* (*gesto*) childlike; (*comportamiento*) childish.

aniquilar *vt* to annihilate.

anís *m* (*bebida*) anisette.

aniversario *m* anniversary.

anoche *adv* last night; (*por la tarde*) yesterday evening; **antes de a.** the night before last.

anochecer [33] **1** *v impers* to get dark. **2** *m* nightfall.

anodino, -a *adj* (*insustancial*) insubstantial; (*soso*) insipid.

anómalo, -a *adj* anomalous.

anonadado, -a *adj* **me quedé/me dejó a.** I was astonished.

anónimo, -a 1 *adj* (*desconocido*) anonymous; **sociedad anónima** corporation. **2** *m* (*carta*) anonymous letter.

anorak m (pl **anoraks**) anorak.

anormal adj abnormal; (inusual) unusual.

anotar vt (apuntar) to note.

anquilosarse vr to stagnate.

ansiar [29] vt to long for.

ansiedad f anxiety; **con a.** anxiously.

ansioso, -a adj (deseoso) eager (por for); (avaricioso) greedy.

antagonismo m antagonism.

antaño adv in the past.

antártico, -a 1 adj Antarctic. **2 m el A.** the Antarctic.

ante¹ m (piel) suede.

ante² prep (delante de) in the presence of; (en vista de) faced with; **a. todo** most of all.

anteanoche adv the night before last.

anteayer adv the day before yesterday.

antecedente 1 adj previous. **2 antecedentes** mpl (historial) record sing; **antecedentes penales** criminal record sing.

antecesor, -a mf (en un cargo) predecessor.

antelación f con un mes de a. a month beforehand.

antemano adv **de a.** beforehand, in advance.

antena f (de radio, televisión, animal) antenna; **a. parabólica** satellite dish; **en a.** on the air.

anteojos mpl (binoculares) binoculars; Am (gafas) glasses, spectacles.

antepecho m (de ventana) sill.

antepenúltimo, -a adj **el capítulo a.** the last chapter but two.

anteproyecto m draft; **a. de ley** draft bill.

anterior adj previous; (delantero) front.

anteriormente adv previously.

antes 1 adv before; (antaño) in the past; **mucho a.** long before; **cuanto a.** as soon as possible; **a. prefiero hacerlo yo** I'd rather do it myself; **a.**

(bien) on the contrary. **2** prep **a. de** before.

antiadherente adj nonstick.

antibiótico, -a adj & m antibiotic.

anticaspa adj anti-dandruff.

anticipar 1 vt (acontecimiento) to bring forward; (dinero) to pay in advance. **2 anticiparse** vr (llegar pronto) to arrive early; **él se me anticipó** he beat me to it.

anticonceptivo, -a adj & m contraceptive.

anticongelante adj & m (de radiador) antifreeze; (de parabrisas) de-icer.

anticonstitucional adj unconstitutional.

anticuado, -a adj antiquated.

anticuario, -a mf antique dealer.

anticuerpo m antibody.

antídoto m antidote.

antier adv Am fam the day before yesterday.

antifaz m mask.

antigüedad f (período histórico) antiquity; (en cargo) seniority; **tienda de antigüedades** antique shop.

antiguo, -a adj old; (pasado de moda) old-fashioned; (anterior) former.

antihistamínico m antihistamine.

antiniebla adj inv **luces a.** foglights.

antipático, -a adj unpleasant.

antirrobo 1 adj inv **alarma a.** burglar alarm; (para coche) car alarm. **2** m burglar alarm; (para coche) car alarm.

antiséptico, -a adj & m antiseptic.

antivirus m inv antivirus system.

antojarse vr **cuando se me antoja** when I feel like it; **se le antojó un helado** he wanted an ice-cream.

antojo m (capricho) whim; (de embarazada) craving.

antorcha f torch.

antropología f anthropology.

anual adj annual.

anudar vt (atar) to knot.

anular vt (matrimonio) to annul; (ley) to repeal.

anunciar [43] *vt (producto etc)* to advertise; *(avisar)* to announce.

anuncio *m (comercial)* advertisement; *(aviso)* announcement; *(cartel)* notice.

anzuelo *m* (fish)hook.

añadir *vt* to add (**a** to).

añejo, -a *adj (vino, queso)* mature.

añicos *mpl* smithereens; **hacer a.** to smash to smithereens.

año *m* year; **el a. pasado** last year; **el a. que viene** next year; **hace años** a long time ago; **los años noventa** the nineties; **todo el a.** all the year (round); **¿cuántos años tienes?** how old are you?; **tiene seis años** he's six years old.

añorar *vt* to long for.

apacible *adj* mild.

apagado, -a *adj (luz, cigarro)* out; *(color)* dull; *(voz)* sad; *(mirada)* expressionless, lifeless; *(carácter, persona)* spiritless.

apagar [42] *vt (fuego)* to put out; *(luz, tele etc)* to switch off.

apagón *m* power cut.

apaisado, -a *adj (papel)* landscape.

aparador *m (mueble)* sideboard.

aparato *m (dispositivo)* device; *(instrumento)* instrument; **a. de radio/televisión** radio/television set; **a. digestivo** digestive system.

aparatoso, -a *adj (pomposo)* ostentatious, showy; *(espectacular)* spectacular; *(grande)* bulky.

aparcamiento *m (en la calle)* parking place; *(parking)* parking lot.

aparcar [44] *vti* to park.

aparecer [33] **1** *vi* to appear; **no aparece en mi lista** he is not on my list; *(en un sitio)* to turn up; **¿apareció el dinero?** did the money turn up?; **no apareció nadie** nobody turned up. **2 aparecerse** *vr* to appear.

aparejador, -a *mf* quantity surveyor.

aparejo *m (equipo)* equipment.

aparentar 1 *vt (simular)* to affect; *(tener aspecto)* **no aparenta esa**

edad she doesn't look that age. **2** *vi* to show off.

apariencia *f* appearance; **en a.** apparently; **guardar las apariencias** to keep up appearances.

apartamento *m* apartment.

apartar 1 *vt (alejar)* to remove; *(guardar)* to put aside. **2** *vi* **¡aparta!** move out of the way! **3 apartarse** *vr (alejarse)* to move away.

aparte 1 *adv* aside; **modestia/bromas a.** modesty/joking apart; **eso hay que pagarlo a.** *(separadamente)* you have to pay for that separately; **punto y a.** full stop, new paragraph. **2** *prep* **a. de eso** *(además)* besides that; *(excepto)* apart from that.

apasionado, -a *adj* passionate.

apasionante *adj* exciting.

apasionar *vt* to excite.

apático, -a 1 *adj* apathetic. **2** *mf* apathetic person.

apearse *vi (de un autobús, tren)* to get off; *(de un coche)* to get out.

apedrear *vt* to throw stones at.

apelar *vi (sentencia)* to appeal; *(recurrir)* to resort (**a** to).

apellidarse *vr* to have as a surname, to be called.

apellido *m* surname; **a. de soltera** maiden name.

apenar 1 *vt* to grieve. **2 apenarse** *vr* to be grieved; *Andes, CAm, Carib, Méx (avergonzarse)* to be ashamed.

apenas *adv (casi no)* hardly, scarcely; **a. hay nieve** there is hardly any snow; **a. llegó, sonó el teléfono** he hardly had arrived when the phone rang.

apéndice *m* appendix.

apendicitis *f* appendicitis.

aperitivo *m (bebida)* apéritif; *(comida)* appetizer.

apertura *f (comienzo)* opening.

apestar *vi* to stink (**a** of).

apetecer [33] *vi* **¿qué te apetece para cenar?** what would you like for supper?; **¿te apetece ir al cine?** do

you want to go to the movie theater?
apetito m appetite; **tengo mucho apetito** I'm really hungry.
apetitoso, -a adj appetizing, tempting; (comida) delicious, tasty.
apiadarse vr to take pity (**de** on).
apilar vt, **apilarse** vr to pile up.
apiñarse vr to crowd together.
apio m celery.
apisonadora f steamroller.
aplacar [44] vt, **aplacarse** vr to calm down.
aplanar vt to level.
aplastar vt to squash.
aplaudir vt to applaud.
aplauso m applause.
aplazamiento m postponement.
aplazar [40] vt to postpone.
aplicado, -a adj hard-working.
aplicar [44] **1** vt to apply. **2 aplicarse** vr (esforzarse) to apply oneself; (usar) to apply.
aplique m wall lamp.
aplomo m aplomb.
apocado, -a adj shy, timid.
apoderado, -a mf representative.
apoderarse vr **a. de** to take possession of.
apodo m nickname.
apogeo m **estar en pleno a.** (fama etc) to be at its height.
apoplejía f apoplexy.
aporrear vt to beat; (puerta) to bang.
aportar vt to contribute.
aposento m (cuarto) room.
aposta adv on purpose.
apostar [2] vti, **apostarse** vr to bet (**por** on).
apoyacabezas m headrest.
apoyar 1 vt to lean; (causa) to support. **2 apoyarse** vr **apoyarse en** to lean on; (basarse) to be based on.
apoyo m support.
apreciar [43] **1** vt to appreciate; (percibir) to see. **2 apreciarse** vr (notarse) to be noticeable.
aprecio m regard; **tener a. a algn** to be fond of sb.
aprender vt to learn.

aprendiz, -a mf apprentice.
aprensivo, -a 1 adj apprehensive. **2** mf apprehensive person.
apresar vt to capture.
apresurar 1 vt (paso etc) to speed up. **2 apresurarse** vr to hurry up.
apretado, -a adj (ropa, cordón) tight; **íbamos todos apretados en el coche** we were all squashed together in the car.
apretar [1] **1** vt (botón) to press; (nudo, tornillo) to tighten; **me aprietan las botas** these boots are too tight for me. **2 apretarse** vr to squeeze together.
apretón m squeeze; **a. de manos** handshake.
apretujar 1 vt to squeeze, to crush. **2 apretujarse** vr to squeeze together, to cram together.
aprieto m tight spot; **poner a algn en un a.** to put sb in an awkward position.
aprisa adv quickly.
aprisionar vt to trap.
aprobación f approval.
aprobado m (nota) pass.
aprobar [2] vt (autorizar) to approve; (estar de acuerdo con) to approve of; (examen) to pass; (ley) to pass.
apropiado, -a adj suitable.
apropiarse [43] vr **a. de** to appropriate.
aprovechado, -a adj (egoísta) self-seeking; (espacio) well-planned; **bien a.** put to good use; **mal a.** (recurso, tiempo) wasted.
aprovechamiento m use.
aprovechar 1 vt to make good use of; (recursos etc) to take advantage of. **2** vi **¡que aproveche!** enjoy your meal! **3 aprovecharse** vr **aprovecharse de algo/algn** to take advantage of sth/sb.
aproximadamente adv approximately.
aproximado, -a adj approximate.
aproximar 1 vt to bring nearer. **2 aproximarse** vr to approach (**a** -).

aptitud f aptitude; **prueba de a.** aptitude test.

apto, -a adj (apropiado) suitable; (capacitado) capable; (examen) passed.

apuesta f bet.

apuesto, -a adj handsome.

apuntador, -a mf (en el teatro) prompter.

apuntalar vt to prop up.

apuntar 1 vt (con arma) to aim; (anotar) to note; (indicar) to suggest. **2 apuntarse** vr (en una lista) to put one's name down; fam to take part (a in).

apuntes mpl notes; **tomar apuntes** to take notes.

apuñalar vt to stab.

apurar 1 vt (terminar) to finish off; (preocupar) to worry. **2 apurarse** vr (preocuparse) to worry; (darse prisa) to hurry.

apuro m (situación difícil) tight spot; (escasez de dinero) hardship; (vergüenza) embarrassment; **pasar apuros** to be hard up; **¡qué a.!** how embarrassing!

aquel, -ella adj dem that; **a. niño** that boy; **aquellos, -as** those; **aquellas niñas** those girls.

aquél, -élla pron dem mf that one; (el anterior) the former; **todo a. que** anyone who; **aquéllos, -as** those; (los anteriores) the former.

aquella adj dem f ver **aquel**.

aquélla pron dem f ver **aquél**.

aquello pron dem neutro that, it.

aquellos, -as adj dem pl ver **aquel**.

aquéllos, -as pron dem mfpl ver **aquél**.

aquí adv (lugar) here; **a. arriba/fuera** up/out here; **a. mismo** right here; **de a. para allá** up and down, to and fro; **hasta a.** this far; **por a., por favor** this way please; **está por a.** it's around here somewhere; (tiempo) **de a. en adelante** from now on.

árabe 1 adj & mf Arab. **2** m (idioma) Arabic.

arado m plow.

aragonés, -esa adj & mf Aragonese.

arancel m customs duty.

arandela f washer.

araña f spider.

arañar vt to scratch.

arañazo m scratch.

arar vti to plow.

arbitrario, -a adj arbitrary.

árbitro, -a mf referee; (de tenis) umpire; (mediador) arbitrator.

árbol m tree; **á. genealógico** family tree.

arbusto m bush.

arcada f (de puente) arch; (náusea) retching.

arcén m verge; (de autopista) hard shoulder.

archipiélago m archipelago.

archivador m filing cabinet.

archivar vt (documento etc) to file (away); (caso, asunto) to shelve.

archivo m file; (archivador) filing cabinet; **archivos** archives; **a. adjunto** (en email) attachment.

arcilla f clay.

arco m (de edificio etc) arch; (de violín, para flechas) bow; **a. iris** rainbow.

arder vi to burn.

ardiente adj (encendido) burning; fig (fervoroso) eager; **capilla a.** chapel of rest.

ardilla f squirrel.

ardor m fervor; **a. de estómago** heartburn.

área f area; (medida) are (100 square meters).

arena f sand; (en plaza de toros) bullring; **playa de a.** sandy beach.

arenisca f sandstone.

arenque m herring.

arete m Andes, Méx earring.

argelino, -a adj & mf Algerian.

argentino, -a adj & mf Argentinian, Argentine.

argolla f (aro) (large) ring; Andes, Méx (alianza) wedding ring.

argot m (popular) slang; (técnico) jargon.

argüir [62] *vt* to argue.

argumentar *vt* to argue.

argumento *m (trama)* plot; *(razonamiento)* argument.

árido, -a *adj* arid.

arisco, -a *adj (persona)* unfriendly; *(áspero)* gruff; *(animal)* unfriendly.

aristócrata *mf* aristocrat.

aritmética *f* arithmetic.

arma *f* weapon; **a. de fuego** firearm; **a. nuclear** nuclear weapon.

armada *f* navy.

armado, -a *adj* armed; **ir a.** to be armed; **lucha armada** armed struggle.

armador, -a *mf* shipowner.

armadura *f (armazón)* frame.

armamento *m (armas)* armaments; **a. nuclear** nuclear weapons.

armar 1 *vt (tropa, soldado)* to arm; *(montar)* to assemble. **2 armarse** *vr* to arm oneself; **armarse de paciencia** to summon up one's patience; **armarse de valor** to pluck up courage.

armario *m (para ropa)* wardrobe; *(de cocina)* cupboard; **a. empotrado** built-in wardrobe/cupboard.

armazón *m* frame; *(de madera)* timberwork.

armisticio *m* armistice.

armonioso, -a *adj* harmonious.

aro *m* hoop; *(servilletero)* napkin ring.

aroma *m* aroma; *(de vino)* bouquet.

arpa** *f* harp.

arpón *m* harpoon.

arqueología *f* archaeology.

arquitectura *f* architecture.

arrabales *mpl* slums.

arraigado, -a *adj* deeply rooted.

arrancar [44] **1** *vt (planta)* to uproot; *(diente, pelo)* to pull out; *(coche, motor)* to start; **a. de raíz** to uproot. **2** *vi (coche, motor)* to start; *(empezar)* to begin.

arrasar *vt* to devastate.

arrastrar 1 *vt* to drag (along); **lo arrastró la corriente** he was swept away by the current. **2 arrastrarse** *vr* to drag oneself.

arrebatar 1 *vt (coger)* to seize. **2**

arrebatarse *vr (enfurecerse)* to become furious; *(exaltarse)* to get carried away.

arrebato *m* outburst.

arreciar [43] *vi (viento, tormenta)* to get worse.

arrecife *m* reef.

arreglado, -a *adj (reparado)* repaired; *(solucionado)* settled; *(habitación)* tidy; *(persona)* smart.

arreglar 1 *vt* to arrange; *(problema)* to sort out; *(habitación)* to tidy; *(papeles)* to put in order; *(reparar)* to repair. **2 arreglarse** *vr (vestirse)* to get ready; *fam* **arreglárselas** to manage.

arreglo *m* arrangement; *(acuerdo)* compromise; *(reparación)* repair; **no tiene a.** it is beyond repair; **con a.** in accordance with.

arremangarse *vr* to roll one's sleeves/trousers up.

arrendar [1] *vt (piso)* to rent; *(dar en arriendo)* to lease; *(tomar en arriendo)* to take on a lease.

arrepentido, -a *adj* regretful.

arrepentirse [5] *vr* **a. de** to regret; *(en confesión)* to repent.

arrestar *vt* to arrest; *(encarcelar)* to put in prison.

arriba 1 *adv* up; *(encima)* on the top; *(en casa)* upstairs; **ahí a.** up there; **de a. abajo** from top to bottom; **mirar a algn de a. abajo** to look sb up and down; **desde a.** from above; **hacia a.** upwards; **más a.** further up; **la parte de a.** the top (part); **vive a.** he lives upstairs; **véase más a.** see above. **2** *interj* up you go!; **¡a. la República!** long live the Republic!; **¡a. las manos!** hands up! **3** *prep Am* **a. (de)** on top of.

arribeño, -a *Am* **1** *adj* highland. **2** *mf* highlander.

arriendo *m* lease.

arriesgado, -a *adj (peligroso)* risky; *(persona)* daring.

arriesgar [42] *vt*, **arriesgarse** *vr* to risk.

arrimar 1 vt to move closer; fam **a. el hombro** to lend a hand. **2 arrimarse** vr to move nearer.

arrinconar vt (poner en un rincón) to put in a corner; (acorralar) to corner.

arrodillarse vr to kneel down.

arrogante adj arrogant.

arrojar 1 vt (tirar) to throw. **2 arrojarse** vr to throw oneself.

arrollador, -a adj overwhelming; (éxito) resounding; (personalidad) captivating.

arrollar 1 vt (atropellar) to run over, to knock down. **2** vi to win easily.

arropar 1 vt to wrap up; (en cama) to tuck in. **2 arroparse** vr to wrap oneself up.

arroyo m stream.

arroz m rice; **a. con leche** rice pudding.

arruga f (en piel) wrinkle; (en ropa) crease.

arrugar [42] **1** vt (piel) to wrinkle; (ropa) to crease; (papel) to crumple (up). **2 arrugarse** vr (piel) to wrinkle; (ropa) to crease.

arruinar 1 vt to ruin. **2 arruinarse** vr to be ruined.

arsenal m arsenal.

arte m o f art; (habilidad) skill; **bellas artes** fine arts.

artefacto m device.

arteria f artery.

artesanal adj handmade.

artesanía f craftsmanship; (objetos) crafts pl.

ártico, -a 1 adj arctic; **el océano a.** the Arctic Ocean. **2** m **el A.** the Arctic.

articulación f (de huesos) joint.

artículo m article.

artificial adj artificial; (sintético) man-made, synthetic.

artillería f artillery.

artista mf artist; **a. de cine** film star.

artritis f arthritis.

arveja f Am pea.

as m ace.

asa** f handle.

asado, -a 1 adj roast; **pollo a.** roast chicken. **2** m roast.

asaltar vt to assault, to attack; (banco) to rob; fig to assail.

asamblea f meeting; **a. general** general meeting.

asar 1 vt to roast. **2 asarse** vr fig to be roasting.

ascender [3] **1** vt (en un cargo) to promote. **2** vi move upward; (temperatura etc) to rise; **a. de categoría** to be promoted; **la factura asciende a ...** the bill adds up to ....

ascenso m promotion; (subida) rise.

ascensor m elevator.

asco m disgust; **me da a.** it makes me (feel) sick; **¡qué a.!** how disgusting!

ascua** f live coal, ember.

aseado, -a adj tidy, neat.

asear 1 vt to tidy up. **2 asearse** vr to wash.

asedio m siege.

asegurador, -a 1 adj insurance. **2** mf insurer.

asegurar 1 vt to insure; (garantizar) to assure; (cuerda) to fasten. **2 asegurarse** vr to insure oneself; **asegurarse de que ...** to make sure that ....

asemejarse vr **a. a** to look like.

asentamiento m settlement.

asentir [5] vi to agree; **a. con la cabeza** to nod.

aseo m (limpieza) tidiness; (cuarto de baño) toilet.

asequible adj affordable; (alcanzable) attainable.

aserrín m sawdust.

asesinar vt to murder; (rey, ministro) to assassinate.

asesinato m murder; (de rey, ministro) assassination.

asesino, -a 1 adj murderous. **2** mf (hombre) murderer; (mujer) murderess; (de político) assassin.

asesor, -a 1 mf advisor; **a. fiscal** tax advisor. **2** adj advisory.

asesorar vt to advise.

asesoría f consultancy.

asfalto m asphalt.

asfixiar [43] *vt*, **asfixiarse** *vr* to asphyxiate.

así 1 *adv (de esta manera)* like this o that, this way; **ponlo a.** put it this way; **a. de grande/alto** this big/tall; **algo a.** something like this o that; **¿no es a.?** isn't that so o right?; *Am* **a. no más** o **nomás** just like that; **a. las seis** o **a.** around six o'clock; **a. como** as well as; **aun a.** and despite that. **2** *conj* **a. pues** ... so ...; **a. que** ... so ....

asiático, -a *adj & mf* Asian.

asiduo, -a 1 *adj* assiduous. **2** *mf* regular customer.

asiento *m* seat; **a. trasero/delantero** back/front seat; **tome a.** take a seat.

asignar *vt* to allocate; *(nombrar)* to appoint.

asignatura *f* subject.

asilo *m* asylum; **a. de ancianos** old people's home.

asimismo *adv* also, as well.

asir [46] *vt* to grasp, to seize.

asistencia *f (presencia)* attendance; *(público)* audience; **falta de a.** absence; **a. médica/técnica** medical/technical assistance.

asistenta *f* cleaning lady.

asistente 1 *adj* **el público a.** the audience; *(en estadio)* the spectators *pl*. **2** *mf (ayudante)* assistant; **a. personal** *(computadora)* personal digital assistant; **a. social** social worker; **los asistentes** the audience; *(en estadio)* the spectators.

asistir 1 *vt* to assist. **2** *vi* to attend (**a -**).

asma *f* asthma.

asno *m* donkey.

asociación *f* association.

asociar [43] **1** *vt* to associate. **2** **asociarse** *vr* to be associated.

asomar 1 *vt* to stick out; **asomó la cabeza por la ventana** he put his head out the window. **2** *vi* to appear. **3 asomarse** *vr* to lean out; **asomarse a la ventana** to lean out of the window.

asombrar 1 *vt* to astonish. **2 asombrarse** *vr* to be astonished; **asombrarse de algo** to be amazed at sth.

asombro *m* astonishment.

asombroso, -a *adj* astonishing.

asorocharse *vr Andes* to suffer from altitude sickness.

aspa *f (de molino)* arm; *(de ventilador)* blade; *(cruz)* cross.

aspecto *m* look; *(de un asunto)* aspect.

áspero, -a *adj* rough; *(carácter)* surly.

aspersor *m* sprinkler.

aspiradora *f* vacuum cleaner.

aspirante *mf* candidate.

aspirar *vt (respirar)* to inhale.

aspirina *f* aspirin.

asquerosidad *f* filthy o revolting thing; **¡que a.!** how revolting!

asqueroso, -a 1 *adj (sucio)* filthy; *(desagradable)* disgusting. **2** *mf* filthy o revolting person.

asterisco *m* asterisk.

astilla *f* splinter.

astillero *m* shipyard.

astringente *adj & m* astringent.

astro *m* star.

astrología *f* astrology.

astronauta *mf* astronaut.

astronave *f* spaceship.

astronomía *f* astronomy.

asturiano, -a *adj & mf* Asturian.

astuto, -a *adj* astute.

asumir *vt* to assume.

asunto *m* subject; **no es a. tuyo** it's none of your business.

asustar 1 *vt* to frighten. **2 asustarse** *vr* to be frightened.

atacar [44] *vt* to attack.

atajar *vi* to take a shortcut (**por** across o through).

atajo *m* shortcut.

atañer *vi (tocar)* to concern.

ataque *m* attack; *(nervios, tos)* fit; **a. cardíaco** o **al corazón** heart attack.

atar 1 *vt (ligar)* to tie; **a. cabos** to put two and two together; *fam* **loco de a.** as mad as a hatter. **2 atarse** *vr fig* to get tied up; **átate los zapatos** do your shoes up.

atardecer [33] **1** v impers to get dark. **2** m evening.

atareado, -a adj busy.

atascar [44] **1** vt (bloquear) to block. **2 atascarse** vr (bloquearse) to become blocked.

atasco m traffic jam.

ataúd m coffin.

atemorizar [40] vt to frighten.

atención 1 f attention; **llamar la a.** to attract attention; **prestar/poner a.** to pay attention (**a** to). **2** interj attention!; (cuidado) watch out!

atender [3] **1** vt to attend to. **2** vi (alumno) to pay attention (**a** to).

atenerse [24] vr **a. a** (reglas) to abide by; **a. a las consecuencias** to bear the consequences; **me atengo a sus palabras** I'm going by what he said; **no saber a qué a.** not to know what to expect.

atentado m attack.

atentamente adv (con atención) attentively; **le saluda a.** (en carta) yours sincerely.

atentar vi **a. a** o **contra** to commit a crime against; **a. contra la vida de algn** to make an attempt on sb's life.

atento, -a adj attentive; (amable) thoughtful; **estar a.** a to be aware of.

ateo, -a 1 adj atheistic. **2** mf atheist.

aterrador, -a adj terrifying.

aterrar 1 vt to terrify. **2 aterrarse** vr to be terrified.

aterrizaje m landing.

aterrizar [40] vi to land.

aterrorizar [40] **1** vt to terrify. **2 aterrorizarse** vr to be terrified.

ático m attic; (vivienda) attic apartment.

atingencia f Am connection.

atizar [40] vt (fuego) to poke.

atlas m inv atlas.

atleta mf athlete.

atletismo m athletics sing.

atmósfera f atmosphere.

atolondrado, -a adj stunned; (atontado) stupid.

atómico, -a adj atomic.

átomo m atom.

atónito, -a adj astonished.

atontado, -a adj (tonto) silly; (aturdido) bewildered.

atorarse vr to get stuck.

atormentar 1 vt to torment. **2 atormentarse** vr to torment oneself.

atornillar vt to screw on.

atracar [44] **1** vt to hold up; (persona) to rob. **2** vi (barco) to come alongside. **3 atracarse** vr (de comida) to stuff oneself (**de** with).

atracción f attraction; **parque de atracciones** amusement park.

atraco m hold-up; **a. a mano armada** armed robbery.

atracón m fam binge.

atractivo, -a 1 adj attractive. **2** m attraction.

atraer [25] vt to attract.

atragantarse vr to choke (**con** on).

atraigo indic pres de **atraer**.

atraje pt indef de **atraer**.

atrancar [44] **1** vt (puerta) to bolt. **2 atrancarse** vr to get stuck.

atrapar vt to catch.

atrás adv (lugar) at the back, behind; hacia/para **a.** backwards; **puerta de a.** back o rear door; **echarse a.** to back out; **venir de muy a.** to go back a long time.

atrasado, -a adj late; (pago) overdue; (reloj) slow; (país) backward.

atrasar 1 vt to put back. **2** vi (reloj) to be slow. **3 atrasarse** vr to lag behind; (tren) to be late.

atraso m delay; (de país) backwardness; **atrasos** (en pago) arrears.

atravesado, -a adj (cruzado) lying crosswise; (persona) difficult; **lo tengo a.** I can't stand him.

atravesar [1] **1** vt (cruzar) to cross; (traspasar) to go through; (poner a través) to put across. **2 atravesarse** vr to get in the way.

atreverse *vr* to dare; **a. a hacer algo** to dare to do sth.

atrevido, -a *adj (osado)* daring; *(insolente)* insolent; *(ropa etc)* daring.

atributo *m* attribute.

atrochar *vi* to take a short cut.

atropellar *vt* to knock down.

atroz *adj (bárbaro)* atrocious; *fam (hambre, frío)* tremendous.

ATS *mf abr de* **ayudante técnico sanitario** nurse.

atuendo *m* attire.

atún *m* tuna.

aturdido, -a *adj* stunned.

aturdir *vt (con un golpe)* to stun; *(confundir)* to bewilder.

audaz *adj* audacious.

audición *f* hearing; *(en el teatro)* audition.

audiencia *f (público)* audience; *(entrevista)* audience; *(tribunal)* high court.

audiovisual *adj* audio-visual.

auditor, -a *mf* auditor.

auge *m* peak; *(económico)* boom; **estar en a.** to be booming.

aula** *f (en colegio)* classroom; *(en universidad)* lecture room.

aulaga *f* gorse.

aullido *m* howl.

aumentar 1 *vt* to increase; *(precios)* to put up; *(producción)* to step up; *(imagen)* to magnify. **2** *vi (precios)* to go up; *(valor)* to appreciate.

aumento *m* increase; *(de imagen)* magnification; **ir en a.** to be on the increase.

aun *adv* even; **a. así** even so.

aún *adv* still; *(en negativas)* yet; **a. está aquí** he's still here; **ella no ha venido a.** she hasn't come yet; **a. más** even more.

aunque *conj* although, though; *(enfático)* even if, even though.

aureola *f* halo.

auricular *m (del teléfono)* receiver; **auriculares** headphones.

aurora *f* dawn.

auscultar *vt* to sound (with a stethoscope).

ausencia *f* absence.

ausentarse *vr (irse)* to go away.

ausente 1 *adj* absent. **2** *mf* absentee.

austero, -a *adj* austere.

australiano, -a *adj & mf* Australian.

austríaco, -a *adj & mf* Austrian.

auténtico, -a *adj* authentic.

autista 1 *adj* autistic. **2** *mf* autistic person.

auto¹ *m RP* car.

auto² *m (sentencia)* writ; **autos** *(pleito)* documents.

autoadhesivo, -a *adj* self-adhesive.

autobiografía *f* autobiography.

autobiográfico, -a *adj* autobiographical.

autobús *m* bus.

autocar *m* coach.

autóctono, -a *adj* indigenous.

autodefensa *f* self-defense.

autoescuela *f* driving school.

autogobierno *m* self-government.

autógrafo *m* autograph.

automático, -a *adj* automatic.

automotor *m* diesel train.

automóvil *m* car.

automovilista *mf* motorist.

automovilístico, -a *adj* car.

autonomía *f* autonomy; *(región)* autonomous region.

autonómico, -a *adj* autonomous.

autopista *f* highway; **autopista(s) de la información** information superhighway.

autopsia *f* autopsy.

autor, -a *mf* author; *(de crimen)* perpetrator.

autoridad *f* authority.

autoritario, -a *adj* authoritarian.

autorizar [40] *vt* to authorize.

autoservicio *m* self-service; *(tienda)* supermarket.

autostop *m* hitch-hiking; **hacer a.** to hitch-hike.

autostopista *mf* hitch-hiker.

autosuficiencia *f* self-sufficiency.

auxiliar [14] **1** *adj & mf* auxiliary. **2** *vt* to assist.

auxilio *m* assistance; **primeros auxilios** first aid *sing.*

avalancha *f* avalanche.

avalar *vt* to guarantee, to endorse.

avance *m* advance.

avanzado, -a *adj* advanced; **de avanzada edad** advanced in years.

avanzar [40] *vt/i* to advance.

avaricia *f* avarice.

avaricioso, -a *adj* greedy.

avaro, -a 1 *adj* miserly. **2** *mf* miser.

avasallar *vt* to subdue.

ave** *f* bird.

avellana *f* hazelnut.

avellano *m* hazelnut tree.

avena *f* oats *pl.*

avenida *f* avenue.

avenido, -a *adj* **bien/mal avenidos** on good/bad terms.

aventajar *vt* (*ir por delante de*) to be ahead, be in front (**a** of); (*superar*) to outdo.

aventar [1] **1** *vt* *Andes, CAm, Méx* (*tirar*) to throw; *CAm, Méx, Perú* (*empujar*) to push, to shove. **2 aventarse** *vr* *Méx* (*tirarse*) to throw oneself; (*atreverse*) **aventarse a hacer algo** to dare to do sthg.

aventura *f* adventure; (*amorosa*) (love) affair.

aventurarse *vr* to venture.

aventurero, -a 1 *adj* adventurous. **2** *mf* adventurous person.

avergonzado, -a *adj* ashamed.

avergonzar [63] **1** *vt* to shame. **2 avergonzarse** *vr* to be ashamed (**de** of).

avería *f* breakdown.

averiar [29] **1** *vt* to break. **2 averiarse** *vr* (*estropearse*) to malfunction; (*coche*) to break down.

averiguar [45] *vt* to find out.

aversión *f* aversion.

avestruz *m* ostrich.

aviación *f* aviation; (*militar*) air force; **accidente de a.** plane crash.

aviador, -ra *mf* aviator; (*piloto militar*) air force pilot.

ávido, -a *adj* avid; **a. de** eager for.

avión *m* airplane; **por a.** (*en carta*) airmail.

avioneta *f* light aircraft.

avisar *vt* (*informar*) to inform; (*advertir*) to warn; (*llamar*) to call for.

aviso *m* notice; (*advertencia*) warning; (*nota*) note; *Am* (*anuncio*) advertisement; **sin previo a.** without notice.

avispa *f* wasp.

avivar *vt* (*fuego*) to stoke (up); (*paso*) to quicken.

axila *f* armpit.

ay *interj* (*dolor*) ouch!

ayer *adv* yesterday; **a. por la mañana/por la tarde** yesterday morning/ afternoon; **a. por la noche** last night; **antes de a.** the day before yesterday.

ayuda *f* help.

ayudante *mf* assistant.

ayudar 1 *vt* to help. **2 ayudarse** *vr* (*unos a otros*) to help; **ayudarse de** to make use of.

ayunas en a. without having eaten breakfast.

ayuntamiento *m* (*institución*) town council; (*edificio*) town hall.

azafata *f* (*de avión*) flight attendant; (*de congresos*) stewardess; (*de concurso*) hostess.

azafrán *m* saffron.

azahar *m* (*del naranjo*) orange blossom.

azar *m* chance; **al a.** at random.

azorado, -a *adj* embarrassed.

azorar 1 *vt* to embarrass. **2 azorarse** *vr* to be embarrassed.

azotar *vt* to beat; (*lluvia*) to beat down on; (*con látigo*) to whip.

azotea *f* flat roof.

azteca *adj & mf* Aztec.

azúcar *m o f* sugar; **a. blanco** refined sugar; **a. moreno** brown sugar.

azucarado, -a *adj* sweetened.

azucarero, -a 1 *m* sugar bowl. **2** *adj* sugar.

azucena *f* lily.

azul *adj & m* blue; **a. celeste** sky blue; **a. marino** navy blue.

azulejo *m* (glazed) tile.

B

baba f dribble.

babero m bib.

babor m port.

babosa f slug.

baboso, -a adj fam slimy; Am (tonto) stupid.

babucha f slipper.

baca f roof rack.

bacalao m cod.

bache m (en carretera) pot hole; (mal momento) bad patch.

bachillerato m high school diploma.

bacon m bacon.

bacteriológico, -a adj bacteriological; **guerra bacteriológica** germ warfare.

baden m (en carretera) bump.

bádminton m badminton.

bafle m loudspeaker.

bahía f bay.

bailar vti to dance.

bailarín, -ina mf dancer.

baile m (danza) dance; (formal) ball.

baja f (disminución) drop; (en batalla) loss; **dar de b. a algn** (despedir) to lay sb off; **darse de b.** (por enfermedad) to take sick leave.

bajada f (descenso) descent; (señal) way down; (cuesta) slope.

bajar 1 vt to come/go down; (descender) to get down; (volumen) to turn down; (voz, telón) to lower; (precios etc) to cut; (cabeza) to lower; (de Internet) to download; **b. la escalera** to come/go downstairs. **2** vi to come/go down; (apearse) to get off; (de un coche) to get out (**de** of); (disminuir) to fall. **3 bajarse** vr to come/go down; (apearse) to get off; (de un coche) to get out (**de** of).

bajinis: por lo bajinis adv fam on the sly.

bajío m Am lowland.

bajo, -a 1 adj low; (persona) short; (sonido) faint; **en voz baja** in a low voice; **planta baja** ground floor; **de baja calidad** of poor quality. **2** adv low; **hablar b.** to speak quietly. **3** prep (lugar) under, underneath; **b. tierra** underground; **b. cero** below zero; **b. juramento** under oath; **b. fianza** on bail.

bajón m (bajada) sharp fall.

bala f bullet; **como una b.** like a shot.

balance m balance; (declaración) balance sheet.

balanza f scales pl; **b. comercial** balance of trade; **b. de pagos** balance of payments.

balazo m (disparo) shot; (herida) bullet wound; **matar a algn de un b.** to shoot sb dead.

balbucear, balbucir vi (adulto) to stutter, stammer; (niño) to babble.

balcón m balcony.

balde m **de b.** free; **en b.** in vain.

baldosa f (ceramic) floor tile.

balear vt Am to shoot.

baleo m Am shootout.

baliza f (boya) buoy; (en aviación) beacon.

ballena f whale.

ballet m ballet.

balneario m health resort.

balón m ball.

baloncesto m basketball.

balonmano m handball.

balonvolea m volleyball.

balsa f raft.

bálsamo m balm.

balsero, -a mf (de Cuba) = refugee fleeing Cuba on a raft.

bambú m (pl bambúes) bamboo.

banana f banana.

banano m (árbol) banana tree; Col (fruto) banana.

banca f (asiento) bench; **la b.** (the) banks; **b. electrónica** electronic banking; **b. por Internet** e-banking.

bancarrota f bankruptcy.

banco m bank; (asiento) bench.

banda f (de música) band; (cinta)

sash; **b. ancha** broadband; **b. sonora** sound track; **(línea de) b.** touchline; **saque de b.** throw-in.
bandada f flock.
bandeja f tray.
bandera f flag.
bandido m bandit.
bando m side.
bandolero m bandit.
banquero, -a mf banker.
banqueta f stool.
banquete m banquet; **b. de bodas** wedding reception.
bañador m (de mujer) swimming suit; (de hombre) swimming trunks pl.
bañar 1 vt to bath. **2 bañarse** vr (en baño) to have a bath; (en mar, piscina) to go for a swim; Am (ducharse) to have a shower.
bañera f bath.
bañista mf swimmer.
baño m bath; (de chocolate etc) coating; (cuarto de baño) bathroom; (lavabo) toilet; **tomar un b.** to take a bath.
bar m bar, pub.
baraja f pack, deck.
barajar vt (cartas) to shuffle; fig (nombres, cifras) to juggle with.
baranda, barandilla f (de escalera) banister; (de balcón) handrail.
baratija f knick-knack.
barato, -a 1 adj cheap. **2** adv cheaply.
barba f (pelo) beard.
barbacoa f barbecue.
barbaridad f atrocity; (disparate) piece of nonsense; **una b.** a lot.
bárbaro, -a 1 adj (germano) barbarian; (cruel) barbaric, barbarous; fam (enorme) massive; RP fam (estupendo) tremendous, terrific. **2** mf barbarian.
barbería f barber's (shop).
barbero m barber.
barbilla f chin.
barbo m barbel.
barbudo, -a adj with a heavy beard.
barca f small boat.
barcaza f lighter.

barco m ship; **b. de vapor** steamer.
barlovento m windward.
barman m barman.
barniz m (en madera) varnish; (en cerámica) glaze.
barómetro m barometer.
barquillo m wafer.
barra f bar; **b. de pan** French loaf; **b. de labios** lipstick; Andes, RP fam (grupo de amigos) gang, group of friends; **b. brava** = group of violent soccer fans.
barraca f (caseta) hut; (en Valencia y Murcia) thatched farmhouse.
barranco m (despeñadero) cliff; (torrentera) ravine.
barrendero, -a mf (street) sweeper.
barreno m (taladro) large drill; (explosivo) charge.
barreño m tub.
barrer vt to sweep.
barrera f barrier.
barriada f Am (de chabolas) shanty town.
barricada f barricade.
barriga f belly, fam tummy.
barril m barrel; **cerveza de b.** draft beer.
barrio m district; **del b.** local; **b. chino** red-light district; **barrios bajos** slums.
barro m (lodo) mud; (arcilla) clay; **objetos de b.** earthenware sing.
bártulos mpl fam bits and pieces.
barullo m (alboroto) row; (confusión) confusion.
basar 1 vt to base (**en** on). **2 basarse** vr (teoría, película) to be based (**en** on).
báscula f scales pl.
base f base; (de argumento, teoría) basis; (de partido) grass roots; **sueldo b.** minimum wage; **b. de datos** database; **a b. de estudiar** by studying; **a b. de productos naturales** using natural products.
básico, -a adj basic.
básquet m basketball.
bastante 1 adj (suficiente) enough; **b. tiempo/comida** enough time/ food; (abundante) quite a lot of; **hace**

b. calor/frío it's quite hot/cold; **bastantes amigos** quite a lot of friends. **2** *adv (suficiente)* enough; *(considerablemente)* fairly, quite; **con esto hay b.** that is enough; **no soy lo b. rico (como) para …** I am not rich enough to …; **me gusta b.** I quite like it; **vamos b. al cine** we go to the cinema quite often.

bastar *vi* to be sufficient o enough; **basta con tres** three will be enough; **¡basta (ya)!** that's enough!

bastardo, -a *adj & mf* bastard.

basto, -a *adj (cosa)* rough; *(persona)* coarse.

bastón *m* stick.

bastos *mpl (in Spanish pack of cards)* ≃ clubs.

basura *f* trash.

basurero *m (persona)* garbage collector; *(lugar)* garbage dump.

bata *f (para casa)* dressing gown; *(de médico etc)* white coat.

batalla *f* battle.

batata *f* sweet potato.

bate *m (de béisbol)* bat.

batería 1 *f* battery; *(percusión)* drums *pl*; **b. de cocina** set of pans. **2** *mf* drummer.

batida *f (de la policía)* raid.

batido, -a 1 *adj (huevo, crema)* whipped. **2** *m* milk shake.

batidora *f* mixer.

batir *vt* to beat; *(huevo)* to beat; *(nata)* to whip; *(récord)* to break.

baudio *m* baud.

baúl *m (caja)* trunk; *Am (de vehículo)* trunk.

bautizar [40] *vt* to baptize, christen.

bautizo *m* baptism.

baya *f* berry.

bayeta *f* floorcloth.

bazar *m* bazaar.

bazo *m* spleen.

bazofia *f fam* garbage.

be *f (letra)* b; *Am* **be baja** o **corta** v *(to distinguish from "b")*; *Am* **be alta** o **grande** o **larga** b *(to distinguish from "v")*.

beato, -a *adj peyorativo* sanctimonious.

bebé *m* baby.

beber *vti* to drink.

bebida *f* drink.

bebido, -a *adj* drunk.

beca *f* grant.

becario, -a *mf* grant holder; *(en oficina)* intern.

becerro *m* calf.

bechamel *f* bechamel; **salsa b.** white sauce.

bedel *m* janitor.

beige *adj & m inv* beige.

béisbol *m* baseball.

belga *adj & mf* Belgian.

bélico, -a *adj* warlike; *(preparativos etc)* war.

belleza *f* beauty.

bello, -a *adj* beautiful.

bellota *f* acorn.

bencina *f Chile* gas.

bencinera *f Chile* gas station.

bendición *f* blessing.

bendito, -a *adj* blessed.

beneficencia *f* charity.

beneficiar [43] **1** *vt* to benefit. **2 beneficiarse** *vr* **beneficiarse de** o **con algo** to profit from sth.

beneficio *m* profit; *(bien)* benefit; **en b. propio** in one's own interest; **un concierto a b. de …** a concert in aid of ….

beneficioso, -a *adj* beneficial.

benevolencia *f* benevolence.

benévolo, -a *adj (persona)* gentle.

benjamín, -ina *mf* youngest child.

berberecho *m (common)* cockle.

berbiquí *m* drill.

berenjena *f* eggplant.

Bermudas 1 *fpl* **las (Islas) B.** Bermuda *sing*. **2** *mpl* o *fpl* **bermudas** *(prenda)* Bermuda shorts.

berrear *vi* to bellow.

berrinche *m fam* tantrum.

berro *m* watercress.

berza *f* cabbage.

besar *vt*, **besarse** *vr* to kiss.

beso *m* kiss.

bestia 1 *f* beast. **2** *mf fam* brute. **3** *adj fig* brutish.

besugo *m (pez)* sea bream.

betún *m (para el calzado)* shoe polish.

biberón *m* baby's bottle.

Biblia *f* Bible.

bibliografía *f* bibliography.

biblioteca *f (edificio)* library; *(estantería)* bookcase.

bicarbonato *m* bicarbonate; **b. sódico** bicarbonate of soda.

bíceps *m inv* biceps.

bicho *m* bug.

bici *f fam* bike.

bicicleta *f* bicycle; **montar en b.** to ride a bicycle.

bidé *m* bidet.

bidón *m* drum.

bien¹ 1 *adv (correctamente)* well; **responder b.** to answer correctly; **hiciste b. en decírmelo** you were right to tell me; **las cosas le van b.** things are going well for him; **¡b.!** good!, great!; **¡muy b.!** excellent!; **¡qué b.!** great!; **vivir b.** to live comfortably; **¡está b.!** *(de acuerdo!)* fine!, all right!; **¡ya está b.!** that's (quite) enough!; **esta falda te está b.** this skirt suits you; **ese libro está muy b.** that book is very good. • *(intensificador)* very; **b. temprano** nice and early; **b. caliente** pretty hot; **más b.** rather. **2** *conj* **o b.** or else; **b. ... o b. ...** either ... or ...; **no b. llegó ...** no sooner had she arrived than ...; **si b.** although.

bien² *m (bondad)* good; **el b. y el mal** good and evil; **por el b. de** for the good of; **lo hace por tu b.** he does it for your sake; **bienes** goods; **bienes inmuebles** real estate; **bienes de consumo** consumer goods.

bienestar *m* well-being.

bienvenida *f* welcome; **dar la b. a algn** to welcome sb.

bienvenido, -a *adj* welcome.

bifurcación *f (de la carretera)* fork.

bigote *m (de persona)* mustache; **bi-** **gotes** *(de animal)* whiskers *pl.*

bilateral *adj* bilateral.

bilingüe *adj* bilingual.

bilis *f* bile.

billar *m (juego)* billiards *sing*; *(mesa)* billiard table; **b. americano** pool; **b. ruso** snooker.

billete *m* ticket; *(de banco)* bill; **b. de ida y vuelta** round-trip ticket; **b. sencillo** *o* **de ida** one-way (ticket); **b. electrónico** *(de avión)* e-ticket; **un b. de mil pesos** a thousand peso note.

billetera *f*, **billetero** *m* wallet.

billón *m* thousand billion.

bingo *m (juego)* bingo; *(sala)* bingo hall.

biografía *f* biography.

biología *f* biology.

biombo *m* (folding) screen.

biopsia *f* biopsy.

bioquímica *f* biochemistry.

biotecnología *f* biotechnology.

bióxido *m* **b. de carbono** carbon dioxide.

biquini *m* bikini.

birria *f fam* garbage.

bisabuela *f* great-grandmother.

bisabuelo *m* great-grandfather; **bisabuelos** great-grandparents.

bisagra *f* hinge.

bisiesto *adj* **año b.** leap year.

bisnieto, -a *mf (niño)* great-grandson; *(niña)* great-granddaughter; **mis bisnietos** my great-grandchildren.

bisonte *m* bison.

bisté, bistec *m* steak.

bisturí *m* scalpel.

bisutería *f* imitation jewelry.

bitácora *f (Internet)* blog.

bizco, -a 1 *adj* cross-eyed. **2** *mf* cross-eyed person.

bizcocho *m* sponge cake.

biznieto, -a *mf* = **bisnieto.**

blanco, -a¹ 1 *adj* white; *(tez)* fair. **2** *mf (hombre)* white man; *(mujer)* white woman; **los blancos** whites.

blanco² *m (color)* white; *(hueco)* blank; *(diana)* target; **pasar la noche**

en b. to have a sleepless night; **me quedé en b.** my mind went blank; **ser el b. de todas las miradas** to be the center of attention.

blancura f whiteness.

blando, -a adj soft.

blanquear vt (encalar) to whitewash.

blasfemar vi to blaspheme (**contra** against).

blindado, -a adj (carro) armoured; (antibalas) bullet-proof; **coche b.** bullet-proof car; **puerta blindada** reinforced door.

bloc m pad; **b. de notas** notepad.

blog m blog.

blogger mf blogger.

bloguear vi to blog.

bloguero, -a mf blogger.

bloque m block; **b. de pisos** block (of apartments).

bloquear vt to block; (sitiar) to blockade.

blusa f blouse.

blusón m loose blouse.

bobada f nonsense; **decir bobadas** to talk nonsense.

bobina f reel.

bobo, -a 1 adj (tonto) stupid, silly; (ingenu) naïve. **2** mf fool.

boca f mouth; **b. abajo** face downward; **b. arriba** face upward; fam **¡cierra la b.!** shut up!; **con la b. abierta** open-mouthed; **se le hizo la b. agua** his mouth watered; **la b. del metro** the entrance to the subway station.

bocacalle f entrance to a street.

bocadillo m sandwich; **un b. de jamón/tortilla** a ham/omelette sandwich.

bocado m bite.

bocanada f (de humo) puff; **una b. de viento** a gust of wind.

bocata m fam sandwich.

bocazas mf inv fam bigmouth.

boceto m (de cuadro etc) sketch; (esquema) outline.

bochinche m fam uproar; **armar un b.** to kick up a row.

bochorno m (tiempo) sultry weather; (calor sofocante) stifling heat; (vergüenza) embarrassment.

bochornoso, -a adj (tiempo) sultry, close, muggy; (calor) stifling; fig (vergonzoso) shameful, embarrassing.

bocina f horn; **tocar la b.** to sound one's horn.

boda f marriage; **bodas de plata** silver wedding sing.

bodega f (en casa) wine cellar; (tienda) wine shop; Am grocery store, grocer's.

body m bodystocking.

bofetada f, **bofetón** m slap on the face; **dar una b./un b. a algn** to slap sb's face.

bohío m Am hut.

boicotear vt to boycott.

boina f beret.

bol m bowl.

bola f ball; (canica) marble; **b. de nieve** snowball; **no dar pie con b.** to be unable to do anything right.

bolera f bowling alley.

boletería f Am (de estadio, estación) ticket office; (de teatro) box office.

boletero, -a mf Am box office attendant.

boletín m bulletin.

boleto m Am ticket; **b. electrónico** (de avión) e-ticket.

boli m biro®.

boliche m (juego) bowling; (bola) jack; (lugar) bowling alley; CSur fam (bar) small bar.

bólido m (coche) racing car.

bolígrafo m ballpoint (pen).

boliviano, -a adj & mf Bolivian.

bollo m (de pan) roll; (abolladura) dent.

bolo m skittle; **bolos** (juego) skittles.

bolsa[1] f bag; **b. de deportes** sports bag; **b. de la compra** shopping bag; **b. de viaje** travel bag.

bolsa[2] f (de valores) Stock Exchange.

bolsillo m (prenda) pocket; **de b.** pocket; **libro de b.** paperback.

bolso m purse.

boludo, -a mf RP fam (estúpido) idiot, twit.

bomba¹ *f* pump; **b. de incendios** fire engine; *Andes, Ven* **b. (de gasolina)** *(surtidor)* gas pump.

bomba² *f (explosivo)* bomb; **b. atómica/de hidrógeno/de neutrones** atom/hydrogen/neutron bomb; **b. de relojería** time bomb; *fam* **pasarlo b.** to have a great time.

bombardear *vt* to bomb.

bombazo *m* bomb blast.

bombero, -a *mf (hombre)* fireman; *(mujer)* firewoman; *(ambos sexos)* firefighter; **cuerpo de bomberos** fire brigade; **parque de bomberos** fire station.

bombilla *f* (light) bulb.

bombillo *m CAm, Carib, Col, Méx* light bulb.

bombín *m* bowler hat.

bombo *m (de percusión)* bass drum; *(de sorteo)* lottery drum; *(de lavadora)* drum.

bombón *m* chocolate.

bombona *f* cylinder.

bonachón, -ona *adj* good-natured.

bonanza *f (tiempo)* fair weather; *(prosperidad)* prosperity.

bondadoso, -a *adj* good-natured.

boniato *m* sweet potato.

bonificación *f* bonus.

bonito, -a¹ *adj* pretty, nice.

bonito² *m* tuna.

bono *m (vale)* voucher; *(título)* bond.

bono-bus *m* bus pass.

boquerón *m* anchovy.

boquete *m* hole.

boquiabierto, -a *adj* open-mouthed; **se quedó b.** he was flabbergasted.

boquilla *f (de cigarro)* tip; *(de pipa)* mouthpiece.

borda *f* gunwale; **arrojar** o **echar por la b.** to throw overboard; **un fuera b.** *(motor)* an outboard motor.

bordado, -a 1 *adj* embroidered. **2** *m* embroidery.

bordar *vt* to embroider.

borde *m (de mesa, camino)* edge; *(de prenda)* hem; *(de vasija)* rim; **al b. del mar** at the seaside.

bordear *vt* to skirt.

bordillo *m* curb.

bordo *m* **a b.** on board; **subir a b.** to go on board.

borrachera *f (embriaguez)* drunkenness; *(curda)* binge; **coger** o **pillar una b.** to get drunk.

borracho, -a 1 *adj (bebido)* drunk; *(bizcocho)* with rum; **estar b.** to be drunk. **2** *mf* drunk.

borrador *m (escrito)* rough copy; *(de pizarra)* duster.

borrar *vt (con goma)* to rub out; *(pizarra)* to clean; *(en pantalla)* to delete.

borrasca *f* area of low pressure.

borrego, -a *mf* yearling lamb; *(persona)* sheep.

borrico *m* ass, donkey; *fam fig* ass, dimwit.

borroso, -a *adj* blurred; **veo b.** I can't see clearly.

bosque *m* wood.

bosquejo *m (de dibujo)* sketch; *(de plan)* draft.

bostezar [40] *vi* to yawn.

bostezo *m* yawn.

bota *f* boot; *(de vino)* wineskin.

botana *f Méx* snack.

botánico, -a *adj* botanic; **jardín b.** botanic gardens *pl*.

botar 1 *vi (saltar)* to jump; *(pelota)* to bounce. **2** *vt (barco)* to launch; *(pelota)* to bounce; *Am (arrojar)* to throw out.

bote¹ *m* jump; *(de pelota)* bounce.

bote² *m (lata)* can, tin; *(para propinas)* jar o box for tips.

bote³ *m (lancha)* boat; **b. salvavidas** lifeboat.

botella *f* bottle.

botellín *m* small bottle.

botijo *m* earthenware pitcher (with spout and handle).

botín *m (de un robo)* loot.

botiquín *m* medicine cabinet; *(portátil)* first aid kit; *(enfermería)* first aid post.

botón *m* button.

botones *m inv (en hotel)* bellboy, bellhop; *(recadero)* errand boy.

boutique *f* boutique.

boxeador *m* boxer.

boxeo *m* boxing.

boya *f (baliza)* buoy; *(corcho)* float.

boy-scout *m* boy scout.

bozal *m* muzzle.

bracear *vi (nadar)* to swim.

bragas *fpl* panties *pl*, knickers *pl*.

braguete *f (de pantalón)* fly, flies *pl*.

braille *m* Braille.

bramido *m* bellowing.

brandy *m* brandy.

brasa *f* ember; **chuletas a la b.** barbecued chops.

brasero *m* brazier.

brasileño, -a, *RP* **brasilero, -a** *adj & mf* Brazilian.

bravo, -a 1 *adj (valiente)* brave; **un toro b.** a fighting bull. **2** *interj* **¡b.!** well done!

braza *f* breast stroke; **nadar a b.** to do the breast stroke.

brazada *f* stroke.

brazalete *m (pulsera)* bracelet; *(insignia)* armband.

brazo *m* arm; **en brazos** in one's arms; **ir del b.** to walk arm in arm; **con los brazos abiertos** with open arms.

brecha *f (en muro)* gap; *(herida)* wound.

brécol *m* broccoli.

breva *f (higo)* early fig; *fam* **¡no caerá esa b.!** no such luck!

breve *adj* brief; **en b., en breves momentos** shortly, soon.

brezo *m* heather.

bribón, -ona 1 *adj* roguish. **2** *mf* rogue.

bricolaje *m* do-it-yourself, DIY.

bridge *m* bridge.

brigada *f* brigade; *(de policías)* squad.

brillante 1 *adj* brilliant. **2** *m* diamond.

brillantina *f* brilliantine.

brillar *vi (resplandecer)* to shine;

(ojos, joyas) to sparkle; *(lentejuelas etc)* to glitter.

brillo *m (resplandor)* shine; *(del sol, de la luna)* brightness; *(de lentejuelas etc)* glittering; *(del cabello, de tela)* sheen; *(de zapatos)* shine; **sacar b. a** to polish.

brincar [44] *vi* to skip.

brindar 1 *vi* to drink a toast; **b. por algn/algo** drink to sb/sth. **2 brindarse** *vr* to volunteer (**a** to).

brindis *m* toast.

brío *m* energy.

brisa *f* breeze; **b. marina** sea breeze.

británico, -a 1 *adj* British; **las Islas Británicas** the British Isles. **2** *mf* Briton; **los británicos** the British.

brocha *f (para pintar)* paintbrush; *(de afeitar)* shaving brush.

broche *m (joya)* brooch; *(de vestido)* fastener.

bróculi *m* broccoli.

broma *f (chiste)* joke; **en b.** as a joke; **¡ni en b.!** not on your life!; **b. pesada** practical joke; **gastar una b.** to play a joke.

bromear *vi* to joke.

bromista 1 *adj* fond of joking o playing jokes. **2** *mf* joker, prankster.

bronca *f (riña)* row; **echar una b. a algn** to bawl sb out.

bronce *m* bronze.

bronceado, -a 1 *adj* (sun)tanned. **2** *m* (sun)tan.

bronceador, -a 1 *adj* **leche bronceadora** suntan lotion. **2** *m* suntan lotion.

broncearse *vr* to get a tan o a suntan.

bronquitis *f inv* bronchitis.

brotar *vi (planta)* to sprout; *(agua)* to gush; *(epidemia)* to break out.

bruces: de bruces *adv* face downwards; **se cayó de b.** he fell flat on his face.

bruja *f* witch.

brújula *f* compass.

bruma *f* mist.

brusco, -a *adj (persona)* brusque; *(repentino)* sudden.

bruto, -a 1 *adj (necio)* stupid; *(grosero)* coarse; *(no neto)* gross; **un diamante en b.** an uncut diamond. **2** *mf* blockhead.

bucear *vi* to swim under water.

bucle *m* curl.

budín *m* pudding.

budista *adj* Buddhist.

buen *adj (delante de un nombre masculino singular)* good; **¡b. viaje!** have a good trip!; *ver* **bueno**.

buenamente *adv* **haz lo que b. puedas** just do what you can; **si b. puedes** if you possibly can.

bueno, -a 1 *adj* good; *(amable) (con* **ser)** good, kind; *(sano) (con* **estar)** well, in good health; **un alumno muy b.** a very good pupil; **lo b.** the good thing; **hoy hace buen tiempo** it's fine today; **un buen número de** a good number of; **una buena cantidad** a considerable amount; **un buen trozo de pastel** a nice o good big piece of cake; **¡en buen lío te has metido!** that's a fine mess you've got yourself into!; **¡buenas!** *(saludos)* hello!; **buenas tardes** *(desde mediodía hasta las cinco)* good afternoon; *(desde las cinco)* good evening; **buenas noches** *(al llegar)* good evening; *(al irse)* good night; **buenos días** good morning; **de buenas a primeras** all at once; **por las buenas** willingly; **por las buenas o por las malas** willy-nilly; **¡buena la has hecho!** that's done it!; **¡estaría b.!** I should hope not!; **librarse de una buena** to get off scot free. **2** *interj* **¡b.!** *(de acuerdo)* all right, OK; *Col, Méx (al teléfono)* hello.

buey *m* ox.

búfalo, -a *mf* buffalo.

bufanda *f* scarf.

bufete *m (despacho de abogado)* lawyer's office.

buhardilla *f* attic.

búho *m* owl.

buitre *m* vulture.

bujía *f (de coche)* spark plug.

bulbo *m* bulb.

bulla *f (ruido)* noise; **armar b.** to make a lot of noise.

bullicio *m* noise.

bulto *m (cosa indistinta)* shape; *(maleta, caja)* piece of luggage; *(hinchazón)* lump; **hacer mucho b.** to be very bulky.

búnker *m* bunker.

buñuelo *m* doughnut.

buque *m* ship; **b. de guerra** warship; **b. de pasajeros** passenger ship.

burbuja *f* bubble.

burdel *m* brothel.

burguesía *f* bourgeoisie.

burla *f* gibe, jeer; **hacer b. de algo** o **algn** to make fun of sth o sb; **hacer b. a algn** to stick one's tongue out at sb.

burladero *m* refuge in bullring.

burlarse *vr* to make fun (**de** of).

burlón, -ona *adj* mocking.

burocracia *f* bureaucracy.

burocrático, -a *adj* bureaucratic.

burro, -a 1 *mf* donkey; *fam (estúpido)* blockhead. **2** *adj fam (necio)* stupid; *(obstinado)* stubborn.

bursátil *adj* stock market.

busca *f* search; **ir en b. de** to go in search of.

buscar [44] **1** *vt* to look o search for; **ir a b. algo** to go and get sth; **fue a buscarme a la estación** she picked me up at the station. **2 buscarse** *vr* fam **buscarse la vida** to try and earn one's living; **se busca** wanted.

búsqueda *f* search.

busto *m* bust.

butaca *f (sillón)* armchair; *(de teatro, cine)* seat; **b. de platea** o **patio** seat in the stalls.

butano *m* **(gas) b.** butane gas.

buzo *m* diver.

buzón *m* mailbox; **echar una carta al b.** to mail a letter; **b. de entrada** *(para correo electrónico)* in-box; **b. de voz** voice mail.

C

cabalgar [42] *vt* to ride.

caballa *f* mackerel.

caballería *f* *(cuerpo)* cavalry; *(cabalgadura)* mount, steed.

caballero *m* gentleman; **ropa de c.** menswear; **caballeros** *(en letrero)* gents.

caballeroso, -a *adj* gentlemanly.

caballo *m* horse; *(de ajedrez)* knight; *(de naipes)* queen; **a c.** on horseback; **montar a c.** to ride; *fig* **a c. entre ...** halfway between ....

cabaña *f (choza)* cabin.

cabaret *m (pl cabarets)* cabaret.

cabecera *f* top, head.

cabecilla *mf* leader.

cabello *m* hair.

caber [9] *vi* to fit; **cabe en el maletero** it fits in the boot; **en este coche/jarro caben ...** this car/jug holds ...; **no cabe duda** there is no doubt; **cabe la posibilidad de que ...** there is a possibility that ...; **no está mal dentro de lo que cabe** it isn't bad, under the circumstances.

cabestrillo *m* sling.

cabeza 1 *f* head; **en c.** in the lead; **por c.** a head, per person; **a la c. de** at the head of; **estar mal de la c.** to be a mental case. **2** *mf* **el o la c. de familia** the head of the family.

cabezota *fam* **1** *adj* pigheaded. **2** *mf* pigheaded person.

cabida *f* capacity.

cabina *f* cabin; **c. telefónica** telephone booth.

cable *m* cable.

cabo *m (extremo)* end; *(rango)* corporal; *(policía)* sergeant; *(de barco)* rope, cable; *(geográfico)* cape; **al c. de** after; **atar cabos** to put two and two together.

cabra *f* goat.

cabré *indic fut de* **caber**.

cabriola *f* skip.

cacahuete *m* peanut.

cacao *m* cacao; *(polvo, bebida)* cocoa.

cacatúa *f* cockatoo.

cacería *f (actividad)* hunting; *(partida)* hunt.

cacerola *f* saucepan.

cacharro *m* earthenware pot *o* jar; *fam (cosa)* thing, piece of junk; **cacharros** *(de cocina)* pots and pans.

cachear *vt* to frisk, search.

cachetada *f Am* slap.

cachete *m (bofetada)* slap; *Am (mejilla)* cheek.

cachimba *f* pipe.

cachivache *m fam* thing, knick-knack.

cacho¹ *m fam (pedazo)* bit, piece.

cacho² *m Andes, Ven (cuerno)* horn.

cachondeo *m fam* laugh; **tomar algo a c.** to take sth as a joke.

cachorro, -a *mf (de perro)* pup, puppy; *(de gato)* kitten; *(de otros animales)* cub, baby.

cacique *m (jefe)* local boss.

caco *m fam* thief.

cacto *m*, **catus** *m inv* cactus.

cada *adj (de dos)* each; *(de varios)* each, every; **c. día** every day; **c. dos días** every second day; **c. vez más** more and more; **¿c. cuánto?** how often?; **cuatro de c. diez** four out of (every) ten.

cadáver *m (de persona)* corpse, body; *(de animal)* body, carcass.

cadena *f* chain; *(correa de perro)* lead, leash; *(canal)* channel; *(de montañas)* range; **trabajo en c.** assembly line work; **c. perpetua** life imprisonment; *(para ruedas)* **cadenas** tire chains.

cadera *f* hip.

caducar [44] *vi* to expire.

caducidad *f* expiration; **fecha de c.** *(en alimentos)* ≃ sell-by date; *(en medicinas)* to be used before.

caer [39] **1** *vi* to fall; *(entender)* to understand, to see; *(hallarse)* to be; **dejar c.** to drop; **ya caigo** I get it; **cae**

por Granada it is somewhere near Granada; **me cae bien/mal** I like/don't like her. **2 caerse** vr to fall (down); **me caí de la moto** I fell off the motorbike; **se le cayó el pañuelo** she dropped her handkerchief.

café m coffee; (cafetería) café; **c. solo/con leche** black/white coffee.

cafeína f caffeine.

cafetera f (para hacerlo) coffeemaker; (para servirlo) coffeepot.

cafetería f snack bar, coffee bar; (en tren) buffet car.

caída f fall; (de pelo, diente) loss; (de gobierno) downfall, collapse.

caigo indic pres de **caer**.

caimán m cayman, alligator.

caja f box; (de embalaje) crate, case; (en tienda) cash desk; (en banco) cashier's desk; (féretro) coffin, casket; **c. fuerte** safe; **c. de cerveza** case of beer; **c. de cambios** gearbox; **c. de ahorros** o **de pensiones** savings bank.

cajero, -a mf cashier; **c. automático** automatic teller machine (ATM).

cajetilla f packet, pack.

cajón m (en un mueble) drawer; (caja grande) crate, chest.

cal f lime; **a c. y canto** hermetically.

calabacín m (pequeño) zucchini; (grande) squash.

calabaza f pumpkin, gourd.

calabozo m (prisión) jail, prison; (celda) cell.

calado, -a adj (mojado) soaked.

calamar m squid inv; **calamares a la romana** squid fried in batter.

calambre m (descarga) electric shock; (en músculo) cramp; **ese cable da c.** that wire is live.

calamidad f calamity.

calar 1 vt (mojar) to soak, to drench. **2** vi (prenda) to let in water. **3 calarse** vr (prenda, techo) to let in water; (mojarse) to get soaked; (coche) to stall; **calarse el sombrero** to pull one's hat down.

calavera f skull.

calcar [44] vt (dibujo) to trace; (imitar) to copy, to imitate.

calcetín m sock.

calcio m calcium.

calco m tracing; **papel de c.** carbon paper.

calculadora f calculator.

calcular vt to calculate; (evaluar) to (make an) estimate; (suponer) to guess.

cálculo m calculation; (matemático) calculus.

caldera f boiler.

caldo m stock, broth; **c. de cultivo** breeding ground.

calefacción f heating; **c. central** central heating.

calendario m calendar.

calentador m heater.

calentar [1] **1** vt (agua, horno) to heat; (comida, habitación) to warm up. **2 calentarse** vr to get hot, heat up.

calentura f fever, temperature.

calidad f quality; **de primera c.** first-class; **vino de c.** good-quality wine.

cálido, -a adj warm.

caliente adj hot; (debate) heated.

calificar [44] vt to describe (**de** as); (examen) to mark, grade.

caligrafía f calligraphy; (modo de escribir) handwriting.

caliza f limestone.

callado, -a adj quiet; **te lo tenías muy c.** you were keeping that quiet.

callar 1 vi (dejar de hablar) to stop talking; (no hablar) to keep quiet, to say nothing; **¡calla!** be quiet!, shut up! **2** vt (noticia) not to mention, to keep to oneself. **3 callarse** vr to be quiet, to shut up; **¡cállate!** shut up!

calle f street, road; (de piscina, pista) lane; **c. de dirección única** one-way street.

callejón m back alley, back street; **c. sin salida** cul-de-sac, dead end.

callejuela f narrow street, lane.

callista mf chiropodist.

callo m callus, corn; **callos** tripe sing.

calma f calm; **¡c.!** calm down!; **en c.** calm; **tómatelo con c.** take it easy.

calmante m painkiller; *(relajante)* tranquillizer.

calmar 1 vt *(persona)* to calm (down); *(dolor)* to soothe, to relieve. **2 calmarse** vr *(persona)* to calm down; *(dolor, viento)* to ease off.

calor m heat; *(entusiasmo)* warmth; **hace c.** it's hot; **tengo c.** I'm hot; **entrar en c.** to warm up.

caloría f calorie.

calumnia f slander.

caluroso, -a adj hot; *(acogida etc)* warm.

calvicie f baldness.

calvo, -a 1 adj bald. **2** m bald man.

calzada f road.

calzado m shoes pl.

calzador m shoehorn.

calzar [40] **1** vt *(poner calzado)* to put shoes on; *(mueble)* to wedge; **¿qué número calzas?** what size shoe do you wear? **2 calzarse** vr **calzarse los zapatos** to put on one's shoes.

calzoncillos mpl briefs, underpants.

calzones mpl trousers.

cama f bed; **estar en** o **guardar c.** to be confined to bed; **hacer la c.** to make the bed; **irse a la c.** to go to bed; **c. doble/sencilla** double/single bed.

cámara 1 f *(aparato)* camera; *(de rueda)* inner tube; **a c. lenta** in slow motion; **c. frigorífica** cold-storage room; **c. web** webcam **2** mf *(hombre)* cameraman; *(mujer)* camerawoman.

camarada mf comrade.

camarera f *(de hotel)* (chamber)-maid.

camarero, -a mf *(de restaurante)* *(hombre)* waiter; *(mujer)* waitress; *(tras la barra)* bartender.

camarón m prawn.

camarote m cabin.

cambiar [43] **1** vt to change; *(intercambiar)* to swap, to exchange; **c. algo de sitio** to move sth. **2** vi to change; **c. de casa** to move (house); **c. de idea** to change one's mind. **3 cambiarse** vr *(de ropa)* to change (clothes); *(de casa)* to move (house).

cambio m change; *(de impresiones)* exchange; *(de divisas)* exchange; **c. de marcha** gear change; **a c. de** in exchange for; **en c.** on the other hand; **¿tienes c. de mil pesos?** have you got change for a thousand pesos?

camello, -a mf camel.

camilla f stretcher.

caminar 1 vi to walk. **2** vt to walk; **caminaron diez kilómetros** they walked (for) ten kilometers.

camino m *(ruta)* route, way; *(vía)* path, track; **ponerse en c.** to set off; **abrirse c.** to break through; **a medio c.** half-way; **estar en c.** to be on the way; **nos coge** o **pilla de c.** it is on the way.

camión m truck; *CAm, Méx (autobús)* bus; **c. cisterna** tanker; **c. de la basura** garbage truck; **c. frigorífico** refrigerated truck.

camionero, -a mf truck driver.

camioneta f van.

camisa f shirt; **en mangas de c.** in one's shirtsleeves; **c. de fuerza** straightjacket.

camiseta f *(de uso interior)* under-shirt; *(de uso exterior)* T-shirt; *(de deporte)* shirt.

camisón m nightgown.

camote m *Andes, CAm, Méx* sweet potato.

campamento m camp.

campana f bell.

campanada f peal of a bell.

campanario m belfry, bell tower.

campanilla f small bell.

campaña f campaign; **c. electoral** election campaign; **c. publicitaria** advertising campaign.

campeón, -ona mf champion; **c. mundial** world champion.

campeonato m championship.

campesino, -a mf *(hombre)* country-man; *(mujer)* countrywoman.

camping m campsite; **hacer** o **ir de c.** to go camping.

campiña f open country.

campista mf camper.

campo *m* country, countryside; *(de fútbol)* pitch; *(de tenis)* court; *(de golf)* course; *(parcela, ámbito)* field; **a c. traviesa** *o* **través** cross-country; **c. de batalla** battlefield; **c. de béisbol** ballpark; **c. de concentración** concentration camp; **c. de trabajo** work camp.

camposanto *m* cemetery.

cana *f (gris)* gray hair; *(blanco)* white hair; **tener canas** to have gray hair.

canal *m (artificial)* canal; *(natural, de televisión)* channel; **C. de la Mancha** English Channel.

canalla *mf* swine, rotter.

canalón *m* gutter.

canapé *m* canapé; *(sofá)* couch, sofa.

canario, -a 1 *adj & mf* Canarian; **Islas Canarias** Canary Islands, Canaries. **2** *m (pájaro)* canary.

canasta *f* basket.

cancela *f* wrought-iron gate.

cancelar *vt* to cancel; *(deuda)* to pay off; *Chile, Ven (compra)* to pay for.

cáncer *m* cancer; **c. de pulmón/mama** lung/breast cancer.

cancerígeno, -a *adj* carcinogenic.

canceroso, -a *adj* cancerous.

cancha *f* ground; *(de tenis, baloncesto)* court.

canciller *mf* chancellor.

cancillería *f Am* foreign ministry.

canción *f* song.

candado *m* padlock.

candela *f Carib* fire.

candelabro *m* candelabra.

candidato, -a *mf* candidate; *(a un puesto)* applicant.

candidatura *f (lista)* list of candidates.

cándido, -a *adj* candid.

candoroso, -a *adj* innocent, pure.

canela *f* cinnamon.

canelones *mpl (pasta)* cannelloni.

cangrejo *m (de mar)* crab; *(de río)* freshwater crayfish.

canguro 1 *m* kangaroo. **2** *mf fam* baby-sitter.

caníbal *adj & mf* cannibal.

canica *f* marble.

caniche *m* poodle.

canícula *f* dog days, midsummer heat.

canillera *f Am (cobardía)* cowardice; *(miedo)* fear.

canillita *m Andes, RP* newspaper boy.

canino, -a 1 *adj* canine. **2** *m (colmillo)* canine.

canoa *f* canoe.

canoso, -a *adj (de pelo blanco)* white-haired; *(de pelo gris)* gray-haired; *(pelo)* white; gray.

cansado, -a *adj (agotado)* tired, weary.

cansancio *m* tiredness, weariness.

cansar 1 *vt* to tire. **2** *vi* to be tiring. **3 cansarse** *vr* to get tired; **se cansó de esperar** he got tired of waiting, he got fed up (with) waiting.

cantaleta *f Am* **la misma c.** the same old story.

cantante *mf* singer. **2** *adj* singing.

cantaor, -a *mf* flamenco singer.

cantar *vti* to sing.

cántaro *m* pitcher; **llover a cántaros** to rain cats and dogs.

cante *m (canto)* singing; **c. hondo, c. jondo** flamenco.

cantera *f (de piedra)* quarry; *(de equipo)* young players *pl*.

cantidad *f* quantity; *(de dinero)* sum; *fam* **c. de gente** thousands of people.

cantina *f* canteen.

cantinero, -a *mf* bar attendant.

canto¹ *m (arte)* singing; *(canción)* song.

canto² *m (borde)* edge; **de c.** on its side.

canturrear *vi* to hum, croon.

caña *f (de cerveza)* draft beer; *(tallo)* cane, stem; *(de pescar)* rod; *Andes, Cuba, RP (aguardiente)* cane spirit, cheap rum; **c. de azúcar** sugar cane.

cañada *f (barranco)* gully, ravine.

cañería *f (piece of) piping; **cañerías** plumbing *sing*.

caño *m (tubería)* pipe; *(tubo)* tube; *(chorro)* spout.

cañón *m* cannon; *(de fusil)* barrel; *(garganta)* canyon.

cañonazo *m* gunshot.

caoba *f* mahogany.

caos *m* chaos.

caótico, -a *adj* chaotic.

capa *f* (*prenda*) cloak, cape; (*de pintura*) layer, coat.

capacidad *f* capacity.

caparazón *m* shell.

capataz *mf* (*hombre*) foreman; (*mujer*) forewoman.

capaz *adj* capable, able; **ser c. de hacer algo** (*tener la habilidad de*) to be able to do sth; (*atreverse a*) to dare to do sth; *Am* **es c. que** it is likely that.

capicúa *adj* **número c.** reversible number; **palabra c.** palindrome.

capilla *f* chapel.

capital 1 *f* capital. **2** *m* (*dinero*) capital. **3** *adj* capital, main; **pena c.** capital punishment.

capitalismo *m* capitalism.

capitalista *adj & mf* capitalist.

capitán, -ana *mf* captain.

capitulación *f* agreement; (*pacto*) capitulation.

capítulo *m* (*de libro*) chapter; (*tema*) subject.

capó *m* (*de coche*) hood.

capota *f* (*de coche*) convertible top.

capote *m* (*de torero*) cape.

capricho *m* (*antojo*) whim, caprice.

caprichoso, -a *adj* whimsical.

cápsula *f* capsule.

captar *vt* (*ondas*) to receive, to pick up; (*comprender*) to understand, to grasp; (*interés etc*) to attract.

captura *f* capture.

capturar *vt* (*criminal*) to capture; (*cazar, pescar*) to catch.

capucha *f* hood.

capullo *m* (*de insecto*) cocoon; (*de flor*) bud.

caqui 1 *adj* (*color*) khaki. **2** *m* (*fruto*) persimmon.

cara 1 *f* face; (*lado*) side; (*de moneda*) right side; *fam* (*desfachatez*) cheek, nerve; **c. a c.** face to face; **tener buena/mala c.** to look good/bad; **(de) c. a** with a view to; **echarle a algn algo**

en c. to reproach sb for sth; **¿c. o cruz?** heads or tails?; **echar algo a c. o cruz** to flip (a coin) for sth; **¡qué c. (más dura) tienes!** you've got a lot of nerve! **2** *m fam* (*desvergonzado*) bold person.

caracol *m* (*animal*) snail; (*cubierta*) shell.

caracola *f* conch.

carácter *m* (*pl* caracteres) character; (*índole*) nature; **tener buen/ mal c.** to be good-natured/bad-tempered.

característica *f* characteristic.

característico, -a *adj* characteristic.

caradura *mf fam* cheeky devil; **¡qué c. eres!** you're so cheeky!

caramba *interj* (*sorpresa*) good grief!; (*enfado*) damn it!

carámbano *m* icicle.

caramelo *m* (*dulce*) candy; (*azúcar quemado*) caramel.

caravana *f* caravan; (*cola*) hatchback.

carbón *m* coal; **c. vegetal** charcoal; **c. mineral** coal.

carbonizar [40] *vt*, **carbonizarse** *vr* to char.

carbono *m* carbon.

carburador *m* carburetor.

carburante *m* fuel.

carcajada *f* guffaw.

cárcel *f* prison, jail.

carcelero, -a *mf* warden.

cardenal *m* cardinal; (*en la piel*) bruise.

cardiaco, -a, cardíaco, -a *adj* cardiac, heart; **ataque c.** heart attack.

cardinal *adj* cardinal; **punto/número c.** cardinal point/number.

cardiólogo, -a *mf* cardiologist.

cardo *m* (*con espinas*) thistle.

carecer [33] *vi* **c. de** to lack.

carencia *f* lack (**de** of).

careta *f* mask; **c. antigás** gas mask.

carezco *indic pres de* **carecer**.

carga *f* (*acción*) loading; (*cosa cargada*) load; (*de avión, barco*) cargo, freight; (*explosiva, eléctrica*) charge; (*obligación*) burden.

cargado, -a adj loaded; (bebida) strong; **un café c.** a strong coffee; **atmósfera cargada** stuffy atmosphere; **c. de deudas** full of debt.

cargador m (de celular) charger.

cargamento m (carga) load; (mercancías) cargo, freight.

cargar [42] **1** vt to load; (mechero, pluma) to fill; (batería) to charge; **cárguelo a mi cuenta** charge it to my account. **2** vi **c. con** (llevar) to carry; **c. con las consecuencias** to suffer the consequences. **3 cargarse** vr to load oneself with; fam (estropear) to smash, to ruin; fam (matar) to kill, to bump off.

cargo m (puesto) post, position; (persona) top person; (débito) charge, debit; (acusación) charge, accusation; **alto c.** (puesto) top job; **estar al c. de** to be in charge of; **correr a c. de** (gastos) to be met by; **hacerse c. de** to take charge of; **hazte c. de mi situación** please try to understand my situation; **con c. a mi cuenta** charged to my account.

cargoso, -a adj CSur annoying.

caricatura f caricature.

caricia f caress, stroke.

caridad f charity.

caries f inv decay, caries.

cariño m (amor) affection; (querido) darling; **coger/tener c. a algo/algn** to grow/to be fond of sth/sb; **con c.** (en carta) love.

cariñoso, -a adj loving, affectionate.

caritativo, -a adj charitable.

cariz m look.

carmín m (de color) **c.** carmine; **c. (de labios)** lipstick.

carnaval m carnival.

carne f flesh; (alimento) meat; **ser de c. y hueso** to be only flesh and blood; **c. de gallina** goose pimples; **c. de cerdo/cordero/ternera/vaca** pork/lamb/veal/beef.

carné, carnet m card; **c. de conducir** driver's license; **c. de identidad** identity card.

carnero m ram; (carne) mutton.

carnicería f butcher's (shop).

caro, -a 1 adj (precios) expensive; (querido) dear. **2** adv **salir c.** to cost a lot; **te costará c.** (amenaza) you'll pay dearly for this.

carpa f (pez) carp; (de circo) big top, marquee; Am (de camping) tent.

carpeta f folder.

carpintería f (oficio) carpentry; (taller) carpenter's (shop).

carpintero, -a mf carpenter.

carraspear vi to clear one's throat.

carrera f run; (de media) run, ladder; (competición) race; (estudios) degree; (profesión) career, profession; **c. de coches** rally, meeting; **echar una c. a algn** to race sb.

carrerilla f **tomar c.** to take a run; **de c.** parrot fashion.

carreta f cart.

carrete m (de hilo) reel; (de película) spool.

carretera f road; **c. de circunvalación** bypass; **c. de acceso** access road; Méx **c. de cuota** toll road.

carretilla f wheelbarrow.

carril m (de trenes) rail; (de carretera) lane.

carrillo m cheek.

carriola f Méx (de bebé) baby carriage.

carro m (carreta) cart; (de máquina de escribir) carriage; Andes, CAm, Carib, Méx car; **c. de combate** tank.

carrocería f bodywork.

carta f letter; (menú) menu; (de baraja) card; **c. certificada/urgente** registered/express letter; **a la c.** à la carte; **c. de vinos** wine list; **tomar cartas en un asunto** to take part in an affair.

cartel m poster.

cartera f (de bolsillo) wallet; (para documentos) briefcase; (de colegial) satchel, schoolbag; Andes, RP (de mujer) purse.

cartero, -a mf (hombre) postman; (mujer) postwoman.

cartilla f (libreta) book; (para leer) first reader; **c. de ahorros** savings book.

cartón m (material) card, cardboard; (de cigarrillos) carton.

cartucho m cartridge; (de papel) cone.

cartulina f card.

casa f (edificio) house; (hogar) home; (empresa) company, firm; **c. de huéspedes** boarding house; **c. de socorro** first aid post.

casado, -a 1 adj married. **2** mf married person; **los recién casados** the newlyweds.

casamiento m marriage; (boda) wedding.

casar 1 vt to marry. **2 casarse** vr to marry, to get married.

cascabel m bell.

cascada f waterfall, cascade.

cascanueces m inv nutcracker.

cascar [44] vt, **cascarse** vr to crack.

cáscara f shell; (de fruta) skin, peel; (de grano) husk.

cascarón m eggshell.

casco m helmet; (de caballo) hoof; (envase) empty bottle; (de barco) hull; **c. urbano** city center; **cascos** (auriculares) headphones.

casero, -a 1 adj (hecho en casa) home-made; (persona) home-loving. **2** mf (dueño) (hombre) landlord; (mujer) landlady.

caseta f hut, booth; (de feria, exposición) stand, stall.

casete 1 m (magnetófono) cassette player o recorder. **2** f (cinta) cassette (tape).

casi adv almost, nearly; **c. nunca** hardly ever; **c. nadie** hardly anyone; **c. me caigo** I almost fell.

casino m casino.

caso m case; **el c. es que ...** the thing is that ...; **el c. Mattei** the Mattei affair; **(en) c. contrario** otherwise; **en c. de necesidad** if need be; **en cualquier c.** in any case; **en el mejor/peor de los casos** at best/worst; **en ese c.** in such a case; **en todo c.** in any case; **hacer c. a o de algn** to pay attention to sb; **no venir al c.** to be beside the point; **pongamos por c.** let's say.

caspa f dandruff.

cassette m o f = **casete**.

castaña f chestnut.

castaño, -a 1 adj chestnut-brown; (pelo, ojos) brown, dark. **2** m (árbol) chestnut.

castellano, -a 1 adj Castilian. **2** mf (persona) Castilian. **3** m (idioma) Spanish, Castilian.

castigar [42] vt to punish; (penalizar) to penalize.

castigo m punishment; (pena) penalty.

castillo m castle.

casual adj accidental, chance.

casualidad f chance, coincidence; **de o por c.** by chance; **dio la c. de que ...** it so happened that ...; **¿tienes un lápiz, por c.?** do you happen to have a pencil?; **¡que c.!** what a coincidence!

casualmente adv by chance.

cataclismo m cataclysm.

catalejo m telescope.

catalogar [42] vt to catalog; (clasificar) to classify.

catálogo m catalog.

catapulta f catapult.

catarata f waterfall; (enfermedad) cataract.

catarro m (common) cold.

catástrofe f catastrophe.

catecismo m catechism.

cátedra f (universidad) chair.

catedral f cathedral.

catedrático, -a mf (de universidad) professor; (de instituto) head of department.

categoría f category; **de c.** (persona) important.

cateto, -a mf (paleto) yokel, bumpkin.

católico, -a adj & mf Catholic.

catorce adj & m inv fourteen.

cauce m (de un río) bed; fig channel.

caucho m rubber; Am (cubierta) tire.

caudal m (de un río) flow; (riqueza) wealth.

caudillo m leader, head.

causa f cause; **a** o **por c. de** because of.

causante 1 adj causal. **2** mf **el c. del incendio** the person who caused the fire.

causar vt to cause; **c. buena/mala impresión** to make a good/bad impression.

cautela f caution.

cautivar vt to capture, to take prisoner.

cautiverio m, **cautividad** f captivity.

cautivo, -a adj & mf captive.

cava 1 f (bodega) wine cellar. **2** m (vino espumoso) champagne.

cavar vt to dig.

caverna f cave.

caviar m caviar.

cavidad f cavity.

cavilar vt to ponder.

cayado m (de pastor) crook.

caza f hunting; (animales) game; (persecución) hunt; **ir de c.** to go hunting; **c. furtiva** poaching; **c. mayor/menor** big/small game.

cazador, -a mf hunter.

cazadora f (waist-length) jacket.

cazar [40] vt to hunt.

cazo m (cacerola) saucepan; (cucharón) ladle.

cazuela f saucepan; (guiso) casserole, stew; **a la c.** stewed.

cebada f barley.

cebo m bait.

cebolla f onion.

cebolleta f spring onion.

cebra f zebra; **paso de c.** crosswalk.

cecear vi to lisp.

ceder 1 vt to give, to hand over; **c. el paso** to give way. **2** vi (cuerda, cable) to give way; (consentir) to give in.

cédula f document, certificate; **c. de identidad** identity card.

cegar [1] vt to blind; (puerta, ventana) to wall up.

ceguera f blindness.

ceja f eyebrow.

celador, -a mf attendant; (de cárcel) warder.

celda f cell.

celebración f (festejo) celebration; (de juicio etc) holding.

celebrar 1 vt to celebrate; (reunión, juicio, elecciones) to hold. **2 celebrarse** vr to take place, be held.

célebre adj famous, well-known.

celeste adj (de cielo) celestial; (color) sky-blue. **2** m sky blue.

celibato m celibacy.

celo m zeal; **en c.** (macho) in rut; (hembra) in heat; **celos** jealousy sing; **tener celos (de algn)** to be jealous (of sb).

celo® m Scotch tape®.

celofán m cellophane.

celoso, -a adj jealous.

célula f cell.

celular 1 adj cellular; **coche c.** police van; Am **teléfono c.** cellphone, mobile phone. **2** m Am cellphone, mobile.

celulitis f inv cellulite.

cementerio m cemetery.

cemento m cement; (hormigón) concrete.

cena f dinner.

cenar 1 vi to have dinner. **2** vt to have for dinner.

cenicero m ashtray.

cenit m zenith.

ceniza f ash.

censo m census; **c. electoral** electoral roll.

censura f censorship; **moción de c.** vote of no confidence.

censurar vt (libro, película) to censor.

centavo m Am cent.

centellear vi to flash, sparkle.

centena f, **centenar** m hundred.

centenario m centenary.

centeno m rye.

centésimo, -a adj & mf hundredth.

centígrado, -a adj centigrade.

centilitro *m* centiliter.

centímetro *m* centimeter.

céntimo *m* cent.

centinela *m* sentry.

centollo *m* spider crab.

central 1 *adj* central. **2** *f (oficina principal)* head office; **c. nuclear/térmica** nuclear/coal-fired power station.

centralismo *m* centralism.

centralita *f* switchboard.

centralizar [40] *vt* to centralize.

centrar 1 *vt* to center; *(esfuerzos, atención)* to concentrate, to center (**en** on). **2 centrarse** *vr* to be centered o based; *(concentrarse)* to concentrate (**en** on).

céntrico, -a *adj* centrally situated.

centrifugar [42] *vt (ropa)* to spin-dry.

centro *m* center; **c. de la ciudad** city center; **c. comercial** shopping center, mall.

ceñido, -a *adj* tight-fitting, clinging.

ceñirse [6] *vr (prenda)* to cling (**a** to); *(atenerse, limitarse)* to limit oneself (**a** to); **c. al tema** to keep to the subject.

cepillar *vt*, **cepillarse** *vr* to brush.

cepillo *m* brush; *(en carpintería)* plane; **c. de dientes** toothbrush; **c. del pelo** hairbrush.

cera *f* wax; *(de abeja)* beeswax; **hacerse la c. en las piernas** to have one's legs waxed.

cerámica *f* ceramics *sing.*

cerca¹ 1 *adv* near, close; **de c.** closely. **2** *prep* **c. de** *(al lado de)* near, close to; *(casi)* nearby, around; **el colegio está c. de mi casa** the school is near my house; **c. de cien personas** about one hundred people.

cerca² *f* enclosure.

cercanía *f* proximity, nearness; **cercanías** outskirts, suburbs; **(tren de) c.** suburban train.

cercano, -a *adj* nearby; **el C. Oriente** the Near East.

cercar [44] *vt (tapiar)* to fence, enclose; *(rodear)* to surround.

cerdo *m* pig; *(carne)* pork.

cereal *m* cereal.

cerebro *m* brain; *(inteligencia)* brains *pl.*

ceremonia *f* ceremony.

cereza *f* cherry.

cerezo *m* cherry tree.

cerilla *f* match.

cero *m* zero; *(en resultado)* nil; **ser un c. a la izquierda** to be useless.

cerrado, -a *adj* closed, shut; *(intransigente)* uncompromising; *(acento)* broad; *(curva)* sharp.

cerradura *f* lock.

cerrar [1] **1** *vt* to shut, to close; *(grifo, gas)* to turn off; *(cremallera)* to do up; *(negocio)* to close down; *(cuenta)* to close; *(sobre)* to seal; **c. con llave** to lock; **c. el paso a algn** to block sb's way. **2** *vi* to close, to shut. **3 cerrarse** *vr* to close, to shut.

cerril *adj (obstinado)* pig-headed, headstrong.

cerro *m* hill.

cerrojo *m* bolt; **echar el c. (de una puerta)** to bolt (a door).

certamen *m* competition, contest.

certeza, certidumbre *f* certainty; **tener la c. de que ...** to be certain that ....

certificado, -a 1 *adj* certified; *(correo)* registered. **2** *m* certificate; **c. médico** medical certificate.

cervecería *f (bar)* pub, bar; *(fábrica)* brewery.

cerveza *f* beer; **c. de barril** draft beer; **c. negra** stout.

cesar 1 *vi* to stop, cease (**de** -); **sin c.** incessantly. **2** *vt (empleado)* to dismiss.

cese *m* cessation, suspension; *(despido)* dismissal.

césped *m* lawn, grass.

cesta *f* basket.

cesto *m* basket.

ceviche *m* = raw fish marinated in lemon and garlic.

chabola *f* shack.

chacal *m* jackal.

chacinería f pork butcher's shop.

chacra f Andes, RP small farm.

chafar vt fam (plan etc) to ruin; (aplastar) to squash.

chal m shawl.

chalado, -a adj fam crazy, nuts (por about).

chalé m (pl chalés) villa.

chaleco m vest; (de punto) sleeveless pullover; **c. salvavidas** life jacket.

chalet m villa.

chalupa f (embarcación) boat, launch; Méx (torta) = small tortilla with a raised rim to contain a filling.

chamaco, -a mf Méx fam kid.

champán, champaña m champagne.

champiñón m mushroom.

champú m shampoo.

chamuscar [44] vt to singe, scorch.

chancaca f CAm syrup cake.

chance m Am opportunity.

chancear vi to joke, horse around.

chanchada f Am fam dirty trick.

chancho, -a mf Am pig.

chancla, chancleta f thong.

chándal m track suit, jogging suit.

chantaje m blackmail; **hacer c. a algn** to blackmail sb.

chantajear vt to blackmail

chantajista mf blackmailer.

chapa f (de metal) sheet; (tapón) bottle top, cap; (de adorno) badge; Col (cerradura) lock.

chapado, -a adj (metal) plated; **c. en oro** gold-plated.

chaparrón m downpour, heavy shower.

chapotear vi to splash about, to paddle.

chapucero, -a adj fam (trabajo) slapdash, shoddy; (persona) bungling.

chapurrear vt (idioma) to speak badly.

chapuza f fam (trabajo mal hecho) shoddy piece of work; (trabajo ocasional) odd job.

chapuzón m (baño corto) dip; **darse un c.** to have a dip.

chaqueta f jacket.

charca f pond, pool.

charco m puddle.

charcutería f delicatessen.

charla f (conversación) talk, chat; (conferencia) informal lecture.

charlar vi to talk, to chat.

charlatán, -ana 1 adj (parlanchín) talkative. **2** mf (parlanchín) chatterbox; (embaucador) charlatan.

charol m patent leather.

chárter adj inv **vuelo c.** charter flight.

chasca f Andes (cabellera) mop of hair, tangled hair.

chasco m fam (decepción) disappointment; **llevarse un c.** to be disappointed.

chasis m inv chassis.

chasqui m Am messenger, courier.

chasquido m (de la lengua) click; (de los dedos) snap; (de látigo, madera) crack.

chat m (charla) chat; (sala) chat room.

chatarra f scrap (metal), scrap iron; (cosa inservible) junk.

chato, -a adj (nariz) snub; (persona) snub-nosed.

chauvinista adj & mf chauvinist.

chaval, -a mf (chico) boy, lad; (chica) girl, lass.

chavo, -a fam **1** mf Méx (chico) guy; (chica) girl. **2** m (dinero) **no tener un c.** to be broke.

chepa f hump.

cheque m check; **c. de viaje** traveler's check.

chequeo m checkup.

chévere adj Andes, CAm, Carib, Méx fam great, fantastic.

chicano, -a adj & mf chicano.

chicha f Andes maize liquor.

chícharo m CAm, Méx pea.

chicharra f cicada.

chichón m bump, lump.

chicle m chewing gum.

chico, -a 1 mf (muchacho) boy, lad; (muchacha) girl, lass. **2** adj (pequeño) small, little.

chicote m Am whip.

chiflado, -a adj fam mad, crazy (por about).

chiflar vt (silbar) to hiss (at), to boo (at); fam **le chiflan las motos** he's really into motorbikes.

chiflido m whistle, whistling.

chillar vi (persona) to scream, to shriek; (ratón) to squeak.

chillido m (de persona) scream, shriek; (de ratón) squeak.

chillón, -ona adj (voz) shrill, high-pitched; (sonido) harsh; (color) loud.

chimenea f fireplace, hearth; (conducto) chimney.

chincheta f thumbtack.

chinchín interj ¡c.! cheers!, (to) your (good) health!

chingana f Perú fam bar.

chip m (pl **chips**) chip.

chipirón m baby squid.

chiquillo, -a mf kid, youngster.

chirimoya f custard apple.

chiringuito m (en playa etc) refreshment stall; (en carretera) roadside snack bar.

chirriar [29] vi (puerta) to creak; (frenos) to screech.

chirrido m (de puerta) creak, creaking; (de frenos) screech.

chisme m (habladuría) piece of gossip; fam (trasto) knick-knack; (cosa) thing.

chismear vi to gossip.

chismoso, -a 1 adj (murmurador) gossipy. **2** mf gossip.

chispa f spark.

chispear vi to spark; (lloviznar) to spit.

chiste m joke; **contar un c.** to tell a joke.

chistoso, -a adj (persona) funny, witty; (anécdota) funny, amusing.

chivatazo m fam (soplo) tip-off; **dar el c.** to squeal.

chivato, -a mf fam (acusica) tell-tale; (delator) grass.

chivo, -a mf (animal) kid, young goat; fig **c. expiatorio** scapegoat.

chocante adj (sorprendente) surprising; (raro) strange.

chocar [44] **1** vi (topar) to crash, to collide; (pelota) to hit, to strike; **c. con** o **contra** to run into, to collide with. **2** vt to knock; (sorprender) to surprise.

chochear vi (viejo) to be senile.

chocolate m chocolate.

chocolatina f bar of chocolate, chocolate bar.

chófer m (pl **chóferes**), Am **chofer** m (pl **choferes**) driver; (particular) chauffeur.

chollo m fam bargain, snip.

chomba f Arg jumper, pullover.

chonta f Am palm tree.

chopo m poplar.

choque m impact; (de coches etc) crash, collision.

chorizo m highly-seasoned pork sausage.

choro m Andes mussel.

chorrear vi to gush, to spurt; (gotear) to drip, to trickle; fam **estoy chorreando** I am soaking wet.

chorro m (de agua etc) spurt; (muy fino) trickle; **salir a chorros** to gush forth.

chovinista 1 adj chauvinistic. **2** mf chauvinist.

choza f hut, shack.

chubasco m heavy shower, downpour.

chubasquero m raincoat.

chuchería f fam candy.

chuleta f chop, cutlet; **c. de cerdo** pork chop.

chulo, -a fam **1** m show-off. **2** adj (bonito) smashing.

chupachup® m lollipop.

chupar 1 vt to suck; (lamer) to lick; (absorber) to soak up, to absorb. **2** vi to suck. **3 chuparse** vr **está para chuparse los dedos** it's really mouthwatering.

chupete m pacifier.

churrasco m barbecued meat.

churrete m dirty mark, grease spot.

churro m cruller.

chutar vi (a gol) to shoot.

cicatriz f scar.

cicatrizar [40] *vti* to heal.

ciclismo *m* cycling.

ciclista 1 *adj* cycling. **2** *mf* cyclist.

ciclo *m* cycle; *(de conferencias etc)* series.

ciclomotor *m* moped.

ciclón *m* cyclone.

ciego, -a 1 *adj* blind; **a ciegas** blindly. **2** *mf* blind person; **los ciegos** the blind *pl.*

cielo *m* sky; *(gloria)* heaven; *(de la boca)* roof.

ciempiés *m inv* centipede.

cien *adj & m inv* hundred; **c. libras** a o one hundred pounds; **c. por c.** one hundred per cent.

ciencia *f* science; **saber algo a c. cierta** to know something for certain; **c. ficción** science fiction.

cieno *m* mud.

científico, -a 1 *adj* scientific. **2** *mf* scientist.

ciento *adj* hundred; **c. tres** one hundred and three; **por c.** per cent.

cierre *m* *(acción)* closing, shutting; *(de fábrica)* shutdown; *(de emisión)* close-down; *(de bolso)* clasp; *(de puerta)* catch; *Am* **c. relámpago** zipper.

cierto, -a 1 *adj* certain; *(verdadero)* true; **lo c. es que ...** the fact is that ...; **por c.** by the way. **2** *adv* certainly.

ciervo, -a *mf* deer; *(macho)* stag; *(hembra)* doe, hind.

cifra *f* *(número)* figure, number; *(suma)* amount.

cigala *f* Norway lobster.

cigarra *f* cicada.

cigarrillo *m* cigarette.

cigarro *m* *(cigarrillo)* cigarette; *(puro)* cigar.

cigüeña *f* stork.

cilindro *m* cylinder.

cima *f* summit.

cimientos *mpl* foundations.

cinco *adj & m inv* five.

cincuenta *adj & m inv* fifty.

cine *m* movie theater; *(arte)* cinema.

cinematográfico, -a *adj* cinema-tographic; **la industria cinemato-gráfica** the movie industry.

cínico, -a 1 *adj* shameless. **2** *mf* shameless person.

cinismo *m* shamelessness.

cinta *f* *(tira)* band, strip; *(para adornar)* ribbon; *(película)* film; **c. adhe-siva/aislante** adhesive/insulating tape; **c. de vídeo** video tape; **c. transportadora** conveyor belt.

cintura *f* waist.

cinturón *m* belt; **c. de seguridad** safety belt.

ciprés *m* cypress.

circo *m* circus.

circuito *m* circuit; **c. cerrado de te-levisión** CCTV, closed-circuit televi-sion.

circulación *f* circulation; *(tráfico)* traffic.

circular 1 *adj & f* circular. **2** *vi* *(moverse)* to circulate; *(líquido)* to flow; *(tren, autobús)* to run; *(rumor)* to go round.

círculo *m* circle.

circuncisión *f* circumcision.

circundante *adj* surrounding.

circunferencia *f* circumference.

circunscripción *f* district.

circunstancia *f* circumstance.

cirio *m* wax candle.

ciruela *f* plum; **c. claudia** green-gage; **c. pasa** prune.

ciruelo *m* plum tree.

cirugía *f* surgery; **c. estética** *o* **plás-tica** plastic surgery.

cirujano, -a *mf* surgeon.

cisne *m* swan.

cisterna *f* cistern, tank.

cita *f* appointment; *(amorosa)* date; *(mención)* quotation.

citar *vt* *(mencionar)* to quote; **me ha citado el dentista** I have an appoint-ment with the dentist.

cítrico, -a 1 *adj* citric, citrus. **2 cítri-cos** *mpl* citrus fruits.

ciudad *f* town; *(grande)* city.

ciudadano, -a 1 *mf* citizen. **2** *adj* civic.

cívico, -a *adj* civic.

civil *adj* civil; *(no militar)* civilian; **matrimonio c.** civil marriage.

civilización *f* civilization.

civilizado, -a *adj* civilized.

civismo *m* civility.

clamoroso, -a *adj* resounding.

clan *m* clan.

clandestino, -a *adj* clandestine.

clara *f (de huevo)* white.

claraboya *f* skylight.

clarear *vi (amanecer)* to dawn; *(despejar)* to clear up.

clarete *adj & m* claret.

claridad *f (luz)* brightness; *(inteligibilidad)* clarity; **con c.** clearly.

clarificar [44] *vt* to clarify.

clarinete *m* clarinet.

claro, -a 1 *adj* clear; *(líquido, salsa)* thin; *(color)* light. **2** *interj* of course!; **¡c. que no!** of course not!; **¡c. que sí!** certainly! **3** *m (en un bosque)* clearing; *(tiempo despejado)* bright spell. **4** *adv* clearly.

clase *f* class; *(tipo)* kind, sort; *(curso)* class; *(aula)* classroom; **c. alta/media** upper/middle class; **primera/segunda c.** first/second class; **toda c. de …** all kinds of ….

clásico, -a 1 *adj* classical; *(típico, en el vestir)* classic. **2** *m* classic.

clasificación *f* classification; *(para campeonato, concurso)* qualification.

clasificar [44] **1** *vt* to classify, to class. **2 clasificarse** *vr* to qualify.

claustrofobia *f* claustrophobia.

cláusula *f* clause.

clausura *f (cierre)* closure.

clausurar *vt* to close.

clavar *vt* to nail; *(clavo)* to hammer in; *(estaca)* to drive in. **2 clavarse** *vr* **clavarse una astilla** to get a splinter.

clave *f* key; **la palabra c.** the key word.

clavel *m* carnation.

clavícula *f* collarbone.

clavo *m* nail; *fig* **dar en el c.** to hit the nail on the head; *(especia)* clove.

claxon *m (pl* **cláxones**) horn; **tocar el c.** to sound the horn.

clemencia *f* mercy, clemency.

clementina *f* clementine.

clérigo *m* priest.

clero *m* clergy.

clic *m* click; **hacer c. (en)** to click (on).

cliché *m (tópico)* cliché; *(negativo)* negative.

cliente *mf* customer, client.

clima *m* climate.

climatizado, -a *adj* air-conditioned.

climatizar [40] *vt* to air-condition.

clínica *f* clinic.

clip *m (para papel)* clip.

cloaca *f* sewer, drain.

clon *m* clone.

clonar *vt* to clone.

cloro *m* chlorine.

cloroformo *m* chloroform.

club *m (pl* **clubs** *o* **clubes**) club; **c. náutico** yacht club.

coacción *f* coercion.

coalición *f* coalition.

coartada *f* alibi.

cobarde 1 *adj* cowardly. **2** *mf* coward.

cobaya *f* guinea pig.

cobertizo *m* shed, shack.

cobertor *m* bedspread.

cobija *f Am* blanket.

cobijar *vt*, **cobijarse** *vr* to shelter.

cobra *f* cobra.

cobrador, -a *mf (de autobús)* (hombre) conductor; *(mujer)* conductress; *(de luz, agua etc)* collector.

cobrar *vt (dinero)* to charge; *(cheque)* to cash; *(salario)* to earn; **c. importancia** to become important.

cobre *m (metal)* copper; *Am (moneda)* copper cent.

cobro *m (pago)* collecting; *(de cheque)* cashing; **llamada a c. revertido** collect call.

coca *f* coca.

cocaína *f* cocaine.

cocción *f* cooking; *(en agua)* boiling; *(en horno)* baking.

cocer [41] *vt*, **cocerse** *vr* *(comida)* to cook; *(hervir)* to boil; *(en horno)* to bake.

cochambroso, -a *adj* squalid.

coche *m* car; **en c.** by car; **c. de bomberos** fire engine; *(vagón)* carriage, coach; **c. cama** sleeper.

cochecito *m* *(de niño)* baby carriage.

cochera *f* garage; *(de autobuses)* depot.

cochino, -a 1 *mf* *(macho)* pig; *(hembra)* sow; *fig* *(persona)* pig. **2** *adj* *(sucio)* filthy.

cocido *m* stew.

cocina *f* kitchen; *(aparato)* cooker; *(arte)* cooking; **c. eléctrica/de gas** electric/gas cooker; **c. casera** home cooking.

cocinar *vti* to cook.

cocinero, -a *mf* cook.

coco *m* coconut.

cocodrilo *m* crocodile.

cocotero *m* coconut palm.

cóctel *m* cocktail.

codazo *m* *(señal)* nudge with one's elbow; *(golpe)* blow with one's elbow.

codicia *f* greed.

codicioso, -a 1 *adj* covetous. **2** *mf* greedy person.

código *m* code.

codo *m* elbow; *fam* **hablar por los codos** to talk nonstop.

coeficiente *m* **c. intelectual** IQ.

coetáneo, -a *adj & mf* contemporary.

coexistir *vi* to coexist.

cofre *m* trunk, chest.

coger [53] **1** *vt* to take; *(del suelo)* to pick (up); *(fruta, flores)* to pick; *(asir)* to seize, to take hold of; *(coche, bus)* to take, to catch; *(pelota, ladrón, resfriado)* to catch; *(atropellar)* to run over. **2 cogerse** *vr* *(agarrarse)* to hold on.

cogote *m* back of the neck.

cohabitar *vi* to live together, to cohabit.

coherente *adj* coherent.

cohete *m* rocket.

cohibido, -a *adj* inhibited.

cohibir 1 *vt* to inhibit. **2 cohibirse** *vr* to feel inhibited.

coincidencia *f* coincidence.

coincidir *vi* to coincide; *(concordar)* to agree; *(encontrarse)* to meet by chance.

cojear *vi* *(persona)* to limp; *(mesa etc)* to wobble.

cojín *m* cushion.

cojinete *m* bearing.

cojo, -a 1 *adj* *(persona)* lame; *(mueble)* rickety. **2** *mf* lame person.

col *f* cabbage; **c. de Bruselas** Brussels sprout.

cola¹ *f* tail; *(de vestido)* train; *(de pelo)* ponytail; *(fila)* line; **a la c.** at the back; **hacer c.** stand in line.

cola² *f* glue.

colaboración *f* collaboration.

colaborador, -a 1 *mf* collaborator. **2** *adj* collaborating.

colaborar *vi* to collaborate.

colada *f* wash, laundry; **hacer la c.** to do the washing.

colador *m* colander, sieve; *(de té, café)* strainer.

colapso *m* collapse; **c. circulatorio** traffic jam.

colar [2] **1** *vt* *(líquido)* to strain. **2 colarse** *vr* to slip in; *(a fiesta)* to gatecrash; *(en una cola)* to cut in line.

colcha *f* bedspread.

colchón *m* mattress.

colchoneta *f* air bed.

colección *f* collection.

coleccionar *vt* to collect.

colecta *f* collection.

colectivo, -a 1 *adj* collective. **2** *m* *(asociación)* association; *Andes (taxi)* long-distance taxi; *Arg (autobús)* bus.

colega *mf* colleague.

colegial, -a 1 *adj* *(escolar)* school. **2** *mf* *(alumno)* schoolboy; *(alumna)* schoolgirl; **los colegiales** the schoolchildren.

colegio *m* *(escuela)* school; **c.**

mayor o **universitario** *(residencia)* residence hall.

cólera¹ f anger, rage.

cólera² m *(enfermedad)* cholera.

colesterol m cholesterol.

colgante 1 m *(joya)* pendant. **2** *adj* hanging.

colgar [2] **1** vt to hang (up); *(colada)* to hang (out); *(ahorcar)* to hang. **2** vi to hang *(de* from); *(teléfono)* to hang up. **3 colgarse** vr *(ahorcarse)* to hang oneself.

cólico m colic.

coliflor f cauliflower.

colilla f cigarette end.

colina f hill.

colindante adj adjoining, adjacent.

colirio m eyedrops.

colisión f collision, crash.

collar m *(adorno)* necklace; *(de perro)* collar.

colmado, -a adj full, filled; *(cucharada)* heaped.

colmena f beehive.

colmillo m eye tooth; *(de carnívoro)* fang; *(de jabalí, elefante)* tusk.

colmo m ¡eso es el c.! that's the last straw!; **para c.** to top it all off.

colocación f *(acto)* positioning; *(situación)* situation; *(empleo)* job.

colocar [44] **1** vt to place, to put; *(emplear)* to give work to. **2 colocarse** vr *(situarse)* to put oneself; *(emplearse)* to take a job *(de* as).

Colón n Columbus.

colonia¹ f colony; *(campamento)* summer camp; *Méx (barrio)* district.

colonia² f *(agua de colonia)* cologne.

colonial adj colonial.

colonizar [40] vt to colonize.

coloquio m discussion.

color m color; **de colores** multicolored.

colorado, -a 1 adj red; **ponerse c.** to blush. **2** m red.

colorante m coloring.

colorear vt to color.

colorete m rouge.

colorido m color.

columna f column; **c. vertebral** spinal column.

columpio m swing.

coma¹ f *(ortográfica)* comma.

coma² m *(estado)* coma.

comadrona f midwife.

comandante m commander, commanding officer; *(de avión)* captain.

comarca f region.

combate m combat; *(de boxeo)* fight; *(batalla)* battle; **fuera de c.** out for the count.

combatir vti to fight.

combinación f combination; *(prenda)* slip.

combinar vt, **combinarse** vr to combine.

combustible 1 m fuel. **2** adj combustible.

comedia f comedy.

comedido, -a adj self-restrained, reserved.

comedor m dining room.

comentar vt *(escribir)* to comment on; *(discutir)* to discuss.

comentario m comment; **sin c.** no comment.

comentarista mf commentator.

comenzar [51] vti to begin, to start; **comenzó a llover** it started raining o to rain; **comenzó diciendo que ...** he started by saying that ....

comer 1 vti o eat; **dar de c. a algn** to feed sb. **2 comerse** vr to eat.

comercial adj commercial.

comercializar [40] vt to market.

comerciante mf merchant.

comerciar [43] vi to trade; **comercia con oro** he trades in gold.

comercio m commerce, trade; *(tienda)* shop.

comestible 1 adj edible. **2** mpl **comestibles** food *sing*.

cometa 1 m comet. **2** f *(juguete)* kite.

cometer vt *(error, falta)* to make; *(delito, crimen)* to commit.

cometido m *(tarea)* task, assignment; *(deber)* duty; **cumplir su c.** to do one's duty.

comezón *m* itch.

comicios *mpl* elections.

cómico, -a 1 *adj (divertido)* comical, funny; **actor c.** comedian. **2** *mf* comic; *(hombre)* comedian; *(mujer)* comedienne.

comida *f (alimento)* food; *(almuerzo, cena)* meal.

comienzo *m* beginning, start; **dar c. (a algo)** to start (sth).

comillas *fpl* inverted commas; **entre c.** in inverted commas.

comilón, -ona 1 *adj* greedy. **2** *mf* big eater.

comilona *f fam* big meal, feast.

comisaría *f* police station.

comisión *f (retribución)* commission; *(comité)* committee.

como 1 *adv (manera)* as; **hazlo c. quieras** do it however you like. ▪ *(comparación)* as; **blanco c. la nieve** as white as snow; **habla c. su padre** he talks like his father. ▪ *(según)* as; **c. decíamos ayer** as we were saying yesterday. ▪ *(en calidad de)* as; **lo compré c. recuerdo** I bought it as a souvenir. ▪ *(aproximadamente)* about; **c. unos diez** about ten. **2** *conj* **c. + subj (si)** if; **c. no estudies vas a suspender** if you don't study hard, you'll fail. ▪ *(porque)* as, since; **c. no venías me marché** as you didn't come I left. ▪ **c. si** as if; **c. si nada** *o* **tal cosa** as if nothing had happened.

cómo *adv* ¿c.? *(¿perdón?)* what? ▪ *(interrogativo)* how; **¿c. estás?** how are you?; **¿a c. están los tomates?** *(a cuánto)* how much are the tomatoes?; *(por qué)* how come?; **¿c. es eso?** how come?; **¿c. fue que no viniste a la fiesta?** how come you didn't come to the party? ▪ *(exclamativo)* how; **¡c. has crecido!** you've really grown a lot!; **¡c. no!** but of course!

cómoda *f* chest of drawers.

comodidad *f* comfort; *(conveniencia)* convenience.

comodín *m* joker.

cómodo, -a *adj* comfortable; *(útil)* handy, convenient.

compacto, -a *adj* compact; **disco c.** compact disc.

compadecer [33] **1** *vt* to feel sorry for, to pity. **2 compadecerse** *vr* to take pity (**de** on).

compadre *m (padrino)* godfather; *Am fam (amigo)* friend, mate.

compañero, -a *mf* companion; **c. de piso** roommate.

compañía *f* company; **hacer c. a algn** to keep sb company.

comparación *f* comparison; **en c.** comparatively; **en c. con** compared to; **sin c.** beyond compare.

comparar *vt* to compare (**con** with).

compartimento, compartimiento *m* compartment.

compartir *vt* to share.

compás *m* (pair of) compasses; *(brújula)* compass; *(ritmo)* rhythm; **al c. de** in time to.

compasión *f* compassion, pity; **tener c. de algn** to feel sorry for sb.

compasivo, -a *adj* compassionate.

compatible *adj* compatible.

compatriota *mf* compatriot; *(hombre)* fellow countryman; *(mujer)* fellow countrywoman.

compensar 1 *vt (pérdida, error)* to make up for; *(indemnizar)* to compensate (for). **2** *vi* to be worthwhile.

competencia *f (rivalidad, empresas rivales)* competition; *(capacidad)* competence; *(incumbencia)* field.

competente *adj* competent.

competición *f* competition.

competir [6] *vi* to compete.

competitivo, -a *adj* competitive.

compinche *mf (cómplice)* accomplice.

complacer [60] *vt* to please.

complejo, -a *adj & m* complex.

complemento *m* complement; *(objeto)* object.

completamente *adv* completely.

completar *vt* to complete.

completo, -a adj (terminado) complete; (lleno) full; **por c.** completely.

complicado, -a adj (complejo) complicated; (implicado) involved.

complicar [44] **1** vt to complicate; (involucrar) to involve (**en** in). **2 complicarse** vr to get complicated.

cómplice mf accomplice.

complot m (pl **complots**) conspiracy, plot.

componer [19] (pp **compuesto**) **1** vt to compose; (reparar) to mend, repair. **2 componerse** vr (consistir) to be made up (**de** of), consist (**de** of).

comportamiento m behavior.

composición f composition.

compota f compote.

compra f (acción) buying; (cosa comprada) purchase, buy; **ir de compras** to go shopping.

comprar vt to buy.

comprender vt (entender) to understand; (contener) to comprise, to include.

comprensión f understanding.

comprensivo, -a adj understanding.

compresa f (para mujer) sanitary napkin.

comprimido, -a 1 m tablet. **2** adj compressed.

comprobante m (de compra) voucher, receipt.

comprobar [2] vt to check.

comprometer 1 vt (arriesgar) to compromise; (obligar) to compel. **2 comprometerse** vr (involucrarse) to involve oneself; (novios) to become engaged; **comprometerse a hacer algo** to undertake to do sth.

compromiso m (obligación) obligation, commitment; (acuerdo) agreement; **por c.** out of a sense of duty; **poner a algn en un c.** to put sb in a difficult situation.

compuesto, -a 1 adj compound; **c. de** composed of. **2** m compound.

compuse pt indef de **componer**.

computadora f computer; **c. portátil** notebook.

comulgar [42] vi to receive Holy Communion; fig **no comulgo con sus ideas** I don't share his ideas.

común adj common; (compartido) shared; **poco c.** unusual; **por lo c.** generally.

comuna f Am (municipalidad) municipality.

comunicación f communication; (oficial) communiqué; (telefónica) connection; (unión) link, connection.

comunicar [44] **1** vt to communicate; **comuníquenoslo lo antes posible** let us know as soon as possible. **2** vi to communicate; (teléfono) to be engaged. **3 comunicarse** vr to communicate.

comunidad f community; **C. Europea** European Community.

comunión f communion.

con prep with; **c. ese frío/niebla** in that cold/fog; **estar c. (la) gripe** to have the flu; **una bolsa c. dinero** a bag (full) of money; **habló c. todos** he spoke to everybody. • (con infinitivo) **c. llamar será suficiente** it will be enough just to phone. • (con que + subj) **bastará c. que lo esboces** a general idea will do; **c. tal (de) que ...** provided that ....

concebir [6] **1** vt (plan, hijo) to conceive; (entender) to understand. **2** vi (mujer) to conceive.

conceder vt to grant; (premio) to award; (admitir) to concede.

concejal, -a mf town councilor.

concentración f concentration; (de manifestantes) gathering.

concentrado m concentrate.

concentrar vt, **concentrarse** vr to concentrate (**en** on).

concepción f conception.

concepto m concept; **bajo/por ningún c.** under no circumstances.

concerniente adj concerning, regarding (**a** -); fml **en lo c. a** with regard to.

concernir [54] v impers (afectar) to concern; (corresponder) to be up to; **en lo que a mí concierne** as far as I am concerned; **en lo que concierne a** with regard/respect to.

concesión f concession; (de premio, contrato) awarding.

concha f (caparazón) shell; (carey) tortoiseshell.

conciencia f conscience; (conocimiento) consciousness, awareness; **a c.** conscientiously.

concienzudo, -a adj conscientious.

concierto m concert; (composición) concerto; (acuerdo) agreement.

conciso, -a adj concise.

concluir [37] vt to conclude.

conclusión f conclusion; **sacar una c.** to draw a conclusion.

concretamente adv specifically.

concretar vt (precisar) to specify, to state explicitly; (fecha, hora) to fix.

concreto, -a 1 adj (preciso, real) concrete; (particular) specific; **en c.** specifically. **2** m Am concrete.

concurrido, -a adj crowded, busy.

concursante mf contestant, competitor.

concursar vi to compete, to take part.

concurso m (competición) competition; (de belleza etc) contest; (televisivo) quiz show.

condecorar vt to decorate.

condena f sentence; (desaprobación) condemnation, disapproval.

condenado, -a 1 adj convicted; **c. a muerte** condemned to death. **2** mf convicted person; (a muerte) condemned person.

condenar vt to convict, find guilty; (desaprobar) to condemn.

condensado, -a adj condensed; **leche condensada** condensed milk.

condensar vt, **condensarse** vr to condense.

condición f condition; **en buenas/malas condiciones** in good/bad condition; **con la c. de que ...** on condition that ....

condimentar vt to season, to flavor.

condimento m seasoning, flavoring.

condominio m Am (edificio) condominium.

condón m condom.

conducir [10] **1** vt (coche) to drive; (electricidad) to conduct. **2** vi to drive; (llevar) to lead; **permiso de c.** driver's license.

conducta f behavior, conduct.

conducto m (tubería) pipe.

conductor, -a mf driver.

conectar vt to connect up; (enchufar) to plug in, to switch on.

conejillo m **c. de Indias** guinea pig.

conejo m rabbit.

conexión f connection.

confección f dressmaking; (de ropa masculina) tailoring; (de plan) making.

conferencia f lecture; (telefónica) long-distance call.

confesar [1] **1** vti to confess. **2** **confesarse** vr to confess; (de pecados) to go to confession; **confesarse culpable** to admit one's guilt.

confiado, -a adj (seguro) self-confident; (crédulo) gullible, unsuspecting.

confianza f (seguridad) confidence; **tener c. en uno mismo** to be self-confident; **de c.** reliable; **tener c. con algn** to be on intimate terms with sb.

confiar [29] **1** vt (entregar) to entrust; (información, secreto) to confide. **2** vi **c. en** to trust; **no confíes en su ayuda** don't count on his help. **3** **confiarse** vr to confide (en, a in).

confidencia f confidence.

confidencial adj confidential.

confidente, -a mf (hombre) confidant; (mujer) confidante; (de la policía) informer.

confirmar vt to confirm.

confiscar [44] vt to confiscate.

confitería f candy store; CSur café.

confitura f preserve, jam.

conflicto m conflict.

conformarse vr **tendrás que conformarte (con esto)** you will have to be content with that.

conforme 1 adj (satisfecho) satisfied; **no estoy c.** I don't agree. **2** conj as. **3** prep **c. a** in accordance with.

confort m (pl **conforts**) comfort.

confortable adj comfortable.

confrontación f confrontation.

confrontar vt to confront; (comparar) to compare, to collate.

confundir 1 vt to confuse (**con** with); (engañar) to mislead; **c. a una persona con otra** to mistake somebody for somebody else. **2 confundirse** vr (equivocarse) to be mistaken; (mezclarse) to mingle; (colores, formas) to blend.

confusión f confusion.

confuso, -a adj confused; (formas, recuerdo) vague.

congelado, -a 1 adj frozen. **2** mpl **congelados** frozen food sing.

congelador m freezer.

congelar 1 vt to freeze. **2 congelarse** vr to freeze.

congoja f sorrow, grief.

congreso m congress, conference; **c. de los Diputados** ≃ Congress.

congrio m conger eel.

conjugación f conjugation.

conjunción f conjunction.

conjunto, -a 1 m (grupo) collection, group; (todo) whole; (pop) group, band; (prenda) outfit; **de c.** overall; **en c.** on the whole. **2** adj joint.

conllevar vt to entail.

conmemoración f commemoration.

conmigo pron pers with me; **él habló c.** he talked to me.

conmoción f commotion, shock; **c. cerebral** concussion.

conmovedor, -a adj touching.

conmover [4] vt to touch, to move.

conmutador m switch; Am switchboard.

cono m cone.

conocedor, -a adj & mf expert; (de vino, arte etc) connoisseur.

conocer [34] **1** vt to know; (por primera vez) to meet; (reconocer) to recognize; **dar (algo/algn) a c.** to make (sth/sb) known. **2 conocerse** vr (dos personas) to know each other; (por primera vez) to meet.

conocido, -a 1 adj known; (famoso) well-known. **2** mf acquaintance.

conocimiento m knowledge; (conciencia) consciousness; **perder/ recobrar el c.** to lose/regain consciousness; **conocimientos** knowledge.

conquista f conquest.

conquistador, -a mf conqueror.

conquistar vt (país, ciudad) to conquer; **c. a algn** to make a conquest of sb.

consabido, -a adj (bien conocido) well-known; (usual) familiar, usual.

consagrar 1 vt (artista) to establish; (vida, tiempo) to devote. **2 consagrarse** vr (dedicarse) to devote oneself (**a** to); (lograr fama) to establish oneself.

consciente adj conscious.

consecuencia f consequence; (coherencia) consistency; **a o como c. de** as a consequence of; **en c.** therefore.

consecuente adj consistent.

consecutivo, -a adj consecutive; **tres días consecutivos** three days in a row.

conseguir [6] vt to get, to obtain; (objetivo) to achieve; (lograr) to manage.

consejero, -a mf (asesor) adviser; (ministro) regional minister.

consejo m (recomendación) advice; (junta) council; (reunión) cabinet meeting; **un c.** a piece of advice; **c.**

de ministros cabinet; **c. de administración** board of directors.
consentido, -a *adj* spoiled.
consentimiento *m* consent.
consentir [5] **1** *vt (tolerar)* to allow, to permit; *(mimar)* to spoil; **no consientas que haga eso** don't allow him to do that. **2** *vi* to consent; **c. en** to agree to.
conserje *m (bedel)* janitor.
conserva *f* tinned *o* canned food.
conservador, -a *adj & mf* conservative; *(derechista)* Conservative.
conservante *m* preservative.
conservar **1** *vt* to conserve, to preserve; *(mantener)* to keep up; *(alimentos)* to preserve. **2 conservarse** *vr (tradición etc)* to survive.
conservatorio *m* conservatory.
considerado, -a *adj (atento)* considerate, thoughtful.
considerar *vt* to consider; **lo considero imposible** I think it's impossible.
consigna *f (para maletas)* checkroom.
consigo[1] *pron pers (tercera persona) (hombre)* with him; *(mujer)* with her; *(cosa, animal)* with it; *(plural)* with them; *(usted)* with you; **hablar c. mismo** to speak to oneself.
consigo[2] *indic pres de* **conseguir**.
consiguiente *adj* consequent; **por c.** therefore, consequently.
consistente *adj (firme)* firm, solid.
consistir *vi* to consist (**en** of).
consola *f* console.
consolar [2] **1** *vt* to console, to comfort. **2 consolarse** *vr* to console oneself.
consomé *m* clear soup, consommé.
consonante *adj & f* consonant.
consorte *mf (cónyuge)* partner, spouse.
conspiración *f* conspiracy, plot.
conspirar *vi* to conspire, to plot.
constancia *f* perseverance; *(testimonio)* proof, evidence.
constante **1** *adj* constant; *(perso-*

na) steadfast. **2** *f* constant feature.
constantemente *adv* constantly.
constar *vi (figurar)* to figure in, be included (in); **me consta que ...** I am absolutely certain that ...; **c. de** *(consistir)* to consist of.
constatar *vt* to state; *(comprobar)* to check.
constipado, -a 1 *adj* **estar c.** to have a cold. **2** *m* cold.
constiparse *vr* to catch a cold.
constitución *f* constitution.
constituir [37] **1** *vt (formar)* to constitute; *(suponer)* to represent; *(fundar)* to constitute, to set up; **estar constituido por** to consist of. **2 constituirse** *vr* to set oneself up (**en** as).
construcción *f* construction; *(sector)* building industry.
constructor, -a 1 *mf* builder. **2** *adj* **empresa constructora** builders *pl*, construction company.
construir [37] *vt* to construct, to build.
consuelo *m* consolation.
cónsul *mf* consul.
consulado *m* consulate.
consulta *f* consultation; *(médica)* surgery; *(despacho)* consulting room; **horas de c.** surgery hours.
consultar *vt* to consult.
consultivo, -a *adj* consultative, advisory.
consultorio *m (médico)* medical center.
consumidor, -a 1 *mf* consumer. **2** *adj* consuming.
consumir 1 *vt* to consume. **2 consumirse** *vr (agua, jugo)* to boil away.
consumo *m* consumption; **bienes de c.** consumer goods; **sociedad de c.** consumer society.
contabilidad *f (profesión)* accountancy; *(de empresa, sociedad)* accounting.
contabilizar [40] *vt (en contabilidad)* to enter in the books; *(en partido)* to score.

contable *mf* accountant.

contactar *vi* c. con to contact.

contacto *m* contact; *(en coche)* ignition; **ponerse en c.** to get in touch.

contado, -a 1 *adj (pocos)* few and far between; **contadas veces** very seldom. **2** *m* **pagar al c.** to pay cash.

contador *m* meter.

contagiar [43] **1** *vt (enfermedad)* to pass on. **2 contagiarse** *vr (enfermar)* to get infected; *(transmitirse)* to be contagious.

contagio *m* contagion.

contagioso, -a *adj* contagious; *(risa)* infectious.

contaminación *f* contamination; *(del aire)* pollution.

contar [2] **1** *vt (sumar)* to count; *(narrar)* to tell. **2** *vi* to count; **c. con** *(confiar en)* to count on; *(tener)* to have.

contemplar *vt* to contemplate; *(considerar)* to consider.

contemporáneo, -a *adj & mf* contemporary.

contenedor *m* container.

contener [24] **1** *vt* to contain; *(reprimir)* to restrain, to hold back. **2 contenerse** *vr* to control oneself, to hold (oneself) back.

contenido *m* content, contents *pl.*

contentar 1 *vt (satisfacer)* to please; *(alegrar)* to cheer up. **2 contentarse** *vr (conformarse)* to make do, to be satisfied *(con* with).

contento, -a *adj* happy, pleased *(con* with).

contestación *f* answer.

contestador *m* c. automático answering machine.

contestar *vt* to answer.

contienda *f* struggle.

contigo *pron pers* with you.

contiguo, -a *adj* adjoining.

continente *m* continent.

continuación *f* continuation; **a c.** next.

continuamente *adv* continuously.

continuar [30] *vti* to continue.

continuo, -a *adj* continuous; *(reiterado)* continual, constant.

contra 1 *prep* against; **en c. de** against. **2** *mpl* **los pros y los contras** the pros and cons.

contrabajo *m* double bass.

contrabandista *mf* smuggler; **c. de armas** gunrunner.

contrabando *m* smuggling; **pasar algo de c.** to smuggle sth in.

contracción *f* contraction.

contracepción *f* contraception.

contracorriente 1 *f* crosscurrent. **2** *adv* **ir (a) c.** to go against the tide.

contradecir [12] *(pp* contradicho) *vt* to contradict.

contradicción *f* contradiction.

contraer [25] **1** *vt* to contract; **c. matrimonio** to get married. **2 contraerse** *vr* to contract.

contraigo *indic pres de* contraer.

contraje *pt indef de* contraer.

contramano: a contramano *adv* in the wrong direction, the wrong way.

contrapeso *m* counterweight.

contraproducente *adj* counterproductive.

contrariamente *adv* c. a ... contrary to ....

contrariar [29] *vt (oponerse a)* to oppose, to go against; *(disgustar)* to upset.

contrariedad *f (contratiempo)* obstacle, setback; *(decepción)* annoyance.

contrario, -a 1 *adj* opposite; **en el lado/sentido c.** on the other side/in the other direction; **al c., por el c.** on the contrary; **de lo c.** otherwise; **todo lo c.** quite the opposite. **2** *mf* opponent, rival. **3** *f* **llevar la contraria** to be contrary.

contrarrestar *vt* to offset, to counteract.

contraseña *f* password.

contrastar *vt* to contrast *(con* with).

contraste *m* contrast.

contratar *vt (empleado)* to hire, to engage.

contratiempo *m* setback, hitch.

contratista *mf* contractor.

contrato *m* contract.

contraventana *f* shutter.

contribución *f* contribution; *(impuesto)* tax.

contribuir [37] *vti* to contribute (**a** to).

contribuyente *mf* taxpayer.

contrincante *mf* rival, opponent.

control *m* control; *(inspección)* check; *(de policía etc)* checkpoint; **c. remoto** remote control.

controlador, -a *mf* **c. (aéreo)** air traffic controller.

controlar 1 *vt* to control. **2 controlarse** *vr* to control oneself.

controversia *f* controversy.

contundente *adj (arma)* blunt; *(argumento)* forceful, convincing.

contusión *f* contusion, bruise.

convalecencia *f* convalescence.

convalidar *vt* to validate; *(documento)* to ratify.

convencer [49] *vt* to convince; **c. a algn de algo** to convince sb about sth.

convencional *adj* conventional.

conveniencia *f (provecho)* convenience; **conveniencias sociales** social proprieties.

conveniente *adj (oportuno)* convenient; *(aconsejable)* advisable; *(precio)* good, fair.

convenio *m* agreement.

convenir [27] *vti (acordar)* to agree; *(ser oportuno)* to suit, to be good for; **c. en** to agree on; **conviene recordar que** it's as well to remember that.

convento *m (de monjas)* convent.

conversación *f* conversation.

conversar *vi* to converse, to talk.

conversión *f* conversion.

convertir [54] **1** *vt* to change, to convert. **2 convertirse** *vr* **convertirse en** to turn into, to become.

convicción *f* conviction.

convidado, -a *adj & mf* guest.

convidar *vt* to invite.

convivencia *f* life together.

convivir *vi* to live together.

convocar [44] *vt* to summon; *(reunión, elecciones)* to call.

convocatoria *f (a huelga etc)* call.

convulsión *f* convulsion.

conyugal *adj* conjugal; **vida c.** married life.

cónyuge *mf* spouse; **cónyuges** married couple *sing,* husband and wife.

coñac *m* brandy, cognac.

cooperación *f* co-operation.

cooperar *vi* to co-operate (**a, en**; **con** with).

cooperativa *f* co-operative.

coordenada *f* co-ordinate.

coordinar *vt* to co-ordinate.

copa *f* glass; *(de árbol)* top; *(premio)* cup; **tomar una c.** to have a drink.

copia *f* copy; **c. de seguridad** *(archivo)* backup; **hacer una c. de seguridad de algo** to back up sth.

copiar [43] *vt* to copy.

copla *f* verse, couplet.

copo *m* flake; **c. de nieve** snowflake; **copos de maíz** cornflakes.

coquetear *vi* to flirt.

coqueto, -a *adj* coquettish.

coraje *m (valor)* courage; *(ira)* anger, annoyance.

coral¹ *m* coral.

coral² *f (composición)* choral, chorale.

Corán *m* Koran.

coraza *f* armor.

corazón *m* heart; *(de fruta)* core; **tener buen c.** to be kind-hearted.

corazonada *f* hunch, feeling.

corbata *f* necktie.

corcho *m* cork; *(de pesca)* float.

cordel *m* rope, cord.

cordero, -a *mf* lamb.

cordial *adj* cordial, warm.

cordillera *f* mountain range.

cordón *m* string; *(de zapatos)* shoelace.

cordura f common sense.

cornada f (de toro) goring.

córner m corner (kick).

corneta f bugle.

cornisa f cornice.

coro m (musical) choir; (en tragedia) chorus; **a c.** all together.

corona f crown; (de flores etc) wreath, garland.

coronación f coronation.

coronel m colonel.

coronilla f crown of the head; fam **estar hasta la c.** to be fed up (de with).

corporación f corporation.

corporal adj corporal; **olor c.** body odor, BO.

corpulento, -a adj corpulent, stout.

corral m corral.

correa f (tira) strap; (de pantalón) belt; (de perro) lead, leash; (de motor) belt.

corrección f (rectificación) correction; (educación) courtesy, politeness.

correcto, -a adj (sin errores) correct; (educado) polite, courteous (con to); (conducta) proper.

corredizo, -a adj (puerta etc) sliding; **nudo c.** slipknot.

corredor, -a mf (deportista) runner; (balconada) gallery.

corregir [58] **1** vt to correct. **2 corregirse** vr (persona) to mend one's ways.

correo m post, mail; **echar al c.** to post; **por c.** by post; **correos** (edificio) post office sing; **c. aéreo** airmail; **c. basura** spam, junk mail; **c. certificado** registered post; **c. electrónico** electronic mail, e-mail; **me envió un c. (electrónico)** (un mensaje) she e-mailed me, she sent me an e-mail.

correr 1 vi to run; (coche) to go fast; (conductor) to drive fast; (viento) to blow; **c. prisa** to be urgent. **2** vt (cortina) to draw; (cerrojo) to close; (mover) to pull up, to draw up; **c. el riesgo** to run the risk. **2 correrse** vr (moverse) to move over.

correspondencia f correspondence.

corresponder 1 vi to correspond (a to; con with); (ajustarse) to go (con with); (incumbir) to concern; (pertenecer) to be one's due; **me dieron lo que me correspondía** they gave me my share. **2 corresponderse** vr (ajustarse) to correspond; (dos cosas) to tally; **no se corresponde con la descripción** it does not match the description.

correspondiente adj corresponding (a to).

corresponsal mf correspondent.

corrida f c. (de toros) bullfight.

corriente 1 adj (común) common; (agua) running; (mes, año) current, present; (cuenta) current; **estar al c.** to be up to date. **2** f current, stream; (de aire) draft; (tendencia) trend, current; fam **seguirle** o **llevarle la c. a algn** to humor sb; **c. (eléctrica)** (electric) current.

corrijo indic pres de **corregir**.

corro m circle, ring; (juego) ring-a-ring-a-roses.

corroborar vt to corroborate.

corromper 1 vt to rot. **2 corromperse** vr to go bad, to rot.

corrosivo, -a adj (sustancia) corrosive; fig (comentario) caustic.

corrupción f corruption.

corrupto, -a adj corrupt.

cortacésped m o f lawnmower.

cortado, -a 1 adj cut (up); (leche) sour; (labios) chapped; fam (tímido) shy. **2** m small coffee with a dash of milk.

cortar 1 vt to cut; (carne) to carve; (árbol) to cut down; (piel) to chap, to crack; (luz, teléfono) to cut off; (paso, carretera) to block. **2 cortarse** vr (herirse) to cut oneself; (leche etc) to curdle; **cortarse el pelo** to have one's hair cut; **se cortó la comunicación** we were cut off.

corte *m* cut; *(sección)* section; **c. de pelo** haircut.

cortés *adj* courteous, polite.

cortesía *f* courtesy, politeness.

corteza *f (de árbol)* bark; *(de queso)* rind; *(de pan)* crust.

cortijo *m* Andalusian farmhouse.

cortina *f* curtain.

corto, -a *adj (distancia, tiempo)* short; **c. de vista** short-sighted; **luz corta** dipped headlights *pl*; **quedarse c.** *(calcular mal)* to underestimate.

cortocircuito *m* short circuit.

cosa *f* thing; *(asunto)* matter, business; **eso es c. tuya** that's your business; **eso es otra c.** that's different; **hace c. de una hora** about an hour ago.

coscorrón *m* knock on the head.

cosecha *f* harvest, crop; *(año del vino)* vintage.

coser *vt* to sew.

cosmético, -a *adj & m* cosmetic.

cosmonauta *mf* cosmonaut.

coso *m (taurino)* bullring; *CSur fam (objeto)* whatnot, thing.

cosquillas *fpl* **hacer c. a algn** to tickle sb; **tener c.** to be ticklish.

costa *f* coast; *(litoral)* coastline; *(playa)* beach, seaside.

costado *m (lado)* side; **de c.** sideways.

costar [2] *vi* to cost; **¿cuánto cuesta?** how much is it?; **c. barato/caro** to be cheap/expensive; **c. trabajo o mucho** to be hard; **me cuesta hablar francés** I find it hard to speak French.

coste *m* cost; **c. de la vida** cost of living.

costear 1 *vt* to afford, to pay for. **2 costearse** *vr* to pay for.

costilla *f (hueso)* rib; *(chuleta)* cutlet.

costo *m* cost.

costoso, -a *adj* costly, expensive.

costra *f* crust; *(de herida)* scab.

costumbre *f (hábito)* habit; *(tradición)* custom; **como de c.** as usual; **tengo la c. de levantarme temprano** I usually get up early; **tenía la c. de …** he used to ….

costura *f* sewing; *(confección)* dressmaking; *(línea de puntadas)* seam; **alta c.** haute couture.

costurero *m* sewing basket.

cotidiano, -a *adj* daily.

cotilla *mf fam* busybody, gossip.

cotillear *vi fam* to gossip (**de** about).

cotilleo *m fam* gossip.

cotización *f* (market) price, quotation.

coto *m* enclosure; **c. de caza** game reserve.

cotorra *f* parrot; *(persona)* chatterbox.

coz *f* kick.

cráneo *m* cranium, skull.

cráter *m* crater.

creación *f* creation.

crear *vt* to create.

creativo, -a *adj* creative.

crecer [33] *vi* to grow.

crecimiento *m* growth.

credencial *adj* credential; **cartas credenciales** credentials.

crédito *m* credit; **dar c. a** to believe.

creencia *f* belief.

creer [36] **1** *vt* to believe; *(pensar)* to think; **creo que no** I don't think so; **creo que sí** I think so; **ya lo creo** I should think so. **2** *vi* to believe. **3 creerse** *vr* **se cree guapo** he thinks he's good-looking.

creíble *adj* credible, believable.

crema *f* cream.

cremallera *f* zipper.

crematorio *m* crematory.

cremoso, -a *adj* creamy.

crepe *f* pancake.

crepúsculo *m* twilight.

cresta *f* crest; *(de gallo)* comb.

cretino, -a 1 *adj* stupid, cretinous. **2** *mf* cretin.

creyente *mf* believer.

crezco *indic pres de* **crecer**.

cría *f (cachorro)* young; *(crianza)* breeding.

criada *f* maid.

criado, -a 1 *adj* **mal c.** spoiled. **2** *mf* servant.

criar [29] *vt (animales)* to breed; *(niños)* to bring up.

criatura *f* (living) creature; *(crío)* baby, child.

criba *f* sieve.

crimen *m (pl* crímenes*)* crime.

criminal *adj & mf* criminal.

crin *f*, **crines** *fpl* mane *sing*.

crío, -a *mf* kid.

criollo, -a *adj & mf* Creole.

crisis *f inv* crisis; **c. nerviosa** nervous breakdown.

crispar *vt* to make tense; **me crispa los nervios** it makes me nervous.

cristal *m* crystal; *(vidrio)* glass; *(de gafas)* lens; *(de ventana)* (window) pane.

cristiano, -a *adj & mf* Christian.

Cristo *m* Christ.

criterio *m (pauta)* criterion; *(opinión)* opinion.

crítica *f* criticism; *(reseña)* review.

criticar [44] **1** *vt* to criticize. **2** *vi (murmurar)* to gossip.

crítico, -a 1 *adj* critical. **2** *mf* critic.

croissant *m* croissant.

crol *m (en natación)* crawl.

cromo *m (metal)* chromium, chrome; *(estampa)* picture card.

cromosoma *m* chromosome.

crónica *f* feature.

crónico, -a *adj* chronic.

cronológico, -a *adj* chronological.

cronometrar *vt* to time.

cronómetro *m* stopwatch.

croqueta *f* croquette.

croquis *m inv* sketch.

cruce *m* crossing; *(de carreteras)* crossroads.

crucero *m (viaje)* cruise; *(barco)* cruiser.

crucifijo *m* crucifix.

crucigrama *m* crossword (puzzle).

crudo, -a 1 *adj (natural)* raw; *(comida)* underdone; *(color)* cream. **2** *m (petróleo)* crude.

cruel *adj* cruel.

crueldad *f* cruelty.

crujiente *adj* crunchy.

crujir *vi (madera)* to creak; *(comida)* to crunch; *(hueso)* to crack.

cruz *f* cross; **C. Roja** Red Cross; **¿cara o c.?** ≃ heads or tails?

cruzado, -a *adj* crossed; *(atravesado)* lying across; **con los brazos cruzados** arms folded.

cruzar [40] **1** *vt* to cross; *(palabra, mirada)* to exchange. **2** *vi (atravesar)* to cross. **2 cruzarse** *vr* to cross; **cruzarse con algn** to pass sb.

cuaderno *m* notebook.

cuadra *f (establo)* stable; *Am* block (of houses).

cuadrado, -a *adj & m* square; **elevar (un número) al c.** to square (a number).

cuadriculado, -a *adj* papel **c.** squared paper.

cuadro *m* square; *(gráfico)* chart, graph; *(pintura)* painting, picture; **tela a cuadros** checked cloth; **c. de mandos** control panel.

cual *pron* **rel el/la c.** *(persona)* who; *(cosa)* which; **con el/la c.** with whom/which; **lo c.** which.

cuál 1 *pron interr* which (one)?; **¿c. quieres?** which one do you want? **2** *adj interr* which.

cualidad *f* quality.

cualquier *adj indef* any; **c. cosa** anything; **en c. momento** at any moment.

cualquiera *(pl* cualesquiera*)* **1** *adj indef (indefinido)* any; *(corriente)* ordinary. **2** *pron indef (persona)* anybody, anyone; *(cosa, animal)* any one; **c. que sea** whatever it is.

cuando *adv & conj* when; **de c. en c.**, **de vez en c.** from time to time; **c. quieras** whenever you want; **c. vengas** when you come; **(aun) c.** even if.

cuándo *adv interr* when; **¿desde c.?** since when; **¿para c. lo quieres?** when do you want it for?

cuanto, -a 1 *adj* **toma cuantos caramelos quieras** take all the sweets you want; **unas cuantas niñas** a few girls. **2** *pron rel* as much as; **coma (todo) c. quiera** eat as much as you want. **3** *pron indef pl* **unos cuantos** a few. **4** *adv (tiempo)* **c. antes** as soon as possible; **en c.** as soon as; **c. más … más** the more … the more; **en c. a** with respect to, regarding.

cuánto, -a 1 *adj & pron interr* how much; **¿cuántas veces?** how many times; **¿c. es?** how much is it? **2** *adv* how! how much! **¡cuánta gente hay!** what a lot of people there are!

cuarenta *adj & m inv* forty.

cuaresma *f* Lent.

cuartel *m (militar)* barracks *pl*; **c. general** headquarters.

cuartilla *f* sheet of paper.

cuarto, -a 1 *m (habitación)* room; *(cuarta parte)* quarter; **c. de baño** bathroom; **c. de estar** living room; **c. de hora** quarter of an hour. **2** *adj & mf* fourth.

cuate *mf Méx fam* pal, buddy.

cuatro *adj & m inv* four.

cuatrocientos, -as *adj & mf* four hundred.

cubalibre *m* rum o gin and coke.

cubano, -a *adj & mf* Cuban.

cubata *m fam* cubalibre.

cubierta *f* cover; *(de rueda)* tire; *(de barco)* deck.

cubierto, -a 1 *adj* covered; *(piscina etc)* indoor; *(cielo)* overcast. **2** *mpl* **cubiertos** cutlery only.

cubo *m* bucket; *(en matemática)* cube; **c. de la basura** trash bin.

cubrecama *m* bedspread.

cubrir *(pp cubierto)* **1** *vt* to cover. **2 cubrirse** *vr (cielo)* to become overcast.

cucaracha *f* cockroach.

cuchara *f* spoon.

cucharada *f* spoonful.

cucharilla *f* teaspoon; **c. de café** coffee spoon.

cucharón *m* ladle.

cuchichear *vi* to whisper.

cuchilla *f* blade; **c. de afeitar** razor blade.

cuchillo *m* knife.

cuchitril *m fam* hovel, hole.

cuco *m* cuckoo.

cucurucho *m (de helado)* cornet; *(envoltorio)* paper cone.

cuello *m* neck; *(de camisa etc)* collar.

cuenco *m* bowl.

cuenta *f (factura)* check; *(de banco)* account; *(cálculo)* count; *(de collar)* bead; **c. corriente** checking account; **caer en la c., darse c.** to realize; **tener en c.** to take into account; **traer c.** to be worthwhile; **en resumidas cuentas** in short; **trabajar por c. propia** to be self-employed.

cuentakilómetros *m inv (distancia)* ≃ milometer; *(velocidad)* speedometer.

cuentapasos *m inv* pedometer.

cuento *m* story; **contar un c.** to tell a story; **c. de hadas** fairy story.

cuerda *f (cordel)* rope; *(de instrumento)* string; *(del reloj)* spring; **dar c. al reloj** to wind up a watch.

cuerdo, -a *adj* sane.

cuerno *m* horn; *(de ciervo)* antler; *fam* **¡vete al c.!** get lost!

cuero *m* leather; **chaqueta de c.** leather jacket; **c. cabelludo** scalp.

cuerpo *m* body; *(cadáver)* corpse; **c. de bomberos** fire brigade; **c. diplomático** diplomatic corps; **c. de policía** police force.

cuervo *m* raven.

cuesta *f* slope; **c. abajo** downhill; **c. arriba** uphill. **2 a cuestas** *adv* on one's back.

cuestión *f (asunto)* matter, question; *(pregunta)* question; **en c. de unas horas** in just a few hours.

cuestionario *m* questionnaire.

cueva *f* cave.

cuezo *indic pres de* **cocer**.

cuidado, -a 1 *adj* careful. **2** *m* care; **con c.** carefully; **tener c.** to be careful; **estar al c. de** to be in charge of; *(persona)* to look after; **me trae sin c.** I couldn't care less; **cuidados intensivos** intensive care *sing*. **3** *interj* **¡c.!** look out!

cuidadoso, -a *adj* careful.

cuidar 1 *vt* to care for, to look after. **2 cuidarse** *vr* **cuídate** take care of yourself.

culebra *f* snake.

culebrón *m* soap opera.

culo *m fam (trasero)* backside; *(de recipiente)* bottom.

culpa *f* blame; *(culpabilidad)* guilt; **echar la c. a algn** to put the blame on sb; **fue c. mía** it was my fault; **por tu c.** because of you.

culpable 1 *adj* guilty; **declararse c.** to plead guilty. **2** *mf* offender, culprit.

culpar *vt* to blame; **c. a algn de un delito** to accuse sb of an offence.

cultivar *vt* to cultivate.

culto, -a 1 *adj* educated; *(palabra)* learned. **2** *m (devoción)* worship; *(religión)* cult.

cultura *f* culture.

culturismo *m* body building.

cumbre *f (de montaña)* summit, top; **(conferencia) c.** summit conference.

cumpleaños *m inv* birthday; **¡feliz c.!** happy birthday!

cumplir 1 *vt* to carry out; *(deseo)* to fulfil; *(promesa)* to keep; **ayer cumplí veinte años** I was twenty (years old) yesterday. **2** *vi (plazo)* to expire, end; **c. con el deber** to do one's duty. **3 cumplirse** *vr (deseo)* to come true; *(plazo)* to expire.

cuna *f* cot.

cundir *vi (extenderse)* to spread; **cundió el pánico** panic spread; **cundió la voz de que ...** rumor had it that ...; **me cunde mucho el trabajo o el tiempo** I seem to get a lot done.

cuneta *f (de la carretera)* gutter.

cuñado, -a *mf (hombre)* brother-in-law; *(mujer)* sister-in-law.

cuota *f (de club etc)* membership fees *pl*; *(porción)* quota, share; *Méx* **carretera de c.** toll road.

cupe *pt indef de* **caber**.

cupiera *subj imperfecto de* **caber**.

cupón *m* coupon, voucher.

cura 1 *m (religioso)* priest. **2** *f (de enfermedad)* cure.

curación *f* cure, treatment.

curandero, -a *mf* quack.

curar 1 *vt* to cure; *(herida)* to dress; *(enfermedad)* to treat. **2** *vi*, **curarse** *vr (sanar)* to recover, to get well; *(herida)* to heal up.

curiosidad *f* curiosity.

curioso, -a 1 *adj (extraño)* strange, odd; *(indiscreto)* curious, inquisitive. **2** *mf (mirón)* onlooker.

currículum *m* **c. vitae** curriculum vitae.

cursi *adj* posh.

cursillo *m* short course; **c. de reciclaje** refresher course.

curso *m (año académico)* year; *(clase)* class; *(de acontecimientos, río)* course; **en el c. de** in the course of; **moneda de c. legal** legal tender.

cursor *m* cursor.

curtir *vt (cuero)* to tan; *(endurecer)* to harden.

curva *f* curve; *(en carretera)* bend; **c. cerrada** sharp bend.

cutis *m* complexion.

cuyo, -a *pron rel & pos (persona)* whose; *(de cosa)* of which; **en c. caso** in which case.

D

D. *abr de* **don** Mister, Mr.

D.ª *abr de* **doña** Mrs; *(señorita)* Miss.

dactilar *adj* **huellas dactilares** fingerprints.

dado *m* dice.

dálmata *mf* Dalmatian.

dama *f (señora)* lady; **damas** *(juego)* checkers.

danés, -esa 1 *adj* Danish. **2** *mf (per-*

sona) Dane. **3** *m (idiom)* Danish; **gran d.** *(perro)* Great Dane.

danza *f* dancing; *(baile)* dance.

dañar *vt (cosa)* to damage; *(persona)* to hurt, to harm.

dañino, -a *adj* harmful, damaging (**para**).

daño *m (a cosa)* damage; *(a persona) (físico)* hurt; *(perjuicio)* harm.

dar [11] **1** *vt* to give; *(noticia)* to tell; *(mano de pintura, cera)* to apply; *(fruto, flores)* to bear; *(beneficio, interés)* to yield; *(hora)* to strike; **dale a la luz** switch the light on; **d. la mano a algn** *(saludo)* to shake hands with sb; **d. los buenos días/las buenas noches a algn** to say good morning/good evening to sb; **me da lo mismo** *or* **me da igual** it's all the same to me; **¿qué más da?** what difference does it make?; **d. de comer** to feed; **d. a conocer** *(noticia)* to release; **d. a entender que ...** to imply that ...; **d. por** *(considerar)* to consider; **d. por descontado/sabido** to take for granted. **2** *vi* **me dio un ataque de tos/risa** I had a coughing fit/an attack of the giggles; **d. a** *(ventana, habitación)* to overlook; *(puerta)* to open onto; **d. con la solución** to hit upon the solution; **d. de sí** *(ropa)* to stretch; **el presupuesto no da para más** the budget will not stretch any further; **d. que hablar** to get people talking. **3 darse** *vr* **se dio la circunstancia de que** it happened that; **se dio a la bebida** he started drinking; **darse con** *o* **contra** to bump into; **darse por satisfecho** to feel satisfied; **darse por vencido** to give in; **se le da bien/mal francés** she's good/bad at French.

dardo *m* dart.

dársena *f* dock.

dátil *m* date.

dato *m* piece of information; **datos** *(de ordenador)* data.

d.C. *abr de* **después de Cristo** Anno Domini, AD.

dcha. *abr de* **derecha** right.

de *prep (pertenencia)* of; **el título de la novela** the title of the novel; **el coche/hermano de Sofía** Sofia's car/brother. ▪ *(procedencia)* from; **vino de Madrid** he came from Madrid. ▪ *(descripción)* **el niño de ojos azules** the boy with blue eyes; **una avenida de quince kilómetros** an avenue fifteen kilometers long; **una botella de litro** a liter bottle; **el señor de la chaqueta** the man in the jacket; **un reloj de oro** a gold watch. ▪ *(contenido)* of; **un saco de patatas** a sack of potatoes. ▪ *(oficio)* by, as; **trabaja de secretaria** she's working as a secretary. ▪ *(acerca de)* about; **curso de informática** computer course. ▪ *(tiempo)* **a las tres de la tarde** at three in the afternoon; **de día** by day; **de noche** at night; **de lunes a jueves** from Monday to Thursday; **de pequeño** as a child. ▪ *(con superlativo)* **el más largo de España** the longest in Spain. ▪ *(causa)* with, because of; **llorar de alegría** to cry with joy; **morir de hambre** to die of hunger. ▪ **de cuatro en cuatro** four at a time; **de semana en semana** every week.

debajo 1 *adv* underneath, below. **2** *prep* **d. de** under(neath); **por d. de lo normal** below normal.

debate *m* debate.

debatir 1 *vt* to debate. **2 debatirse** *vr* to struggle.

deber¹ *m* duty; *(en el colegio)* **deberes** homework *sing*.

deber² **1** *vt (dinero, explicación)* to owe. **2** *vi* **debe irse ahora** she has to leave now; **la factura debe pagarse mañana** the bill must be paid tomorrow; **deberías vistar a tus padres** you ought to visit your parents; **debería haber ido ayer** I should have gone yesterday; **no debiste hacerlo** you shouldn't have done it; **deben de estar fuera** they must be out. **3 deberse** *vr* **deberse a** to be due to.

debidamente adv duly.
debido, -a adj d. a due to.
débil adj weak; (luz) dim; **punto d.** weak spot.
debilitar 1 vt to weaken. **2 debilitarse** vr to weaken, to grow weak.
debutar vi to make one's debut.
década f en la d. de los noventa during the nineties.
decadencia f decadence.
decaer [39] vi to deteriorate.
decano, -a mf dean.
decena f (about) ten; **una d. de veces** (about) ten times; **por decenas** in tens.
decenio m decade.
decente adj decent; (decoroso) modest.
decepción f disappointment.
decepcionante adj disappointing.
decepcionar vt to disappoint.
decidido, -a adj determined.
decidir 1 vti to decide. **2 decidirse** vr decidirse (a hacer algo) to make up one's mind (to do sth); **decidirse por algo** to decide on sth.
décima f tenth.
decimal adj & m decimal.
décimo, -a 1 adj & mf tenth. **2** m (parte) tenth.
decir [12] (pp dicho) **1** vt to say; **d. una mentira/la verdad** to tell a lie/ the truth; **dígame** (al teléfono) hello; **esta película no me dice nada** this film doesn't appeal to me; **querer d.** to mean; (locuciones) **es d.** that is (to say); **por así decirlo** so to speak; **digamos** let's say; **digo yo** in my opinion; **ni que d. tiene** needless to say; **¡no me digas!** really! **2 decirse** vr **¿cómo se dice 'mesa' en inglés?** how do you say 'mesa' in English?; **se dice que ...** they say that ....
decisión f decision; (resolución) termination; **tomar una d.** to make a decision; **con d.** decisively.
decisivo, -a adj decisive.
declaración f declaration; **d. de (la) renta** tax return; (afirmación)

statement; **hacer declaraciones** to comment.
declarar 1 vt to declare; (afirmar) to state; **d. la guerra a** to declare war on. **2** vi (en juicio) to testify. **3 declararse** vr (guerra, incendio) to break out; **declararse a favor/en contra de** to declare oneself in favor of/ against; **declararse en huelga** to go on strike; **declararse a algn** to declare one's love for sb.
decoración f decoration.
decorador, -a mf decorator; (en teatro) set designer.
decorar vt to decorate.
decorativo, -a adj decorative.
decretar vt to decree.
decreto m decree.
decreto-ley m decree.
dedal m thimble.
dedicar [44] **1** vt to dedicate; (tiempo, esfuerzos) to devote (a to). **2 dedicarse** vr **¿a qué se dedica Vd.?** what do you do for a living?; **los fines de semana ella se dedica a pescar** on weekends she spends her time fishing.
dedicatoria f dedication.
dedo m (de la mano) finger; (del pie) toe; **d. anular/corazón/índice/meñique** ring/middle/index/little finger; **d. pulgar, d. gordo** thumb.
deducir [10] **1** vt to deduce. **2 deducirse** vr **de aquí se deduce que ...** from this it follows that ....
defecar [44] vi to defecate.
defecto m defect.
defectuoso, -a adj defective.
defender [3] **1** vt to defend (contra against; de from). **2 defenderse** vr to defend oneself.
defensa 1 f defense; **en d. propia, en legítima d.** in self-defense. **2** m (en equipo) defender.
defensor, -a mf defender; **abogado d.** counsel for the defense; **el defensor del pueblo** the ombudsman.
deficiente 1 adj deficient. **2** m (nota) fail.

definición *f* definition.

definir *vt* to define.

definitivamente *adv (para siempre)* for good, once and for all; *(con toda seguridad)* definitely.

definitivo, -a *adj* definitive; **en definitiva** in short.

deformar 1 *vt* to deform; *(cara)* to disfigure; *(la verdad, una imagen)* to distort. **2 deformarse** *vr* to become distorted.

deforme *adj* deformed; *(objeto)* misshapen.

defraudar *vt* to disappoint; **d. a Hacienda** to evade taxes.

defunción *f* demise.

degenerado, -a *adj & mf* degenerate.

degenerar *vi* to degenerate.

degollar [2] *vt* to behead.

degradante *adj* degrading.

degradar *vt* to degrade.

degustación *f* tasting.

dejar 1 *vt* to leave; *(prestar)* to lend; *(abandonar)* to give up; *(permitir)* to let, to allow; **déjame en paz** leave me alone; **dejé el tabaco y la bebida** I gave up smoking and drinking; **d. caer** to drop; **d. entrar/salir** to let in/out; **d. triste** to make sad; **d. preocupado/sorprendido** to worry/ surprise. **2** *v aux* **d. de +** *inf* to stop; *(renunciar)* to give up; **no deja de llamarme** she's always calling me. **3 dejarse** *vr* **me he dejado las llaves dentro** I've left the keys inside; **dejarse barba** to grow a beard; **dejarse llevar por** to be influenced by.

del *(contracción de* **de + el***) ver* **de**.

delantal *m* apron.

delante 1 *adv* in front; **la entrada de d.** the front entrance; **por d.** in front; **se lo lleva todo por d.** he destroys everything in his path; **tiene toda la vida por d.** he has his whole life ahead of him. **2** *prep* **d. de** in front of; *(en serie)* ahead of.

delantero, -a 1 *adj* front. **2** *m (en fútbol)* forward; **d. centro** center forward.

delatar *vt* to inform against.

delegación *f (acto, delegados)* delegation; *(oficina)* local office.

delegado, -a *mf* delegate.

delegar [42] *vt* to delegate (**en** to).

deletrear *vt* to spell (out).

delfín *m* dolphin.

delgado, -a *adj* slim; *(capa)* fine.

deliberado, -a *adj* deliberate.

deliberar *vi* to deliberate (on).

delicadeza *f (finura)* daintiness; *(tacto)* tactfulness; **falta de d.** tactlessness.

delicado, -a *adj* delicate.

delicioso, -a *adj (comida)* delicious; *(agradable)* delightful.

delimitar *vt* to delimit.

delincuencia *f* crime.

delincuente *mf* criminal.

delineante *mf (hombre)* draftsman; *(mujer)* draftswoman.

delinquir [48] *vi* to break the law, to commit an offense.

delirar *vi* to be delirious.

delirio *m* delirium.

delito *m* crime.

delta *m* delta.

demacrado, -a *adj* emaciated.

demanda *f (judicial)* lawsuit.

demandar *vt* to sue.

demás 1 *adj* **los/las d.** the rest of. **2** *pron* **lo/los/las d.** the rest; **por lo d.** otherwise, apart from that.

demasiado, -a 1 *adj (singular)* too much; *(plural)* too many. **2** *adv* too (much); **es d. grande/caro** it is too big/dear; **fumas/trabajas d.** you smoke/work too much.

demencia *f* insanity.

democracia *f* democracy.

demócrata 1 *adj* democratic. **2** *mf* democrat.

democrático, -a *adj* democratic.

demográfico, -a *adj* demographic; **crecimiento d.** population growth.

demoledor, -a *adj* devastating.

demonio *m* devil.

demora *f* delay.

demorar 1 vt to delay, to hold up. **2 demorarse** vr (retrasarse) to be delayed, to be held up.

demostrar [2] vt (mostrar) to show; (evidenciar) to prove.

denegar [1] vt to refuse.

denigrante adj humiliating.

denominación f denomination.

denominar vt to name.

denotar vt to denote.

densidad f density.

denso, -a adj dense.

dentadura f teeth; **d. postiza** false teeth pl, dentures pl.

dental adj dental.

dentera f me da d. it sets my teeth on edge.

dentífrico, -a 1 adj pasta/crema dentífrica toothpaste. **2** m toothpaste.

dentista mf dentist.

dentro 1 adv (en el interior) inside; **aquí d.** in here; **por d.** (on the) inside. **2** prep **d. de** (lugar) inside; **d. de poco** shortly, soon; **d. de un mes** in a month's time.

denuncia f (a la policía) report; (crítica) denunciation.

denunciar [43] vt (delito) to report (**a** to).

departamento m department; (territorial) province; Am (piso) apartment.

depender vi to depend (**de** on); (económicamente) to be dependent (**de** on).

dependienta f shop assistant.

dependiente 1 adj dependent (**de** on). **2** m shop assistant.

depilación f depilation.

depilar vt to remove the hair from; (cejas) to pluck.

depilatorio, -a adj & m depilatory; **crema depilatoria** hair-remover.

deportar vt to deport.

deporte m sport; **hacer d.** to go out for sports.

deportista 1 mf (hombre) sportsman; (mujer) sportswoman. **2** adj sporty.

deportivo, -a 1 adj sports; **club d./ chaqueta deportiva** sports club/ jacket. **2** m (coche) sports car.

depositar 1 vt (colocar) to put. **2 depositarse** vr to settle.

depósito m (dinero) deposit; (de agua, gasolina) tank.

depresión f depression.

deprimente adj depressing.

deprimir 1 vt to depress. **2 deprimirse** vr to get depressed.

deprisa adv quickly.

depuradora f purifier.

derecha f (mano) right hand; (lugar) right, right-hand side; **a la d.** on the right, on the right-hand side; (en política) **la d.** the right.

derecho, -a 1 adj (de la derecha) right; (recto) straight. **2** m (privilegio) right; (carrera) law; **derechos civiles/humanos** civil/human rights; **tener d.** a to be entitled to; **no hay d.** it's not fair. **3** adv **siga todo d.** go straight ahead.

derivar 1 vi to drift; **d. de** to derive from. **2 derivarse** vr to stem (**de** from).

dermatólogo, -a mf dermatologist.

derramar 1 vt to spill; (lágrimas) to shed. **2 derramarse** vr to spill.

derrame m d. petrolero o de petróleo oil spill.

derrapar vi to skid.

derretir [6] vt, **derretirse** vr to melt; (hielo, nieve) to thaw.

derribar vt (demoler) to knock down; (gobierno) to bring down.

derrochar vt to waste.

derroche m waste.

derrota f defeat.

derrotar vt to defeat.

derruir [37] vt to demolish.

derrumbar 1 vt (edificio) to knock down. **2 derrumbarse** vr to collapse; (techo) to fall in.

desabrido, -a adj (tono) harsh; (persona) irritable.

desabrochar 1 vt to undo. **2 des-**

abrocharse *vr (prenda)* to come undone; **desabróchate la camisa** undo your shirt.

desacertado, -a *adj* unwise.

desaconsejar *vt* to advise against.

desacreditar *vt (desprestigiar)* to discredit; *(criticar)* to disparage.

desactivar *vt (bomba)* to defuse.

desacuerdo *m* disagreement.

desafiante *adj* defiant.

desafiar [29] *vt* to challenge.

desafinado, -a *adj* out of tune.

desafinar 1 *vi* to sing out of tune; *(instrumento)* to play out of tune. **2 desafinarse** *vr* to go out of tune.

desafío *m* challenge.

desafortunado, -a *adj* unfortunate.

desagradable *adj* unpleasant.

desagradar *vt* to displease.

desagradecido, -a 1 *adj* ungrateful. **2** *mf* ungrateful person.

desagrado *m* displeasure.

desagüe *m (cañería)* drainpipe; *(vaciado)* drain.

desaguisado *m* mess.

desahogado, -a *adj (acomodado)* well-off; *(espacioso)* spacious.

desahogarse [42] *vr* to let off steam.

desahuciar [43] *vt (desalojar)* to evict; *(enfermo)* to deprive of all hope.

desairar *vt* to slight.

desajuste *m* disorder, imbalance.

desalentar [1] **1** *vt* to dishearten. **2 desalentarse** *vr* to get discouraged.

desaliento *m* discouragement.

desaliñado, -a *adj* untidy.

desalmado, -a *adj* heartless.

desalojar *vt (inquilino)* to evict; *(público)* to move on; *(lugar)* to evacuate; *(abandonar)* to abandon.

desamparado, -a *adj (persona)* helpless.

desangrarse *vr* to lose (a lot of) blood.

desanimado, -a *adj (persona)* downhearted; *(fiesta etc)* dull.

desanimar 1 *vt* to dishearten. **2 desanimarse** *vr* to lose heart.

desánimo *m* dejection.

desapacible *adj* unpleasant.

desaparecer [33] *vi* to disappear.

desaparición *f* disappearance.

desapercibido, -a *adj* pasar d. to go unnoticed.

desaprovechar *vt (dinero, tiempo)* to waste.

desarmar *vt (desmontar)* to dismantle; *(ejército)* to disarm.

desarme *m* disarmament; **d. nuclear** nuclear disarmament.

desarraigado, -a *adj* rootless.

desarreglar *vt* to mess up.

desarrollado, -a *adj* developed.

desarrollar 1 *vt* to develop. **2 desarrollarse** *vr (persona, enfermedad)* to develop; *(tener lugar)* to take place.

desarrollo *m* development; **países en vías de d.** developing countries.

desarticular *vt* to dismantle.

desasir [46] **1** *vt* to release. **2 desasirse** *vr* to get loose; **desasirse de** to free oneself of.

desasosiego *m* uneasiness.

desastrado, -a *adj* scruffy.

desastre *m* disaster.

desastroso, -a *adj* disastrous.

desatar 1 *vt* to untie, undo. **2 desatarse** *vr (zapato, cordón)* to come undone.

desatascar [44] *vt* to clear.

desatornillar *vt* to unscrew.

desatrancar [44] *vt* to unblock; *(puerta)* to unbolt.

desautorizar [40] *vt* to disallow; *(huelga etc)* to ban.

desavenencia *f* disagreement.

desayunar 1 *vi* to have breakfast. **2** *vt* to have for breakfast.

desayuno *m* breakfast.

desbarajuste *m* confusion.

desbaratar *vt* to ruin.

desbordar 1 *vt* to overflow. **2** *vi* to overflow (**de** with). **3 desbordarse** *vr* to overflow.

descabellado, -a *adj* crazy.

descafeinado, -a *adj* decaffeinated.

descalabro *m* misfortune.

descalificar [44] *vt* to disqualify.

descalzarse [40] *vr* to take one's shoes off.

descalzo, -a *adj* barefoot.

descaminado, -a *adj fig* **ir d.** to be on the wrong track.

descampado *m* garbage dump.

descansado, -a *adj (persona)* rested; *(vida, trabajo)* restful.

descansar *vi* to rest, to have a rest; *(poco tiempo)* to take a break.

descansillo *m* landing.

descanso *m* rest; *(en teatro, cine)* interval; *(en deporte)* half-time; **un día de d.** a day off.

descapotable *adj & m* convertible.

descarado, -a 1 *adj (insolente)* rude; *(desvergonzado)* shameless. **2** *mf* rude person.

descarga *f* unloading; *(eléctrica, explosiva)* discharge; *(de Internet)* download.

descargar [42] **1** *vt* to unload; *(golpe)* to deal; *(de Internet)* to download. **2** *vi (tormenta)* to burst. **3** **descargarse** *vr* to go flat.

descaro *m* cheek.

descarrilar *vi* to be derailed.

descartar *vt* to rule out.

descato *m* lack of respect (**a** for).

descender [3] **1** *vi (temperatura, nivel)* to fall; **d. de** to descend from. **2** *vt* to lower.

descendiente *mf* descendant.

descenso *m* descent; *(de temperatura)* fall.

descifrar *vt* to decipher; *(mensaje)* to decode; *(misterio)* to solve.

descolgar [2] *vt (el teléfono)* to pick up; *(cuadro, cortinas)* to take down.

descolorido, -a *adj* faded.

descomponer [19] *(pp* **descompuesto) 1** *vt* to break down; *(corromper)* to decompose. **2** **descomponerse** *vr (corromperse)* to

decompose; *(ponerse nervioso)* to lose one's cool.

descomposición *f (de carne)* decomposition.

descompuse *pt indef de* **descomponer**.

descomunal *adj* massive.

desconcertar [1] **1** *vt* to disconcert. **2** **desconcertarse** *vr* to be bewildered.

desconcierto *m* chaos, confusion.

desconectar *vt* to disconnect.

desconfiado, -a *adj* distrustful.

desconfiar [29] *vi* to distrust (**de** -).

descongelar *vt* to defrost.

desconocer [34] *vt* not to know.

desconocido, -a 1 *adj* unknown; *(irreconocible)* unrecognizable. **2 m lo d.** the unknown. **3** *mf* stranger.

desconsiderado, -a 1 *adj* inconsiderate, thoughtless. **2** *mf* inconsiderate *o* thoughtless person.

desconsolado, -a *adj* disconsolate.

descontado, -a *adj fam* **dar por d.** to take for granted; **por d.** needless to say, of course.

descontar [2] *vt* to deduct.

descontento, -a 1 *adj* unhappy. **2** *m* dissatisfaction.

descontrolarse *vr* to lose control.

desconvocar *vt* to call off.

descorchar *vt* to uncork.

descorrer *vt* to draw back.

descortés *adj* impolite, discourteous.

descoser *vt* to unpick.

descoyuntar *vt* to dislocate.

descrédito *m* disrepute.

descremado, -a *adj* skimmed.

describir *(pp* **descrito)** *vt* to describe.

descripción *f* description.

descuartizar [40] *vt* to cut into pieces.

descubierto, -a 1 *adj* open. **2** *m* **al d.** in the open; **poner al d.** to bring out into the open.

descubrimiento *m* discovery.

descubrir *(pp* **descubierto)** *vt* to discover; *(conspiración)* to uncover; *(placa)* to unveil.

descuento *m* discount.

descuidado, -a *adj (negligente)* careless; *(desaseado)* untidy; *(desprevenido)* off one's guard.

descuidar 1 *vt* to neglect, to overlook. **2** *vi* **descuida, voy yo** don't worry, I'll go. **3 descuidarse** *vr (despistarse)* to be careless; **como te descuides, llegarás tarde** if you don't watch out, you'll be late.

descuido *m* oversight; *(negligencia)* carelessness; **por d.** inadvertently.

desde *adv (tiempo)* since; *(lugar)* from; **no lo he visto d. hace un año** I haven't seen him for a year; **d. siempre** always; **d. luego** of course; **d. que** ever since.

desdén *m* disdain.

desdeñar *vt* to disdain.

desdichado, -a 1 *adj* unfortunate. **2** *mf* poor devil.

desdoblar *vt* to unfold.

desear *vt* to desire; *(querer)* to want; **¿qué desea?** can I help you?; **estoy deseando que vengas** I'm looking forward to your coming; **te deseo buena suerte/feliz Navidad** I wish you good luck/a Merry Christmas.

desechable *adj* disposable.

desechar *vt (tirar)* to discard; *(idea, proyecto)* to drop.

desembalar *vt* to unpack.

desembarcar [44] **1** *vt (mercancías)* to unload; *(personas)* to disembark. **2** *vi* to disembark.

desembarco, desembarque *m (de mercancías)* unloading; *(de personas)* disembarkation.

desembocadura *f* mouth.

desembocar [44] *vi (río)* to flow (en into); *(calle, situación)* to lead (en to).

desembolsar *vt* to pay out.

desembolso *m* expenditure.

desembrollar *vt fam (aclarar)* to clear up; *(desenredar)* to disentangle.

desempaquetar *vt* to unpack.

desempatar *vi* to break the deadlock.

desempate *m* play-off.

desempeñar *vt (cargo)* to hold; *(función)* to fulfill; *(papel)* to play.

desempleado, -a 1 *adj* unemployed, out of work. **2** *mf* unemployed person; **los desempleados** the unemployed.

desempleo *m* unemployment; **cobrar el d.** to be on welfare.

desencadenar 1 *vt (provocar)* to unleash. **2 desencadenarse** *vr (viento, pasión)* to rage; *(conflicto)* to break out.

desencaminado, -a *adj* = **descaminado.**

desencanto *m* disillusion.

desenchufar *vt* to unplug.

desenfadado, -a *adj* free and easy.

desenfocado, -a *adj* out of focus.

desenfrenado, -a *adj* frantic, uncontrolled; *(vicio, pasión)* unbridled.

desenganchar *vt* to unhook; *(vagón)* to uncouple.

desengañar 1 *vt* **d. a algn** to open sb's eyes. **2 desengañarse** *vr* to be disappointed; *fam* **¡desengáñate!** get real!

desengaño *m* disappointment.

desengrasar *vt* to remove the grease from.

desenlace *m* outcome; *(de historia)* ending.

desenmascarar *vt* to unmask.

desenredar *vt* to disentangle.

desenrollar *vt* to unroll; *(cable)* to unwind.

desenroscar [44] *vt* to unscrew.

desentenderse [3] *vr* **se desentendió de mi problema** he didn't want to have anything to do with my problem.

desentonar *vi* to be out of tune; *(colores etc)* not to match; *(persona,* *comentario)* to be out of place.

desentrañar *vt* to unravel.

desentrenado, -a *adj* out of training.

desenvolver [4] (*pp* **desenvuelto**) **1** *vt* to unwrap. **2 desenvolverse** *vr* (*persona*) to manage.

desenvuelto, -a *adj* relaxed.

deseo *m* wish; (*sexual*) desire.

deseoso, -a *adj* eager; **estar d. de** be eager to.

desequilibrado, -a 1 *adj* unbalanced. **2** *mf* unbalanced person.

desértico, -a *adj* desert.

desertor, -a *mf* deserter.

desesperado, -a *adj* (*sin esperanza*) desperate; (*exasperado*) exasperated.

desesperante *adj* exasperating.

desesperar 1 *vt* to drive to despair; (*exasperar*) to exasperate. **2 desesperarse** *vr* to despair.

desestabilizar [40] *vt* to destabilize.

desestimar *vt* to reject.

desfachatez *f* cheek.

desfallecer [33] *vi* (*debilitarse*) to feel faint; (*desmayarse*) to faint.

desfasado, -a *adj* outdated; (*persona*) old-fashioned, behind the times.

desfavorable *adj* unfavorable.

desfigurar *vt* (*cara*) to disfigure.

desfiladero *m* narrow pass.

desfilar *vi* to march in single file; (*soldados*) to march past.

desfile *m* (*militar*) parade; **d. de modas** fashion show.

desganado, -a *adj* (*apático*) apathetic; **estar d.** (*inapetente*) to have no appetite.

desgarbado, -a *adj* ungraceful, ungainly.

desgarrador, -a *adj* blood-curdling.

desgarrar *vt* to tear.

desgastar *vt*, **desgastarse** *vr* to wear away.

desgaste *m* wear.

desgracia *f* misfortune; **por d.** unfortunately.

desgraciadamente *adv* unfortunately.

desgraciado, -a 1 *adj* unfortunate; (*infeliz*) unhappy. **2** *mf* unfortunate person.

desgravación *f* deduction; **d. fiscal** tax deduction.

desgravar *vt* to deduct.

deshabitado, -a *adj* uninhabited.

deshacer [15] (*pp* **deshecho**) **1** *vt* (*paquete*) to undo; (*maleta*) to unpack; (*destruir*) to destroy; (*disolver*) to dissolve; (*derretir*) to melt. **2 deshacerse** *vr* to come undone; **deshacerse de algn/algo** to get rid of sb/sth; (*disolverse*) to dissolve; (*derretirse*) to melt.

deshidratar *vt* to dehydrate.

deshielo *m* thaw.

deshonesto, -a *adj* dishonest; (*indecente*) indecent.

deshonrar *vt* to dishonor; (*a la familia etc*) to bring disgrace on.

deshora a d. *adv* at an inconvenient time; **comer a d.** to eat at odd times.

deshuesar *vt* (*carne*) to bone; (*fruta*) to stone.

desierto, -a 1 *m* desert. **2** *adj* (*deshabitado*) uninhabited; (*vacío*) deserted.

designar *vt* to designate; (*fecha, lugar*) to fix.

desigual *adj* uneven.

desigualdad *f* inequality; (*del terreno*) unevenness.

desilusión *f* disappointment.

desilusionar *vt* to disappoint.

desinfectante *adj* & *m* disinfectant.

desinfectar *vt* to disinfect.

desinflar 1 *vt* to deflate; (*rueda*) to let down. **2 desinflarse** *vr* to go flat.

desintegrar *vt*, **desintegrarse** *vr* to disintegrate.

desinterés *m* (*indiferencia*) lack of interest, apathy; (*generosidad*) unselfishness.

desinteresado, -a *adj* selfless.

desintoxicar [44] **1** *vt* to detoxicate; *(de alcohol)* to dry out. **2 desintoxicarse** *vr* to detoxicate oneself; *(de alcohol)* to dry out.

desistir *vi* to desist.

deslenguado, -a *adj (insolente)* insolent.

desliz *m* slip.

deslizar [40] **1** *vi* to slide. **2 deslizarse** *vr (patinar)* to slide; *(bajar)* to slide down.

deslumbrador, -a, deslumbrante *adj* dazzling; *fig* stunning.

deslumbrar *vt* to dazzle.

desmadrarse *vr fam* to go wild.

desmandarse *vr* to get out of hand.

desmano: a desmano *adv* out of the way; **me coge a d.** it is out of my way.

desmantelar *vt* to dismantle.

desmaquillador, -a 1 *m* make-up remover. **2** *adj* **leche desmaquilladora** cleansing cream.

desmaquillarse *vr* to remove one's make-up.

desmayarse *vr* to faint.

desmayo *m* fainting fit; **tener un d.** to faint.

desmedido, -a *adj* out of proportion.

desmejorar(se) *vi & vr* to deteriorate.

desmemoriado, -a *adj* forgetful.

desmentir [5] *vt* to deny.

desmenuzar [40] *vt* to crumble.

desmesurado, -a *adj* excessive.

desmontable *adj* that can be taken apart.

desmontar *vt* to dismantle.

desmoralizar [40] *vt* to demoralize.

desmoronarse *vr* to crumble.

desnatado, -a *adj (leche)* skim milk.

desnivel *m* drop.

desnudar *vt*, **desnudarse** *vr* to undress.

desnudista *adj & mf* nudist.

desnudo, -a *adj* naked.

desnutrido, -a *adj* undernourished.

desobedecer [33] *vt* to disobey.

desobediente 1 *adj* disobedient. **2** *mf* disobedient person.

desocupado, -a *adj (vacío)* empty; *(ocioso)* free.

desocupar *vt* to empty, to vacate.

desodorante *adj & m* deodorant.

desolar [2] *vt* to devastate.

desollar [2] **1** *vt* to skin. **2 desollarse** *vr* to scrape; **me desollé el brazo** I scraped my arm.

desorbitado, -a *adj (precio)* exorbitant.

desorden *m* mess; **d. público** civil disorder.

desordenado, -a *adj* untidy.

desordenar *vt* to make untidy, to mess up.

desorganizar [40] *vt* to disorganize, to disrupt.

desorientar *vt* to disorientate. **2 desorientarse** *vr* to lose one's bearings.

despabilado, -a *adj (sin sueño)* wide awake; *(listo)* quick.

despachar *vt (asunto)* to get through; *(en tienda)* to serve.

despacho *m (oficina)* office; *(en casa)* study.

despacio *adv (lentamente)* slowly.

desparramar *vt*, **desparramarse** *vr* to scatter; *(líquido)* to spill.

despavorido, -a *adj* terrified.

despectivo, -a *adj* derogatory.

despedida *f* goodbye.

despedir [6] **1** *vt (empleado)* to sack; *(decir adiós a)* to say goodbye to; *(olor, humo etc)* to give off. **2 despedirse** *vr (decir adiós)* to say goodbye (**de** to).

despegado, -a *adj* unstuck; *(persona)* couldn't-care-less.

despegar [42] **1** *vt* to detach. **2** *vi (avión)* to take off. **3 despegarse** *vr* to come unstuck.

despegue *m* takeoff.

despeinado, -a *adj* dishevelled.

despejado, -a *adj* clear; *(cielo)* cloudless.

despejar 1 *vt* to clear. **2 despejarse** *vr (cielo)* to clear; *(persona)* to clear one's head.

despeje *m (de balón)* clearance.

despensa *f* pantry.

despeñarse *vr* to go over a cliff.

desperdiciar [43] *vt* to waste; *(oportunidad)* to throw away.

desperdicio *m* waste; **desperdicios** *(basura)* trash *sing; (desechos)* leftovers.

desperdigar [42] *vt*, **desperdigarse** *vr* to scatter.

desperezarse [40] *vr* to stretch (oneself).

desperfecto *m (defecto)* flaw; *(daño)* damage.

despertador *m* alarm clock.

despertar [1] *vt*, **despertarse** *vr* to wake (up).

despiadado, -a *adj* merciless.

despido *m* dismissal.

despierto, -a *adj (desvelado)* awake; *(listo)* quick.

despilfarrar *vt* to squander.

despilfarro *m* squandering.

despistado, -a 1 *adj* scatterbrained. **2** *mf* scatterbrain.

despistar 1 *vt (hacer perder la pista a)* to lose. **2 despistarse** *vr (perderse)* to get lost; *(distraerse)* to switch off.

desplazamiento *m (viaje)* journey.

desplazar [40] **1** *vt* to displace. **2 desplazarse** *vr* to travel.

despojar *vt* to strip (**de** of); *fig* to deprive (**de** of).

desposar *vt* to marry.

déspota *mf* despot, tyrant.

despreciar [43] *vt (desdeñar)* to scorn; *(rechazar)* to reject.

desprecio *m (desdén)* scorn, disdain; *(desaire)* slight, snub.

desprender 1 *vt (separar)* to remove; *(olor, humo etc)* to give off. **2 desprenderse** *vr (soltarse)* to come

off; **desprenderse de** to rid oneself (**de** of).

despreocupado, -a *adj (tranquilo)* unconcerned; *(descuidado)* careless; *(estilo)* casual.

despreocuparse *vr (tranquilizarse)* to stop worrying; *(desentenderse)* to be unconcerned, to be indifferent (**de** to).

desprestigiar [43] *vt* to discredit.

desprestigio *m* discredit, loss of reputation; **campaña de d.** smear campaign.

desprevenido, -a *adj* unprepared; **coger** o **pillar a algn d.** to catch sb unawares.

desproporcionado, -a *adj* disproportionate.

desprovisto, -a *adj* lacking (**de** -).

después 1 *adv* afterwards, later; *(entonces)* then; *(seguidamente, lugar)* next; **poco d.** soon after. **2** *prep* **d. de** after. **3** *conj* **d. de que** after.

destacar [44] **1** *vt* to stress. **2 destacar(se)** *vi & vr* to stand out.

destapador *m Am* bottle opener.

destapar *vt* to take the lid off; *(botella)* to open. **2 destaparse** *vr* to get uncovered.

destartalado, -a *adj* rambling; *(desvencijado)* ramshackle.

destello *m* sparkle.

desteñir [6] **1** *vti* to discolor. **2 desteñirse** *vr* to fade.

desternillarse *vi* **d. (de risa)** to split one's sides laughing.

desterrar [1] *vt* to exile.

destiempo: a destiempo *adv* at the wrong time o moment.

destierro *m* exile.

destilería *f* distillery.

destinar *vt (dinero etc)* to assign; *(empleado)* to appoint.

destino *m (rumbo)* destination; *(sino)* fate; *(de empleo)* post; **el avión con d. a Bilbao** the plane to Bilbao.

destituir [37] *vt* to remove from office.

destornillador *m* screwdriver.

destreza f skill.

destrozar [40] vt (destruir) to destroy; (abatir) to shatter.

destrozo m destruction; **destrozos** damage.

destrucción f destruction.

destructivo, -a adj destructive.

destruir [37] vt to destroy.

desuso m disuse; **caer en d.** to fall into disuse.

desvalijar vt (robar) to rob; (casa, tienda) to burgle.

desván m loft.

desvanecerse [33] vr (disiparse) to vanish; (desmayarse) to faint.

desvariar [29] vi to talk nonsense.

desvelar 1 vt to keep awake. **2 desvelarse** vr to make every effort.

desvencijarse vr to fall apart.

desventaja f disadvantage; (inconveniente) drawback; **estar en d.** to be at a disadvantage.

desvergonzado, -a 1 adj (indecente) shameless; (descarado) insolent. **2** mf (sinvergüenza) shameless person; (fresco) insolent person.

desvergüenza f (indecencia) shamelessness; (atrevimiento) insolence; (acto impertinente) insolent o rude remark; **tuvo la d. de negarlo** he had the cheek to deny it.

desvestir [6] vt, **desvestirse** vr to undress.

desviar [29] **1** vt (río, carretera) to divert; (golpe, conversación) to deflect. **2 desviarse** vr to go off course; (coche) to turn off.

desvío m diversion.

detallado, -a adj detailed.

detallar vt to give the details of.

detalle m detail; (delicadeza) nice thought.

detallista adj perfectionist.

detectar vt to detect.

detective mf detective; **d. privado** private detective.

detener [24] **1** vt to stop; (arrestar) to arrest. **2 detenerse** vr to stop.

detenidamente adv carefully.

detenido, -a 1 adj (parado) stopped; (arrestado) detained; (minucioso) thorough. **2** mf detainee.

detenimiento m **con d.** carefully, thoroughly.

detergente adj & m detergent.

deteriorar 1 vt to spoil. **2 deteriorarse** vr (estropearse) to get damaged.

determinado, -a adj (preciso) definite; (resuelto) resolute.

determinar 1 vt (fecha etc) to set; (decidir) to decide on. **2 determinarse** vr **determinarse a** to make up one's mind to.

detestar vt to hate.

detrás 1 adv behind. **2** prep **d. de** behind.

detuve pt indef de **detener**.

deuda f debt; **d. pública** national debt.

deudor, -a mf debtor.

devaluar [30] vt to devalue.

devastador, -a adj devastating.

devastar vt to devastate, to ravage.

devoción f devoutness; (al trabajo etc) devotion.

devolución f return; (de dinero) refund.

devolver [4] (pp **devuelto**) **1** vt to give back; (dinero) to refund. **2** vi (vomitar) to vomit. **3 devolverse** vr Am to go/come back.

devorar vt to devour.

devoto, -a 1 adj devout. **2** mf pious person; (seguidor) devotee.

devuelto, -a pp de **devolver**.

DF m abr de **Distrito Federal** (en México) Mexico City.

di pt indef de **dar**; imperativo de **decir**.

día m day; **¿qué d. es hoy?** what's the date today?; **d. a d.** day by day; **de d.** by day; **durante el d.** during the daytime; **un d. sí y otro no** every other day; **pan del d.** fresh bread; **hoy (en) d.** nowadays; **el d. de mañana** in the future; **d. festivo** holiday; **d. laborable** working day; **d.**

libre day off; **es de d.** it is daylight; **hace buen/mal d.** it's a nice/rotten day.

diabético, -a *adj & mf* diabetic.

diablo *m* devil.

diadema *f* tiara.

diagnosticar [44] *vt* to diagnose.

diagnóstico *m* diagnosis.

diagonal *adj & f* diagonal; **en d.** diagonally.

dial *m* dial.

dialogar [42] *vi* to have a conversation; *(para negociar)* to talk.

diálogo *m* dialog.

diamante *m* diamond.

diámetro *m* diameter.

diana *f (blanco)* bull's eye.

diapositiva *f* slide.

diariamente *adv* daily.

diario, -a 1 *adj* daily; **a d.** daily. **2** *m* (daily) newspaper; *(memorias)* diary.

diarrea *f* diarrhea.

dibujante *mf* drawer; *(de cómic)* cartoonist; *(delineante) (hombre)* draftsman; *(mujer)* draftswoman.

dibujar *vt* to draw.

dibujo *m* drawing; **dibujos animados** cartoons.

diccionario *m* dictionary.

dicho, -a *adj* said; **mejor d.** or rather; **d. y hecho** no sooner said than done; **dicha persona** the above-mentioned person.

dichoso, -a *adj (feliz)* happy; *fam (maldito)* damned.

diciembre *m* December.

dictado *m* dictation.

dictadura *f* dictatorship.

dictáfono® *m* Dictaphone®.

dictar *vt* to dictate; *(ley)* to enact.

didáctico, -a *adj* didactic.

diecinueve *adj & m inv* nineteen.

dieciocho *adj & m inv* eighteen.

dieciséis *adj & m inv* sixteen.

diecisiete *adj & m inv* seventeen.

diente *m* tooth; **d. de ajo** clove of garlic; **d. de leche** milk tooth; **dientes postizos** false teeth.

diera *subj imperfecto de* **dar**.

diesel *adj & m* diesel.

diestro, -a 1 *adj (hábil)* skillful. **2** *m* bullfighter.

dieta *f (paga)* diet; **estar a d.** to be on a diet; **dietas** expenses.

diez *adj & m inv* ten.

diferencia *f* difference; **a d. de** unlike.

diferenciar [43] **1** *vt* to differentiate (**entre** between). **2 diferenciarse** *vr* to differ (**de** from).

diferente 1 *adj* different (**de** than). **2** *adv* differently.

diferido, -a *adj* **en d.** recorded.

difícil *adj* difficult; **d. de creer/hacer** difficult to believe/do; **es d. que venga** it is unlikely that she'll come.

dificultad *f* difficulty; *(aprieto)* problem.

dificultar *vt* to make difficult.

dificultoso, -a *adj* difficult, hard.

difundir *vt*, **difundirse** *vr* to spread.

difunto, -a *mf* deceased.

digerir [5] *vt* to digest; *fig* to assimilate.

digestión *f* digestion.

digestivo, -a *adj* easy to digest.

digital *adj* digital; **huellas digitales** fingerprints.

dígito *m* digit.

dignarse *vr* to deign (**a** to), to condescend (**a** to).

dignidad *f* dignity.

digno, -a *adj (merecedor)* worthy; *(decoroso)* decent.

digo *indic pres de* **decir**.

dije *pt indef de* **decir**.

dilatar *vt*, **dilatarse** *vr* to expand.

dilema *m* dilemma.

diluir [37] *vt*, **diluirse** *vr* to dilute.

diluyo *indic pres de* **diluir**.

dimensión *m* dimension; **de grandes dimensiones** very large.

dimisión *f* resignation; **presentar la d.** to hand in one's resignation.

dimitir *vi* to resign (**de** from).

dinámico, -a *adj* dynamic.

dinamita *f* dynamite.

dinamo f, **dínamo** f dynamo.
dinastía f dynasty.
dinero m money; **d. efectivo** o en **metálico** cash.
dinosaurio m dinosaur.
dios m god; **¡D. mío!** my God!; **¡por D.!** for goodness sake!
diploma m diploma.
diplomacia f diplomacy.
diplomarse vr to graduate.
diplomático, -a 1 adj diplomatic. **2** mf diplomat.
diptongo m diphthong.
diputación f **d. provincial** ≃ county council.
diputado, -a mf & (hombre) Congressman; (mujer) Congresswoman; **Congreso de los Diputados** ≃ Congress.
dique m dike.
diré fut de **decir**.
dirección f direction; (señas) address; (destino) destination; (de vehículo) steering; (dirigentes) management; (cargo) directorship; (de un partido) leadership; **d. prohibida** no entry; **calle de d. única** one-way street.
directa f (marcha) top gear.
directamente adv directly.
directiva f board of directors.
directo, -a adj direct; **en d.** live.
director, -a mf director; (de colegio) (hombre) headmaster; (mujer) headmistress; (de periódico) editor; **d. de cine** (film) director; **d. de orquesta** conductor; **d. gerente** managing director.
dirigir [57] **1** vt to direct; (empresa) to manage; (negocio, colegio) to run; (orquesta) to conduct; (partido) to lead; (periódico) to edit; **d. la palabra a algn** to speak to sb. **2 dirigirse** vr **dirigirse a** o **hacia** (ir) to make one's way towards; (hablar) to speak to.
discapacidad f disability.
discernir [54] vt to discern.
disciplina f discipline.

discípulo, -a mf disciple.
disco m disk; (de música) record; **d. compacto** compact disk; **d. duro** hard disk; **d. óptico** optical disk.
discontinuo, -a adj discontinuous; **línea discontinua** (en carretera) broken line.
discoteca f discotheque.
discrepar vi (disentir) to disagree (de with; en on).
discreto, -a adj discreet.
discriminación f discrimination.
disculpa f excuse; **dar disculpas** to make excuses; **pedir disculpas a algn** to apologize to sb (por for).
discurrir vi to think.
discurso m speech; **dar** o **pronunciar un d.** to make a speech.
discusión f argument.
discutir 1 vi to argue (de about). **2** vt to discuss.
diseñar vt to design.
diseño m design.
disfrazar [40] **1** vt to disguise. **2 disfrazarse** vr to disguise oneself.
disfrutar 1 vi (gozar) to enjoy oneself; (poseer) to enjoy (de -). **2** vt to enjoy.
disgustado, -a adj upset, displeased.
disgustar 1 vt to upset. **2 disgustarse** vr (molestarse) to get upset; (dos amigos) to quarrel.
disgusto m (preocupación) upset; (desgracia) trouble; **llevarse un d.** to get upset; **dar un d. a algn** to upset sb; **a d.** unwillingly.
disimular vt to conceal.
disimulo m pretense.
disipar 1 vt (niebla) to drive away; (temor, duda) to dispel. **2 disiparse** vr (niebla, temor etc) to disappear.
disketera f disk drive.
dislocar [44] vt to dislocate.
disminuir [37] **1** vt to reduce. **2** vi to diminish.
disolvente adj & m solvent.
disolver [4] (pp disuelto) vt to dissolve.

disparar 1 vt (pistola etc) to fire; (flecha, balón) to shoot. **2 dispararse** vr (arma) to go off; (precios) to rocket.

disparate m (dicho) nonsense; **decir disparates** to talk nonsense; (acto) foolish act.

disparo m shot.

dispersar vt, **dispersarse** vr to disperse.

disponer [19] (pp **dispuesto**) **1** vt (arreglar) to arrange; (ordenar) to order. **2** vi **d. de** to have at one's disposal. **3 disponerse** vr to get ready.

disponible adj available.

disposición f (colocación) layout; (orden) law; **a su d.** at your service.

dispositivo m device.

disputa f (discusión) argument; (contienda) contest.

disputar 1 vt (premio) to compete for; (partido) to play. **2 disputarse** vr (premio) to compete for.

disquete m diskette, floppy disk.

disquetera f disk drive.

distancia f distance.

distante adj distant.

distinguir [59] **1** vt (diferenciar) to distinguish; (reconocer) to recognize. **2** vi (diferenciar) to discriminate. **3 distinguirse** vr to distinguish oneself.

distintivo, -a 1 adj distinctive. **2** m distinctive mark.

distinto, -a adj different.

distracción f entertainment; (pasatiempo) pastime; (descuido) absentmindedness.

distraer [25] **1** vt (atención) to distract; (divertir) to entertain. **2 distraerse** vr (divertirse) to amuse oneself; (abstraerse) to let one's mind wander.

distraído, -a adj entertaining; (abstraído) absent-minded.

distribuidor, -a 1 adj distributing. **2** mf distributor.

distribuir [37] vt to distribute; (trabajo) to share out.

distrito m district. **d. postal** postal district.

disturbio m riot.

disuadir vt to dissuade.

disuelto, -a pp de **disolver**.

divagar [42] vi to digress, to wander.

diván m couch.

diversión f fun.

diverso, -a adj different; **diversos** various.

divertido, -a adj funny.

divertir [54] **1** vt to amuse. **2 divertirse** vr to enjoy oneself.

dividir vt, **dividirse** vr to divide (**en** into).

divino, -a adj divine.

divisa f foreign currency.

división f division.

divorciado, -a 1 adj divorced. **2** mf (hombre) divorcé; (mujer) divorcée.

divorciarse [43] vr to get divorced.

divorcio m divorce.

divulgación f (de ciencia) popularization.

divulgar [42] vt (noticia) to spread; (ciencia) to popularize.

DNI m abr de **Documento Nacional de Identidad** Identity Card, ID card.

dóberman m Doberman (pinscher).

dobladillo m hem.

doblar 1 vt to double; (plegar) to fold up; (torcer) to bend; (la esquina) to go round. **2** vi (girar) to turn. **3 doblarse** vr (plegarse) to fold; (torcerse) to bend.

doble 1 adj double. **2** m double; **gana el d. que tú** she earns twice as much as you do.

doce adj & m inv twelve.

docena f dozen.

docente adj teaching; **centro d.** educational center.

dócil adj docile.

doctor, -a mf doctor.

doctorado m doctorate, PhD.

documentación f documentation; (DNI, de conducir etc) papers pl.

documental adj & m documentary.

documento m document; **d. nacional de identidad** identity card.

dogo m bulldog.

dólar m dollar.

doler [4] vi to ache; **me duele la cabeza** I've got a headache.

dolor m pain; (pena) grief; **d. de cabeza** headache; **d. de muelas** toothache.

domar vt to tame; (caballo) to break in.

doméstico, -a adj domestic; **animal d.** pet.

domicilio m residence; (señas) address.

dominante adj dominant; (déspota) domineering.

dominar 1 vt to dominate; (situación) to control; (idioma) to speak very well. **2** vi to dominate; (resaltar) to stand out. **3 dominarse** vr to control oneself.

domingo m Sunday; **D. de Resurrección** o **Pascua** Easter Sunday.

dominical 1 adj Sunday. **2** m (suplemento) Sunday supplement.

dominicano, -a adj & mf Dominican; **República Dominicana** Dominican Republic.

dominio m (poder) control; (de un idioma) command; (territorio) dominion.

dominó, dómino m dominoes pl.

don¹ m (habilidad) gift; **tener el d. de** to have a knack for.

don² m Señor **D. José García** MrJosé Garcia; **D. Fulano de Tal** Mr So-and-So.

donante mf donor; **d. de sangre** blood donor.

donar vt (sangre etc) to donate.

donativo m donation.

dónde adv where (in questions); **¿por d. se va a la playa?** which way is it to the beach?

donde adv rel where; **a** o **en d.** where; **de** o **desde d.** from where.

doña f Señora **D. Leonor Benítez** Mrs Leonor Benítez.

dorada f (pez) gilthead bream.

dorado, -a adj golden.

dormido, -a adj asleep; **quedarse d.** to fall asleep; (no despertarse) to oversleep.

dormilón, -ona fam **1** adj sleepyheaded. **2** mf sleepyhead.

dormir [7] **1** vi to sleep. **2** vt **d. la siesta** to have an afternoon nap. **3 dormirse** vr to fall asleep; **se me ha dormido el brazo** my arm has gone to sleep.

dormitorio m (de una casa) bedroom; (de colegio, residencia) dormitory.

dorsal 1 adj **espina d.** spine. **2** m (de camiseta) number.

dorso m back; **instrucciones al d.** instructions over; **véase al d.** see overleaf.

dos 1 adj two. **2** m inv two; **los d.** both; **nosotros/vosotros d.** both of us/you.

doscientos, -as adj & mf two hundred.

dosis f inv dose.

dotar vt **d. de** to provide with.

doy indic pres de **dar**.

Dr. abr de **doctor** doctor, Dr.

Dra. abr de **doctora** doctor, Dr.

dragón m dragon.

drama m drama.

dramático, -a adj dramatic.

drástico, -a adj drastic.

droga f drug; **d. blanda/dura** soft/hard drug.

drogadicto, -a mf drug addict.

drogar [42] **1** vt to drug. **2 drogarse** vr to take drugs.

droguería f hardware and household goods shop.

ducha f shower; **darse/tomar una d.** to take/have a shower.

ducharse vr to take a shower.

duda f doubt; **sin d.** without a doubt; **no cabe d.** (there is) no doubt.

dudar 1 vi to doubt; (vacilar) to hesitate (en to). **2** vt to doubt.

dudoso, -a adj (poco honrado) dubious; **ser d.** (incierto) to be uncertain o doubtful; **estar d.** (indeciso) to be undecided.

dueña *f* owner; *(de pensión)* landlady.

dueño *m* owner; *(de casa etc)* landlord.

dulce 1 *adj (sabor)* sweet; *(carácter, voz)* gentle; *(agua)* fresh. **2** *m (pastel)* cake; *(caramelo)* candy.

duna *f* dune.

duodécimo, -a *adj & mf* twelfth.

duplicar [44] **1** *vt* to duplicate; *(cifras)* to double. **2 duplicarse** *vr* to double.

duración *f* duration.

duradero, -a *adj* durable, lasting.

durante *prep* during.

durar *vi* to last.

durazno *m Am (fruto)* peach; *(árbol)* peach tree.

dureza *f* hardness; *(severidad)* severity; *(callosidad)* corn.

duro, -a 1 *adj* hard; *(resistente)* tough. **2** *adv* hard.

E

e *conj (before words beginning with* **i** *or* **hi***)* and.

ébano *m* ebony.

echar 1 *vt* to throw; *(carta)* to post; *(vino, agua)* to pour; *(expulsar)* to throw out; *(despedir)* to sack; *(humo, olor etc)* to give off; **e. una mano** to give a hand; **e. una mirada/una ojeada** to have a look/a quick look; **e. gasolina al coche** to put gas in the car; **e. de menos** *o* **en falta** to miss. **2** *vi* (+ **a** + *infinitivo*) *(empezar)* to begin to; **echó a correr** he ran off. **3 echarse** *vr (tumbarse)* to lie down; *(lanzarse)* to throw oneself; (+ **a** + *infinitivo*) *(empezar)* to begin to; *fig* **echarse atrás** to get cold feet; **echarse a llorar** to burst into tears; **echarse a perder** *(comida)* to go bad.

eclesiástico, -a 1 *adj* ecclesiastical. **2** *m* clergyman.

eclipse *m* eclipse.

eco *m* echo.

ecológico, -a *adj* ecological.

ecologista 1 *adj* ecological. **2** *mf* ecologist.

economía *f* economy; *(ciencia)* economics *sing.*

económico, -a *adj* economic; *(barato)* economical.

economizar [40] *vti* to economize.

ecuación *f* equation.

ecuador *m* equator.

ecuánime *adj (temperamento)* even-tempered; *(juicio)* impartial.

ecuatoriano, -a *adj & mf* Ecuadorian.

ecuestre *adj* equestrian.

edad *f* age; **¿qué e. tienes?** how old are you?; **E. Media** Middle Ages *pl.*

edición *f (publicación)* publication; *(conjunto de ejemplares)* edition.

edicto *m* edict.

edificar [44] *vt* to build.

edificio *m* building.

edil, -a *mf* town councilor.

editar *vt (libro, periódico)* to publish; *(disco)* to release; *(en ordenador)* to edit.

editor, -a 1 *adj* publishing. **2** *mf* publisher. **3** *m* **e. de textos** text editor.

editorial 1 *adj* publishing. **2** *f* publishing house. **3** *m* editorial.

edredón *m* duvet, eiderdown.

educación *f* education; *(formación)* upbringing; **buena/mala e.** *(modales)* good/bad manners; **falta de e.** bad manners.

educado, -a *adj* polite.

educar [44] *vt (hijos)* to raise.

educativo, -a *adj* educational.

edulcorante *m* sweetener.

efectivamente *adv* yes indeed!

efectivo, -a 1 *adj* effective; **hacer e. un cheque** to cash a check. **2** *m* **en e.** in cash.

efecto *m (resultado)* effect; *(impresión)* impression; **efectos personales** personal belongings; **en e.** yes indeed!

efectuar [30] *vt* to carry out; *(viaje)* to make; *(pedido)* to place.

efervescente *adj* effervescent; **aspirina e.** soluble aspirin.

eficacia *f (de persona)* efficiency; *(de remedio, medida)* effectiveness.

eficaz *adj (persona)* efficient; *(remedio, medida)* effective.

eficiencia *f* efficiency.

eficiente *adj* efficient.

efusivo, -a *adj* effusive.

egipcio, -a *adj & mf* Egyptian.

egoísmo *m* egoism.

egoísta 1 *adj* selfish. **2** *mf* ego(t)ist.

egresar *vi Am* to leave school; to graduate.

ej. *abr de* ejemplo example.

eje *m (de rueda)* axle; *(de máquina)* shaft.

ejecutar *vt (ajusticiar)* to execute; *(sinfonía)* to perform.

ejecutiva *f (gobierno)* executive.

ejecutivo, -a 1 *adj* executive; **el poder e.** the government. **2** *mf* executive.

ejemplar 1 *m (de libro)* copy; *(de revista, periódico)* issue; *(especimen)* specimen. **2** *adj* exemplary.

ejemplo *m* example; **por e.** for example; **dar e.** to set an example.

ejercer [49] *vt (profesión etc)* to practice; *(influencia)* to exert.

ejercicio *m* exercise; *(de profesión)* practice; **hacer e.** to take exercise.

ejercitar *vt* to practice.

ejército *m* army.

el 1 *art def m* the; **el Sr. García** Mr. Garcia. ▪ *(no se traduce)* **el hambre/destino** hunger/fate. ▪ *(con partes del cuerpo, prendas de vestir)* **me he cortado el dedo** I've cut my finger; **métetelo en el bolsillo** put it in your pocket. ▪ *(con días de la semana)* **el lunes** on Monday. **2** *pron* the one; **el de las once** the eleven o'clock one; **el que tienes en la mano** the one you've got in your hand; **el que quieras** whichever one you want; **el de tu amigo** your friend's.

él *pron pers (sujeto) (persona)* he; *(animal, cosa)* it; *(complemento) (persona)* him; *(animal, cosa)* it.

elaboración *f (de un producto)* production.

elaborar *vt (producto)* to produce.

elasticidad *f* elasticity; *fig* flexibility.

elástico, -a *adj & m* elastic.

elección *f* choice; *(votación)* election.

electorado *m* electorate *pl.*

electoral *adj* electoral; **campaña e.** election campaign; **colegio e.** polling station.

electricidad *f* electricity.

electricista *mf* electrician.

eléctrico, -a *adj* electric.

electrocutar *vt* to electrocute.

electrodoméstico *m* (domestic) electrical appliance.

electrónico, -a *adj* electronic.

elefante *m* elephant.

elegancia *f* elegance.

elegante *adj* elegant.

elegir [58] *vt* to choose; *(en votación)* to elect.

elemental *adj (fundamental)* basic; *(simple)* elementary.

elemento *m* element; *(componente)* component.

elepé *m* LP (record).

elevación *f* elevation; *(de precios)* rise.

elevado, -a *adj* high; *(edificio)* tall.

elevalunas *m inv* **e. eléctrico** electric windows *pl.*

elevar 1 *vt* to raise. **2 elevarse** *vr (subir)* to rise; **elevarse a** *(cantidad)* to come to.

elijo *indic pres de* **elegir.**

eliminar *vt* to eliminate.

eliminatoria *f* heat, qualifying round.

eliminatorio, -a *adj* qualifying.

ella *pron pers (sujeto)* she; *(animal, cosa)* it, she; *(complemento)* her; *(animal, cosa)* it, her.

ellas *pron pers fpl (sujeto)* they; *(complemento)* them.

ello *pron pers neutro* it; **por e.** for that reason.

ellos *pron pers mpl (sujeto)* they; *(complemento)* them.

elocuente *adj* eloquent.

elogiar [43] *vt* to praise.

elote *m CAm, Méx* tender corncob.

eludir *vt* to avoid.

e-mail *m* e-mail.

embajada *f* embassy.

embajador, -a *mf* ambassador.

embalaje *m* packing.

embalse *m* reservoir; *(presa)* dam.

embarazada 1 *adj* pregnant. **2** *f* pregnant woman.

embarazo *m (preñez)* pregnancy; *(turbación)* embarrassment.

embarazoso, -a *adj* embarrassing.

embarcación *f* boat.

embarcadero *m* quay.

embarcar [44] **1** *vt* to ship. **2** *vi* to go on board. **3 embarcarse** *vr* to go on board (**en** -); *(en avión)* to board (**en** -).

embargar [42] *vt (bienes)* to seize, to impound; *fig* **le embarga la emoción** he's overwhelmed with joy.

embarque *m (de persona)* boarding; *(de mercancías)* loading; **tarjeta de e.** boarding card.

embellecer [33] *vt* to embellish.

embestida *f* onslaught; *(de toro)* charge.

embestir [6] *vt (a torero)* to charge; *(atacar)* to attack.

emblema *m* emblem.

embobado, -a *adj* fascinated.

embobarse *vr* to be fascinated *o* besotted (**con, de** by).

émbolo *m* piston.

embolsar *vt*, **embolsarse** *vr* to pocket.

emborrachar *vt*, **emborracharse** *vr* to get drunk.

emboscada *f* ambush.

embotellamiento *m* traffic jam.

embotellar *vt* to bottle; *(tráfico)* to block.

embrague *m* clutch.

embriagar [42] **1** *vt* to intoxicate. **2 embriagarse** *vr* to get drunk.

embriaguez *f* intoxication.

embrollar 1 *vt* to confuse. **2 embrollarse** *vr* to get confused.

embrujado, -a *adj (sitio)* haunted.

embudo *m* funnel.

embuste *m* lie.

embustero, -a *mf* cheat.

embutido *m* sausage.

emergencia *f* emergency; **salida de e.** emergency exit; **en caso de e.** in an emergency.

emigración *f* emigration.

emigrante *adj & mf* emigrant.

emigrar *vi* to emigrate.

emisión *f* emission; *(de radio, TV)* broadcasting.

emisora *f (de radio)* radio station; *(de televisión)* television station.

emitir *vt* to emit; *(luz, calor)* to give off; *(opinión, juicio)* to express; *(programa)* to transmit.

emoción *f* emotion; *(excitación)* excitement; **¡qué e.!** how exciting!

emocionado, -a *adj* deeply moved *o* touched.

emocionante *adj (conmovedor)* moving; *(excitante)* exciting.

emocionar 1 *vt (conmover)* to move; *(excitar)* to thrill. **2 emocionarse** *vr (conmoverse)* to be moved; *(excitarse)* to get excited.

emotivo, -a *adj* emotional.

empacar [44] *vt Am (mercancías)* to pack.

empacho *m (de comida)* indigestion.

empalagoso, -a *adj (dulce)* sickly sweet.

empalizada *f* fence.

empalmar 1 *vt (unir)* to join; *(cuerdas, cables)* to splice. **2** *vi* to converge; *(trenes)* to connect.

empanada *f* pie.

empanadilla *f* pastry.

empañar *vt*, **empañarse** *vr (cristales)* to steam up.

empapar 1 *vt (mojar)* to soak; *(absorber)* to soak up. **2 empaparse** *vr (persona)* to get soaked; *fam fig* to take in (**de** -).

empapelar *vt* to wallpaper.

empaquetar *vt* to pack.

emparedado *m* sandwich.

empastar *vt (diente)* to fill.

empaste *m (de diente)* filling.

empatar *vi* to draw; *Am (unir)* to join.

empate *m* draw.

empedrado, -a 1 *adj* cobbled. **2** *m (adoquines)* cobblestones *pl*.

empeine *m (de pie, de zapato)* instep.

empellón *m* shove.

empeñar 1 *vt* to pawn. **2 empeñarse** *vr (insistir)* to insist (**en** on); *(endeudarse)* to get into debt.

empeño *m (insistencia)* insistence; *(deuda)* pledge.

empeoramiento *m* deterioration, worsening.

empeorar 1 *vi* to deteriorate. **2** *vt* to make worse. **3 empeorarse** *vr* to deteriorate.

emperador *m* emperor.

empezar [51] *vti* to begin, start (**a hacer algo** to do sth).

empinado, -a *adj (cuesta)* steep.

empinar 1 *vt* to raise. **2 empinarse** *vr (persona)* to stand on tiptoe.

emplazamiento *m (colocación)* location.

empleado, -a *mf* employee; *(de oficina, banco)* clerk.

emplear *vt (usar)* to use; *(contratar)* to employ; *(dinero, tiempo)* to spend.

empleo *m* employment; *(oficio)* job; *(uso)* use; **modo de e.** instructions for use.

emplomar *vt Am (diente)* to fill.

empobrecer [33] **1** *vt* to impoverish. **2 empobrecerse** *vr* to become impoverished.

empobrecimiento *m* impoverishment.

empollón, -ona *mf fam* grind.

emporio *m Am* department store.

empotrado, -a *adj* fitted.

emprendedor, -a *adj* enterprising.

emprender *vt* to undertake; *fam* **emprenderla con algn** to pick on sb.

empresa *f* firm; *(tarea)* undertaking.

empresarial *adj (de empresa)* business; *(espíritu)* entrepreneurial; **(ciencias) empresariales** business studies.

empresario, -a *mf (hombre)* businessman; *(mujer)* businesswoman; *(patrón)* employer.

empujar *vt* to push, to shove.

empujón *m* push, shove.

emulsión *f* emulsion.

en *prep (posición)* in; at; *(sobre)* on; **en Madrid/Bolivia** in Madrid/Bolivia; **en casa/el trabajo** at home/work; **en la mesa** on the table. ▪ *(movimiento)* into; **entrar en la casa** to go into the house. ▪ *(tiempo)* in; on; at; **en 1940** in 1940; *Am* **en la mañana** in the morning; **cae en martes** it falls on a Tuesday; **en ese momento** at that moment. ▪ *(transporte)* by; **en coche/tren** by car/train. ▪ *(modo)* **en español** in Spanish; **en broma** jokingly; **en serio** seriously. ▪ *(reducción, aumento)* by; **los precios aumentaron en un diez por ciento** the prices went up by ten percent. ▪ *(tema, materia)* at, in; **bueno en deportes** good at sports; **experto en política** expert in politics. ▪ *(división, separación)* in; **lo dividió en tres partes** he divided it in three. ▪ *(con infinitivo)* **fue rápido en responder** he was quick to answer.

enaguas *fpl* petticoat *sing*.

enamorado, -a 1 *adj* in love. **2** *mf* person in love.

enamorar 1 *vt* to win the heart of. **2 enamorarse** *vr* to fall in love (**de** with).

enano, -a *adj & mf* dwarf.

encabezamiento *m (de carta)*

heading; *(de periódico)* headline.

encabezar [40] *vt (carta, lista)* to head; *(periódico)* to lead; *(rebelión, carrera, movimiento)* to lead.

encajar 1 *vt (ajustar)* to insert; **e. un golpe a algn** to land sb a blow. **2** *vi (ajustarse)* to fit; **e. con** to fit (in) with.

encaje *m* lace.

encallar *vi* to run aground.

encantado, -a *adj (contento)* delighted; *(embrujado)* enchanted; **e. de conocerle** pleased to meet you.

encantador, -a *adj* charming.

encantar *vt (hechizar)* to cast a spell on; **me encanta nadar** I love swimming.

encanto *m* charm; **ser un e.** to be charming.

encapricharse *vr* to set one's mind on (**con** on).

encaramarse *vr* to climb up.

encarar 1 *vt* to face. **2 encararse** *vr* **encararse con** to face up to.

encarcelar *vt* to imprison.

encarecer [33] **1** *vt* to put up the price of. **2 encarecerse** *vr* to go up (in price).

encarecidamente *adv* earnestly, insistently.

encargado, -a 1 *mf* manager; *(responsable)* person in charge. **2** *adj* in charge.

encargar [42] **1** *vt* to entrust with; *(mercancías)* to order. **2 encargarse** *vr* **encargarse de** to see to.

encargo *m* order; *(recado)* errand; *(tarea)* job.

encariñarse *vr* to become fond (**con** of).

encarnado, -a *adj (rojo)* red.

encarnizado, -a *adj* fierce.

encauzar [40] *vt* to channel.

encendedor *m* lighter.

encender [3] **1** *vt (luz, radio, tele)* to switch on, to put on; *(cigarro, vela, fuego)* to light; *(cerilla)* to strike. **2 encenderse** *vr (fuego)* to catch; *(lámpara etc)* to go o come on.

encendido *m* ignition.

encerado *m (pizarra)* blackboard.

encerrar [1] **1** *vt* to shut in; *(con llave)* to lock in. **2 encerrarse** *vr* to shut oneself in; *(con llave)* to lock oneself in.

enchaquetado, -a *adj* smartly dressed.

encharcar [44] *vt*, **encharcarse** *vr* to flood.

enchufado, -a 1 *adj fig fam* **estar e.** to have good connections. **2** *mf (favorito)* pet.

enchufar *vt* to plug in; *(unir)* to join.

enchufe *m (hembra)* socket; *(macho)* plug; *fam* contact.

encía *f* gum.

enciclopedia *f* encyclopedia.

encima 1 *adv* on top; *(arriba)* above; *(en el aire)* overhead; *(además)* besides. **2** *prep* **e. de** *(sobre)* on; *(además)* besides; **ahí e.** up there; **por e.** above; **leer un libro por e.** to skim through a book.

encina *f* holm oak.

encinta *adj* pregnant.

enclenque *adj (débil)* puny; *(enfermizo)* sickly.

encoger [53] **1** *vti* to contract; *(prenda)* to shrink. **2 encogerse** *vr (contraerse)* to contract; *(prenda)* to shrink; **encogerse de hombros** to shrug (one's shoulders).

encolar *vt (papel)* to paste; *(madera)* to glue.

encolerizar [40] **1** *vt* to infuriate. **2 encolerizarse** *vr* to become furious.

encono *m* spitefulness.

encontrar [2] **1** *vt (hallar)* to find; *(a persona)* to meet; *(problema)* to come up against. **2 encontrarse** *vr (sentirse)* to feel, to be; *(estar)* to be; **encontrarse a gusto** to feel comfortable; **encontrarse con algn** to meet sb.

encontronazo *m (choque)* clash.

encorvarse *vr* to bend (over).

encrucijada *f* crossroads.

encuadernar *vt* to bind.

encubrir *vt* to conceal.

encuentro *m* meeting; *(deportivo)* match.

encuesta *f (sondeo)* (opinion) poll; *(investigación)* investigation.

encuestar *vt* to poll.

endeble *adj* weak.

endémico, -a *adj* endemic.

enderezar [40] **1** *vt (poner derecho)* to straighten out; *(poner vertical)* to set upright. **2 enderezarse** *vr* to straighten up.

endeudarse *vr* to get into debt.

endiablado, -a *adj* mischievous.

endibia *f* endive.

endosar *vt (cheque)* to endorse; *fam (tarea)* to lumber with.

endulzar [40] *vt* to sweeten.

endurecer [33] *vt,* **endurecerse** *vr* to harden.

enemigo, -a *adj & mf* enemy.

enemistad *f* hostility, enmity.

enemistar **1** *vt* to set at odds. **2 enemistar** *vr* to become enemies; **enemistarse con algn** to fall out with sb.

energético, -a *adj* energy.

energía *f* energy; **e. nuclear** nuclear power; **e. vital** vitality.

enérgico, -a *adj* energetic; *(tono)* emphatic.

enero *m* January.

enfadado, -a *adj* angry.

enfadar **1** *vt* to make angry. **2 enfadarse** *vr* to get angry (**con** with); *(dos personas)* to fall out.

enfado *m* anger.

énfasis *m inv* emphasis.

enfático, -a *adj* emphatic.

enfatizar [40] *vt* to emphasize, to stress.

enfermar *vi,* **enfermarse** *vr Am* to fall ill.

enfermedad *f* illness; *(contagiosa)* disease.

enfermería *f* infirmary.

enfermero, -a *mf (mujer)* nurse; *(hombre)* male nurse.

enfermizo, -a *adj* unhealthy.

enfermo, -a 1 *adj* ill. **2** *mf* ill person; *(paciente)* patient.

enfocar [44] *vt (imagen)* to focus; *(tema)* to approach; *(con linterna)* to shine a light on.

enfrentamiento *m* clash.

enfrentar 1 *vt (situación, peligro)* to confront; *(enemistar)* to set at odds. **2 enfrentarse** *vr* **enfrentarse con** *o* **a** *(encararse)* to confront.

enfrente 1 *adv* opposite; **la casa de e.** the house opposite. **2** *prep* **e. de** opposite.

enfriamiento *m (proceso)* cooling; *(catarro)* chill.

enfriar [29] **1** *vt* to cool (down). **2 enfriarse** *vr* to get cold; *(resfriarse)* to catch a cold.

enfurecer [33] **1** *vt* to enrage. **2 enfurecerse** *vr* to get furious.

engalanar 1 *vt* to deck out, to adorn. **2 engalanarse** *vr* to dress up, to get dressed up.

enganchar 1 *vt* to hook. **2 engancharse** *vr (ropa)* to get caught; *(persona)* to get hooked.

engañar 1 *vt* to deceive; *(estafar)* to cheat; *(mentir a)* to lie to; *(al marido, mujer)* to be unfaithful to. **2 engañarse** *vr* to deceive oneself.

engaño *m* deceit; *(estafa)* fraud; *(mentira)* lie.

engañoso, -a *adj (palabras)* deceitful; *(apariencias)* deceptive.

engarzar [40] *vt (unir)* to link; *(engastar)* to mount.

engatusar *vt fam* to coax; **e. a algn para que haga algo** to coax sb into doing sth.

engendrar *vt fig* to engender.

englobar *vt* to include.

engordar 1 *vt* to make fat. **2** *vi* to put on weight; *(comida, bebida)* to be fattening.

engorro *m* nuisance.

engranaje *m* gearing.

engrasar *vt (lubricar)* to lubricate; *(manchar)* to make greasy.

engreído, -a *adj* conceited.

engrudo *m* paste.

engullir *vt* to gobble up.

enharinar *vt* to cover with flour.

enhebrar *vt* to thread.

enhorabuena *f* congratulations *pl*; **dar la e. a algn** to congratulate sb.

enigma *m* enigma.

enjabonar *vt* to soap.

enjambre *m* swarm.

enjaular *vt (animal)* to cage.

enjuagar [42] *vt* to rinse.

enjugar [42] *vt*, **enjugarse** *vr (secar)* to mop up; *(lágrimas)* to wipe away.

enjuiciar [43] *vt (criminal)* to prosecute.

enjuto, -a *adj* lean, skinny.

enlace *m* connection; *(casamiento)* marriage.

enlatado, -a *adj* canned.

enlatar *vt* to can.

enlazar [40] *vti* to connect (**con** with).

enloquecedor, -a *adj* maddening.

enloquecer [33] **1** *vi* to go mad. **2** *vt* to drive mad. **3 enloquecerse** *vr* to go mad.

enmarañar 1 *vt (pelo)* to tangle; *(complicar)* to complicate. **2 enmarañarse** *vr (pelo)* to get tangled.

enmarcar [44] *vt* to frame.

enmascarar *vt (problema, la verdad)* to disguise.

enmendar [1] **1** *vt (corregir)* to put right. **2 enmendarse** *vr (persona)* to mend one's ways.

enmienda *f* correction; *(de ley)* amendment.

enmohecerse [33] *vr (metal)* to rust; *(comida)* to get moldy.

enmoquetar *vt* to carpet.

enmudecer [33] *vi* to fall silent; *(por sorpresa etc)* to be dumbstruck.

ennegrecer [33] *vt*, **ennegrecerse** *vr* to turn black.

enojado, -a *adj* angry.

enojar 1 *vt* to anger. **2 enojarse** *vr* to get angry.

enojo *m* anger, annoyance.

enorgullecer [33] **1** *vt* to fill with pride. **2 enorgullecerse** *vr* to be proud (**de** of).

enorme *adj* enormous.

enraizado, -a *adj* rooted.

enraizar [40] *vi*, **enraizarse** *vr (planta, costumbre)* to take root.

enrarecerse [33] *vr (aire)* to become rarefied.

enredadera *f* climbing plant.

enredar 1 *vt (enmarañar)* to entangle; *fig (implicar)* to involve (**en** in). **2 enredarse** *vr (enmarañarse)* to get tangled up; *fig (involucrarse)* to get involved, to get entangled (**con** with).

enredo *m (maraña)* tangle; *fig (lío)* muddle, mess.

enrejado *m (de ventana)* lattice.

enrevesado, -a *adj* complicated, difficult.

enriquecer [33] **1** *vt* to make rich; *fig* to enrich. **2 enriquecerse** *vr* to become rich; *fig* to become enriched.

enrojecer [33] **1** *vt* to redden, to turn red. **2** *vi (ruborizarse)* to blush.

enrollado, -a *adj* rolled up.

enrollar 1 *vt* to roll up; *(cable)* to coil; *(hilo)* to wind up. **2 enrollarse** *vr fam (hablar)* to go on and on.

enroscar [44] **1** *vt* to coil (round); *(tornillo)* to screw in; *(tapón)* to screw on. **2 enroscarse** *vr* to coil.

ensaimada *f* kind of spiral pastry from Majorca.

ensalada *f* salad.

ensaladera *f* salad bowl.

ensaladilla rusa *f* Russian salad.

ensamblaje *m* assembly.

ensamblar *vt* to assemble.

ensanchar 1 *vt* to widen; *(ropa)* to let out. **2 ensancharse** *vr* to widen.

ensangrentado, -a *adj* bloodstained.

ensañarse *vr* to be brutal (**con** with); *(cebarse)* to delight in tormenting (**con** -).

ensayar *vt* to try out; *(obra, canción)* to rehearse.

ensayo *m* trial; *(de obra)* rehearsal; **e. general** dress rehearsal.

enseguida, en seguida *adv (inmediatamente)* at once, straight away; *(poco después)* in a minute, soon.

ensenada *f* inlet.

enseñanza *f (educación)* education; *(de idioma etc)* teaching.

enseñar *vt* to teach; *(mostrar)* to show; *(señalar)* to point out; **e. a algn a hacer algo** to teach sb how to do sth.

ensimismado, -a *adj (absorbido)* engrossed; *(abstraído)* lost in thought.

ensimismarse *vr (absorberse)* to become engrossed; *(abstraerse)* to be lost in thought.

ensombrecer [33] **1** *vt* to cast a shadow over. **2 ensombrecerse** *vr* to darken.

ensopar *vt Am* to soak.

ensordecedor, -a *adj* deafening.

ensuciar [43] *vt*, **ensuciarse** *vr* to get dirty.

ensueño *m* dream.

entablar *vt (conversación)* to begin; *(amistad)* to strike up.

entallado, -a *adj (vestido)* close-fitting; *(camisa)* fitted.

entender [3] **1** *vt (comprender)* to understand; **dar a algn a e. que ...** to give sb to understand that .... **2** *vi (comprender)* to understand; **e. de** *(saber)* to know about. **3 entenderse** *vr (comprenderse)* to be understood.

entendimiento *m* understanding.

enteramente *adv* entirely.

enterarse *vr* to find out; **me he enterado de que ...** I understand ...; **ni me enteré** I didn't even realize it.

entereza *f* strength of character.

enternecedor, -a *adj* moving.

enternecer [33] **1** *vt* to move. **2 enternecerse** *vr* to be moved.

entero, -a *adj (completo)* entire, whole.

enterrador *m* gravedigger.

enterrar [1] *vt* to bury.

entidad *f* organization, entity.

entierro *m* burial; *(ceremonia)* funeral.

entonar *vt (canción)* to intone, to sing.

entonces *adv* then; **por aquel e.** at that time.

entornar *vt (ojos etc)* to half-close; *(puerta)* to leave ajar.

entorno *m* environment.

entorpecer [33] *vt (obstaculizar)* to hinder.

entrada *f* entrance; *(billete)* ticket; *(recaudación)* takings *pl*; *(plato)* starter; **entradas** *(en la frente)* receding hairline.

entrañable *adj (lugar)* intimate, close; *(persona)* affectionate, warm-hearted.

entrar 1 *vi* to enter; *(venir dentro)* to come in; *(ir dentro)* to go in; *(encajar)* to fit; **me entró dolor de cabeza** I got a headache; **me entraron ganas de reír** I felt like laughing. **2** *vt (datos)* to enter.

entre *prep (dos)* between; *(más de dos)* among(st).

entreabierto, -a *adj (ojos etc)* half-open; *(puerta)* ajar.

entreacto *m* interval.

entrecejo *m* space between the eyebrows.

entrecortado, -a *adj (voz)* faltering.

entrecot *m* fillet steak.

entredicho *m* **estar en e.** to be suspect; **poner algo en e.** to bring sth into question.

entrega *f (de productos)* delivery; *(de premios)* presentation; *(devoción)* selflessness.

entregar [42] **1** *vt (dar)* to hand over; *(deberes etc)* to hand in; *(mercancía)* to deliver. **2 entregarse** *vr (rendirse)* to give in; **entregarse a** to devote oneself to.

entrelazar [40] *vt*, **entrelazarse** *vr* to entwine.

entremedias *adv* in between.

entremés *m* hors d'oeuvres.

entremeterse *vr* = **entrometerse**.

entremezclarse *vr* to mix, to mingle.

entrenador, -a *mf* trainer.

entrenamiento *m* training.

entrenar *vi*, **entrenarse** *vr* to train.

entresuelo *m* mezzanine.

entretanto *adv* meanwhile.

entretención *f Am* entertainment.

entretener [24] **1** *vt (divertir)* to entertain; *(retrasar)* to delay; *(detener)* to detain. **2 entretenerse** *vr (distraerse)* to amuse oneself; *(retrasarse)* to be held up.

entretenido, -a *adj* entertaining.

entretenimiento *m* entertainment.

entretiempo *adj* ropa de e. lightweight clothing.

entrever [28] *vt* to glimpse, to catch sight of; *fig* dejó e. que ... she hinted that ...

entrevista *f* interview.

entrevistador, -a *mf* interviewer.

entrevistar 1 *vt* to interview. **2 entrevistarse** *vr* entrevistarse con **algn** to have an interview with sb.

entristecer [33] **1** *vt* to sadden. **2 entristecerse** *vr* to be sad *(por about)*.

entrometerse *vr* to meddle *(en in, with)*.

entumecerse [33] *vr* to go numb.

enturbiar [43] **1** *vt* to make cloudy. **2 enturbiarse** *vr* to become cloudy.

entusiasmar 1 *vt* to fill with enthusiasm. **2 entusiasmarse** *vr* to get enthusiastic *(con about)*.

entusiasmo *m* enthusiasm; con e. enthusiastically.

enumerar *vt* to enumerate.

envasar *vt (embotellar)* to bottle; *(empaquetar)* to pack; *(enlatar)* to can, to tin.

envase *m (recipiente)* container; *(botella vacía)* empty.

envejecer [33] *vti* to age.

envejecimiento *m* aging.

envenenar *vt* to poison.

envergadura *f* de gran e. large-scale.

enviar [29] *vt* to send.

envidia *f* envy; tener e. de algn to envy sb.

envidiable *adj* enviable.

envidiar [43] *vt* to envy.

envidioso, -a *adj* envious.

envío *m* sending; *(remesa)* consignment; *(paquete)* parcel; gastos de e. postage and packing.

enviudar *vi (hombre)* to become a widower; *(mujer)* to become a widow.

envoltorio *m*, **envoltura** *f* wrapping.

envolver [4] *(pp envuelto)* **1** *vt (con papel)* to wrap; *(en complot etc)* to involve *(en in)*. **2 envolverse** *vr* to wrap oneself up *(en in)*.

enyesar *vt* to put in plaster.

epidemia *f* epidemic.

episodio *m* episode.

época *f* time; *(periodo)* period.

equilibrar *vt* to balance.

equilibrio *m* balance.

equilibrista *mf* tightrope walker; *Am* opportunist.

equipaje *m* luggage; hacer el e. to pack.

equipar *vt* to equip *(con, de with)*.

equiparar *vt* to compare *(con with)*.

equipo *m (de expertos, jugadores)* team; *(aparatos)* equipment; *(ropas)* outfit; e. de alta fidelidad hi-fi stereo system.

equitación *f* horseriding.

equitativo, -a *adj* equitable.

equivalente *adj* equivalent.

equivaler [26] *vi* to be equivalent *(to a)*.

equivocación *f* error.

equivocado, -a *adj* mistaken.

equivocar [44] **1** *vt* to mix up. **2 equivocarse** *vr* to make a mistake.

equívoco, -a *adj* misleading.

era *pt imperfecto de* **ser**.

eras *pt imperfecto de* **ser**.

eres *indic pres de* **ser**.

erguir [55] *vt* to erect.

erizarse [40] *vr* to stand on end.

erizo *m* hedgehog; **e. de mar, e. ma-rino** sea urchin.

ermita *f* shrine.

erosión *f* erosion.

erosionar *vt* to erode.

erótico, -a *adj* erotic.

erradicar [44] *vt* to eradicate.

errante *adj* wandering.

errar [50] **1** *vt* to miss, to get wrong. **2** *vi (vagar)* to wander, to roam; *(fallar)* to err.

errata *f* misprint.

erróneo, -a *adj* erroneous.

error *m* mistake.

eructar *vi* to belch.

eructo *m* belch, burp.

erudito, -a 1 *adj* erudite. **2** *mf* scholar.

erupción *f (de volcán)* eruption; *(en la piel)* rash.

es *indic pres de* **ser**.

esa *adj dem* that.

ésa *pron dem ver* **ése**.

esbelto, -a *adj* slender.

esbozar [40] *vt* to sketch, to outline.

escabeche *m* brine.

escabullirse *vr* to scurry off.

escala *f* scale; *(parada) (de barco)* port of call; *(escalera)* ladder; **a gran e.** on a large scale; **hacer e. en** to stop over in.

escalada *f* climb.

escalador, -a *mf* climber.

escalar *vt* to climb.

escaldar *vt* to scald.

escalera *f* stair; *(escala)* ladder; **e. de incendios** fire escape; **e. mecáni-ca** escalator.

escalerilla *f* steps *pl*.

escalfar *vt* to poach.

escalinata *f* stoop.

escalofriante *adj* hair-raising, bloodcurdling.

escalofrío *m* shiver.

escalón *m* step; **e. lateral** *(en le-trero)* ramp.

escalonar *vt* to space out.

escama *f (de animal)* scale; *(de ja-bón)* flake.

escamotear *vt* to cheat out of.

escampar *vi* to clear up.

escandalizar [40] **1** *vt* to scan-dalize. **2 escandalizarse** *vr* to be shocked (**de** at, by).

escándalo *m (alboroto)* racket; *(desvergüenza)* scandal; **armar un e.** to kick up a fuss.

escandaloso, -a *adj (ruidoso)* noisy, rowdy; *(ofensivo)* scandalous.

escanear *vt* to scan.

escáner *m* scanner.

escaño *m (parlamentario)* seat.

escapada *f (de prisión)* escape.

escapar 1 *vi* to escape. **2 escaparse** *vr* to escape; *(gas etc)* to leak.

escaparate *m* shop window.

escapatoria *f* escape; **no tener e.** to have no way out.

escape *m (huida)* escape; *(de gas etc)* leak; **tubo de e.** exhaust (pipe).

escarabajo *m* beetle.

escarbar *vt (suelo)* to scratch.

escarcha *f* frost.

escarlata *adj* scarlet.

escarlatina *f* scarlet fever.

escarmentar [1] *vi* to learn one's lesson.

escarmiento *m* lesson.

escarola *f* escarole.

escarpado, -a *adj (paisaje)* craggy.

escasear *vi* to be scarce.

escasez *f* scarcity.

escaso, -a *adj* scarce; *(dinero)* tight; *(conocimientos)* scant.

escatimar *vt* to skimp on; **no esca-timó esfuerzos para ...** he spared no efforts to ...

escayola *f* plaster of Paris; *(para brazo etc)* plaster.

escayolar *vt (brazo etc)* to put in plaster.

escena *f* scene; *(escenario)* stage.

escenario m (en teatro) stage; (de película) setting.

escéptico, -a adj & mf sceptic.

esclarecer [33] vt to shed light on.

esclavo, -a adj & mf slave.

esclusa f lock.

escoba f brush.

escocer [41] vi to sting.

escocés, -a 1 adj Scottish, Scots; **falda escocesa** kilt. **2** mf Scot.

escoger [53] vt to choose.

escolar 1 adj (curso, año) school. **2** mf (niño) schoolboy; (niña) schoolgirl.

escollo m reef; (obstáculo) pitfall.

escolta f escort.

escoltar vt to escort.

escombros mpl debris sing.

esconder vt, **esconderse** vr to hide (de from).

escondidas: a escondidas adv secretly.

escondite m (lugar) hiding place; (juego) hide-and-seek.

escondrijo m hiding place.

escopeta f shotgun; **e. de aire comprimido** air gun.

escorpión m scorpion.

escotado, -a adj low-cut.

escote m low neckline.

escotilla f hatch.

escozor m stinging.

escribir (pp **escrito**) **1** vt to write; **e. a máquina** to type. **2 escribirse** vr (dos personas) to write to each other.

escrito, -a 1 adj written; **por e.** in writing. **2** m (documento) document.

escritor, -a mf writer.

escritorio m (mueble) writing desk; (en computadora) desktop.

escritura f (documento) document.

escrúpulo m (recelo) scruple; **una persona sin escrúpulos** an unscrupulous person.

escrupuloso, -a adj squeamish; (honesto) scrupulous; (meticuloso) painstaking.

escrutinio m (de votos) count.

escuadra f (instrumento) square; (militar) squad; (de barcos) squadron.

escuálido, -a adj emaciated.

escuchar 1 vt to listen to; (oír) to hear. **2** vi to listen.

escudarse vr fig **e. en algo** to hide behind sth.

escudo m (arma defensiva) shield; (blasón) coat of arms.

escuela f school; **e. de idiomas** language school.

escueto, -a adj plain.

escuezo indic pres de **escocer**.

esculcar [44] vt Am (registrar) to search.

escultor, -a mf (hombre) sculptor; (mujer) sculptress; (de madera) woodcarver.

escultura f sculpture.

escupidera f (recipiente) spittoon, cuspidor; (orinal) chamberpot.

escupir 1 vi to spit. **2** vt to spit out.

escurreplatos m inv dish rack.

escurridizo, -a adj slippery.

escurridor m colander; (escurreplatos) dish rack.

escurrir 1 vt (plato, vaso) to drain; (ropa) to wring out; **e. el bulto** to wriggle out. **2 escurrirse** vr (resbalarse) to slip.

ese, -a adj dem that; **esos, -as** those.

ése, -a pron dem mf that one; **ésos, -as** those (ones); fam **¡ni por ésas!** no way!

esencia f essence.

esencial adj essential; **lo e.** the main thing.

esencialmente adv essentially.

esfera f sphere; (de reloj de pulsera) dial; (de reloj de pared) face.

esforzarse [2] vr to endeavor (**por** to).

esfuerzo m effort.

esfumarse vr fam to beat it.

esgrima f fencing.

esgrimir vt to wield.

esguince m sprain.

eslabón m link.

eslogan m (pl **eslóganes**) slogan.

esmalte *m* enamel; *(de uñas)* nail polish.

esmeralda *f* emerald.

esmerarse *vr* to be careful; *(esforzarse)* to go to great lengths.

esmero *m* great care.

esmoquin *m* *(pl* **esmóquines)** tuxedo.

esnob *(pl* **esnobs) 1** *adj (persona)* snobbish; *(restaurante etc)* posh. **2** *mf* snob.

eso *pron dem neutro* that; ¡**e. es!** that's it!; **por e.** that's why; **a e. de las diez** around ten.

esos, -as *adj dem pl* those.

ésos, -as *pron dem mfpl* those.

espabilado, -a *adj (despierto)* wide awake; *(listo)* clever.

espabilar *vt*, **espabilarse** *vr* to wake up.

espacial *adj* spatial; **nave e.** spaceship.

espacio *m* space; *(de tiempo)* length; *(programa)* program.

espacioso, -a *adj* spacious.

espada *f* sword; **pez e.** swordfish.

espaguetis *mpl* spaghetti *sing.*

espalda *f* back; *(en natación)* backstroke; **espaldas** back *sing*; **a espaldas de algn** behind sb's back; **por la e.** from behind; **volver la e. a algn** to turn one's back on sb.

espantajo *m* *(muñeco)* scarecrow.

espantapájaros *m inv* scarecrow.

espantar 1 *vt (asustar)* to frighten; *(ahuyentar)* to frighten away. **2 espantarse** *vr* to become frightened (**de** of).

espantoso, -a *adj* dreadful.

español, -a 1 *adj* Spanish. **2** *mf* Spaniard; **los españoles** the Spanish. **3** *m (idioma)* Spanish.

esparadrapo *m* sticking plaster.

esparcir [52] **1** *vt (papeles, semillas)* to scatter; *(rumor)* to spread. **2 esparcirse** *vr* to be scattered.

espárrago *m* asparagus.

espátula *f* spatula.

especia *f* spice.

especial *adj* special; **en e.** especially.

especialidad *f* specialty.

especialista *mf* specialist.

especializarse [40] *vr* to specialize (**en** in).

especialmente *adv (exclusivamente)* specially; *(muy)* especially.

especie *f* species *inv*; *(clase)* kind.

específicamente *adv* specifically.

especificar [44] *vt* to specify.

específico, -a *adj* specific.

espectacular *adj* spectacular.

espectáculo *m* show.

espectador, -a *mf* spectator; *(en teatro, cine)* member of the audience; **los espectadores** the audience *sing*; *(de televisión)* viewers.

especulación *f* speculation.

espejismo *m* mirage.

espejo *m* mirror; **e. retrovisor** rearview mirror.

espeluznante *adj* horrifying.

espera *f* wait; **en e. de** waiting for; **a la e. de** expecting; **sala de e.** waiting room.

esperanza *f* hope; **e. de vida** life expectancy.

esperanzador, -a *adj* encouraging.

esperar 1 *vi (aguardar)* to wait; *(tener esperanza)* to hope. **2** *vt (aguardar)* to wait for; *(tener esperanza)* to hope for; *(estar a la espera de, bebé)* to expect; **espero que sí** I hope so; **espero que vengas** I hope you'll come.

esperma *m* sperm; *Am (vela)* candle.

espesar *vt*, **espesarse** *vr* to thicken.

espeso, -a *adj (bosque, niebla)* dense; *(líquido)* thick; *(masa)* stiff.

espesor *m* thickness; **tres metros de e.** three meters thick.

espía *mf* spy.

espiar [29] **1** *vi* to spy. **2** *vt* to spy on.

espiga *f (de trigo)* ear.

espigado, -a *adj* slender.

espina f (de planta) thorn; (de pescado) bone; **e. dorsal** spine.

espinaca f spinach.

espinazo m spine.

espinilla f shin; (en la piel) spot.

espionaje m spying.

espiral adj & f spiral.

espirar vi to breathe out.

espíritu m spirit; (alma) soul.

espiritual adj spiritual.

espléndido, -a adj (magnífico) splendid; (generoso) lavish.

esplendor m splendor.

espliego m lavender.

esponja f sponge.

espontáneo, -a adj spontaneous.

esposado, -a adj (con esposas) handcuffed.

esposas fpl handcuffs.

esposo, -a mf spouse; (hombre) husband; (mujer) wife.

esprint m sprint.

espuela f spur.

espuma f foam; (de cerveza) head; (de jabón) lather; **e. de afeitar** shaving foam.

espumoso, -a adj frothy; (vino) sparkling.

esqueleto m skeleton.

esquema m diagram.

esquemático, -a adj (escueto) schematic; (con diagramas) diagrammatic.

esquí m (objeto) ski; (deporte) skiing; **e. acuático** water-skiing.

esquiador, -a mf skier.

esquiar [29] vi to ski.

esquimal adj & mf Eskimo.

esquina f corner.

esquivar vt (a una persona) to avoid; (un golpe) to dodge.

esta adj dem this.

está indic pres de **estar**.

ésta pron dem f this (one).

estabilidad f stability.

estable adj stable.

establecer [33] **1** vt to establish; (récord) to set. **2 establecerse** vr (instalarse) to settle.

establecimiento m establishment.

establo m cow shed.

estaca f stake; (de tienda de campaña) peg.

estación f station; (del año) season; **e. de servicio** service station; **e. de esquí** ski resort; **e. de trabajo** work station.

estacionamiento m (acción) parking.

estacionar vt, **estacionarse** vr to park.

estacionario, -a adj stationary.

estada f, **estadía** f Am stay.

estadio m (deportivo) stadium; (fase) stage.

estadística f statistics sing; **una e.** a statistic.

estado m state; **e. civil** marital status; **e. de cuentas** statement of account.

estadounidense 1 adj United States, American. **2** mf United States citizen.

estafa f swindle.

estafar vt to swindle.

estafeta f **e. de Correos** sub post office.

estallar vi to burst; (bomba) to explode; (guerra) to break out.

estallido m explosion; (de guerra) outbreak.

estampa f illustration.

estampado, -a 1 adj (tela) printed. **2** m (de tela) print.

estampilla f Am (postage) stamp.

estancar [44] **1** vt (agua) to hold back; (paralizar) to block; (negociaciones) to bring to a standstill. **2 estancarse** vr to stagnate.

estancia f (permanencia) stay; (habitación) room; Am (hacienda) ranch.

estanco m tobacconist's.

estándar (pl **estándares**) adj & m standard.

estanque m pond.

estante m shelf; (para libros) bookcase.

estantería f shelves.

estaño m tin.

estar [13] vi to be; ¿está tu madre? is your mother in?; ¿cómo estás? how are you?; está escribiendo she is writing; estamos a 2 de noviembre it is the 2nd of November; están a 20 pesos el kilo they're 20 pesos a kilo; ¿estamos? OK?; e. de más not to be needed. ▪ (+ para) estará para las seis it will be finished by six; hoy no estoy para bromas I'm in no mood for jokes today; el tren está para salir the train is just about to leave. ▪ (+ por) está por hacer it has still to be done; eso está por ver it remains to be seen. ▪ (+ con) to have; e. con la gripe to have the flu. ▪ (+ sin) to have no. 2 estarse vr ¡estáte quieto! keep still!

estatal adj state.

estatua f statue.

estatura f height.

estatuto m statute; (de empresa etc) rules pl.

este 1 adj eastern; (dirección) easterly. **2** m east; **al e. de** to the east of.

esté subj pres de estar.

este, -a adj dem this; **estos, -as** these.

éste, -a pron dem mf this one; **aquél ... é.** the former ... the latter; **éstos, -as** these (ones); **aquéllos ... éstos** the former ... the latter.

estela f (de barco) wake; (de avión) vapor trail.

estepa f steppe.

estera f rush mat.

estercolero m dunghill.

estéreo adj & m stereo.

estereofónico, -a adj stereophonic.

estereotipo m stereotype.

estéril adj sterile.

esterilla f small mat.

esterlina adj **libra e.** pound (sterling).

esternón m breastbone.

estero m Am marsh.

esteticienne, esteticista f beautician.

estético, -a adj aesthetic; **cirugía estética** plastic surgery.

estiércol m manure.

estilarse vr to be in vogue.

estilo m style; (modo) manner; (en natación) stroke.

estilográfica f (pluma) e. fountain pen.

estima f esteem.

estimación f (estima) esteem; (valoración) evaluation; (cálculo aproximado) estimate.

estimado, -a adj respected; **E. Señor** (en carta) Dear Sir.

estimar vt (apreciar) to esteem; (considerar) to think; (valuar) to value.

estimativo, -a adj approximate, estimated.

estimulante 1 adj stimulating. **2** m stimulant.

estimular vt to stimulate.

estímulo m stimulus.

estirar vt, **estirarse** vr to stretch.

estival adj summer.

esto pron dem (esta cosa) this, this thing; (este asunto) this matter.

estocada f stab.

estofado m stew.

estómago m stomach; **dolor de e.** stomach ache.

estoque m sword.

estorbar 1 vt (dificultar) to hinder. **2** vi to be in the way.

estorbo m (obstáculo) obstacle.

estornudar vi to sneeze.

estornudo m sneeze.

estos, -as adj dem pl these.

éstos, -as pron dem mfpl these.

estoy indic pres de estar.

estragos mpl **hacer e. en** to wreak havoc with o on.

estrangular vt to strangle.

estraperlo m black market.

estratagema f ruse.

estratégico, -a adj strategic.

estrechamente adv (íntimamente) closely.

estrechamiento *m* narrowing; **'e. de calzada'** *(en letrero)* 'road narrows'.

estrechar 1 *vt* to make narrow; **e. la mano a algn** to shake sb's hand; *(lazos de amistad)* to tighten. **2 estrecharse** *vr* to narrow.

estrechez *f* narrowness; **pasar estrecheces** to be hard up.

estrecho, -a 1 *adj* narrow; *(ropa, zapato)* tight; *(amistad, relación)* close. **2** *m* strait.

estrella *f* star; **e. de cine** film star; **e. de mar** starfish; **e. fugaz** shooting star.

estrellado, -a *adj (en forma de estrella)* star-shaped; *(cielo)* starry; *(huevos)* scrambled.

estrellar 1 *vt fam* to smash. **2 estrellarse** *vr (chocar)* to crash (**contra** into).

estremecedor, -a *adj* bloodcurdling.

estremecer [33] *vt,* **estremecerse** *vr* to shake.

estrenar *vt* to use for the first time; *(ropa)* to wear for the first time; *(obra, película)* to premiere.

estreno *m (teatral)* first performance; *(de película)* premiere.

estreñido, -a *adj* constipated.

estreñimiento *m* constipation.

estrépito *m* din.

estrepitoso, -a *adj (fracaso)* spectacular.

estrés *m* stress.

estresado, -a *adj (persona)* stressed.

estresante *adj* stressful.

estribillo *m (en canción)* chorus; *(en poema)* refrain.

estribo *m* stirrup; *fig* **perder los estribos** to fly off the handle.

estribor *m* starboard.

estricto, -a *adj* strict.

estropajo *m* scourer.

estropear 1 *vt (máquina, cosecha)* to damage; *(fiesta, plan)* to spoil; *(pelo, manos)* to ruin. **2 estropearse**

vr to be ruined; *(máquina)* to break down.

estropicio *m fam (destrozo)* damage; *(ruido)* crash, clatter.

estructura *f* structure; *(armazón)* framework.

estruendo *m* roar.

estrujar *vt (limón etc)* to squeeze; *(apretar)* to crush.

estuche *m* case.

estudiante *mf* student.

estudiantil *adj* student.

estudiar [43] *vti* to study.

estudio *m* study; *(encuesta)* survey; *(sala)* studio; *(apartamento)* studio (apartment).

estudioso, -a 1 *adj* studious. **2** *mf* specialist.

estufa *f* heater.

estupefaciente *m* drug.

estupefacto, -a *adj* astounded.

estupendamente *adv* marvelously.

estupendo, -a *adj* marvelous; **¡e.!** great!

estupidez *f* stupidity.

estúpido, -a 1 *adj* stupid. **2** *mf* idiot.

estuve *pt indef de* **estar**.

ETA *f abr de* **Euzkadi Ta Askatasuna** *(Patria Vasca y Libertad)* ETA.

etapa *f* stage.

etcétera *adv* etcetera.

eterno, -a *adj* eternal.

ético, -a *adj* ethical.

etílico, -a *adj* **alcohol e.** ethyl alcohol.

etiqueta *f (de producto)* label; *(ceremonia)* etiquette; **de e.** formal.

étnico, -a *adj* ethnic.

EU *f abr de* **Unión Europea** European Union, EU.

eucalipto *m* eucalyptus.

eufórico, -a *adj* euphoric.

euro *m* euro.

europeo, -a *adj & mf* European.

euskera *m* Basque.

eutanasia *f* euthanasia.

evacuación *f* evacuation.

evacuar [47] *vt* to evacuate.

evadir 1 *vt (respuesta, peligro, impuestos)* to avoid; *(responsabilidad)* to shirk. **2 evadirse** *vr* to escape.

evaluación *f* evaluation; *(en colegio)* assessment.

evaluar [30] *vt* to evaluate, to assess.

evangelio *m* gospel.

evaporación *f* evaporation.

evaporar *vt*, **evaporarse** *vr* to evaporate.

evasión *f (fuga)* escape; *(escapismo)* escapism; **e. de capitales** flight of capital.

evasiva *f* evasive answer.

evasivo, -a *adj* evasive.

evento *m (acontecimiento)* event; *(incidente)* unforeseen event.

eventual *adj (posible)* possible; *(trabajo, obrero)* casual.

evidencia *f* obviousness; **poner a algn en e.** to show sb up.

evidenciar [43] *vt* to show, to demonstrate.

evidente *adj* obvious.

evidentemente *adv* obviously.

evitar *vt* to avoid; *(problema futuro)* to prevent; *(desastre)* to avert.

evocar [44] *vt (traer a la memoria)* to evoke.

evolución *f* evolution; *(desarrollo)* development.

evolucionar *vi* to develop; *(especies)* to evolve.

ex *prefijo* former, ex-; **ex alumno** former pupil; **ex marido** ex-husband; *fam* **mi ex** my ex.

exabrupto *m* sharp comment.

exacerbar 1 *vt (agravar)* to exacerbate. **2 exacerbarse** *vr (irritarse)* to feel exasperated.

exactamente *adv* exactly.

exactitud *f* accuracy; **con e.** precisely.

exacto, -a *adj* exact; ¡e.! precisely!

exageración *f* exaggeration.

exagerado, -a *adj* exaggerated; *(excesivo)* excessive.

exagerar *vti* to exaggerate.

exaltarse *vr (acalorarse)* to get carried away.

examen *m* examination, exam; **e. de conducir** driving test.

examinador, -a *mf* examiner.

examinar 1 *vt* to examine. **2 examinarse** *vr* to sit for an examination.

exasperante *adj* exasperating.

exasperar 1 *vt* to exasperate. **2 exasperarse** *vr* to become exasperated.

excavación *f* excavation; *(en arqueología)* dig.

excavadora *f* digger.

excavar *vt* to excavate, to dig.

excedencia *f (de empleado)* leave (of absence); *(de profesor)* sabbatical.

excedente *adj & m* surplus.

exceder 1 *vt* to exceed. **2 excederse** *vr* to go too far.

excelencia *f* excellence.

excelente *adj* excellent.

excéntrico, -a *adj* eccentric.

excepción *f* exception; **a e. de** except for.

excepcional *adj* exceptional.

excepto *adv* except (for).

exceptuar [30] *vt* to except.

excesivo, -a *adj* excessive.

exceso *m* excess; **e. de velocidad** speeding.

excitación *f (sentimiento)* excitement; *(acción)* excitation.

excitante *adj* exciting.

excitar 1 *vt* to excite. **2 excitarse** *vr* to get excited.

exclamación *f* exclamation.

exclamar *vti* to exclaim.

excluir [37] *vt* to exclude.

exclusive *adv (en fechas)* exclusive.

exclusivo, -a *adj* exclusive.

excremento *m* excrement.

exculpar *vt* to exonerate.

excursión *f* excursion.

excursionista *mf* tripper; *(a pie)* hiker.

excusa *f (pretexto)* excuse; *(disculpa)* apology.

excusado *m (retrete)* toilet.
excusar 1 *vt (justificar)* to excuse; *(eximir)* to exempt (**de** from). **2 excusarse** *vr (disculparse)* to apologize.
exención *f* exemption.
exento, -a *adj* exempt (**de** from).
exhalar *vt* to breathe out.
exhaustivo, -a *adj* exhaustive.
exhausto, -a *adj* exhausted.
exhibición *f* exhibition.
exhibir 1 *vt (mostrar)* to exhibit; *(lucir)* to show off. **2 exhibirse** *vr* to show off.
exigencia *f* demand; *(requisito)* requirement.
exigente *adj* demanding.
exigir [57] *vt* to demand.
exilado, -a 1 *adj* exiled. **2** *mf* exile.
exilar 1 *vt* to exile. **2 exilarse** *vr* to go into exile.
exiliado, -a *adj & mf* = **exilado**.
exiliar [43] *ot* = **exilar**.
exilio *m* exile.
existencia *f (vida)* existence; **existencias** stocks.
existente *adj* existing.
existir *vi* to exist.
éxito *m* success; **con é.** successfully; **tener é.** to be successful.
exitoso, -a *adj* successful.
éxodo *m* exodus.
exorbitante *adj* exorbitant.
exótico, -a *adj* exotic.
expandir *vt*, **expandirse** *vr* to expand.
expansión *f* expansion; *(de noticia)* spreading; *(diversión)* relaxation.
expatriar [29] **1** *vt* to exile, to banish. **2 expatriarse** *vr* to leave one's country.
expectación *f (interés)* excitement.
expectativa *f* expectancy.
expedición *f* expedition.
expediente *m (informe)* record; *(ficha)* file; **e. académico** student's record.
expedir [6] *vt (pasaporte etc)* to issue.
expendeduría *f* tobacconist's.

expensas *fpl* **a e. de** at the expense of.
experiencia *f* experience; *(experimento)* experiment.
experimentado, -a *adj* experienced.
experimental *adj* experimental.
experimentar 1 *vi* to experiment. **2** *vt* to undergo; *(aumento)* to show; *(pérdida)* to suffer; *(sensación)* to experience.
experimento *m* experiment.
experto, -a *adj & mf* expert.
expirar *vi* to expire.
explanada *f* esplanade.
explicación *f* explanation.
explicar [44] *vt* to explain. **2 explicarse** *vr (persona)* to explain (oneself); **no me lo explico** I can't understand it.
exploración *f* exploration.
explorador, -a *mf* explorer.
explorar *vt* to explore.
explosión *f* explosion; **hacer e.** to explode.
explosionar *vti* to explode, to blow up.
explosivo, -a *adj & m* explosive.
explotación *f* exploitation.
explotar 1 *vi (bomba)* to explode, to go off. **2** *vt* to exploit.
exponer [19] *(pp* **expuesto**) **1** *vt (mostrar)* to exhibit; *(presentar)* to put forward; *(arriesgar)* to expose. **2 exponerse** *vr* to expose oneself (**a** to).
exportación *f* export.
exportar *vt* to export.
exposición *f* exhibition.
exprés *adj* express; **olla e.** pressure cooker; **café e.** espresso (coffee).
expresamente *adv* expressly.
expresar 1 *vt* to express; *(manifestar)* to state. **2 expresarse** *vr* to express oneself.
expresión *f* expression.
expresivo, -a *adj* expressive.
expreso, -a 1 *adj* express. **2** *m* express (train). **3** *adv* on purpose.

exprimidor *m* juicer.

exprimir *vt (limón)* to squeeze; *(zumo)* to squeeze out.

expulsar *vt* to expel; *(jugador)* to send off.

expuse *pt indef de* **exponer**.

exquisito, -a *adj* exquisite; *(comida)* delicious; *(gusto)* refined.

extender [3] **1** *vt* to extend; *(agrandar)* to enlarge; *(mantel, mapa)* to spread (out); *(mano, brazo)* to stretch (out); *(crema, mantequilla)* to spread. **2 extenderse** *vr (en el tiempo)* to last; *(en el espacio)* to stretch; *(rumor, noticia)* to spread.

extendido, -a *adj* extended; *(mapa, plano)* open; *(mano, brazo)* outstretched; *(costumbre, rumor)* widespread.

extensión *f (de libro etc)* length; *(de terreno)* expanse.

extenso, -a *adj (terreno)* extensive; *(libro, película)* long.

extenuar [30] **1** *vt* to exhaust. **2 extenuarse** *vr* to exhaust oneself.

exterior **1** *adj (de fuera)* outer; *(puerta)* outside; *(política, deuda)* foreign; **Ministerio de Asuntos Exteriores** State Department. **2** *m (parte de fuera)* outside; *(extranjero)* abroad.

exteriormente *adv* outwardly.

exterminar *vt* to exterminate.

externalización *f* outsourcing.

externo, -a *adj* external.

extinguir [59] **1** *vt (fuego)* to extinguish; *(raza)* to wipe out. **2 extinguirse** *vr (fuego)* to go out; *(especie)* to become extinct.

extintor *m* fire extinguisher.

extirpar *vt (tumor)* to remove; *fig* to eradicate, to stamp out.

extorsión *f* extortion.

extorsionar *vt* to extort.

extra **1** *adj* extra; *(superior)* top quality; **horas e.** overtime; **paga e.** bonus. **2** *mf* extra.

extracto *m* extract; **e. de cuenta** statement of account.

extraer [25] *vt* to extract.

extranjero, -a **1** *adj* foreign. **2** *mf* foreigner. **3** *m* abroad; **en el e.** abroad.

extrañar **1** *vt (sorprender)* to surprise; *Am (echar de menos)* to miss. **2 extrañarse** *vr* **extrañarse de** *(sorprenderse)* to be surprised at.

extrañeza *f (sorpresa)* surprise; *(singularidad)* strangeness.

extraño, -a **1** *adj* strange. **2** *mf* stranger.

extraoficial *adj* unofficial.

extraordinario, -a *adj* extraordinary.

extrarradio *m* suburbs *pl*.

extraterrestre *mf* alien.

extravagante *adj* outlandish.

extravertido, -a *adj & mf* = **extrovertido**.

extraviar [29] **1** *vt* to mislay. **2 extraviarse** *vr* to be missing.

extremeño, -a *adj & mf* Estremaduran.

extremidad *f (extremo)* tip; *(miembro)* limb.

extremo, -a **1** *m (de calle, cable)* end; *(máximo)* extreme; **en último e.** as a last resort; *f* **e. derecha/izquierda** outside-right/-left. **2** *adj* extreme; **E. Oriente** Far East.

extrovertido, -a *adj & mf* extrovert.

exuberante *adj* exuberant; *(vegetación)* lush.

F

fabada *f* stew of beans, pork sausage and bacon.

fábrica *f* factory.

fabricación *f* manufacture.

fabricante *mf* manufacturer.

fabricar [44] *vt* to manufacture.

fabuloso, -a *adj* fabulous.

facción *f* faction; **facciones** *(rasgos)* features.

facha *f fam* look.

fachada *f* façade.

facial *adj* facial.

fácil *adj* easy; **es f. que …** it's (quite) likely that ….

facilidad *f (sencillez)* easiness; *(soltura)* ease; **facilidades de pago** easy terms.

facilitar *vt (simplificar)* to make easy *o* easier; **f. algo a algn** to provide sb with sth.

fácilmente *adv* easily.

facsímil, facsímile *m* facsimile.

factible *adj* feasible.

factor *m* factor.

factoría *f* factory.

factura *f* invoice.

facturación *f (en aeropuerto)* check-in; *(en estación)* registration.

facturar *vt (en aeropuerto)* to check in; *(en estación)* to register.

facultad *f* faculty.

faena *f (tarea)* task; *(en corrida)* performance.

faisán *m* pheasant.

faja *f (corsé)* corset.

fajo *m (de billetes)* wad.

falda *f (prenda)* skirt; *(de montaña)* slope; **f. pantalón** culottes *pl.*

falla *f Am (defecto)* fault.

fallar 1 *vi* to fail; **le falló la puntería** he missed his target. **2** *vt* to miss.

fallecer [33] *vi* to pass away, die.

fallecimiento *m* demise.

fallo *m (error)* mistake; *(del corazón, de los frenos)* failure.

falsear *vt (hechos, la verdad)* to distort.

falsificar [44] *vt* to falsify; *(cuadro, firma, moneda)* to forge.

falso, -a *adj* false; *(persona)* insincere.

falta *f (carencia)* lack; *(escasez)* shortage; *(ausencia)* absence; *(error)* mistake; *(defecto)* fault, defect; *(fútbol)* foul; *(tenis)* fault; **sin f.** without

fail; **echar algo/a algn en f.** to miss sth/sb; **f. de ortografía** spelling mistake; **hacer f.** to be necessary; **(nos) hace f. una escalera** we need a ladder; **harán f. dos personas para mover el piano** it'll take two people to move the piano; **no hace f. que …** there is no need for ….

faltar *vi (no estar)* to be missing; *(escasear)* to be lacking *o* needed; *(quedar)* to be left; **¿quién falta?** who is missing?; **le falta confianza en sí mismo** he lacks confidence in himself; **¡lo que me faltaba!** that's all I needed!; **¡no faltaría** *o* **faltaba más!** *(por supuesto)* (but) of course!; **¿cuántos kilómetros faltan para Managua?** how many kilometers is it to Managua?; **ya falta poco para las vacaciones** it won't be long now until the holidays; **f. a la verdad** not to tell the truth.

fama *f* fame; *(reputación)* reputation.

familia *f* family.

familiar 1 *adj (de la familia)* family; *(conocido)* familiar. **2** *mf* relation, relative.

familiarizarse [40] *vr* to familiarize oneself (**con** with).

famoso, -a *adj* famous.

fan *mf* fan.

fanático, -a 1 *adj* fanatical. **2** *mf* fanatic.

fanfarrón, -ona 1 *adj* boastful. **2** *mf* show-off.

fango *m (barro)* mud.

fantasía *f* fantasy.

fantasma *m* ghost.

fantástico, -a *adj* fantastic.

fardo *m* bundle.

farmacéutico, -a 1 *adj* pharmaceutical. **2** *mf* pharmacist.

farmacia *f* pharmacy.

fármaco *m* medicine, medication.

faro *m (torre)* lighthouse; *(de coche)* headlight.

farol *m (luz)* lantern; *(en la calle)* streetlight, streetlamp.

farola *f* streetlight, streetlamp.

farsante *mf* fake, impostor.

fascículo *m* installment.

fascinar *vt* to fascinate.

fascista *adj & mf* fascist.

fase *f* phase, stage.

fastidiar [43] **1** *vt (molestar)* to annoy, to bother. **2 fastidiarse** *vr (aguantarse)* to put up with it; **que se fastidie** that's his tough luck; **fastidiarse el brazo** to hurt one's arm.

fastidio *m* nuisance.

fastuoso, -a *adj (acto)* splendid, lavish.

fatal 1 *adj (muy malo)* awful; *(mortal)* fatal. **2** *adv* awfully; **lo pasó f.** he had a rotten time.

fatiga *f (cansancio)* fatigue.

fatigar [42] *vt*, **fatigarse** *vr* to tire.

fauna *f* fauna.

favor *m* favor; **¿puedes hacerme un f.?** can you do me a favor?; **estar a f. de** to be in favor of; **por f.** please; **haga el f. de sentarse** please sit down.

favorable *adj* favorable.

favorecedor, -a *adj* flattering.

favorecer [33] *vt* to favor; *(sentar bien)* to flatter.

favorito, -a *adj & mf* favorite.

fe *f* faith; **fe de bautismo/matrimonio** baptism/marriage certificate.

fealdad *f* ugliness.

febrero *m* February.

fecha *f* date; **f. de caducidad** sell-by date; **hasta la f.** so far.

fechar *vt* to date.

fecundación *f* fertilization.

federación *f* federation.

felicidad *f* happiness; **(muchas) felicidades** *(en cumpleaños)* many happy returns.

felicitación *f* tarjeta de f. greeting card.

felicitar *vt* to congratulate (**por** on); **¡te felicito!** congratulations!

feligrés, -a *mf* parishioner.

feliz *adj (contento)* happy; **¡felices Navidades!** Merry Christmas!

felpa *f (tela)* plush; **oso** *o* **osito de f.** teddy bear.

felpudo *m* mat.

femenino, -a *adj* feminine; *(equipo, ropa)* women's; **sexo f.** female sex.

feminista *adj & mf* feminist.

fémur *m* femur.

fenomenal 1 *adj* phenomenal; *fam (fantástico)* great. **2** *adv fam* wonderfully.

fenómeno *m* phenomenon; *(prodigio)* genius; *(monstruo)* freak.

feo, -a *adj* ugly.

féretro *m* coffin.

feria *f* fair; **f. de muestras/del libro** trade/book fair.

feriado, -a *Am* **1** *adj* día f. (public) holiday. **2** *m* (public) holiday.

fermentar *vi* to ferment.

feroz *adj* fierce, ferocious.

ferretería *f* hardware store.

ferrocarril *m* railroad.

ferroviario, -a *adj* railway, rail.

ferry *m* ferry.

fértil *adj* fertile.

fertilizante *m* fertilizer.

fertilizar [40] *vt* to fertilize.

fervor *m* fervor.

festejar *vt* to celebrate.

festín *m* feast.

festival *m* festival.

festividad *f* festivity.

festivo, -a 1 *adj (ambiente etc)* festive; **día f.** holiday. **2** *m* holiday.

feto *m* fetus.

fiable *adj* reliable, trustworthy.

fiador, -a *mf* guarantor.

fiambre *m* cold meat.

fiambrera *f* lunch box.

fianza *f (depósito)* deposit; *(jurídica)* bail.

fiarse [29] *vr* to trust (**de** -).

fibra *f* fiber.

ficción *f* fiction.

ficha *f (de archivo)* filing card; *(en juegos)* counter; *(de ajedrez)* piece.

fichaje *m* signing.

fichar **1** *vt* to put on file; *(deportista)* to sign up. **2** *vi (en el trabajo) (al entrar)* to clock in; *(al salir)* to clock out; *(deportista)* to sign.

fichero m card index; (de ordenador) file.

ficticio, -a adj fictitious.

fidelidad f faithfulness; **alta f.** high fidelity, hi-fi.

fideo m noodle.

fiebre f fever; **tener f.** to have a temperature.

fiel 1 adj (leal) faithful, loyal. **2** mpl **los fieles** the congregation.

fieltro m felt.

fiera f wild animal.

fierro m Am (hierro) iron; (navaja) knife.

fiesta f (entre amigos) party; (vacaciones) holiday; (festividad) celebration.

figura f figure.

figurar 1 vi (aparecer) to figure. **2** figurarse vr to imagine; **ya me lo figuraba** I thought as much; **¡figúrate, figúrese!** just imagine!

fijador m (gomina) gel.

fijamente adv mirar f. to stare.

fijar 1 vt to fix. **2** fijarse vr (darse cuenta) to notice; (poner atención) to pay attention, to watch.

fijo, -a adj fixed; (trabajo) steady.

fila f file; (de cine, teatro) row; **en f. india** in single file.

filántropo, -a mf philanthropist.

filarmónico, -a adj philharmonic.

filatelia f stamp collecting, philately.

filete m fillet.

filial 1 adj (de hijos) filial. **2** f (empresa) subsidiary.

filmar vt to film.

film(e) m film.

filo m edge.

filosofía f philosophy.

filosófico, -a adj philosophical.

filósofo, -a mf philosopher.

filtración f filtration; (de noticia) leak(ing).

filtrar 1 vt to filter; (noticia) to leak. **2** filtrarse vr (líquido) to seep; (noticia) to leak out.

filtro m filter.

fin m (final) end; (objetivo) purpose, aim; **dar** o **poner f. a** to put an end to; **en f.** anyway; **¡por** o **al f.!** at last!; **f. de semana** weekend; **al f. y al cabo** when all's said and done; **a f. de** in order to, so as to.

final 1 adj final. **2** m end; **al f.** in the end; **a finales de octubre** at the end of October. **3** f (de campeonato) final.

finalizar [40] vti to end, to finish.

finalmente adv finally.

financiación f financing.

financiar [43] vt to finance.

financiero, -a adj financial.

financista mf Am financier.

finanzas fpl finances.

finca f (de campo) country house.

fingir [57] **1** vt to feign. **2** vi to pretend.

fino, -a 1 adj (hilo, capa) fine; (flaco) thin; (educado) refined, polite; (oído) sharp, acute. **2** m (vino) type of dry sherry.

firma f signature; (empresa) firm.

firmar vt to sign.

firme 1 adj firm; **tierra f.** terra firma. **2** adv hard.

firmemente adv firmly.

fiscal 1 adj fiscal, tax. **2** mf district attorney.

fisco m treasury.

fisgar [42] vi fam to snoop, to pry.

fisgón, -ona mf snooper.

física f physics sing.

físico, -a adj physical.

fisioterapia f physiotherapy.

flaco, -a adj (delgado) skinny.

flamante adj (nuevo) brand-new; (vistoso) splendid, brilliant.

flamenco, -a 1 adj (música) flamenco; (de Flandes) Flemish. **2** m (música) flamenco.

flan m caramel custard.

flanco m flank, side.

flaquear vi (fuerzas, piernas) to weaken, to give way.

flaqueza f weakness.

flash m flash.

LA FECHA Y LA HORA

Días de la semana
Monday · Tuesday · Wednesday · Thursday · Friday · Saturday · Sunday
Meses del año
January · February · March · April · May · June · July · August · September · October · November · December
Los días y meses se escriben con mayúscula inicial en inglés. Las fechas se indican con números ordinales (**el tres de marzo** the third of March).

¿Qué día es hoy?
What day is it today?

¿A qué fecha estamos hoy?
What's today's date?

Es miércoles doce de abril.
It's Wednesday April 12th.

Nací en mil novecientos ochenta.
I was born in 1980.

¿Hasta cuándo se van a quedar aquí?
How long are you staying?

Llegamos aquí el fin de semana pasado.
We got here last weekend.

¡Hasta el sábado!
See you on Saturday!

Tómeselo tres veces al día.
Take it three times a day.

¿Qué hora es?
What's the time?

Son casi las doce de la mañana./ Es casi medianoche.
It's nearly midday/midnight.

Son las siete menos cuarto.
It's a quarter to seven.

Llegaré sobre las ocho.
I'll be there about eight.

Mi avión llegó con dos horas de retraso.
My plane arrived two hours late.

No tengo tiempo (de...).
I don't have time (to...).

Es viernes.
It's Friday.

Estamos a quince de abril.
It's April 15th.

Mañana es jueves.
It's Thursday tomorrow.

Vine a México hace unos años.
I came to Mexico a few years ago.

Nos vamos el domingo/el (día) ocho.
We leave on Sunday/the 8th.

Estuve todo el día esperando.
I waited all day.

¡Hasta la semana que viene!
See you next week!

Les veo cada dos semanas.
I see them every two weeks.

Son las dos.
It's 2 o'clock.

Son las cuatro y media/las cuatro treinta.
It's half four/four-thirty.

Son las siete y veinte.
It's twenty after seven.

Nos vemos dentro de media hora.
I'll see you in half an hour.

Llegué pronto/tarde/a tiempo.
I got there early/late/on time.

Es hora de irse.
It's time to go.

flauta f flute.

flecha f arrow.

flechazo m (enamoramiento) love at first sight.

fleco m fringe.

flema f phlegm.

flemático, -a adj phlegmatic.

flemón m gumboil.

flequillo m bangs pl.

fletar vt to charter.

flexible adj flexible.

flexión f flexion.

flexionar vt to bend; (músculo) to flex.

flexo m reading lamp.

flirtear vi to flirt.

flojear vi (ventas etc) to fall off, to go down; (piernas) to weaken, to grow weak; (memoria) to fail; Andes fam (holgazanear) to laze around o about.

flojera f fam weakness, faintness.

flojo, -a adj (tornillo, cuerda etc) loose, slack; (perezoso) lazy, idle.

flor f flower.

flora f flora.

floreado, -a adj flowery.

florecer [33] vi (plantas) to flower; (negocio) to flourish, to thrive.

floreciente adj flourishing, prosperous.

florero m vase.

floristería f florist's (shop).

flota f fleet.

flotador m (para nadar) rubber ring.

flotar vi to float.

flote m a f. afloat.

flotilla f flotilla.

fluctuar [30] vi to fluctuate.

fluidez f fluency.

fluido, -a 1 adj fluid; (estilo etc) fluent. **2** m liquid.

fluir [37] vi to flow.

flujo m flow; (de la marea) rising tide.

flúor m fluorine.

fluorescente adj fluorescent.

fluvial adj river.

FMI m abr de **Fondo Monetario Internacional** International Monetary Fund, IMF.

fobia f phobia (**a** of).

foca f seal.

foco m (lámpara) spotlight, floodlight; Andes, Méx (bombilla) (electric light) bulb; Am (de coche) (car) headlight; Am (farola) street light.

fofo, -a adj soft; (persona) flabby.

fogata f bonfire.

fogón m (de cocina) ring.

folio m sheet of paper.

folklórico, -a adj música folklórica folk music.

follaje m foliage.

folletín m (relato) newspaper serial.

folleto m leaflet; (turístico) brochure.

follón m fam (alboroto) ruckus; (enredo, confusión) mess.

fomentar vt to promote.

fomento m promotion.

fonda f inn.

fondear vi to anchor.

fondista mf (corredor) long-distance runner.

fondo¹ m (parte más baja) bottom; (de habitación) back; (de pasillo) end; (segundo término) background; **a f.** thoroughly; **al f. de la calle** at the end of the street; **en el f. es bueno** deep down he's kind; **música de f.** background music.

fondo² m (dinero) fund; **cheque sin fondos** bad check.

fonético, -a adj phonetic.

fontanero, -a mf plumber.

footing m jogging; **hacer f.** to go jogging.

forastero, -a mf outsider.

forcejear vi to wrestle.

forense 1 adj forensic. **2** mf (médico) f. forensic surgeon.

forestal adj forest; **repoblación f.** re-afforestation.

forjar vt to forge.

forma f form, shape; (manera) way; **¿qué f. tiene?** what shape is it?; **de**

esta f. in this way; **de f. que** so that; **de todas formas** anyway, in any case; **estar en f.** to be in shape; **estar en baja f.** to be out of shape.

formación f formation; *(enseñanza)* training; **f. profesional** vocational training.

formal adj formal; *(serio)* serious; *(fiable)* reliable.

formalizar [40] vt *(hacer formal)* to formalize; *(contrato)* to legalize.

formar 1 vt to form; **f. parte de algo** to be a part of sth; *(enseñar)* to educate, to train. **2 formarse** vr to be formed, to form.

formatear vt to format.

formato m format; *(del papel)* size.

formidable adj *(estupendo)* terrific.

fórmula f formula.

formular vt *(quejas, peticiones)* to make; *(deseo)* to express; *(pregunta)* to ask; *(una teoría)* to formulate.

formulario m form.

forrar vt *(por dentro)* to line; *(por fuera)* to cover.

forro m *(por dentro)* lining; *(por fuera)* cover.

fortalecer [33] vt to fortify, to strengthen.

fortificar [44] vt to fortify.

fortísimo, -a adj very strong.

fortuito, -a adj fortuitous.

fortuna f *(suerte)* luck; *(capital)* fortune; **por f.** fortunately.

forzado, -a adj forced; **trabajos forzados** hard labor.

forzar [2] vt to force.

forzosamente adv necessarily.

forzoso, -a adj obligatory, compulsory.

fosa f *(sepultura)* grave; *(hoyo)* pit.

fósforo m *(cerilla)* match.

fósil adj & m fossil.

foso m *(hoyo)* pit.

foto f photo.

fotocopia f photocopy.

fotocopiadora f photocopier.

fotocopiar [43] vt to photocopy.

fotografía f photograph; **hacer fotografías** to take photographs.

fotografiar [29] vt to photograph, to take a photograph of.

fotógrafo, -a mf photographer.

FP f abr de **Formación Profesional** vocational training.

frac m *(pl* **fracs** o **fraques** *)* dress coat, tails *pl.*

fracasar vi to fail.

fracaso m failure.

fraccionar vt, **fraccionarse** vr to break up.

fractura f fracture.

fragancia f fragrance.

frágil adj *(quebradizo)* fragile; *(débil)* frail.

fragmento m fragment; *(de novela etc)* passage.

fraile m friar, monk.

frambuesa f raspberry.

francamente adv frankly.

francés, -esa 1 adj French. **2** mf *(hombre)* Frenchman; *(mujer)* Frenchwoman. **3** m *(idioma)* French.

franco, -a¹ adj *(persona)* frank; **puerto f.** free port.

franco² m *(moneda)* franc.

franela f flannel.

franja f *(de terreno)* strip; *(de bandera)* stripe.

franqueo m postage.

frasco m small bottle, flask.

frase f *(oración)* sentence; *(expresión)* phrase.

fraterno, -a adj fraternal, brotherly.

fraude m fraud.

frazada f Am blanket.

frecuencia f frequency; **con f.** frequently.

frecuentar vt to frequent.

frecuente adj frequent.

frecuentemente adv frequently, often.

fregadero m *(kitchen)* sink.

fregar [1] vt *(lavar)* to wash; *(suelo)* to mop; *Am* to annoy.

fregón, -ona adj Am annoying.

fregona f mop.

freidora f (deep) fryer.

freír [56] (pp **frito**) vt to fry.

frenar vti to brake.

frenazo m sudden braking.

frenético, -a adj frantic.

freno m brake; **pisar/soltar el f.** to press/release the brake; **f. de mano** handbrake.

frente 1 m front; **chocar de f.** to crash head on; **hacer f. a algo** to face up to sth. **2** f (de la cara) forehead; **f. a f.** face to face. **3** prep **f. a** opposite.

fresa f strawberry.

fresco, -a 1 adj (frío) cool; (comida, fruta) fresh; (descarado) rude. **2** m (frescor) fresh air; (caradura) cheek; **hace f.** it's chilly.

frescor m freshness.

frescura f freshness; (desvergüenza) nerve.

fresón m (large) strawberry.

fríamente adv coolly.

fricción f friction.

friegaplatos mf inv (persona) dishwasher.

frígido, -a adj frigid.

frigorífico m refrigerator, fridge.

frijol, fríjol m kidney bean.

frío, -a 1 adj cold; (indiferente) cold, cool. **2** m cold; **hace f.** it's cold.

friolento, -a adj Am sensitive to the cold.

friolero, -a adj sensitive to the cold, chilly.

frívolo, -a adj frivolous.

frontera f frontier.

fronterizo, -a adj frontier, border; **países fronterizos** neighboring countries.

frontón m pelota.

frotar 1 vt to rub. **2 frotarse** vr **f. las manos** to rub one's hands together.

fruncir [52] vt **f. el ceño** to frown.

frustrar 1 vt to frustrate. **2 frustrarse** vr (esperanza) to fail; (persona) to be frustrated o disappointed.

fruta f fruit; **f. del tiempo** fresh fruit.

frutería f fruit shop.

frutero m fruit dish o bowl.

frutilla f Bol, CSur, Ecuad strawberry.

fruto m fruit; **frutos secos** nuts.

fucsia f fuchsia.

fuego m fire; (lumbre) light; **fuegos artificiales** fireworks; **¿me da f., por favor?** have you got a light, please?

fuel, fuel-oil m diesel.

fuente f (artificial) fountain; (recipiente) dish; (origen) source; (de caracteres) font.

fuera¹ 1 adv outside; **desde f.** from (the) outside; **por f.** on the outside; **la puerta de f.** the outer door. **2** prep **f. de** out of; **f. de serie** extraordinary.

fuera² 1 subj imperfecto de **ir**. 2 subj imperfecto de **ser**.

fuerte 1 adj strong; (dolor) severe; (sonido) loud; (comida) heavy. **2** m (fortaleza) fort. **3** adv **¡abrázame f.!** hold me tight!; **¡habla más f.!** speak up!; **¡pégale f.!** hit him hard!

fuerza f (fortaleza) strength; (cuerpo) force; **a la f.** (por obligación) of necessity; (con violencia) by force; **por f.** of necessity; **Fuerzas Armadas** Armed Forces.

fuese 1 subj imperfecto de **ir**. 2 subj imperfecto de **ser**.

fuete m Am whip.

fuga f (huida) escape; (de gas etc) leak.

fugarse [42] vr to escape.

fui 1 pt indef de de **ir**. 2 pt indef de **ser**.

fulano, -a mf so-and-so; (hombre) what's his name; (mujer) what's her name; **Doña Fulana de tal** Mrs So-and-so.

fullería f cheating; **hacer fullerías** to cheat.

fullero, -a 1 adj cheating. **2** mf cheat.

fulminante adj (muerte, enfermedad) sudden; (mirada) withering.

fumador, -a m smoker; **los no fumadores** non-smokers.

fumar 1 vti to smoke; **no f.** (en letrero) no smoking. **2 fumarse** vr **f.**

un cigarro to smoke a cigarette.
función f function; *(cargo)* duties
pl; *(de teatro, cine)* performance.
funcionamiento m operation;
poner/entrar en f. to put/come into
operation.
funcionar vi to work; **no funciona**
(en letrero) out of order.
funcionario, -a mf civil servant.
funda f cover; *(de gafas etc)* case; **f.
de almohada** pillowcase.
fundación f foundation.
fundamental adj fundamental.
fundamento m basis, grounds pl;
sin f. unfounded.
fundar 1 vt *(crear)* to found. **2 fun-
darse** vr *(empresa)* to be founded;
(teoría, afirmación) to be based.
fundir vt, **fundirse** vr *(derretirse)* to
melt; *(bombilla, plomos)* to blow;
(unirse) to merge.
fúnebre adj *(mortuorio)* funeral;
coche f. hearse.
funeral m funeral.
funeraria f funeral parlor.
fungir vi Am to act (**de** as).
funicular m funicular (railway).
furgoneta f van.
furia f fury.
furioso, -a adj furious.
furor m fury.
furtivo, -a adj furtive; **cazador/
pescador f.** poacher.
furúnculo m boil.
fusible m fuse.
fusil m gun, rifle.
fusilar vt to shoot, to execute.
fusión f *(de metales)* fusion; *(del hielo)* thawing, melting; *(de empresas)*
merger.
fusionar vt, **fusionarse** vr *(metales)*
to fuse; *(empresas)* to merge.
fútbol m soccer; **f. americano**
football.
futbolín m table football.
futbolista mf football/soccer
player.
futuro, -a 1 adj future. **2** m future.

G

gabardina f *(prenda)* raincoat.
gabinete m *(despacho)* study; *(de
gobierno)* cabinet.
gacho, -a adj con la cabeza gacha
hanging one's head.
gafas fpl glasses, spectacles; **g. de
sol** sunglasses.
gafe m ser (un) g. to be a jinx.
gaita f bagpipes pl.
gajes mpl fam irón g. del oficio oc-
cupational hazards.
gajo m *(de naranja, pomelo etc)*
segment.
gala f *(espectáculo)* gala; **de g.** dressed up; *(ciudad)* decked out.
galán m handsome young man;
(personaje) leading man.
galante adj gallant.
galápago m turtle.
galardón m prize.
galardonar vt to award a prize to.
galería f *(corredor)* covered balcony; *(museo)* art gallery.
Gales m (el país de) G. Wales.
galés, -esa 1 adj Welsh. **2** mf
(hombre) Welshman; *(mujer)* Welsh-
woman; **los galeses** the Welsh. **3** m
(idioma) Welsh.
galgo m greyhound.
Galicia f Galicia.
galimatías m inv gibberish.
gallego, -a 1 adj Galician; Am
Spanish. **2** mf Galician; Am Spaniard.
3 m *(idioma)* Galician.
galleta f cracker.
gallina f hen.
gallinero m henhouse.
gallo m cock.
galopante adj *(inflación etc)*
galloping.
galopar vi to gallop.
galope m gallop; **a g. tendido** flat
out.

gama *f* range.

gamba *f* prawn.

gamberro, -a 1 *mf* hooligan. **2** *adj* uncouth.

gamo *m* fallow deer.

gamuza *f (trapo)* chamois *o* shammy leather.

gana *f (deseo)* wish (**de** for); *(apetito)* appetite; **de buena g.** willingly; **de mala g.** reluctantly; **tener ganas de (hacer) algo** to feel like (doing) sth.

ganadero, -a *mf* livestock farmer.

ganado *m* livestock.

ganador, -a 1 *adj* winning. **2** *mf* winner.

ganancia *f* profit.

ganar 1 *vt (sueldo)* to earn; *(premio)* to win; *(aventajar)* to beat. **2 ganarse** *vr* to earn.

ganchillo *m* crochet work.

gancho *m* hook; *Am (para el pelo)* hairpin; *Andes, CAm, Méx, Ven (para la ropa)* hanger.

ganga *f* bargain.

ganso, -a *mf* goose; *(macho)* gander; *fam* dolt.

garabato *m* scrawl.

garaje *m* garage.

garantía *f* guarantee.

garantizar [40] *vt (cosa)* to guarantee; *(a persona)* to assure.

garbanzo *m* garbanzo (bean).

garfio *m* hook.

garganta *f* throat; *(desfiladero)* narrow pass.

gargantilla *f* short necklace.

gárgara *f Am (elixir)* gargling solution; **gárgaras** gargling *sing*; **hacer gárgaras** to gargle.

garra *f* claw; *(de ave)* talon; *fig* **tener g.** to be compelling.

garrafa *f* carafe.

garrafal *adj* monumental.

garrapata *f* tick.

garrote *m (porra)* club.

gas *m* gas; *(en bebida)* fizz; **g. ciudad** town gas; **gases (nocivos)** fumes; **g. de escape** exhaust fumes; **agua con g.** fizzy water.

gasa *f* gauze.

gaseosa *f* lemonade.

gasoducto *m* gas pipeline.

gasoil, gasóleo *m* diesel oil.

gasolina *f* gasoline.

gasolinera *f* gas station.

gastar 1 *vt (consumir) (dinero, tiempo)* to spend; *(gasolina, electricidad)* to consume; *(malgastar)* to waste; *(ropa)* to wear; **g. una broma a algn** to play a practical joke on sb. **2 gastarse** *vr (zapatos etc)* to wear out.

gasto *m* expenditure; **gastos** expenses.

gatas: a gatas *adv* on all fours.

gatear *vi* to crawl.

gatillo *m (de armas)* trigger.

gato *m* cat; *(de coche)* jack.

gauchada *f CSur* favor.

gaucho, -a 1 *adj RP fam (servicial)* helpful, obliging. **2** *mf* gaucho.

gaveta *f (cajón)* drawer; *Am (guantera)* glove compartment.

gaviota *f* seagull.

gay *adj inv & m (pl gays)* gay.

gazpacho *m* gazpacho.

gel *m* gel; **g. (de ducha)** shower gel.

gelatina *f (ingrediente)* gelatin; *(para postre)* jelly.

gema *f* gem.

gemelo, -a 1 *adj & mf* (identical) twin. **2** *mpl* **gemelos** *(de camisa)* cufflinks; *(anteojos)* binoculars.

gemido *m* groan.

gemir [6] *vi* to groan.

generación *f* generation.

general *adj* general; **por lo** *o* **en g.** in general.

generalizar [40] **1** *vt* to generalize. **2 generalizarse** *vr* to become widespread *o* common.

generalmente *adv* generally.

generar *vt* to generate.

género *m (clase)* kind, sort; *(mercancía)* article; *(gramatical)* gender.

generoso, -a *adj* generous (**con, para** to).

genético, -a *adj* genetic.

genial *adj* brilliant.

genio *mf inv* genius; *(mal carácter)* temper; **estar de mal g.** to be in a bad mood.

genocidio *m* genocide.

gente *f* people *pl*; *Am* respectable people.

gentuza *f* riffraff.

genuino, -a *adj (puro)* genuine; *(verdadero)* authentic.

geografía *f* geography.

geología *f* geology.

geometría *f* geometry.

geranio *m* geranium.

gerente *mf* manager.

gérmen *m* germ.

gerundio *m* gerund.

gestación *f* gestation.

gesticular *vi* to gesticulate.

gestión *f (administración)* management; **gestiones** *(negociaciones)* negotiations; *(trámites)* formalities.

gestionar *vt* to take steps to acquire *o* obtain; *(negociar)* to negotiate.

gesto *m (mueca)* face; *(con las manos)* gesture.

gestor, -a *mf* ≃ solicitor.

gigabyte *m* gigabyte.

gigante, -a *adj & m* giant.

gigantesco, -a *adj* gigantic.

gil, -ila *mf CSur fam* twit, idiot.

gimnasia *f* gymnastics *pl*.

gimnasio *m* gym, gymnasium.

gimotear *vi* to whine.

ginebra *f (bebida)* gin.

ginecólogo, -a *mf* gynecologist.

gira *f (musical, teatral)* tour.

girar *vi (dar vueltas)* to spin; **g. a la derecha/izquierda** to turn right/left.

girasol *m* sunflower.

giratorio, -a *adj* revolving.

giro *m (vuelta)* turn; *(frase)* turn of phrase; *(libranza)* draft; **g. telegráfico** giro *o* money order; **g. postal** postal *o* money order.

gitano, -a *adj & mf* gypsy.

glaciar *m* glacier.

glándula *f* gland.

global *adj* comprehensive.

globalización *f* globalization.

globo *m* balloon; *(esfera)* globe.

gloria *f (fama)* glory; *(cielo)* heaven.

glorieta *f (plazoleta)* small square; *(encrucijada de calles)* roundabout, traffic circle.

glosario *m* glossary.

glotón, -ona 1 *adj* greedy. **2** *mf* glutton.

glucosa *f* glucose.

gobernación *f* government; **Ministerio de la Gobernación** ≃ Department of the Interior.

gobernador, -a *mf* governor.

gobernante 1 *adj* ruling. **2** *mpl* **los gobernantes** the rulers.

gobernar [1] *vt* to govern; *(un país)* to rule.

gobierno *m* government; *(mando)* running.

gofio *m (en América y Canarias)* roasted maize meal.

gol *m* goal.

golf *m* golf; **palo de g.** golf club.

golfo, -a¹ *mf* good for nothing.

golfo² *m* gulf.

golondrina *f* swallow.

golosina *f* candy.

goloso, -a *adj* sweet-toothed.

golpe *m* blow; *(llamada)* knock; *(puñetazo)* punch; *(choque)* bump; *(desgracia)* blow; **de g.** all of a sudden; **g. de estado** coup d'état.

golpear *vt* to hit; *(con el puño)* to punch; *(puerta, cabeza)* to bang.

goma *f* rubber; *(elástico)* rubber band; *Cuba, CSur (para ruedas)* tire; **g. de borrar** eraser.

gomal *m Am* rubber plantation.

gomero *m Am* gum tree; *(recolector)* rubber collector.

gordo, -a 1 *adj (carnoso)* fat; *(grueso)* thick. **2** *mf* fat person, *fam* fatty; *Am fam (como apelativo)* **¿cómo estás, gorda?** hey, how are you doing? **3** *m* **el g.** *(de lotería)* first prize.

gorila *m* gorilla.

gorra *f* cap.

gorrión *m* sparrow.

gorro *m* cap.

gota *f* drop; **g. a g.** drop by drop; **ni g.** not a bit.

gotear *v impers* to drip; **el techo gotea** there's a leak in the ceiling.

gotera *f* leak.

gozar [40] **1** *vt* to enjoy. **2** *vi (disfrutar)* to enjoy (**de** -).

gozne *m* hinge.

grabación *f* recording.

grabado *m (arte)* engraving; *(dibujo)* drawing.

grabadora *f* tape recorder.

grabar *vt (sonidos, imágenes)* to record; *(en ordenador)* to save.

gracia *f (chiste)* joke; *(indulto)* pardon; **hacer** *o* **tener g.** to be funny.

gracias *fpl* thanks; **muchas** *o* **muchísimas g.** thank you very much.

gracioso, -a 1 *adj (divertido)* funny. **2** *mf (personaje)* comic character.

grada *f (peldaño)* step; **gradas** *(estadio)* terracing.

grado *m* degree; **de buen g.** willingly.

gradual *adj* gradual.

gradualmente *adv* gradually.

graduar [30] **1** *vt (regular)* to regulate. **2 graduarse** *vr (soldado, alumno)* to graduate; **g. la vista** to have one's eyes tested.

gráfico, -a 1 *adj* graphic. **2** *mf* graph; **gráficos** *(de ordenador)* graphics.

gragea *f* pill.

gral. *abr de* **General** Gen.

gramática *f* grammar.

gramo *m* gram.

gran *adj ver* **grande**.

granada *f (fruto)* pomegranate; *(explosivo)* grenade.

granate 1 *adj inv* maroon. **2** *m* maroon.

grande *adj (before singular noun* **gran** *is used) (tamaño)* big, large; *fig (persona)* great; *(cantidad)* large; **pasarlo en g.** to have a great time.

granel: a granel *adv* loose.

granero *m* granary.

granito *m* granite.

granizada *f*, **granizado** *m* iced drink.

granizo *m* hail.

granja *f* farm.

granjear(se) *vt & vr* to gain.

granjero, -a *mf* farmer.

grano *m* grain; *(de café)* bean; *(espinilla)* spot.

granuja *m* **1** *(pilluelo)* rascal. **2** *(estafador)* con-man.

grapa *f* staple.

grapadora *f* stapler.

grasa *f* grease; **grasas saturadas** saturated fats.

grasiento, -a *adj* greasy.

graso, -a *adj (pelo)* greasy; *(materia)* fatty.

gratis *adv* free.

gratitud *f* gratitude.

gratuito, -a *adj (de balde)* free (of charge); *(arbitrario)* gratuitous.

grava *f (guijas)* gravel; *(en carretera)* gravel *pl*.

gravar *vt (impuestos)* to tax.

grave *adj (importante)* serious; *(muy enfermo)* seriously ill; *(voz, nota)* low.

gravedad *f* seriousness; *(fuerza)* gravity.

gravilla *f (en carretera)* gravel *pl*.

griego, -a 1 *adj & mf* Greek. **2** *m (idioma)* Greek.

grieta *f* crack; *(en la piel)* chap.

grifo *m* faucet.

grillo *m* cricket.

gringo, -a *adj & mf* gringo, yankee.

gripe *f* flu.

gris *adj & m* gray.

grisáceo, -a *adj* grayish.

gritar *vti* to shout.

grito *m* shout.

grosella *f (fruto)* redcurrant; **g. negra** blackcurrant; **g. silvestre** gooseberry.

grosería *f (ordinariez)* rude word *o* expression.

grosero, -a *adj (tosco)* coarse; *(maleducado)* rude.

grosor *m* thickness.

grotesco, -a *adj* grotesque.

grúa *f (en construcción)* crane; *(para coches)* tow truck.

grueso, -a 1 *adj* thick; *(persona)* stout. **2** *m (parte principal)* bulk.

grumo *m* lump.

gruñido *m* grunt.

gruñir *vi* to grunt.

gruñón, -ona *adj* grumpy.

grupo *m* group.

gruta *f* cave.

guacamol, guacamole *m Am* avocado sauce.

guachafita *f Am* uproar.

guacho, -a *adj & mf Am* orphan.

guagua¹ *f (en Canarias y Cuba)* bus.

guagua² *f Am* baby.

guajiro, -a *mf Cuba fam (campesino)* peasant.

guante *m* glove.

guantera *f (en coche)* glove compartment.

guapo, -a 1 *adj* good-looking; *(mujer)* beautiful, pretty; *(hombre)* handsome. **2** *m Am (matón)* bully.

guaraca *f Am* sling.

guarango, -a *adj Am* rude.

guarda *mf* guard; **g. jurado** security guard.

guardacoches *mf inv* parking attendant.

guardacostas *m inv (persona)* coastguard; *(embarcación)* coastguard vessel.

guardaespaldas *mf inv* bodyguard.

guardameta *mf* goalkeeper.

guardar *vt (conservar, reservar)* to keep; *(un secreto)* to keep; *(poner en un sitio)* to put away; *(en ordenador)* to save.

guardarropa *m (cuarto)* cloakroom; *(armario)* wardrobe.

guardería infantil *f* nursery (school).

guardia 1 *f (vigilancia)* watch; *(turno de servicio)* duty; **la g. civil** the civil guard. **2** *mf (hombre)* policeman; *(mujer)* policewoman.

guardián, -ana *mf (hombre)* watchman; *(mujer)* watchwoman.

guarecerse [33] *vr* to take shelter o refuge (**de** from).

guarro, -a 1 *adj* filthy. **2** *mf* pig.

guaso, -a *adj Am* peasant.

guasón, -ona 1 *adj* humorous. **2** *mf* joker.

guata *f (relleno)* padding; *Am (barriga)* paunch.

guayabera *f CAm, Carib, Col* short jacket.

guayabo, -a *mf Am (chica bonita)* pretty young girl; *(chico guapo)* good-looking boy.

güero, -a *adj Méx fam* blond, blonde.

guerra *f* war; **g. civil/fría/mundial/ nuclear** civil/cold/world/nuclear war.

guerrilla *f (partida armada)* guerrilla force o band; *(lucha)* guerrilla warfare.

guía 1 *mf (persona)* guide. **2** *f (libro)* guide; **la g. de teléfonos** the telephone directory.

guiar [29] **1** *vt (indicar el camino)* to guide; *(automóvil)* to drive. **2 guiarse** *vr* to be guided (**por** by).

guijarro *m* pebble.

guindilla *f* chili.

guiñapo *m (andrajo)* rag.

guiñar *vt* i to wink.

guiño *m* wink.

guión *m (de cine, televisión)* script; *(ortográfico)* hyphen; *(esquema)* sketch.

guirnalda *f* garland.

guisante *m* pea.

guisar *vt* to cook.

guiso *m* dish; *(guisado)* stew.

guita *f* rope.

guitarra 1 *f* guitar. **2** *mf* guitarist.

gula *f* gluttony.

gusano *m* worm; *(oruga)* caterpillar.

gustar 1 *vt* **me gusta el vino** I like wine; **me gustaban los caramelos** I used to like sweets; **me gusta nadar** I like swimming; **me gustaría ir** I would like to go. **2** *vi* **g. de** to enjoy.

gusto *m* taste; **con (mucho) g.** with (great) pleasure; **tanto g.** pleased to meet you; **estar a g.** to feel comfortable o at ease; **ser de buen/mal g.** to be in good/bad taste; **tener buen/mal g.** to have good/bad taste.

H

ha *indic pres de* **haber**.

haba *f* broad bean.

habano *m* Havana (cigar).

haber [14] **1** *v aux (en tiempos compuestos)* to have; **lo he visto** I have seen it; **ya lo había hecho** I had already done it. ▪ **h. de** + *infinitivo (obligación)* to have to; **has de ser bueno** you must be good. **2** *v impers (special form of present tense:* **hay)** *(existir, estar) (singular used also with plural nouns)* **hay** there is o are; **había** there was o were; **habrá una fiesta** there will be a party; **había una vez ...** once upon a time ...; **no hay de qué** you're welcome; **¿qué hay?** how are things? ▪ **hay que** + *infinitivo* it is necessary to.

habichuela *f* kidney bean.

hábil *adj (diestro)* skillful; **días hábiles** working days.

habitación *f (cuarto)* room; *(dormitorio)* bedroom; **h. individual/doble** single/double room.

habitante *mf* inhabitant.

hábito *m (costumbre)* habit; *(de monje)* habit.

habitual *adj* usual, habitual.

habituar [30] **1** *vt* to accustom (**a** to). **2 habituarse** *vr* to get used (**a** to), to become accustomed (**a** to).

hablador, -a *adj (parlanchín)* talkative.

hablar 1 *vi* to speak, to talk; **h. con**

algn to speak to sb; **¡ni h.!** no way!; *fam* **¡quién fue a h.!** look who's talking! **2** *vt (idioma)* to speak. **3 hablarse** *vr* to speak o talk to one another; **'se habla español'** 'Spanish spoken'.

habré *indic fut de* **haber**.

hacer [15] **1** *vt* to do; *(crear, fabricar)* to make; **hazme un favor** do me a favor; **¿qué haces?** *(en este momento)* what are you doing?; *(para vivir)* what do you do (for a living)?; **tengo mucho que h.** I have a lot to do; **lo hizo con sus propias manos** he made it with his own hands; **h. la cama** to make the bed; **h. la cena** to make dinner; **el negro le hace más delgado** black makes him look slimmer; **ya no puedo leer como solía hacerlo** I can't read as well as I used to; **¡bien hecho!** well done! **2** *vi (actuar)* to play; **hizo de Desdémona** she played Desdemona; **h. por o para** + *infinitivo* to try to; **haz por venir** try and come. **3** *v impers* **hace calor/frío** it's hot/cold; **hace mucho (tiempo)** a long time ago; **hace dos días que no lo veo** I haven't seen him for two days; **hace dos años que vivo en Chicago** I've been living in Chicago for two years. **4 hacerse** *vr (volverse)* to become, to grow; *(simular)* to pretend; **hacerse el dormido** to pretend to be sleeping; **hacerse con** *(apropiarse)* to get hold of; **hacerse a** *(habituarse)* to get used to.

hacha *f (herramienta)* ax.

hachís *m* hashish.

hacia *prep (dirección)* towards; to; *(aproximadamente)* at about, at around; **h. abajo** down, downwards; **h. adelante** forwards; **h. arriba** up, upwards; **h. atrás** back, backwards.

hacienda *f* ranch.

hada *f* fairy; **cuento de hadas** fairy tale.

hago *indic pres de* **hacer**.

halagar [42] *vt* to flatter.

halago *m* flattery.

halcón m falcon.

hallar 1 vt (encontrar) to find; (descubrir) to discover. **2 hallarse** vr (estar) to be, to find oneself; (estar situado) to be situated.

hallazgo m (descubrimiento) discovery; (cosa encontrada) find.

hamaca f hammock.

hambre f (apetito) hunger; (inanición) starvation; (catástrofe) famine; **tener h.** to be hungry.

hambriento, -a adj starving.

hamburguesa f hamburger.

han indic pres de **haber**.

haré indic fut de **hacer**.

harina f flour.

hartar 1 vt (cansar, fastidiar) to annoy; (atiborrar) to satiate. **2 hartarse** vr (saciar el apetito) to eat one's fill; (cansarse) to get fed up (**de** with).

harto, -a adj (lleno) full; (cansado) fed up; **estoy h. de trabajar** I'm fed up with working.

has indic pres de **haber**.

hasta 1 prep (lugar) up to, as far as; (tiempo) until, up to; (con cantidad) up to, as many as; (incluso) even; **h. la fecha** up to now; **h. luego** see you later. **2** conj **h. que** until.

hay indic pres de **haber**.

haya subj pres de **haber**.

haz imperativo de **hacer**.

hazmerreír m laughing stock.

he indic pres de **haber**.

hebilla f buckle.

hebra f thread.

hebreo, -a 1 adj Hebrew. **2** mf Hebrew.

hechizo m (embrujo) spell.

hecho, -a 1 adj made, done; (carne) done; (ropa) ready-made. **2** m (realidad) fact; (acto) act, deed; (suceso) event, incident; **de h.** in fact.

hectárea f hectare.

heder [3] vi to stink, to smell foul.

hedor m stink, stench.

helada f frost.

heladería f ice-cream parlor.

helado, -a 1 m ice cream. **2** adj (muy frío) freezing cold; fig **quedarse h.** (atónito) to be flabbergasted.

helar [1] **1** vt (congelar) to freeze. **2** v impers to freeze; **anoche heló** there was a frost last night. **3 helarse** vr (congelarse) to freeze.

helecho m fern.

hélice f (de avión, barco) propeller.

helicóptero m helicopter.

hembra f (animal, planta) female; (mujer) woman.

hemorragia f hemorrhage.

hemos indic pres de **haber**.

hendidura f crack.

heno m hay.

herbolario m (tienda) herbalist's (shop).

heredar vt to inherit.

heredero, -a mf (hombre) heir; (mujer) heiress.

herencia f inheritance, legacy; (biológica) heredity.

herida f (lesión) injury; (corte) wound.

herido, -a 1 adj injured, hurt. **2** mf injured person.

herir [5] **1** vt (físicamente) (lesionar) to injure; (cortar) to wound. **2 herirse** vr to injure o hurt oneself.

hermana f sister.

hermanastro, -a mf (hombre) stepbrother; (mujer) stepsister.

hermano m brother; **primo h.** first cousin; **hermanos** brothers and sisters.

herméticamente adv **h. cerrado** hermetically sealed.

hermético, -a adj (cierre) hermetic, airtight; fig (grupo) secretive.

hermoso, -a adj beautiful, lovely; (grandioso) fine.

hermosura f beauty.

héroe m hero.

heroína f (mujer) heroine; (droga) heroin.

herradura f horseshoe.

herramienta f tool.

hervir [5] **1** vt (hacer bullir) to boil. **2** vi (bullir) to boil.

heterogéneo, -a adj heterogeneous.

hice pt indef de **hacer**.

hiciste pt indef de **hacer**.

hidratante adj moisturizing; **crema/leche h.** moisturizing cream/lotion.

hidráulico, -a adj hydraulic.

hidroavión m hydroplane.

hiedra f ivy.

hielo m ice.

hiena f hyena.

hierba f grass; **mala h.** weed.

hierbabuena f mint.

hierro m iron.

hígado m liver.

higiene f hygiene.

higiénico, -a adj hygienic; **papel h.** toilet paper.

higo m fig; fam fig **hecho un h.** wizened, crumpled.

hija f daughter.

hijastro, -a mf (hombre) stepson; (mujer) stepdaughter.

hijo m son; **hijos** children.

hilera f line, row.

hilo m thread; (grueso) yarn; (fibra) linen; **perder el h.** to lose the thread; **h. musical** background music.

himno m hymn; **h. nacional** national anthem.

hincapié m hacer **h. en** (insistir) to insist on; (subrayar) to emphasize.

hincar [44] **1** vt (clavar) to drive (in). **2 hincarse** vr **hincarse de rodillas** to kneel (down).

hincha 1 mf (de equipo) fan, supporter. **2** f (antipatía) grudge, dislike.

hinchado, -a adj swollen.

hinchar 1 vt (inflar) to inflate, to blow up. **2 hincharse** vr to swell (up); fam (hartarse) to stuff oneself.

hindú adj & mf Hindu.

hipermercado m hypermarket.

hípico, -a adj horse.

hipnotizar [40] vt to hypnotize.

hipo m tener **h.** to have the hiccups.

hipócrita 1 adj hypocritical. **2** mf hypocrite.

hipopótamo m hippopotamus.

hipoteca f mortgage.

hipótesis f inv hypothesis.

hispánico, -a adj Hispanic.

hispano, -a 1 adj Hispanic. **2** mf Spanish American, Hispanic.

hispanohablante 1 adj Spanish-speaking. **2** mf Spanish speaker.

histérico, -a adj hysterical.

historia f (estudio del pasado) history; (narración) story.

historial m record; (antecedentes) background.

histórico, -a adj historical; (de gran importancia) historic, memorable.

historieta f (tira cómica) comic strip.

hizo indic indef de **hacer**.

hocico m (de animal) snout.

hogar m (casa) home; (de la chimenea) hearth.

hoguera f bonfire.

hoja f leaf; (de papel) sheet; (de cuchillo, espada) blade; (impreso) hand-out.

hojalata f tin.

hojaldre m puff pastry.

hojear vt (libro) to leaf through.

hola interj hello!

holgado, -a adj (ropa) loose, baggy; (económicamente) comfortable; (espacio) roomy.

holgazán, -ana 1 adj lazy. **2** mf lazybones inv.

hollín m soot.

hombre 1 m man; **h. de negocios** businessman. **2** interj (saludo) hey!; ¡**sí h.!**, ¡**h. claro!** (enfático) sure!, you bet!

hombrera f shoulder pad.

hombro m shoulder; **a hombros** on one's shoulders; **encogerse de hombros** to shrug one's shoulders; **mirar a algn por encima del h.** to look down one's nose at sb.

homenaje m homage, tribute.

homicida 1 *mf (hombre)* murderer; *(mujer)* murderess. **2** *adj* homicidal.
homicidio *m* homicide.
homogéneo, -a *adj* homogeneous, uniform.
homosexual *adj & mf* homosexual.
hondo, -a *adj* deep; **plato h.** soup dish.
honesto, -a *adj (honrado)* honest; *(recatado)* modest.
hongo *m* fungus; *(sombrero)* derby (hat); **h. venenoso** toadstool.
honor *m* honor; **palabra de h.** word of honor.
honorario, -a 1 *adj* honorary. **2** *mpl* **honorarios** fees.
honra *f (dignidad)* dignity; *(honor)* honor; **¡a mucha h.!** and proud of it!
honradez *f* honesty.
honrado, -a *adj (de fiar)* honest.
honrar *vt (respetar)* to honor; *(enaltecer)* to be a credit to.
honroso, -a *adj (loable)* honorable.
hora *f* hour; *(cita)* appointment; **media h.** half an hour; **h. punta** rush hour; **horas extra** overtime (hours); **¿qué h. es?** what time is it?; **a última h.** at the last moment; **pedir h.** *(al médico etc)* to ask for an appointment.
horario *m* schedule.
horca *f* gallows *pl*.
horchata *f* sweet milky drink made from chufa nuts.
horizonte *m* horizon.
hormiga *f* ant.
hormigón *m* concrete.
hormigueo *m* pins and needles *pl*, tingling o itching sensation.
hormiguero *m* anthill.
hormona *f* hormone.
horno *m (de cocina)* oven; *(para metales)* furnace; *(para cerámica etc)* kiln; **pescado al h.** baked fish.
horóscopo *m* horoscope.
horquilla *f (del pelo)* hair-grip.
horrendo, -a *adj* horrifying, horrible.
horrible *adj* horrible.

horror *m* horror; **¡qué h.!** how awful!; *fam* **tengo h. a las motos** I hate motorbikes.
horrorizar [40] *vt* to horrify; *(dar miedo)* to terrify.
horroroso, -a *adj* horrifying; *(que da miedo)* terrifying; *fam (muy feo)* hideous; *fam (malísimo)* awful.
hortaliza *f* vegetable.
hortera *f am (persona)* flashy; *(cosa)* tacky.
hospedaje *m* lodgings *pl*, accommodations.
hospedar 1 *vt* to put up. **2 hospedarse** *vr* to stay (**en** at).
hospicio *m (para huérfanos)* orphanage.
hospital *m* hospital.
hospitalizar [40] *vt* to send into hospital, to hospitalize.
hostal *m* guest house.
hostelería *f (negocio)* catering business; *(estudios)* hotel management.
hostería *f Am* hostel, inn.
hostil *adj* hostile.
hotel *m* hotel.
hoy *adv (día)* today; **h. (en) día** nowadays.
hoyo *m* hole.
hube *pt indef de* **haber**.
hubiera *subj imperfecto de* **haber**.
hucha *f* piggy bank.
hueco, -a 1 *adj (vacío)* empty, hollow; *(sonido)* resonant. **2** *m (cavidad)* hollow, hole; *(sitio no ocupado)* empty space.
huele *indic pres de* **oler**.
huelga *f* strike; **estar en** o **de h.** to be on strike; **hacer h.** to go on strike.
huella *f (del pie)* footprint; *(coche)* track; **h. dactilar** fingerprint; *fig (vestigio)* trace.
huérfano, -a *adj & mf* orphan.
huerta *f (parcela)* truck garden; *(región)* irrigated area used for cultivation.
huerto *m (de verduras)* vegetable garden; *(de frutales)* orchard.
hueso *m (del cuerpo)* bone; *(de fru-*

to) pit; *Am (enchufe)* contact.

huésped, -a *mf* guest; **casa de huéspedes** guesthouse.

huevo *m* egg; **h. duro** hard-boiled egg; **h. frito** fried egg; **h. pasado por agua**, *Am* **h. tibio** soft-boiled egg; **huevos revueltos** scrambled eggs.

huevón, -ona *muy fam mf Andes, Arg, Ven* dork.

huida *f* flight, escape.

huir [37] *vi (escaparse)* to run away (**de** from); *(evadirse)* to escape (**de** from).

hule *m (tela impermeable)* oilcloth; *(de mesa)* tablecloth; *Am* rubber.

humanitario, -a *adj* humanitarian.

humano, -a 1 *adj (relativo al hombre)* human; *(compasivo)* humane; **ser h.** human being. **2** *m* human (being).

humeante *adj (chimenea)* smoky, smoking.

humedad *f (atmosférica)* humidity; *(de lugar)* dampness.

humedecer [33] **1** *vt* to moisten, to dampen. **2 humedecerse** *vr* to become damp o moist.

húmedo, -a *adj (casa, ropa)* damp; *(clima)* humid, damp.

humildad *f (de persona)* humility; *(de cosa)* humbleness.

humilde *adj* humble; *(familia)* poor.

humillante *adj* humiliating.

humillar 1 *vt* to humiliate. **2 humillarse** *vr* **humillarse ante algn** to humble oneself before sb.

humo *m* smoke; *(gas)* fumes *pl*; *(vapor)* vapor, steam.

humor *m (genio)* mood; *(gracia)* humor; **estar de buen** o **mal h.** to be in a good o bad mood; **sentido del h.** sense of humor.

hundimiento *m (de edificio)* collapse; *(de barco)* sinking; *(de tierra)* subsidence; *(ruina)* downfall.

hundir 1 *vt (barco)* to sink; *(derrumbar)* to bring o knock down. **2 hun-**dirse *vr (barco)* to sink; *(edificio, empresa)* to collapse.

huracán *m* hurricane.

huraño, -a *adj* unsociable.

hurgar [42] **1** *vi (fisgar)* to poke one's nose (**en** in). **2** *vt (fuego etc)* to poke.

hurto *m* petty theft.

huyo *indic pres de* **huir**.

I

ibérico, -a *adj* Iberian.

iberoamericano, -a *adj & mf* Latin American.

iceberg *m (pl* **icebergs***)* iceberg.

icono *m* icon.

ida *f* **billete de i. y vuelta** round trip ticket.

idea *f* idea; **hacerse a la i. de** to get used to the idea of; **ni i.** no idea; **cambiar de i.** to change one's mind.

ideal *adj & m* ideal.

idear *vt (inventar)* to devise; *(concebir)* to think up.

idéntico, -a *adj* identical.

identidad *f* identity; **carnet de i.** identity card.

identificación *f* identification.

identificar [44] **1** *vt* to identify. **2 identificarse** *vr* to identify oneself; *(simpatizar)* to identify (**con** with).

idilio *m (romance)* romance.

idioma *m* language.

idiota 1 *adj* stupid. **2** *mf* idiot.

idiotez *f* **decir/hacer una i.** to say/ to do something stupid.

ídolo *m* idol.

idóneo, -a *adj* suitable.

iglesia *f (edificio)* church; **la I.** the Church.

ignorante 1 *adj (sin instrucción)* ignorant; *(no informado)* unaware (**de** of). **2** *mf* ignoramus.

ignorar 1 *vt (algo)* not to know;

(algn) to ignore. **2 ignorarse** *vr* to be unknown.

igual 1 *adj (lo mismo)* the same; *(equivalente)* equal; **i. que** the same as; **a partes iguales** fifty-fifty; **al i. que** just like; **por i.** equally; **6 más 7 i. a 13** 6 plus 7 equals 13. **2 m** equal. **3** *adv* **lo haces i. que yo** you do it the same way I do; **es i.** it doesn't matter.

igualar *vt* to make equal; *(nivelar)* to level.

igualdad *f* equality; *(identidad)* sameness; **en i. de condiciones** on equal terms.

igualmente *adv* equally; *(también)* also, likewise; **¡gracias! — ¡i.!** thank you! — the same to you!

ilegal *adj* illegal.

ilegalmente *adv* illegally.

ilegible *adj* illegible, unreadable.

ilegítimo, -a *adj* illegitimate.

ileso, -a *adj* unharmed.

ilícito, -a *adj* unlawful.

ilimitado, -a *adj* unlimited.

iluminación *f (alumbrado)* illumination.

iluminar *vt* to illuminate.

ilusión *f (esperanza)* hope; *(esperanza vana)* illusion; *(emoción)* excitement; **hacerse ilusiones** to build up one's hopes; **me hace i. verla** I'm looking forward to seeing her; **¡qué i.!** how exciting!

ilusionar 1 *vt (esperanzar)* **i. a algn** to build up sb's hopes; *(entusiasmar)* to excite. **2 ilusionarse** *vr (esperanzarse)* to build up one's hopes; *(entusiasmarse)* to be excited (**con** about).

ilustración *f (grabado)* illustration; *(erudición)* learning.

ilustrar *vt* to illustrate.

ilustre *adj* distinguished.

imagen *f* image; *(de televisión)* picture.

imaginación *f* imagination.

imaginar 1 *vt* to imagine. **2 imaginarse** *vr* to imagine; **me imagino que sí** I suppose so.

imaginario, -a *adj* imaginary.

imán *m* magnet.

imbatible *adj* unbeatable.

imbécil 1 *adj* stupid. **2 mf** imbecile.

imitar *vt* to imitate; *(gestos)* to mimic.

impacientar 1 *vt* **i. a algn** to exasperate sb. **2 impacientarse** *vr* to get impatient (**por** at).

impaciente *adj (deseoso)* impatient; *(intranquilo)* anxious.

impactar *vt* to shock, to stun.

impactante *adj* **una noticia i.** a sensational piece of news.

impacto *m* impact.

impar *adj* odd.

imparable *adj* unstoppable.

imparcial *adj* impartial.

impartir *vt (clases)* to give.

impasible *adj* impassive.

impecable *adj* impeccable.

impedimento *m* impediment; *(obstáculo)* hindrance.

impedir [6] *vt (obstaculizar)* to impede; *(imposibilitar)* to prevent, to stop.

impenetrable *adj* impenetrable.

impensable *adj* unthinkable.

imperante *adj (gobernante)* ruling; *(predominante)* prevailing.

imperativo, -a 1 *adj* imperative. **2** *m* imperative.

imperdible *m* safety pin.

imperdonable *adj* unforgivable, inexcusable.

imperfecto, -a *adj* imperfect; *(defectuoso)* defective; *(tiempo verbal)* imperfect.

imperio *m* empire.

impermeable 1 *adj* impervious; *(ropa)* waterproof. **2 m** raincoat.

impertinente *adj (insolente)* impertinent; *(inoportuno)* irrelevant.

ímpetuoso, -a *adj (violento)* violent; *(fogoso)* impetuous.

implacable *adj* implacable.

implicar [44] *vt (involucrar)* to involve (**en** in); *(conllevar)* to imply.

implícito, -a *adj* implicit.

implorar *vt* to implore.

imponente adj (impresionante) imposing; (sobrecogedor) stunning.

imponer [19] (pp impuesto) **1** vt to impose; (impresionar) to be impressive; **i. respeto** to inspire respect. **2 imponerse** vr (prevalecer) to prevail; (ser necesario) to be necessary.

importación f (mercancía) import; (acción) importing; **artículos de i.** imported goods.

importancia f importance; (tamaño) size.

importante adj important; (grande) significant.

importar¹ 1 vi (tener importancia) to be important; **no importa** it doesn't matter; **eso no te importa a tí** that doesn't concern you; **¿te importa si fumo?** do you mind if I smoke? **2** vt (valer) to amount to.

importar² vt to import.

importe m amount.

importunar vt to bother, to pester.

imposibilitar vt (impedir) to make impossible; (incapacitar) to disable.

imposible adj impossible; **me es i. hacerlo** I can't (possibly) do it.

impostor, -a mf impostor.

impotencia f powerlessness.

imprenta f (taller) printer's; (aparato) printing press.

imprescindible adj essential.

impresentable adj unpresentable.

impresión f (efecto, opinión) impression; (acto, de revista etc) printing; (edición) edition.

impresionante adj impressive.

impresionar vt (causar admiración) to impress; (sorprender) to stun.

impresionismo m impressionism.

impreso, -a 1 adj printed. **2** m (papel, folleto) printed matter; (formulario) form; **i. de solicitud** application form.

impresora f printer; **i. de chorro de tinta** ink-jet (printer); **i. láser** laser (printer); **i. matricial** dot matrix (printer).

imprevisible adj unforeseeable.

imprevisto, -a 1 adj unforeseen. **2** m unforeseen event.

imprimir (pp impreso) vt to print.

impropio, -a adj (inadecuado) inappropriate.

improvisado, -a adj (espontáneo) improvised; (provisional) makeshift.

improvisar vt to improvise.

imprudencia f rashness; (indiscreción) indiscretion.

imprudente adj imprudent, unwise; (indiscreto) indiscreet.

impuesto m tax; **i. sobre la renta** income tax; **libre de impuestos** tax-free.

impulsar vt to drive.

impulso m impulse.

impunemente adv with impunity.

impureza f impurity.

impuse pt indef de **imponer**.

inacabable adj endless.

inaccesible adj inaccessible.

inaceptable adj unacceptable.

inadaptado, -a 1 adj maladjusted. **2** mf misfit.

inadecuado, -a adj unsuitable.

inadmisible adj inadmissible.

inadvertido, -a adj unnoticed; **pasar i.** to escape notice, to pass unnoticed.

inagotable adj (recursos etc) inexhaustible; (persona) tireless.

inaguantable adj unbearable.

inalámbrico, -a adj wireless.

inalcanzable adj unattainable, unachievable.

inapreciable adj (valioso) invaluable; (insignificante) insignificant.

inasequible adj (producto) unaffordable; (meta) unattainable; (persona) unapproachable.

inaudito, -a adj unprecedented.

inauguración f inauguration.

inaugurar vt to inaugurate.

inca adj & mf Inca.

incalculable adj incalculable.

incandescente adj white hot.

incansable adj tireless.

incapacidad *f* inability; *(incompetencia)* incompetence.

incapacitar *vt* to incapacitate; *(inhabilitar)* to disqualify.

incapaz *adj* incapable (**de** of).

incendiar [43] **1** *vt* to set fire to. **2 incendiarse** *vr* to catch fire.

incendio *m* fire; **i. forestal** forest fire.

incentivo *m* incentive.

incertidumbre *f* uncertainty.

incidente *m* incident.

incierto, -a *adj* uncertain.

incinerar *vt (basura)* to incinerate; *(cadáveres)* to cremate.

incipiente *adj* incipient.

incitar *vt* to incite.

inclinación *f (de terreno)* slope; *(del cuerpo)* stoop; *(reverencia)* bow.

inclinar 1 *vt* to incline; *(cabeza)* to nod. **2 inclinarse** *vr* to lean; *(al saludar)* to bow; *(optar)* **inclinarse a** to be inclined to.

incluir [37] *vt* to include; *(contener)* to contain; *(adjuntar)* to enclose.

inclusive *adv (incluido)* inclusive; *(incluso)* even; **hasta la lección ocho i.** up to and including lesson eight.

incluso *adv* even.

incógnita *f (misterio)* mystery.

incoherente *adj* incoherent.

incoloro, -a *adj* colorless.

incombustible *adj* incombustible.

incomodar 1 *vt (causar molestia)* to inconvenience, to put out; *(fastidiar)* to bother, to annoy. **2 incomodarse** *vr (tomarse molestias)* to put oneself out, to go out of one's way; *(disgustarse)* to get annoyed o angry.

incomodidad *f* discomfort; *(molestia)* inconvenience.

incómodo, -a *adj* uncomfortable.

incompatible *adj* incompatible.

incompetencia *f* incompetence.

incompetente 1 *adj* incompetent. **2** *mf* incompetent person.

incompleto, -a *adj* incomplete; *(inacabado)* unfinished.

incomprensible *adj* incomprehensible.

incomunicado, -a *adj (aislado)* isolated; *(en la cárcel)* in solitary confinement; **el pueblo se quedó i.** the town was cut off.

inconcebible *adj* inconceivable.

incondicional *adj* unconditional; *(apoyo)* wholehearted; *(amigo)* faithful; *(partidario)* staunch.

inconexo, -a *adj (incoherente)* incoherent, confused.

inconfundible *adj* unmistakable.

incongruente *adj* incongruous.

inconsciencia *f* unconsciousness; *(irresponsabilidad)* irresponsibility.

inconsciente 1 *adj (con estar) (desmayado)* unconscious; *(con ser) (despreocupado)* unaware (**de** of); *(irreflexivo)* thoughtless.

inconsistente *adj (argumento)* weak.

inconstante *adj* fickle.

incontrolable *adj* uncontrollable.

inconveniencia *f* inconvenience; *(impropiedad)* unsuitability.

inconveniente 1 *adj* inconvenient; *(inapropiado)* unsuitable. **2** *m (objeción)* objection; *(desventaja)* disadvantage; *(problema)* difficulty.

incordiar [43] *vt fam* to bother, to pester.

incordio *m fam* nuisance, pain.

incorporación *f* incorporation.

incorporar 1 *vt* to incorporate (**en** into); *(levantar)* to help to sit up. **2 incorporarse** *vr (en la cama)* to sit up; **incorporarse a** *(sociedad)* to join; *(trabajo)* to start.

incorrecto, -a *adj (equivocado)* incorrect.

incorregible *adj* incorrigible.

incrédulo, -a 1 *adj* incredulous. **2** *mf* disbeliever.

increíble *adj* incredible.

incrementar 1 *vt* to increase. **2 incrementarse** *vr* to increase.

inculto, -a 1 *adj* uneducated. **2** *mf* ignoramus.

incultura f ignorance, lack of culture.

incumplimiento m *(de un deber)* non-fulfillment; *(de una orden)* failure to execute.

incumplir vt not to fulfill; *(deber)* to fail to fulfill; *(promesa, contrato)* to break; *(orden)* to fail to carry out.

incurrir vi to fall (**en** into).

indagar [42] vt to investigate.

indebido, -a adj *(desconsiderado)* undue; *(ilegal)* unlawful.

indecente adj indecent.

indeciso, -a 1 adj hesitant. **2** m *(en encuesta)* don't know.

indefenso, -a adj defenseless.

indefinidamente adv indefinitely.

indefinido, -a adj *(indeterminado)* indefinite; *(impreciso)* vague; *(tiempo verbal)* indefinite.

indemnización f *(acto)* indemnification; *(compensación)* compensation.

indemnizar [40] vt to compensate (**por** for).

independencia f independence.

independiente adj *(libre)* independent; *(individualista)* self-reliant.

independientemente adv independently (**de** of); *(aparte de)* irrespective (**de** of).

indescriptible adj indescribable.

indeseable adj & mf undesirable.

indeterminado, -a adj indefinite; *(impreciso)* vague; *(artículo)* indefinite.

indicación f *(señal)* indication; *(instrucción)* instruction.

indicador m indicator.

indicar [44] vt to indicate.

indicativo, -a adj indicative (**de** of); *(modo)* i. indicative (mode).

índice m *(de libro)* index; *(relación)* rate; **í. de natalidad/mortalidad** birth/death rate; **(dedo) í.** index finger.

indicio m indication (**de** of).

índico, -a adj Indian; **Océano I.** Indian Ocean.

indiferente adj indifferent; **me es i.** it makes no difference to me.

indígena 1 adj indigenous (**de** to). **2** mf native (**de** of).

indigestión f indigestion.

indignación f indignation.

indignar 1 vt to infuriate. **2** indignarse vr to be indignant (**por** at, about).

indigno, -a adj unworthy (**de** of); *(despreciable)* wretched, dreadful.

indio, -a adj & mf Indian.

indirecta f fam insinuation.

indirecto, -a adj indirect.

indiscreto, -a adj indiscreet.

indiscutible adj indisputable.

indispensable adj indispensable.

indisponer [19] *(pp indispuesto)* **1** vt to make ill. **2 indisponerse** vr to become ill.

indispuse pt indef de **indisponer**.

indistintamente adv **pueden escribir en inglés o en español i.** you can write in English or Spanish, it doesn't matter which.

individual adj individual; **habitación i.** single room.

individuo m individual.

índole f *(carácter)* character; *(clase, tipo)* kind.

inducir [10] vt to lead.

indudable adj indubitable; **es i. que** there is no doubt that.

induje pt indef de **inducir**.

indultar vt to pardon.

indumentaria f clothing.

industria f industry.

industrial 1 adj industrial. **2** mf manufacturer.

industrialización f industrialization.

induzco indic pres de **inducir**.

ineficacia f *(ineptitud)* inefficiency; *(inutilidad)* ineffectiveness.

ineficaz adj *(inepto)* inefficient; *(inefectivo)* ineffective.

ineludible *adj* inescapable, unavoidable.

ineptitud *f* ineptitude, incompetence.

inepto, -a 1 *adj* inept. **2** *mf* incompetent person.

inequívoco, -a *adj* unmistakable, unequivocal.

inerte *adj (inanimado)* inert; *(inmóvil)* motionless.

inesperado, -a *adj (fortuito)* unexpected; *(imprevisto)* sudden.

inestabilidad *f* instability.

inevitable *adj* inevitable.

inexistente *adj* non-existent.

inexperiencia *f* lack of experience.

inexplicable *adj* inexplicable.

infalible *adj* infallible.

infame *adj (vil)* infamous, vile; *(despreciable)* dreadful, awful.

infancia *f* childhood.

infantería *f* infantry.

infantil *adj* literatura i. *(para niños)* children's literature. **2** *(aniñado)* childlike; *(peyorativo)* childish.

infarto *m* i. (de miocardio) heart attack.

infección *f* infection.

infectar 1 *vt* to infect. **2 infectarse** *vr* to become infected (**de** with).

infeliz 1 *adj* unhappy; *(desdichado)* unfortunate. **2** *mf fam* simpleton.

inferior 1 *adj (más bajo)* lower; *(calidad)* inferior; *(cantidad)* lower. **2** *mf (persona)* subordinate.

infestado, -a *adj* i. de infested with; **i. de turistas** swarming with tourists.

infidelidad *f* unfaithfulness.

infierno *m* hell; *(horno)* inferno; *fam* ¡vete al i.! go to hell!

infinidad *f* infinity; *(sinfín)* great number; **en i. de ocasiones** on countless occasions.

infinitivo, -a *adj & m* infinitive.

infinito, -a 1 *adj* infinite. **2** *m* infinity.

inflable *adj* inflatable.

inflación *f* inflation.

inflamable *adj* flammable.

inflamación *f* inflammation.

inflamar 1 *vt* to inflame; *(encender)* to set on fire. **2 inflamarse** *vr* to become inflamed; *(incendiarse)* to catch fire.

inflar 1 *vt* to inflate. **2 inflarse** *vr* to inflate.

inflexible *adj* inflexible.

influencia *f* influence; **ejercer** o **tener i. sobre algn** to have an influence on sb.

influir [37] **1** *vt* to influence. **2** *vi* to have influence; **i. en** o **sobre** to influence.

información *f* information; *(servicio telefónico)* directory enquiries *pl*.

informal *adj (reunión, cena)* informal; *(comportamiento)* casual; *(persona)* unreliable.

informar 1 *vt (enterar)* to inform (**de** of); *(dar informes)* to report. **2 informarse** *vr (procurarse noticias)* to find out (**de** about); *(enterarse)* to inquire (**de** about).

informática *f* information technology, IT.

informático, -a 1 *adj* computer, computing. **2** *mf* (computer) technician.

informe *m* report; **informes** references.

infracción *f* infringement.

infraestructura *f* infrastructure.

infringir [57] *vt* i. una ley to break a law.

infundir *vt* to infuse; *(idea etc)* to instil.

infusión *f* infusion.

ingeniero, -a *mf* engineer; **i. de caminos** civil engineer; **i. técnico** technician.

ingenio *m (talento)* talent; *(inventiva)* inventiveness; *(agudeza)* wit.

ingenioso, -a *adj* ingenious; *(vivaz)* witty.

ingenuo, -a 1 *adj* naïve. **2** *mf* naïve person.

ingerir [5] *vt (comida)* to ingest, to consume; *(líquidos, alcohol)* to drink, to consume.

ingle *f* groin.

inglés, -esa 1 *adj* English. **2** *mf (hombre)* Englishman; *(mujer)* Englishwoman; **los ingleses** the English. **3** *m (idioma)* English.

ingratitud *f* ingratitude.

ingrediente *m* ingredient.

ingresar 1 *vt (dinero)* to pay in; *(enfermo)* to admit; **la ingresaron en el hospital** she was admitted to the hospital. **2** *vi* to enter.

ingreso *m (dinero)* deposit; *(entrada)* entry (**en** into); *(admisión)* admission (**en** to); **ingresos** *(sueldo, renta)* income *sing, (beneficios)* revenue *sing.*

inhalador *m* inhaler.

inhalar *vt* to inhale.

inhumano, -a *adj* inhumane; *(cruel)* inhuman.

inicial *adj & f* initial.

iniciar [43] **1** *vt (empezar)* to begin, to start; *(discusión)* to initiate; *(una cosa nueva)* to pioneer. **2 iniciarse** *vr* to begin, to start.

iniciativa *f* initiative; **por i. propia** on one's own initiative.

inicio *m* beginning, start.

ininterrumpido, -a *adj* uninterrupted.

injerirse *vr* to interfere (**en** in).

injuria *f* insult.

injusticia *f* injustice.

injustificado, -a *adj* unjustified.

injusto, -a *adj* unjust.

inmaduro, -a *adj* immature.

inmediaciones *fpl* neighbourhood *sing.*

inmediatamente *adv* immediately, at once.

inmediato, -a *adj (en el tiempo)* immediate; *(en el espacio)* next (**a** to); **de i.** at once.

inmejorable *adj (trabajo)* excellent; *(precio)* unbeatable.

inmenso, -a *adj* immense.

inmigración *f* immigration.

inmigrante *adj & mf* immigrant.

inminente *adj* imminent.

inmiscuirse [37] *vr* to interfere (**en** in).

inmobiliaria *f* real estate company.

inmoral *adj* immoral.

inmortal *adj & mf* immortal.

inmóvil *adj* motionless.

inmovilizar [40] *vt* to immobilize.

inmueble *m* building.

inmune *adj* immune (**a** to).

inmunidad *f* immunity (**contra** to).

inmunizar [40] *vt* to immunize (**contra** against).

inmutarse *vr* **ni se inmutó** he didn't turn a hair.

innato, -a *adj* innate.

innecesario, -a *adj* unnecessary.

innegable *adj* undeniable.

innovación *f* innovation.

innumerable *adj* countless.

inocencia *f* innocence; *(ingenuidad)* naïvety.

inocentada *f* ≃ April Fools' joke.

inocente 1 *adj* innocent. **2** *mf* innocent (person).

inocuo, -a *adj* innocuous.

inofensivo, -a *adj* harmless.

inolvidable *adj* unforgettable.

inoportuno, -a *adj* inappropriate.

inoxidable *adj* **acero i.** stainless steel.

inquietante *adj* worrying.

inquietar 1 *vt* to worry. **2 inquietarse** *vr* to worry (**por** about).

inquieto, -a *adj (preocupado)* worried (**por** about); *(intranquilo)* restless.

inquietud *f (preocupación)* worry; *(agitación)* restlessness.

inquilino, -a *mf* tenant.

insaciable *adj* insatiable.

insatisfecho, -a *adj* dissatisfied.

inscribir *(pp* inscrito*)* **1** *vt (registrar)* to register; *(matricular)* to enroll; *(grabar)* to inscribe. **2 inscribirse** *vr (registrarse)* to register; *(hacerse miembro)* to join; *(matricu-*

larse) to enroll; **inscribirse en un club** to join a club.

inscripción f *(matriculación)* enrollment; *(escrito etc)* inscription.

insecticida m insecticide.

insecto m insect.

inseguridad f *(falta de confianza)* insecurity; *(duda)* uncertainty; *(peligro)* lack of safety.

inseguro, -a adj *(poco confiado)* insecure; *(dubitativo)* uncertain; *(peligroso)* unsafe.

insensato, -a 1 adj foolish. **2** mf fool.

insensible adj *(indiferente)* unfeeling; *(imperceptible)* imperceptible; *(miembro)* numb.

inseparable adj inseparable.

insertar vt to insert.

inservible adj useless.

insignia f badge.

insignificante adj insignificant.

insinuar [30] vt to insinuate.

insistir vi to insist (**en** on).

insolación f sunstroke.

insolente adj insolent.

insólito, -a adj *(poco usual)* unusual; *(extraño)* strange, odd.

insomnio m insomnia.

insoportable adj unbearable.

insospechado, -a adj unsuspected.

insostenible adj untenable.

inspección f inspection.

inspeccionar vt to inspect.

inspector, -a mf inspector; **i. de Hacienda** tax inspector.

inspiración f inspiration; *(inhalación)* inhalation.

inspirar 1 vt to inspire; *(inhalar)* to inhale. **2 inspirarse** vr **inspirarse en** to be inspired by.

instalación f installation; **instalaciones deportivas** sports facilities.

instalar 1 vt to install; *(erigir)* to set up. **2 instalarse** vr to settle (down).

instancia f *(solicitud)* request; **a instancia(s) de** at the request of; **en última i.** as a last resort.

instantáneamente adv instantly.

instantáneo, -a adj instantaneous; **café i.** instant coffee.

instante m instant; **a cada i.** constantly; **al i.** immediately.

instaurar vt to found.

instigar [42] vt to instigate.

instintivo, -a adj instinctive.

instinto m instinct; **por i.** instinctively.

institución f institution.

instituto m institute; *(colegio)* high school.

institutriz f governess.

instrucción f *(educación)* education; **instrucciones para el** o **de uso** instructions o directions for use.

instructivo, -a adj instructive.

instruir [37] vt to instruct; *(enseñar)* to educate.

instrumento m instrument.

insubordinarse vr to rebel (**contra** against).

insuficiente 1 adj insufficient. **2** m *(nota)* fail.

insulso, -a adj insipid.

insultar vt to insult.

insulto m insult.

insuperable adj *(inmejorable)* unsurpassable; *(problema)* insurmountable.

insurrección f insurrection.

intacto, -a adj intact.

integral adj integral; **pan i.** wholewheat bread.

integrante 1 adj integral; **ser parte i. de** to be an integral part of. **2** mf member.

integrar 1 vt to integrate; *(formar)* to compose. **2 integrarse** vr to integrate (**en** with).

integridad f integrity.

íntegro, -a adj *(entero)* whole; *(honrado)* upright; **versión íntegra** unabridged version.

intelectual adj & mf intellectual.

inteligencia f intelligence.

inteligente adj intelligent.

inteligible adj intelligible.

intemperie *f* **a la i.** in the open (air).

intención *f* intention; **con i.** deliberately; **tener la i. de hacer algo** to intend to do sth.

intencionadamente *adv* on purpose.

intencionado, -a *adj* deliberate.

intensidad *f* intensity; *(del viento)* force.

intensificar [44] *vt,* **intensificarse** *vr* to intensify; *(relación)* to strengthen.

intenso, -a *adj* intense.

intentar *vt* to try.

intento *m* attempt; **i. de suicidio** attempted suicide.

intercambiar [43] *vt* to exchange.

interceder *vi* to intercede.

interceptar *vt (detener)* to intercept; *(carretera)* to block; *(tráfico)* to hold up.

interés *m* interest; *(provecho personal)* self-interest; **tener i. en** *o* **por** to be interested in; **tipos de i.** interest rates.

interesante *adj* interesting.

interesar **1** *vt (tener interés)* to interest; *(concernir)* to concern. **2** *vi (ser importante)* to be of interest. **2 interesarse** *vr* **interesarse por** *o* **en** to be interested in.

interferencia *f* interference; *(en radio, televisión)* jamming.

interfono *m* intercom.

interior **1** *adj* inner; **ropa i.** underwear; *(política, vuelo)* domestic; *(región)* inland. **2** *m* inside; *(de un país)* interior; **Ministerio del I.** Department of the Interior.

interjección *f* interjection.

interlocutor, -a *mf* speaker.

intermediario, -a *mf* intermediary, middleman.

intermedio, -a **1** *adj* intermediate. **2** *m (en televisión)* break.

interminable *adj* endless.

intermitente **1** *adj* intermittent. **2** *m (de automóvil)* indicator.

internacional *adj* international.

internado *m (colegio)* boarding school.

internauta *mf* Net user.

Internet *f* Internet; **está en I.** it's on the Internet.

interno, -a **1** *adj* internal; *(política)* domestic. **2** *mf (alumno)* boarder.

interpretación *f* interpretation.

interpretar *vt* to interpret; *(papel)* to play; *(obra)* to perform; *(concierto)* to perform; *(canción)* to sing.

intérprete *mf (traductor)* interpreter; *(actor, músico)* performer; *(cantante)* singer.

interrogación *f* interrogation; **(signo de) i.** question mark.

interrogante *f fig* question mark.

interrogar [42] *vt* to question; *(con amenazas)* to interrogate.

interrogatorio *m* interrogation.

interrumpir *vt* to interrupt; *(tráfico)* to block.

interruptor *m* switch.

interurbano, -a *adj* intercity; **conferencia interurbana** long-distance call.

intervalo *m* interval.

intervenir [27] **1** *vi (mediar)* to intervene *(en* in); *(participar)* take part *(en* in). **2** *vt (teléfono)* to tap.

interviú *m (pl* interviús*)* interview.

intestino *m* intestine.

intimidar *vt* to intimidate.

íntimo, -a *adj* intimate; *(vida)* private; *(amigo)* close.

intolerante **1** *adj* intolerant. **2** *mf* intolerant person.

intoxicación *f* poisoning; **i. alimenticia** food poisoning.

intranquilizarse *vr* to get worried.

intranquilo, -a *adj (preocupado)* worried; *(agitado)* restless.

intransigente *adj* intransigent.

intransitivo, -a *adj* intransitive.

intriga *f* intrigue; *(trama)* plot.

intrigar [42] **1** *vt (interesar)* to intrigue. **2** *vi (maquinar)* to plot.

intrínseco, -a *adj* intrinsic.

introducir [10] *vt* to introduce; *(meter)* to insert.

introvertido, -a 1 *adj* introverted. **2** *mf* introvert.

intruso, -a *mf* intruder.

intuición *f* intuition.

intuir [37] *vt* to know by intuition.

inundación *f* flood.

inusitado, -a *adj* unusual.

inútil 1 *adj* useless; *(esfuerzo, intento)* pointless. **2** *mf fam* good-for-nothing.

inutilizar [40] *vt* to make useless.

invadir *vt* to invade; **los estudiantes invadieron la calle** students poured out onto the street.

inválido, -a 1 *adj (nulo)* invalid; *(minusválido)* disabled. **2** *mf* disabled person.

invariable *adj* invariable.

invasión *f* invasion.

invencible *adj (enemigo)* invincible; *(obstáculo)* insurmountable.

invención *f (invento)* invention; *(mentira)* fabrication.

inventar *vt (crear)* to invent; *(excusa, mentira)* to concoct.

inventario *m* inventory.

invento *m* invention.

invernadero *m* greenhouse.

invernal *adj* winter.

inversión *f* inversion; *(de dinero)* investment.

inverso, -a *adj* **en sentido i.** in the opposite direction; **en orden i.** in reverse order.

invertir [5] *vt (orden)* to invert; *(dinero)* to invest (**en** in); *(tiempo)* to spend (**en** on).

investigación *f (policial etc)* investigation; *(científica)* research.

investigar [42] *vt (indagar)* to investigate; *(científicamente)* to research.

invierno *m* winter.

invisible *adj* invisible.

invitado, -a 1 *adj* invited. **2** *mf* guest.

invitar *vt* to invite; **me invitó a una copa** he treated me to a drink.

involucrarse *vr* to get involved (**en** in).

involuntario, -a *adj* involuntary; *(impremeditado)* unintentional.

inyección *f* injection; **poner una i.** to give an injection.

inyectar *vt* to inject (**en** into); **i. algo a algn** to inject sb with sth.

ir [16] **1** *vi* to go; **¡vamos!** let's go!; **¡ya voy!** (I'm coming!; **¿cómo le va el nuevo trabajo?** how is he doing in his new job?; **el negro no te va** black doesn't suit you; **ir con falda** to wear a skirt; **ir de blanco/de uniforme** to be dressed in white/in uniform; **va para abogado** he's studying to be a lawyer; **ir por la derecha** to keep (to the) right; **ve (a) por agua** go and fetch some water; **voy por la página noventa** I've got as far as page ninety; **en lo que va de año** so far this year; **ir a parar** to end up; **¡qué va!** of course not!; **va a lo suyo** he looks after his own interests; **¡vamos a ver!** let's see!; **¡vaya!** fancy that; **¡vaya moto!** what a bike! **2** *v aux* **ir andando** to go on foot; **va mejorando** she's improving; **ya van rotos tres** three (of them) have already been broken; **iba a decir que …** I was going to say that …; **va a llover** it's going to rain. **3** **irse** *vr (marcharse)* to go away; **me voy** I'm off; **¡vámonos!** let's go!; **¡vete!** go away!; **¡vete a casa!** go home!; **¿por dónde se va a …?** which is the way to …?

ira *f* rage.

iraní *adj & mf (pl iraníes)* Iranian.

iraquí *adj & mf (pl iraquíes)* Iraqi.

irascible *adj* irascible.

iris *m inv* **arco i.** rainbow.

irlandés, -esa 1 *adj* Irish. **2** *mf (hombre)* Irishman; *(mujer)* Irishwoman; **los irlandeses** the Irish. **3** *m (idioma)* Irish.

ironía *f* irony.

irónico, -a *adj* ironic.

irracional *adj* irrational.

irreal *adj* unreal.

irregular *adj* irregular.

irremediable *adj* incurable.

irresistible *adj (impulso, persona)* irresistible; *(insoportable)* unbearable.

irresponsable *adj* irresponsible.

irrisorio, -a *adj* derisory, ridiculous.

irritación *f* irritation.

irritante *adj* irritating.

irritar 1 *vt* to irritate. **2 irritarse** *vr* to become irritated.

irrompible *adj* unbreakable.

irrumpir *vi* to burst (**en** into).

isla *f* island.

islámico, -a *adj* Islamic.

israelí *adj & mf (pl* **israelíes)** Israeli.

italiano, -a 1 *adj* Italian. **2** *mf (persona)* Italian. **3** *m (idioma)* Italian.

itinerario *m* itinerary.

IVA *m abr de* **impuesto sobre el valor añadido** value-added tax, VAT.

izqda., izqdª *abr de* **izquierda** left.

izqdo., izqdº *abr de* **izquierdo** left.

izquierda *f* left; *(mano)* left hand; **a la i.** on the left; **girar a la i.** to turn left.

izquierdo, -a *adj* left.

J

jabalí *m (pl* **jabalíes)** wild boar.

jabalina *f* javelin.

jabón *m* soap; **j. de afeitar/tocador** shaving/toilet soap.

jabonera *f* soap dish.

jaca *f* gelding.

jacaré *m Am* caiman.

jacinto *m* hyacinth.

jactarse *vr* to boast (**de** about).

jadear *vi* to pant.

jalar 1 *vt Andes, CAm, Carib, Méx (tirar)* to pull; *fam (comer)* to wolf down. **2 jalarse** *vr fam (comerse)* to wolf down, to scoff.

jalea *f* jelly.

jaleo *m (alboroto)* ruckus; *(confusión)* muddle.

jalón *m Am* lift.

jamás *adv* never; **j. he estado allí** I have never been there; **el mejor libro que j. se ha escrito** the best book ever written; **nunca j.** never again.

jamón *m* ham; **j. de York/serrano** boiled/cured ham.

japonés, -esa *adj & mf* Japanese; **los japoneses** the Japanese.

jaque *m* check; **j. mate** checkmate; **j. al rey** check.

jaqueca *f* migraine.

jarabe *m* syrup; **j. para la tos** cough mixture.

jardín *m* garden; **j. botánico** botanical garden; **j. de infancia** nursery school.

jardinero, -a *mf* gardener.

jarra *f* pitcher.

jarro *m (recipiente)* jug; *(contenido)* jugful.

jarrón *m* vase.

jaula *f* cage.

jazmín *m* jasmine.

J.C. *abr de* **Jesucristo** Jesus Christ, J.C.

jeep *m* jeep.

jefa *f* manager.

jefatura *f (cargo, dirección)* leadership; *(sede)* central office.

jefe *m* head; *(de empresa)* manager; *(de partido)* leader; **J. de Estado** Head of State.

jengibre *m* ginger.

jerarquía *f* hierarchy; *(categoría)* rank.

jerez *m* sherry.

jerga *f (técnica)* jargon; *(vulgar)* slang.

jeringa *f* syringe.

jeringuilla *f* (hypodermic) syringe.

jeroglífico *m* hieroglyphic; *(juego)* rebus.

jersey m (pl **jerseis**) pullover.

Jesucristo m Jesus Christ.

Jesús 1 m Jesus. **2** interj (al estornudar) bless you!

jíbaro, -a m Am peasant.

jícara f Am gourd.

jilguero m goldfinch.

jinete m horseman, rider.

jirafa f giraffe.

jirón m (trozo desgarrado) strip; (pedazo suelto) scrap; **hecho jirones** in tatters.

JJOO mpl abr de **Juegos Olímpicos** Olympic Games.

jornada f **j. (laboral)** (día de trabajo) working day; **trabajo de media j./j. completa** part-time/full-time work.

jornal m day's wage.

jornalero, -a mf day laborer.

joroba f hump.

jorobado, -a 1 adj hunchbacked. **2** mf hunchback.

joven 1 adj young; **de aspecto j.** young-looking. **2** mf (hombre) young man; (mujer) young woman; **de j.** as a young man/woman; **los jóvenes** young people.

joya f jewel; **ser una j.** (persona) to be a gem.

joyería f (tienda) jewelry shop.

joyero, -a 1 mf jeweler. **2** m jewel case.

jubilado, -a 1 adj retired. **2** mf retired person; **los jubilados** retired people.

judía f bean; **j. verde** green bean.

judío, -a 1 adj Jewish. **2** mf Jew.

judo m judo.

juego m game; (conjunto de piezas) set; (apuestas) gambling; **j. de azar** game of chance; **j. de cartas** card game; **Juegos Olímpicos** Olympic Games; **terreno de j.** field; **fuera de j.** offside; **j. de café/té** coffee/tea service; **ir a j. con** to match.

juerga f fam rave-up; **ir de j.** to go on a binge.

jueves m inv Thursday; **J. Santo** Holy Thursday.

juez, -a mf judge; **j. de línea** linesman.

jugada f move; fam dirty trick.

jugador, -a mf player; (apostador) gambler.

jugar [32] **1** vi to play; **j. a(l) fútbol** to play football; **j. sucio** to play dirty. **2** vt to play; (apostar) to bet. **3** **jugarse** vr (arriesgar) to risk; (apostar) to bet.

jugo m juice.

juguete m toy; **pistola de j.** toy gun.

juicio m (facultad mental) judgement; (sensatez) reason; (opinión) opinion; (en tribunal) trial; **a j. de** in the opinion of; **a mi j.** in my opinion; **perder el j.** to go mad.

julio m July.

junco m rush.

jungla f jungle.

junio m June.

júnior adj junior.

junta f (reunión) meeting; (dirección) board; (gobierno militar) junta.

juntar 1 vt (unir) to join; (piezas) to assemble; (dinero) to raise. **2** **juntarse** vr (unirse) to join; (ríos, caminos) to meet; (personas) to gather.

junto, -a 1 adj together. **2** adv **j. con** together with; **j. a** next to.

jurado m jury.

juramento m oath; **bajo j.** under oath.

jurar 1 vi to swear. **2** vt to swear; **j. el cargo** to take the oath of office.

jurídico, -a adj legal.

justamente adv **¡j.!** precisely!; **j. detrás de** right behind.

justicia f justice; **tomarse la j. por su mano** to take the law into one's own hands.

justificado, -a adj justified.

justificante m written proof.

justificar [44] **1** vt to justify. **2** **justificarse** vr to justify oneself.

justo, -a 1 adj just; (apretado) (ropa) tight; (exacto) accurate; **un trato j.** a fair deal; **estamos justos de tiempo**

we're pressed for time; **llegamos en el momento j. en que salían** we arrived just as they were leaving; **lo j.** just enough. **2** adv (exactamente) precisely; **j. al lado de** right beside.

juvenil adj young; **ropa j.** (de joven) young people's clothes; **delincuencia j.** juvenile delinquency.

juventud f (edad) youth; (jóvenes) young people.

juzgado m court.

juzgar [42] vt to judge; **a j. por ...** judging by ....

K

karaoke m karaoke.

kárate m karate.

kilo m (medida) kilo.

kilogramo m kilogram.

kilometraje m ≃ mileage.

kilómetro m kilometer.

kiosco m kiosk.

kiwi m (fruto) kiwi (fruit).

kleenex® m tissue.

L

la¹ 1 art def f the. **2** pron dem the one; **la del vestido azul** the one in the blue dress.

la² pron pers f (persona) her; (usted) you; (cosa) it; **la invitaré** I'll invite her along; **ya la avisaremos, señora** we'll let you know, madam; **no la dejes abierta** don't leave it open.

labio m lip.

labor f job; (de costura) needlework.

laborable adj día l. working day.

laboral adj industrial; **accidente l.** industrial accident; **jornada l.** working day.

laboratorio m laboratory.

labrar 1 vt (tierra) to till; (madera) to carve; (piedra) to cut; (metal) to work. **2 labrarse** vr fig **labrarse un porvenir** to build a future for oneself.

laca f hairspray; **l. de uñas** nail polish.

ladear 1 vt (inclinar) to tilt; (cabeza) to lean. **2 ladearse** vr (inclinarse) to lean, to tilt; (desviarse) to go off to one side.

ladera f slope.

ladino, -a 1 adj (astuto) crafty; CAm, Méx, Ven (no blanco) non-white. **2** mf CAm, Méx, Ven (no blanco) = non-white Spanish-speaking person.

lado m side; **a un l.** aside; **al l.** close by, nearby; **al l. de** next to; **ponte de l.** stand sideways; **por todos lados** on all sides; **por otro l.** (además) moreover; **por un l. ..., por otro l. ...** on the one hand ..., on the other hand ....

ladrar vi to bark.

ladrillo m brick.

ladrón, -ona mf thief.

lagartija f small lizard.

lagarto m lizard.

lago m lake.

lágrima f tear.

laguna f small lake.

lamentar 1 vt to regret; **lo lamento** I'm sorry. **2 lamentarse** vr to complain.

lamer vt to lick.

lámina f sheet.

lámpara f lamp; (bombilla) bulb.

lana f wool; Andes, Méx fam (dinero) dough, cash.

lancha f motorboat; **l. motora** speedboat; **l. neumática** rubber dinghy; **l. salvavidas** lifeboat.

langosta f lobster; (insecto) locust.

langostino m king prawn.

lanza f spear.

lanzar [40] **1** vt (arrojar) to throw; (grito) to let out; (ataque, producto) to launch. **2 lanzarse** vr to throw oneself.

lapicera f CSur ballpoint (pen); **l. fuente** fountain pen.

lápiz m pencil; **l. de labios** lipstick; **l. de ojos** eyeliner.

largo, -a adj long; **a lo l. de** (espacio) along; (tiempo) through; **a la larga** in the long run. **2** m (longitud) length; **¿cuánto tiene de l.?** fam how long is it?; fam **esto va para l.** this is going to last a long time. **3** adv fam **¡l. (de aquí)!** clear off!

largometraje m feature film.

las¹ 1 art def fpl the. **2** pron dem **l. que** (personas) those who; (objetos) those that; **toma l. que quieras** take whichever ones you want.

las² pron pers fpl (ellas) them; (ustedes) you; **no l. rompas** don't break them; **l. llamaré mañana** (a ustedes) I'll call you tomorrow.

láser m inv laser.

lástima f pity; **¡qué l.!** what a pity!; **es una l. que …** it's a pity (that) ….

lata¹ f (envase) tin, can; (hojalata) tin(plate); **en l.** tinned, canned.

lata² f fam drag; **dar la l.** to be a nuisance.

lateral adj side; **escalón l.** (en letrero) ramp.

latido m beat.

látigo m whip.

latín m Latin.

latinomericano, -a adj & mf Latin American.

latir vi to beat.

latón m brass.

laucha f Am mouse.

laurel m bay leaf.

lava f lava.

lavable adj washable.

lavabo m (pila) washbasin; (cuarto de aseo) washroom; (retrete) toilet.

lavadero m (de coches) carwash.

lavado m washing; **l. en seco** dry-cleaning.

lavadora f washing machine.

lavanda f lavender.

lavandería f laundromat; (atendida por personal) laundry.

lavaplatos m inv dishwasher.

lavar vt to wash.

lavavajillas m inv dishwasher.

laxante adj & m laxative.

lazo m (adorno) bow; (nudo) knot; **lazos** (vínculo) links.

le 1 pron pers mf (objeto indirecto) (a él) (to/for) him; (a ella) (to/for) her; (a cosa) (to/for) it; (a usted) (to/for) you; **lávale la cara** wash his face; **le compraré uno** I'll buy one for her; **¿qué le pasa a usted?** what's the matter with you? **2** pron pers m (objeto directo) (él) him; (usted) you; **no le oigo** I can't hear him; **no quiero molestarle** I don't wish to disturb you.

leal adj faithful.

lección f lesson.

leche f milk; **dientes de l.** milk teeth; **l. descremada** o **desnatada** skim milk.

lechuga f lettuce.

lechuza f owl.

lector, -a mf (persona) reader; (de colegio) (language) assistant.

lectura f reading.

leer [36] vt to read.

legal adj legal.

legalizar [40] vt to legalize; (documento) to authenticate.

legislación f legislation.

legítimo, -a adj legitimate; (auténtico) real; **en legítima defensa** in self-defense; **oro l.** pure gold.

legumbres fpl pulses.

lejano, -a adj far-off.

lejía f bleach.

lejos adv far (away); **a lo l.** in the distance; **de l.** from a distance; fig **sin ir más l.** to take an obvious example.

lema m motto.

lencería f (prendas) lingerie; (ropa blanca) linen (goods pl).

lengua f tongue; (idioma) language; **l. materna** mother tongue.

lenguado f sole.

lenguaje m language; **l. corporal** body language.

lente 1 f lens; **lentes de contacto** contact lenses. **2** mpl **lentes** Am glasses, spectacles; **lentes de contacto** contact lenses.

lenteja f lentil.

lentejuela f sequin.

lentilla f contact lens.

lento, -a adj slow; **a fuego l.** on a low heat.

leña f firewood.

leño m log.

león m lion.

leopardo m leopard.

leotardos mpl thick tights.

les pron pers mfpl (a ellos/ellas) them; (a ustedes) you; **dales el dinero** give them the money; **l. he comprado un regalo** I've bought you/them a present; **l. esperaré** I shall wait for you/them; **no quiero molestarles** I don't wish to disturb you/them.

lesión f (física) injury.

lesionar vt to injure.

letal adj lethal.

letargo m lethargy.

letra f letter; (escritura) (hand)writing; (de canción) lyrics pl; **l. de imprenta** block capitals; **l. mayúscula** capital letter; **l. minúscula** small letter; **l. (de cambio)** bill of exchange; (carrera) **letras** arts.

letrero m (aviso) notice; (cartel) poster.

levadura f yeast; **l. en polvo** baking powder.

levantamiento m lifting; (insurrección) uprising; **l. de pesos** weightlifting.

levantar 1 vt to lift; (mano, voz) to raise; (edificio) to erect; (ánimos) to raise. **2 levantarse** vr to get up; (ponerse de pie) to stand up.

levante m **(el) L.** Levante, the regions of Valencia and Murcia.

leve adj (ligero) light; (de poca importancia) slight.

levemente adv slightly.

ley f law; **aprobar una l.** to pass a bill; **oro de l.** pure gold; **plata de l.** sterling silver.

leyenda f (relato) legend; (bajo ilustración) caption.

liar [29] **1** vt (envolver) to wrap up; (cigarrillo) to roll; (enredar) to muddle up; (confundir) to confuse. **2 liarse** vr (embarullarse) to get muddled up.

liberal 1 adj liberal; (generoso) generous; (carácter) open-minded; **profesión l.** profession. **2** mf liberal.

liberalizar [40] vt to liberalize.

liberar vt (país) to liberate; (prisionero) to release.

libertad f freedom; **(en) l. bajo palabra/fianza** (on) parole/bail; **(en) l. condicional** (on) parole.

libio, -a adj & mf Libyan.

libra f pound; **l. esterlina** pound sterling.

librar 1 vt to free; (preso) to release. **2 librarse** vr to escape; **librarse de algn** to get rid of sb.

libre adj free; (sin restricción) open to the public; **entrada l.** admission free; **l. de impuestos** tax-free.

librería f (tienda) bookstore; (estante) bookcase.

libreta f notebook.

libro m book; **l. de texto** textbook.

licencia f (permiso) permission; (documentos) licence; Am driver's license.

licenciado, -a mf graduate; Am lawyer; **l. en Ciencias** Bachelor of Science.

licenciar [43] **1** vt (soldado) to discharge; (estudiante) to confer a degree on. **2 licenciarse** vr (estudiante) to graduate.

licenciatura f (título) (bachelor's)

degree (course); *(carrera)* degree (course).

licor *m* liquor.

licuadora *f* liquidizer.

líder *mf* leader.

liderar *vt* to lead, to head.

liderato, liderazgo *m* leadership; *(en deportes)* top *o* first position.

lidia *f* bullfighting.

lidiar [43] *vt* to fight.

liebre *f* hare.

liga *f* league.

ligar [42] **1** *vt* to join. **2** *vi fam* **l. con una chica** to flirt with a girl.

ligeramente *adv (levemente)* lightly; *(un poco)* slightly.

ligereza *f* flightness; *(frivolidad)* flippancy; *(acto)* indiscretion; *(rapidez)* speed.

ligero, -a 1 *adj (peso)* light; *(veloz)* quick; *(leve)* slight; **l. de ropa** lightly clad; **brisa/comida ligera** light breeze/meal. **2** *adv* **ligero** *(rápido)* fast.

liguero *m* garter belt.

lija *f* sandpaper; **papel de l.** sandpaper.

lima *f (herramienta)* file; **l. de uñas** nailfile.

limar *vt* to file.

limitar 1 *vt* to restrict. **2** *vi* **l. con** to border on.

límite *m* limit; *(de país)* border; **fecha l.** deadline; **velocidad l.** maximum speed.

limón *m* lemon.

limonada *f* lemon squash.

limonero *m* lemon tree.

limosna *f* alms; **pedir l.** to beg.

limpiabotas *m inv* bootblack, shoeshine.

limpiaparabrisas *m inv* windshield wiper.

limpiar [43] *vt* to clean; *(con un trapo)* to wipe; *(zapatos)* to polish.

limpieza *f (calidad)* cleanliness; *(acción)* cleaning.

limpio, -a 1 *adj (aseado)* clean; *(neto)* net; **juego l.** fair play. **2** *adv*

limpio fairly; **jugar l.** to play fair.

lindar *vi* **l. con** to border on.

lindo, -a 1 *adj (bonito)* pretty; **de lo l.** a great deal. **2** *adv Am (bien)* nicely.

línea *f* line; **l. aérea** airline; **en líneas generales** roughly speaking; **guardar la l.** to watch one's figure.

lino *m (fibra)* linen.

linterna *f* torch.

lío *m (paquete)* bundle; *(embrollo)* mess; **hacerse un l.** to get mixed up; **meterse en líos** to get into trouble.

lipotimia *f* fainting fit.

liquidación *f (saldo)* clearance sale; *(de deuda, cuenta)* settling.

liquidar 1 *vt (deuda, cuenta)* to settle; *(mercancías)* to sell off. **2** *vr* **liquidarse a algn** *(matar)* to bump sb off.

líquido, -a 1 *adj* liquid; *(cantidad)* net. **2** *m* liquid.

lirio *m* iris.

lirio, -a 1 *adj* crippled. **2** *mf* cripple.

liso, -a *adj (superficie)* smooth; *(pelo, falda)* straight; *(tela)* self-colored; *Am (desvergonzado)* rude.

lista *f (relación)* list; *(franja)* stripe; **l. de espera** waiting list; *(en avión)* standby; **pasar l.** to call the register; **de/a listas** striped.

listín *m* **l. telefónico** telephone directory.

listo, -a *adj* **ser l.** to be clever; **estar l.** to be ready.

litera *f (cama)* bunk bed; *(en tren)* couchette.

literatura *f* literature.

litigio *m* lawsuit.

litoral 1 *m* coast. **2** *adj* coastal.

litro *m* liter.

llaga *f* sore; *(herida)* wound.

llama *f* flame; **en llamas** in flames.

llamada *f* call; **l. interurbana** long-distance call.

llamado, -a 1 *adj* so-called. **2** *m Am (telefónico)* call; *(a la puerta)* knock; *(con timbre)* ring; *(llamamiento)* appeal, call; **hacer un l.** to make a phone call.

llamamiento m appeal.

llamar 1 vt to call; **l. (por teléfono)** to call; **l. la atención** to attract attention. **2** vi (a la puerta) to knock. **3 llamarse** vr to be called; **¿cómo te llamas?** what's your name?

llano, -a 1 adj (superficie) flat. **2** m plain.

llanta f (de rueda) wheel rim; Am tire.

llanto m crying.

llanura f plain.

llave f key; (interruptor) switch; (herramienta) spanner; **cerrar con l.** to lock; (de coche) **l. de contacto** ignition key; **l. inglesa** adjustable spanner; **l. de paso** stopcock; **l. USB** memory stick.

llavero m key ring.

llegada f arrival; (meta) finish.

llegar [42] vi to arrive; **l. a Madrid** to arrive in Madrid; **¿llegas al techo?** can you reach the ceiling?; **l. a +** infinitivo to go so far as to; **l. a ser** to become.

llenar 1 vt to fill; (satisfacer) to satisfy. **2** vi (comida) to be filling. **3 llenarse** vr to fill (up).

lleno, -a adj full (up).

llevar 1 vt to take; (hacia el oyente) to bring; (transportar) to carry; (prenda) to wear; (negocio) to be in charge of; **llevo dos años aquí** I've been here for two years; **esto lleva mucho tiempo** this takes a long time. **2** v aux **l. +** gerundio to have been + present participle; **llevo dos años estudiando español** I've been studying Spanish for two years. ▪ **l. +** participio pasado to have + past participle; **llevaba escritas seis cartas** I had written six letters. **3 llevarse** vr to take away; (premio) to win; (estar de moda) to be fashionable; **llevarse bien con algn** to get along well with sb.

llorar vi to cry.

lloriquear vi to whimper, to snivel.

llover [4] v impers to rain.

llovizna f drizzle.

lloviznar v impers to drizzle.

lluvia f rain.

lluvioso, -a adj rainy.

lo¹ art def neutro the; **lo mismo** the same thing; **lo mío** mine; **lo tuyo** yours.

lo² pron pers m & neutro (cosa) it; **debes hacerlo** you must do it; (no se traduce) **no se lo dije** I didn't tell her; **lo que ...** what ...; **lo cual ...** which ...; **lo de ...** the business of ...; **cuéntame lo del juicio** tell me about the trial.

lobo m wolf; **como boca de l.** pitch-dark.

local 1 adj local. **2** m (recinto) premises pl.

localidad f (pueblo) locality; (asiento) seat.

localizar [40] vt (encontrar) to find; (fuego, dolor) to localize.

loción f lotion.

loco, -a 1 adj mad; **a lo l.** crazily; **l. por** crazy about; **volverse l.** to go mad. **2** mf (hombre) madman; (mujer) madwoman.

locomotora f locomotive.

locura f madness.

locutor, -a mf presenter.

locutorio m telephone booth.

lodo m mud.

lógico, -a adj logical; **era l. que ocurriera** it was bound to happen.

lograr vt to get, to obtain; (premio) to win; (meta) to achieve; **l. hacer algo** to manage to do something.

lombriz f earthworm.

lomo m back; (para filete) loin.

lona f canvas.

loncha f slice.

lonchería f Méx snack bar.

longaniza f spicy (pork) sausage.

longitud f length; **dos metros de l.** two meters long; **salto de l.** long jump.

lonja f market.

loquería *f Am* mental hospital.
lord *m* (*pl* **lores**) lord.
loro *m* parrot.
los¹ 1 *art def mpl* the. **2** *pron* **l. que** (*personas*) those who; (*cosas*) the ones (that); **toma l. que quieras** take whichever ones you want; **esos son l. míos/tuyos** these are mine/yours.
los² *pron pers mpl* them; **¿l. has visto?** have you seen them?
losa *f* slab.
lote *m* (*de productos*) lot; *Am* (*terreno*) plot (of land).
lotería *f* lottery; **tocarle la l. a algn** to win a prize in the lottery.
loza *f* (*material*) earthenware; (*vajilla*) crockery.
lubricante *m* lubricant.
lucha *f* fight; (*deporte*) wrestling; **l. libre** free-style o all-in wrestling.
luchar *vi* to fight; (*como deporte*) to wrestle.
lucir [35] **1** *vi* (*brillar*) to shine. **2** *vt* (*ropa*) to sport. **3 lucirse** *vr* (*hacer buen papel*) to do very well; (*pavonearse*) to show off.
luego 1 *adv* (*después*) then, next; (*más tarde*) later (on); **¡hasta l.!** so long!; *Am* **l. de** after; **desde l.** of course. **2** *conj* therefore.
lugar *m* place; **en primer l.** in the first place; **en l. de** instead of; **sin l. a dudas** without a doubt; **tener l.** to take place; **dar l. a** to give rise to.
lujo *m* luxury.
lujoso, -a *adj* luxurious.
lujuria *f* lust.
lumbre *f* fire.
luminoso, -a *adj* luminous; *fig* bright.
luna *f* moon; (*espejo*) mirror; *fig* **estar en la l.** to have one's head in the clouds; **l. llena** full moon; **l. de miel** honeymoon.
lunar *m* (*en la ropa*) dot; (*en la piel*) mole.
lunes *m inv* Monday.
lupa *f* magnifying glass.

lustre *m* shine.
luto *m* mourning.
luz *f* light; **apagar la l.** to put out the light; **dar a l.** (*parir*) to give birth to; **luces de cruce** dipped headlights; **luces de posición** sidelights; **luces largas** headlights; **traje de luces** bullfighter's costume.
luzco *indic pres de* **lucir**.

M

macabro, -a *adj* macabre.
macana *f Am* (*palo*) club; (*trasto*) rubbish.
macanear *vt Am* to make up.
macarrones *mpl* macaroni *sing.*
macedonia *f* fruit salad.
maceta *f* flowerpot.
machacar [44] *vt* to crush.
machista *adj & m* male chauvinist.
macho 1 *adj* male; *fam* (*viril*) manly. **2** *m* male; *fam* (*hombre viril*) macho.
machote *m Am* rough draft.
macizo, -a 1 *adj* solid. **2** *m* massif.
macuto *m* haversack.
madeja *f* hank.
madera *f* wood; (*de construcción*) lumber; **de m.** wooden.
madrastra *f* stepmother.
madre 1 *f* mother; **m. de familia** housewife; **m. política** mother-in-law; **m. soltera** unmarried mother. **2** *interj* **¡m. mía!** good heavens!
madrina *f* (*de bautizo*) godmother; (*de boda*) ≃ bridesmaid.
madrugada *f* small hours *pl*; **de m.** in the small hours; **las tres de la m.** three o'clock in the morning.
madrugador, -a 1 *adj* early rising. **2** *mf* early riser.
madrugar [42] *vi* to get up early.
madurar *vi* (*persona*) to mature; (*fruta*) to ripen.

madurez f maturity; (de fruta) ripeness.

maduro, -a adj mature; (fruta) ripe; **de edad madura** middle-aged.

maestro, -a 1 mf teacher; (especialista) master; (músico) maestro. **2** adj **obra maestra** masterpiece.

magdalena f ≃ cupcake.

magia f magic; **por arte de m.** as if by magic.

magnetofón, magnetófono m tape recorder.

magnífico, -a adj magnificent.

mago, -a mf wizard; **los (tres) Reyes Magos** the Three Wise Men, the Three Kings.

magro, -a 1 m (de cerdo) lean meat. **2** adj (sin grasa) lean.

magullar 1 vt to bruise. **2 magullarse** vr to get bruised.

mahonesa f mayonnaise.

maíz m corn.

majestad f majesty.

majo, -a adj (bonito) pretty; nice; fam (simpático) nice.

mal 1 m evil; (daño) harm; (enfermedad) illness. **2** adj bad; **un m. año** a bad year; ver **malo**. **3** adv badly; **menos m. que ...** it's a good job (that) ...; **no está (nada) m.** it is not bad (at all); **te oigo/veo (muy) m.** I can hardly hear/see you.

malabarista mf juggler.

malcriado, -a adj spoiled.

malcriar [29] vt to spoil.

maldad f badness; (acción perversa) evil thing.

maldecir [12] vti to curse.

maldición 1 f curse. **2** interj damnation!

maldito, -a adj fam (molesto) damned; **¡maldita sea!** damn it!

maleducado, -a 1 adj bad-mannered. **2** mf bad-mannered person.

malentendido m misunderstanding.

malestar m (molestia) discomfort; (inquietud) uneasiness.

maleta f suitcase; **hacer la m.** to pack one's case.

maletero m (de coche) trunk.

maletín m briefcase.

maleza f (arbustos) undergrowth; (malas hierbas) weeds pl.

malgastar vt to waste.

malhablado, -a 1 adj foul-mouthed. **2** mf foul-mouthed person.

malhechor, -a mf wrongdoer.

malhumor m bad mood; **de m.** in a bad mood.

malicia f (mala intención) malice; (astucia) cunning; (maldad) badness.

malintencionado, -a 1 adj ill-intentioned. **2** mf ill-intentioned person.

malla f (red) mesh; Am (bañador) swimsuit; (mallas) leotard.

malo, -a adj bad; (persona) (malvado) wicked; (travieso) naughty; (enfermo) ill; (cosa) bad; (perjudicial) harmful; **por las malas** by force; **lo m. es que ...** the problem is that ....

maloliente adj foul-smelling.

malpensado, -a 1 adj nasty-minded. **2** mf nasty-minded person.

malta f malt.

maltratado, -a adj battered.

maltratar vt to ill-treat.

malvado, -a 1 adj evil, wicked. **2** mf villain, evil person.

malvender vt to sell at a loss.

malvivir vi to live badly.

mama f (de mujer) breast; (de animal) teat; (mamá) mum.

mamá f fam mum, mummy.

mamadera f Am feeding bottle.

mamar vt to suck.

mamífero, -a mf mammal.

mampara f screen.

manada f (de vacas, elefantes) herd; (de ovejas) flock; (de lobos, perros) pack; (de leones) pride.

manantial m spring.

mancha f stain.

manchar 1 vt to stain. **2 mancharse** vr to get dirty.

manco, -a 1 adj (de un brazo) one-armed; (de una mano) one-handed. **2** mf (de un brazo) one-armed person; (de una mano) one-handed person.

mancornas fpl Am cufflinks.

mandado m (recado) errand; **hacer un m.** to run an errand.

mandar vt (ordenar) to order; (dirigir) to be in charge of; (ejército) to command; (enviar) to send; **m. (a) por** to send for; **m. algo por correo** to send sth by post.

mandarina f mandarin.

mandíbula f jaw.

mando m (autoridad) command; (control) controls pl; **cuadro o tablero de mandos** dashboard; **m. a distancia** remote control.

manecilla f (de reloj) hand.

manejar 1 vt (máquina, situación) to handle; (dirigir) to manage; Am (coche) to drive. **2 manejarse** vr to manage.

manejo m (uso) handling, use; (de un negocio) management; Am (de un coche) driving; **de fácil m.** easy-to-use.

manera f way, manner; **de cualquier m.** (mal) carelessly; (en cualquier caso) in any case; **de esta m.** in this way; **de ninguna m.** certainly not; **de todas maneras** anyway; **de m. que** so; **de tal m. que** in such a way that; **maneras** manners; **con buenas maneras** politely.

manga f sleeve; (de riego) hose; (vuelta) leg; (en tenis) set; **de m. corta/larga** short-/long-sleeved; **sin mangas** sleeveless; fig **sacarse algo de la m.** to pull sth out of one's hat.

mango m handle.

manguera f hose.

maní m (pl **manises**) Am peanut.

maniático, -a 1 adj fussy. **2** mf fusspot.

manicomio m mental hospital.

manifestación f demonstration; (expresión) expression.

manifestante mf demonstrator.

manifestar [1] **1** vt (declarar) to state; (mostrar) to show. **2 manifestarse** vr (por la calle) to demonstrate.

manilla f (de reloj) hand; Am (palanca) lever.

manillar m handlebar.

maniobra f maneuver.

manipular vt to manipulate; (máquina) to handle.

maniquí m dummy.

manivela f crank.

manjar m delicacy, dish.

mano f hand; **a m.** (sin máquina) by hand; (asequible) at hand; **escrito a m.** hand-written; **hecho a m.** hand-made; **estrechar la m. a algn** to shake hands with sb; **de segunda m.** second-hand; **¡manos a la obra!** hands on the wheel!; **equipaje de m.** hand luggage; **a m. derecha/izquierda** on the right/left(-hand side); **m. de pintura** coat of paint; **m. de obra** labor (force).

manojo m bunch.

manopla f mitten.

manso, -a adj (animal) tame.

manta f blanket.

manteca f fat; **m. de cacao/cacahuete** cocoa/peanut butter.

mantecado m shortcake.

mantel m tablecloth.

mantener [24] **1** vt (conservar) to keep; (entrevista, reunión) to have; (familia) to support; (sostener) to hold up; **m. la línea** to keep in trim. **2 mantenerse** vr (sostenerse) to stand; (sustentarse) to live (**de** on); **mantenerse firme** (perseverar) to hold one's ground.

mantenimiento m (de máquina) maintenance; (alimento) sustenance.

mantequilla f butter.

manto m cloak.

mantón m shawl.

mantuve pt indef de **mantener**.

manual 1 adj manual; **trabajos ma-**

nuales handicrafts. **2** *m (libro)* manual.

manufactura *f* manufacture.

manzana *f* apple; *(de edificios)* block.

manzanilla *f (infusión)* camomile tea; *(vino)* manzanilla.

maña *f (astucia)* cunning; *(habilidad)* skill.

mañana 1 *f (parte de día)* morning; **de m.** early in the morning; **por la m.** in the morning. **2** *m* **el m.** tomorrow. **3** *adv* tomorrow; **¡hasta m.!** see you tomorrow!; **m. por la m.** tomorrow morning; **pasado m.** the day after tomorrow.

mañoso, -a *adj* skillful.

mapa *m* map.

maquillaje *m* make-up.

maquillar 1 *vt* to make up. **2 maquillarse** *vr (ponerse maquillaje)* to put one's make-up on; *(usar maquillaje)* to wear make-up.

máquina *f* machine; **escrito a m.** typewritten; **hecho a m.** machine-made; **m. de afeitar (eléctrica)** (electric) shaver; **m. de coser** sewing machine; **m. de escribir** typewriter; **m. fotográfica** *o* **de fotos** camera.

maquinaria *f* machinery; *(mecanismo)* mechanism.

maquinilla *f* **m. de afeitar** safety razor.

mar *m o f* sea; **en alta m.** on the high seas; *fam* **está la m. de guapa** she's looking really beautiful; **llover a mares** to rain cats and dogs.

maratón *m o f* marathon.

maravilla *f* marvel; **de m.** wonderfully; **¡qué m. de película!** what a wonderful film!

maravilloso, -a *adj* wonderful, marvellous.

marca *f* mark; *(de producto)* brand; *(récord)* record; **m. registrada** registered trademark.

marcador *m (tablero)* scoreboard; *(persona)* scorer; *(rotulador)* felt-tip pen; *Méx (fluorescente)* highlighter pen.

marcar [44] *vt* to mark; *(número)* to dial; *(indicar)* to indicate; *(gol, puntos)* to score; *(cabello)* to set.

marcha *f* march; *(de coche)* gear; **hacer algo sobre la m.** to do sth as one goes along; **estar en m.** *(vehículo)* to be in motion; *(máquina)* to be working; **poner en m.** to start; **m. atrás** reverse (gear).

marchar 1 *vi (ir)* to walk; *(aparato)* to be on; **m. bien** *(negocio)* to be going well. **2 marcharse** to leave, to go away.

marchitar *vt*, **marchitarse** *vr* to shrivel, to wither.

marco *m (de cuadro etc)* frame; *(moneda)* mark.

marea *f* tide; **m. alta/baja** high/low tide; **m. negra** oil slick.

marear 1 *vt* to make sick; *(en el mar)* to make seasick; *(en un avión)* to make airsick; *(en un coche)* to make carsick; *(aturdir)* to make dizzy; *fam (fastidiar)* to annoy. **2 marearse** *vr* to get sick/seasick/airsick/carsick; *(quedar aturdido)* to get dizzy.

marejada *f* swell.

mareo *m (náusea)* sickness; *(en el mar)* seasickness; *(en un avión)* airsickness; *(en un coche)* carsickness; *(aturdimiento)* dizziness.

marfil *m* ivory.

margarina *f* margarine.

margarita *f* daisy.

margen *m* edge; *(de folio)* margin; *fig* **mantenerse al m.** not to get involved.

marginado, -a 1 *adj* excluded. **2** *mf* dropout.

marginar *vt (a una persona)* to exclude.

marido *m* husband.

marihuana, marijuana, mariguana *f* marijuana.

marinero *m* sailor.

marioneta *f* marionette.

mariposa *f* butterfly.

mariquita *f* ladybird.

marisco *m* shellfish; **mariscos** seafood.

marítimo, -a *adj* maritime; **paseo m.** promenade.

mármol *m* marble.

marqués *m* marquis.

marrano, -a 1 *adj (sucio)* filthy. **2** *mf (animal)* pig; *fam* slob.

marrón *adj & m* brown.

marroquí *adj & mf (pl* **marroquíes)** Moroccan.

Marte *m* Mars.

martes *m inv* Tuesday.

martillo *m* hammer.

mártir *mf* martyr.

marzo *m* March.

más 1 *adv* more; **m. gente de la que esperas** more people than you're expecting; **m. de** more than, over; **cada día o vez m.** more and more; **es m.** what's more, furthermore; **lo m. posible** as much as possible; **m. bien** rather; **m. o menos** more or less; **m. aún** even more; **¿qué m. da?** what's the difference? ▪ *(comparativo)* **es m. alta/inteligente que yo** she's taller/more intelligent than me. ▪ *(superlativo)* **el m. bonito/caro** the prettiest/most expensive. ▪ *(exclamación)* **¡qué casa m. bonita!** what a lovely house!; **¡está m. guapa!** she looks so beautiful! ▪ *(después de pron interr e indef)* **else; ¿algo m.?** anything else?; **no, nada m.** no, nothing else; **¿quién m.?** who else?; **nadie/alguien m.** nobody/somebody else. ▪ **por m. +** *(adj/adv +) que + subj* however (much); **por m. fuerte que sea** however strong he may be. **2** *m inv* **los/las m.** most people. **3** *prep (en sumas)* plus.

masa *f* mass; *(de cosas)* bulk; *(de pan etc)* dough; **medios de comunicación de masas** mass media.

masaje *m* massage; **dar masaje(s) (a)** to massage.

mascar [44] *vti* to chew.

máscara *f* mask; **m. de gas** gas mask.

mascarilla *f* mask; **m. de oxígeno** oxygen mask; *(cosmética)* face pack.

mascota *f* mascot.

masculino, -a *adj male; (para hombre)* men's; *(género)* masculine.

máster *m* master's degree.

masticar [44] *vt* to chew.

mástil *m* mast.

mastín *m* mastiff.

mata *f (matorral)* shrub.

matador *m* matador, bullfighter.

matanza *f* slaughter.

matar *vt* to kill.

mate¹ *adj (sin brillo)* matt.

mate² *m* mate; **jaque m.** checkmate.

matemática *f*, **matemáticas** *fpl* mathematics *sing*.

materia *f* matter; *(tema)* question; *(asignatura)* subject; **m. prima** raw material; **índice de materias** table of contents.

material 1 *adj* material. **2** *m* material; **m. escolar/de construcción** teaching/building materials *pl*; **m. de oficina** office equipment.

materialmente *adv* physically.

maternal *adj* maternal.

maternidad *f* maternity, motherhood.

materno, -a *adj* maternal; **abuelo m.** maternal grandfather; **lengua materna** mother tongue.

matiz *m (de color)* shade.

matizar [40] *vt* to clarify, to explain.

matorral *m* thicket.

matrero, -a *mf Am (bandolero)* bandit.

matrícula *f* registration; *(de coche) (número)* registration number; *(placa)* license plate.

matricular *vt*, **matricularse** *vr* to register.

matrimonio *m* marriage; *(pareja casada)* married couple; **m. civil/religioso** civil/church wedding; **contraer m.** to marry; **cama de m.** double bed.

matriz *f* matrix; *(útero)* womb.

matrona *f (comadrona)* midwife.

maullar *vi* to mew.

maxilar 1 *adj* maxillary. **2** *m* jaw.

máximo, -a 1 adj maximum. **2** m maximum; **al m.** to the utmost; **como m.** (como mucho) at the most; (lo más tarde) at the latest.

mayo m May.

mayonesa f mayonnaise.

mayor adj (comparativo) (tamaño) bigger (**que** than); (edad) older, elder; (superlativo) (tamaño) biggest; (edad) oldest, eldest; (adulto) grown-up; (maduro) mature; (principal) major; **la m. parte** the majority; **la m. parte de las veces** most often; **ser m. de edad** to be of age; **al por m.** wholesale.

mayoría f majority; **la m. de los niños** most children; **m. de edad** majority.

mayorista 1 adj wholesale. **2** mf wholesaler; **precios de m.** wholesale prices.

mayoritario, -a adj majority; **un gobierno m.** a majority government.

mayúscula f capital letter.

mazapán m marzipan.

me pron pers (objeto directo) me; **no me mires** don't look at me. ▪ (objeto indirecto) me, to me, for me; **¿me das un caramelo?** will you give me a sweet?; **me lo dio** he gave it to me. ▪ (pron reflexivo) myself; **me he cortado** I've cut myself; **me voy/muero** (no se traduce) I'm off/dying.

mecánico, -a 1 adj mechanical. **2** mf mechanic.

mecanismo m mechanism.

mecanografía f typing.

mecanografiar [29] vt to type.

mecanógrafo, -a mf typist.

mecedora f rocking chair.

mecer [49] **1** vt to rock. **2 mecerse** vr to rock.

mecha f (de vela) wick; (de pelo) streak.

mechero m (cigarette) lighter.

mechón m (de pelo) lock; (de lana) tuft.

medalla f medal.

media f stocking; Am (calcetín) sock; (promedio) average; **a medias** (incompleto) unfinished; (entre dos) half and half.

medialuna f Am (pasta) croissant.

mediano, -a adj (tamaña) medium-sized.

medianoche f midnight.

mediante prep by means of.

medicación f medication.

medicamento m medicine.

medicina f medicine; **estudiante de m.** medical student.

médico, -a 1 mf doctor; **m. de cabecera** family doctor. **2** adj medical.

medida f measure; (dimensión) measurement; **a (la) m.** (ropa) made-to-measure; **a m. que avanzaba** as he advanced; **adoptar o tomar medidas** to take steps.

medieval adj medieval.

medio, -a 1 adj half; (intermedio) middle; (normal) average; **una hora y media** an hour and a half; **a media mañana/tarde** in the middle of the morning/afternoon; **clase media** middle class; **salario m.** average wage. **2** adv half; **está m. muerta** she is half dead. **3** m (mitad) half; (centro) middle; **en m. (de)** (en el centro) in the middle (of); (entre dos) in between; **medios de transporte** means of transport; **por m. de** by means of; **medios de comunicación** (mass) media; **m. ambiente** environment.

medioambiental adj environmental.

mediocre adj mediocre.

mediodía m (hora exacta) midday; (período aproximado) early afternoon; (sur) south.

medir [6] **1** vt to measure. **2** vi to measure; **mide 2 metros** he is 2 meters tall; **mide dos metros de alto/ancho/largo** it is two meters high/wide/long.

médula f marrow; **m. ósea** bone marrow.

megabyte m megabyte.

megafonía f public-address system.

mejicano, -a adj & mf Mexican.

mejilla f cheek.

mejillón m mussel.

mejor 1 adj (comparativo) better (**que** than); (superlativo) best; **tu m. amiga** your best friend; **lo m.** the best thing. **2** adv (comparativo) better (**que** than); (superlativo) best; **cada vez m.** better and better; **m. dicho** or rather; **es el que m. canta** he is the one who sings the best; **a lo m.** (quizás) perhaps; (ojalá) hopefully.

mejora f improvement.

mejorar 1 vti to improve. **2 mejorarse** vr to get better; **¡que te mejores!** get well soon!

melancolía f melancholy.

melancólico, -a adj melancholic.

melena f (head of) hair; (de león) mane.

mellado, -a adj (sin dientes) gap-toothed.

mellizo, -a adj & mf twin.

melocotón m peach.

melodía f tune.

melón m melon.

membrana f membrane.

membrillo m quince.

memoria f memory; (informe) report; **memorias** (biografía) memoirs; **aprender/saber algo de m.** to learn/know sth by heart.

memorizar [40] vt to memorize.

mencionar vt to mention.

mendigo, -a mf beggar.

mendrugo m crust (of stale bread).

menear 1 vt to shake; (cola) to wag. **2 menearse** vr to shake.

menestra f vegetable stew.

menguar [45] vti to diminish.

menopausia f menopause.

menor 1 adj (comparativo) (de tamaño) smaller (**que** than); (de edad) younger (**que** than); (superlativo) (de tamaño) smallest; (de intensidad) least, slightest; (de edad) youngest;

ser m. de edad to be a minor, to be under age; **al por m.** retail. **2** mf minor.

menos 1 adj (comparativo) (con singular) less; (con plural) fewer; **m. dinero/leche/tiempo que** less money/milk/time than; **m. libros que** fewer books than; **tiene m. años de lo que parece** he's younger than he looks; (superlativo) **fui el que perdí m. dinero** I lost the least money. **2** adv **m. de** (con singular) less than; (con plural) fewer than, less than. ▪ (superlativo) (con singular) least; **el m. inteligente de la clase** the least intelligent boy in the class. ▪ (con plural) the fewest; **ayer fue cuando vinieron m. personas** yesterday was when the fewest people came. ▪ (locuciones) **a m. que** + subj unless; **al o por lo m.** at least; **echar a algn de m.** to miss sb; **¡m. mal!** just as well!; **ni mucho m.** far from it. **3** prep except; (en restas) minus.

menosprecio m contempt.

mensaje m message.

mensajería f **m. instantánea** instant messaging.

mensajero, -a mf messenger.

mensual adj monthly.

mensualidad f (pago) monthly payment; (sueldo) monthly salary o wage.

menta f mint; (licor) crème de menthe.

mental adj mental.

mentalidad f mentality; **de m. abierta/cerrada** open-/narrow-minded.

mentalizar [40] **1** vt (concienciar) to make aware. **2 mentalizarse** vr (concienciarse) to become aware; (hacerse a la idea) to come to terms (a with).

mente f mind.

mentir [5] vi to lie.

mentira f lie.

mentón m chin.

menú m menu.

menudo, -a 1 adj minute; **¡m. lío/ susto!** what a mess/fright! **2** adv **a m.** often.

meñique adj & m (dedo) m. little finger.

mercado m market; **M. Común** Common Market.

mercadotecnia f marketing.

mercancías fpl goods.

mercantil adj commercial.

merecer [33] vt **1** to deserve; (uso impers) **no merece la pena hacerlo** it's not worthwhile doing it. **2 merecerse** vr to deserve.

merecido, -a 1 adj deserved; **lo tiene m.** (castigo) it serves him right. **2** m just deserts pl.

merendar [1] vt to have for tea. **2** vi to have tea.

merendero m (en el campo) picnic spot.

merezco indic pres de **merecer**.

meridional adj southern.

merienda f afternoon snack.

mérito m merit.

merluza f hake.

mermelada f jam; (de agrios) marmalade; **m. de fresa** strawberry jam; **m. de naranja** orange marmalade.

mes m month; **el m. pasado/que viene** last/next month.

mesa f table; (de despacho etc) desk; **poner/recoger la m.** to set/clear the table.

mesada f Am (dinero) monthly payment; RP (para adolescentes) (monthly) allowance.

mesero, -a mf CAm, Col, Méx (hombre) waiter; (mujer) waitress.

meseta f plateau.

mesilla f **m. de noche** bedside table.

mesón m old-style tavern.

meta f (objetivo, portería) goal; (de carrera) finishing line.

metal m metal.

metálico, -a 1 adj metallic. **2** m **pagar en m.** to pay (in) cash.

meteorológico, -a adj meteorological; **parte m.** weather report.

meter 1 vt (poner) to put (en in); (comprometer) to involve (en in). **2 meterse** vr (entrar) to go/come in; (entrometerse) to meddle; (estar) **¿dónde te habías metido?** where have you been (all this time)?; **meterse con algn** (en broma) to get at sb.

método m method.

metralleta f submachine-gun.

métrico, -a adj metric; **sistema m.** metric system.

metro m meter; (tren) subway.

mexicano, -a adj & mf Mexican.

mezcla f (producto) mixture; (acción) mixing.

mezclar 1 vt to mix; (involucrar) to involve. **2 mezclarse** vr (cosas) to get mixed up; (gente) to mingle.

mezquino, -a adj (tacaño) mean; (escaso) miserable.

mezquita f mosque.

mi adj my; **mis cosas/libros** my things/books.

mí pron pers me; **a mí me dio tres** he gave me three; **compra otro para mí** buy one for me too; **por mí mismo** by myself.

mía adj & pron pos f ver **mío**.

microbús m minibus.

micrófono m microphone.

microonda f **un (horno) microondas** a microwave (oven).

microprocesador m microprocessor.

miedo m (pavor) fear; (temor) apprehension; **una película de m.** a horror film; **tener m. de algo/algn** to be afraid of sth/sb.

miedoso, -a adj fearful.

miel f honey.

miembro m (socio) member; (de cuerpo) limb.

mientras 1 conj while; (cuanto) **m. más/menos ...** the more/less .... **2** adv **m. (tanto)** meanwhile, in the meantime.

miércoles m inv Wednesday; **M. de Ceniza** Ash Wednesday.

miga f (de pan etc) crumb.

mil adj & m thousand; **m. pesos** a o one thousand pesos.

milagro m miracle.

milagroso, -a adj miraculous.

milésimo, -a adj & mf thousandth.

mili f military service; **hacer la m.** to do one's military service.

milímetro m millimeter.

militar 1 adj military. **2** mf soldier.

milla f mile.

millar m thousand.

millón m million.

millonario, -a adj & mf millionaire.

mimar vt to spoil.

mimbre f wicker.

mina f mine; (de lápiz) lead.

mineral 1 adj mineral. **2** m ore.

minero, -a 1 mf miner. **2** adj mining.

miniatura f miniature.

minifalda f miniskirt.

mínimo, -a 1 adj (muy pequeño) minute; (en matemáticas) minimum. **2** m minimum; **como m.** at least.

ministerio m department.

ministro, -a mf minister; **primer m.** Prime Minister.

minoría f minority; **m. de edad** minority.

minúsculo, -a adj minute; **letra minúscula** small letter.

minusválido, -a 1 adj disabled. **2** mf disabled person.

minuto m minute.

mío, -a 1 adj pos of mine; **un amigo m.** a friend of mine; **no es asunto m.** it is none of my business. **2** pron pos mine.

miope mf short-sighted person.

mirada f look; **lanzar** o **echar una m. a** to glance at.

mirar 1 vt to look at; (observar) to watch; (cuidar) **mira que no le pase nada** see that nothing happens to him. **2** vi **la casa mira al norte** the house faces north.

mirlo m blackbird.

misa f mass.

miserable adj (mezquino) (perso-

na) despicable; (sueldo etc) miserable; (pobre) wretched.

miseria f (pobreza extrema) extreme poverty; (insignificancia) pittance; (tacañería) meanness.

misión f mission.

mismo, -a 1 adj same; (uso enfático) **yo m.** I myself; **por eso m.** that is why; **por uno** o **sí m.** by oneself; **aquí m.** right here. **2** pron same; **es el m. de ayer** it's the same one as yesterday; **lo m.** the same (thing); **dar** o **ser lo m.** to make no difference. **3** adv **así m.** likewise.

misterio m mystery.

mitad f half; (centro) middle; **a m. de camino** half-way there; **a m. de precio** half price; **en la m. del primer acto** half-way through the first act.

mitote m Am uproar.

mixto adj mixed.

mobiliario m furniture.

moca m mocha.

mochila f rucksack.

moco m snot; **sonarse los mocos** to blow one's nose.

mocoso, -a mf fam brat.

moda f fashion; **a la m., de m.** in fashion; **pasado de m.** old-fashioned.

modales mpl manners.

modelo 1 adj inv & m model. **2** mf (fashion) model; **desfile de modelos** fashion show.

módem m modem.

moderado, -a adj moderate.

modernizar [40] vt, **modernizarse** vr to modernize.

moderno, -a adj modern.

modesto, -a adj modest.

modificar [44] vt to modify.

modisto, -a mf fashion designer.

modo m (manera) way, manner; (en lingüística) mood; **m. de empleo** instructions for use; **modos** manners.

mofarse vr to laugh (**de** at).

moflete m chubby cheek.

mohoso, -a adj moldy; (oxidado) rusty.

mojar 1 *vt* to wet; *(humedecer)* to dampen. **2 mojarse** *vr* to get wet.
molde *m* mold.
moldeador *m (de pelo)* wave.
mole *f* mass.
moler [4] *vt* to grind.
molestar 1 *vt (incomodar)* to disturb; *(causar malestar)* to hurt; **¿le molestaría esperar fuera?** would you mind waiting outside? **2 molestarse** *vr (tomarse la molestia)* to bother; *(ofenderse)* to take offense.
molestia *f* bother; *(dolor)* slight pain.
molesto, -a *adj (irritante)* annoying; **estar m. con algn** *(enfadado)* to be annoyed with sb.
molino *m* mill; **m. de viento** windmill.
momentáneo, -a *adj* momentary.
momento *m (instante)* moment; *(periodo)* time; **al m.** at once; **de m.** for the time being; **en cualquier m.** at any time.
monasterio *m* monastery.
mondar 1 *vt* to peel. **2 mondarse** *vr fam* **mondarse (de risa)** to laugh one's head off.
moneda *f (pieza)* coin; *(dinero)* currency; **m. suelta** small change.
monedero *m* purse.
monetario, -a *adj* monetary.
monigote *m (persona)* wimp; *(dibujo)* rough sketch (of a person).
monitor, -a *mf* monitor; *(profesor)* instructor.
monja *f* nun.
monje *m* monk.
mono, -a 1 *m* monkey; *(prenda) (de trabajo)* overalls *pl*; *(de vestir)* catsuit. **2** *adj fam (bonito)* pretty.
monopolio *m* monopoly.
monótono, -a *adj* monotonous.
monstruo *m* monster; *(genio)* genius.
montaje *m (instalación)* fitting; *(ensamblaje)* assembling.
montaña *f* mountain; **m. rusa** big dipper.

montañismo *m* mountaineering.
montañoso, -a *adj* mountainous.
montar 1 *vi (en bici, a caballo)* to ride; *(en coche, tren)* to travel; *(subirse)* to get in. **2** *vt (colocar)* to put on; *(máquina etc)* to assemble; *(negocio)* to set up. **3 montarse** *vr (subirse)* to get on; *(en coche)* to get in.
monte *m (montaña)* mountain; *(con nombre propio)* mount.
montón *m* heap; **un m. de** a load of.
montura *f (cabalgadura)* mount; *(de gafas)* frame.
monumento *m* monument.
moño *m* bun.
moqueta *f* fitted carpet.
mora *f (zarzamora)* blackberry.
morado, -a *adj & m* purple.
moral 1 *adj* moral. **2** *f (ética)* morals *pl*; *(ánimo)* morale.
morboso, -a *adj (malsano)* morbid.
morcilla *f* black pudding.
mordaz *adj* biting.
morder [4] *vt* to bite.
mordida *f Am (soborno)* bribe.
mordisco *m* bite.
moreno, -a 1 *adj (pelo)* dark-haired; *(piel)* dark-skinned; *(bronceado)* tanned; **ponerse m.** to get a suntan; **pan/azúcar m.** brown bread/sugar. **2** *mf (persona) (de pelo)* dark-haired person; *(mujer)* brunette; *(de piel)* dark-skinned person.
morgue *f Am* morgue.
moribundo, -a 1 *adj* moribund. **2** *mf* dying person.
morir [7] **1** *vi* to die; **m. de frío/hambre/cáncer** to die of cold/hunger/cancer. **2 morirse** *vr* to die; **morirse de hambre** to starve to death; *fig* to be starving; **morirse de aburrimiento** to be bored to death; **morirse de risa** to die laughing.
moro, -a *adj & mf* Moor; *fam (musulmán)* Muslim; *(árabe)* Arab.
morocho, -a *adj Am (moreno)* swarthy.
morro *m (hocico)* snout.

mortadela f mortadella.

mortal adj mortal; (mortífero) fatal; **un accidente m.** a fatal accident.

mortalidad f mortality; **índice de m.** death rate.

mortandad f death toll.

mosca f fly; fam **estar m.** (suspicaz) to be suspicious; fam **por si las moscas** just in case.

moscardón m blowfly.

mosquitero m (red) mosquito net.

mosquito m mosquito.

mostaza f mustard.

mostrador m (de tienda) counter; (de bar) bar.

mostrar 1 vt to show. **2 mostrarse** vr to be; **se mostró muy comprensiva** she was very understanding.

mota f speck.

mote[1] m (apodo) nickname.

mote[2] m Am boiled salted corn.

motín m (amotinamiento) mutiny; (disturbio) riot.

motivo m (causa) reason; **motivos** grounds; **con m. de** on the occasion of; **sin m.** for no reason at all.

moto f motorbike.

motocicleta f motorbike.

motociclista mf motorcyclist.

motoneta f Am (motor) scooter.

motor m (grande) engine; (pequeño) motor; **m. de reacción** jet engine.

motora f motorboat.

motorista mf motorcyclist.

mover [4] **1** vt to move; (hacer funcionar) to drive. **2 moverse** vr to move.

móvil 1 adj mobile; **teléfono m.** mobile phone; **unidad m.** (de radio, TV) outside broadcast unit. **2** m (de delito) motive; (teléfono) mobile.

movimiento m movement; (en física) motion; (actividad) activity; **(poner algo) en m.** (to set sth) in motion.

moza f young girl.

mozo m boy; (de estación) porter; (de hotel) bellboy.

MP3 m abr de **MPEG1 Audio Layer** **reproductor de M.** MP3 player.

mucamo, -a mf Am servant.

muchacha f girl.

muchacho m boy.

muchedumbre f crowd.

mucho, -a 1 adj sing lots of; (en frases negativas e interrogativas) much; **hay m. tonto suelto** there are lots of idiots around; **no tengo m. dinero** I don't have much money; **¿bebes m. café?** do you drink a lot of coffee?; **m. tiempo** a long time; **tengo m. sueño/mucha sed** I am very sleepy/thirsty. ▪ **muchos, -as** lots of; (en frases negativas e interrogativas) many; **no hay muchas chicas** there aren't many girls; **¿tienes muchos amigos?** do you have many friends?; **tiene muchos años** he is very old. **2** pron lots; **¿cuánta leche queda? — mucha** how much milk is there left? — a lot; **muchos, -as** lots; **¿cuántos libros tienes? — muchos** how many books have you got? — lots; **muchos creemos que ...** many of us believe that .... **3** adv a lot; **lo siento m.** I'm very sorry; **como m.** at the most; **con m.** by far; **m. antes/después** long before/after; **¡ni m. menos!** no way!; **por m. (que)** + subj however much; **hace m. que no viene por aquí** he has not been to see us for a long time.

mudanza f move; **estar de m.** to be moving; **camión de m.** removal van.

mudar 1 vt (ropa) to change; (plumas, pelo) to molt; (de piel) to shed. **2 mudarse** vr **mudarse de casa/ropa** to move house/to change one's clothes.

mudo, -a 1 adj (que no habla) dumb. **2** mf mute.

mueble m piece of furniture; **muebles** furniture sing; **con/sin muebles** furnished/unfurnished.

muela f molar; **dolor de muelas** toothache; **m. del juicio** wisdom tooth.

muelle[1] m spring.

muelle² m *(en puerto)* dock.

muerte f death; **dar m. a algn** to kill sb; **odiar a algn a m.** to loathe sb; **un susto de m.** the fright of one's life.

muerto, -a 1 adj dead; **m. de hambre** starving; **m. de frío** frozen to death; **m. de miedo** scared stiff; **m. de risa** laughing one's head off; **(en) punto m.** (in) neutral. **2** mf *(difunto)* dead person; **hacerse el m.** to pretend to be dead.

muestra f *(espécimen)* sample; *(modelo a copiar)* model; *(prueba, señal)* sign; **dar muestras de** to show signs of; **m. de cariño/respeto** token of affection/respect.

mugido m *(de vaca)* moo; *(de toro)* bellow.

mugre f filth.

mugriento, -a adj filthy.

mujer f woman; *(esposa)* wife; **m. de la limpieza** cleaning lady; **m. de su casa** houseproud woman.

muleta f *(prótesis)* crutch; *(de torero)* muleta.

mulo, -a mf mule.

multa f fine; *(de tráfico)* ticket.

multicopista f duplicator.

multicultural adj multicultural.

multinacional adj & f multinational.

múltiple adj multiple.

multiplicación f multiplication.

multiplicar [44] **1** vti to multiply (**por** by). **2 multiplicarse** vr to multiply.

multisalas f multiplex.

multitud f *(de personas)* crowd; *(de cosas)* multitude.

mundial 1 adj worldwide; **campeón m.** world champion; **de fama m.** world-famous. **2** m world championship.

mundialmente adv **m. famoso** world-famous.

mundo m world; **todo el m.** everyone.

munición f ammunition.

municipal adj municipal; *(policía)* local.

municipio m municipality; *(ayuntamiento)* town council.

muñeca f wrist; *(juguete, muchacha)* doll.

muñeco m *(juguete)* (little) boy doll; **m. de trapo** rag doll; **m. de nieve** snowman.

murciélago m bat.

murmullo m murmur.

murmurar vi *(criticar)* to gossip; *(susurrar)* to whisper; *(producir murmullo)* to murmur.

muro m wall.

músculo m muscle.

musculoso, -a adj muscular.

museo m museum.

musgo m moss.

música f music; **m. clásica** classical music.

musical adj musical.

músico, -a mf musician.

muslo m thigh.

musulmán, -ana adj & mf Muslim.

mutilado, -a mf disabled person.

mutuo, -a adj mutual.

muy adv very; **m. bueno/malo** very good/bad; **¡m. bien!** very good!; **M. señor mío** Dear Sir; **m. de mañana/noche** very early/late.

N

nº abr de **número** number, no.

nabo m turnip.

nácar m mother-of-pearl.

nacer [60] vi to be born; *(pelo)* to begin to grow; *(río)* to rise; **nací en Montoro** I was born in Montoro.

nacimiento m birth; *(de río)* source; *(belén)* Nativity scene; **lugar de n.** place of birth.

nación f nation; **las Naciones Unidas** the United Nations.

nacional 1 adj national; (producto, mercado, vuelo) domestic. **2** mf national.

nacionalidad f nationality.

nada 1 pron nothing; (con verbo) not … anything, nothing; **no sé n.** I don't know anything; **yo no digo n.** I'm saying nothing, I'm not saying anything; **más que n.** more than anything; **sin decir n.** without saying anything; **casi n.** hardly anything; **gracias — de n.** thanks — don't mention it; **para n.** not at all; **como si n.** just like that; **n. de eso** nothing of the kind; **n. de n.** nothing at all; **n. más verla** as soon as he saw her. **2** adv not at all; **no me gusta n.** I don't like it at all.

nadar vi to swim; **n. a braza** to do the breaststroke.

nadador, -a mf swimmer.

nadie pron no one, nobody; (con verbo) not … anyone o anybody; **no conozco a n.** I don't know anyone o anybody; **más que n.** more than anyone; **sin decírselo a n.** without telling anyone; **casi n.** hardly anyone.

nafta f Am (gasolina) gasoline.

nailon m nylon; **medias de n.** nylons.

naipe m playing card.

nalga f buttock.

nana f lullaby.

naranja 1 f orange. **2** adj & m (color) orange.

naranjada f orangeade.

naranjo m orange tree.

narcotraficante mf drug trafficker.

narcotráfico m drug trafficking.

nariz f nose; **narices** nose sing, fam **meter las narices en algo** to poke one's nose into sth.

nata f cream; (de leche hervida) skin; **n. batida/montada** whipped cream.

natación f swimming.

natal adj mi país n. my native country; **su pueblo n.** his home town.

natillas fpl custard sing.

nativo, -a adj & mf native.

nato, -a adj born.

natural 1 adj natural; (fruta, flor) fresh; (bebida) at room temperature; **de tamaño n.** life-size. **2** mf native.

naturaleza f nature; **en plena n.** in unspoilt countryside.

naturalidad f (sencillez) naturalness; (espontaneidad) ease; **con n.** straightforwardly.

naturalizar [40] **1** vt to naturalize. **2** **naturalizarse** vr to become naturalized.

naturalmente adv naturally; **¡n.!** of course!

naturismo m naturism.

naufragar [42] vi (barco) to be wrecked.

naufragio m shipwreck.

náusea f nausea; **me da n.** it makes me sick; **sentir náuseas** to feel sick.

náutico, -a adj nautical.

navaja f (cuchillo) penknife; **n. de afeitar** razor.

nave f ship; (de iglesia) nave; **n. (espacial)** spaceship; **n. industrial** plant.

navegable adj navigable.

navegar [42] vi to sail; (en avión) to navigate, to fly; **n. por Internet** to surf the Net.

Navidad(es) f(pl) Christmas; **árbol de Navidad** Christmas tree; **Feliz Navidad/Felices Navidades** Merry Christmas.

navideño, -a adj Christmas.

navío m ship.

neblina f mist.

necesario, -a adj necessary; **es n. hacerlo** it has to be done; **es n. que vayas** you must go; **no es n. que vayas** it's not necessary for you to go; **si fuera n.** if need be.

neceser m make-up bag.

necesidad f need; **por n.** of necessity; **tener n. de** to need.

necesitado, -a 1 adj (pobre) needy, poor; **n. de** in need of. **2** mpl **los necesitados** the needy.

necesitar vt to need.

necio, -a 1 adj silly. **2** mf fool.

nectarina f nectarine.

neerlandés, -esa 1 adj Dutch. **2** mf (hombre) Dutchman; (mujer) Dutchwoman; **los neerlandeses** the Dutch. **3** m (idioma) Dutch.

nefasto, -a adj (perjudicial) harmful; (funesto) ill-fated.

negación f negation; (negativa) denial; (gramatical) negative.

negar [1] **1** vt to deny; (rechazar) to refuse; **negó haberlo robado** he denied stealing it; **le negaron la beca** they refused him the grant. **2 negarse** vr to refuse (**a** to).

negativo, -a adj & m negative.

negligencia f negligence.

negociación f negotiation.

negociante mf dealer; (hombre) businessman; (mujer) businesswoman.

negociar [43] **1** vt to negotiate. **2** vi (comerciar) to do business.

negocio m business; (transacción) deal; (asunto) affair; **hombre de negocios** businessman; **mujer de negocios** businesswoman.

negro, -a 1 adj black; **verlo todo n.** to be very pessimistic. **2** mf (hombre) black; (mujer) black (woman); fam **trabajar como un n.** to work like a dog. **3** m (color) black.

nene, -a mf (niño) baby boy; (niña) baby girl.

neocelandés, -esa 1 adj New Zealand. **2** mf New Zealander.

neoyorkino, -a 1 adj New York. **2** mf New Yorker.

neozelandés, -esa adj & mf = **neocelandés**.

nervio m nerve; (de la carne) sinew; **nervios** nerves; **ataque de nervios** a fit of hysterics; **ser un manojo de nervios** to be a bundle of nerves.

nervioso, -a adj nervous; **poner n. a algn** to get on sb's nerves.

neto, -a adj (peso, cantidad) net.

neumático, -a 1 adj pneumatic. **2** m tire; **n. de recambio** spare tire.

neumonía f pneumonia.

neurótico, -a adj & mf neurotic.

neutral adj neutral.

neutro, -a adj (imparcial) neutral; (género) neuter.

nevada f snowfall.

nevar [1] v impers to snow.

nevera f (frigorífico) fridge; (portátil) cool box.

ni conj no ... ni, ni ... ni neither ... nor, not ... or; **ni se te ocurra** don't even think about it.

nicaragüense, nicaragüeño, -a adj & mf Nicaraguan.

nido m nest.

niebla f fog; **hay mucha n.** it is very foggy.

nieto, -a mf (niño) grandson; (niña) granddaughter; **mis nietos** my grandchildren.

nieve f snow.

nigeriano, -a adj & mf Nigerian.

ningún adj (delante de m sing) ver **ninguno**.

ninguno, -a 1 adj (con verbo) not ... any; **en ninguna parte** nowhere; **de ningún modo** no way. **2** pron (persona) nobody, no one; **n. de los dos** neither of the two; **n. de ellos** none of them; (cosa) not ... any of them; (enfático) none of them; **n. me gusta** I don't like any of them; **no vi n.** I saw none of them.

niña f girl; (pupila) pupil.

niñera f nanny.

niñez f childhood.

niño, -a mf child; (bebé) baby; (muchacho) (small) boy; (muchacha) (little) girl; **de n.** as a child; **niños** children.

nitrógeno m nitrogen.

nivel m (altura) level; (categoría) standard; **a n. del mar** at sea level; **n. de vida** standard of living.

no adv not; (como respuesta) no; **no vi a nadie** I did not see anyone, I didn't see anyone; **aún no** not yet; **ya no** no longer; **¿por qué no?** why not?; **no fumar/aparcar** *(en letrero)* no smoking/parking; **no sea que +** *subj* in case; **es rubia, ¿no?** she's blonde, isn't she?; **llegaron anoche, ¿no?** they arrived yesterday, didn't they?

noble 1 *adj* noble. **2** *mf (hombre)* nobleman; *(mujer)* noblewoman; **los nobles** the nobility *sing.*

noche *f* evening; *(después de las diez)* night; **de n., por la n.** at night; **esta n.** tonight; **mañana por la n.** tomorrow night/evening; **buenas noches** *(saludo)* good evening; *(despedida)* good night.

nochebuena *f* Christmas Eve.

nochevieja *f* New Year's Eve.

nocturno, -a *adj* night; **clases nocturnas** evening classes.

nombrar *vt* to name.

nombre *m* name; *(sustantivo)* noun; **n. de pila** Christian name; **n. y apellidos** full name; **n. propio** proper noun.

nordeste *adj & m* northeast.

nórdico, -a 1 *adj (del norte)* northern; *(escandinavo)* Nordic. **2** *mf* Nordic person.

noreste *adj & m* northeast.

norma *f* norm.

normal *adj* normal; **lo n.** the usual.

normalizar [40] **1** *vt* to normalize. **2 normalizarse** *vr* to return to normal.

noroeste *adj & m* northwest.

norte *m* north; **al n. de** to the north of.

norteafricano, -a *adj & mf* North African.

norteamericano, -a *adj & mf* (North) American.

noruego, -a 1 *adj* Norwegian. **2** *mf* Norwegian. **3** *m (idioma)* Norwegian.

nos *pron pers* us; *(con verbo reflexivo)* ourselves; *(con verbo recíproco)* each other; **n. hemos divertido mucho** we enjoyed ourselves a lot; **n. queremos mucho** we love each other very much.

nosotros, -as *pron pers (sujeto)* we; *(complemento)* us; **con n.** with us.

nostalgia *f* nostalgia; *(morriña)* homesickness.

nota *f* note; *(de examen)* mark, grade; **sacar buenas notas** to get good grades.

notable 1 *adj (apreciable)* noticeable; *(digno de notar)* outstanding. **2** *m (nota)* very good.

notar 1 *vt (percibir)* to notice. **2 notarse** *vr (percibirse)* to show; **no se nota** it doesn't show.

notaría *f (despacho)* notary's office.

notario, -a *mf* notary (public).

noticia *f* news *sing*; **una n.** a piece of news; **una buena n.** (some) good news.

noticiario, *Am* **noticiero** *m* television news *sing.*

notificar [44] *vt* to notify.

novato, -a 1 *adj (persona)* inexperienced. **2** *mf (principiante)* novice.

novecientos, -as *adj & m* nine hundred.

novedad *f (cosa nueva)* novelty; *(cambio)* change; *(cualidad)* newness.

novela *f* novel; *(corta)* story.

novelista *mf* novelist.

noveno, -a *adj & m* ninth; **novena parte** ninth.

noventa *adj & m inv* ninety.

novia *f (amiga)* girlfriend; *(prometida)* fiancée; *(en boda)* bride.

noviembre *m* November.

novillada *f* bullfight with young bulls.

novillo, -a *mf (toro)* young bull; *(vaca)* young cow; **hacer novillos** to play hooky.

novio *m (amigo)* boyfriend; *(prometido)* fiancé; *(en boda)* bridegroom; **los novios** the bride and groom.

nube *f* cloud.

nublado, -a *adj* cloudy, overcast.

nublarse *vr* to cloud over.

nuboso, -a *adj* cloudy.

nuca *f* back of the neck.
nuclear *adj* nuclear; **central n.** nuclear power station.
núcleo *m* nucleus; *(parte central)* core.
nudillo *m* knuckle.
nudista *adj & mf* nudist.
nudo *m* knot; **hacer un n.** to tie a knot.
nuera *f* daughter-in-law.
nuestro, -a 1 *adj pos* our; **un amigo n.** a friend of ours. **2** *pron pos* ours; **este libro es n.** this book is ours.
nuevamente *adv* again.
nueve *adj & m inv* nine.
nuevo, -a *adj* new.
nuez *f* walnut; **n. (de Adán)** Adam's apple.
nulo, -a *adj (sin valor)* null and void, invalid; *(inepto)* useless; **voto n.** invalid vote; **crecimiento n.** zero growth.
numérico, -a *adj* digital.
número *m* number; *(de zapatos)* size; **n. e matrícula** license number.
numeroso, -a *adj* numerous.
nunca *adv* never; *(enfático)* not … ever; **no he estado n. en España** I've never been to Spain; **yo no haría n. eso** I wouldn't ever do that; **casi n.** hardly ever; **más que n.** more than ever; **n. jamás** never ever; *(futuro)* never again.
nupcial *adj* wedding, nuptial; **marcha n.** wedding march.
nutrición *f* nutrition.
nutrir 1 *vt* to nourish, to feed. **2 nutrirse** *vr* to feed **(de, con** on).
nutritivo, -a *adj* nutritious; **valor n.** nutritional value.
ñame *m Am* yarn.
ñapa *f Am* bonus.
ñato, -a *adj Am* snub-nosed.
ñoño, -a 1 *adj Am (soso)* dull. **2** *mf* dullard.

O

o *conj* or; **o … o** either … or; **o sea** in other words.
oasis *m inv* oasis.
obedecer [33] *vt* to obey.
obediencia *f* obedience.
obediente *adj* obedient.
obesidad *f* obesity.
obeso, -a *adj* obese.
obispo *m* bishop.
objetar 1 *vt* **no tengo nada que o.** I've got no objections. **2** *vi* to be a conscientious objector.
objetivo, -a 1 *m (fin, meta)* objective; *(de cámara)* lens. **2** *adj* objective.
objeto *m* object; *(fin)* purpose; **con o. de …** in order to ….
obligación *f (deber)* obligation; **por o.** out of a sense of duty.
obligar [42] *vt* to force.
obligatorio, -a *adj* obligatory.
obra *f (trabajo)* work; **o. maestra** masterpiece; *(acto)* deed; *(construcción)* building site; **'carretera en o.'** 'roadworks'.
obrar *vi (proceder)* to act; **o. bien/mal** to do the right/wrong thing.
obrero, -a 1 *mf* worker. **2** *adj* working; **clase obrera** working class.
obsceno, -a *adj* obscene.
obscuro, -a *adj* dark; *(origen, idea)* obscure.
obsequio *m* gift.
observador, -a 1 *mf* observer. **2** *adj* observant.
observar *vt (mirar)* to watch; *(notar)* to notice; *(cumplir)* to observe.
observatorio *m* observatory.
obsesión *f* obsession.
obsesionarse *vr* to get obsessed.
obsesivo, -a *adj* obsessive.
obsoleto, -a *adj* obsolete.
obstaculizar [40] *vt* to obstruct, to get in the way of.

obstáculo *m* obstacle.
obstante: no obstante *adv* nevertheless.
obstinado, -a *adj* obstinate.
obstinarse *vr* to persist (**en** in).
obstruir [37] **1** *vt (salida, paso)* to block. **2 obstruirse** *vr* to get blocked up.
obtener [24] *vt (alcanzar)* to obtain, to get.
obvio, -a *adj* obvious.
oca *f* goose.
ocasión *f (momento)* occasion; *(oportunidad)* opportunity; *(saldo)* bargain; **en cierta o.** once; **aprovechar la o.** to make the most of an opportunity.
ocasional *adj (eventual)* occasional; **de forma o.** occasionally.
ocasionar *vt* to cause.
occidental *adj* western.
occidente *m* West.
océano *m* ocean.
ochenta *adj & m inv* eighty.
ocho *adj & m inv* eight.
ochocientos, -as *adj & mf* eight hundred.
ocio *m* leisure.
ocioso, -a *adj (inactivo)* idle; *(inútil)* pointless.
octavilla *f (panfleto)* hand-out, leaflet.
octavo, -a *adj & mf* eighth.
octubre *m* October.
oculista *mf* ophthalmologist.
ocultar **1** *vt* to conceal; **o. algo a algn** to hide sth from sb. **2 ocultarse** *vr* to hide.
oculto, -a *adj* concealed, hidden.
ocupación *f (tarea)* occupation.
ocupado, -a *adj (persona)* busy; *(asiento)* taken; *(aseos, teléfono)* engaged; *(puesto de trabajo)* filled.
ocupante *mf* occupant; *(ilegal)* squatter.
ocupar **1** *vt* to occupy; *(espacio, tiempo)* to take up; *(cargo)* to hold. **2 ocuparse** *vr* **ocuparse de** *(cuidar)* to look after; *(encargarse)* to see to.

ocurrencia *f (agudeza)* witty remark; *(idea)* idea.
ocurrente *adj* witty.
ocurrir **1** *v impers* to happen; **¿qué te ocurre?** what's the matter with you? **2 ocurrirse** *vr* **no se me ocurre nada** I can't think of anything.
odiar [43] *vt* to hate.
odio *m* hatred.
odioso, -a *adj* hateful.
odontólogo, -a *mf* dental surgeon.
oeste *adj & m* west.
ofender **1** *vt* to offend. **2 ofenderse** *vr* to take offense (**con, por** at).
ofensa *f* offense.
ofensiva *f* offensive.
ofensivo, -a *adj* offensive.
oferta *f* offer; *(presupuesto)* bid.
ofertar *vt* to offer.
oficial, -a **1** *adj* official. **2** *m (rango)* officer; *(obrero)* skilled worker.
oficialismo *m Am (gobierno)* government.
oficialista *Am* **1** *adj* pro-government. **2** *mf* government supporter.
oficina *f* office; **o. de turismo** tourist office; **o. de correos** post office.
oficinista *mf* office worker.
oficio *m (ocupación)* occupation; *(profesión)* trade.
ofimática *f* office automation.
ofrecer [33] **1** *vt* to offer; *(aspecto)* to present. **2 ofrecerse** *vr (prestarse)* to offer; *(situación)* to present itself.
ofrezco *indic pres de* **ofrecer**.
oftalmólogo, -a *mf* ophthalmologist.
oídas: de oídas *adv* by hearsay.
oído *m (sentido)* hearing; *(órgano)* ear.
oír [17] *vt* to hear; **¡oye!** hey!; **¡oiga!** excuse me!
ojal *m* buttonhole.
ojalá **1** *interj* let's hope so! **2** *conj + subj* **¡o. sea cierto!** I hope it is true!
ojeada *f* **echar una o.** to have a quick look (**a** at).
ojeras *fpl* bags under the eyes.

ojo 1 *m* eye; *(de cerradura)* keyhole; **calcular a o.** to guess. **2** *interj* careful!

ojota *f* *Méx (sandalia)* sandal; *RP (chancleta)* thong.

ola *f* wave.

oleaje *m* swell.

óleo *m* oil; **pintura** *o* **cuadro al ó.** oil painting.

oleoducto *m* pipeline.

oler [4] **1** *vt* to smell. **2** *vi (exhalar)* to smell; **o. a** to smell of; **o. bien/mal** to smell good/bad.

olfatear *vt (oler)* to sniff; *fig (indagar)* to pry into.

olfato *m* sense of smell.

olimpiada *f* Olympic Games *pl*; **las olimpiadas** the Olympic Games.

olímpicamente *adv* **paso o. de estudiar** I don't give a damn about studying.

olímpico, -a *adj* Olympic.

oliva *f* olive; **aceite de o.** olive oil.

olivo *m* olive (tree).

olla *f* saucepan; **o. exprés** *o* **a presión** pressure cooker.

olmo *m* elm.

olor *m* smell.

olvidadizo, -a *adj* forgetful.

olvidar 1 *vt* to forget; *(dejar)* to leave. **2 olvidarse** *vr* **olvidarse de algo** to forget sth.

olvido *m (desmemoria)* oblivion; *(lapsus)* oversight.

ombligo *m* navel.

omisión *f* omission.

omitir *vt* to omit.

omnipotente *adj* almighty.

omoplato, omóplato *m* shoulder blade.

once *adj & m inv* eleven.

onda *f* wave; **o. larga/media/corta** long/medium/short wave; *fam* **¡qué buena o.!** that's cool! *Méx, RP fam* **¿qué o.?** *(¿qué tal?)* how's it going?, how are things?

ondulado, -a *adj (pelo)* wavy; *(paisaje)* rolling.

ONU *f abr de* **Organización de las**

Naciones Unidas United Nations (Organization), UN(O).

opaco, -a *adj* opaque.

opcional *adj* optional.

ópera *f* opera.

operación *f* operation; *(financiera)* transaction.

operador, -a *mf* operator; *(de la cámara) (hombre)* cameraman; *(mujer)* camerawoman.

operar 1 *vt* to operate (**a** on). **2 operarse** *vr* to have an operation (**de** for); *(producirse)* to take place.

opinar *vi (pensar)* to think; *(declarar)* to give one's opinion.

opinión *f* opinion; **cambiar de o.** to change one's mind.

oponente *mf* opponent.

oponer [19] *(pp* **opuesto) 1** *vt (resistencia)* to offer. **2 oponerse** *vr (estar en contra)* to be against.

oporto *m (vino)* port.

oportunidad *f* opportunity.

oportuno, -a *adj* timely; *(conveniente)* appropriate.

oposición *f* opposition; *(examen)* competitive examination.

opresión *f* oppression.

oprimir *vt (pulsar)* to press; *(subyugar)* to oppress.

optar *vi (elegir)* to choose (**entre** between); *(aspirar)* to apply (**a** for); **opté por ir yo mismo** I decided to go myself; **puede o. a medalla** he's in with a chance of winning a medal.

optativo, -a *adj* optional.

óptica *f (tienda)* optician's (shop).

óptico, -a 1 *adj* optical. **2** *mf* optician.

optimista 1 *adj* optimistic. **2** *mf* optimist.

óptimo, -a *adj* excellent; *(condiciones)* optimum.

opuesto, -a *adj (contrario)* contrary; *(de enfrente)* opposite; **en direcciones opuestas** in opposite directions.

opuse *pt indef de* **oponer**.

oración *f (plegaria)* prayer.

oral *adj* oral; **por vía o.** to be taken orally.

órale *interj Méx fam (vamos)* come on!; *(de acuerdo)* right!, sure!

orar *vi* to pray.

orden 1 *m* order; **o. público** law and order; **por o. alfabético** in alphabetical order; **del o. de** in the order of. **2** *f* order; *(judicial)* warrant; **¡a la o.!** sir!

ordenado, -a *adj* tidy.

ordenador *m* computer; **o. de sobremesa** desktop (computer); **o. doméstico** home computer; **o. portátil** notebook

ordenanza 1 *m (empleado)* office boy. **2** *f* regulations *pl.*

ordenar *vt (organizar)* to put in order; *(habitación)* to tidy up; *(mandar)* to order; *Am (encargar)* to order.

ordeñar *vt* to milk.

ordinario, -a *adj (corriente)* ordinary; *(grosero)* common.

orégano *m* oregano.

oreja *f* ear.

orfanato, orfelinato *m* orphanage.

orgánico, -a *adj* organic.

organismo *m* organism; *(institución)* body.

organización *f* organization.

organizador, -a 1 *adj* organizing. **2** *mf* organizer.

organizar [40] **1** *vt* to organize. **2 organizarse** *vr (armarse)* to happen.

órgano *m* organ.

orgullo *m (propia estima)* pride; *(arrogancia)* arrogance.

orgulloso, -a *adj* **estar o.** *(satisfecho)* to be proud; **ser o.** *(arrogante)* to be arrogant.

orientación *f (dirección)* orientation; *(guía)* guidance.

oriental 1 *adj* eastern. **2** *mf* Oriental.

orientar 1 *vt (indicar camino)* to give directions to; **una casa orientada al sur** a house facing south. **2 orientarse** *vr (encontrar el camino)* to get one's bearings.

oriente *m* East; **el Extremo** *o* **Lejano/Medio/Próximo O.** the Far/Middle/Near East.

orificio *m* hole; *(del cuerpo)* orifice.

origen *m* origin; **dar o. a** to give rise to.

original *adj & mf* original.

originar 1 *vt* to cause, to give rise to. **2 originarse** *vr* to originate.

orilla *f (borde)* edge; *(del río)* bank; *(del mar)* shore.

orinal *m* chamberpot; *fam* potty.

orinar 1 *vi* to urinate. **2 orinarse** *vr* to wet oneself.

oriundo, -a *adj* native of; **ser o. de** to come from.

oro *m* gold; **de o.** golden; **o. de ley** fine gold.

orquesta *f* orchestra; *(de verbena)* dance band.

ortiga *f* (stinging) nettle.

ortodoxo, -a *adj* orthodox.

ortografía *f* spelling.

ortográfico, -a *adj* spelling.

ortopédico, -a *adj* orthopedic.

oruga *f* caterpillar.

orzuelo *m* sty(e).

os *pron pers (complemento directo)* you; *(complemento indirecto)* (to) you; *(con verbo reflexivo)* yourselves; *(con verbo recíproco)* each other; **os veo mañana** I'll see you tomorrow; **os daré el dinero** I'll give you the money; **os escribiré** I'll write to you.

osadía *f (audacia)* daring; *(desvergüenza)* impudence.

osado, -a *adj (audaz)* daring; *(desvergonzado)* shameless.

osar *vi* to dare.

oscilar *vi (variar)* to fluctuate.

oscuras: a oscuras *adv* in the dark.

oscurecer [33] **1** *vi impers* to get dark. **2** *vt (ensombrecer)* to darken. **3 oscurecerse** *vr (nublarse)* to become cloudy.

oscuridad *f* darkness; *fig* obscurity.

oscuro, -a *adj* dark; *(origen, idea)* obscure.

osito *m* **o. (de peluche)** teddy bear.

CÓMO EXPRESAR LA OPINIÓN

¿Qué opina/opinas? or **¿Qué le/te parece?**
What do you think?

Me gustó mucho./Me gusta mucho.
I really like it/liked it.

¡Estuvo muy bien!/¡Fue increíble!
It was great/amazing!

No estuvo mal.
It was OK.

La visita al castillo estuvo bastante interesante.
The tour of the castle was quite interesting.

Me encanta el tequila/el esquí.
I love tequila/skiing.

Odio la nieve/ir de compras.
I hate snow/shopping.

Prefiero un café.
I'd rather have coffee.

¿Cuál prefiere/prefieres?
Which do you prefer?

Creo que eso estaría bien.
I think that would be nice.

Estoy de acuerdo (con usted/contigo).
I agree (with you).

Tiene(s) toda la razón.
You're absolutely right.

Seguro que hará bueno mañana.
I'm sure it'll be nice tomorrow.

Es verdad.
That's true.

He cambiado de idea.
I've changed my mind.

No lo sé.
I don't know.

¿De verdad?/ Ah ¿sí?
Really?

¡Qué sorpresa!
What a surprise!

¿Le/Te gustó el museo?
Did you like the art gallery?

No me gusta./No me gustó nada.
I don't like it./didn't like it at all.

Fue un poco aburrido/demasiado turístico.
It was a bit boring/too touristy.

La comida no tiene nada de particular.
The food's nothing special.

Nos lo pasamos muy bien.
We had a great time!

No me gusta el jazz/ir en bici.
I don't like jazz/cycling.

¡Está delicioso(a)/asqueroso(a)!
This is delicious/disgusting!

Prefiero los hoteles pequeños a los grandes.
I prefer small hotels to big ones.

Prefiero el(la) más grande/el(la) más pequeño(a).
I prefer the bigger/smaller one.

Creo que es posible./Creo que no es posible.
I think/I don't think it's possible.

No estoy de acuerdo (con usted/contigo).
I disagree (with you).

¡Claro (que no)!
Of course (not)!

¿Está/Estás seguro(a)?
Are you sure?

No le/te creo.
I don't believe you.

No estoy seguro(a).
I'm not sure.

Depende.
It depends.

¡Qué raro!
That's strange!

¡Qué pena!
What a pity!

oso *m* bear; **o. polar** polar bear.

ostentación *f* ostentation.

osteópata *mf* osteopath.

ostra *f* oyster; **aburrirse como una o.** to be bored stiff.

OTAN *f abr de* **Organización del Tratado del Atlántico Norte** North Atlantic Treaty Organization, NATO.

otoño *m* autumn, fall.

otorgar [42] *vt* (premio) to award (**a** to).

otorrinolaringólogo, -a *mf* ear, nose and throat specialist.

otro, -a 1 *adj indef* **otro/otra ...** another ...; **otros/otras ...** other ...; **el otro/la otra ...** the other ...; **otra cosa** something else; **otra vez** again. **2** *pron indef* another (one); **otros/ otras** others; **el otro/la otra** the other (one); **los otros/las otras** the others.

ovacionar *vt* to give an ovation to.

oval, ovalado, -a *adj* oval.

oveja *f* sheep; (hembra) ewe; **la o. negra** the black sheep.

overol *m Am* overalls *pl.*

ovillo *m* ball (of wool).

OVNI *m abr de* **objeto volador no identificado** UFO.

oxidado, -a *adj* rusty.

oxidar 1 *vt* (metales) to rust. **2 oxidarse** *vr* (metales) to rust.

oxígeno *m* oxygen.

oye *indic pres & imperativo de* **oír**.

ozono *m* ozone; **capa de o.** ozone layer.

P

pabellón *m* (en feria) stand; (bloque) wing; **p. de deportes** sports center.

paciencia *f* patience.

paciente *adj & mf* patient.

pacificar [44] *vt* to pacify.

pacotilla *f* **de p.** second-rate.

pactar *vt* to agree.

padecer [33] *vti* to suffer; **padece del corazón** he suffers from heart trouble.

padrastro *m* stepfather; (pellejo) hangnail.

padre 1 *m* father; **padres** parents. **2** *adj Méx* (genial) great.

padrenuestro *m* Lord's Prayer.

padrino *m* (de bautizo) godfather; (de boda) best man; **padrinos** godparents.

padrón *m* census.

paella *f* paella (rice dish made with vegetables, meat and/or seafood).

pág *abr de* **página** page, p.

paga *f* (salario) wage; **p. extra** bonus.

pagar [42] *vti* to pay; (recompensar) to repay; **p. en metálico** *o* **al contado** to pay cash.

página *f* page; **p. web** web page.

pago *m* payment; **p. adelantado** *o* **anticipado** advance payment.

paila *f Am* (frying) pan.

país *m* country; **P. Vasco** Basque Country; **P. Valenciano** Valencia.

paisaje *m* landscape.

paisano, -a 1 *adj* of the same country. **2** *mf* (hombre) fellow countryman; (mujer) fellow countrywoman; **en traje de p.** in plain clothes.

paja *f* straw.

pajar *m* (almacén) straw loft; (en el exterior) straw rick.

pajarita *f* bow tie; (de papel) paper bird.

pájaro *m* bird; **p. carpintero** woodpecker.

pajita, pajilla *f* (drinking) straw.

pakistaní *adj & mf* (pl pakistaníes) Pakistani.

pala *f* shovel; (de jardinero) spade; (de ping-pong, frontón) bat; (de remo) blade.

palabra *f* word; **dirigir la p. a algn**

to address sb; **juego de palabras** pun; **p. de honor** word of honor.
palabrota *f* swearword.
palacio *m (grande)* palace; *(más pequeño)* mansion.
paladar *m* palate.
paladear *vt* to savor.
palanca *f* lever; *(manecilla)* handle; **p. de cambio** gearshift.
palangana *f* washbasin.
palco *m* box.
palestino, -a *adj & mf* Palestinian.
paleta *f (espátula)* slice; *(de pintor)* palette; *(de albañil)* trowel; *(de pingpong)* bat.
paletilla *f* shoulder blade.
paleto, -a **1** *adj* boorish. **2** *mf* country bumpkin.
paliar [43] *vt* to alleviate.
palidecer [33] *vi (persona)* to turn pale.
palidez *f* paleness.
pálido, -a *adj* pale.
palillero *m* toothpick case.
palillo *m (mondadientes)* toothpick; **palillos chinos** chopsticks; *(de tambor)* drumstick.
paliza *f* beating; **darle a algn una p.** to give sb a thrashing.
palma *f* palm; *(árbol)* palm tree; **hacer palmas** to applaud.
palmada *f (golpe)* slap.
palmera *f* palm tree.
palmo *m*; **a p. a p.** inch by inch.
palo *m* stick; *(vara)* rod; *(de escoba)* broomstick; *(golpe)* blow; *(madera)* wood; *(de portería)* woodwork; *(de golf)* club.
paloma *f* pigeon; *(como símbolo)* dove.
palomar *m* pigeon house.
palomitas (de maíz) *fpl* popcorn *sing.*
palpable *adj* palpable.
palpar *vt* to feel.
palpitar *vi* to palpitate.
palurdo, -a *adj* boorish.
pamela *f* broad-brimmed hat.
pampa *f* pampa, pampas *pl.*

pan *m* bread; **p. de molde** loaf of sliced bread; **p. integral** wholewheat bread; **p. rallado** breadcrumbs *pl.*
pana *f* corduroy.
panadería *f* bakery.
panameño, -a *adj & mf* Panamanian.
pancarta *f* placard; *(en manifestación)* banner.
panda[1] *m* panda.
panda[2] *f (de amigos)* gang.
pandereta *f* tambourine.
pandilla *f* gang.
panecillo *m* bread roll.
panera *f* breadbasket.
panfleto *m* pamphlet.
pánico *m* panic; **sembrar el p.** to cause panic.
panorama *m* panorama.
pantaletas *fpl Am* panties.
pantalla *f (monitor)* screen; *(de lámpara)* shade.
pantalones *mpl* trousers *pl*; **p. vaqueros** jeans *pl.*
pantano *m (natural)* marsh; *(artificial)* reservoir.
pantera *f* panther.
pantorrilla *f* calf.
pantufla *f* slipper.
panty *m (pair of)* tights *pl.*
panza *f fam* belly.
pañal *m* diaper.
paño *m* cloth.
pañuelo *m* handkerchief; *(pañoleta)* shawl.
Papa *m* **el P.** the Pope.
papa *f (patata)* potato.
papá *m fam* dad, daddy.
papada *f* double chin.
papagayo *m* parrot.
papel *m* paper; *(hoja)* piece of paper; *(rol)* role; **papeles** *(documentos)* identification papers; **p. higiénico** toilet paper; **p. de aluminio** aluminum foil; **p. pintado** wallpaper.
papelera *f (en despacho)* wastepaper basket; *(en calle)* trash can.
papelería *f (tienda)* stationer's.

papeleta f (de rifa) ticket; (de votación) ballot.

paperas fpl mumps sing.

papilla f mush; (de niños) baby food.

paquete m packet; (postal) parcel.

paquistaní adj & mf (pl paquistaníes) Pakistani.

par 1 adj (número) even. **2** m (pareja) pair; (dos) couple; **de p. en p.** wide open.

para prep for; (finalidad) to, in order to; (tiempo) by; (a punto de) **está p. salir** it's about to leave; **p. terminar antes** (in order) to finish earlier; **p. entonces** by then; **¿p. qué?** what for?; **ir p. viejo** to be getting old; **no es p. tanto** it's not as bad as all that; **p. mí** in my opinion.

parabólico, -a adj antena parabólica satellite dish.

parabrisas m inv windshield.

paracaidista mf parachutist; (soldado) paratrooper.

parachoques m inv bumper, fender.

parada f stop; **p. de autobús** bus stop; **p. de taxis** taxi rank.

paradero m (lugar) whereabouts pl; (apeadero) stop.

parado, -a 1 adj stopped; (quieto) still; (fábrica) at a standstill; (desempleado) unemployed; Am (de pie) standing; fig **salir bien/mal p.** to come off well/badly. **2** mf unemployed person.

parador m roadside inn; **p. nacional o de turismo** luxury hotel.

paraguas m inv umbrella.

paraíso m paradise.

paraje m spot, place.

paralelo, -a adj & m parallel.

paralítico, -a adj & mf paralytic.

paralizar [40] **1** vt to paralyze; (circulación) to stop. **2 paralizarse** vr to come to a standstill.

parapente m paragliding, parapenting.

parapeto m parapet; (de defensa) barricade.

parar 1 vt to stop; (balón) to save. **2** vi to stop; **sin p.** nonstop; **fue a p. a la cárcel** he ended up in jail. **3 pararse** vr to stop; Am (ponerse en pie) to stand up.

pararrayos m inv lightning rod.

parásito, -a adj & m parasite.

parcela f plot.

parche m patch; (emplasto) plaster.

parchís m ≃ ludo.

parcial adj (partidario) biased; (no completo) partial; **a tiempo p.** part-time.

parcialmente adv partly.

pardo, -a adj (marrón) brown; (gris) dark gray.

parecer [33] **1** vi to seem; **parece que no arranca** it looks as if it won't start; **como te parezca** whatever you like; **¿te parece?** is that okay with you?; **¿qué te parece?** what do you think of it? **2 parecerse** vr to be alike; **parecerse a** to look like.

parecido, -a 1 adj similar; **bien p.** good-looking. **2** m resemblance.

pared f wall.

pareja f pair; (hombre y mujer) couple; (de baile, juego) partner; **por parejas** in pairs; **hacen buena p.** they make a nice couple.

parentesco m relationship.

paréntesis m inv bracket; **entre p.** in brackets.

parezco indic pres de **parecer**.

pariente mf relative, relation.

parir 1 vt to give birth to. **2** vi to give birth.

parlamento m parliament.

paro m (huelga) strike; (desempleo) unemployment; **estar en p.** to be unemployed; **cobrar el p.** to be on the dole.

parpadear vi (ojos) to blink; (luz) to flicker.

párpado m eyelid.

parque m park; (de niños) playpen; **p. de atracciones** amusement park; **p. zoológico** zoo; **p. nacional/natural** national park/nature reserve.

parqueadero m Carib, Col, Pan parking lot.

parquear vti Am to park.

parquímetro m parking meter.

parra f grapevine.

párrafo m paragraph.

parranda f fam spree.

parrilla f grill; **pescado a la p.** grilled fish.

párroco m parish priest.

parroquia f parish; (iglesia) parish church.

parte 1 f (sección) part; (en una repartición) share; (lugar) place; (en juicio) party; **en o por todas partes** everywhere; **por mi p.** as far as I am concerned; **de p. de …** on behalf of …; **¿de p. de quién?** who's calling?; **en gran p.** to a large extent; **en p.** partly; **la mayor p.** the majority; **por otra p.** on the other hand. **2** m (informe) report.

participación f participation; (acción) share; (notificación) notification.

participante 1 adj participating. **2** mf participant.

participar 1 vi to take part, participate (en in). **2** vt (notificar) to notify.

participio m participle.

particular 1 adj (concreto) particular; (privado) private; (raro) peculiar. **2** mf (individuo) private individual.

partida f (salida) departure; (remesa) batch; (juego) game; (certificado) certificate; **p. de nacimiento** birth certificate.

partidario, -a 1 adj **ser/no ser p. de algo** to be for/against sth. **2** mf supporter.

partido m party; (fútbol) match, game; **sacar p. de** to profit from.

partir 1 vt to break; (dividir) to split; (cortar) to cut. **2** vi (marcharse) to leave; **a p. de** from. **3 partirse** vr to split (up); **partirse de risa** to split one's sides laughing.

partitura f score.

parto m labor, childbirth.

pasa f raisin.

pasadizo m corridor.

pasado, -a 1 adj (último) last; (anticuado) old-fashioned; (alimento) bad; (cocido) cooked; **p. (de moda)** out of date; **p. mañana** the day after tomorrow. **2** m past.

pasaje m passage; (calle) alley; (pasajeros) passengers pl; (billete) ticket.

pasajero, -a 1 adj passing. **2** mf passenger.

pasamanos m inv (barra) handrail; (de escalera) banister.

pasaporte m passport.

pasar 1 vt to pass; (página) to turn; (trasladar) to move; (tiempo) to spend, to pass; (padecer) to suffer; (cruzar) to cross; (límite) to go beyond; **p. hambre** to go hungry. **2** vi to pass; (entrar) to come in; **p. a** (continuar) to go on to; **p. de largo** to go by (without stopping). **3** v impers (suceder) to happen; **¿qué pasa aquí?** what's going on here?; **¿qué te pasa?** what's the matter?; **pase lo que pase** come what may. **4 pasarse** vr (comida) to go off; (excederse) to go too far; **se me pasó la ocasión** I missed my chance; **se le pasó llamarme** he forgot to phone me; **pasarse el día haciendo algo** to spend the day doing sth; **pasárselo bien/mal** to have a good/bad time.

pasarela f (puente) footbridge; (de barco) gangway; (de moda) catwalk.

pasatiempo m pastime, hobby.

pascua f Easter; **pascuas** (Navidad) Christmas sing; **¡Felices Pascuas!** Merry Christmas!

pasear 1 vi to go for a walk. **2** vt (perro) to walk. **3 pasearse** vr to go for a walk.

paseo m walk; (en bicicleta, caballo) ride; (en coche) drive; (avenida) avenue; **dar un p.** to go for a walk/ride/drive.

pasillo m corridor.

pasión f passion.

pasivo, -a *adj* passive; *(inactivo)* inactive.

pasmado, -a *adj (asombrado)* astounded, amazed; *(atontado)* flabbergasted; **dejar p.** to astonish; **quedarse p.** to be amazed.

paso *m* step; *(modo de andar)* gait; *(ruido al andar)* footstep; *(camino)* way; *(acción)* passage; *(de montaña)* mountain pass; **abrirse p.** to force one's way through; **'ceda el p.'** 'give way'; **'prohibido el p.'** 'no entry'; **p. de peatones** pedestrian crossing, crosswalk; **el p. del tiempo** the passage of time; **estar de p.** to be just passing through.

pasta *f* paste; *(italiana)* pasta; *(galleta)* biscuit; *fam (dinero)* dough; **p. de dientes** o **dentífrica** toothpaste.

pastel *m* cake; *(de carne, fruta)* pie.

pastelería *f* pastry shop, bakery.

pastilla *f* tablet; *(de jabón)* bar; **pastillas para la tos** cough drops.

pastor, -a 1 *mf (hombre)* shepherd; *(mujer)* shepherdess; **p. alemán** Alsatian. **2** *m (sacerdote)* pastor.

pastoso, -a *adj* pasty; *(lengua)* furry.

pata *f* leg; **patas arriba** upside down; **mala p.** bad luck; **meter la p.** to put one's foot in it.

patada *f* kick; *(en el suelo)* stamp.

patalear *vi* to stamp one's feet (with rage).

patán *m* bumpkin.

patata *f* potato; **patatas fritas** French fries; *(de bolsa)* potato chips.

paté *m* pâté.

patentar *vt* to patent.

patente 1 *f (de invención)* patent; *(autorización)* license; *CSur (matrícula)* license plate. **2** *adj (evidente)* patent, obvious.

paternal *adj* paternal.

paterno, -a *adj* paternal.

patilla *f (de gafas)* leg; **patillas** *(pelo)* sideburns.

patín *m* skate; *(hidropedal)* pedal boat; **p. de ruedas/de hielo** roller/ice skate.

patinaje *m* skating; **p. artístico** figure skating; **p. sobre hielo/ruedas** ice-/roller-skating.

patinar *vi* to skate; *(sobre ruedas)* to roller-skate; *(sobre hielo)* to ice-skate; *(deslizarse)* to slide; *(resbalar)* to slip; *(vehículo)* to skid.

patinete *m* scooter.

patio *m (de una casa)* patio; *(de recreo)* playground; **p. de butacas** stalls.

pato *m* duck.

patoso, -a *adj* clumsy, awkward.

patria *f* homeland.

patrimonio *m (bienes)* wealth; *(heredado)* inheritance.

patriotismo *m* patriotism.

patrocinador, -a 1 *adj* sponsoring. **2** *mf* sponsor.

patrocinar *vt* to sponsor.

patrón, -ona 1 *mf (jefe)* boss; *(de pensión) (hombre)* landlord; *(mujer)* landlady. **2** *m* pattern.

patronal 1 *adj* employers'. **2** *f* employers' organization.

patronato, patronazgo *m (institución benéfica)* foundation; *(protección)* patronage.

patrono, -a *mf* boss; *(empresario)* employer.

patrulla *f* patrol.

paulatino, -a *adj* gradual.

pausa *f* pause; *(musical)* rest.

pauta *f* guidelines *pl*.

pavimento *m (de calle)* paving.

pavo *m* turkey.

pavor *m* terror.

payaso *m* clown.

payo, -a *mf* non-Gipsy.

paz *f* peace; *(sosiego)* peacefulness; **¡déjame en p.!** leave me alone!

PC *m abr de* **personal computer** PC.

PDA *m abr de* **personal digital assistant** PDA.

peaje *f* toll; **autopista de p.** turnpike.

peatón *m* pedestrian.

peca *f* freckle.

pecado *m* sin.

pecador, -a *mf* sinner.

pecar [44] *vi* to sin.

pecera *f* fishtank.

pecho *m* chest; *(de mujer, animal)* breast; **dar el p. (a un bebé)** to breast-feed (a baby).

pechuga *f (de ave)* breast.

pectoral *adj* chest.

peculiar *adj (raro)* peculiar; *(característico)* characteristic.

pedagógico, -a *adj* pedagogical.

pedal *m* pedal.

pedante 1 *adj* pedantic. **2** *mf* pedant.

pedazo *m* piece, bit; **hacer pedazos** to smash to pieces; *(papel, tela)* to tear to pieces.

pediatra *mf* pediatrician.

pedido *m (remesa)* order.

pedir [6] *vt* to ask (for); *(en bar etc)* to order; *(mendigar)* to beg; **p. algo a algn** to ask sb for sth; **p. prestado** to borrow; **p. cuentas** to ask for an explanation.

pedrada *f (golpe)* blow from a stone; *(lanzamiento)* throw of a stone.

pega *f fam (objeción)* objection; **de p.** *(falso)* sham.

pegajoso, -a *adj (pegadizo)* sticky.

pegamento *m* glue.

pegar [42] **1** *vt (adherir)* to stick; *(con pegamento)* to glue; *(golpear)* to hit; *fam* **no pegó ojo** he didn't sleep a wink; **p. un grito** to shout; **p. un salto** to jump. **2** *vi (adherirse)* to stick; *(armonizar)* to match; *(sol)* to beat down. **3 pegarse** *vr (adherirse)* to stick; *(pelearse)* to fight; *(comida)* to get burnt; *(arrimarse)* to get close; **pegarse un tiro** to shoot oneself; **se me ha pegado el sol** I've got a touch of the sun.

pegatina *f* sticker.

peinado *m* hairstyle, *fam* hairdo.

peinar 1 *vt (pelo)* to comb. **2 peinarse** *vr* to comb one's hair.

peine *m* comb.

pelado, -a *adj (fruta, patata)* peeled; *(cabeza)* shorn.

pelapatatas *m inv* potato peeler.

pelar 1 *vt (cortar el pelo a)* to cut the hair of; *(fruta, patata)* to peel. **2 pelarse** *vr (cortarse el pelo)* to get one's hair cut.

peldaño *m* step; *(de escalera de mano)* rung.

pelea *f* fight; *(riña)* row.

pelear 1 *vi* to fight; *(reñir)* to quarrel. **2 pelearse** *vr* to fight; *(reñir)* to quarrel; *(enemistarse)* to fall out.

peletería *f (tienda)* fur shop.

película *f* movie; *(fotográfica)* film; **p. de miedo** *o* **terror** horror movie; **p. del Oeste** Western.

peligrar *vi* to be in danger; **hacer p.** to endanger, to jeopardize.

peligro *m* danger; *(riesgo)* risk; **correr (el) p. de …** to run the risk of …; **poner en p.** to endanger.

peligroso, -a *adj* dangerous.

pelirrojo, -a 1 *adj* red-haired; *(anaranjado)* ginger-haired. **2** *mf* redhead.

pellejo *m (piel)* skin; **jugarse el p.** to risk one's neck.

pellizco *m* pinch.

pelma *mf*, **pelmazo, -a** *mf (persona)* bore.

pelo *m* hair; *(de animal)* coat; **cortarse el p. (uno mismo)** to cut one's hair; *(en la peluquería)* to have one's hair cut; **tomar el p. a algn** to pull sb's leg; **por los pelos** by the skin of one's teeth.

pelota *f* ball; **hacer la p. a algn** to suck up to sb.

pelotón *m* squad.

pelotudo, -a *adj Am* slack.

peluca *f* wig.

peluche *m* **osito de p.** teddy bear.

peludo, -a *adj* hairy.

peluquería *f* hairdresser's (shop).

peluquero, -a *mf* hairdresser.

pelusa, pelusilla *f* fluff; *(de planta)* down; *fam* jealousy (among children).

pena *f (tristeza)* sorrow; **¡qué p.!** what a pity!; **no merece** *o* **vale la p.**

(ir) it's not worthwhile (going); **a duras penas** with great difficulty; **p. de muerte** o **capital** death penalty.

penalti m (pl **penaltis**) penalty.

pendejo m Am jerk.

pendiente 1 adj (por resolver) pending; (colgante) hanging (**de** from); asignatura **p.** (en colegio) subject not yet passed; **estar p. de** (esperar) to be waiting for; (vigilar) to be on the lookout for. **2** m (joya) earring. **3** f slope.

penetrante adj penetrating; (frío, voz, mirada) piercing.

penetrar 1 vt to penetrate. **2** vi (entrar) to enter (**en** -).

penicilina f penicillin.

península f peninsula.

penique m penny, pl pence.

penitenciario, -a adj prison.

penoso, -a adj (lamentable) sorry, distressing; (laborioso) laborious, difficult; CAm, Carib, Col, Méx (vergonzoso) shy.

pensamiento m thought; (flor) pansy.

pensar [1] **1** vi to think (**en** of, about; **sobre** about, over); **sin p.** (con precipitación) without thinking; (involuntariamente) involuntarily. **2** vt (considerar) to think about; (proponerse) to intend; (concebir) to make; fam ¡ni pensarlo! not on your life!

pensativo, -a adj thoughtful.

pensión f (residencia) boarding house; (hotel) guesthouse; (paga) allowance; **media p.** half board; **p. completa** full board.

pensionista mf pensioner.

penúltimo, -a adj & mf penultimate.

penumbra f half-light.

penuria f scarcity, shortage.

peña f rock; (de amigos) club.

peñón m rock; **el P. de Gibraltar** the Rock of Gibraltar.

peón m unskilled laborer; (en ajedrez) pawn.

peor adj & adv (comparativo) worse;

(superlativo) worst; **en el p. de los casos** if the worst comes to the worst.

pepinillo m gherkin.

pepino m cucumber.

pepita f (de fruta) pip, seed; (de metal) nugget.

pequeño, -a 1 adj small, little; (bajo) short. **2** mf child; **de p.** as a child.

pera f pear.

peral m pear tree.

percance m mishap.

percatarse vr **p. de** to realize.

percepción f perception.

percha f (colgador) (coat)hanger.

perchero m clothes rack.

percibir vt (notar) to perceive; (cobrar) to receive.

percusión f percussion.

perdedor, -a 1 adj losing. **2** mf loser.

perder [3] **1** vt to lose; (tren, autobús, oportunidad) to miss; (tiempo) to waste. **2** vi to lose; **echar (algo) a p.** to spoil (sth); **echarse a p.** to be spoiled; **salir perdiendo** to come off worst. **3 perderse** vr (extraviarse) (persona) to get lost; **se me ha perdido la llave** I've lost my key.

pérdida f loss; (de tiempo, esfuerzos) waste.

perdiz f partridge.

perdón m pardon; **¡p.!** sorry!; **pedir p.** to apologize.

perdonar vt to forgive; (eximir) to pardon; **¡perdone!** sorry!; **perdonarle la vida a algn** to spare sb's life.

perecedero, -a adj perishable; **artículos perecederos** perishables.

perecer [33] vi to perish.

peregrino, -a 1 mf pilgrim. **2** adj **ideas peregrinas** crazy ideas.

perejil m parsley.

perenne adj perennial.

pereza f laziness.

perezoso, -a adj lazy.

perfección f perfection; **a la p.** to perfection.

perfeccionar vt to perfect; (mejorar) to improve.

perfeccionista adj & mf perfectionist.

perfectamente adv perfectly; ¡p.! (de acuerdo) agreed!, all right!

perfecto, -a adj perfect.

perfil m profile; (contorno) outline; de p. in profile.

perfilar 1 vt (dar forma) to shape, to outline. **2 perfilarse** vr to take shape.

perforar vt to perforate.

perfumar 1 vt to perfume. **2 perfumarse** vr to put on perfume.

perfume m perfume.

pericia f expertise.

periferia f periphery; (alrededores) outskirts pl.

periférico m peripheral.

perilla f (barba) goatee; fam **venir de perilla(s)** to be very handy, to be just the thing.

periódico, -a 1 m newspaper. **2** adj periodic.

periodista mf journalist.

periodo, período m period.

periquito m budgerigar, fam budgie.

perjudicar [44] vt to harm; (intereses) to prejudice.

perjudicial adj harmful.

perjuicio m damage.

perla f pearl.

permanecer [33] vi to remain, to stay.

permanente 1 adj permanent. **2** f (de pelo) perm; **hacerse la p.** to have one's hair permed.

permiso m (autorización) permission; (licencia) license; **p. de conducir** driver's license.

permitir 1 vt to permit, to allow. **2 permitirse** vr (costearse) to afford; **'no se permite fumar'** 'no smoking'.

pero conj but.

perpendicular adj & f perpendicular.

perpetrar vt to perpetrate, to commit.

perpetuo, -a adj perpetual; **cadena perpetua** life imprisonment.

perplejo, -a adj perplexed.

perra f bitch.

perrera f kennel; (para muchos perros) kennels pl.

perro m dog; fam **vida de perros** dog's life; **p. caliente** hot dog.

persecución f pursuit; (represión) persecution.

perseguir [6] vt to pursue; (seguir) to run after; (reprimir) to persecute.

perseverar vi to persevere; (durar) to last.

persiana f blinds pl.

persignarse vr to cross oneself.

persistente adj persistent.

persistir vi to persist.

persona f person; fam **p. mayor** grown-up.

personaje m character; (celebridad) celebrity.

personal 1 adj personal. **2** m (plantilla) personnel.

personalidad f personality.

perspectiva f perspective; (futuro) prospect.

perspicaz adj perspicacious.

persuadir vt to persuade.

persuasión f persuasion.

pertenecer [33] vi to belong (a to).

pertinaz adj persistent; (obstinado) obstinate.

perturbación f disturbance.

perturbado, -a adj (mentally) deranged o unbalanced.

perturbar vt (el orden) to disturb.

peruano, -a adj & mf Peruvian.

perverso, -a adj perverse.

pervertir [5] vt to pervert.

pesa f weight; **levantamiento de pesas** weightlifting.

pesadez f heaviness; (de estómago) fullness; (fastidio) drag.

pesadilla f nightmare.

pesado, -a adj heavy; (aburrido) tedious.

pésame m dar el p. to offer one's condolences.

pesar 1 *vt* to weigh; *(entristecer)* to grieve. **2** *vi* to weigh; *(ser pesado)* to be heavy. **3** *m (pena)* sorrow; *(arrepentimiento)* regret; **a p. de** in spite of.

pesca *f* fishing.

pescadería *f* fish shop.

pescadilla *f* young hake.

pescado *m* fish.

pescador, -a 1 *adj* fishing. **2** *mf (hombre)* fisherman; *(mujer)* fisherwoman.

pescar [44] *vti* to fish.

pescuezo *m fam* neck.

pese: pese a (que) *prep* in spite of (the fact that).

peseta *f* peseta.

pesimismo *m* pessimism.

pesimista 1 *adj* pessimistic. **2** *mf* pessimist.

pésimo, -a *adj* awful.

peso *m* weight; **p. bruto/neto** gross/net weight; **de p.** *(razón)* convincing.

pestaña *f* eyelash.

peste *f (hedor)* stench; *(epidemia)* plague.

pesticida *m* pesticide.

pestillo *m* bolt.

petaca *f (para cigarrillos)* cigarette case; *(para bebidas)* flask; *Am (maleta)* suitcase.

pétalo *m* petal.

petardo *m* firecracker.

petición *f* request.

petróleo *m* oil.

petrolero *m* oil tanker.

pez *m* fish.

pezón *m* nipple.

pezuña *f* hoof.

piadoso, -a *adj (devoto)* pious; *(compasivo)* compassionate; **mentira piadosa** white lie.

pianista *mf* pianist.

piano *m* piano.

pibe, -a *mf Am (niño)* kid.

picadero *m* riding school.

picado, -a 1 *adj (carne)* ground; *(fruta)* bad; *(diente)* decayed; *(mar)* choppy. **2** *m* **caer en p.** to plummet.

picador *m* picador.

picadora *f* mincer.

picadura *f (de insecto, serpiente)* bite; *(de avispa, abeja)* sting; *(en fruta)* spot.

picante *adj* hot; *(chiste etc)* risqué.

picaporte *m (aldaba)* door knocker; *(pomo)* door handle.

picar [44] **1** *vt (insecto, serpiente)* to bite; *(avispas, abejas)* to sting; *(comer)* *(aves)* to peck (at); *(persona)* to pick at; *(anzuelo)* to bite; *(perforar)* to prick; *(carne)* to mince. **2** *vi (escocer)* to itch; *(herida)* to smart; *(el sol)* to burn; *(estar picante)* to be hot; *(pez)* to bite; *fig (dejarse engañar)* to swallow it. **3 picarse** *vr (fruta)* to spot; *(dientes)* to decay; *(enfadarse)* to get cross.

pícaro, -a 1 *adj (travieso)* mischievous; *(astuto)* crafty. **2** *mf* rogue.

pico *m (de ave)* beak, bill; *(punta)* corner; *(de montaña)* peak; *(herramienta)* pick; **cincuenta y p.** fifty odd; **las dos y p.** a little after two.

picor *m* tingling.

pie *m* foot; *(de instrumento)* stand; *(de copa)* stem; *(de una ilustración)* caption; **a p.** on foot; **de p.** standing up; **de pies a cabeza** from head to foot; **en p.** standing; **hacer p.** to touch the bottom; **perder p.** to get out of one's depth; **al p. de la letra** to the letter.

piedad *f* piety; *(compasión)* pity.

piedra *f* stone; *(de mechero)* flint.

piel *f* skin; *(de patata)* peel; *(cuero)* leather; *(con pelo)* fur; **p. de gallina** goose pimples *pl*.

pienso *m* fodder.

piercing *m* piercing.

pierna *f* leg.

pieza *f* piece, part; *(habitación)* room; *(teatral)* play; **p. de recambio** spare part.

pijama *m* pajamas *pl*.

pila *f* battery; *(montón)* pile; *(de la cocina)* sink; **nombre de p.** Christian name.

píldora f pill.

pileta f (pila) sink; Am (piscina) swimming pool.

pillar 1 vt (coger) to catch; (alcanzar) to catch up with; **lo pilló un coche** he was run over by a car. **2 pillarse** vr to catch; **pillarse un dedo/una mano** to catch one's finger/hand.

pillo, -a 1 adj (travieso) naughty; (astuto) cunning. **2** mf rogue.

piloto 1 mf (de avión, barco) pilot; (de coche) driver; (de moto) rider **2** m (luz) pilot lamp **3** adj inv **piso p.** show apartment.

pimentón m red pepper.

pimienta f pepper.

pimiento m (fruto) pepper; (planta) pimiento.

pinar m pine wood.

pincel m paintbrush.

pinchadiscos mf inv disc jockey, DJ.

pinchar 1 vt (punzar) to jag; (balón, globo) to burst; (rueda) to puncture. **2** vi (coche) to get a puncture.

pinchazo m (punzadura) prick; (de rueda) puncture; (de dolor) sharp pain.

pincho m (púa) barb; **p. moruno** shish kebab.

ping-pong m table tennis.

pingüino m penguin.

pino m pine; fig **hacer el p.** to do a handstand.

pinole m Am corn drink.

pinta f (medida) pint; fam (aspecto) look.

pintada f graffiti.

pintar 1 vt (dar color) to paint; (dibujar) to draw. **2 pintarse** vr (maquillarse) to put make-up on.

pintor, -a mf painter.

pintoresco, -a adj (lugar) picturesque; (persona) eccentric.

pintura f painting; (materia) paint.

pinza f (para depilar) tweezers pl; (para tender) clothes pin; (de animal) pincer.

piña f (de pino) pine cone; (ananás) pineapple.

piñón m pine seed.

piojo m louse.

pipa f (de fumar) pipe; (de fruta) seed; (de girasol) sunflower seed.

pipí m fam pee, wee-wee; **hacer p.** to pee, to wee-wee.

piragua f canoe.

piragüismo m canoeing.

pirámide f pyramid.

piraña f piranha.

pirata adj & mf pirate.

piratear vt to pirate.

piropo m **echar un p.** to pay a compliment.

pis m fam wee-wee, pee; **hacer p.** to wee-wee, to have a pee.

pisada f footstep; (huella) footprint.

pisapapeles m inv paperweight.

pisar vt to step on.

piscifactoría f fish farm.

piscina f swimming pool.

piscolabis m inv fam snack.

piso m apartment; (planta) floor; (de carretera) surface.

pisotear vt (aplastar) to stamp on; (pisar) to trample on.

pisotón m **me dio un p.** he stood on my foot.

pista f track; (rastro) trail; (indicio) clue; **p. de baile** dance floor; **p. de esquí** ski slope; **p. de patinaje** ice rink; **p. de tenis** tennis court; **p. de aterrizaje** landing strip; **p. de despegue** runway.

pistacho m pistachio (nut).

pistola f pistol.

pitar 1 vt (silbato) to blow. **2** vi to whistle; (coche) to toot one's horn.

pitido m whistle.

pitillo m cigarette.

pito m whistle; (de vehículo) horn.

pizarra f (encerado) blackboard; (piedra) slate.

pizarrón m Am blackboard.

pizca f little bit; **ni p.** not a bit.

placa f plate; (conmemorativa) plaque.

placentero, -a adj pleasant, agreeable.

placer [33] *m* pleasure; **tengo el p. de …** it gives me great pleasure to ….

plácido, -a *adj* placid, easy-going.

plaga *f* plague.

plagiar [43] *vt (copiar)* to plagiarize; *Andes, CAm, Méx (secuestrar)* to kidnap.

plagiario, -a *mf Am (secuestrador)* kidnapper.

plagio *m* plagiarism.

plan *m (proyecto)* plan; *(programa)* program; **p. de estudios** syllabus; **estar a p.** to be on a diet.

plana *f* page; **primera p.** front page.

plancha *f* iron; *(de metal)* plate; *(de cocina)* hotplate; **sardinas a la p.** grilled sardines.

planchar *vt* to iron.

planeta *m* planet.

planificación *f* planning.

planificar [44] *vt* to plan.

planilla *f Am* application form.

plano, -a 1 *m (de ciudad)* map; *(proyecto)* plan. **2** *adj* flat.

planta *f* plant; *(del pie)* sole; *(piso)* floor, story; **p. baja** first floor.

plantado, -a *adj fam* **dejar a algn p.** to stand sb up.

plantar 1 *vt (árboles, campo)* to plant; *(poner)* to put, to place. **2 plantarse** *vr* to stand; *(llegar)* to arrive.

planteamiento *m* approach.

plantear 1 *vt (problema)* to raise; *(proponer)* to put forward; *(exponer)* to present. **2 plantearse** *vr (considerar)* to consider; *(problema)* to arise.

plantilla *f (personal)* staff; *(de zapato)* insole.

plantón *m fam* **dar un p. a algn** to stand sb up.

plasmar 1 *vt (reproducir)* to capture; *(expresar)* to express. **2 plasmarse** *vr* **plasmarse en** to take the shape of.

plástico, -a *adj & m* plastic.

plastificar [44] *vt* to coat o cover with plastic.

plastilina® *f* Plasticine®.

plata *f* silver; *(objetos de plata)* silverware; *Am* money; **p. de ley** sterling silver.

plataforma *f* platform.

plátano *m (fruta)* banana; *(árbol)* plane tree.

plática *f CAm, Méx* chat, talk.

platicar [44] *vi CAm, Méx* to chat, to talk.

platillo *m* saucer; **p. volante** flying saucer.

platina *f (de tocadiscos)* deck.

plato *m* plate, dish; *(parte de una comida)* course; *(guiso)* dish; *(de balanza)* tray; *(de tocadiscos)* turntable; **de primer p.** for starters; **p. combinado** one-course meal.

playa *f* beach; *(costa)* seaside; *Am* **p. de estacionamiento** parking lot.

playera *f* sneaker; *Am (camiseta)* teeshirt.

plaza *f* square; *(mercado)* marketplace; *(de vehículo)* seat; *(laboral)* post; **p. de toros** bullring.

plazo *m (periodo)* period; *(término)* deadline; **a corto/largo p.** in the short term/in the long run; **comprar a plazos** buy on an installment plan.

plegable *adj* folding.

plegar [1] *vt* to fold.

plegaria *f* prayer.

pleito *m* lawsuit; **poner un p. (a algn)** to sue (sb).

pleno, -a 1 *adj* full. **2** *m* plenary meeting.

pliego *m* sheet of paper.

pliegue *m* fold; *(de vestido)* pleat.

plomero *m Am* plumber.

plomo *m (metal)* lead; *(fusible)* fuse.

pluma *f* feather; *(de escribir)* fountain pen.

plumero *m* feather duster.

plumier *m* pencil box.

plural *adj & m* plural.

pluriempleo *m* moonlighting.

población *f (ciudad)* town; *(pueblo)* village; *(habitantes)* population.

poblado, -a 1 adj populated. **2** m village.

pobre 1 adj poor; **¡p.!** poor thing! **2** mf poor person; **los pobres** the poor.

pobreza f (indigencia) poverty; (escasez) scarcity.

pocho, -a adj (fruta) overripe.

pocillo m Am cup.

poco, -a 1 m **un p.** a little; **un p. de azúcar** a little sugar. **2** adj not much, little; **p. sitio/tiempo** not much space/time, little space/time; **pocos, -as** not many, few; **pocas personas** not many people, few people; **unos, -as pocos, -as** a few. **3** pron not much; **pocos, -as** few, not many; **queda p.** there isn't much left. **4** adv (con verbo) not (very) much, little; (con adj) not very; **p. generoso** not very generous; **un p. tarde/frío** a little late/cold; **dentro de p.** soon; **p. a p.** little by little; **p. antes/después** shortly before/afterwards; **por p.** almost.

podcast m podcast.

poder¹ m power.

poder² [18] **1** vt to be able to; **no puede hablar** she can't speak; **no podré llamar** I won't be able to phone. ▪ (permiso) may, can; **¿se puede (entrar)?** may o can I (come in)?; **aquí no se puede fumar** you can't smoke here. ▪ (posibilidad) may, might; **puede que no lo sepan** they may o might not know; **no puede ser** that's impossible; **puede (ser) (que sí)** maybe, perhaps. ▪ (deber) **podrías haberme advertido** you might have warned me. **2** vi to cope (con with).

poderoso, -a adj powerful.

podómetro m pedometer.

podré indic fut de **poder**.

podrido, -a adj rotten.

podrir vt defectivo de **pudrir**.

poesía f (género) poetry; (poema) poem.

poeta mf poet.

póker m poker.

polaco, -a 1 adj Polish. **2** mf Pole. **3** m (idioma) Polish.

polea f pulley.

polémica f controversy.

polémico, -a adj controversial.

polen m pollen.

policía 1 f police(force). **2** mf (hombre) policeman; (mujer) policewoman.

policíaco, -a, policiaco, -a, policial adj police; **novela/película policíaca** detective story/film.

polideportivo m sports center.

poliéster m polyester.

polietileno m polyethylene.

polígono m polygon; **p. industrial** industrial estate.

polilla f moth.

politécnico, -a adj & m polytechnic.

política f politics sing; (estrategia) policy.

políticamente adv **p. correcto(a)** politically correct

político, -a 1 adj political; (pariente) in-law; **su familia política** her in-laws. **2** mf politician.

póliza f (sello) stamp; **p. de seguros** insurance policy.

pollera f RP (occidental) skirt; Andes (indígena) = long skirt worn by Indian women.

polo m pole; (helado) Popsicle®; (deporte) polo; **P. Norte/Sur** North/South Pole.

polución f pollution.

polvera f powder compact.

polvo m dust; **limpiar** o **quitar el p.** to dust; **en p.** powdered; **polvo(s) de talco** talcum powder; fam **estar hecho p.** (deprimido) to be depressed.

pólvora f gunpowder.

polvoriento, -a adj dusty.

polvorón m sweet pastry.

pollo m chicken.

pomada f ointment.

pomelo m (fruto) grapefruit; (árbol) grapefruit tree.

pómez *adj inv* **piedra p.** pumice (stone).

pomo *m (de puerta)* knob.

pómulo *m* cheekbone.

ponche *m* punch.

poncho *m* poncho.

pondré *indic fut de* **poner**.

poner [19] *vt* to put; *(mesa, huevo)* to lay; *(gesto)* to make; *(multa)* to impose; *(telegrama)* to send; *(negocio)* to set up; *(encender)* to switch on; *(película)* to put on; *(+ adjetivo)* to make; **p. triste a algn** to make sb sad; **¿qué llevaba puesto?** what was he wearing?; *(decir)* **¿qué pone aquí?** what does it say here? **2 ponerse** *vr* to put oneself; *(vestirse)* to put on; *(+ adjetivo)* to become; *(sol)* to set; **ponerse al teléfono** to answer the phone; **ponerse a** to start to; **ponerse a trabajar** to get down to work.

poney *m* pony.

pongo *indic pres de* **poner**.

poniente *m (occidente)* West.

popa *f* stern.

popular *adj (música, costumbre)* folk; *(famoso)* popular.

popularidad *f* popularity.

póquer *m* poker.

por *prep (agente)* by; **pintado p. Picasso** painted by Picasso; **p. qué** why. ▪ *(causa)* because of; **p. necesidad/amor** out of need/love. ▪ *(tiempo)* **p. la mañana/noche** in the morning/at night; **p. ahora** for the time being. ▪ *(en favor de)* for; **lo hago p. mi hermano** I'm doing it for my brother('s sake). ▪ *(lugar)* **pasamos p. Córdoba** we went through Cordoba; **p. ahí** over there; **¿p. dónde vamos?** which way are we taking?; **mirar p. la ventana** to look out of the window; **entrar p. la ventana** to get in through the window. ▪ *(medio)* **p. avión/correo** by plane/post. ▪ *(a cambio de)* for; **cambiar algo p. algo** to exchange sth for sth. ▪ *(distributivo)* **p. cabeza** per

person; **p. hora/mes** per hour/month. ▪ *(multiplicación)* **dos p. tres, seis** two times three is six; **un diez p. ciento** ten percent. ▪ *(con infinitivo)* in order to. ▪ **p. más/muy ... que sea** no matter how ... he/she is; **p. mí** as far as I'm concerned.

porcelana *f* porcelain.

porcentaje *m* percentage.

porche *m* porch.

porción *f* portion.

pormenor *m* detail; **venta al p.** retail.

porno *adj inv* porn.

pornográfico, -a *adj* pornographic.

poro *m* pore.

porque *conj* because; **¡p. no!** just because!

porqué *m* reason.

porquería *f (suciedad)* dirt; *(birria)* garbage.

porra *f (de policía)* nightstick; *fam* **¡vete a la p.!** get lost!

porrazo *m* thump.

porrón *m* glass bottle with a spout coming out of its base, used for drinking wine.

portada *f (de libro etc)* cover; *(de periódico)* front page; *(de disco)* sleeve; *(fachada)* facade.

portaequipajes *m inv (maletero)* trunk; *(baca)* roof rack.

portal *m* entrance hall; *(porche)* porch; *(puerta de la calle)* main door.

portaminas *m inv* propelling pencil.

portamonedas *m inv* purse.

portarse *vr* to behave.

portátil *adj* portable.

portazo *m* slam of a door; **dar un p.** to slam the door.

portento *m (cosa)* marvel; *(persona)* genius.

portería *f* porter's lodge; *(de fútbol etc)* goal.

portero, -a 1 *mf (de vivienda)* caretaker; *(guardameta)* goalkeeper **2** *m* **p. automático** entryphone.

portorriqueño, -a *adj & mf* Puerto Rican.

portugués, -a *adj & mf* Portuguese.

porvenir *m* future.

posada *f* inn.

posar 1 *vi (para retrato etc)* to pose. **2** *vt* to put down. **3 posarse** *vr* to settle.

posdata *f* postscript.

poseer [36] *vt* to possess.

posibilidad *f* possibility; *(oportunidad)* chance.

posible *adj* possible; **de ser p.** if possible; **lo antes p.** as soon as possible; **es p. que venga** he might come.

posición *f* position.

positivo, -a *adj* positive.

posponer [19] *vt (aplazar)* to postpone; *(relegar)* to relegate.

postal 1 *adj* postal. **2** *f* postcard.

poste *m* pole; *(de portería)* post.

póster *m* poster.

posterior *adj (lugar)* rear; *(tiempo)* subsequent (**a** to).

posteriormente *adv* subsequently.

postgraduado, -a *adj & mf* postgraduate.

postigo *m (de puerta)* wicket; *(de ventana)* shutter.

postizo, -a *adj* false; **dentadura postiza** dentures *pl.*

postre *m* dessert.

póstumo, -a *adj* posthumous.

postura *f* position.

potable *adj* drinkable; **agua p./no p.** drinking water/not drinking water.

potaje *m* hotpot.

potencia *f* power; **en p.** potential.

potencial *adj & m* potential.

potenciar [43] *vt* to promote, to strengthen.

potente *adj* powerful.

potro *m* colt; *(de gimnasia)* horse.

poyo *m* stone bench.

pozo *m* well; *(minero)* shaft.

práctica *f* practice; **en la p.** in practice.

practicante 1 *adj (de religión)* practicing. **2** *mf* medical assistant.

practicar [44] *vti* to practice; *(operación)* to carry out.

práctico, -a *adj* practical; *(útil)* handy.

pradera *f*, **prado** *m* meadow.

pragmático, -a *adj* pragmatic. **2** *mf* pragmatist.

preámbulo *m (introducción)* preamble; *(rodeo)* circumlocution.

precalentamiento *m* warm-up.

precario, -a *adj* precarious.

precaución *f (cautela)* caution; *(medida)* precaution; **con p.** cautiously.

precaver 1 *vt* to guard against. **2 precaverse** *vr* to take precautions (**de, contra** against).

precavido, -a *adj* cautious.

precedente 1 *adj* preceding. **2** *m* precedent; **sin p.** unprecedented.

preceder *vt* to precede.

precepto *m* precept.

precintar *vt* to seal off.

precinto *m* seal.

precio *m* price.

preciosidad *f (cosa)* lovely thing; *(persona)* darling.

precioso, -a *adj (hermoso)* lovely, beautiful; *(valioso)* precious.

precipicio *m* precipice.

precipitación *f (prisa)* haste; *(lluvia)* rainfall.

precipitado, -a *adj (apresurado)* hurried; *(irreflexivo)* rash.

precipitar 1 *vt (acelerar)* to hurry; *(arrojar)* to hurl down. **2 precipitarse** *vr (persona)* to hurl oneself; *(acontecimientos)* to gather speed; *(actuar irreflexivamente)* to rush.

precisamente *adv (con precisión)* precisely; *(exactamente)* exactly.

precisar *vt (especificar)* to specify; *(necesitar)* to require.

precisión *f (exactitud)* precision;

(aclaración) clarification; **con p.** precisely.

preciso, -a *adj (necesario)* necessary; *(exacto)* accurate; *(claro)* clear.

precoz *adj (persona)* precocious.

predecesor, -a *mf* predecessor.

predecir [12] *(pp predicho) vt* to predict.

predicado *m* predicate.

predicar [44] *vt* to preach.

predicción *f* prediction.

predigo *indic pres de* **predecir**.

predije *pt indef de* **predecir**.

predilecto, -a *adj* favorite.

predisponer [19] *(pp predispuesto) vt* to predispose.

predominante *adj* predominant.

predominar *vi* to predominate.

predominio *m* predominance.

preescolar *adj* preschool.

preferencia *f* preference.

preferible *adj* preferable; **es p. que no vengas** you'd better not come.

preferido, -a *adj & mf* favorite.

preferir [5] *vt* to prefer.

prefijo *m (telefónico)* area code; *(gramatical)* prefix.

pregunta *f* question; **hacer una p.** to ask a question; **preguntas más frecuentes** *(en página web)* frequently asked questions, FAQ.

preguntar 1 *vti* to ask; **p. algo a algn** to ask sb sth; **p. por algn** to ask about sb. **2 preguntarse** *vr* to wonder.

prehistórico, -a *adj* prehistoric.

prejuicio *m* prejudice.

preliminar *adj & m* preliminary.

prematuro, -a *adj* premature.

premeditado, -a *adj* premeditated.

premiar [43] *vt* to award a prize (**a** to); *(recompensar)* to reward.

premio *m* prize; *(recompensa)* reward.

prenatal *adj* prenatal.

prenda *f* garment.

prender 1 *vt (sujetar)* to fasten; *(con alfileres)* to pin; **p. fuego a** to set fire to. **2** *vi (fuego)* to catch; *(madera)* to catch fire. **2 prenderse** *vr* to catch fire.

prensa *f* press.

prensar *vt* to press.

preñado, -a *adj* pregnant.

preocupación *f* worry.

preocupado, -a *adj* worried.

preocupar 1 *vt* to worry. **2 preocuparse** *vr* to worry (**por** about); **no te preocupes** don't worry.

preparación *f* preparation; *(formación)* training.

preparado, -a 1 *adj (dispuesto)* ready, prepared; *(capacitado)* trained, qualified; **comidas preparadas** ready-cooked meals. **2** *m* preparation.

preparar 1 *vt* to prepare. **2 prepararse** *vr* to get ready.

preparativo *m* preparation.

preposición *f* preposition.

presa *f* prey; *(embalse)* dam; *fig* **ser p. de** to be a victim of.

presagiar [43] *vt* to predict.

presagio *m (señal)* omen; *(premonición)* premonition.

prescindir *vi* **p. de** to do without.

presencia *f* presence; **p. de ánimo** presence of mind.

presenciar [43] *vt* to witness.

presentación *f* presentation; *(de personas)* introduction.

presentador, -a *mf* presenter.

presentar 1 *vt* to present; *(una persona a otra)* to introduce. **2 presentarse** *vr (comparecer)* to present oneself; *(inesperadamente)* to turn up; *(ocasión, oportunidad)* to arise; *(candidato)* to stand; *(darse a conocer)* to introduce oneself (**a** to).

presente 1 *adj* present; **tener p.** *(tener en cuenta)* to bear in mind. **2** *m* present.

presentimiento *m* premonition.

preservar *vt* to preserve (**de** from; **contra** against).

preservativo *m* condom.

presidente, -a *mf* president; *(de una reunión)* chairperson.

presidiario, -a *mf* prisoner.

presidio *m* prison.

presidir *vt* to head; *(reunión)* to chair.

presión *f* pressure; **a** *o* **bajo p.** under pressure.

presionar *vt* to press; *fig* to pressurize.

préstamo *m* loan.

prestar 1 *vt* to lend, to loan; ¿me **prestas tu pluma?** can I borrow your pen?; *(atención)* to pay; *(ayuda)* to give; *(servicio)* to do. **2 prestarse** *vr (ofrecerse)* to offer oneself (**a** to); **prestarse a** *(dar motivo)* to cause; **se presta a (crear) malentendidos** it makes for misunderstandings.

prestidigitador, -a *mf* conjuror.

prestigio *m* prestige.

presumido, -a 1 *adj* conceited. **2** *mf* vain person.

presumir 1 *vt (suponer)* to presume. **2** *vi (ser vanidoso)* to show off.

presunto, -a *adj* supposed; *(culpable)* alleged.

presuntuoso, -a *adj (vanidoso)* conceited; *(pretencioso)* pretentious.

presuponer [19] *(pp* **presupuesto)** *vt* to presuppose.

presupuesto *m* budget; *(cálculo)* estimate.

pretender *vt (intentar)* to try; *(aspirar a)* to try for; *(cortejar)* to court.

pretendiente, -a 1 *mf (al trono)* pretender **2** *m (amante)* suitor.

pretérito *m* preterite.

pretexto *m* pretext.

prevenir [27] *vt (precaver)* to prevent; *(evitar)* to avoid; *(advertir)* to warn.

prever [28] *(pp* **previsto)** *vt* to forecast.

previo, -a *adj* prior; **sin p. aviso** without notice.

previsible *adj* predictable.

previsión *f (predicción)* forecast;

(precaución) precaution; **p. del tiempo** weather forecast; **en p. de** as a precaution against; *Andes, RP* **p. social** social security.

previsto, -a *adj* forecast.

primario, -a *adj* primary.

primavera *f* spring.

primer *adj (delante de m)* first.

primera *f (en tren)* first class; *(marcha)* first (gear).

primero, -a 1 *adj* first; **de primera necesidad** basic. **2** *mf* first; **a primero(s) de mes** at the beginning of the month. **3** *adv* first.

primitivo, -a *adj* primitive; *(tosco)* rough.

primo, -a 1 *mf* cousin; **p. hermano** first cousin. **2** *adj* **materia prima** raw material.

primogénito, -a *adj & mf* first-born.

primoroso, -a *adj* exquisite.

princesa *f* princess.

principal *adj* main, principal; **puerta p.** front door.

príncipe *m* prince.

principiante 1 *adj* novice. **2** *mf* beginner.

principio *m* beginning, start; *(fundamento)* principle; **a principio(s) de** at the beginning of; **al p., en un p.** at first; **en p.** in principle; **principios** basics.

pringar [42] **1** *vt (ensuciar)* to make greasy. **2 pringarse** *vr (ensuciarse)* to get greasy.

pringoso, -a *adj (grasiento)* greasy.

prioridad *f* priority.

prisa *f* hurry; **date p.** hurry up; **tener p.** to be in a hurry; **de** *o* **a p.** in a hurry.

prisión *f* prison.

prisionero, -a *mf* prisoner.

prismáticos *mpl* binoculars.

privado, -a *adj* private.

privar 1 *vt (despojar)* to deprive (**de** of). **2 privarse** *vr (abstenerse)* to go without.

privilegio *m* privilege.

pro 1 *m* advantage; **los pros y los**

contras the pros and cons. **2** *prep* in favor of.

proa *f* prow.

probable *adj* probable, likely; **es p. que llueva** it'll probably rain.

probador *m* fitting room.

probar [2] **1** *vt* to try; *(comprobar)* to check; *(demostrar)* to prove. **2** *vi* to try. **3 probarse** *vr* *(ropa)* to try on.

probeta *f* test tube.

problema *m* problem.

procedente *adj (adecuado)* appropriate; *(en juicio)* proper; **p. de** coming from.

proceder 1 *vi (actuar)* to act; *(ser oportuno)* to be advisable; **p. de** *(provenir)* to come from; **p. a** *(continuar)* to go on to. **2** *m (comportamiento)* behavior.

procedimiento *m* procedure.

procesador *m* processor; **p. de textos** word processor.

procesar *vt* to prosecute; *(información)* to process.

procesión *f* procession.

proceso *m* process; *(juicios)* trial; **p. de datos** data processing.

proclamar *vt* to proclaim.

procurar *vt (intentar)* to attempt; *(proporcionar)* to manage) to get; **procura que no te vean** make sure they don't see you.

prodigio *m* prodigy, miracle; **hacer prodigios** to work wonders; **niño p.** child prodigy.

prodigioso, -a *adj (sobrenatural)* prodigious; *(maravilloso)* wonderful.

producción *f (acción)* production; *(producto)* product; **p. en cadena/serie** assembly-line/mass production.

producir [10] **1** *vt* to produce; *(fruto, cosecha, rendir)* to yield; *(originar)* to bring about. **2 producirse** *vr* to take place.

productivo, -a *adj* productive; *(beneficioso)* profitable.

producto *m* product; *(producción)* produce.

productor, -a 1 *adj* producing. **2** *mf* producer.

profesión *f* profession.

profesional *adj & mf* professional.

profesor, -a *mf* teacher; *(de universidad)* lecturer.

profesorado *m (grupo de profesores)* staff.

profetizar [40] *vt* to prophesy.

prófugo, -a *adj & mf* fugitive.

profundidad *f* depth; **un metro de p.** one meter deep.

profundizar [40] *vt (cavar)* to deepen; *fig (examinar)* to study in depth.

profundo, -a *adj* deep; *(idea, sentimiento)* profound.

progenitor, -a *mf* **progenitores** *(padres)* parents.

programa *m* program; *(informático)* program; *(de estudios)* syllabus.

programación *f* programming.

programar *vt* to program; *(para ordenador)* to program.

progresar *vi* to make progress.

progresista *adj & mf* progressive.

progresivamente *adv* progressively.

progresivo, -a *adj* progressive.

progreso *m* progress.

prohibido, -a *adj* forbidden; **'prohibida la entrada'** 'no admittance'; **p. aparcar/fumar** no parking/smoking.

prohibir *vt* to forbid.

prójimo, -a *mf* one's fellow man.

proliferar *vi* to proliferate.

prólogo *m* prologue.

prolongar [42] **1** *vt (alargar)* to extend. **2 prolongarse** *vr (continuar)* to carry on.

promedio *m* average.

promesa *f* promise.

prometedor, -a *adj* promising.

prometer 1 *vt* to promise. **2** *vi* to be promising. **3 prometerse** *vr* to get engaged.

prometido, -a 1 *adj* promised. **2** *mf (hombre)* fiancé; *(mujer)* fiancée.

promocionar vt to promote.

promover [4] vt (cosas, personas) to promote; (juicio, querella) to initiate; (causar) to cause, to give rise to.

pronombre m pronoun.

pronosticar [44] vt to forecast.

pronóstico m (del tiempo) forecast; (médico) prognosis.

pronto, -a 1 adj quick, prompt. **2** adv (deprisa) quickly; (temprano) early; **de p.** suddenly; **por de o lo p.** (para empezar) to start with; ¡**hasta p.!** see you soon!

pronunciación f pronunciation.

pronunciar [43] vt to pronounce; (discurso) to deliver.

propaganda f (política) propaganda; (comercial) advertising; (postal) junk mail.

propagar [42] **1** vt to spread. **2 propagarse** vr to spread.

propiamente adv **p. dicho** strictly speaking.

propiedad f (posesión) ownership; (cosa poseída) property; **con p.** properly.

propietario, -a mf owner.

propina f tip.

propio, -a adj (de uno) own; (correcto) suitable; (característico) typical; (mismo) (hombre) himself; (mujer) herself; (animal, cosa) itself; **el p. autor** the author himself; **propios, -as** themselves.

proponer [19] (pp propuesto) **1** vt to propose. **2 proponerse** vr to intend.

proporción f proportion; **proporciones** (tamaño) size sing.

proporcional adj proportional.

proporcionar vt (dar) to give; (suministrar) to supply.

proposición f (propuesta) proposal.

propósito m (intención) intention; **a p.** (por cierto) by the way; (adrede) on purpose.

propuesta f suggestion.

propuse pt indef de **proponer**.

prórroga f (prolongación) extension; (en partido) overtime; (aplazamiento) postponement.

prorrogar [42] vt (prolongar) to extend; (aplazar) to postpone.

prosa f prose.

proseguir [6] vti to carry on.

prospecto m leaflet.

prosperar vi (negocio, país) to prosper; (propuesta) to be accepted.

próspero, -a adj prosperous.

prostitución f prostitution.

prostituta f prostitute.

protagonista mf main character.

protección f protection; **p. de escritura** write protection.

protector, -a 1 adj protective. **2** mf protector.

proteger [53] vt to protect.

protesta f protest.

protestante adj & mf Protestant.

protestar vi to protest; (quejarse) to complain.

protocolo m protocol.

protuberante adj bulging.

provecho m benefit; ¡**buen p.!** enjoy your meal!; **sacar p. de algo** to benefit from sth.

proveedor, -a mf supplier; **p. de acceso (a Internet)** Internet access provider.

proveer [36] (pp provisto) vt to supply.

provenir [27] vi **p. de** to come from.

proverbio m proverb.

provincia f province.

provisional adj provisional.

provisto, -a adj **p. de** equipped with.

provocación f provocation.

provocador, -a 1 mf instigator. **2** adj provocative.

provocar [44] vt (causar) to cause; (instigar) to provoke; **Am si no le provoca** if he doesn't feel like it.

provocativo, -a adj provocative.

próximamente adv soon.

proximidad f closeness; **en las proximidades de** in the vicinity of.

próximo, -a adj (cercano) near, close; (siguiente) next.

proyección f projection; (de película) showing.

proyectar vt (luz) to project; (planear) to plan; (película) to show.

proyectil m projectile.

proyecto m project.

proyector m projector.

prudencia f prudence; (moderación) care.

prudente adj prudent; (conductor) careful.

prueba f (argumento) proof; (examen etc) test; **a p. de agua/balas** waterproof/bullet-proof.

psicoanálisis m inv psycho-analysis.

psicología f psychology.

psicológico, -a adj psychological.

psicólogo, -a mf psychologist.

psicópata mf psychopath.

psiquiatra mf psychiatrist.

psiquiátrico, -a 1 adj psychiatric. **2** m mental hospital.

psíquico, -a adj psychic.

pta(s)., pts abr de **peseta(s)** peseta(s).

púa f (de planta) thorn; (de animal) spine; (de peine) tooth.

pub m (pl **pubs, pubes**) pub.

publicación f publication.

publicar [44] vt to publish; (divulgar) to publicize.

publicidad f advertising; (conocimiento público) publicity.

público, -a 1 adj public. **2** m public; (de teatro) audience; (de estadio) spectators pl.

puchero m (olla) cooking pot; (cocido) stew; **hacer pucheros** to pout.

pucho m Am dog-end.

pude pt indef de **poder**.

pudiente adj rich, wealthy.

pudor m modesty.

pudoroso, -a adj modest.

pudrir vt defective, **pudrirse** vr to rot.

pueblo m village; (small) town; (gente) people.

puente m bridge; **p. aéreo** (civil) air shuttle service.

puerco, -a 1 adj filthy. **2** m pig; f sow.

puericultura f pediatrics sing.

pueril adj childish.

puerro m leek.

puerta f door; (verja) gate.

puerto m (de mar, ordenador) port; (de montaña) (mountain) pass; **p. deportivo** marina.

puertorriqueño, -a adj & mf Puerto Rican.

pues conj (puesto que) as, since; (por lo tanto) therefore; (entonces) so; (para reforzar) ¡**p. claro que sí!** but of course!; **p. como iba diciendo** well, as I was saying; ¡**p. no!** certainly not!

puestero, -a mf Am stallholder.

puesto, -a 1 conj **p. que** since, as. **2** m (lugar) place; (empleo) post; (tienda) stall; **p. de trabajo** job. **3** adj (colocado) put; **llevar p.** (ropa) to have on, to wear.

pugna f fight.

pulcro, -a adj (extremely) neat.

pulga f flea.

pulgada f inch.

pulgar m thumb.

pulir vt (metal, madera) to polish.

pulmón m lung.

pulpería f Am store.

pulpo m octopus.

pulsación f pulsation; (en mecanografía) keystroke.

pulsar vt (timbre, botón) to press; (tecla) to hit.

pulsera f (aro) bracelet; **reloj de p.** wristwatch.

pulso m pulse; (mano firme) steady hand; **echarse un p.** to arm-wrestle.

pulverizador m spray, atomizer.

puma m puma.

puna f Am high moor; (mal) mountain sickness.

punta f (extremo) tip; (extremo afilado) point; (de cabello) end; **sacar p. a**

un lápiz to sharpen a pencil; **tecnología p.** state-of-the-art technology; **hora p.** rush hour.

puntapié *m* kick.

puntería *f* aim; **tener buena/mala p.** to be a good/bad shot.

puntiagudo, -a *adj* sharp.

puntilla *f (encaje)* lace; **dar la p.** to finish (the bull) off; **de puntillas** on tiptoe.

punto *m* point; *(marca)* dot; *(lugar)* point; *(de costura, sutura)* stitch; **a p.** ready; **a p. de** on the point of; **hasta cierto p.** to a certain extent; **p. muerto** neutral; **p. de vista** point of view; **p. y seguido** period; **p. y coma** semicolon; **dos puntos** colon; **p. y aparte** full stop, new paragraph; **las ocho en p.** eight o'clock sharp; **hacer p.** to knit.

puntuación *f (ortográfica)* punctuation; *(deportiva)* score; *(nota)* mark.

puntual 1 *adj* punctual. **2** *adv* punctually.

puntualidad *f* punctuality.

puntualizar [40] *vt* to make it clear.

puntuar [30] **1** *vt (al escribir)* to punctuate; *(calificar)* to mark. **2** *vi (marcar)* to score; *(ser puntuable)* to count.

punzante *adj (objeto)* sharp; *(dolor)* acute, piercing.

puñado *m* handful.

puñal *m* dagger.

puñalada *f* stab.

puñetazo *m* punch.

puño *m* fist; *(de camisa etc)* cuff; *(de herramienta)* handle.

pupa *f (herida)* sore.

pupila *f* pupil.

pupitre *m* desk.

puré *m* purée; **p. de patata** mashed potatoes *pl.*

pureza *f* purity.

purificar [44] *vt* to purify.

puritano, -a 1 *adj* puritanical. **2** *mf* puritan.

puro, -a 1 *adj (sin mezclas)* pure;

(mero) sheer; **aire p.** fresh air; **la pura verdad** the plain truth. **2** *m (cigarro)* cigar.

púrpura *adj inv* purple.

puse *pt indef de* **poner.**

puzzle *m* jigsaw puzzle.

P.V.P. *m abr de* **precio de venta al público** recommended retail price.

Pza., Plza. *abr de* **plaza** square, Sq.

Q

que¹ *pron rel (sujeto, persona)* who, that; *(cosa)* that, which. ▪ *(complemento, persona) no se traduce o* that; *(cosa) no se traduce o* that, which; **la chica q. conocí** the girl (that) I met; **el coche q. compré** the car (that *o* which) I bought. ▪ **lo q.** what. ▪ *(con infinitivo)* **hay mucho q. hacer** there's a lot to do.

que² *conj no se traduce o* that; **dijo que llamaría** he said (that) he would call. ▪ *(consecutivo) no se traduce o* that; **habla tan bajo q. no se le oye** he speaks so quietly (that) he can't be heard. ▪ *(en comparativas)* than; **mejor q. tú** better than you. ▪ *(causal)* because; **date prisa q. no tenemos mucho tiempo** hurry up, because we haven't got much time. ▪ *(enfático)* **¡q. no!** no! ▪ *(deseo, mandato) (+ subj)* **¡q. te diviertas!** enjoy yourself! ▪ *(final)* so that; **ven q. te dé un beso** come and let me give you a kiss. ▪ *(disyuntivo)* whether; **me da igual q. suba o no** I couldn't care whether he comes up or not. ▪ *(locuciones)* **q. yo sepa** as far as I know; **yo q. tú** if I were you.

qué 1 *pron interr* what; **¿q. quieres?** what do you want? ▪ *(exclamativo) (+ adj)* how; *(+ n)* what a; **¡q. bonito!** how pretty!; **¡q. lástima!** what a pity!

2 *adj interr* which; ¿q. libro quieres? which book do you want?

quebrada *f Am* stream.

quebrar [1] **1** *vt (romper)* to break. **2** *vi (empresa)* to go bankrupt. **2 quebrarse** *vr* to break.

quedar 1 *vi (restar)* to be left; *(con amigo)* to arrange to meet; *(acordar)* to agree (**en** to); *(estar situado)* to be; **quedan dos** there are two left; **quedaría muy bien allí** it would look very nice there; **q. en ridículo** to make a fool of oneself; **q. bien/mal** to make a good/bad impression. **2 quedarse** *vr (permanecer)* to stay; **quedarse sin dinero/pan** to run out of money/bread; **quedarse con hambre** to be still hungry; **quedarse (con)** *(retener)* to keep; **quédese (con) el cambio** keep the change.

quehacer *m* chore.

queja *f* complaint; *(de dolor)* groan.

quejarse *vr* to complain (**de** about).

quemadura *f* burn.

quemar 1 *vt* to burn. **2** *vi* to be burning hot. **3 quemarse** *vr fig* to burn oneself out.

quemazón *f* smarting.

quepo *indic pres de* **caber.**

querella *f* lawsuit.

querer [20] **1** *vt* to want; *(amar)* to love; **sin q.** without meaning to; ¡por lo que más quieras! for heaven's sake!; ¿quiere pasarme el pan? would you pass me the bread?; **q. decir** to mean; **no quiso darme permiso** he refused me permission. **2 quererse** *vr* to love each other.

querido, -a *adj* dear.

querré *indic fut de* **querer.**

queso *m* cheese.

quicio *m (de puerta)* doorpost; **sacar de q. (a algn)** to infuriate (sb).

quien *pron rel* **el hombre con q. vino** the man she came with; *(formal)* the man with whom she came. ▪ *(in-*

definido) **q. quiera venir** whoever wants to come; **hay q. dice lo contrario** thre are some people who say the opposite.

quién *pron interr* who; ¿q. es? who is it?; ¿para q. es? who is it for?; ¿de q. es esa bici? whose bike is that?

quienquiera *pron indef (pl* **quienesquiera)** whoever.

quieto, -a *adj* still; ¡estáte q.! keep still!

quilo *m* = **kilo.**

química *f (ciencia)* chemistry.

químico, -a 1 *adj* chemical. **2** *m (científico)* chemist.

quince *adj & m inv* fifteen.

quiniela *f* sports lottery.

quinientos, -as *adj & mf* five hundred.

quinqué *m* oil lamp.

quintal *m (medida)* 46 kg; **q. métrico** = 100 kg.

quinto, -a *adj & mf* fifth.

quiosco *m* kiosk; **q. de periódicos** newspaper stand.

quirófano *m* operating room.

quirúrgico, -a *adj* surgical.

quise *pt de* **querer.**

quitaesmaltes *m inv* nail varnish remover.

quitamanchas *m inv* stain remover.

quitanieves *m* **(máquina) q.** snowplow.

quitar 1 *vt* to remove, to take away; *(ropa)* to take off; *(dolor)* to relieve; *(sed)* to quench; *(hambre)* to take away; *(robar)* to steal; *(tiempo)* to take up; *(asiento)* to take. **2** *vi* ¡quita! get out of the way! **3 quitarse** *vr (apartarse)* to move away; *(mancha)* to come out; *(dolor)* to go away; *(ropa, gafas)* to take off; **quitarse de fumar** to give up smoking; **quitarse a algn de encima** to get rid of sb.

quizá(s) *adv* perhaps, maybe.

R

rábano m radish.
rabia f (ira) rage; (enfermedad) rabies sing; **¡qué r.!** how annoying!; **me da r.** it makes me mad.
rabiar [43] vi (enfadarse) to rage; **hacer r. a algn** to make sb see red.
rabioso, -a adj rabid; (enfadado) furious.
rabo m (de animal) tail; (de fruta) stalk.
racha f (período) spell; (de viento) gust.
racial adj racial.
racimo m bunch.
ración f portion.
racionar vt to ration.
racismo m racism.
racista adj & mf racist.
radar m (pl **radares**) radar.
radiación f radiation.
radiactividad f radioactivity.
radiactivo, -a adj radioactive.
radiador m radiator.
radiante adj radiant (**de** with).
radical adj radical.
radio¹ f (aparato) radio.
radio² m (de circunferencia) radius; (de rueda) spoke.
radioactividad f radioactivity.
radiocasete m radio cassette.
radiografía f (imagen) X-ray.
ráfaga f (de viento) gust; (de disparos) burst.
raído, -a adj (gastado) worn.
raíz f (pl **raíces**) root; **r. cuadrada** square root; **a r. de** as a result of.
raja f (corte) cut; (hendidura) crack.
rajar 1 vt (tela) to tear; (hender) to crack. **2 rajarse** vr (tela) to tear; (partirse) to crack; fam (echarse atrás) to back out; (acobardarse) to chicken out.
rallado, -a adj queso r. grated cheese; **pan r.** breadcrumbs pl.

rallador m grater.
rallar vt to grate.
ralo, -a adj thin.
rama f branch.
ramillete m (de flores) posy.
ramo m (de flores) bunch; (sector) branch.
rampa f ramp.
rana f frog.
rancho m (granja) ranch.
rancio, -a adj (comida) stale.
rango m rank; (jerarquía elevada) high social standing.
ranura f slot; **r. de expansión** expansion slot.
rapar vt to crop.
rapaz 1 adj predatory; **ave r.** bird of prey. **2** mf (muchacho) lad; (muchacha) lass.
rape m (pez) angler fish; **cortado al r.** close-cropped.
rapidez f speed.
rápido, -a 1 adj quick, fast. **2** adv quickly. **3** m (tren) fast train.
raptar vt to kidnap.
rapto m (secuestro) kidnapping.
raqueta f (de tenis) racket; (de ping-pong) paddle.
raquítico, -a adj (delgado) emaciated; fam (escaso) meager.
raro, -a adj rare; (extraño) strange.
rascacielos m inv skyscraper.
rascar [44] vt (con las uñas) to scratch.
rasgar [42] vt to tear.
rasgo m feature.
rasguño m scratch.
raso, -a 1 adj (llano) flat; (cielo) clear. **2** m satin.
raspa f (de pescado) bone.
raspar 1 vt (limar) to scrape (off). **2** vi (ropa, tela) to chafe.
rastrear vt (zona) to comb.
rastrillo m rake; (mercadillo) flea market.
rastro m trace; (en el suelo) trail.
rasurar vt, **rasurarse** vr to shave.
rata f rat.
ratero, -a mf pickpocket.

ratificar [44] *vt* to ratify.
rato *m (momento)* while; **a ratos** at times; **al poco r.** shortly after; **pasar un buen/mal r.** to have a good/bad time; **ratos libres** free time *sing.*
ratón *m (también de ordenador)* mouse.
raya *f (línea)* line; *(del pantalón)* crease; *(del pelo)* part; **camisa a rayas** striped shirt.
rayar *vt* to scratch.
rayo *m* ray; *(relámpago)* (flash of) lightning.
raza *f (humana)* race; *(de animal)* breed.
razón *f* reason; *(proporción)* rate; **uso de r.** power of reasoning; **dar la r. a algn** to say that sb is right; **tener r.** to be right.
razonable *adj* reasonable.
razonar 1 *vt (argumentar)* to reason out. **2** *vi (discurrir)* to reason.
reacción *f* reaction; **avión de r.** jet (plane).
reaccionar *vi* to react.
reactor *m* reactor; *(avión)* jet (plane).
reajuste *m* readjustment.
real¹ *adj (efectivo, verdadero)* real.
real² *adj (regio)* royal.
realidad *f* reality; **en r.** in fact.
realismo *m* realism.
realizador, -a *mf* producer.
realizar [40] **1** *vt (hacer)* to carry out; *(ambición)* to achieve. **2 realizarse** *vr (persona)* to fulfill oneself; *(sueño)* to come true.
realmente *adv* really.
realzar [40] *vt (recalcar)* to highlight; *(belleza, importancia)* to heighten.
reanimar *vt*, **reanimarse** *vr* to revive.
reanudar 1 *vt* to renew. **2 reanudarse** *vr* to resume.
rebaja *f (descuento)* reduction; **rebajas** sales.
rebajar 1 *vt (precio)* to cut; *(tanto por ciento)* to take off. **2 rebajarse** *vr (humillarse)* to humble oneself.

rebanada *f* slice.
rebaño *m* herd; *(de ovejas)* flock.
rebasar *vt (exceder)* to exceed.
rebeca *f* cardigan.
rebelarse *vr* to rebel.
rebelde 1 *mf* rebel. **2** *adj* rebellious.
rebelión *f* rebellion.
rebobinar *vt* to rewind.
rebosar *vi* to overflow.
rebotar *vi (pelota)* to bounce; *(bala)* to ricochet.
rebuznar *vi* to bray.
recado *m (mandado)* errand; *(mensaje)* message; **dejar un r.** to leave a message.
recalcar [44] *vt* to stress.
recalentar [1] *vt (comida)* to reheat.
recámara *f (de rueda)* tube; *(habitación)* dressing room; *CAm, Col, Méx (dormitorio)* bedroom.
recambio *m (repuesto)* spare (part); *(de pluma etc)* refill; **rueda de r.** spare wheel.
recapacitar *vt* to think over.
recargado, -a *adj (estilo)* over-elaborate.
recargar [42] *vt (batería)* to recharge; *(adornar mucho)* to over-elaborate; *(celular)* to recharge.
recatado, -a *adj (prudente)* cautious; *(modesto)* modest.
recaudador, -a *mf* tax collector.
recaudar *vt* to collect.
recelar *vi* **r. de** to distrust.
receloso, -a *adj* suspicious.
recepción *f* reception.
recepcionista *mf* receptionist.
receptor, -a 1 *mf (persona)* recipient. **2** *m (aparato)* receiver.
receta *f* recipe; **r. (médica)** prescription.
recetar *vt* to prescribe.
rechazar [40] *vt* to reject.
rechinar *vi (metal)* to squeak; *(dientes)* to chatter.
rechoncho, -a *adj* chubby.
recibidor *m* entrance hall.
recibimiento *m* reception.
recibir 1 *vt* to receive; *(acoger)* to

welcome. **2 recibirse** *vr Am* **recibirse de** to qualify as.

recibo *m (factura)* bill; *(resguardo)* receipt.

reciclar *vt* to recycle.

recién *adv* recently; *Am (hace poco)* recently. **r. casados** newlyweds; **r. nacido** newborn baby.

reciente *adj* recent.

recientemente *adv* recently.

recinto *m (cercado)* enclosure; **r. comercial** shopping precinct.

recio, -a *adj (robusto)* sturdy; *(grueso)* thick; *(voz)* loud.

recipiente *m* container.

recíproco, -a *adj* reciprocal.

recitar *vt* to recite.

reclamación *f (demanda)* claim; *(queja)* complaint.

reclamar 1 *vt* to claim. **2** *vi* to protest (**contra** against).

reclinar 1 *vt* to lean (**sobre** on). **2 reclinarse** *vr* to lean back.

recluir [37] *vt* to shut away.

recluso, -a *mf* inmate.

recobrar 1 *vt* to recover; *(conocimiento)* to regain; **r. el aliento** to get one's breath back. **2 recobrarse** *vr* to recover.

recodo *m* bend.

recoger [53] **1** *vt* to pick up; *(datos etc)* to collect; *(ordenar, limpiar)* to clean; *(cosecha)* to gather. **2 recogerse** *vr* **r. el pelo** to put one's hair up

recogida *f* collection; *(cosecha)* harvest.

recomendación *f* recommendation; *(para persona)* reference.

recomendar [1] *vt* to recommend.

recompensa *f* reward.

reconciliar [43] **1** *vt* to reconcile. **2 reconciliarse** *vr* to be reconciled.

reconfortante *adj* comforting.

reconocer [34] *vt* to recognize; *(admitir)* to admit; *(paciente)* to examine.

reconocimiento *m* recognition; *(médico)* examination.

reconstituyente *m* tonic.

reconstruir [37] *vt* to reconstruct.

recopilación *f* compilation.

recopilar *vt* to compile.

récord *m* record.

recordar [2] *vt* to remember; **r. algo a algn** to remind sb of sth.

recorrer *vt (distancia)* to travel; *(país)* to tour; *(ciudad)* to walk round.

recorrido *m (trayecto)* journey; *(itinerario)* route.

recortar *vt* to cut out.

recorte *m* cutting; *(de pelo)* trim.

recostar [2] **1** *vt* to lean. **2 recostarse** *vr (tumbarse)* to lie down.

recreo *m* recreation; *(en colegio)* break, playtime.

recriminar *vt* to recriminate; *(reprochar)* to reproach.

recrudecer [33] *vt*, **recrudecerse** *vr* to worsen.

recta *f (de carretera)* straight stretch.

rectangular *adj* rectangular.

rectángulo *m* rectangle.

rectificar [44] *vt* to rectify; *(corregir)* to remedy.

recto, -a **1** *adj (derecho)* straight; *(ángulo)* right. **2** *adv* straight (on).

rector, -a *mf* rector.

recuerdo *m (memoria)* memory; *(regalo etc)* souvenir; **recuerdos** regards.

recuperación *f* recovery.

recuperar 1 *vt (salud)* to recover; *(conocimiento)* to regain; *(tiempo, clases)* to make up. **2 recuperarse** *vr* to recover.

recurrir *vi (sentencia)* to appeal; **r. a** *(a algn)* to turn to; *(a algo)* to resort to.

recurso *m* resource; *(de sentencia)* appeal.

red *f* net; *(sistema)* network; **r. local** local area network, LAN.

redacción *f (escrito)* composition; *(acción)* writing.

redactar *vt* to draft.

redactor, -a *mf* editor.

redondel *m (círculo)* ring.

redondo, -a *adj* round; *(rotundo)* categorical.

reducción *f* reduction.

reducir [10] **1** *vt (disminuir)* to reduce. **2 reducirse** *vr (disminuirse)* to diminish; *(limitarse)* to confine oneself (**a** to).

reembolso *m* reimbursement; **contra r.** cash on delivery.

reemplazar [40] *vt* to replace (**con** with).

ref. *abr de* **referencia** reference, ref.

refaccionar *vt Am* to repair.

refectorio *m* refectory.

referencia *f* reference.

referéndum *m (pl* **referéndums)** referendum.

referente *adj* **r. a** concerning, regarding.

referir [5] **1** *vt* to tell. **2 referirse** *vr (aludir)* to refer (**a** to).

refilón: de refilón *adv* briefly.

refinería *f* refinery.

reflector *m* spotlight.

reflejar 1 *vt* to reflect. **2 reflejarse** *vr* to be reflected (**en** in).

reflejo, -a 1 *m (imagen)* reflection; *(destello)* gleam; **reflejos** *(en el cabello)* highlights. **2** *adj (movimiento)* reflex.

reflexión *f* reflection.

reflexionar *vi* to think (**sobre** about).

reflexivo, -a *adj (persona)* thoughtful; *(verbo etc)* reflexive.

reforma *f* reform; *(reparación)* repair.

reformar *vt* to reform; *(edificio)* to renovate.

reformatorio *m* reform school.

reforzar [2] *vt* to strengthen.

refrán *m* saying.

refregar [1] *vt* to rub vigorously.

refrescante *adj* refreshing.

refrescar [44] **1** *vt* to refresh. **2** *vi (bebida)* to be refreshing. **3 refrescarse** *vr* to cool down.

refresco *m* soft drink.

refrigeración *f* refrigeration; *(aire acondicionado)* air conditioning.

refrigerado, -a *adj (local)* air-conditioned.

refrigerador *m* refrigerator, fridge.

refrigerio *m* snack, refreshments *pl.*

refuerzo *m* strengthening.

refugiarse [43] *vr* to take refuge.

refugio *m* refuge.

refunfuñar *vi* to grumble.

regadera *f* watering can.

regalar *vt (dar)* to give (as a present).

regaliz *m* licorice.

regalo *m* present.

regañadientes: a regañadientes *adv* reluctantly.

regañar 1 *vt* to tell off. **2** *vi* to nag.

regar [1] *vt* to water.

regata *f* regatta.

regatear *vi* to haggle; *(en fútbol)* to dribble.

regazo *m* lap.

regeneración *f* regeneration.

régimen *m (pl* **regímenes)** regime; *(dieta)* diet; **estar a r.** to be on a diet.

regio, -a *adj (real)* regal; *Am (magnífico)* majestic.

región *f* region.

regional *adj* regional.

regir [58] **1** *vt* to govern. **2** *vi* to be in force. **3 regirse** *vr* to be guided, to go (**por** by).

registrado, -a *adj* **marca registrada** registered trademark.

registrar 1 *vt (examinar)* to inspect; *(cachear)* to frisk; *(inscribir)* to register. **2 registrarse** *vr (detectarse)* to be recorded; *(inscribirse)* to register.

registro *m* inspection; *(inscripción)* registration.

regla *f (norma)* rule; *(instrumento)* ruler; *(periodo)* period; **por r. general** as a (general) rule.

reglamentario, -a *adj* statutory.

reglamento *m* regulations *pl.*

regocijar *vt* to delight.

regocijo *m (placer)* delight; *(alborozo)* rejoicing.

regresar *vi* to return.

regreso *m* return.

regular 1 *vt* to regulate; *(ajustar)* to adjust. **2** *adj* regular; *(mediano)* so-so; **vuelo r.** scheduled flight. **3** *adv* so-so.

regularidad *f* regularity; **con r.** regularly.

regularizar [40] *vt* to regularize.

rehabilitar *vt* to rehabilitate; *(edificio)* to convert.

rehacer [15] *(pp* **rehecho**) **1** *vt* to redo. **2 rehacerse** *vr (recuperarse)* to recover.

rehén *m* hostage.

rehogar [42] *vt* to brown.

rehuir [37] *vt* to shun.

rehusar *vt* to refuse.

reina *f* queen.

reinar *vi* to reign.

reincidir *vi* to relapse (**en** into).

reincorporarse *vr* **r. al trabajo** to return to work.

reino *m* kingdom; **el R. Unido** the United Kingdom.

reinserción *f* reintegration.

reinsertar *vt*, **reinsertarse** *vr* to reintegrate.

reír [56] *vi*, **reírse** *vr* to laugh (**de** at).

reiterar *vt* to reiterate.

reivindicación *f* demand.

reivindicar [44] *vt* to demand.

reja *f (de ventana)* grating.

rejilla *f* grill; *(de horno)* gridiron; *(por equipaje)* luggage rack.

rejoneador, -a *mf* bullfighter on horseback.

relación *f* relationship; *(conexión)* connection; **relaciones públicas** public relations.

relacionado, -a *adj* related (**con** to).

relacionar 1 *vt* to relate (**con** to). **2 relacionarse** *vr* to be related; *(alternar)* to get acquainted.

relajación *f* relaxation.

relajante *adj* relaxing.

relajar *vt*, **relajarse** *vr* to relax.

relamerse *vr* to lick one's lips.

relámpago *m* flash of lightning.

relatar *vt* to tell, to relate.

relativo, -a *adj* relative (**a** to).

relato *m* story.

relax *m* relaxation.

relegar [42] *vt* to relegate.

relevante *adj* important.

relevar *vt (sustituir)* to take over from.

relevo *m* relief; *(en carrera)* relay.

religión *f* religion.

religioso, -a 1 *adj* religious. **2** *mf (hombre)* monk; *(mujer)* nun.

relinchar *vi* to neigh.

rellano *m* landing.

rellenar *vt (impreso etc)* to fill in; *(llenar)* to pack (**de** with).

relleno, -a 1 *m (de aves)* stuffing; *(de pasteles)* filling. **2** *adj* stuffed.

reloj *m* clock; *(de pulsera)* watch.

relojería *f (tienda)* watchmaker's.

reluciente *adj* shining.

relucir [35] *vi* to shine.

reluzco *indic pres de* **relucir**.

remache *m* rivet.

remangar [42] *vt*, **remangarse** *vr (mangas, pantalones)* to roll up; *(camisa)* to tuck up.

remar *vi* to row.

rematar *vt* to finish off.

remate *m (final)* finish; *(en fútbol)* shot at goal; **para r.** to crown it all; **de r.** utter.

remediar [43] *vt* to remedy; *(enmendar)* to repair; **no pude remediarlo** I couldn't help it.

remedio *m (cura)* remedy; *(solución)* solution; **¡qué r.!** what else can I do!; **no hay más r.** there's no choice; **sin r.** without fail.

remendar [1] *vt (ropa)* to patch.

remesa *f (de mercancías)* consignment.

remiendo *m (arreglo)* mend; *(parche)* patch.

remilgado, -a *adj (melindroso)* fussy.

remite m (en carta) sender's name and address.

remitente mf sender.

remitir 1 vt (enviar) to send. **2** vi (fiebre, temporal) to subside.

remo m oar.

remodelación f (modificación) reshaping; (reorganización) reorganization.

remojar vt to soak (**en** in).

remojón m fam **darse un r.** to go for a dip.

remolacha f red beet.

remolcador m tug.

remolcar [44] vt to tow.

remolino m (de agua) whirlpool; (de aire) whirlwind.

remolón, -ona adj **hacerse el r.** to shirk, to slack.

remolonear vi to shirk, to slack.

remolque m (acción) towing; (vehículo) trailer.

remordimiento m remorse.

remoto, -a adj remote.

remover [4] vt (tierra) to turn over; (líquido) to shake up; (comida etc) to stir.

remplazar [40] vt = **reemplazar**.

remuneración f remuneration.

remunerar vt to remunerate.

renacer [60] vi to be reborn; fig (revivir) to revive, to come back to life.

renacuajo m tadpole; fam (niño pequeño) shrimp.

rencor m resentment; **guardar r. a algn** to have a grudge against sb.

rencoroso, -a adj resentful.

rendido, -a adj (muy cansado) exhausted.

rendija f crack.

rendimiento m (de máquina, motor) performance.

rendir [6] **1** vt (fruto, beneficios) to yield; (cansar) to exhaust. **2** vi (dar beneficios) to pay. **3 rendirse** vr to surrender.

RENFE f abr de **Red Nacional de Ferrocarriles Españoles** Spanish railroad network.

renglón m line.

reno m reindeer.

renombre m renown.

renovación f (de contrato, pasaporte) renewal.

renovar [2] vt to renew; (edificio) to renovate.

renta f (ingresos) income; (beneficio) interest; (alquiler) rent.

rentable adj profitable.

renunciar [43] vi (dimitir) to resign; (no aceptar) to decline; **r. a** to give up.

reñido, -a adj (disputado) hard-fought.

reñir [6] **1** vt (regañar) to tell off. **2** vi (discutir) to argue; (pelear) to fight.

reo mf (acusado) accused; (culpable) culprit.

reojo: de reojo adv **mirar algo de r.** to look at sth out of the corner of one's eye.

reparar 1 vt to repair. **2** vi **r. en** (darse cuenta de) to notice.

reparo m **no tener reparos en** not to hesitate to; **me da r.** I am embarrassed.

repartidor, -a mf distributor.

repartir vt (dividir) to share out; (regalo, premio) to give out; (correo) to deliver.

reparto m distribution; (distribución) handing out; (de mercancías) delivery; (de actores) cast.

repasar vt to revise.

repaso m revision.

repecho m short steep slope.

repeler vt (repugnar) to disgust.

repente: de repente adv suddenly.

repentino, -a adj sudden.

repercutir 1 vt (subida de precio) to pass on. **2** vi **r. en** to affect.

repertorio m repertoire.

repetición f repetition.

repetir [6] **1** vt to repeat; (plato) to have a second helping of. **2** vi (en colegio) to repeat a year. **3 repetirse** vr (hecho) to recur.

repicar [44] *vti (campanas)* to ring.

repisa *f* shelf.

replegarse [1] *vr* to fall back.

repleto, -a *adj* full (up); **r. de** packed with.

réplica *f* answer; *(copia)* replica.

replicar [44] **1** *vt (objetar)* to argue. **2** *vi* to reply.

repoblar [2] *vt* to repopulate; *(bosque)* to reforest.

repollo *m* cabbage.

reponer [19] **1** *vt* to replace. **2 reponerse** *vr* **reponerse de** to recover from.

reportaje *m* report; *(noticias)* news item.

reportar 1 *vt (beneficios)* to bring; *Am (informar)* to report. **2 reportarse** *vr Am (presentarse)* to report (**a** to).

reportero, -a *mf* reporter.

reposar *vti* to rest (**en** on).

reposo *m* rest.

repostar *vti (gasolina)* to fill up.

repostería *f* confectionery.

reprender *vt* to reprimand.

represalia *f (usu pl)* reprisals *pl*, retaliation.

representante *mf* representative.

representar *vt* to represent; *(significar)* to mean; *(obra)* to perform.

represión *f* repression.

represivo, -a *adj* repressive.

reprimenda *f* reprimand.

reprimir *vt* to repress.

reprochar *vt* **r. algo a algn** to reproach sb for sth.

reproducción *f* reproduction.

reproducir [10] *vt*, **reproducirse** *vr* to reproduce.

reptil *m* reptile.

república *f* republic.

repuesto *m (recambio)* spare (part); **rueda de r.** spare wheel.

repugnante *adj* disgusting.

repugnar *vt* to disgust.

repulsivo, -a *adj* repulsive.

repuse *pt indef de* **reponer**.

reputación *f* reputation.

requesón *m* cottage cheese.

requisar *vt* to requisition.

requisito *m* requirement.

res *f* animal.

resaca *f* hangover.

resaltar *vi (sobresalir)* to project; *fig* to stand out.

resbaladizo, -a *adj* slippery.

resbalar *vi*, **resbalarse** *vr* to slip.

resbalón *m* slip.

rescatar *vt (liberar)* to rescue.

rescate *m* rescue; *(dinero pagado)* ransom.

rescindir *vt (contrato)* to cancel.

rescoldo *m* embers *pl*.

resecarse [44] *vr* to dry up, to become parched.

reseco, -a *adj* parched.

resentido, -a *adj* resentful.

resentimiento *m* resentment.

reserva *f (de entradas etc)* booking; *(provisión)* reserve.

reservado, -a *adj* reserved.

reservar *vt (billetes etc)* to reserve, to book; *(guardar)* to keep.

resfriado, -a 1 *m (catarro)* cold; **coger un r.** to catch (a) cold. **2** *adj* **estar r.** to have a cold.

resfriarse *vr* to catch (a) cold.

resguardo *m (recibo)* receipt.

residencia *f* residence; **r. de ancianos** old people's home.

residencial *adj* residential.

residente *adj & mf* resident.

residir *vi* to reside (**en** in).

resignado, -a *adj* resigned.

resignarse *vr* to resign oneself (**a** to).

resina *f* resin.

resistencia *f* resistance; *(aguante)* endurance; *(de bombilla etc)* element.

resistente *adj* resistant (**a** to); *(fuerte)* tough, hardy.

resistir 1 *vi* to resist; *(soportar)* to hold (out). **2** *vt (situación, persona)* to put up with; *(tentación)* to resist. **2 resistirse** *vr* to resist; *(oponerse)* to offer resistance; *(negarse)* to refuse.

resolver [4] (*pp* **resuelto**) **1** *vt* (*solucionar*) to solve; (*asunto*) to settle. **2 resolverse** *vr* (*solucionarse*) to be solved.

resonar [2] *vi* to resound; (*tener eco*) to echo.

resoplar *vi* (*respirar*) to breathe heavily; (*de cansancio*) to puff and pant.

resorte *m* (*muelle*) spring; (*medio*) means.

respaldar *vt* to support, to back (up).

respaldo *m* (*de asiento*) back.

respecto *m* **al r., a este r.** in this respect; **con r. a, r. a** with regard to.

respetable *adj* respectable.

respetar *vt* to respect.

respeto *m* respect.

respetuoso, -a *adj* respectful.

respingo *m* start.

respiración *f* (*acción*) breathing; (*aliento*) breath.

respirar *vti* to breathe.

resplandecer [33] *vi* to shine.

resplandor *m* (*brillo*) brightness; (*muy intenso*) brilliance; (*de fuego*) blaze.

responder 1 *vt* to answer. **2** *vi* (*a una carta*) to reply; (*reaccionar*) to respond; (*corresponder*) to answer; (*protestar*) to answer back.

responsabilidad *f* responsibility.

responsabilizar [40] **1** *vt* to make responsible (**de** for); (*culpar*) hold responsible (**de** for). **2 responsabilizarse** *vr* to claim responsibility (**de** for).

responsable 1 *adj* responsible. **2** *mf* **el/la r.** (*de robo etc*) the perpetrator.

respuesta *f* answer, reply; (*reacción*) response.

resquicio *m* chink.

resta *f* subtraction.

restablecer [33] **1** *vt* to re-establish; (*el orden*) to restore. **2 restablecerse** *vr* (*mejorarse*) to recover.

restaguardia *f* rearguard.

restante *adj* remaining.

restar *vt* to subtract.

restaurante *m* restaurant.

restaurar *vt* to restore.

resto *m* rest; (*en resta*) remainder; **restos** remains; (*de comida*) leftovers.

restregar [1] *vt* to scrub.

restricción *f* restriction.

restringir [57] *vt* to restrict.

resucitar *vti* to revive.

resuello *m* gasp.

resultado *m* result; (*consecuencia*) outcome.

resultar *vi* (*ser*) to turn out; **me resultó fácil** it turned out to be easy for me.

resumen *m* summary; **en r.** in short.

resumir *vt* to sum up.

resurgir [57] *vi* to reappear.

retahíla *f* series *sing*.

retal *m* (*pedazo*) scrap.

retar *vt* to challenge.

retardarse *vr* to be delayed.

retazo *m* (*pedazo*) scrap.

retención *f* retention; **r. de tráfico** (traffic) hold-up.

retener [24] *vt* (*conservar*) to retain; (*detener*) to detain.

reticente *adj* reticent, reserved.

retirada *f* withdrawal.

retirar 1 *vt* (*apartar, alejar*) to take away; (*dinero*) to withdraw. **2 retirarse** *vr* (*apartarse*) to withdraw; (*irse, jubilarse*) to retire.

retiro *m* (*lugar tranquilo*) retreat.

reto *m* challenge.

retoque *m* final touch.

retorcer [41] **1** *vt* (*cuerda, hilo*) to twist; (*ropa*) to wring (out). **2 retorcerse** *vr* to become twisted.

retorcido, -a *adj fig* twisted.

retornar 1 *vt* to return, to give back. **2** *vi* to return, to come back, to go back.

retorno *m* return.

retortijón *m* (*dolor*) stomach cramp.

retraído, -a *adj* reserved.

retransmisión f broadcast.
retrasado, -a 1 adj (tren etc) late; (reloj) slow; **estar r.** (en el colegio) to be behind. **2** mf **r. (mental)** mentally retarded person.
retrasar 1 vt (retardar) to slow down; (atrasar) to postpone; (reloj) to put back. **2 retrasarse** vr to be delayed; (reloj) to be slow.
retraso m (demora) delay; **con r.** late; **una hora de r.** an hour behind schedule.
retratar 1 vt (pintar) to paint a portrait of; (fotografiar) to take a photograph of; fig (describir) to describe, to depict. **2 retratarse** vr to have one's photograph taken.
retrato m (pintura) portrait; (fotografía) photograph.
retrete m toilet.
retribución f (pago) pay; (recompensa) reward.
retroceder vi to back away.
retroceso m (movimiento) backward movement.
retrógrado, -a adj & mf (reaccionario) reactionary.
retrospectivo, -a adj & f retrospective.
retrovisor m rear-view mirror.
retumbar vi (resonar) to resound; (tronar) to thunder.
retuve pt indef de **retener**.
reúma, reumatismo m rheumatism.
reunión f meeting.
reunir 1 vt to gather together; (dinero) to raise; (cualidades) to possess; (requisitos) to fulfill. **2 reunirse** vr to meet.
revalorizar [40] vt, **revalorizarse** vr (moneda) to revalue.
revancha f revenge; (partido) return match.
revelar vt to reveal; (película) to develop.
reventa f (de entradas) touting.
reventar [1] vti, **reventarse** vr to burst.

reventón m (de neumático) blowout.
reverencia f (de hombre) bow; (de mujer) curtsy.
reversible adj reversible.
reverso m back.
revés m (reverso) reverse; (contrariedad) setback; **al** o **del r.** (al contrario) the other way round; (la parte interior en el exterior) inside out; (boca abajo) upside down; (la parte de detrás delante) back to front.
revisar vt to check; (coche) to service.
revisión f checking; (de coche) service; **r. médica** checkup.
revisor, -a mf corrector, inspector.
revista f magazine.
revitalizar [40] vt to revitalize.
revivir vti to revive.
revolcarse vr to roll about.
revoltijo, revoltillo m jumble.
revoltoso, -a adj (travieso) mischievous.
revolución f revolution.
revolucionar vt to revolutionize.
revolver [4] (pp revuelto) **1** vt (desordenar) to mess up; **me revuelve el estómago** it turns my stomach. **2 revolverse** vr (agitarse) to roll; (el mar) to become rough.
revólver m (pl revólveres) revolver.
revuelo m (agitación) stir.
revuelta f revolt.
revuelto, -a adj (desordenado) in a mess; (tiempo) unsettled; (mar) rough; (huevos) scrambled.
rey m king; **(el día de) Reyes** Epiphany, January 6.
rezagarse vr to fall behind.
rezar [40] **1** vi (orar) to pray. **2** vt (oración) to say.
rezumar vt to ooze.
ría f estuary.
riada f flood.
ribera f (de río) bank; (zona) riverside.
rico, -a 1 adj ser r. to be rich; estar r.

(delicioso) to be delicious. **2** *mf* rich person; **los ricos** the rich.

ridiculizar [40] *vt* to ridicule.

ridículo, -a 1 *adj* ridiculous. **2** *m* ridicule; **hacer el r., quedar en r.** to make a fool of oneself; **poner a algn en r.** to make a fool of sb.

riego *m* irrigation.

rienda *f* rein.

riesgo *m* risk; **correr el r. de** to run the risk of.

rifa *f* raffle.

rifar *vt* to raffle (off).

rifle *m* rifle.

rigidez *f* rigidity; *(severidad)* inflexibility.

rígido, -a *adj* rigid, stiff; *fig (severo)* strict, inflexible.

rigor *m* rigor; *(severidad)* severity.

rigurosamente *adv* rigorously; *(meticulosamente)* meticulously; *(severamente)* severely.

riguroso, -a *adj* rigorous; *(severo)* severe.

rimar *vti* to rhyme (**con** with).

rímel *m* mascara.

rincón *m* corner.

rinoceronte *m* rhinoceros.

riña *f (pelea)* fight; *(discusión)* row.

riñón *m* kidney.

río *m* river; **r. abajo** downstream; **r. arriba** upstream.

riqueza *f* wealth.

risa *f* laugh; *(carcajadas)* laughter; **me da r.** it makes me laugh; **morirse** *o* **mondarse de r.** to die laughing.

risueño, -a *adj (sonriente)* smiling.

ritmo *m* rhythm; *(paso)* rate.

rito *m* rite; *(ritual)* ritual.

ritual *adj & m* ritual.

rival *adj & mf* rival.

rivalizar [40] *vi* to rival (**en** in).

rizado, -a *adj (pelo)* curly; *(mar)* choppy.

rizar [40] *vt,* **rizarse** *vr (pelo)* to curl.

rizo *m (de pelo)* curl.

robar *vt (objeto)* to steal; *(banco, persona)* to rob; *(casa)* to burgle.

roble *m* oak (tree).

robo *m* robbery, theft; *(en casa)* burglary; **r. a mano armada** armed robbery; **r. de identidad** identity theft.

robot *m (pl* robots*)* robot; **r. de cocina** food processor.

robustecer [33] *vt* to strengthen.

robusto, -a *adj* robust.

roca *f* rock.

roce *m (fricción)* friction; *(en la piel)* chafing; *(contacto ligero)* brush.

rociar [29] *vt* to sprinkle.

rocío *m* dew.

rocoso, -a *adj* rocky.

rodaja *f* slice.

rodaje *m* shooting.

rodar [64] **1** *vt (película etc)* to shoot. **2** *vi* to roll.

rodear 1 *vt* to surround. **2 rodearse** *vr* to surround oneself (**de** with).

rodeo *m (desvío)* detour; *(al hablar)* evasiveness; rodeo; **no andarse con rodeos** to get straight to the point.

rodilla *f* knee; **de rodillas** kneeling; **hincarse** *o* **ponerse de rodillas** to kneel down.

rodillera *f (de pantalón)* knee patch; *(para la rodilla)* knee pad.

roer [38] *vt (hueso)* to gnaw; *(galleta)* to nibble at.

rogar [2] *vt (pedir)* to ask; *(implorar)* to beg; **hacerse de r.** to play hard to get.

roído, -a *adj* gnawed, eaten away.

rojizo, -a *adj* reddish.

rojo, -a 1 *adj* red; **estar en números rojos** to be in the red. **2** *m (color)* red.

rollizo, -a *adj* chubby.

rollo *m* roll; *fam (pesadez)* drag.

romance *m (aventura amorosa)* romance.

romántico, -a *adj & mf* romantic.

rombo *m* diamond; *(en geometría)* rhombus.

rompecabezas *m inv (juego)* (jigsaw) puzzle.

rompeolas *m inv* breakwater, jetty.

romper *(pp* roto*)* **1** *vt* to break; *(papel, tela)* to tear; *(vajilla, cristal)* to smash; *(pantalones)* to split; *(rela-*

ciones) to break off. **2** *vi* to break; **r. a llorar** to burst out crying. **3 romperse** *vr* to break; *(papel, tela)* to tear; **romperse la cabeza** to rack one's brains.

ron *m* rum.

roncar [44] *vi* to snore.

roncha *f (en la piel)* swelling.

ronco, -a *adj* hoarse; **quedarse r.** to lose one's voice.

ronda *f* round; *(patrulla)* patrol; *(carretera)* ring road; *(paseo)* avenue.

rondar *vti (merodear)* to prowl around; *(estar cerca de)* to be about.

ronquido *m* snore.

ronronear *vi* to purr.

roñoso, -a *adj (mugriento)* filthy; *(tacaño)* mean.

ropa *f* clothes *pl*, clothing; **r. interior** underwear.

ropero *m (armario)* **r.** wardrobe, closet.

rosa 1 *adj inv (color)* pink; **novela r.** romantic novel. **2** *f (flor)* rose. **3** *m (color)* pink.

rosado, -a 1 *adj (color)* pink; *(vino)* rosé. **2** *m (vino)* rosé.

rosal *m* rosebush.

rosbif *m* roast beef.

rosco *m (pastel)* ring-shaped pastry.

rosquilla *f* ring-shaped pastry; **venderse como rosquillas** to sell like hot cakes.

rostro *m (cara)* face; *fam* **tener mucho r.** to have a lot of nerve.

roto, -a 1 *adj* broken; *(papel)* torn; *(gastado)* worn out; *(ropa)* in tatters. **2** *m (agujero)* hole.

rótula *f* kneecap.

rotulador *m* felt-tip pen.

rótulo *m (letrero)* sign; *(titular)* heading.

rotundo, -a *adj* categorical; **éxito r.** resounding success.

rotura *f (ruptura)* breaking; *(de hueso)* fracture.

rozadura *f* scratch.

rozar [40] **1** *vt* to brush against. **2** *vi* to rub. **3 rozarse** *vr* to brush (**con** against).

Rte. *abr de* **remite, remitente** sender.

rubí *m (pl* **rubíes)** ruby.

rubio, -a 1 *adj (pelo, persona)* blond; **tabaco r.** Virginia tobacco. **2** *mf* blond; *f* blonde.

ruborizarse [40] *vr* to blush.

rudimentario, -a *adj* rudimentary.

rudo, -a *adj* rough.

rueda *f* wheel; **r. de recambio** spare wheel; **r. de prensa** press conference.

ruedo *m* bullring.

ruego *m* request.

rugido *m (de animal)* roar.

rugir [57] *vi* to roar.

rugoso, -a *adj* rough.

ruido *m* noise; *(sonido)* sound; **hacer r.** to make a noise.

ruidoso, -a *adj* noisy.

ruin *adj (vil)* vile; *(tacaño)* mean.

ruina *f* ruin.

ruiseñor *m* nightingale.

ruleta *f* roulette.

rulo *m (para el pelo)* roller.

rumba *f* rumba.

rumbo *m* direction; *(con)* **r. a** bound for.

rumor *m* rumor; *(murmullo)* murmur.

rumorearse *v impers* to be rumored.

ruptura *f* breaking; *(de relaciones)* breaking-off.

rural *adj* rural.

ruso, -a *adj & mf* Russian.

rústico, -a *adj* rustic.

ruta *f* route.

rutina *f* routine.

S

S.A. abr de Sociedad Anónima ≃ PLC, ≃ Ltd, ≃ Inc.

sábado m Saturday.

sábana f sheet; fam **se pegaron las sábanas** I overslept.

sabañón m chilblain.

sabelotodo mf inv know-all.

saber¹ m knowledge.

saber² [21] vt to know; (tener habilidad) to be able to; (enterarse) to learn; **que yo sepa** as far as I know; **vete tú a s.** goodness knows; **a s.** namely; **¿sabes cocinar?** can you cook? **2** vi (tener sabor) to taste (a of); (soler) to be accustomed to; **sabe a fresa** it tastes of strawberries.

sabiduría f wisdom.

sabiendas: a sabiendas adv lo hizo a s. he did it in the full knowledge of what he was doing; **a s. de que ...** knowing full well that ...

sabio, -a 1 adj (prudente) wise. **2** m scholar.

sable m sabre.

sabor m (gusto) flavor; **con s. a limón** lemon-flavored.

saborear vt (degustar) to taste.

sabotaje m sabotage.

sabotear vt to sabotage.

sabré indic fut de **saber**.

sabroso, -a adj tasty; (delicioso) delicious.

sacacorchos m inv corkscrew.

sacapuntas m inv pencil sharpener.

sacar [44] **1** vt to take out; (con más fuerza) to pull out; (obtener) to get; (conclusiones) to draw; (entrada) to buy; (libro, disco) to bring out; (fotografía) to take; **s. la lengua** to stick one's tongue out; **s. provecho de algo** to benefit from sth.

sacarina f saccharin.

sacerdote m priest.

saciar [43] vt (sed) to quench; (deseos, hambre) to satisfy.

saciedad f satiety; **repetir algo hasta la s.** to repeat sth ad nauseam.

saco m sack; Am (chaqueta) jacket; **s. de dormir** sleeping bag.

sacrificar [44] **1** vt to sacrifice. **2** sacrificarse vr to make sacrifices.

sacrificio m sacrifice.

sacudida f shake; (espasmo) jolt; (de terremoto) tremor.

sacudir vt (agitar) to shake; (alfombra, sábana) to shake out; (arena, polvo) to shake off; (golpear) to beat.

sádico, -a 1 adj sadistic. **2** mf sadist.

saeta f (dardo) dart.

safari m (cacería) safari; (parque) safari park.

sagaz adj (listo) clever; (astuto) shrewd.

sagrado, -a adj sacred.

sal¹ f salt; **s. de mesa** table salt; **s. gorda** cooking salt.

sal² imperativo de **salir**.

sala f room; (en un hospital) ward; **s. de estar** living room; **s. de espera** waiting room; **s. de exposiciones** exhibition hall; **s. de fiestas** nightclub.

salado, -a adj (con sal) salted; (con exceso de sal) salty; (infortunado) unlucky; **agua salada** salt water.

salario m salary.

salchicha f sausage.

salchichón m (salami-type) sausage.

saldar vt (cuenta) to settle; (deuda) to pay off.

saldo m (de cuenta) balance; **saldos** sales.

saldré indic fut de **salir**.

salero m (recipiente) saltcellar.

salgo indic pres de **salir**.

salida f (partida) departure; (puerta etc) exit, way out; (de carrera) start; (de un astro) rising; (perspectiva) opening; (en ordenador) output;

callejón sin s. dead end; **s. de emergencia** emergency exit; **te vi a la s. del cine** I saw you leaving the cinema; **s. del sol** sunrise.

salir [22] **1** *vi (de un sitio, tren etc)* to leave; *(venir de dentro, revista, disco)* to come out; *(novios)* to go out; *(aparecer)* to appear; *(ley)* to come in; *(trabajo, vacante)* to come up; *(resultar)* to turn out (to be); *(problema)* to work out; **salió de la habitación** she left the room; **¿cómo te salió el examen?** how did your exam go?; **s. ganando** to come out on top; **s. barato/caro** to work out cheap/expensive; **esta cuenta no me sale** I can't work this calculation out. **2 salirse** *vr (líquido, gas)* to leak (out); **salirse de lo normal** to be out of the ordinary; **salirse con la suya** to get one's own way.

saliva *f* saliva.

salivar *vi* to salivate.

salmón 1 *m (pescado)* salmon. **2** *adj inv (color)* salmon pink.

salmonete *m (pescado)* red mullet.

salobre *adj (agua)* brackish; *(gusto)* salty.

salón *m (en una casa)* lounge; **s. de actos** assembly hall; **s. de belleza** beauty salon; **s. del automóvil** motor show.

salpicar [44] *vt (rociar)* to splash; **me salpicó el abrigo de barro** he splashed mud on my coat.

salsa *f* sauce; *(de carne)* gravy.

saltamontes *m inv* grasshopper.

saltar 1 *vt (obstáculo, valla)* to jump (over). **2** *vi* to jump; *(romperse)* to break; *(plomos)* to blow; *(desprenderse)* to come off; **s. a la vista** to be obvious. **2 saltarse** *vr (omitir)* to skip; *(no hacer caso)* to ignore; **saltarse el semáforo** to run the lights; **se me saltaron las lágrimas** tears came to my eyes.

salto *m (acción)* jump, leap; **a saltos** in leaps and bounds; **dar** *o* **pegar un s.** to jump, to leap; **de un s.** in a flash;

s. de altura high jump; **s. de longitud** long jump; **s. mortal** somersault.

salud *f* health; **beber a la s. de algn** to drink to sb's health; **¡s.!** cheers!

saludable *adj (sano)* healthy.

saludar *vt (decir hola a)* to say hello to; **saluda de mi parte a** give my regards to; **le saluda atentamente** *(en una carta)* yours faithfully.

saludo *m* greeting; **un s. de** best wishes from.

salvado *m* bran.

salvaguardar *vt* to safeguard (**de** from).

salvajada *f* brutal act.

salvaje *adj (planta, animal)* wild; *(pueblo, tribu)* savage.

salvam(i)ento *m* rescue.

salvar 1 *vt* to save (**de** from); *(obstáculo)* to clear; *(dificultad)* to overcome. **2 salvarse** *vr (sobrevivir)* to survive; *(escaparse)* to escape (**de** from); **¡sálvese quien pueda!** every man for himself!

salvavidas *m inv* life preserver.

salvo, -a 1 *adj* safe; **a s.** safe. **2** *adv (exceptuando)* except (for). **3** *conj* **s. que** unless.

san *adj* saint; *ver* **santo**.

sanar 1 *vt (curar)* to heal. **2** *vi (persona)* to recover; *(herida)* to heal.

sanción *f* sanction.

sancionar *vt (castigar)* to penalize.

sancochar *vt* to parboil; *Am* to boil meat in water and salt.

sandalia *f* sandal.

sándalo *m* sandalwood.

sandía *f* watermelon.

sandwich *m* sandwich.

sanear *vt (terrenos)* to drain; *(empresa)* to reorganize.

sangrar *vi* to bleed.

sangre *f* blood; **donar s.** to give blood; **a s. fría** in cold blood.

sangría *f (bebida)* sangria.

sangriento, -a *adj (cruel)* cruel.

sanguíneo, -a *adj* blood; **grupo s.** blood group.

sanidad f health; **Ministerio de S.** Department of Health.

sano, -a adj healthy; **s. y salvo** safe and sound.

santería f (religión) santería, = form of religion common in the Caribbean in which people allegedly have contact with the spirit world; Am (tienda) = shop selling religious mementoes such as statues of saints.

santiguarse [45] vr to cross oneself.

santo, -a 1 adj holy. **2** mf saint; (día onomástico) saint's day; **se me fue el s. al cielo** I completely forgot; **¿a s. de qué?** why on earth?

santuario m shrine.

sapo m toad.

saque m (en tenis) service; (en fútbol) **s. inicial** kick-off; **s. de esquina** corner kick.

saquear vt (casas y tiendas) to loot.

sarampión m measles.

sarcástico, -a adj sarcastic.

sardina f sardine.

sargento m sergeant.

sarpullido m rash.

sarro m (en los dientes) tartar; (en la lengua) fur.

sartén f frying pan, skillet.

sastre m tailor.

satélite m satellite; **televisión vía s.** satellite television.

satén m satin.

sátira f satire.

satisfacción f satisfaction.

satisfacer [15] (pp satisfecho) vt to satisfy; (deuda) to pay.

satisfecho, -a adj satisfied; **me doy por s.** that's good enough for me.

sauce m willow; **s. llorón** weeping willow.

sauna f sauna.

saxofón m saxophone.

sazonar vt to season.

se¹ pron (reflexivo) (a él mismo) himself; (a ella misma) herself; (animal) itself; (a usted mismo) yourself; (a ellos/ellas mismos/mismas) them-

selves; (a ustedes mismos) yourselves; **se afeitó** he shaved; **se compró un nuevo coche** he bought himself a new car. ▪ (recíproco) one another, each other. ▪ (voz pasiva) **el vino se guarda en cubas** wine is kept in casks. ▪ (impersonal) **nunca se sabe** you never know; **se habla inglés** English spoken; **se dice que…** it is said that….

se² pron pers (a él) (to o for) him; (a ella) (to o for) her; (a usted o ustedes) (to o for) you; (a ellos) (to o for) them; **se lo diré en cuanto les vea** I'll tell them as soon as I see them; **¿se lo explico?** shall I explain it to him/her etc?

sé¹ indic pres de **saber**.

sé² imperativo de **ser**.

sea subj pres de **ser**.

secador m dryer; **s. de pelo** hairdryer.

secadora f tumble dryer.

secar [44] **1** vt to dry. **2 secarse** vr to dry; (marchitarse) to dry up; **secarse las manos** to dry one's hands.

sección f section.

seco, -a adj dry; (tono) curt; (golpe, ruido) sharp; **frutos secos** dried fruit; **limpieza en s.** dry-cleaning; **frenar en s.** to pull up sharply.

secretaría f (oficina) secretary's office.

secretario, -a mf secretary.

secreto, -a 1 adj secret; **en s.** in secret. **2** m secret.

secta f sect.

sector m sector; (zona) area.

secuencia f sequence.

secuestrar vt (persona) to kidnap; (avión) to hijack.

secuestro m (de persona) kidnapping; (de avión) hijacking.

secundar vt to back.

secundario, -a adj secondary.

sed f thirst; **tener s.** to be thirsty.

seda f silk.

sedal m fishing line.

sedante adj & m sedative.

sede f headquarters; (de gobierno) seat.

SALUDOS Y PRESENTACIONES

Hola ¿cómo está/estás?
Hello, how are you?

Hola, ¿qué tal?
Hi, how's it going?

Bien, gracias, ¿y usted/tú?
Fine thank you, how are you?

Bien, ¿y tú?
Good, and you?

Buenos días./Buenas tardes.
Good morning/afternoon.

Buenas noches.
Good evening.

¿Cómo se llama?/¿Cómo te llamas?
What's your name?

Me llamo Eve.
My name's Eve.

Me llamo Brian, y esta es Kim, mi mujer.
I'm Brian and this is my wife Kim.

Encantado(a).
Nice to meet you.

¿Qué edad tiene/tienes?
How old are you?

Tengo quince/veinticinco años.
I'm 15/25 (years old).

¿De dónde es/eres?
Where are you from?

Soy de Estados Unidos./Soy estadounidense.
I'm from the United States./I'm American.

¿Dónde vive/vives?
Where do you live?

Vivo cerca de San Francisco.
I live near San Francisco.

¿A qué se dedica/te dedicas?
What do you do?

Soy profesor(ora)/estudiante.
I'm a teacher/a student.

Estoy en secundaria.
I'm at high school.

Soy madre y ama de casa.
I'm a stay-at-home mom.

Trabajo para una compañía de seguros.
I work for an insurance company.

Estoy jubilado(a).
I'm retired.

¿Tiene/Tienes hermanos?
Do you have any brothers and sisters?

Tengo una hermana mayor y dos hermanos pequeños.
I've got an older sister and two little brothers.

¿Tiene/Tienes hijos?
Do you have kids?

Tengo un hijo de tres años que se llama Josh.
I have a three-year-old son named Josh.

¿Está/Estás casado(a)?
Are you married?

Estoy divorciado(a)/separado(a)/viudo(a).
I'm divorced/separated/widowed.

¿A qué se dedica/te dedicas en su/tu tiempo libre?
What do you do in your spare time?

Me gusta leer/ir al cine.
I like reading/going to the movies.

Juego al baloncesto./Hago yoga.
I play basketball./I do yoga.

Estoy haciendo un curso de español.
I'm taking Spanish classes.

Hasta pronto/luego.
See you soon/later!

¡Buen viaje!
Have a good trip!

Deberíamos seguir en contacto. Este es mi email.
We should keep in touch, here's my e-mail address.

sedentario, -a adj sedentary.

sedimento m sediment.

sedoso, -a adj silky.

seducir [10] vt to seduce.

seductor, -a 1 adj seductive. **2** mf seducer.

segar [1] vt to cut.

seglar 1 adj secular. **2** mf lay person; m layman; f laywoman.

segmento m segment.

seguida: en seguida adv immediately, straight away.

seguido adv straight; Am (a menudo) often; **todo s.** straight ahead.

seguir [6] **1** vt to follow; (camino) to continue. **2** vi to follow; **siguió hablando** he went on o kept on speaking; **sigo resfriado** I've still got the cold.

según 1 prep according to; (en función de) depending on; (tal como) just as; **estaba s. lo dejé** it was just as I had left it. **2** conj (a medida que) as; **s. iba leyendo** as I read. **3** adv ¿vendrás? — **s.** are you coming? — it depends.

segundo, -a[1] adj second.

segundo[2] m (tiempo) second.

seguramente adv (probablemente) most probably; (seguro) surely.

seguridad f security; (física) safety; (confianza) confidence; (certeza) sureness; **s. en carretera** road safety; **s. en sí mismo** self-confidence; **con toda s.** most probably; **tener la s. de que** to be certain that; **S. Social** ≃ Social Security.

seguro, -a 1 adj (cierto) sure; (libre de peligro) safe; (protegido) secure; (fiable) reliable; (firme) steady; **estoy s. de que...** I am sure that...; **está segura de ella misma** she has self-confidence. **2** m (de accidentes etc) insurance; (dispositivo) safety device; **s. de vida** life insurance. **3** adv definitely.

seis adj & m inv six.

seiscientos, -as adj & mf six hundred.

seleccionador, -a mf selector; (en fútbol) manager.

seleccionar vt to select.

selecto, -a adj select.

self-service m self-service restaurant.

sello m (de correos) stamp; (para documentos) seal.

selva f jungle.

semáforo m traffic lights pl.

semana f week; **S. Santa** Holy Week.

semanal adj & m weekly.

semanario m weekly magazine.

sembrar [1] vt to sow; **s. el pánico** to spread panic.

semejante 1 adj (parecido) similar. **2** m (prójimo) fellow being.

semestre m semester.

semifinal f semifinal.

semilla f seed.

seminario m (en colegio) seminar; (para sacerdotes) seminary.

sémola f semolina.

senado m senate.

senador, -a mf senator.

sencillo, -a adj (fácil) simple; (natural) unaffected; (billete) single; (sin adornos) plain.

senda f, **sendero** m path.

seno m (pecho) breast; (interior) heart.

sensación f sensation; **tengo la s. de que...** I have a feeling that...; **causar s.** to cause a sensation.

sensacional adj sensational.

sensato, -a adj sensible.

sensible adj sensitive; (perceptible) perceptible.

sensiblemente adv noticeably.

sensiblero, -a adj over-sentimental, mawkish.

sensualidad f sensuality.

sentar [1] **1** vt to sit; (establecer) to establish. **2** vi (color, ropa) to suit; **el pelo corto te sienta mal** short hair doesn't suit you; **s. bien/mal a** (comida) to agree/disagree with; **la sopa te sentará bien** the soup will do you good. **3 sentarse** vr to sit (down).

sentencia f (condena) sentence.

sentido m sense; (significado) meaning; (dirección) direction; (conciencia) consciousness; **s. común** common sense; **no tiene s.** it doesn't make sense; **(de) s. único** one-way; **perder el s.** to faint.

sentimental 1 adj sentimental; **vida s.** love life. **2** mf sentimental person.

sentimiento m feeling; (pesar) sorrow.

sentir [5] **1** vt to feel; (lamentar) to regret; **lo siento (mucho)** I'm very sorry; **siento molestarle** I'm sorry to bother you. **2 sentirse** vr to feel; **me siento mal** I feel ill.

seña f mark; (gesto, indicio) sign; **hacer señas a algn** to signal to sb; **señas** (dirección) address.

señal f sign; (marca) mark; (vestigio) trace; **s. de llamada** dial tone; **s. de tráfico** road sign.

señalar vt (indicar) to indicate; (identificar, comunicar) to point out; **s. con el dedo** to point at.

señor m (hombre) man; (caballero) gentleman; (con apellido) Mr; (tratamiento de respeto) sir; **el Sr. Gutiérrez** Mr Gutiérrez.

señora f (mujer) woman; (trato formal) lady; (con apellido) Mrs; (tratamiento de respeto) madam; (esposa) wife; **¡señoras y señores!** ladies and gentlemen!; **la Sra. Salinas** Mrs Salinas.

señorita f (joven) young woman; (trato formal) young lady; (tratamiento de respeto) Miss; **la S. Padilla** Miss Padilla.

sepa subj pres de **saber**.

separación f separation; (espacio) space.

separar 1 vt to separate; (desunir) to detach; (dividir) to divide; (apartar) to move away. **2 separarse** vr to separate; (apartarse) to move away (**de** from).

septentrional adj northern.

septiembre m September.

séptimo, -a adj & mf seventh.

sepultura f grave.

sequía f drought.

séquito m entourage.

ser¹ m being; **s. humano** human being; **s. vivo** living being.

ser² [23] vi to be; **ser músico** to be a musician; **s. de** (procedencia) to be from; (+ material) to be made of; (+ poseedor) to belong to; **el perro es de Miguel** the dog belongs to Miguel; **hoy es dos de noviembre** today is the second of November; **son las cinco de la tarde** it's five o'clock; **¿cuántos estaremos en la fiesta?** how many of us will there be at the party?; **¿cuánto es?** how much is it?; **el estreno será mañana** tomorrow is the opening night; **es que…** it's just that…; **como sea** anyhow; **lo que sea** whatever; **o sea** that is (to say); **por si fuera poco** to top it all; **sea como sea** be that as it may; **a no s. que** unless; **de no s. por…** had it not been for…. ■ (auxiliar en pasiva) to be; **fue asesinado** he was murdered.

sereno, -a adj calm.

serial m serial.

serie f series sing; **fabricación en s.** mass production.

seriedad f (severidad) seriousness; (gravedad) gravity; **falta de s.** irresponsibility.

serio, -a adj serious; **en s.** seriously.

sermón m sermon.

seropositivo, -a adj HIV-positive.

serpiente f snake; **s. de cascabel** rattlesnake; **s. pitón** python.

serrín m sawdust.

serrucho m handsaw.

servicial adj helpful.

servicio m service; (retrete) rest room; **s. a domicilio** delivery service; **s. militar** military service.

servidor, -a 1 m server. **2** mf (criado) servant.

servilleta f napkin.

servilletero m serviette ring, napkin ring.

servir [6] **1** vt to serve. **2** vi to serve; (valer) to be suitable; **ya no sirve** it's no use; **¿para qué sirve esto?** what is this (used) for?; **s. de** to serve as. **3 servirse** vr (comida etc) to help oneself.

sesenta adj & m inv sixty.

sesión f (reunión) session; (pase) showing.

seso m brain.

seta f (comestible) mushroom; **s. venenosa** toadstool.

setecientos, -as adj & mf seven hundred.

setenta adj & m inv seventy.

setiembre m September.

seto m hedge.

seudónimo m pseudonym; (de escritor) pen name.

severidad f severity; (rigurosidad) strictness.

sexo m sex; (órgano) genitals pl.

sexto, -a adj & mf sixth.

sexual adj sexual; **vida s.** sex life.

si conj if; **como si** as if; **ya no si** not now; **me preguntó si me gustaba** he asked me if o whether I liked it.

sí¹ pron pers (sing) (él) himself; (ella) herself; (cosa) itself; (pl) themselves; (uno mismo) oneself; **por sí mismo** by himself.

sí² adv yes; **porque sí** just because; **¡que sí!** yes, I tell you!; **un día sí y otro no** every other day; (uso enfático) **sí que me gusta** of course I like it; **¡eso sí que no!** certainly not!

sico- = psico-.

sida m AIDS.

siderúrgico, -a adj iron and steel.

sidra f cider.

siempre 1 adv always; **como s.** as usual; **a la hora de s.** at the usual time; **para s.** forever. **2** conj **s. que** (cada vez que) whenever; (a condición de que) provided, as long as; **s. y cuando** provided, as long as.

sien f temple.

sierra f saw; (montañosa) mountain range.

siesta f siesta; **dormir la s.** to have a siesta.

siete adj & m inv seven.

sigilo m secrecy.

sigilosamente adv (secretamente) secretly.

sigiloso, -a adj secretive.

sigla f acronym.

siglo m century.

significado m meaning.

significar [44] vt to mean.

significativo, -a adj significant; (expresivo) meaningful.

signo m sign; **s. de interrogación** question mark.

sigo indic pres de **seguir**.

siguiente adj following, next; **al día s.** the following day.

sílaba f syllable.

silbar vi to whistle.

silbato m whistle.

silbido m whistle.

silencio m silence.

silencioso, -a adj (persona) quiet; (motor etc) silent.

silicona f silicone.

silla f chair; (de montura) saddle; **s. de ruedas** wheelchair.

sillín m saddle.

sillón m armchair.

silueta f silhouette; (de cuerpo) figure.

silvestre adj wild.

símbolo m symbol.

simétrico, -a adj symmetrical.

simiente f seed.

similar adj similar.

similitud f similarity.

simio m monkey.

simpatía f (de persona, lugar) charm; **tenerle s. a algn** to like sb.

simpático, -a adj nice.

simpatizar [40] vi to sympathize (con with); (llevarse bien) to hit it off (con with), to get along well (con with).

simple 1 *adj* simple; *(mero)* mere. **2** *m (persona)* simpleton.

simulacro *m* sham.

simular *vt* to simulate.

simultanear *vt* to combine; **simultanea el trabajo y los estudios** he's working and studying at the same time.

simultáneo, -a *adj* simultaneous.

sin *prep* without; **cerveza s.** alcohol-free beer; **s. más ni más** without further ado.

sinagoga *f* synagogue.

sinceridad *f* sincerity.

sincero, -a *adj* sincere.

sincronizar [40] *vt* to synchronize.

sindicato *m* labor union.

sinfonía *f* symphony.

singular 1 *adj* singular; *(excepcional)* exceptional; *(raro)* odd. **2** *m (número)* singular; **en s.** in the singular.

siniestro, -a 1 *adj* sinister. **2** *m* disaster.

sino *conj* but; **nadie s. él** no one but him; **no quiero s. que me oigan** I only want them to listen (to me).

sinónimo, -a 1 *adj* synonymous. **2** *m* synonym.

sinsabor *m (usu pl)* trouble, worry.

sintético, -a *adj* synthetic.

sintetizar [40] *vt* to synthesize.

síntoma *m* symptom.

sintonía *f (de programa)* tuning.

sintonizador *m (de radio)* tuning knob.

sintonizar [40] *vt (radio)* to tune in.

sinuoso, -a *adj (camino)* winding.

sinvergüenza 1 *adj (desvergonzado)* shameless; *(descarado)* rude. **2** *mf (desvergonzado)* rogue; *(caradura)* cheeky devil.

siquiera *adv (por lo menos)* at least; **ni s.** not even.

sirena *f* mermaid; *(señal acústica)* siren.

sirviente, -a *mf* servant.

sistema *m* system; **por s.** as a rule; **s. nervioso** nervous system; **s. operativo** operating system.

sitio *m (lugar)* place; *(espacio)* room; **en cualquier s.** anywhere; **hacer s.** to make room; **s. web** web site.

situación *f* situation; *(ubicación)* location.

situar [30] **1** *vt* to locate. **2 situarse** *vr* to be situated.

slogan *m* slogan.

smoking *m* tuxedo.

s/n. *abr de* **sin número**.

snob *adj & mf =* **esnob**.

sobaco *m* armpit.

soberanía *f* sovereignty.

soberano, -a *adj & mf* sovereign.

soberbia *f* pride.

soberbio, -a *adj* proud; *(magnífico)* splendid.

sobornar *vt* to bribe.

soborno *m (acción)* bribery; *(dinero etc)* bribe.

sobra *f* **de s.** *(no necesario)* superfluous; **tener de s.** to have plenty; **saber algo de s.** to know sth only too well; **sobras** *(restos)* leftovers.

sobrante 1 *adj* remaining. **2** *m* surplus.

sobrar *vi* to be more than enough; *(quedar)* to be left over; **sobran tres sillas** there are three chairs too many; **ha sobrado carne** there's still some meat left (over).

sobrasada *f* sausage spread.

sobre¹ *m (para carta)* envelope; *(de sopa etc)* packet.

sobre² *prep (encima)* on, on top of; *(por encima)* over, above; *(acerca de)* about, on; *(aproximadamente)* about; **s. todo** above all.

sobrecogedor, -a *adj* awesome.

sobrecoger [53] *vt (conmover)* to shock.

sobredosis *f inv* overdose.

sobreentenderse *vr* **se sobreentiende** that goes without saying.

sobrehumano, -a *adj* superhuman.

sobrellevar *vt* to endure, to bear.

sobrenatural *adj* supernatural.

sobrenombre *m* nickname.

sobrepasar 1 *vt* to exceed. **2 sobrepasarse** *vr* to go too far.

sobreponerse *vr (superar)* to overcome; *(animarse)* to pull oneself together.

sobresaliente 1 *m (nota)* A. **2** *adj (que destaca)* excellent.

sobresalir [22] *vi* to protrude; *fig (destacar)* to stand out.

sobresaltar 1 *vt* to startle. **2 sobresaltarse** *vr* to be startled, to start.

sobresalto *m (movimiento)* start; *(susto)* fright.

sobrevenir [27] *vi* to happen unexpectedly.

sobreviviente 1 *adj* surviving. **2** *mf* survivor.

sobrevivir *vi* to survive.

sobrevolar [2] *vt* to fly over.

sobrina *f* niece.

sobrino *m* nephew.

sobrio, -a *adj* sober.

socarrón, -ona *adj (sarcástico)* sarcastic.

socavón *m (bache)* pothole.

sociable *adj* sociable.

social *adj* social.

socialista *adj & mf* socialist.

sociedad *f* society; *(empresa)* company.

socio, -a *mf (miembro)* member; *(de empresa)* partner; **hacerse s. de un club** to join a club.

sociológico, -a *adj* sociological.

socorrer *vt* to assist.

socorrista *mf* lifeguard.

socorro *m* assistance; **¡s.!** help!; **puesto de s.** first-aid post.

soda *f (bebida)* soda water.

soez *adj* vulgar.

sofá *m (pl sofás)* sofa; **s. cama** sofa bed.

sofisticado, -a *adj* sophisticated.

sofocado, -a *adj* suffocated; **estar s.** to be out of breath; *(preocupado)* to be upset.

sofocante *adj* stifling.

sofocar [44] **1** *vt (ahogar)* to suffocate; *(incendio)* to extinguish. **2 so-**

focarse *vr (ahogarse)* to suffocate; *(irritarse)* to get upset.

sofoco *m fig (vergüenza)* embarrassment; **le dio un s.** *(disgusto)* it gave her quite a turn.

sofocón *m fam* shock; **llevarse un s.** to get upset.

soga *f* rope.

soja *f* soybean.

sol *m* sun; *(luz)* sunlight; *(luz y calor)* sunshine; **hace s.** it's sunny; **tomar el s.** to sunbathe; **al o bajo el s.** in the sun.

solamente *adv* only; **no s.** not only; **s. que** except that.

solapa *f (de chaqueta)* lapel; *(de sobre, bolsillo, libro)* flap.

solar¹ *adj* solar; **luz s.** sunlight.

solar² *m (terreno)* plot; *(en obras)* building site.

soldado *m* soldier.

soldar [2] *vt (cable)* to solder; *(chapa)* to weld.

soleado, -a *adj* sunny.

soledad *f (estado)* solitude; *(sentimiento)* loneliness.

solemne *adj (majestuoso)* solemn.

soler [4] *vi defectivo* to be in the habit of; **solemos ir en coche** we usually go by car; **solía pasear por aquí** he used to walk round here.

solicitar *vt (información etc)* to request; *(trabajo)* to apply for.

solicitud *f (petición)* request; *(de trabajo)* application.

solidaridad *f* solidarity.

sólido, -a *adj* solid.

solitario, -a *adj (que está solo)* solitary; *(que se siente solo)* lonely.

sollozar [40] *vi* to sob.

sollozo *m* sob.

solo, -a 1 *adj* only; *(solitario)* lonely; **una sola vez** only once; **se enciende s.** it switches itself on automatically; **a solas** alone, by oneself. **2** *m (musical)* solo.

sólo *adv* only; **tan s.** only; **no s....** **sino (también)** not only... but (also); **con s., (tan) s. con** just by.

solomillo m sirloin.

soltar [2] **1** vt (desasir) to let go of; (prisionero) to release; (humo, olor) to give off; (carcajada) to let out; **¡suéltame!** let me go! **2 soltarse** vr (desatarse) to come loose; (perro etc) to get loose; (desprenderse) to come off.

soltero, -a **1** adj single. **2** m (hombre) bachelor. **3** f (mujer) single woman.

solterón, -ona **1** m (hombre) old bachelor. **2** f (mujer) old maid.

soltura f (agilidad) agility; (seguridad) confidence, assurance; **habla italiano con s.** he speaks Italian fluently.

soluble adj soluble; **café s.** instant coffee.

solución f solution.

solucionar vt to solve; (arreglar) to settle.

solvencia f (financiera) solvency; (fiabilidad) reliability; **fuentes de toda s.** completely reliable sources.

sombra f (sombra) shade; (silueta proyectada) shadow; **s. de ojos** eyeshadow.

sombrero m (prenda) hat; **s. de copa** top hat; **s. hongo** derby hat.

sombrilla f sunshade.

sombrío, -a adj (oscuro) dark; (tenebroso) gloomy.

someter **1** vt to subject; (rebeldes) to put down; **s. a prueba** to put to the test. **2 someterse** vr (subordinarse) to submit; (rendirse) to surrender; **someterse a un tratamiento** to undergo treatment.

somnífero m sleeping pill.

somnoliento, -a adj sleepy.

sonar [2] **1** vi to sound; (timbre, teléfono) to ring; **suena bien** it sounds good; **tu nombre/cara me suena** your name/face rings a bell. **2 sonarse** vr **sonarse (la nariz)** to blow one's nose.

sondeo m (encuesta) poll.

sonido m sound.

sonoro, -a adj (resonante) resounding; **banda sonora** soundtrack.

sonreír [56] vi, **sonreírse** vr to smile; **me sonrió** he smiled at me.

sonrisa f smile.

sonrojarse vr to blush.

sonso, -a adj Am foolish, silly.

soñador, -a mf dreamer.

soñar [2] vti to dream; **s. con** to dream of o about.

soñoliento, -a adj sleepy.

sopa f soup.

sopera f soup tureen.

sopesar vt to try the weight of; fig to weigh up.

soplar **1** vi (viento) to blow. **2** vt (polvo etc) to blow away; (para enfriar) to blow on; (para apagar) to blow out; (para inflar) to blow up.

soplo m (acción) puff; (de viento) gust.

soplón, -ona mf fam (niño) telltale; (delator) informer.

soportable adj bearable.

soportar vt (sostener) to support; (tolerar) to endure; (aguantar) to put up with.

soporte m support.

sorber vt (beber) to sip; (absorber) to soak up.

sorbete m sorbet.

sorbo m sip; (trago) gulp.

sórdido, -a adj sordid.

sordo, -a **1** adj (persona) deaf; (ruido, dolor) dull. **2** mf deaf person.

sordomudo, -a **1** adj deaf and dumb. **2** mf deaf and dumb person.

sorprender vt to surprise; (coger desprevenido) to take by surprise.

sorpresa f surprise; **coger por s.** to take by surprise.

sorpresivo, -a adj Am unexpected.

sortear vt to draw lots for; (rifar) to raffle (off).

sorteo m draw; (rifa) raffle.

sortija f ring.

sosegado, -a adj (tranquilo) calm, quiet; (pacífico) peaceful.

sosegar [1] **1** vt to calm. **2 sosegarse** vr to calm down.

soso, -a *adj* lacking in salt; *(persona)* dull.

sospecha *f* suspicion.

sospechar 1 *vi (desconfiar)* to suspect; **s. de algn** to suspect sb. **2** *vt (pensar)* to suspect.

sospechoso, -a 1 *adj* suspicious. **2** *mf* suspect.

sostén *m (apoyo)* support; *(prenda)* bra, brassiere.

sostener [24] **1** *vt* to hold; *(sustentar)* to hold up; **s. que...** to maintain that.... **2 sostenerse** *vr (mantenerse)* to support oneself; *(permanecer)* to remain.

sostuve *pt indef de* **sostener**.

sota *f (de baraja)* jack.

sotana *f* cassock.

sótano *m* basement.

soviético, -a *adj & mf* Soviet; **la Unión Soviética** the Soviet Union.

soy *indic pres de* **ser**.

spray *m (pl sprays)* spray.

Sr. *abr de* **Señor** Mister, Mr.

Sra. *abr de* **Señora** Mrs, Ms.

Srta. *abr de* **Señorita** Miss.

standard *adj & m* standard.

su *adj pos (de él)* his; *(de ella)* her; *(de usted, ustedes)* your; *(de animales o cosas)* its; *(impersonal)* one's; *(de ellos)* their.

suave *adj* smooth; *(luz, voz etc)* soft; *(templado)* mild.

suavidad *f* smoothness; *(dulzura)* softness; *(de tiempo)* mildness.

suavizante *m (para el pelo)* (hair) conditioner; *(para la ropa)* fabric softener.

suavizar [40] **1** *vt* to smooth (out). **2 suavizarse** *vr (temperatura)* to get milder.

subalterno, -a *adj & mf* subordinate.

subasta *f* auction.

subcampeón, -ona *mf* runner-up.

subconsciente *adj & m* subconscious.

subdesarrollado, -a *adj* underdeveloped.

subdirector, -a *mf* assistant director.

súbdito, -a *mf* subject.

subestimar *vt* to underestimate.

subir 1 *vt* to go up; *(llevar arriba)* to take up, to bring up; *(precio, salario, voz)* to raise; *(volumen)* to turn up. **2** *vi (ir arriba)* to go/come up; *(al autobús, barco etc)* to get on; *(aumentar)* to go up; **s. a** *(un coche)* to get into. **3 subirse** *vr* to climb up; *(al autobús, avión, tren, bici)* to get on; *(cremallera)* to do up; *(mangas)* to roll up; **subirse a** *(un coche)* to get into.

súbitamente *adv* suddenly.

súbito, -a *adj* sudden.

subjetivo, -a *adj* subjective.

sublevarse *vr* to rebel.

sublime *adj* sublime.

submarinismo *m* skin-diving.

submarino, -a 1 *adj* underwater. **2** *m* submarine.

subnormal 1 *adj* mentally handicapped. **2** *mf* mentally handicapped person.

subordinado, -a *adj & mf* subordinate.

subrayar *vt* to underline; *fig (recalcar)* to stress.

subscribir *(pp* **subscrito)** *vt =* **suscribir**.

subscripción *f* subscription.

subsecretario, -a *mf* undersecretary.

subsidiario, -a *adj* subsidiary.

subsidio *m* allowance; **s. de desempleo** unemployment benefit.

subsistencia *f* subsistence.

subterráneo, -a *adj* underground.

suburbio *m (barrio pobre)* slum; *(barrio periférico)* suburb.

subvención *f* subsidy.

suceder 1 *vi (ocurrir) (uso impers)* to happen; **¿qué sucede?** what's going on?; **s. a** *(seguir)* to follow. **2 sucederse** *vr* to follow one another.

sucesión *f (serie)* succession.

sucesivamente *adv* **y así s.** and so on.

sucesivo, -a *adj (siguiente)* following; **en lo s.** from now on.
suceso *m (acontecimiento)* event; *(incidente)* incident.
sucesor, -a *mf* successor.
suciedad *f* dirt; *(calidad)* dirtiness.
sucio, -a *adj* dirty.
suculento, -a *adj* succulent.
sucumbir *vi* to succumb.
sucursal *f (de banco etc)* branch.
sudadera *f* sweatshirt.
sudafricano, -a *adj & mf* South African.
sudamericano, -a *adj & mf* South American.
sudar *vti* to sweat.
sudeste *adj & m* southeast.
sudoeste *adj & m* southwest.
sudor *m* sweat.
sudoroso, -a *adj* sweaty.
sueco, -a 1 *adj* Swedish. **2** *mf (persona)* Swede. **3** *m (idioma)* Swedish.
suegra *f* mother-in-law.
suegro *m* father-in-law; **mis suegros** my in-laws.
suela *f* sole.
sueldo *m* wages *pl.*
suelo *m (superficie)* ground; *(de interior)* floor.
suelto, -a 1 *adj* loose; *(en libertad)* free; *(huido)* at large; *(desatado)* undone; **dinero s.** loose change. **2** *m (dinero)* (loose) change.
sueño *m* sleepiness; *(cosa soñada)* dream; **tener s.** to be sleepy.
suerte *f (fortuna)* luck; **por s.** fortunately; **tener s.** to be lucky; **¡que tengas s.!** good luck!
suéter *m* sweater.
suficiente 1 *adj (bastante)* sufficient, enough. **2** *m (nota)* pass.
suficientemente *adv* sufficiently; **no es lo s. rico como para…** he isn't rich enough to….
sufragar [42] **1** *vt (gastos)* to pay, to defray. **2** *vi Am* to vote *(***por** for).
sufragio *m (voto)* vote.
sufrido, -a *adj (persona)* long-suffering.

sufrimiento *m* suffering.
sufrir 1 *vi* to suffer. **2** *vt (accidente)* to have; *(dificultades, cambios)* to experience; *(aguantar)* to put up with.
sugerencia *f* suggestion.
sugerir [5] *vt* to suggest.
sugestión *f* suggestion.
suicida 1 *mf (persona)* suicide. **2** *adj* suicidal.
suicidarse *vr* to commit suicide.
suicidio *m* suicide.
suizo, -a 1 *adj* Swiss. **2** *mf (persona)* Swiss. **3** *m (pastel)* eclair.
sujetador *m* bra, brassiere.
sujetar 1 *vt (agarrar)* to hold; *(fijar)* to hold down; *(someter)* to restrain. **2 sujetarse** *vr (agarrarse)* to hold on.
sujeto, -a 1 *m* subject; *(individuo)* fellow. **2** *adj (atado)* secure.
suma *f (cantidad)* sum; *(cálculo)* addition.
sumamente *adv* extremely, highly.
sumar *vt (cantidades)* to add (up).
sumergir [57] **1** *vt* to submerge; *(hundir)* to sink. **2 sumergirse** *vr* to submerge; *(hundirse)* to sink.
sumidero *m* drain.
suministrar *vt* to supply; **s. algo a algn** to supply sb with sth.
suministro *m* supply.
sumiso, -a *adj* submissive.
supe *pt indef de* **saber**.
súper *m (gasolina)* premium; *fam (supermercado)* supermarket.
superar *vt (obstáculo etc)* to overcome; *(prueba)* to pass; *(aventajar)* to surpass.
superdotado, -a 1 *adj* exceptionally gifted. **2** *mf* genius.
superficial *adj* superficial.
superficie *f* surface; *(área)* area.
superfluo, -a *adj* superfluous.
superior 1 *adj (posición)* top, upper; *(cantidad)* greater (**a** than); *(calidad)* superior; *(estudios)* higher. **2** *m (jefe)* superior.
supermercado *m* supermarket.
supermodelo *f* supermodel.
superponer [19] *vt* to superimpose.

supersónico, -a adj supersonic.

supersticioso, -a adj superstitious.

supervisar vt to supervise.

supervivencia f survival.

súpito, -a adj Am sudden.

suplantar vt to supplant.

suplementario, -a adj supplementary.

suplemento m supplement.

suplente adj & mf (sustituto) substitute, deputy; (jugador) substitute.

suplicar [44] vt to beg.

suplicio m (tortura) torture; (tormento) torment.

suplir vt (reemplazar) to replace; (compensar) to make up for.

suponer [19] (pp supuesto) vt to suppose; (significar) to mean; (implicar) to entail; **supongo que sí** I suppose so.

supositorio m suppository.

supremo, -a adj supreme.

suprimir vt (ley) to abolish; (restricción) to lift; (palabra) to delete.

supuesto, -a adj (asumido) supposed; (presunto) alleged; **¡por s.!** of course!; **dar algo por s.** to take sth for granted.

supuse pt indef de **suponer**.

sur adj & m south.

suramericano, -a adj & mf South American.

surco m (en tierra) furrow; (en disco) groove.

sureste adj & m southeast.

surf(ing) m surfing.

surfista mf surfer.

surgir [57] vi (problema, dificultad) to crop up; (aparecer) to arise.

suroeste adj & m southwest.

surtido, -a 1 adj (variado) assorted. **2** m selection.

surtidor m spout; **s. de gasolina** gas pump.

surtir vt to supply, to provide; **s. efecto** to have the desired effect.

susceptible adj susceptible; (quisquilloso) touchy; **s. de (capaz)** capable of.

suscitar vt (provocar) to cause; (rebelión) to stir up; (interés etc) to arouse.

suscribir (pp suscrito) **1** vt to subscribe to, to endorse; fml (firmar) to sign. **2 suscribirse** vr to subscribe (**a** to).

suscripción f subscription.

suspender 1 vt (reunión) to adjourn; (examen) to fail; (colgar) to hang; **me han suspendido** I've failed (the exam). **2** vi (en colegio) **he suspendido** I've failed.

suspense m suspense; **novela/película de s.** thriller.

suspensión f (levantamiento) hanging (up); (de coche) suspension.

suspenso m (nota) fail.

suspicacia f suspiciousness.

suspicaz adj suspicious; (desconfiado) distrustful.

suspirar vi to sigh.

suspiro m sigh.

sustancia f substance.

sustantivo m noun.

sustento m (alimento) sustenance.

sustituir [37] vt to substitute.

sustituto, -a mf substitute.

susto m fright; **llevarse o darse un s.** to be frightened.

sustraer [25] vt to subtract; (robar) to steal.

susurrar vi to whisper.

sutil adj (diferencia, pregunta) subtle; (aroma) delicate.

suyo, -a adj & pron pos (de él) his; (de ella) hers; (de animal o cosa) its; (de usted, ustedes) yours; (de ellos, ellas) theirs.

T

tabaco m tobacco; (cigarrillos) cigarettes pl; **t. rubio** Virginia tobacco.

taberna f bar.

tabique m (pared) partition (wall).

tabla 190 **tanto**

tabla f board; (de vestido) pleat; (de sumar etc) table; **t. de surf** surfboard; **t. de windsurf** sailboard.

tablero m (tablón) panel; (en juegos) board; **t. de mandos** (de coche) dash(board).

tableta f (de chocolate) bar.

tablón m plank; (en construcción) beam; **t. de anuncios** notice bulletin board.

taburete m stool.

tacaño, -a 1 adj mean. **2** mf miser.

tachar vt to cross out.

tacho m Am bucket.

taco m (tarugo) plug; (de jamón, queso) cube; (palabrota) swearword.

tacón m heel; **zapatos de t.** high-heeled shoes.

táctica f tactics pl.

táctico, -a adj tactical.

tacto m (sentido) touch; (delicadeza) tact.

tajada f slice.

tajante adj incisive.

tal 1 adj (semejante) such; (más sustantivo singular contable) such a; (indeterminado) such and such; **en tales condiciones** in such conditions; **nunca dije t. cosa** I never said such a thing; **t. vez** perhaps, maybe; **como si t. cosa** as if nothing had happened. **2** adv **t. (y) como** just as; **¿qué t.?** how are things?; **¿qué t. ese vino?** how do you find this wine? **3** conj as; **con t. (de) que** + subj so long as, provided. **4** pron (cosa) something; (persona) someone, somebody.

taladrar vt to drill; (pared) to bore through; (papeles) to punch.

taladro m (herramienta) drill.

talante m (carácter) disposition; **de mal t.** unwillingly.

talar vt (árboles) to fell.

talco m talc; **polvos de t.** talcum powder.

talega f sack.

talento m talent.

Talgo m fast passenger train.

talla f (de prenda) size; (estatura) height.

tallar vt (madera, piedra) to carve; (piedras preciosas) to cut; (metales) to engrave.

tallarines mpl noodles, tagliatelle sing.

talle m (cintura) waist.

taller m (obrador) workshop; **t. de reparaciones** (garaje) garage.

tallo m stem.

talón m heel; (cheque) check.

talonario m (de cheques) check book.

tamaño m size; **de gran t.** large; **del t. de** as big as.

tambalearse vr (persona) to stagger; (mesa) to wobble.

también adv too, also; **yo t.** me too.

tambor m drum.

tampoco adv (en afirmativas) nor, neither; (en negativas) not either; **no lo sé, yo t.** I don't know, neither o nor do I.

tampón m tampon.

tan adv so; **¡es t. listo!** he's so clever; **¡qué gente t. agradable!** such nice people; **¡qué vestido t. bonito!** such a beautiful dress. • (consecutivo) so (that); **iba t. deprisa que no lo ví** he was going so fast that I couldn't see him. • (comparativo) **t. ... como** as ... as; **t. alto como tú** as tall as you (are). • **t. sólo** only.

tanga m thong.

tango m tango.

tanque m tank.

tantear 1 vt fig **t. a algn** to sound sb out; **t. el terreno** to see how the land lies. **2** vi (deporte) to (keep) score.

tanto, -a 1 m (punto) point; **un t. para cada uno** so much for each; **t. por ciento** percentage; **estar al t.** (informado) to be informed; (pendiente) to be on the lookout. **2** adj (en singular) so much; **tantos, -as** so many; **t. dinero** so much money; **¡ha pasado t. tiempo!** it's been so long!; **tantas manzanas** so many apples; **cincuen-**

SUGERENCIAS, INVITACIONES Y DESEOS

¿Qué quiere/quieres hacer?
What do you want to do?

¿Quiere/Quieres ir a un restaurante?
Do you want to go to a restaurant?

¿Y si vamos a dar un paseo?
How about going for a walk?

Nos vemos al mediodía/en la puerta del cine.
Let's meet at noon/outside the movie theater.

No quiero ir al museo.
I don't want to go to the museum.

Me tomaría or **Me provoca un helado.**
I feel like an ice-cream.

¿Qué prefiere/prefieres hacer?
What would you rather do?

Me gustaría aprender castellano.
I'd like to learn Spanish.

Me da lo mismo.
I don't mind.

¡Me encantaría!
I'd love to!

No tengo ganas.
I don't feel like it.

¿Está/Estás libre mañana por la noche?
Are you free tomorrow night?

Muy amable.
That's very kind of you.

¿Tomamos un café?
Shall we go for a coffee?

¿Quiere/Quieres or **Le/Te provoca ir a tomar algo?**
Would you like to go for a drink?

¡Vamos a darnos un baño!
Let's go for a swim!

Me gustaría ir a la playa.
I'd like to go to the beach.

Prefiero ir de compras.
I'd rather go shopping.

No tengo ganas de ir al mercado.
I don't feel like going to the market.

Creo que deberíamos salir sobre las 6.30.
I think we should leave around 6.30.

No me importaría vivir aquí.
I wouldn't mind living here.

Usted decide./Tú decides.
It's up to you.

Es buena idea.
That's a good idea.

Lo siento, no puedo.
I'm sorry, I can't.

Lo siento, ya tengo planes.
I'm afraid I already have plans.

Gracias por invitarme.
Thank you for inviting me.

ta y tantas personas fifty odd people; **t. ... como** as much... as; **tantos, -as... como** as many... as. **3** *pron (en singular)* so much; **tantos, -as** so many; **otro t.** the same again; **no es** o **hay para t.** it's not that bad; **otros tantos** as many again; **uno de tantos** run-of-the-mill. **4** *adv (cantidad)* as much; *(tiempo)* so long; *(frecuencia)* so often; **t. mejor/peor** so much the better/worse; **t. ... como** both... and; **t. tú como yo** both you and I; **por lo t.** therefore.

tapa *f (cubierta)* lid; *(de libro)* cover; *(aperitivo)* appetizer.

tapadera *f* cover.

tapar 1 *vt* to cover; *(botella etc)* to put the lid on; *(con ropas o mantas)* to wrap up; *(ocultar)* to hide; *(vista)* to block. **2 taparse** *vr (cubrirse)* to cover oneself; *(abrigarse)* to wrap up.

tapete *m* (table) cover.

tapia *f* wall; *(cerca)* garden wall.

tapizar [40] *vt* to upholster.

tapón *m (de lavabo etc)* plug; *(de botella)* cap; *(de tráfico)* traffic jam.

taponar 1 *vt (tubería, hueco)* to plug; *(herida)* to tampon. **2 taponarse** *vr* **se me han taponado los oídos** my ears are blocked up.

taquigrafía *f* shorthand.

taquilla *f* ticket office; *(de cine, teatro)* box-office.

tararear *vt* to hum.

tardar 1 *vt* **tardé dos horas en venir** it took me two hours to get here. **2** *vi (demorar)* to take long; **no tardes** don't be long; **a más t.** at the latest. **3 tardarse** *vr* **¿cuánto se tarda en llegar?** how long does it take to get there?

tarde 1 *f (hasta las cinco)* afternoon; *(después de las cinco)* evening. **2** *adv* late; **(más) t. o (más) temprano** sooner or later.

tarea *f* task; **tareas** *(de ama de casa)* housework *sing*; *(de estudiante)* homework *sing*.

tarifa *f (precio)* rate; *(en transportes)* fare; *(lista de precios)* price list.

tarjeta *f* card; **t. postal** postcard; **t. de crédito** credit card.

tarro *m (vasija)* jar; *Am (lata)* tin.

tarta *f* tart; *(pastel)* cake.

tartamudear *vi* to stutter, to stammer.

tartamudo, -a 1 *adj* stuttering, stammering. **2** *mf* stutterer, stammerer.

tartera *f* lunch box.

tasa *f (precio)* fee; *(impuesto)* tax; *(índice)* rate; **tasas académicas** course fees; **t. de natalidad/mortalidad** birth/death rate.

tasar *vt (valorar)* to value; *(poner precio)* to fix the price of.

tasca *f* bar.

tatarabuelo, -a *mf (hombre)* great-great-grandfather; *(mujer)* great-great-grandmother; **tatarabuelos** great-great-grandparents.

tataranieto, -a *mf (hombre)* great-great-grandson; *(mujer)* great-great-granddaughter; **tataranietos** great-great-grandchildren.

tatuaje *m* tattoo.

tatuar [30] *vt* to tattoo.

taurino, -a *adj* bullfighting.

taxi *m* taxi.

taxista *mf* taxi driver.

taza *f* cup; **una t. de café** *(recipiente)* a coffee cup; *(contenido)* a cup of coffee.

tazón *m* bowl.

te *pron pers* **1** *(complemento directo)* you; *(complemento indirecto)* (to o for) you; *(reflexivo)* yourself; **no quiero verte** I don't want to see you; **te compraré uno** I'll buy you one; **te lo dije** I told you so; **lávate** wash yourself; **no te vayas** don't go.

té *m (pl* **tés)** tea.

teatro *m* theatre; **obra de t.** play.

tebeo *m* children's comic.

techo *m (de habitación)* ceiling; *(tejado)* roof.

tecla *f* key.

teclado *m* keyboard; **t. numérico** numeric keypad.

técnica *f (tecnología)* technology; *(método)* technique; *(habilidad)* skill.

técnico, -a *adj* technical. **2** *mf* technician.

tecnología *f* technology; **tecnologías de la información** information technology, IT.

tedio *m* tedium.

teja *f* tile.

tejado *m* roof.

tejanos *mpl* jeans.

tejer *vt (en el telar)* to weave; *(hacer punto)* to knit.

tejido *m* fabric.

tela *f* cloth; **t. de araña** cobweb; **t. metálica** gauze.

telaraña *f* spider's web.

tele *f fam* TV, telly.

telecabina *f* cable car.

telediario *m* television news bulletin.

telefax *m* fax.

teleférico *m* cable car.

telefilm(e) *m* TV film.

telefonear *vti* to telephone, to phone.

teléfono *m* telephone, phone; **t. celular** *or* **móvil** cellphone; **t. portátil** portable telephone; **te llamó por t.** she phoned you; **al t.** on the phone.

telegrama *m* telegram.

telenovela *f* television serial.

teleobjetivo *m* telephoto lens.

telescopio *m* telescope.

telesilla *m* chair lift.

telespectador, -a *mf* TV viewer.

telesquí *m* ski lift.

teletienda *f* home shopping program.

televidente *mf* TV viewer.

televisión *f* television; **t. digital** digital television; **t. por cable** cable television; **ver la t.** to watch television.

televisivo, -a *adj* television.

televisor *m* television set.

télex *m inv* telex.

telón *m* curtain.

tema *m* subject.

temblar [1] *vi (de frío)* to shiver; *(de miedo)* to tremble (**de** with); *(voz, pulso)* to shake.

temblor *m* tremor; **t. de tierra** earth tremor.

temer 1 *vt* to fear. **2** *vi* to be afraid. **3 temerse** *vr* to fear; **¡me lo temía!** I was afraid this would happen!

temerario, -a *adj* reckless.

temible *adj* fearful, frightful.

temor *m* fear; *(recelo)* worry.

témpano *m* ice block.

temperamento *m* temperament.

temperatura *f* temperature.

tempestad *f* storm.

templado, -a *adj (agua)* lukewarm; *(clima)* mild.

templo *m* temple.

temporada *f* season; *(período)* period; **t. alta** high season; **t. baja** low season.

temporal 1 *adj* temporary. **2** *m* storm.

temprano, -a *adj & adv* early.

tenaz *adj* tenacious.

tenaza *f,* **tenazas** *fpl (herramienta)* pliers.

tendencia *f* tendency.

tender [3] **1** *vt (extender)* to spread out; *(para secar)* to hang out; *(trampa)* to set; *(mano)* to hold out; *Am (cama)* to make; *Am (mesa)* to set, to lay. **2** *vi* **t. a** to tend to. **3 tenderse** *vr* to stretch out.

tendero *mf* shopkeeper.

tendón *m* tendon.

tenebroso, -a *adj (sombrío)* dark; *(siniestro)* sinister.

tenedor *m* fork.

tener [24] **1** *vt* to have, to have got; **va a t. un niño** she's going to have a baby. ▪ *(sostener)* to hold; **tenme el bolso un momento** hold my bag a minute. ▪ **t. calor/frío** to be hot/cold; **t. cariño a algn** to be fond of sb; **t. miedo** to be frightened. ▪ *(edad)* to be; **tiene dieciocho (años)**

EL TELÉFONO

¿Bueno? *(Méx)/*¿Hola? *(RP)/*¿Aló?
(Andes, Carib) Hello?

Hola Claire, soy Alex.
Hi Claire, it's Alex.

Aló, Alan Wright al aparato.
Hello, Alan Wright speaking.

Soluciones Avanzadas, ¡buenos días!
*Good morning/afternoon, Soluciones
Avanzadas!*

Hola, ¿me puede comunicar con el departamento de servicio al cliente, por favor?
Hello, could you put me through to Customer Services, please?

¿Podría hablar con Julio Rey, por favor? Soy Steve Brown de parte de CPS.
Can I speak to Julio Rey, please? This is Steve Brown from CPS.

Soy yo.
Speaking!

¿De parte de quién?
Who's calling, please?

¿Puede repetirlo/deletrearlo?
Could you repeat that/spell it?

Un momento, por favor. Voy a buscarlo.
Just a moment, I'll get him/her.

No cuelgue, lo comunico *(Méx)/*le paso.
Hold the line please, I'll put you through.

Lo siento, está en una reunión/ no
está.
*I'm afraid she's in a meeting/she's not
here.*

Da ocupado, ¿quiere esperar?
The line's busy, would you like to hold?

No contestan.
There's no reply.

¿Quiere dejarle un mensaje?
Would you like to leave a message?

Por favor deje su mensaje después de
la señal.
Please leave a message after the tone.

No gracias, luego vuelvo a llamar.
No thanks, I'll call back later.

¿Puede/Puedes decirle que le llamé?
Could you tell him/her I called?

¿Le puede decir que me llame lo antes posible?
Can you ask him/her to call me back as soon as possible?

Mi número es el cuarenta y dos, treinta y cinco, cincuenta y nueve, cero uno.
My number is 42-35-59-01.

Gracias por llamar.
Thank you for calling.

Luego le/te llamo.
Talk to you later!

¿Me da/das su teléfono?
Can I take your number?

Me puede/puedes llamar a mi celular.
You can reach me on my cellphone.

Luego le/te mando un mensaje/SMS.
I'll text you later.

No hay señal aquí.
I can't get a signal in here.

No me quedan muchos minutos.
I don't have many minutes left.

Necesito recargar mi celular.
I need to charge my cellphone.

Se equivocó de número.
You've got the wrong number.

Perdón, debo de haber marcado el
número equivocado.
*Sorry, I must have dialled the wrong
number.*

Casi no le/te oigo.
I can barely hear you.

Se cortó.
We got cut off.

¿Hay un teléfono público por aquí?
Is there a payphone around here?

Quisiera hacer una llamada por cobrar.
I'd like to call collect.

he's eighteen (years old); ▪ *(medida)* **la casa tiene cien metros cuadrados** the house is 100 square meters. ▪ *(contener)* to hold. ▪ *(mantener)* to keep; **me tuvo despierto toda la noche** he kept me up all night. ▪ *(considerar)* to consider; **ten por seguro que lloverá** you can be sure it'll rain. ▪ **t. que** to have (got) to; **tengo que...** I have to..., I must.... **2 tenerse** *vr* **tenerse en pie** to stand (up).

tenga *subj pres de* **tener**.

tengo *indic pres de* **tener**.

teniente *mf* lieutenant.

tenis *m* tennis.

tenista *mf* tennis player.

tenor *m* tenor.

tensión *f* tension; *(eléctrica)* voltage; **t. arterial** blood pressure.

tenso, -a *adj (cuerda, cable)* taut; *(persona, relaciones)* tense.

tentación *f* temptation.

tentar [1] *vt (incitar)* to tempt; *(atraer)* to attract.

tentativa *f* attempt.

tentempié *m (pl* **tentempiés)** *(comida)* snack; *(juguete)* tumbler.

tenue *adj (luz, sonido)* faint.

teñir [6] **1** *vt (pelo etc)* to dye. **2 teñirse** *vr* **teñirse el pelo** to dye one's hair.

teoría *f* theory; **en t.** theoretically.

terapia *f* therapy.

tercer *adj* third; **el t. mundo** the third world.

tercero, -a *adj & mf* third.

tercio *m* (one) third; *(cerveza)* medium-sized bottle of beer.

terciopelo *m* velvet.

terco *adj* stubborn.

tergiversar *vt* to distort; *(declaraciones)* to twist.

terminal 1 *adj* terminal. **2** *f* terminal; *(de autobús)* terminal. **3** *m (de ordenador)* terminal.

terminar 1 *vt* to finish. **2** *vi (acabarse)* to finish; *(ir a parar)* to end up (**en** in); **terminó por comprarlo**

he ended up buying it. **3 terminarse** *vr* to finish; *(vino, comida)* to run out.

término *m (final)* end; *(palabra)* term; **en términos generales** generally speaking; **por t. medio** on average.

termo *m* thermos (flask).

termómetro *m* thermometer.

termostato *m* thermostat.

ternera *f* calf; *(carne)* veal.

ternura *f* tenderness.

terraplén *m* embankment.

terremoto *m* earthquake.

terreno *m (tierra)* land; *(campo)* field; *(deportivo)* ground; *(ámbito)* field.

terrestre *adj (de la tierra)* terrestrial; *(transporte, ruta)* by land.

terrible *adj* terrible.

territorio *m* territory.

terrón *m (de azúcar)* lump.

terror *m* terror; **película de t.** horror film.

terrorismo *m* terrorism.

terrorista *adj & mf* terrorist.

terso, -a *adj (liso)* smooth.

tertulia *f* get-together.

tesis *f inv* thesis; *(opinión)* point of view.

tesoro *m* treasure.

test *m* test.

testamento *m* will; **hacer t.** to make one's will.

testarudo, -a *adj* obstinate.

testificar [44] *vi* to testify.

testigo *mf* witness.

testimonio *m* testimony; *(prueba)* evidence.

tétano *m* tetanus.

tetera *f* teapot.

tetina *f* (rubber) teat.

texto *m* text; **libro de t.** textbook.

tez *f* complexion.

ti *pron pers* you; **es para ti** it's for you; **piensas demasiado en ti mismo** you think too much about yourself.

tía *f* aunt; *fam (mujer)* woman.

tibio, -a *adj* tepid.

tiburón *m* shark.

tic *m* (*pl* **tics**) twitch; **t. nervioso** nervous twitch.

tiempo *m* time; (*meteorológico*) weather; (*de partido*) half; (*verbal*) tense; **a t.** in time; **a su (debido) t.** in due course; **al mismo t.** at the same time; **al poco t.** soon afterwards; **con t.** in advance; **¿cuánto t.?** how long?; **¿cuánto t. hace?** how long ago?; **estar a t. de** to still have time to; **¿nos da t. de llegar?** have we got (enough) time to get there?; **t. libre** free time; **¿qué t. hace?** what's the weather like?; **hace buen/mal t.** the weather is good/bad.

tienda *f* store; **ir de tiendas** to go shopping; **t. (de campaña)** tent.

tienta *f* **a tientas** by touch; **andar a tientas** to feel one's way; **buscar (algo) a tientas** to grope (for sth).

tierno, -a *adj* tender; (*reciente*) fresh.

tierra *f* land; (*planeta*) earth; (*suelo*) ground; **tocar t.** to land.

tieso, -a *adj* (*rígido*) stiff; (*erguido*) upright.

tiesto *m* flowerpot.

tifus *m inv* typhus (fever).

tigre *m* tiger; *Am* jaguar.

tijeras *fpl* pair of scissors *sing*, scissors.

tila *f* lime tea.

timar *vt* to swindle.

timbre *m* (*de puerta*) bell; (*sonido*) timbre.

timidez *f* shyness.

tímido, -a *adj* shy.

timo *m* swindle.

timón *m* (*de barco, avión*) rudder; (*de coche*) steering wheel.

tímpano *m* eardrum.

tinieblas *fpl* darkness *sing*.

tino *m* (*puntería*) **tener buen t.** to be a good shot.

tinta *f* ink; **t. china** Indian ink.

tinte *m* dye.

tintero *m* inkwell.

tintinear *vi* (*vidrio*) to clink; (*campana*) to tinkle.

tinto 1 *adj* (*vino*) red. **2** *m* (*vino*) red.

tintorería *f* dry-cleaner's.

tío *m* uncle; *fam* guy; **mis tíos** (*tío y tía*) my uncle and aunt.

tiovivo *m* merry-go-round.

típico, -a *adj* typical; (*baile, traje*) traditional.

tipo *m* (*clase*) type, kind; *fam* (*persona*) guy; (*figura*) (*de hombre*) build; (*de mujer*) figure; **jugarse el t.** to risk one's neck; **t. bancario** *o* **de descuento** bank rate; **t. de cambio/interés** exchange/interest rate.

tira *f* strip.

tirabuzón *m* ringlet.

tirachinas *m inv* slingshot.

tirada *f* print run.

tiranía *f* tyranny.

tirante 1 *adj* (*cable etc*) taut. **2** *m* (*de vestido etc*) strap; **tirantes** suspenders.

tirar 1 *vt* (*echar*) to throw, to fling; (*dejar caer*) to drop; (*desechar*) to throw away; (*derribar*) to knock down. **2** *vi* **t. de** (*cuerda, puerta*) to pull; (*disparar*) to shoot; **ir tirando** to get by; **tira a la izquierda** turn left. **3 tirarse** *vr* (*lanzarse*) to throw oneself; (*tumbarse*) to lie down; **tirarse de cabeza al agua** to dive into the water.

tirita® *f* Band-Aid®.

tiritar *vi* to shiver.

tiro *m* (*lanzamiento*) throw; (*disparo, ruido*) shot; (*de chimenea*) draft; **t. al blanco** target shooting; **t. al plato** clay pigeon shooting.

tirón *m* pull; (*de bolso*) snatch; *fam* **de un t.** in one go.

tiroteo *m* shooting.

titubear *vi* (*dudar*) to hesitate.

titulado, -a *adj* (*licenciado*) graduate; (*diplomado*) qualified.

titular¹ 1 *mf* (*persona*) holder. **2** *m* (*periódico*) headline.

titular² 1 *vt* (*poner título*) to call. **2 titularse** *vr* (*película etc*) to be called.

título *m* title; *(diploma)* diploma; *(titular)* headline.

tiza *f* chalk.

tiznar *vt* to blacken (with soot).

toalla *f* towel.

toallero *m* towel rail.

tobillo *m* ankle.

tobogán *m* slide; *(en piscina)* chute.

tocadiscos *m inv* record player.

tocador *m (mueble)* dressing table; *(habitación)* dressing room.

tocar [44] **1** *vt* to touch; *(instrumento, canción)* to play; *(timbre, campana)* to ring; *(bocina)* to blow; *(tema, asunto)* to touch on. **2** *vi (entrar en contacto)* to touch; **¿a quién le toca?** *(en juegos)* whose turn is it?; **me tocó el gordo** *(en rifa)* I won the jackpot. **3 tocarse** *vr (una cosa con otra)* to touch each other.

tocino *m* lard; **t. de cielo** sweet made with egg yolk.

tocólogo, -a *m* obstetrician.

todavía *adv (aún)* still; *(en negativas)* yet; *(para reforzar)* even, still; **t. la quiere** he still loves her; **t. no** not yet; **t. más/menos** even more/less.

todo, -a 1 *adj* all; *(cada)* every; **t. el mundo** everybody; **t. el día** all day, the whole day; **t. ciudadano de más de dieciocho años** every citizen over eighteen years of age; **todos, -as** all; **t. los niños** all the children; **t. los martes** every Tuesday. **2** *pron* all, everything; **t. aquél o el que quiera** anybody who wants (to); **todos, -as** all of them; **hablé con todos** I spoke to everybody; **todos aprobamos** we all passed; **ante t.** first of all; **del t.** completely; **después de t.** after all; **eso es t.** that's all; **hay de t.** there are all sorts; **lo sé t.** I know all about it; **t. lo contrario** quite the opposite; **t. lo más** at the most. **3** *adv* completely; **t. sucio** all dirty.

todoterreno *m* four-wheel drive (vehicle), SUV.

toldo *m (cubierta)* awning; *(en la playa)* sunshade; *Am (cabaña)* tent.

tolerante *adj* tolerant.

tolerar *vt* to tolerate.

toma *f (acción)* taking; **t. de corriente** socket.

tomado, -a *adj Am (borracho)* drunk.

tomar 1 *vt* to take; *(comer, beber)* to have; **toma** here (you are); **t. el sol** to sunbathe; **t. en serio/broma** to take seriously/as a joke. **2 tomarse** *vr (comer)* to eat; *(beber)* to drink; **no te lo tomes así** don't take it like that.

tomate *m* tomato; **salsa de t.** *(de lata)* tomato sauce; *(de botella)* ketchup.

tómbola *f* tombola.

tomo *m* volume.

tonel *m* cask.

tonelada *f* ton; **t. métrica** tonne.

tónico, -a 1 *m* tonic. **2** *f (bebida)* tonic (water); **tónica general** overall trend.

tono *m* tone; **un t. alto/bajo** a high/ low pitch.

tontería *f* silliness; *(dicho, hecho)* silly thing; *(insignificancia)* trifle.

tonto, -a 1 *adj* silly. **2** *mf* fool.

topacio *m* topaz.

toparse *vr* **t. con** to bump into; *(dificultades)* to run up against.

tope *m (límite)* limit; **estar hasta los topes** to be full up; **fecha t.** deadline.

tópico *m* cliché.

top model *f* supermodel.

topo *m (animal)* mole; *(espía)* spy, inside informer.

topónimo *m* place name.

torbellino *m (de viento)* whirlwind.

torcer [41] **1** *vt (tobillo)* to sprain; *(esquina)* to turn; *(inclinar)* to slant. **2** *vi* to turn. **3 torcerse** *vr (doblarse)* to twist; *(tobillo, mano)* to sprain; *(desviarse)* to go off to the side.

torear *vi* to fight.

torero, -a *mf* bullfighter.

tormenta *f* storm.

tormento *m (tortura)* torture; *(padecimiento)* torment.

tornillo *m* screw.

torno *m* *(de alfarero)* wheel; **en t. a** around.

toro *m* bull; ¿**te gustan los toros?** do you like bullfighting?

toronja *f* grapefruit.

torpe *adj* *(sin habilidad)* clumsy; *(tonto)* thick; *(movimiento)* slow.

torre *f* tower; *(en ajedrez)* rook.

torrente *m* torrent.

tórrido, -a *adj* torrid.

torso *m* torso.

torta *f* *(pastel)* cake; *(golpe)* slap.

tortazo *m* *(bofetada)* slap.

tortícolis *f inv* crick in the neck.

tortilla *f* omelet; *Am* tortilla; **t. francesa/española** (plain)/potato omelet.

tortuga *f* turtle.

tortuoso, -a *adj* tortuous.

tortura *f* torture.

tos *f* cough. **t. ferina** whooping cough.

tosco, -a *adj* *(basto)* rough; *(persona)* uncouth.

toser *vi* to cough.

tostada *f* **una t.** some toast, a slice of toast.

tostador *m* toaster.

tostar [2] *vt* *(pan)* to toast; *(café)* to roast.

total **1** *adj* total. **2** *m* *(todo)* whole; *(cantidad)* total; **en t.** in all. **3** *adv* anyway; *(para resumir)* in short.

totalidad *f* whole; **la t. de** all of; **en su t.** as a whole.

tóxico, -a **1** *adj* toxic. **2** *m* poison.

toxicómano, -a **1** *adj* addicted to drugs. **2** *mf* drug addict.

tozudo, -a *adj* stubborn.

traba *f* *(obstáculo)* hindrance.

trabajador, -a **1** *mf* worker. **2** *adj* hard-working.

trabajar **1** *vi* to work; **t. de camarera** to work as a waitress. **2** *vt* to work (on).

trabajo *m* work; *(esfuerzo)* effort; **un t.** a job; **t. eventual** casual labor; **trabajos manuales** arts and crafts.

trabalenguas *m inv* tongue twister.

trabar **1** *vt* *(conversación, amistad)* to start. **2 trabarse** *vr* **se le trabó la lengua** he got tongue-tied.

tractor *m* tractor.

tradición *f* tradition.

tradicional *adj* traditional.

traducción *f* translation.

traducir [10] **1** *vt* to translate (**a** into). **2 traducirse** *vr* to result (**en** in).

traductor, -a *mf* translator.

traer [25] **1** *vt* to bring; *(llevar consigo)* to carry; *(problemas)* to cause; *(noticia)* to feature; **trae** give it to me. **2 traerse** *vr* *(llevar consigo)* to bring along.

traficante *mf* *(de drogas etc)* trafficker.

traficar [44] *vi* *(ilegalmente)* to traffic (**con** in).

tráfico *m* traffic; **t. de drogas** drug traffic.

tragaperras *f inv* *(máquina)* **t.** slot machine.

tragar [42] *vt*, **tragarse** *vr* to swallow.

tragedia *f* tragedy.

trágico, -a *adj* tragic.

trago *m* *(bebida)* swig; **de un t.** in one go; **pasar un mal t.** to have a bad time.

traición *f* betrayal.

traicionar *vt* to betray.

traidor, -a **1** *adj* treacherous. **2** *mf* traitor.

traigo *indic pres de* **traer**.

traje¹ *m* *(de hombre)* suit; *(de mujer)* dress; **t. de baño** swimsuit; **t. de chaqueta** two-piece suit; **t. de novia** wedding dress.

traje² *pt indef de* **traer**.

trama *f* plot.

tramar *vt* to plot.

trámite *m* *(paso)* step; *(formalidad)* formality.

tramo *m* *(de carretera)* stretch; *(de escalera)* flight.

trampa f (de caza) trap; (engaño) fiddle; **hacer trampa(s)** to cheat.

trampilla f trap door.

trampolín m springboard.

tramposo, -a 1 adj deceitful. **2** mf cheat.

tranquilizante m tranquillizer.

tranquilizar [40] **1** vt to calm down; **lo dijo para tranquilizarme** he said it to reassure me. **2 tranquilizarse** vr (calmarse) to calm down.

tranquilo, -a adj (persona, lugar) calm; (agua) still; (conciencia) clear; (despreocupado) placid, easy-going; **fam tú t.** don't you worry.

transatlántico, -a 1 m (ocean) liner. **2** adj transatlantic.

transbordador m (car) ferry; **t. espacial** space shuttle.

transbordo m (de trenes) **hacer t.** to change.

transcurrir vi (tiempo) to pass, to go by; (acontecer) to take place.

transcurso m **en el t. de** in the course of.

transeúnte mf (peatón) passer-by.

transferencia f transference; (de dinero) transfer; **t. bancaria** bank transfer.

transferir [5] vt to transfer.

transformación f transformation.

transformador m transformer.

transformar 1 vt to transform. **2 transformarse** vr to turn (en into).

transfusión f transfusion.

transición f transition.

transistor m transistor.

transitado, -a adj (carretera) busy.

transitivo, -a adj transitive.

tránsito m (tráfico) traffic; (movimiento) passage; **pasajeros en t.** passengers in transit.

transitorio, -a adj transitory.

transmisión f transmission; (emisión) broadcast.

transmisor m transmitter.

transmitir vt to pass on; (emitir) to transmit.

transparentarse vr to be trans-

parent; **se le transparentaban las bragas** you could see her panties.

transparente adj transparent.

transpiración f perspiration.

transplante m transplant.

transportar vt to transport; (pasajeros) to carry; (mercancías) to ship.

transporte m transport.

transversal adj cross.

tranvía m streetcar.

trapo m (viejo, roto) rag; (bayeta) cloth; **t. de cocina** dishcloth; **t. del polvo** duster.

tráquea f trachea.

tras prep (después de) after; (detrás) behind.

trascendencia f (importancia) significance.

trascendental, trascendente adj significant.

trascurrir vi = transcurrir.

trasero, -a 1 adj back, rear; **en la parte trasera** at the back. **2** m fam bottom.

trasladar 1 vt (cosa) to move; (trabajador) to transfer. **2 trasladarse** vr to move.

traslado m (de casa) move; (de personal) transfer.

trasmano: a trasmano adv out of reach; **(me) coge a t.** it's out of my way.

trasnochar vi to stay up (very) late.

traspapelarse vr to get mislaid o misplaced.

trasparentarse vr = transparentarse.

traspasar vt (atravesar) to go through; (río) to cross; (negocio, local) to transfer; **'se traspasa'** 'for sale'.

traspié m (pl traspiés) stumble; **dar un t.** to trip.

trastero m (cuarto) **t.** junk room.

trastienda f back room.

trasto m thing; (cosa inservible) piece of junk.

trastocar [44] vt = trastornar.

trastornado, -a *adj (loco)* mad, unhinged.

trastornar 1 *vt (planes)* to disrupt; *fig (persona)* to unhinge. **2 trastornarse** *vr (enloquecer)* to go mad.

trastorno *m (molestia)* trouble; **t. mental** mental disorder.

tratado *m (pacto)* treaty; *(estudio)* treatise.

tratamiento *m* treatment; *(de textos etc)* processing.

tratar 1 *vt* to treat; *(asunto)* to discuss; *(manejar)* to handle; *(textos etc)* to process; **me trata de 'tú'** he calls me 'tu'. **2** *vi* **t. de** *(intentar)* to try to; **t. de** *o* **sobre** *o* **acerca de** to be about. **3 tratarse** *vr (relacionarse)* to be on speaking terms; **se trata de** *(es cuestión de)* it's a question of; *(es)* it is.

tratativas *fpl CSur* negotiation.

trato *m (contacto)* contact; *(acuerdo)* agreement; *(comercial)* deal; **malos tratos** ill-treatment *sing*; **¡t. hecho!** it's a deal!

traumático, -a *adj* traumatic.

través 1 *prep* **a t. de** *(superficie)* across, over; *(agujero etc)* through; *(por medio de)* through; **a t. del periódico** through the newspaper. **2** *adv* **de t.** *(transversalmente)* crosswise; *(de lado)* sideways.

travesaño *m* crosspiece; *(en fútbol)* crossbar.

travesía *f (viaje)* crossing.

travestí, travesti *mf* transvestite.

travesura *f* mischief.

travieso, -a *adj* mischievous.

trayecto *m (distancia)* distance; *(recorrido)* route; *(viaje)* journey.

trazar [40] *vt (línea)* to draw; *(plano)* to design.

trébol *m* trefoil; *(en naipes)* club.

trece *adj & m inv* thirteen.

trecho *m (distancia)* distance; *(tramo)* stretch.

tregua *f* truce.

treinta *adj & m inv* thirty.

tremendo, -a *adj (terrible)* terrible;

(muy grande) enormous; *(excelente)* tremendous.

tren *m* train.

trenca *f (prenda)* duffle coat.

trenza *f (de pelo)* braid.

trepar *vti* to climb.

tres *adj & m inv* three; **t. en raya** tick-tack-toe.

trescientos, -as *adj & mf* three hundred.

tresillo *m* three-piece suite.

treta *f* ruse.

triángulo *m* triangle; *fig* **t. amoroso** love triangle.

tribu *f* tribe.

tribuna *f (plataforma)* dais; *(en estadio)* stand.

tribunal *m* court; *(de examen)* board of examiners; **T. Supremo** Supreme Court.

tributo *m* tribute; *(finanzas)* tax.

triciclo *m* tricycle.

trienio *m* three-year period.

trigésimo, -a *adj & mf* thirtieth; **t. primero** thirty-first.

trigo *m* wheat.

trimestral *adj* quarterly.

trimestre *m* quarter; *(escolar)* term.

trinchar *vt (carne)* to carve.

trinchera *f* trench.

trineo *m* sledge; *(grande)* sleigh.

tripa *f (intestino)* gut; *fam* tummy; **dolor de t.** stomachache.

triple *adj & m inv* triple.

triplicar [44] *vt* to triple, to treble.

trípode *m* tripod.

tripulación *f* crew.

tripulante *mf* crew member.

tripular *vt* to man.

triquiñuela *f* dodge.

triste *adj (infeliz)* sad; *(sombrío)* gloomy.

tristeza *f* sadness.

triturar *vt* to grind (up).

triunfador, -a 1 *adj* winning. **2** *mf* winner.

triunfar *vi* to triumph.

triunfo *m (victoria)* triumph; *(deportiva)* win; *(éxito)* success.

trivial *adj* trivial.

triza *f* **hacer trizas** to tear to shreds.

trocar [64] *vt* to transform, to turn (**en** into).

trocear *vt* to cut up (into pieces).

trofeo *m* trophy.

tromba *f* **t. de agua** violent downpour.

trombón *m* trombone.

trompa *f* (*instrumento*) horn; (*de elefante*) trunk; *fam* **estar t.** to be sloshed.

trompeta *f* trumpet.

tronchar 1 *vt* (*rama, tronco*) to cut down. **2 troncharse** *vr* **troncharse de risa** to split one's sides laughing.

tronco *m* (*torso, de árbol*) trunk; (*leño*) log.

trono *m* throne.

tropa *f* **tropas** troops.

tropel *m* **en t.** in a mad rush.

tropezar [1] *vi* (*tropicar*) to stumble (**con** on); **t. con algn/dificultades** to run into sb/difficulties.

tropezón *m* (*traspié*) stumble; **dar un t.** to trip.

tropical *adj* tropical.

trópico *m* tropics *pl*.

tropiezo[1] *m* (*obstáculo*) trip.

tropiezo[2] *indic pres de* **tropezar**.

trotar *vi* to trot.

trote *m* trot; **al t.** at a trot.

trozo *m* piece.

trucha *f* trout.

truco *m* (*ardid*) trick; (*manera de hacer algo*) knack; **coger el t. (a algo)** to get the knack *o* hang (of sth).

trueno *m* thunder; **un t.** a thunderclap.

trufa *f* truffle.

tu *adj pos* your; **tu libro** your book; **tus libros** your books.

tú *pron pers* you.

tubería *f* (*de agua*) pipes *pl*; (*de gas, petróleo*) pipeline.

tubo *m* tube; (*tubería*) pipe; **t. de ensayo** test tube; **t. de escape** exhaust (pipe).

tuerca *f* nut.

tuerto, -a 1 *adj* blind in one eye. **2** *mf* person who is blind in one eye.

tuerzo *indic pres de* **torcer**.

tulipán *m* tulip.

tullido, -a *adj* crippled.

tumba *f* grave.

tumbar 1 *vt* to knock down. **2 tumbarse** *vr* (*acostarse*) to lie down.

tumbona *f* easy chair; (*de lona*) deckchair.

tumor *m* tumor.

tumulto *m* commotion.

túnel *m* tunnel; **el t. del Canal de la Mancha** the Channel Tunnel.

túnica *f* tunic.

tupé *m* (*pl* **tupés**) (*flequillo*) fringe.

tupido, -a *adj* thick.

turba *f* (*combustible*) peat.

turbado, -a *adj* (*alterado*) disturbed; (*desconcertado*) confused.

turbar 1 *vt* (*alterar*) to unsettle; (*desconcertar*) to baffle. **2 turbarse** *vr* (*preocuparse*) to become upset; (*desconcertarse*) to become confused.

turbio, -a *adj* (*agua*) cloudy; (*negocio etc*) dubious.

turbulencia *f* turbulence.

turco, -a 1 *adj* Turkish. **2** *mf* (*persona*) Turk; *fig* **cabeza de t.** scapegoat. **3** *m* (*idioma*) Turkish.

turismo *m* tourism; (*coche*) car; **ir de t.** to go touring.

turista *mf* tourist.

turístico, -a *adj* tourist; **de interés t.** of interest to tourists.

turnarse *vr* to take turns.

turno *m* (*en juegos etc*) turn; (*de trabajo*) shift; **t. de día/noche** day/night shift.

turquesa *adj & f* turquoise.

turrón *m* nougat.

tutear 1 *vt* to address as 'tú'. **2 tutearse** *vr* to call (each other) 'tú'.

tutela *f* guidance.

tutor, -a *mf* (*de huérfano*) guardian; (*de estudiante*) tutor.

tuve *pt indef de* **tener**.

tuyo, -a 1 *adj pos* (*con personas*) of

yours; *(con objetos)* one of your; **¿es amigo t.?** is he a friend of yours?; **un libro t.** one of your books. **2** *pron pos* yours.

U

u *conj (before words beginning with* **o** *or* **ho)** or.
ubicación *f* location.
ubicar [44] **1** *vt (situar)* to locate. **2** **ubicarse** *vr (en un lugar)* to be located.
Ud. *abr de* **usted** you.
Uds. *abr de* **ustedes** you.
UE *f abr de* **Unión Europa** European Union, EU.
úlcera *f* ulcer.
últimamente *adv* recently.
ultimar *vt (terminar)* to finalize; *(matar)* to finish off.
ultimátum *m (pl* **ultimátums)** ultimatum.
último, -a *adj* last; *(más reciente)* latest; *(más alto)* top; *(más bajo)* lowest; *(definitivo)* final; *(más lejano)* back; **por ú.** finally; **a. últimos de mes** at the end of the month; **últimas noticias** latest news; **el u. piso** the top apartment; **el u. de la lista** the lowest on the list; **la última fila** the back row.
ultraderecha *f* extreme right.
ultramarinos *mpl* groceries; **tienda de u.** greengrocer.
ultrasónico, -a *adj* ultrasonic.
ultravioleta *adj inv* ultraviolet.
ulular *vi (viento)* to howl; *(búho)* to hoot.
umbral *m* threshold.
un, -a 1 *art indef* a, *(antes de vocal)* an; **unos, -as** some. **2** *adj (delante de m sing)* one; **un chico y dos chicas** one boy and two girls.

unánime *adj* unanimous.
unanimidad *f* unanimity; **por u.** unanimously.
undécimo, -a *adj* eleventh.
únicamente *adv* only.
único, -a *adj (solo)* only; *(extraordinario)* unique; **hijo ú.** only child; **lo ú. que quiero** the only thing I want.
unidad *f* unit; *(cohesión)* unity; **u. de disquete** disk drive.
unido, -a *adj* united; **están muy unidos** they are very attached to one another; **una familia muy unida** a very close family.
unificación *f* unification.
uniforme 1 *m (prenda)* uniform. **2** *adj* uniform; *(superficie)* even.
unilateral *adj* unilateral.
unión *f* union.
unir *vt,* **unirse** *vr* to unite.
unísono *m* al **u.** in unison.
universal *adj* universal.
universidad *f* university.
universitario, -a 1 *adj* university. **2** *mf* university student.
universo *m* universe.
uno, -a 1 *m inv* one; **el u. de mayo** the first of May. **2** *f (hora)* **es la una** it's one o'clock. **3** *adj* **unos, -as** some; **unas cajas** some boxes; **debe haber unos/unas veinte** there must be around twenty. **4** *pron* one; *(persona)* someone, somebody; *(impers)* you, one; **u. (de ellos)**, **una (de ellas)** one of them; **unos cuantos** a few; **se miraron el u. al otro** they looked at each other; **de u. en u.** one by one; **u. tras otro** one after the other; **vive con u.** she's living with some man; **u. tiene que...** you have to....
untar *vt* to smear; *(mantequilla)* to spread.
uña *f* nail; **morderse** *o* **comerse las uñas** to bite one's nails.
uperizado, -a *adj* **leche uperizada** UHT milk.
urbanismo *m* town planning.
urbanización *f (barrio)* housing

estate; *(proceso)* urbanization.
urbano, -a *adj* urban.
urbe *f* large city.
urgencia *f* urgency; *(emergencia)* emergency.
urgente *adj* urgent; **correo u.** express mail.
urgir [57] *vi* to be urgent.
urna *f (para votos)* ballot box.
urraca *f* magpie.
uruguayo, -a *adj & mf* Uruguayan.
usado, -a *adj (ropa)* second-hand.
usar 1 *vt* to use; *(prenda)* to wear. **2 usarse** *vr* to be used.
usina *f Am (central eléctrica)* power station.
uso *m* use; **u. externo** for external use only; **u. tópico** local application; **haga u. del casco** wear a helmet.
usted *(pl* **ustedes)** *pron pers* you; **¿quién es u.?, ¿quiénes son ustedes?** who are you?
usual *adj* usual.
usuario, -a *mf* user.
utensilio *m* utensil; *(herramienta)* tool.
útil *adj* useful; *(día)* working.
utilidad *f* utility; **tener u.** to be useful.
utilitario, -a 1 *m (coche)* utility vehicle. **2** *adj* utilitarian.
utilización *f* use.
utilizar [40] *vt* to use.
utópico, -a *adj & mf* utopian.
uva *f* grape; **u. blanca** green grape.
UVI *f abr de* **unidad de vigilancia intensiva** intensive care unit.

V

vaca *f* cow; *(carne)* beef.
vacaciones *fpl* vacation; *(viaje)* holiday; **estar/irse de v.** to be/go on holiday.

vacante 1 *adj* vacant. **2** *f* vacancy.
vaciar [29] *vt,* **vaciarse** *vr* to empty.
vacilar *vi (dudar)* to hesitate; *(voz)* to falter; **sin v.** without hesitation.
vacío, -a 1 *adj* empty; *(hueco)* hollow; *(sin ocupar)* vacant. **2** *m* void; *(hueco)* gap; *(espacio)* (empty) space.
vacuna *f* vaccine.
vacunación *f* vaccination.
vacunar 1 *vt* to vaccinate (**contra** against); *fig* to inure. **2 vacunarse** *vr* to get oneself vaccinated.
vacuno, -a *adj* bovine; **ganado v.** cattle.
vado *m (de un río)* ford; **v. permanente** keep clear.
vagabundo, -a 1 *adj (errante)* wandering. **2** *mf* wanderer; *(sin casa)* hobo.
vagar [42] *vi* to wander about.
vago, -a 1 *adj (perezoso)* lazy; *(indefinido)* vague. **2** *mf (holgazán)* layabout.
vagón *m (para pasajeros)* car; *(para mercancías)* freight car.
vaho *m (de aliento)* breath; *(vapor)* vapor.
vaina *f (de guisante etc)* pod; *Am (molestia)* nuisance.
vainilla *f* vanilla.
vajilla *f* dishes *pl*.
valdré *indic fut de* **valer**.
vale¹ *interj* all right, OK.
vale² *m (comprobante)* voucher; *(pagaré)* IOU (I owe you).
valer [26] **1** *vt* to be worth; *(costar)* to cost; **no vale nada** it is worthless; **no vale la pena (ir)** it's not worthwhile (going); **¿cuánto vale?** how much is it? **2** *vi (servir)* to be useful; *(ser válido)* to count; **más vale** it is better; **más vale que te vayas ya** you had better leave now. **3 valerse** *vr* **valerse por sí mismo** to be able to manage on one's own.
valgo *indic pres de* **valer**.
válido, -a *adj* valid.
valiente *adj (valeroso)* brave.

valioso, -a adj valuable.

valla f (cerca) fence; (muro) wall; **v. publicitaria** billboard.

valle m valley.

valor m value; (precio) price; (valentía) courage; **objetos de v.** valuables; **sin v.** worthless.

valoración f appraisal.

valorar vt to value.

vals m waltz.

válvula f valve; **v. de seguridad** safety valve.

vampiro m vampire.

vandalismo m vandalism.

vanguardia f vanguard; (artística) avant-garde.

vanidad f vanity.

vanidoso, -a adj conceited.

vano, -a adj (vanidoso) vain; (esfuerzo, esperanza) futile; **en v.** in vain.

vapor m (de agua hirviendo) steam; (gas) vapor; **al v.** steamed; **v. de agua** water vapor.

vaporizador m vaporizer.

vaquero, -a 1 m cowboy. **2** adj **pantalón v.** jeans pl. **3** mpl **vaqueros** (prenda) jeans.

vara f rod.

variable adj & f variable.

variado, -a adj varied.

variante f (carretera) detour.

variar [29] vti to vary; (con ironía) **para v.** just for a change.

varicela f chickenpox.

variedad f variety; (espectáculo) variedades variety show.

varilla f (vara) rod; (de abanico, paraguas) rib.

varios, -as adj several.

variz f varicose vein.

varón m (hombre) man; (chico) boy.

vas indic pres de **ir**.

vascuence m (idioma) Basque.

vaselina f Vaseline®.

vasija f pot.

vaso m (para beber) glass.

vaticinar vt to predict.

vatio m watt.

vaya¹ interj **¡v. lío!** what a mess!

vaya² subj pres de **ir**.

Vd., Vds. abr de usted, ustedes you.

ve 1 imperativo de **ir**. **2** indic pres de **ver**.

vecindad f, **vecindario** m (área) neighborhood; (vecinos) residents pl.

vecino, -a 1 mf (persona) neighbor; (residente) resident. **2** adj neighboring.

vega f fertile plain.

vegetación f vegetation; (en nariz) **vegetaciones** adenoids.

vegetal adj & m vegetable.

vegetariano, -a adj & mf vegetarian.

vehemente adj vehement.

vehículo m vehicle.

veinte adj & m inv twenty.

vejez f old age.

vejiga f bladder.

vela¹ f candle; **pasar la noche en v.** to have a sleepless night.

vela² f (de barco) sail.

velador m Am (mesilla de noche) bedside table.

velar 1 vt (difrento) to hold a wake; (enfermo) to watch over. **2** vi (no dormir) to stay awake. **3 velarse** vr to blur.

velatorio m vigil.

velero m sailing boat.

veleta f weather vane.

vello m hair.

velo m veil.

velocidad f (rapidez) speed; (marcha) gear; **v. máxima** speed limit.

velocímetro m speedometer.

veloz adj rapid.

vena f vein.

venado m deer; (carne) venison.

vencedor, -a 1 mf winner. **2** adj winning.

vencer [49] **1** vt to defeat; (dificultad) to overcome. **2** vi (pago, deuda) to be payable; (plazo) to expire.

vencido, -a adj (derrotado) defeated; (equipo etc) beaten; **darse por v.** to give up.

venda *f* bandage.

vendaje *m* dressing.

vendar *vt* to bandage; **v. los ojos a algn** to blindfold sb.

vendaval *m* gale.

vendedor, -a *mf* seller; *(hombre)* salesman; *(mujer)* saleswoman.

vender *vt*, **venderse** *vr* to sell; **se vende** for sale.

vendimia *f* grape harvest.

vendré *indic fut de* **venir**.

veneno *m* poison; *(de serpiente)* venom.

venenoso, -a *adj* poisonous.

venéreo, -a *adj* venereal.

venezolano, -a *adj & mf* Venezuelan.

venga *subj pres de* **venir**.

venganza *f* vengeance, revenge.

vengarse [42] *vr* to avenge oneself; **v. de algn** to take revenge on sb.

vengo *indic pres de* **venir**.

venir [27] **1** *vi* to come; **el año que viene** next year; *fam* **¡venga ya!** *(expresa incredulidad)* come off it!; *(vamos)* come on!; **v. grande/pequeño** *(ropa)* to be too big/small; **v. mal/bien** to be inconvenient/convenient. ▪ *(en pasivas)* **esto vino provocado por...** this was brought about by... ▪ **esto viene ocurriendo desde hace mucho tiempo** this has been going on for a long time now. **2 venirse** *vr* **venirse abajo** to collapse.

venta *f* sale; *(posada)* country inn; **en v.** for sale; **a la v.** on sale; **v. a plazos/al contado** credit/cash sale; **v. al por mayor/al por menor** wholesale/retail.

ventaja *f* advantage; **llevar v. a** to have the advantage over.

ventana *f* window; *(de la nariz)* nostril.

ventanilla *f* window; *(de la nariz)* nostril.

ventilador *m* ventilator; *(de coche)* fan.

ventilar *vt* to ventilate.

ventisca *f* blizzard; *(de nieve)* snowstorm.

ver [28] **1** *vt* to see; *(televisión)* to watch; **a v.** let's see; **a v. si escribes** I hope you'll write; **(ya) veremos** we'll see; **no tener nada que v. con** to have nothing to do with. **2 verse** *vr* *(imagen etc)* to be seen; *(encontrarse con algn)* to see each other; **¡nos vemos!** see you later!; *Am* **te ves divina** you look divine.

veraneante *mf* vacationist, tourist.

veranear *vi* to spend one's summer vacation.

veraniego, -a *adj* summer.

verano *m* summer.

veras: de veras *adv* really.

verbena *f* street o night party.

verbo *m* verb.

verdad *f* truth; **es v.** it is true; **¡de v!** really!; truly!; **un amigo de v.** a real friend; *(en frase afirmativa)* **está muy bien, ¿(no es) v.?** it is very good, isn't it?; *(en frase negativa)* **no te gusta, ¿v.?** you don't like it, do you?

verdaderamente *adv* truly.

verdadero, -a *adj* true.

verde 1 *adj* green; *(fruta)* unripe; *(chiste, película)* blue. **2** *m (color)* green.

verdoso, -a *adj* greenish.

verdura *f* vegetables *pl.*

vereda *f* path; *Am (acera)* sidewalk.

veredicto *m* verdict.

vergonzoso, -a *adj (penoso)* disgraceful; *(tímido)* shy.

vergüenza *f* shame; *(timidez)* shyness; **¿no te da v.?** aren't you ashamed?; **es una v.** it's a disgrace; **me da v.** I'm too embarrassed.

verificar [44] *vt* to check.

verja *f (reja)* grating; *(cerca)* railing; *(puerta)* iron gate.

vermut, vermú *m (pl* **vermús)** vermouth.

verosímil *adj* probable, likely; *(creíble)* credible.

verruga *f* wart.

versión *f* version.

verso *m (poesía)* verse.

vertebrado, -a *adj & m* vertebrate.

vertedero *m (de basura)* tip.

verter [3] *vt* to pour (out); *(basura)* to dump.

vertical *adj* vertical.

vertiente *f (de montaña, tejado)* slope; *Am (manantial)* spring.

vertiginoso, -a *adj (velocidad)* breakneck.

vértigo *m* vertigo; **me da v.** it makes me dizzy.

vespa® *f* (motor) scooter.

vespino® *m* moped.

vestíbulo *m (de casa)* hall; *(de edificio público)* foyer.

vestido, -a 1 *m (de mujer)* dress. **2** *adj* dressed.

vestigio *m* trace.

vestir [6] **1** *vt (a algn)* to dress; *(llevar puesto)* to wear. **2** *vi* to dress; **ropa de (mucho) v.** formal dress. **3** **vestirse** *vr* to get dressed, to dress; **vestirse de** to wear; *(disfrazarse)* to dress up as.

vestuario *m (conjunto de vestidos)* wardrobe; *(para teatro)* costumes *pl*; *(camerino)* dressing room; *(en estadio)* changing room.

veterano, -a *adj & mf* veteran.

veterinario, -a 1 *mf* vet, veterinarian. **2** *f* veterinary medicine.

veto *m* veto.

vez *f* time; *(turno)* turn; **una v.** once; **dos veces** twice; **cinco veces** five times; **a o algunas veces** sometimes; **cada v.** each o every time; **cada v. más** more and more; **de v. en cuando** now and again; **¿le has visto alguna v.?** have you ever seen him?; **otra v.** again; **a la v.** at the same time; **tal v.** perhaps, maybe; **de una v.** in one go; **en v. de** instead of.

vía 1 *f (del tren)* track; *(camino)* road; **(por) v. oral** to be taken orally; **por v. aérea/marítima** by air/sea. **2** *prep (a través de)* via.

viajar *vi* to travel.

viaje *m* journey, trip; *(largo, en barco)* voyage; **¡buen v.!** have a good trip!; **estar de v.** to be away (on a trip); **v. de negocios** business trip; **v. de novios** honeymoon.

viajero, -a *mf* traveler; *(en transporte público)* passenger.

víbora *f* viper.

vibración *f* vibration.

vibrar *vti* to vibrate.

vicepresidente, -a *mf* vice president; *(de compañía, comité)* vice-chairman, vice president.

viceversa *adv* vice versa.

vicio *m* vice; *(mala costumbre)* bad habit.

vicioso, -a 1 *adj (persona)* depraved; **círculo v.** vicious circle. **2** *mf* depraved person.

víctima *f* victim.

victoria *f* victory.

vid *f* vine.

vida *f* life; **en mi v.** never in my life; **ganarse la v.** to earn one's living; **¿qué es de tu v.?** how's life?

vídeo *m* video; **grabar en v.** to video.

videocámara *f* video camera.

videoclub *m* video club.

videojuego *m* video game.

vidriera *f* stained-glass window; *Am (escaparate)* shop window.

vidrio *m* glass.

viejo, -a 1 *adj* old; **hacerse v.** to grow old; **un v. amigo** an old friend. **2** *mf (hombre)* old man; *(mujer)* old woman; **los viejos** old people; *fam* **mis viejos** my parents.

viento *m* wind; **hace o sopla mucho v.** it is very windy.

vientre *m* belly.

viernes *m inv* Friday; **V. Santo** Good Friday.

vietnamita *adj & mf* Vietnamese.

viga *f (de madera)* beam; *(de hierro)* girder.

vigencia *f* validity; **entrar en v.** to come into force.

vigésimo, -a *adj & mf* twentieth.

vigilante *m* guard; *(nocturno)* night watchman.

vigilar 1 *vt* to watch; *(lugar)* to guard. **2** *vi* to keep watch.

vigor *m* vigor; *(fuerza)* strength; **en v.** in force.

vil *adj* vile.

villa *f* *(población)* town; *(casa)* villa.

villancico *m* (Christmas) carol.

vinagre *m* vinegar.

vinagreras *fpl* oil and vinegar cruets.

vinagreta *f* vinaigrette.

vincha *f Am* headband.

vínculo *m* link.

vine *pt indef de* **venir**.

vino *m* wine; **v. blanco/tinto** white/red wine; **v. rosado** rosé.

viña *f* vineyard.

viñedo *m* vineyard.

viñeta *f* illustration.

violación *f* *(de persona)* rape; *(de ley, derecho)* violation.

violar *vt* *(persona)* to rape; *(ley, derecho)* to violate.

violencia *f* violence.

violento, -a *adj* violent; *(situación)* embarrassing; **sentirse v.** to feel awkward.

violeta 1 *adj* violet. **2** *m (color)* violet. **3** *f (flor)* violet.

violín *m* violin.

violonc(h)elo *m* cello.

virar *vt* to turn round.

virgen *adj* *(persona, selva)* virgin; *(aceite, lana)* pure; *(cinta)* blank.

viril *adj* virile.

virtud *f* virtue; *(propiedad)* ability.

virtuoso, -a *adj* virtuous; *(músico)* virtuoso.

viruela *f* smallpox.

virus *m inv* virus.

visa *f Am* visa.

visado *m* visa.

visera *f* *(de gorra)* peak; *(de casco)* visor.

visibilidad *f* visibility.

visible *adj* visible.

visillo *m* small net curtain.

visión *f* vision; *(vista)* sight.

visita *f* visit; *(invitado)* visitor; **hacer una v.** to pay a visit; **estar de v.** to be visiting.

visitante 1 *mf* visitor. **2** *adj (equipo)* away.

visitar *vt* to visit.

vislumbrar *vt* to glimpse.

visón *m* mink.

víspera *f* *(día anterior)* day before; *(de festivo)* eve.

vista *f* sight; *(panorama)* view; **a la v.** visible; **a primera** *o* **simple v.** on the face of it; **en v. de** in view of, considering; **corto de v.** short-sighted; **conocer a algn de v.** to know sb by sight; **perder de v. a** to lose sight of; **¡hasta la v.!** see you!; **con vista(s) al mar** overlooking the sea.

vistazo *m* glance; **echar un v. a algo** *(ojear)* to have a (quick) look at sth.

visto, -a 1 *adj* **está v. que** it is obvious that ; **por lo v.** apparently; **estar bien v.** to be well looked upon; **estar mal v.** to be frowned upon. **2** *m* **v. bueno** approval.

vitalicio, -a *adj* lifelong.

vitalidad *f* vitality.

vitamina *f* vitamin.

viticultor, -a *mf* wine grower.

vitorear *vt* to cheer.

vitrina *f* *(aparador)* display cabinet; *(de exposición)* showcase; *Am (escaparate)* shop window.

viudo, -a *mf* *(hombre)* widower; *(mujer)* widow.

viva *interj* hurrah!

vivaracho, -a *adj* lively.

vivaz *adj* vivacious; *(perspicaz)* quick-witted.

víveres *mpl* provisions.

vivero *m* *(de plantas)* nursery.

vivienda *f* housing; *(casa)* house; *(piso)* apartment.

vivir 1 *vi* to live. **2** *vt* *(guerra, experiencia)* to live through.

vivo, -a *adj* alive; *(vivaz)* lively; *(lis-*

vocabulario *m* vocabulary.

vocación *f* vocation.

vocal 1 *f* vowel. **2** *m* member. **3** *adj* vocal.

voceador, -a *mf Am* vendor.

vocero, -a *mf Am* spokesperson; *(hombre)* spokesman; *(mujer)* spokeswoman.

vociferar *vi* to shout.

vodka *m* vodka.

volandas: en vandas *adv* flying through the air.

volante 1 *m* steering wheel; *(de vestido)* frill; **ir al v.** to be at the wheel. **2** *adj* flying; **platillo v.** flying saucer.

volantín *m Am (cometa)* small kite.

volar [2] **1** *vi* to fly; *fam* **lo hizo volando** he did it in a flash. **2** *vt (explotar)* to blow up; *(caja fuerte)* to blow open; *(terreno)* to blast. **3 volarse** *vr (papel etc)* to be blown away.

volcán *m* volcano.

volcar [2] **1** *vt (cubo etc)* to knock over; *(barco, bote)* to capsize; *(vaciar)* to empty out. **2** *vi (coche)* to turn over; *(barca)* to capsize. **3 volcarse** *vr (vaso, jarra)* to fall over; *(coche)* to turn over; *(barca)* to capsize.

voleibol *m* volleyball.

voltaje *m* voltage.

voltear 1 *vt CSur (derribar)* to knock over; *Andes, CAm, Carib, Méx (cabeza)* to turn; **v. la espalda a algn** to turn one's back on sb. **2 voltearse** *vr Andes, CAm, Carib, Méx (volverse)* to turn around.

voltereta *f* somersault.

voltio *m* volt.

volumen *m* volume.

voluminoso, -a *adj* voluminous; *(enorme)* massive.

voluntad *f* will; **fuerza de v.** willpower; **tiene mucha v.** he is very strong-willed.

voluntario, -a 1 *adj* voluntary; **ofrecerse v.** to volunteer. **2** *mf* volunteer.

volver [4] *(pp* **vuelto)** **1** *vi* to return; *(venir de vuelta)* to come back; *(ir de vuelta)* to go back; **v. en sí** to come round; **v. a hacer algo** to do sth again. **2** *vt (convertir)* to make; *(dar vuelta a)* to turn; *(boca abajo)* to turn upside down; *(de fuera adentro)* to turn inside out; *(de atrás adelante)* to turn back to front; *(cinta, disco)* to turn over; **volverle la espalda a algn** to turn one's back on sb; **al v. la esquina** on turning the corner. **3 volverse** *vr* to turn; *(venir de vuelta)* to come back; *(ir de vuelta)* to go back; *(convertirse)* to become; **volverse loco** to go mad.

vomitar 1 *vi* to vomit; **tengo ganas de v.** I feel sick. **2** *vt* to bring up.

voraz *adj* voracious.

vos *pron pers pl Am* you.

vosotros, -as *pron pers pl* you.

votación *f (voto)* vote; *(acción)* voting.

votante *mf* voter.

votar *vi* to vote; **v. a algn** to vote for sb.

voto *m* vote.

voy *indic pres de* **ir**.

voz *f* voice; *(grito)* shout; **en v. alta** aloud; **en v. baja** in a low voice; **a media v.** in a low voice; **a voces** shouting; **dar voces** to shout; **no tener ni v. ni voto** to have no say in the matter.

vuelo *m* flight; **v. chárter/regular** charter/scheduled flight; **una falda de v.** a full skirt.

vuelta *f (regreso)* return; *(viaje)* return journey; *(giro)* turn; *(en carreras)* lap; *(ciclista)* tour; *(dinero)* change; **a v. de correo** by return post; **estar de v.** to be back; **dar media v.** to turn round; **la cabeza me da vueltas** my head is spinning; **no le des más vueltas** stop worrying about it; **dar una v.** *(a pie)* to go for a walk; *(en coche)* to go for a drive.

vuelto *m Am* change.

vuestro, -a 1 *adj pos (antes del sustantivo)* your; *(después del sustanti-*

vo) of yours. **2** *pron pos* yours; **lo v.** what is yours.

vulgar *adj* vulgar.

vulnerable *adj* vulnerable.

W

walkman® *m* Walkman®.

WAP *m abr de* **Wireless Application Protocol** WAP.

wáter *m (pl* **wáteres)** toilet.

Web *f* la Web the Web

web *m o f* website

whisky *m* whiskey.

windsurf(ing) *m* windsurfing.

wireless *adj* wireless.

X

xenofobia *f* xenophobia.

Y

y *conj* and; **son las tres y cuarto** it's a quarter past three; **¿y qué?** so what?; **¿y tú?** what about you?; **¿y eso?** how come?; *ver* **e**.

ya 1 *adv* already; *(ahora mismo)* now; **ya lo sabía** I already knew; **¡hazlo ya!** do it at once!; **ya mismo** right away; **ya hablaremos luego** we'll talk about it later; **ya verás** you'll see; **ya no** no longer; **ya no viene por aquí** he doesn't come round here

any more; **ya era hora** about time too; **ya lo creo** I should think so; **¡ya voy!** coming!; **¡ya está!** that's it! **2** *conj* **ya que** since.

yacaré *m Am* alligator.

yacer [61] *vi* to lie.

yacimiento *m* deposit.

yanqui 1 *adj* Yankee. **2** *mf* Yank.

yarda *f* yard.

yate *m* yacht.

yedra *f* ivy.

yegua *f* mare.

yema *f (de huevo)* yolk; *(de planta)* bud; *(pastel)* sweet made from sugar and egg yolk; **y. del dedo** fingertip.

yendo *gerundio de* **ir.**

yerba *f* = **hierba.**

yerbatero, -a *mf Am (curandero)* witch doctor who uses herbs.

yerno *m* son-in-law.

yerro *indic pres de* **errar.**

yeso *m* plaster.

yo *pron pers* I; **entre tú y yo** between you and me; **¿quién es? — soy yo** who is it? — it's me; **yo no** not me; **yo que tú** if I were you; **yo mismo** I myself.

yoga *m* yoga.

yogur *m* yogurt.

yuca *f* yucca.

yudo *m* judo.

yugo(e)slavo, -a *adj & mf* Yugoslav, Yugoslavian.

Z

zafarse *vr* to get away (**de** from).

zafiro *m* sapphire.

zalamero, -a 1 *mf* crawler. **2** *adj* crawling.

zamarra *f (prenda)* sheepskin jacket.

zambo, -a *adj* knock-kneed; *Am* half Indian and half Negro.

zambullirse *vr* to jump.

zanahoria *f* carrot.

zancada *f* stride.

zancadilla *f* ponerle la z. a algn to trip sb up.

zanco *m* stilt.

zancudo *m Am* mosquito.

zanja *f* ditch.

zapatería *f* shoe shop.

zapatero, -a *mf (vendedor)* shoe shop owner; *(fabricante)* shoemaker; *(reparador)* cobbler.

zapatilla *f* slipper; **zapatillas de deporte** trainers.

zapato *m* shoe.

zarandear *vt* to shake.

zarcillo *m (pendiente)* earring.

zarpa *f* claw.

zarpar *vi* to set sail.

zarza *f* bramble.

zarzamora *f (zarza)* blackberry bush; *(fruto)* blackberry.

zarzuela *f* Spanish operetta; **la Z.** royal residence in Madrid.

zigzag *m (pl* **zigzags** *o* **zigzagues)** zigzag.

zócalo *m (de pared)* baseboard.

zodiaco, zodíaco *m* zodiac; **signo del z.** sign of the zodiac.

zona *f* zone.

zoo *m* zoo.

zoológico, -a 1 *adj* zoological; **parque z.** zoo. **2** *m* zoo.

zopilote *m Am* buzzard.

zoquete *mf fam* blockhead.

zorra *f* vixen.

zorro *m* fox.

zueco *m* clog.

zumbar *vi* to buzz; **me zumban los oídos** my ears are buzzing.

zumbido *m* buzzing.

zumo *m* juice.

zurcir [52] *vt* to darn.

zurdo, -a 1 *mf (persona)* left-handed person. **2** *adj* left-handed.

SPANISH VERBS

Models for regular conjugation

TOMAR to take

INDICATIVE

PRESENT	FUTURE	CONDITIONAL
1. tomo	tomaré	tomaría
2. tomas	tomarás	tomarías
3. toma	tomará	tomaría
1. tomamos	tomaremos	tomaríamos
2. tomáis	tomaréis	tomaríais
3. toman	tomarán	tomarían

IMPERFECT	PRETERITE	PERFECT
1. tomaba	tomé	he tomado
2. tomabas	tomaste	has tomado
3. tomaba	tomó	ha tomado
1. tomábamos	tomamos	hemos tomado
2. tomabais	tomasteis	habéis tomado
3. tomaban	tomaron	han tomado

FUTURE PERFECT	CONDITIONAL PERFECT	PLUPERFECT
1. habré tomado	habría tomado	había tomado
2. habrás tomado	habrías tomado	habías tomado
3. habrá tomado	habría tomado	había tomado
1. habremos tomado	habríamos tomado	habíamos tomado
2. habréis tomado	habríais tomado	habíais tomado
3. habrán tomado	habrían tomado	habían tomado

SUBJUNCTIVE

PRESENT	IMPERFECT	PERFECT/PLUPERFECT
1. tome	tom-ara/ase	haya/hubiera* tomado
2. tomes	tom-aras/ases	hayas/hubieras tomado
3. tome	tom-ara/ase	haya/hubiera tomado

* the alternative form 'hubiese' etc is also possible.

1. tomemos	tom-áramos/ásemos	hayamos/hubiéramos tomado
2. toméis	tom-arais/aseis	hayáis/hubierais tomado
3. tomen	tom-aran/asen	hayan/hubieran tomado

IMPERATIVE	**INFINITIVE**	**PARTICIPLE**
(tú) toma	**PRESENT**	**PRESENT**
(Vd) tome	tomar	tomando
(nosotros) tomemos		
(vosotros) tomad	**PERFECT**	**PAST**
(Vds) tomen	haber tomado	tomado

COMER to eat

INDICATIVE

PRESENT	**FUTURE**	**CONDITIONAL**
1. como	comeré	comería
2. comes	comerás	comerías
3. come	comerá	comería
1. comemos	comeremos	comeríamos
2. coméis	comeréis	comeríais
3. comen	comerán	comerían

IMPERFECT	**PRETERITE**	**PERFECT**
1. comía	comí	he comido
2. comías	comiste	has comido
3. comía	comió	ha comido
1. comíamos	comimos	hemos comido
2. comíais	comisteis	habéis comido
3. comían	comieron	han comido

FUTURE PERFECT	**CONDITIONAL PERFECT**	**PLUPERFECT**
1. habré comido	habría comido	había comido
2. habrás comido	habrías comido	habías comido
3. habrá comido	habría comido	había comido
1. habremos comido	habríamos comido	habíamos comido
2. habréis comido	habríais comido	habíais comido
3. habrán comido	habrían comido	habían comido

PRESENT	IMPERFECT	PERFECT/PLUPERFECT
1. coma	com-iera/iese	haya/hubiera* comido
2. comas	com-ieras/ieses	hayas/hubieras comido
3. coma	com-iera/iese	haya/hubiera comido
1. comamos	com-iéramos/iésemos	hayamos/hubiéramos comido
2. comáis	com-ierais/ieseis	hayáis/hubierais comido
3. coman	com-ieran/iesen	hayan/hubieran comido

* the alternative form 'hubiese' etc is also possible

IMPERATIVE	INFINITIVE	PARTICIPLE
(tú) come	**PRESENT**	**PRESENT**
(Vd) coma	comer	comiendo
(nosotros) comamos		
(vosotros) comed	**PERFECT**	**PAST**
(Vds) coman	haber comido	comido

PARTIR to leave

INDICATIVE

PRESENT	FUTURE	CONDITIONAL
1. parto	partiré	partiría
2. partes	partirás	partirías
3. parte	partirá	partiría
1. partimos	partiremos	partiríamos
2. partís	partiréis	partiríais
3. parten	partirán	partirían

IMPERFECT	PRETERITE	PERFECT
1. partía	partí	he partido
2. partías	partiste	has partido
3. partía	partió	ha partido
1. partíamos	partimos	hemos partido
2. partíais	partisteis	habéis partido
3. partían	partieron	han partido

FUTURE PERFECT	CONDITIONAL PERFECT	PLUPERFECT
1. habré partido	habría partido	había partido
2. habrás partido	habrías partido	habías partido
3. habrá partido	habría partido	había partido
1. habremos partido	habríamos partido	habíamos partido
2. habréis partido	habríais partido	habíais partido
3. habrán partido	habrían partido	habían partido

PRESENT	IMPERFECT	PERFECT/PLUPERFECT
parta	parti-era/ese	haya/hubiera* partido
partas	parti-eras/eses	hayas/hubieras partido
parta	parti-era/ese	haya/hubiera partido
partamos	parti-éramos/ésemos	hayamos/hubiéramos partido
partáis	parti-erais/eseis	hayáis/hubierais partido
partan	parti-eran/esen	hayan/hubieran partido

* the alternative form 'hubiese' etc is also possible

<table>

IMPERATIVE	INFINITIVE	PARTICIPLE
(tú) parte	**PRESENT**	**PRESENT**
(Vd) parta	partir	partiendo
(nosotros) partamos		
(vosotros) partid	**PERFECT**	**PAST**
(Vds) partan	haber partido	partido

Models for irregular conjugation

[1] pensar PRES pienso, piensas, piensa, pensamos, pensáis, piensan; PRES SUBJ piense, pienses, piense, pensemos, penséis, piensen; IMPERAT piensa, piense, pensemos, pensad, piensen

[2] contar PRES cuento, cuentas, cuenta, contamos, contáis, cuentan; PRES SUBJ cuente, cuentes, cuente, contemos, contéis, cuenten; IMPERAT cuenta, cuente, contemos, contad, cuenten

[3] perder PRES pierdo, pierdes, pierde, perdemos, perdéis, pierden; PRES SUBJ pierda, pierdas, pierda, perdamos, perdáis, pierdan; IMPERAT pierde, pierda, perdamos, perded, pierdan

[4] morder PRES muerdo, muerdes, muerde, mordemos, mordéis, muerden; PRES SUBJ muerda, muerdas, muerda, mordamos, mordáis, muerdan; IMPERAT muerde, muerda, mordamos, morded, muerdan

[5] sentir PRES siento, sientes, siente, sentimos, sentís, sienten; PRES SUBJ sienta, sientas, sienta, sintamos, sintáis, sientan; PRES P sintiendo; IMPERAT siente, sienta, sintamos, sentid, sientan

[6] vestir PRES visto, vistes, viste, vestimos, vestís, visten; PRES SUBJ vista, vistas, vista, vistamos, vistáis, vistan; PRES P vistiendo; IMPERAT viste, vista, vistamos, vestid, vistan

[7] dormir PRES duermo, duermes, duerme, dormimos, dormís, duermen; PRES SUBJ duerma, duermas, duerma, durmamos, durmáis, duerman; PRES P durmiendo; IMPERAT duerme, duerma, durmamos, dormid, duerman

[8] andar PRET anduve, anduviste, anduvo, anduvimos, anduvisteis, anduvieron; IMPERF SUBJ anduviera/anduviese

[9] caber PRES quepo, cabes, cabe, cabemos, cabéis, caben; PRES SUBJ quepa, quepas, quepa, quepamos, quepáis, quepan; FUT cabré; COND cabría; PRET cupe, cupiste, cupo, cupimos, cupisteis, cupieron; IMPERF SUBJ cupiera/cupiese; IMPERAT cabe, quepa, quepamos, cabed, quepan

[10] conducir PRES conduzco, conduces, conduce, conducimos, conducís, conducen; PRES SUBJ conduzca, conduzcas, conduzca, conduzcamos, conduzcáis, conduzcan; PRET conduje, condujiste, condujo, condujimos, condujisteis, condujeron; IMPERAT conduce, conduzca, conduzcamos, conducid, conduzcan

[11] dar PRES doy, das, da, damos, dais, dan; PRES SUBJ dé, des, dé, demos, deis, den; PRET di, diste, dio, dimos, disteis, dieron; IMPERF SUBJ diera/diese; IMPERAT da, dé, demos, dad, den

[12] decir PRES digo, dices, dice, decimos, decís, dicen; PRES SUBJ diga, digas, diga, digamos, digáis, digan; FUT diré; COND diría; PRET dije, dijiste, dijo, dijimos, dijisteis, dijeron; IMPERF SUBJ dijera/dijese; PRES P diciendo; PP dicho; IMPERAT di, diga, digamos, decid, digan

[13] ESTAR to be

INDICATIVE

PRESENT	FUTURE	CONDITIONAL
1. estoy	estaré	estaría
2. estás	estarás	estarías
3. está	estará	estaría
1. estamos	estaremos	estaríamos
2. estáis	estaréis	estaríais
3. están	estarán	estarían

IMPERFECT	PRETERITE	PERFECT
1. estaba	estuve	he estado
2. estabas	estuviste	has estado
3. estaba	estuvo	ha estado
1. estábamos	estuvimos	hemos estado
2. estabais	estuvisteis	habéis estado
3. estaban	estuvieron	han estado

FUTURE PERFECT	CONDITIONAL PERFECT	PLUPERFECT
1. habré estado	habría estado	había estado
2. habrás estado	habrías estado	habías estado
3. habrá estado	habría estado	había estado
1. habremos estado	habríamos estado	habíamos estado
2. habréis estado	habríais estado	habíais estado
3. habrán estado	habrían estado	habían estado

SUBJUNCTIVE

PRESENT	IMPERFECT	PERFECT/PLUPERFECT
1. esté	estuv-iera/iese	haya/hubiera* estado
2. estés	estuv-ieras/ieses	hayas/hubieras estado
3. esté	estuv-iera/iese	haya/hubiera estado
1. estemos	estuv-iéramos/iésemos	hayamos/hubiéramos estado
2. estéis	estuv-ierais/ieseis	hayáis/hubierais estado
3. estén	estuv-ieran/iesen	hayan/hubieran estado

IMPERATIVE / INFINITIVE / PARTICIPLE

IMPERATIVE	INFINITIVE	PARTICIPLE
(tú) está	**PRESENT**	**PRESENT**
(Vd) esté	estar	estando
(nosotros) estemos		
(vosotros) estad	**PERFECT**	**PAST**
(Vds) estén	haber estado	estado

* the alternative form 'hubiese' etc is also possible

(6)

[14] HABER to have (*auxiliary*)

INDICATIVE

PRESENT	FUTURE	CONDITIONAL
1. he	habré	habría
2. has	habrás	habrías
3. ha/hay*	habrá	habría
1. hemos	habremos	habríamos
2. habéis	habréis	habríais
3. han	habrán	habrían

IMPERFECT	PRETERITE	PERFECT
1. había	hube	
2. habías	hubiste	
3. había	hubo	ha habido*
1. habíamos	hubimos	
2. habíais	hubisteis	
3. habían	hubieron	

FUTURE PERFECT	CONDITIONAL PERFECT	PLUPERFECT
1.		
2.		
3. habrá habido*	habría habido*	había habido*
1.		
2.		
3.		

SUBJUNCTIVE

PRESENT	IMPERFECT	PERFECT/PLUPERFECT
1. haya	hub-iera/iese	
2. hayas	hub-ieras/ieses	
3. haya	hub-iera/iese	haya/hubiera** habido*
1. hayamos	hub-iéramos/iésemos	
2. hayáis	hub-ierais/ieseis	
3. hayan	hub-ieran/iesen	

INFINITIVE

PRESENT
haber
PERFECT
haber habido*

PARTICIPLE

PRESENT
habiendo
PAST
habido

* 'haber' is an auxiliary verb used with the participle of another verb to form compound tenses (eg he bebido – I have drunk). 'hay' means 'there is/are' and all third person singular forms in their respective tenses have this meaning. The forms highlighted with an asterisk are used only for this latter construction.

** the alternative form 'hubiese' is also possible.

(7)

[15] hacer PRES hago, haces, hace, hacemos, hacéis, hacen; PRES SUBJ haga, hagas, haga, hagamos, hagáis, hagan; FUT haré; COND haría; PRET hice, hiciste, hizo, hicimos, hicisteis, hicieron; IMPERF SUBJ hiciera/hiciese; PP hecho; IMPERAT haz, haga, hagamos, haced, hagan

[16] ir PRES voy, vas, va, vamos, vais, van; PRES SUBJ vaya, vayas, vaya, vayamos, vayáis, vayan; IMPERF iba, ibas, iba, íbamos, ibais, iban; PRET fui, fuiste, fue, fuimos, fuisteis, fueron; IMPERF SUBJ fuera/fuese; PRES P yendo; IMPERAT ve, vaya, vamos, id, vayan

[17] oír PRES oigo, oyes, oye, oímos, oís, oyen; PRES SUBJ oiga, oigas, oiga, oigamos, oigáis, oigan; IMPERF oí, oíste, oyó, oímos, oísteis, oyeron; IMPERF SUBJ oyera/oyese; PRES P oyendo; PP oído; IMPERAT oye, oiga, oigamos, oíd, oigan

[18] poder PRES puedo, puedes, puede, podemos, podéis, pueden; PRES SUBJ pueda, puedas, pueda, podamos, podáis, puedan; FUT podré; COND podría; PRET pude, pudiste, pudo, pudimos, pudisteis, pudieron; IMPERF SUBJ pudiera/pudiese; PRES P pudiendo; IMPERAT puede, pueda, podamos, poded, puedan

[19] poner PRES pongo, pones, pone, ponemos, ponéis, ponen; PRES SUBJ ponga, pongas, ponga, pongamos, pongáis, pongan; FUT pondré; PRET puse, pusiste, puso, pusimos, pusisteis, pusieron; IMPERF SUBJ pusiera/pusiese; PP puesto; IMPERAT pon, ponga, pongamos, poned, pongan

[20] querer PRES quiero, quieres, quiere, queremos, queréis, quieren; PRES SUBJ quiera, quieras, quiera, queramos, queráis, quieran; FUT querré; COND querría; PRET quise, quisiste, quiso, quisimos, quisisteis, quisieron; IMPERF SUBJ quisiera/quisiese; IMPERAT quiere, quiera, queramos, quered, quieran

[21] saber PRES sé, sabes, sabe, sabemos, sabéis, saben; PRES SUBJ sepa, sepas, sepa, sepamos, sepáis, sepan; FUT sabré; COND sabría; PRET supe, supiste, supo, supimos, supisteis, supieron; IMPERF SUBJ supiera/supiese; IMPERAT sabe, sepa, sepamos, sabed, sepan

[22] salir PRES salgo, sales, sale, salimos, salís, salen; PRES SUBJ salga, salgas, salga, salgamos, salgáis, salgan; FUT saldré; COND saldría; IMPERAT sal, salga, salgamos, salid, salgan

[23] ser PRES soy, eres, es, somos, sois, son; PRES SUBJ sea, seas, sea, seamos, seáis, sean; IMPERF era, eras, era, éramos, erais, eran; PRET fui, fuiste, fue, fuimos, fuisteis, fueron; IMPERF SUBJ fuera/fuese; IMPERAT sé, sea, seamos, sed, sean

[24] tener PRES tengo, tienes, tiene, tenemos, tenéis, tienen; PRES SUBJ tenga, tengas, tenga, tengamos, tengáis, tengan; FUT tendré; COND tendría; PRET tuve, tuviste, tuvo, tuvimos, tuvisteis, tuvieron; IMPERF SUBJ tuviera/tuviese; IMPERAT ten, tenga, tengamos, tened, tengan

[25] traer PRES traigo, traes, trae, traemos, traéis, traen; PRES SUBJ traiga, traigas, traiga, traigamos, traigáis, traigan; PRET traje, trajiste, trajo, trajimos, trajisteis, trajeron; IMPERF SUBJ trajera/trajese; IMPERAT trae, traiga, traigamos, traed, traigan

[26] valer PRES valgo, vales, vale, valemos, valéis, valen; PRES SUBJ valga, valgas, valga, valgamos, valgáis, valgan; FUT valdré; COND valdría; IMPERAT vale, valga, valgamos, valed, valgan

[27] venir PRES vengo, vienes, viene, venimos, venís, vienen; PRES SUBJ venga, vengas, venga, vengamos, vengáis, vengan; FUT vendré; COND vendría; PRET vine, viniste, vino, vinimos, vinisteis, vinieron; IMPERF SUBJ viniera/viniese; PRES P viniendo; IMPERAT ven, venga, vengamos, venid, vengan

[28] ver PRES veo, ves, ve, vemos, veis, ven; PRES SUBJ vea, veas, vea, veamos, veáis, vean; IMPERF veía, veías, veía, veíamos, veíais, veían; PRET vi, viste, vio, vimos, visteis, vieron; IMPERF SUBJ viera/viese; IMPERAT ve, vea, veamos, ved, vean

[29] desviar PRES desvío, desvías, desvía, desviamos, desviáis, desvían; PRES SUBJ desvíe, desvíes, desvíe, desviemos, desviéis, desvíen; IMPERAT desvía, desvíe, desviemos, desviéis, desvíen

[30] continuar PRES continúo, continúas, continúa, continuamos, continuáis, continúan; PRES SUBJ continúe, continúes, continúe, continuemos, continuéis, continúen; IMPERAT continúa, continúe, continuemos, continuad, continúen

[31] adquirir PRES adquiero, adquieres, adquiere, adquirimos, adquirís, adquieren; PRES SUBJ adquiera, adquiras, adquiera, adquiramos, adquiráis, adquieran; IMPERAT adquiere, adquiera, adquiramos, adquirid, adquieran

[32] jugar PRES juego, juegas, juega, jugamos, jugáis, juegan; PRES SUBJ juegue, juegues, juegue, juguemos, juguéis, jueguen; IMPERAT juega, juegue, juguemos, jugad, jueguen

[33] agradecer PRES agradezco, agradeces, agradece, agradecemos, agradecéis, agradecen; PRES SUBJ agradezca, agradezcas, agradezca, agradezcamos, agradezcáis, agradezcan; IMPERAT agradece, agradezca, agradezcamos, agradeced, agradezcan

[34] conocer PRES conozco, conoces, conoce, conocemos, conocéis, conocen; PRES SUBJ conozca, conozcas, conozca, conozcamos, conozcáis, conozcan; IMPERAT conoce, conozca, conozcamos, conoced, conozcan

[35] lucir PRES luzco, luces, luce, lucimos, lucís, lucen; PRES SUBJ luzca, luzcas, luzca, luzcamos, luzcáis, luzcan; IMPERAT luce, luzca, luzcamos, lucid, luzcan

[36] leer PRET leí, leíste, leyó, leímos, leísteis, leyeron; IMPERF SUBJ leyera/leyese; PRES P leyendo; PP leído; IMPERAT lee, lea, leamos, leed, lean

[37] huir PRES huyo, huyes, huye, huimos, huís, huyen; PRES SUBJ huya, huyas, huya, huyamos, huyáis, huyan; PRET huí, huiste, huyó, huimos, huisteis, huyeron; IMPERF SUBJ huyera/huyese; PRES P huyendo; PP huido; IMPERAT huye, huya, huyamos, huid, huyan

[38] roer PRES roo/roigo/royo, roes, roe, roemos, roéis, roen; PRES SUBJ roa/roiga/roya, roas, roa, roamos, roáis, roan; PRET roí, roíste, royó, roímos, roísteis, royeron; IMPERF SUBJ royera/royese; PRES P royendo; PP roído; IMPE-RAT roe, roa, roamos, roed, roan

[39] caer PRES caigo, caes, cae, caemos, caéis, caen; PRES SUBJ caiga, caigas, caiga, caigamos, caigáis, caigan; PRES P cayendo; PP caído; IMPERAT cae, caiga, caigamos, caed, caigan

[40] cazar PRET cacé, cazaste, cazó, cazamos, cazasteis, cazaron; PRES SUBJ cace, caces, cacen, cacemos, cacéis, cacen

[41] cocer PRES cuezo, cueces, cuece, cocemos, cocéis, cuecen; PRES SUBJ cueza, cuezas, cueza, cozamos, cozáis, cuezan; IMPERAT cuece, cueza, cozamos, coced, cuezan

[42] llegar PRET llegué, llegaste, llegó, llegamos, llegasteis, llegaron; PRES SUBJ llegue, llegues, llegue, lleguemos, lleguéis, lleguen

[43] cambiar PRES cambio, cambias, cambia, cambiamos, cambiáis, cambian; PRES SUBJ cambie, cambies, cambie, cambiemos, cambiéis, cambien; IMPERAT cambia, cambie, cambiemos, cambiad, cambien

[44] sacar PRET saqué, sacaste, sacó, sacamos, sacasteis, sacaron; PRES SUBJ saque, saques, saque, saquemos, saquéis, saquen; IMPERAT saca, saque, saquemos, sacad, saquen

[45] averiguar PRET averigüé, averiguaste, averiguó, averiguamos, averiguasteis, averiguaron; PRES SUBJ averigüe, averigües, averigüe, averigüemos, averigüéis, averigüen; IMPERAT averigua, averigüe, averigüemos, averiguad, averigüen

[46] asir PRES asgo, ases, ase, asimos, asís, asen; PRES SUBJ asga, asgas, asga, asgamos, asgáis, asgan; IMPERAT ase, asga, asgamos, asid, asgan

[47] adecuar PRES adecuo, adecuas, adecua, adecuamos, adecuáis, adecuan; PRES SUBJ adecue, adecues, adecue, adecuemos, adecuéis, adecuen; IMPERAT adecua, adecuen, adecuemos, adecuad, adecuen

[48] delinquir PRES delinco, delinques, delinque, delinquimos, delinquís, delinquen; PRES SUBJ delinca, delincas, delinca, delincamos, delincáis, delincan; IMPERAT delinque, delinca, delincamos, delinquid, delincan

[49] mecer PRES mezo, meces, mece, mecemos, mecéis, mecen; PRES SUBJ meza, mezas, meza, mezamos, mezáis, mezan; IMPERAT mece, meza, mezamos, meced, mezan

[50] errar PRES yerro, yerras, yerra, erramos, erráis, yerran; PRES SUBJ yerre, yerres, yerre, erremos, erréis, yerren; IMPERAT yerra, yerre, erremos, errad, yerren

[51] comenzar PRES comienzo, comienzas, comienza, comenzamos, comenzáis, comienzan; PRES SUBJ comience, comiences, comience, comencemos, comencéis, comiencen; IMPERAT comienza, comience, comencemos, comenzad, comiencen

[52] zurcir PRES zurzo, zurces, zurce, zurcimos, zurcís, zurcen; PRES SUBJ zurza, zurzas, zurza, zurzamos, zurzáis, zurzan; **IMPERAT** zurce, zurza, zurzamos, zurcid, zurzan

[53] proteger **PRES** protejo, proteges, protege, protegemos, protegéis, protegen; **PRES SUBJ** proteja, protejas, proteja, protejamos, protejáis, protejan; **IMPERAT** protege, proteja, protejamos, proteged, protejan

[54] discernir **PRES** discierno, disciernes, discierne, discernimos, discernís, disciernen; **PRES SUBJ** discierna, disciernas, discierna, discernamos, discernáis, disciernan; **IMPERAT** discierne, discierna, discernamos, discernid, disciernan

[55] erguir **PRES** irgo/yergo, irgues/yergues, irgue/yergue, erguimos, erguís, irguen/yerguen; **PRET** erguí, erguiste, irguió, erguimos, erguisteis, irguieron; **PRES SUBJ** irga/yerga, irgas/yergas, irga/yerga, irgamos/yergamos, irgáis/yergáis, irgan/yergan; **IMPERF SUBJ** irguiera/irguiese; **IMPERAT** irgue/yergue, irga/yerga, irgamos/yergamos, erguid, irgan/yergan

[56] reír **PRES** río, ríes, ríe, reímos, reís, ríen; **PRET** reí, reíste, rió, reímos, reísteis, rieron; **PRES SUBJ** ría, rías, ría, riamos, riáis, rían; **IMPERF SUBJ** riera/riese; **IMPERAT** ríe, ría, riamos, reíd, rían

[57] dirigir **PRES** dirijo, diriges, dirige, dirigimos, dirigís, dirigen; **PRES SUBJ** dirija, dirijas, dirija, dirijamos, dirijáis, dirijan; **IMPERAT** dirige, dirija, dirijamos, dirigid, dirijan

[58] regir **PRES** rijo, riges, rige, regimos, regís, rigen; **PRES SUBJ** rija, rijas, rija, rijamos, rijáis, rijan; **IMPERAT** rige, rija, rijamos, regid, rijan

[59] distinguir **PRES** distingo, distingues, distingue, distinguimos, distinguís, distinguen; **PRES SUBJ** distinga, distingas, distinga, distingamos, distingáis, distingan; **IMPERAT** distingue, distinga, distingamos, distinguid, distingan

[60] nacer **PRES** nazco, naces, nace, nacemos, nacéis, nacen; **PRES SUBJ** nazca, nazcas, nazca, nazcamos, nazcáis, nazcan; **IMPERAT** nace, nazca, nazcamos, naced, nazcan

[61] yacer **PRES** yazco/yazgo/yago, yaces, yace, yacemos, yacéis, yacen; **PRES SUBJ** yazca/yazga/yaga; **IMPERAT** yace/yaz, yazca/yazga/yaga, yazcamos/yazgamos/yagamos, yaced, yazcan/yazgan/yagan

[62] argüir **PRES** arguyo, arguyes, arguye, argüimos, argüís, arguyen; **PRET** argüí, argüiste, arguyó, argüimos, argüisteis, arguyeron; **PRES SUBJ** arguya, arguyas, arguya, arguyamos, arguyáis, arguyan; **IMPERF SUBJ** arguyera/arguyese; **IMPERAT** arguye, arguya, arguyamos, argüid, arguyan

[63] avergonzar **PRES** avergüenzo, avergüenzas, avergüenza, avergonzamos, avergonzáis, avergüenzan; **PRET** avergoncé, avergonzaste, avergonzó, avergonzamos, avergonzasteis, avergonzaron; **PRES SUBJ** avergüence, avergüences, avergüence, avergoncemos, avergoncéis, avergüencen; **IMPERAT** avergüenza, avergüence, avergoncemos, avergonzad, avergüencen

[64] trocar **PRES** trueco, truecas, trueca, trocamos, trocáis, truecan; **PRET**

troqué, trocaste, trocó, trocamos, trocasteis, trocaron; **PRES SUBJ** trueque, trueques, trueque, troquemos, troquéis, truequen; **IMPERAT** trueca, trueque, troquemos, trocad, truequen

[65] oler **PRES** huelo, hueles, huele, olemos, oléis, huelen; **PRES SUBJ** huela, huelas, huela, olamos, oláis, huelan; **IMPERAT** huele, huela, olamos, oled, huelan

VERBOS IRREGULARES INGLESES

INFINITIVE	PAST SIMPLE	PAST PARTICIPLE
arise	arose	arisen
awake	awoke	awoken
be	was, were	been
bear	bore	borne
beat	beat	beaten
become	became	become
begin	began	begun
bend	bent	bent
bet	bet, betted	bet, betted
bid *(offer)*	bid	bid
bind	bound	bound
bite	bit	bitten
bleed	bled	bled
blow	blew	blown
break	broke	broken
breed	bred	bred
bring	brought	brought
broadcast	broadcast	broadcast
build	built	built
burn	burnt, burned	burnt, burned
burst	burst	burst
buy	bought	bought
cast	cast	cast
catch	caught	caught
choose	chose	chosen
cling	clung	clung
come	came	come
cost	cost	cost
creep	crept	crept
cut	cut	cut
deal	dealt	dealt
dig	dug	dug
dive	dove	dived
do	did	done
draw	drew	drawn

INFINITIVE	PAST SIMPLE	PAST PARTICIPLE
dream	dreamt, dreamed	dreamt, dreamed
drink	drank	drunk
drive	drove	driven
eat	ate	eaten
fall	fell	fallen
feed	fed	fed
feel	felt	felt
fight	fought	fought
find	found	found
flee	fled	fled
fling	flung	flung
fly	flew	flown
forbid	forbad(e)	forbidden
forecast	forecast	forecast
foresee	foresaw	foreseen
forget	forgot	forgotten
forgive	forgave	forgiven
freeze	froze	frozen
get	got	gotten
give	gave	given
go	went	gone
grind	ground	ground
grow	grew	grown
hang	hung, hanged	hung, hanged
have	had	had
hear	heard	heard
hide	hid	hidden
hit	hit	hit
hold	held	held
hurt	hurt	hurt
keep	kept	kept
kneel	knelt, kneeled	knelt, kneeled
know	knew	known
lay	laid	laid
lead	led	led
lean	leant, leaned	leant, leaned
leap	leapt, leaped	leapt, leaped
learn	learnt, learned	learnt, learned
leave	left	left
lend	lent	lent
let	let	let
lie	lay	lain

INFINITIVE	PAST SIMPLE	PAST PARTICIPLE
light	lit, lighted	lit, lighted
lose	lost	lost
make	made	made
mean	meant	meant
meet	met	met
mislay	mislaid	mislaid
mislead	misled	misled
mistake	mistook	mistaken
misunderstand	misunderstood	misunderstood
mow	mowed	mown, mowed
outdo	outdid	outdone
overcome	overcame	overcome
overdo	overdid	overdone
overtake	overtook	overtaken
pay	paid	paid
put	put	put
quit	quit	quit
read	read	read
redo	redid	redone
rend	rent	rent
rewind	rewound	rewound
ride	rode	ridden
ring	rang	rung
rise	rose	risen
run	ran	run
saw	sawed	sawn, sawed
say	said	said
see	saw	seen
seek	sought	sought
sell	sold	sold
send	sent	sent
set	set	set
sew	sewed	sewn, sewed
shake	shook	shaken
shear	sheared	shorn, sheared
shed	shed	shed
shine	shone	shone
shoot	shot	shot
show	showed	shown, showed
shrink	shrank, shrunk	shrunk
shut	shut	shut
sing	sang	sung

INFINITIVE	PAST SIMPLE	PAST PARTICIPLE
sink	sank	sunk
sit	sat	sat
sleep	slept	slept
slide	slid	slid
sling	slung	slung
slink	slunk	slunk
slit	slit	slit
smell	smelt, smelled	smelt, smelled
sneak	sneaked, snuck	sneaked, snuck
sow	sowed	sown, sowed
speak	spoke	spoken
speed	sped, speeded	sped, speeded
spell	spelt, spelled	spelt, spelled
spend	spent	spent
spill	spilt, spilled	spilt, spilled
spin	spun	spun
spit	spat	spat
split	split	split
spoil	spoilt, spoiled	spoilt, spoiled
spread	spread	spread
spring	sprang	sprung
stand	stood	stood
steal	stole	stolen
stick	stuck	stuck
sting	stung	stung
stink	stank	stunk
stride	strode	stridden
strike	struck	struck, stricken
string	strung	strung
strive	strove	striven
swear	swore	sworn
sweep	swept	swept
swell	swelled	swollen, swelled
swim	swam	swum
swing	swung	swung
take	took	taken
teach	taught	taught
tear	tore	torn
tell	told	told
think	thought	thought
thrive	thrived, throve	thrived
throw	threw	thrown
thrust	thrust	thrust

INFINITIVE	PAST SIMPLE	PAST PARTICIPLE
tread	trod	trodden
undergo	underwent	undergone
understand	understood	understood
undertake	undertook	undertaken
undo	undid	undone
upset	upset	upset
wake	woke	woken
wear	wore	worn
weave	wove	woven
weep	wept	wept
wet	wet, wetted	wet, wetted
win	won	won
wind	wound	wound
withdraw	withdrew	withdrawn
withhold	withheld	withheld
wring	wrung	wrung
write	wrote	written

COUNTRIES AND REGIONS
PAÍSES Y REGIONES

Africa (African)	África f (africano, -a)
Albania (Albanian)	Albania f (albanés, -esa)
Algeria (Algerian)	Argelia f (argelino, -a)
America (American)	América f (americano, -a)
Antarctica, the Antarctic (Antarctic)	la Antártida, el Antártico (antártico, -a)
Arabia (Arab, Arabic)	Arabia f (árabe)
the Arctic (Arctic)	el Ártico m (ártico, -a)
Argentina (Argentinian, Argentine)	Argentina f (argentino, -a)
Asia (Asian)	Asia f (asiático, -a)
Australia (Australian)	Australia f (australiano, -a)
Austria (Austrian)	Austria f (austríaco, -a)
Belgium (Belgian)	Bélgica f (belga)
Bolivia (Bolivian)	Bolivia f (boliviano, -a)
Brazil (Brazilian)	Brasil m (brasileño, -a, brasilero, -a)
Bulgaria (Bulgarian)	Bulgaria f (búlgaro, -a)
Burma (Burmese)	Birmania f (birmano, -a)
Canada (Canadian)	Canadá m (canadiense)

Central America (*Central American*)	Centroamérica *f* (*centroamericano, -a*)
Chile (*Chilean*)	Chile *m* (*chileno, -a*)
China (*Chinese*)	China *f* (*chino, -a*)
Colombia (*Colombian*)	Colombia *f* (*colombiano, -a*)
Costa Rica (*Costa Rican*)	Costa Rica *f* (*costarricense, costarriqueño, -a*)
Crete (*Cretan*)	Creta *f* (*cretense*)
Cuba (*Cuban*)	Cuba *f* (*cubano, -a*)
Cyprus (*Cypriot*)	Chipre *m* (*chipriota*)
Czech Republic (*Czech*)	República Checa *f* (*checo, -a*)
Denmark (*Danish*)	Dinamarca *f* (*danés, -esa*)
Dominican Republic (*Dominican*)	República Dominicana *f* (*dominicano, -a*)
Ecuador (*Ecuadorian*)	Ecuador *m* (*ecuatoriano, -a*)
Egypt (*Egyptian*)	Egipto *m* (*egipcio, -a*)
El Salvador (*Salvadoran, Salvadorian*)	El Salvador *m* (*salvadoreño, -a*)
England (*English*)	Inglaterra *f* (*inglés, -esa*)
Ethiopia (*Ethiopian*)	Etiopía *f* (*etíope, etíope*)
Europe (*European*)	Europa *f* (*europeo, -a*)
Finland (*Finnish*)	Finlandia *f* (*finlandés, -a*)
France (*French*)	Francia *f* (*francés, -esa*)
Germany (*German*)	Alemania *f* (*alemán, -ana*)
Gibraltar (*Gibraltarian*)	Gibraltar *m* (*gibraltareño, -a*)
Great Britain (*British*)	Gran Bretaña *f* (*británico, -a*)
Greece (*Greek*)	Grecia *f* (*griego, -a*)
Holland (*Dutch*)	Holanda *f* (*holandés, -esa*)
Honduras (*Honduran*)	Honduras *f* (*hondureño, -a*)
Hungary (*Hungarian*)	Hungría *f* (*húngaro, -a*)
Iceland (*Icelandic*)	Islandia *f* (*islandés, -esa*)
India (*Indian*)	India *f* (*indio, -a*)
Indonesia (*Indonesian*)	Indonesia *f* (*indonesio, -a*)
Iran (*Iranian*)	Irán *m* (*iraní*)
Iraq (*Iraqi*)	Irak, Iraq *m* (*iraquí*)
Ireland (*Irish*)	Irlanda *f* (*irlandés, -esa*)
Israel (*Israeli*)	Israel *m* (*israelí*)
Italy (*Italian*)	Italia *f* (*italiano, -a*)
Jamaica (*Jamaican*)	Jamaica *f* (*jamaicano, -a*)
Japan (*Japanese*)	Japón *m* (*japonés, -esa*)
Kenya (*Kenyan*)	Kenia *f* (*keniano, -a*)
Korea (*Korean*)	Corea *f* (*coreano, -a*)

Latin America *(Latin American)*	Latinoamérica f *(latinoamericano, -a);* Hispanoamérica f *(hispanoamericano, -a);* Iberoamérica f *(iberoamericano, -a)*
Latvia *(Latvian)*	Letonia f *(letón, -ona)*
the Lebanon *(Lebanese)*	Líbano m *(libanés, -esa)*
Libya *(Libyan)*	Libia f *(libio, -a)*
Lithuania *(Lithuanian)*	Lituania f *(lituano, -a)*
Luxembourg	Luxemburgo m *(luxemburgués)*
Malaysia *(Malay)*	Malasia f *(malasio, -a)*
Mexico *(Mexican)*	México, Méjico m *(mexicano, -a, mejicano, -a)*
Mongolia *(Mongolian)*	Mongolia f *(mongol, -a)*
Morocco *(Moroccan)*	Marruecos m *(marroquí)*
the Netherlands, the Low Countries *(Dutch)*	Países Bajos mpl *(neerlandés, -esa)*
Nicaragua *(Nicaraguan)*	Nicaragua f *(nicaragüense, nicaragüeño, -a)*
North Africa *(North African)*	África f del Norte *(norteafricano, -a)*
North America *(North American)*	Norteamérica f *(norteamericano, -a)*
Northern Ireland *(Northern Irish)*	Irlanda del Norte f *(norirlandés, -esa)*
Norway *(Norwegian)*	Noruega f *(noruego, -a)*
Pakistan *(Pakistani)*	Pakistán, Paquistán m *(paquistaní)*
Palestine *(Palestinian)*	Palestina f *(palestino, -a)*
Panama *(Panamanian)*	Panamá m *(panameño, -a)*
Paraguay *(Paraguayan)*	Paraguay m *(paraguayo, -a)*
Peru *(Peruvian)*	Perú m *(peruano, -a)*
(the) Philippines *(Philippine, Filipino)*	Filipinas fpl *(filipino, -a)*
Poland *(Polish)*	Polonia f *(polaco, -a)*
Portugal *(Portuguese)*	Portugal m *(portugués, -esa)*
Puerto Rico *(Puerto Rican)*	Puerto Rico m *(portorriqueño, -a, puertorriqueño, -a)*
Rumania, Romania *(Rumanian, Romanian)*	Rumanía f *(rumano, -a)*
Russia *(Russian)*	Rusia f *(ruso, -a)*
Saudi Arabia *(Saudi Arabian, Saudi)*	Arabia Saudita f *(saudita, saudí)*
Scandinavia *(Scandinavian)*	Escandinavia f *(escandinavo, -a)*
Scotland *(Scottish, Scots)*	Escocia f *(escocés, -esa)*

Slovakia *(Slovak)*	Eslovaquia f *(eslovaco, -a)*
South Africa *(South African)*	Sudáfrica f *(sudafricano, -a)*
South America *(South American)*	Sudamérica f *(sudamericano, -a);*
	Suramérica f *(suramericano, -a)*
Spain *(Spanish)*	España f *(español, -a)*
Sweden *(Swedish)*	Suecia f *(sueco, -a)*
Switzerland *(Swiss)*	Suiza f *(suizo, -a)*
Syria *(Syrian)*	Siria f *(sirio, -a)*
Thailand *(Thai)*	Tailandia f *(tailandés, -esa)*
Tunisia *(Tunisian)*	Túnez m *(tunecino, -a)*
Turkey *(Turkish)*	Turquía f *(turco, -a)*
Ukraine *(Ukrainian)*	Ucrania f *(ucraniano, -a)*
the United States *(United States,*	Estados Unidos mpl
American)	*(estadounidense)*
Uruguay *(Uruguayan)*	Uruguay m *(uruguayo, -a)*
Venezuela *(Venezuelan)*	Venezuela f *(venezolano, -a)*
Vietnam *(Vietnamese)*	Vietnam m *(vietnamita)*
Wales *(Welsh)*	Gales m (el país m de) *(galés, -esa)*
the West Indies *(West Indian)*	Antillas f *(antillano, -a)*

A

a *indef art (before vowel or silent h* **an)** un, una; **he has a big nose** tiene la nariz grande; **half a liter/an hour** medio litro/media hora; **he's a teacher** es profesor; **60 cents a kilo** 60 centavos el kilo; **three times a week** tres veces a la semana.

a·ban·don *vt* abandonar.

ab·bey abadía *f.*

ab·bre·vi·a·tion abreviatura *f.*

a·bil·i·ty capacidad *f.*

a·ble *adj (capable)* capaz; **to be a. to do sth** poder hacer algo.

a·ble-bod·ied *adj* sano, -a.

ab·nor·mal *adj* anormal.

ab·nor·mal·ly *adv* anormalmente.

a·board 1 *adv* a bordo; **to go a.** *(ship)* embarcarse; *(train)* subir. **2** *prep* a bordo de.

a·bol·ish *vt* abolir.

a·bor·tion aborto *m*; **to have an a.** abortar.

a·bout 1 *adv (approximately)* más o menos; **he's a. 40** tendrá unos 40 años; **it's a. time you got up** ya es hora de que te levantes. **2** *prep (concerning)* acerca de; **a program a. New York** un programa sobre Nueva York; **to speak a. sth** hablar de algo; **what's it all a.?** ¿de qué se trata?; **how a. a game of tennis?** ¿qué te parece un partido de tenis? • **it's a. to start** está a punto de empezar.

a·bove 1 *adv* arriba; **the apartment a.** el piso de arriba; **a policy imposed from a.** una política impuesta desde arriba. **2** *prep (higher than)* encima de; *(greater than)* superior a; **100 meters a. sea level** 100 metros sobre el nivel del mar; **it's a. the door** está encima de la puerta; **a. all** sobre todo; **he's not a. stealing** es capaz incluso de robar.

a·bove-men·tioned *adj* susodicho, -a.

a·breast *adv* **to keep a. of things** mantenerse al día.

a·broad *adv* en el extranjero; **to go a.** irse al extranjero.

a·brupt *adj (manner)* brusco, -a; *(change)* súbito, -a.

a·brupt·ly *adv (act)* bruscamente; *(speak)* con aspereza.

ab·scess absceso *m.*

ab·sence *(of person)* ausencia *f*; *(of thing)* falta *f.*

ab·sent *adj* ausente.

ab·sent-mind·ed *adj* distraído, -a.

ab·so·lute *adj* absoluto, -a; *(failure)* total; *(truth)* puro, -a.

ab·so·lute·ly *adv* completamente; **a. not** en absoluto; **you're a. right** tienes toda la razón; **a.!** ¡desde luego!

ab·sorb *vt (liquid)* absorber; **to be absorbed in sth** estar absorto, -a en algo.

ab·surd *adj* absurdo, -a.

a·buse 1 *n (ill-treatment)* malos tratos *mpl*; *(misuse)* abuso *m*; *(insults)* injurias *fpl.* **2** *vt (ill-treat)* maltratar; *(misuse)* abusar de; *(insult)* injuriar.

a·bu·sive *adj (insulting)* grosero, -a.

ac·a·dem·ic 1 *adj* académico, -a; *(career)* universitario, -a; **a. year** año *m* escolar. **2** *n* académico, -a *mf.*

ac·cel·er·ate *vi* acelerar.

ac·cel·er·a·tor acelerador *m.*

ac·cent acento *m.*

ac·cept *vt* aceptar; *(theory)* admitir.

ac·cept·a·ble *adj* admisible.

ac·cess acceso *m.*

ac·ces·si·ble *adj* accesible; *(person)* asequible.

ac·ces·so·ry *(to crime)* cómplice *mf*, **accessories** accesorios *mpl*; *(for outfit)* complementos *mpl.*

ac·cess time tiempo *m* de acceso.

ac·ci·dent accidente *m*; **by a.** por casualidad.

ac·ci·den·tal *adj* fortuito, -a; *(unintended)* imprevisto, -a.

ac·ci·den·tal·ly *adv (by chance)* por casualidad.

ac·com·mo·date *vt (guests)* alojar; **to a. sb's wishes** complacer a algn.

ac·com·mo·da·tion(s) alojamiento *m*.

ac·com·pa·ny *vt* acompañar.

ac·com·plish *vt (aim)* conseguir; *(task, mission)* llevar a cabo.

ac·cord **of his own a.** espontáneamente.

ac·cor·dance **in a. with** de acuerdo con.

ac·cord·ing·ly *adv* en consecuencia.

ac·cord·ing to *prep* según.

ac·cor·di·on acordeón *m*.

ac·count *(report)* informe *m*; *(at bank, in business)* cuenta *f*; **on a. of** a causa de; **to take a. of, to take into a.** tener en cuenta; **accounts department** servicio *m* de contabilidad; **current a.** cuenta *f* corriente.

▸**account for** *(explain)* explicar.

ac·count·ant contable *mf*.

ac·cu·mu·late **1** *vt* acumular. **2** *vi* acumularse.

ac·cu·rate *adj (number)* exacto, -a; *(answer)* correcto, -a; *(observation)* acertado, -a; *(translation)* fiel.

ac·cu·rate·ly *adv* con precisión.

ac·cu·sa·tion acusación *f*.

ac·cuse *vt* acusar.

ac·cused *n* **the a.** el/la acusado(a).

ac·cus·tomed *adj* **to be a. to sth** estar acostumbrado a algo; **to get a. to sth** acostumbrarse a algo.

ace *(card & fig)* as *m*; *(in tennis)* ace *m*.

ache **1** *n* dolor *m*. **2** *vi* doler; **my back aches** me duele la espalda.

a·chieve *vt (attain)* conseguir; *(accomplish)* llevar a cabo.

a·chieve·ment *(attainment)* logro *m*; *(feat)* hazaña *f*.

a·cid **1** *adj* ácido, -a. **2** *n* ácido *m*.

a·cid rain lluvia *f* ácida.

ac·knowl·edge *vt (recognize)* reconocer; *(letter)* acusar recibo de; *(greet)* saludar.

ac·ne acné *m*.

a·corn bellota *f*.

a·cous·tics *npl* acústica *f* sing.

ac·quaint *vt* **to be acquainted with sb** conocer a algn; **to be acquainted with sth** estar al corriente de algo.

ac·quain·tance conocimiento *m*; *(person)* conocido, -a *mf*; **to make sb's a.** conocer a algn.

ac·quire *vt* adquirir.

a·cre acre *m (approx 40,47 áreas)*.

ac·ro·bat·ic *adj* acrobático, -a.

a·cross **1** *adv* a través; **to go a.** atravesar; **to run a.** atravesar corriendo. **2** *prep* a través de; *(at the other side of)* al otro lado de; **they live a. the road** viven enfrente; **to go a. the street** cruzar la calle.

a·cryl·ic *adj* acrílico, -a.

act **1** *n (action)* acto *m*; *(parliamentary)* ley *f*; *(of play)* acto *m*; **a. of God** caso *m* de fuerza mayor. **2** *vt (part)* interpretar; *(character)* representar; **to a. the fool** hacer el tonto. **3** *vi (pretend)* fingir; *(behave)* comportarse; *(take action)* actuar; *(work)* funcionar.

▸**act for** *vt* obrar en nombre de.

▸**act out** *vt* exteriorizar.

▸**act up** *vi fam (machine)* funcionar mal; *(child)* dar guerra.

ac·tion *(deed)* acción *f*, *(in war)* acción *f* de combate; **to be out of a.** *(person)* estar fuera de servicio; *(machine)* estar estropeado, -a; **to take a.** tomar medidas.

ac·ti·ve *adj* activo, -a; *(energetic)* vigoroso, -a; *(interest)* vivo, -a.

ac·tiv·i·ty actividad *f*, *(on street etc)* bullicio *m*.

ac·tor actor *m*.

ac·tress actriz *f*.

ac·tu·al *adj* verdadero, -a.

ac·tu·al·ly *adv (really)* en efecto; *(even)* incluso.

a·cute *adj (angle)* agudo, -a; *(pain)* intenso, -a; *(hearing)* muy fino, -a.

AD *abbr of Anno Domini* después de Cristo, d.C.

ad *fam* anuncio *m.*

a·dapt 1 *vt* adaptar (**to** a). **2** *vi* adaptarse.

a·dapt·a·ble *adj* he's very a. se amolda fácilmente a las circunstancias.

a·dap·ter, a·dap·tor *(plug)* ladrón *m.*

add 1 *vt (numbers)* sumar; *(one thing to another)* añadir. **2** *vi (count)* sumar.

▸ **add in** *vt (include)* incluir.

▸ **add to** *vt* aumentar.

▸ **add together** *vt (numbers)* sumar.

▸ **add up 1** *vt (numbers)* sumar. **2** *vi* it doesn't a. up no tiene sentido.

ad·dict adicto, -a *mf*; **drug a.** drogadicto, -a *mf*; **television a.** teleadicto, -a *mf.*

ad·dict·ed *adj* adicto, -a.

ad·dic·tion *(to gambling etc)* vicio *m*; *(to drugs)* adicción *f.*

ad·di·tion adición *f*; **in a. to** además de.

ad·di·tion·al *adj* adicional.

ad·di·tive aditivo *m.*

ad·dress 1 *n (on letter)* dirección *f*; *(speech)* discurso *m.* **2** *vt (letter)* dirigir; *(speak to)* dirigirse (**to** a).

ad·e·noids *npl* vegetaciones *fpl* (adenoideas).

ad·e·quate *adj (enough)* suficiente; *(satisfactory)* adecuado, -a.

ad·e·quate·ly *adv* suficientemente.

ad·here *vi (stick)* pegarse (**to** a).

▸ **adhere to** *vt (policy)* adherirse a; *(contract)* cumplir con.

ad·he·sive 1 *adj* adhesivo, -a. **2** *n* adhesivo *m.*

ad·ja·cent *adj (building)* contiguo, -a; *(land)* colindante; **a. to** contiguo, -a a.

ad·jec·tive adjetivo *m.*

ad·just 1 *vt (machine etc)* ajustar; *(methods)* variar. **2** *vi (person)* adaptarse (**to** a).

ad·just·a·ble *adj* ajustable.

ad·just·ment *(by person)* adaptación *f*; *(change)* modificación *f.*

ad·lib *vi* improvisar.

ad·min·is·ter *vt (country)* gobernar; *(justice)* administrar.

ad·min·is·tra·tion *(of country)* gobierno *m*; *(of justice)* administración *f.*

ad·min·is·tra·tive *adj* administrativo, -a.

ad·mi·ral almirante *m.*

ad·mi·ra·tion admiración *f.*

ad·mire *vt* admirar.

ad·mis·sion *(to school etc)* ingreso *m*; *(price)* entrada *f*; *(of fact)* reconocimiento *m.*

ad·mit *vt (person)* dejar entrar; *(crime, guilt)* confesar.

ad·mit·tance *(entry)* entrada *f.*

ad·o·les·cent adolescente *mf.*

a·dopt *vt* adoptar.

a·dopt·ed *adj* **a. child** hijo, -a *mf* adoptivo, -a.

a·dop·tion adopción *f.*

a·dor·a·ble *adj* adorable.

a·dore *vt* adorar.

a·dult 1 *n (person)* adulto, -a *mf.* **2** *adj (film, education)* para adultos.

ad·vance 1 *n (movement)* avance *m*; *(progress)* progreso *m*; **in a.** de antemano. **2** *adj (before time)* adelantado, -a; **a. payment** pago *m* por adelantado. **3** *vt (troops)* avanzar; *(time, date)* adelantar; *(idea)* proponer; *(loan)* prestar. **4** *vi (move forward, make progress)* avanzar.

ad·vanced *adj (developed)* avanzado, -a; *(student)* adelantado, -a; *(course)* superior.

ad·van·tage ventaja *f*; **to take a. of sb** abusar de algn; **to take a. of sth** aprovechar algo.

ad·ven·ture aventura *f.*

ad·ven·tur·ous *adj (character)* aventurero, -a; *(bold)* atrevido, -a.

ad·verb adverbio *m.*

ad·ver·tise 1 *vt* anunciar. **2** *vi* hacer publicidad; *(in newspaper)* poner un anuncio; **to a. for sth/sb** buscar algo/a algn mediante un anuncio.

ad·ver·tise·ment anuncio *m*; **ad·vertisements** publicidad *f sing*.

ad·vice consejos *mpl*; **a piece of a.** un consejo.

ad·vis·a·ble *adj* aconsejable.

ad·vise *vt* aconsejar; *(on business etc)* asesorar.

▸**advise against** *vt* desaconsejar.

ad·vis·er consejero, -a *mf*; *(in business etc)* asesor, -a *mf*.

ad·vo·cate 1 *n (supporter)* defensor, -a *mf*. **2** *vt* abogar por.

aer·i·al antena *f*.

aer·o·bics aerobic *m*.

aer·o·plane avión *m*.

aer·o·sol aerosol *m*.

aes·thet·ic *adj* estético, -a.

af·fair *(matter)* asunto *m*; **business affairs** negocios *mpl*; **love a.** aventura *f* amorosa.

af·fect *vt (person, health)* afectar; *(prices, future)* influir en.

af·fec·tion afecto *m*.

af·fec·tion·ate *adj* cariñoso, -a.

af·flu·ent *adj (society)* opulento, -a; *(person)* rico, -a.

af·ford *vt (be able to buy)* permitirse el lujo de.

af·ford·a·ble *adj (price etc)* asequible.

a·float *adv* **to keep a.** mantenerse a flote.

a·fraid *adj* **to be a.** tener miedo (**of** *sb* a algn; **of** *sth* de algo); **I'm a. of it** me da miedo; **I'm a. not/so** me temo que no/sí.

Af·ri·can *adj & n* africano, -a *(mf)*.

af·ter 1 *adv* después; **the day a.** el día siguiente. **2** *prep (later)* después de; *(behind)* detrás de; **the day a. tomorrow** pasado mañana; **a. you!** ¡pase usted!; **they asked a. you** preguntaron por ti; **what's he a.?** ¿qué pretende?; **he takes a. his uncle** se parece a su tío. **3** *conj* después (de) que; **a. it happened** después de que ocurrió.

af·ter·ef·fects *npl* consecuencias *fpl*; *(of drug)* efectos *mpl* secundarios.

af·ter·noon tarde *f*; **good a.!** ¡buenas tardes!; **in the a.** por la tarde.

after-sales ser·vice servicio *m* posventa.

af·ter·shave loción *f* para después del afeitado.

af·ter·wards *adv* después.

a·gain *adv* otra vez; **a. and a.** repetidas veces; **to do sth a.** volver a hacer algo; **never a.!** ¡nunca más!; **now and a.** de vez en cuando.

a·gainst *prep* contra; **a. the law** ilegal.

age 1 *n* edad *f*, *fam (long time)* eternidad *f*; **underage** menor de edad; **old a.** vejez *f*; **the Iron A.** la Edad del Hierro. **2** *vti* envejecer.

ag·ed[1] *adj* de or a la edad de; *(old)* anciano, -a.

ag·ed[2] *npl* **the a.** los ancianos.

a·gen·cy agencia *f*.

a·gen·da orden *m* del día.

a·gent agente *mf*; *(representative)* representante *mf*.

ag·gra·vate *vt (worsen)* agravar; *(annoy)* molestar.

ag·gres·sion agresión *f*.

ag·gres·sive *adj* agresivo, -a.

ag·ile *adj* ágil.

ag·i·tat·ed *adj* inquieto, -a.

a·go *adv* **a week a.** hace una semana; **how long a.?** ¿hace cuánto tiempo?

ag·o·ny dolor *m* muy fuerte; *(mental)* angustia *f*.

a·gree *vi (be in agreement)* estar de acuerdo; *(reach agreement)* ponerse de acuerdo; **to a. to do sth** consentir en hacer algo; **onions don't a. with me** la cebolla no me sienta bien.

▸**agree (up)on** *vt (decide)* ponerse de acuerdo en.

a·gree·a·ble *adj (pleasant)* agradable; *(person)* simpático, -a; *(in agreement)* de acuerdo.

a·greed *adj (time, place)* acordado, -a.

a·gree·ment *(arrangement)* acuerdo *m*; *(contract etc)* contrato *m*.

ag·ri·cul·tur·al *adj* agrícola.

ag·ri·cul·ture agricultura *f.*

a·head *adv* delante; *(early)* antes; **go a.!** ¡adelante!; **to be a.** *(in race etc)* llevar la ventaja; **to look a.** pensar en el futuro.

aid 1 *n* ayuda *f*; *(rescue)* auxilio *m*; **in a. of** a beneficio de. **2** *vt* ayudar.

AIDS SIDA *m.*

aim 1 *n* *(with weapon)* puntería *f*; *(objective)* propósito *m.* **2** *vti* *(gun)* apuntar (**at** a, hacia).

▸ **aim at** *vt* *(target)* apuntar a.

▸ **aim to** *vt* **to a. to do sth** tener la intención de hacer algo.

air 1 *n* aire *m*; **to travel by a.** viajar en avión; **to be on the a.** *(program)* estar emitiendo. **2** *vt* *(bed, clothes)* airear; *(room)* ventilar.

air-con·di·tioned *adj* climatizado, -a.

air con·di·tion·ing aire *m* acondicionado.

air·craft *inv* avión *m.*

air·craft car·ri·er portaaviones *m inv.*

air·fare precio *m* de billete de avión.

air force fuerzas *fpl* aéreas.

air fresh·en·er ambientador *m.*

air·line línea *f* aérea.

air·line tick·et billete *m* de avión.

air·mail correo *m* aéreo; **by a.** por avión.

air·plane avión *m.*

air·port aeropuerto *m.*

air raid ataque *m* aéreo.

air·sick·ness mareos *mpl* (del avión).

air·tight *adj* hermético, -a.

air traf·fic con·trol control *m* de tráfico aéreo.

air traf·fic con·trol·ler controlador *m* aéreo.

aisle *(in church)* nave *f*; *(in theater)* pasillo *m.*

a·jar *adj & adv* entreabierto, -a.

a·larm 1 *n* alarma *f*; *(fear)* inquietud *f.* **2** *vt* alarmar.

a·larm clock despertador *m.*

al·bum álbum *m.*

al·co·hol alcohol *m.*

al·co·hol·ic *adj & n* alcohólico, -a *(mf).*

a·lert 1 *adj* alerta; *(lively)* despabilado, -a. **2** *n* alerta *m.*

al·ge·bra álgebra *f.*

Al·ge·ri·an *adj & n* argelino, -a *(mf).*

a·li·as 1 *n* *(pl aliases)* alias *m.* **2** *adv* alias.

al·i·bi coartada *f.*

a·li·en *adj & n* extranjero, -a *(mf)*; *(from space)* extraterrestre *mf.*

a·light *adj* *(on fire)* ardiendo, -a.

a·like 1 *adj* *(similar)* parecidos, -as; *(the same)* iguales. **2** *adv* *(in the same way)* de la misma manera, igualmente.

a·live *adj* vivo, -a; *fig (teeming)* lleno, -a (**with** de).

all 1 *adj* todo, -a, todos, -as; **a. year** *(during)* todo el año; **a. kinds of things** todo tipo de cosas; **at a. times** siempre; **a. six of us were there** los seis estábamos allí. **2** *pron* todo, -a, todos, -as; **after a.** al fin y al cabo; **a. who saw it** todos los que lo vieron; **it's a. you can do** es lo único que puedes hacer; **I don't like it at a.** no me gusta en absoluto; **most of a., above a.** sobre todo; **once and for a.** de una vez para siempre; **thanks — not at a.** gracias — de nada; **a. in a.** en conjunto; **that's a.** ya está; **the score was one a.** empataron a uno; **it's still 3 a.** siguen empatados a tres. **3** *adv* **a. by myself** completamente solo, -a; **a. at once** *(suddenly)* de repente; *(altogether)* de una vez; **a. the better** tanto mejor; **a. the same** de todos modos; **if it's a. the same to you** si no te importa. **4** *n* **to give one's a.** darse por completo.

all-a·round *adj* *(athlete etc)* completo, -a.

al·le·giance lealtad *f* (**to** a).

al·ler·gic *adj* alérgico, -a (**to** a).

al·ley callejón *m.*

al·ley·way callejón *m.*

al·li·ance alianza f.

al·lied adj (country) aliado, -a; (matters) afín.

al·li·ga·tor caimán m.

al·lo·cate vt destinar (**to** para).

al·lot·ment (land) parcela f.

all-out adj (effort) supremo, -a; (attack) concentrado, -a.

al·low vt (permit) permitir; (a request) acceder a; (allot) (time) dejar; (money) destinar; **you're not allowed to do that** no puedes hacer eso; **I wasn't allowed to go** no me dejaron ir.

▶ **allow for** vt tener en cuenta.

al·low·ance (payment) subsidio m; (discount) descuento m; **to make allowances for sb** disculpar a algn; **travel a.** dietas fpl de viaje.

all-pur·pose adj (tool) multiuso, de uso universal.

all-right 1 adj (okay) bien; **thank you very much — that's a.** muchas gracias — de nada. **2** adv (well) bien; (definitely) sin duda; (okay) de acuerdo.

al·ly aliado, -a mf.

al·mond almendra f.

al·most adv casi.

a·lone 1 adj solo, -a; **let a.** ni mucho menos; **leave it a.!** ¡no lo toques!; **leave me a.** déjame en paz. **2** adv solamente.

a·long 1 adv come a.! ¡anda, ven!; **with** junto con. **2** prep (the length of) a lo largo de; **to walk a. the street** andar por la calle.

a·long·side 1 adv de costado. **2** prep al lado de.

a·loud adv en voz alta.

al·pha·bet alfabeto m.

al·pha·bet·i·cal adj alfabético, -a.

al·pha·bet·i·cal·ly adv por orden alfabético.

Alps npl **the A.** los Alpes.

al·read·y adv ya.

al·right adj & adv = **all right**.

al·so adv también.

al·tar altar m.

al·ter 1 vt (plan) cambiar; (law, draft etc) modificar. **2** vi cambiar(se).

al·ter·a·tion (to plan) cambio m; (to law etc) modificación f; (to timetable) revisión f.

al·ter·nate 1 adj alterno, -a; **on a. days** cada dos días. **2** vt alternar; **a alternates with b** a alterna con b.

al·ter·nate·ly adv **a. hot and cold** ahora caliente, ahora frío.

al·ter·na·tive 1 adj alternativo, -a. **2** n alternativa f; **I have no a.** no tengo más remedio.

al·ter·na·tive·ly adv o bien.

al·though conj aunque.

al·to·geth·er adv (in total) en total; (completely) completamente.

a·lu·mi·num aluminio m.

al·ways adv siempre.

am 1st person sing pres of **be**.

a.m. abbr of ante meridiem de la mañana; **2 a.m.** las dos de la mañana.

am·a·teur 1 n aficionado, -a mf. **2** adj aficionado, -a; (pejorative) chapucero, -a.

a·maze vt asombrar; **to be amazed at sth** quedar pasmado, -a de algo.

a·maz·ing adj asombroso, -a.

am·bas·sa·dor embajador, -a mf.

am·ber 1 adj (traffic light) amarillo, -a, ámbar. **2** n ámbar.

am·big·u·ous adj ambiguo, -a.

am·bi·tion ambición f.

am·bi·tious adj ambicioso, -a.

am·bu·lance ambulancia f; **a. driver** ambulanciero m.

a·mend vt (law) enmendar; (error) subsanar.

A·mer·i·can adj & n (of USA) norteamericano, -a (mf), estadounidense (mf); (of continent) americano, -a (mf).

a·mid(st) prep entre, en medio de.

am·mu·ni·tion municiones fpl.

a·mong(st) prep entre.

am·o·rous adj (person) ligón, -ona; (feelings, relationship) amoroso, -a.

a·mount cantidad f; (of money) suma f; (of bill) importe m.

▶**amount to** *vt* ascender a; *(be equivalent to)* equivaler a.

am·ple *adj (enough)* bastante; *(more than enough)* abundante; *(large)* amplio, -a.

am·pli·fi·er amplificador *m*.

am·pu·tate *vt* amputar.

a·muse *vt* divertir.

a·muse·ment diversión *f*.

a·muse·ment park parque *m* de atracciones.

a·mus·ing *adj* divertido, -a.

an *indef art see* **a**.

a·nal·y·sis *(pl analyses)* análisis *m inv*.

an·a·lyst *n* analista *mf*; *(psychoanalyst)* psicoanalista *mf*.

an·a·lyze *vt* analizar.

an·ar·chy anarquía *f*.

a·nat·o·my anatomía *f*.

an·ces·tor antepasado *m*.

an·chor *n* 1 ancla *f*. 2 *vt* anclar; *fig (fix securely)* sujetar.

an·cho·vy anchoa *f*.

an·cient *adj* antiguo, -a.

and *conj* y; *(before stressed i-, hi-)* e; **a hundred a. one** ciento uno; **a. so on** etcétera; **come a. see us** ven a vernos; **she cried a. cried** no paró de llorar; **try a. help me** trata de ayudarme; **wait a. see** espera a ver; **worse a. worse** cada vez peor.

an·es·thet·ic anestesia *f*.

an·gel ángel *m*.

an·ger cólera *f*.

an·gle ángulo *m*; *(point of view)* punto *m* de vista.

an·gler pescador, -a *mf* de caña.

an·gling pesca *f* con caña.

an·gri·ly *adv* furiosamente.

an·gry *adj* enfadado, -a; **to get a.** enfadarse.

an·i·mal *adj & n* animal *(m)*.

an·kle tobillo *m*; **a. socks** calcetines *mpl* cortos.

an·nex *(building)* (edificio *m*) anexo *m*.

an·ni·ver·sa·ry aniversario *m*.

an·nounce *vt* anunciar; *(news)* comunicar.

an·nounce·ment anuncio *m*; *(news)* comunicación *f*; *(statement)* declaración *f*.

an·nounc·er *(on TV)* locutor, -a *mf*.

an·noy *vt* molestar; **to get annoyed** molestarse.

an·noy·ing *adj* molesto, -a.

an·nu·al 1 *adj* anual. 2 *n (book)* anuario *m*.

an·nu·al·ly *adv* anualmente.

a·non·y·mous *adj* anónimo, -a.

an·o·rak anorak *m*.

an·oth·er 1 *adj* otro, -a; **a. one** otro, -a; **a. 15** otros quince. 2 *pron* otro, -a; **to love one a.** quererse el uno al otro.

an·swer 1 *n (to letter etc)* contestación *f*; *(to question)* respuesta *f*; *(to problem)* solución *f*; **there's no a.** *(on telephone)* no contestan; *(at door)* no abren. 2 *vt* contestar a; *(problem)* resolver; *(door)* abrir; *(phone)* contestar. 3 *vi* contestar.

▶**answer back** *vi* replicar; **don't a. back!** ¡no repliques!

▶**answer for** *vt* responder de; **he's got a lot to a. for** es responsable de muchas cosas.

▶**answer to** *vt (name)* responder a; *(description)* corresponder a.

an·swer·ing ma·chine contestador *m* automático.

ant hormiga *f*.

Ant·arc·tic 1 *adj* antártico, -a; **A. Ocean** océano *m* Antártico. 2 *n* the **A.** La Antártida.

an·te·lope antílope *m*.

an·ten·na *(pl antennae)* antena *f*.

an·them national a. himno *m* nacional.

an·thol·o·gy antología *f*.

an·ti·bi·ot·ic *adj & n* antibiótico, -a *(m)*.

an·ti·bod·y anticuerpo *m*.

an·tic·i·pate *vt (expect)* esperar; *(problems)* anticipar.

an·tic·i·pa·tion *(excitement)* ilusión *f*.

an·tics *npl* payasadas *fpl*; *(naughtiness)* travesuras *fpl*.

an·ti·freeze anticongelante *m*.

an·ti·his·ta·mine *n* antihistamínico *m*.

an·tique 1 *adj* antiguo, -a. **2** *n* antigüedad *f*.

an·tique deal·er anticuario, -a *mf*.

an·tique shop tienda *f* de antigüedades.

an·ti·sep·tic *adj & n* antiséptico, -a *(m)*.

anx·i·e·ty *(concern)* inquietud *f*; *(worry)* preocupación *f*; *(eagerness)* ansia *f*.

anx·ious *adj (concerned)* inquieto, -a; *(worried)* preocupado, -a; *(fearful)* angustiado, -a; *(eager)* ansioso, -a.

anx·ious·ly *adv (to wait)* con impaciencia.

an·y 1 *adj (in questions, conditionals)* algún, -una; **are there a. seats left?** ¿quedan plazas?; **is there a. water left?** ¿queda agua?; **if you see a. blouses you like** si ves algunas blusas que te gusten. ▪ *(in negative clauses)* ningún, -una; **there aren't a. others** no hay otros. ▪ *(no matter which)* cualquier, -a; *(every)* todo, -a; **a. doctor will say the same** cualquier médico te dirá lo mismo; **at a. moment** en cualquier momento; **in a. case** de todas formas. **2** *pron (in questions, conditionals)* alguno, -a; **do they have a.?** ¿tienen alguno?; **I need some paper, do you have a.?** necesito papel, ¿tienes?; **if you see a., let me know** si ves alguno, -a, dímelo. ▪ *(in negative clauses)* ninguno, -a; **I don't want a.** no quiero ninguno, -a. ▪ *(no matter which)* cualquiera; **a. of them will do** cualquiera vale. **3** *adv* **is there a. more?** ¿hay más?; **not a. more/longer** ya no; **is that a. better?** ¿está mejor así?

an·y·bod·y *pron (in questions, conditionals)* alguien; *(in negative clauses)* nadie; *(no matter who)* cualquiera; **bring a. you like** trae a quien quieras.

an·y·how *adv (in spite of that)* de todas formas; *(changing the subject)* bueno; *(carelessly)* de cualquier forma.

an·y·one *pron* = **anybody**.

an·y·place *adv* = **anywhere**.

an·y·thing *pron (in questions, conditionals)* algo, alguna cosa; *(in negative clauses)* nada; *(no matter what)* cualquier cosa; **a. but that** cualquier cosa menos eso; **a. else?** ¿algo más?; **hardly a.** casi nada; **to run/work like a.** correr/trabajar a más no poder.

an·y·way *adv* = **anyhow**.

an·y·where *adv (in questions, conditionals) (position)* en alguna parte; *(movement)* a alguna parte; **could it be a. else?** ¿podría estar en otro sitio? ▪ *(in negative clauses) (position)* en ninguna parte; *(movement)* a ninguna parte. ▪ *(no matter where)* en cualquier parte; **go a. you like** ve a donde quieras.

a·part *adv* **you should keep them a.** debes mantenerlos aparte; **to fall a.** deshacerse; **to take sth a.** desmontar algo; **with his feet a.** con los pies separados; **a. from** aparte de.

a·part·ment piso *m*; **a. complex** bloque *m* de pisos.

ape mono *m*.

a·pé·ri·tif aperitivo *m*.

a·pol·o·get·ic *adj* **he was very a.** pidió mil perdones.

a·pol·o·gize *vi* disculparse *(for por)*.

a·pol·o·gy disculpa *f*.

a·pos·tro·phe apóstrofo *m*.

ap·pall *vt* horrorizar.

ap·pall·ing *adj (horrifying)* horroroso, -a; *(very bad)* fatal.

ap·pa·ra·tus aparato *m*; *(equipment)* equipo *m*.

ap·par·ent *adj (obvious)* evidente;

(seeming) aparente; **to become a.** ponerse de manifiesto.

ap·par·ent·ly *adv (seemingly)* por lo visto.

ap·peal 1 *n (request)* solicitud *f;* *(plea)* súplica *f; (interest)* interés *m;* *(in law)* apelación *f.* **2** *vi (plead)* rogar **(to** a); **to a. for** help solicitar ayuda; **it doesn't a. to me** no me dice nada.

ap·pear *vi (become visible)* aparecer; *(publicly)* presentarse; *(seem)* parecer; **so it appears** según parece.

ap·pear·ance *(becoming visible)* aparición *f; (publicly)* presentación *f; (of book etc)* publicación *f; (look)* aspecto *m;* **to all appearances** al parecer.

ap·pen·di·ci·tis apendicitis *f.*

ap·pen·dix *(pl* appendices*)* apéndice *m.*

ap·pe·tite apetito *m; (sexual)* deseo *m;* **he's lost his a. for this sort of job** se le han quitado las ganas de un trabajo de este tipo.

ap·pe·tiz·ing *adj* apetitoso.

ap·plaud *vti* aplaudir.

ap·plause aplausos *mpl,* aplauso *m.*

ap·ple manzana *f;* **a. pie** tarta *f* de manzana; **a. tree** manzano *m.*

ap·pli·ance dispositivo *m.*

ap·pli·ca·ble *adj* aplicable **(to** a).

ap·pli·cant *(for post)* candidato, -a *mf.*

ap·pli·ca·tion *(of cream)* aplicación *f; (for post etc)* solicitud *f;* **a. form** solicitud *f.*

ap·ply 1 *vt* aplicar; *(brake)* echar; *(law)* recurrir a; *(force)* usar; **to a. oneself to sth** dedicarse a algo. **2** *vi (for job)* presentar una solicitud.

▸**apply for** *vt (post, information)* solicitar.

ap·point·ment *(to post)* nombramiento *m; (meeting)* cita *f.*

ap·prais·al evaluación *f.*

ap·pre·ci·ate 1 *vt (be thankful for)* agradecer; *(understand)* entender; *(value)* apreciar. **2** *vi (increase in value)* apreciarse.

ap·pre·ci·a·tion *(of help, advice)* agradecimiento *m; (of difficulty)* comprensión *f; (increase in value)* apreciación *f.*

ap·pren·tice aprendiz, -a *mf.*

ap·pren·tice·ship aprendizaje *m.*

ap·proach 1 *n (coming near)* acercamiento *m; (to town)* acceso *m; (to problem)* enfoque *m.* **2** *vt (come near to)* acercarse a; *(problem)* abordar. **3** *vi* acercarse.

ap·pro·pri·ate *adj (suitable)* apropiado, -a; *(convenient)* oportuno, -a.

ap·pro·pri·ate·ly *adv* adecuadamente.

ap·prov·al aprobación *f,* **on a.** sin compromiso de compra.

ap·prove *vt* aprobar.

▸**approve of** *vt (conduct, decision, idea)* aprobar.

ap·prox·i·mate *adj* aproximado, -a.

ap·prox·i·mate·ly *adv* aproximadamente.

a·pri·cot albaricoque *m.*

A·pril abril *m;* **A. Fools' Day** día *m* uno de abril, ≃ día de los Inocentes (28 de diciembre).

a·pron delantal *m.*

apt *adj (suitable)* apropiado, -a; *(description)* exacto, -a; **to be a. to do sth** *(liable)* tener tendencia a hacer algo.

ap·ti·tude capacidad *f.*

a·quar·i·um acuario *m.*

Ar·ab *adj & n* árabe *(mf).*

A·ra·bi·an *adj* árabe.

A·ra·bic 1 *adj* árabe; **A. numerals** numeración *f* arábiga. **2** *n (language)* árabe *m.*

ar·bi·trar·y *adj* arbitrario, -a.

arc arco *m.*

ar·cade arcada *f,* **shopping a.** galerías *fpl* (comerciales); **amusement a.** salón *m* de juegos.

arch 1 *n (of bridge etc)* arco *m; (roof)* bóveda *f.* **2** *vt (back)* arquear.

arch·er arquero, -a *mf.*

arch·er·y tiro *m* con arco.

ar·chi·tect arquitecto, -a *mf.*

ar·chi·tec·ture arquitectura *f.*

Arc·tic the A. el Ártico.

are *2nd person sing pres, 1st, 2nd, 3rd person pl pres of* **be**.

ar·e·a zona *f; (of surface)* superficie *f.*

ar·e·a code prefijo *m* local.

a·re·na *n (stadium)* estadio *m; (circus)* pista *f.*

Ar·gen·tin·i·an *adj & n* argentino, -a *(mf).*

ar·gue 1 *vi (quarrel)* discutir; *(reason)* argumentar. **2** *vt* discutir; *(point of view)* mantener; **to a. that ...** sostener que ....

ar·gu·ment *(quarrel)* discusión *f,* disputa *f; (reason)* argumento *m* **(for** a favor de; **against** en contra de).

a·rise* *vi (get up)* levantarse; *(problem, need)* surgir.

ar·ith·me·tic aritmética *f.*

arm 1 *n* brazo *m; (of garment)* manga *f;* **arms** *(weapons)* armas *fpl.* **2** *vt* armar.

arm·band brazalete *m; (for swimming)* manguito *m.*

arm·chair sillón *m.*

ar·mor *(of tank etc)* blindaje *m;* **(suit of)** a. armadura *f.*

ar·mored car coche *m* blindado.

arm·pit axila *f.*

ar·my ejército *m.*

a·round 1 *adv* alrededor; **all a.** por todos lados. **2** *prep* alrededor de; *(approximately)* aproximadamente; **a. the corner** a la vuelta de la esquina; **a. here** por aquí; **there's nobody a.** no hay nadie; **to rush a.** correr de un lado para otro.

a·rouse *vt* despertar; *(sexually)* excitar.

ar·range 1 *vt (order)* ordenar; *(hair, flowers)* arreglar; *(music)* adaptar; *(plan)* organizar; *(agree on)* quedar en; **to a. a time** fijar una hora. **2** *vi* **I shall a. for him to be there** lo arreglaré para que pueda asistir.

ar·range·ment *(display)* colocación *f; (of music)* adaptación *f; (agreement)* acuerdo *m;* **arrangements** *(plans)* planes *mpl.*

ar·rears *npl* atrasos *mpl;* **to be paid in a.** cobrar con retraso; **salaries are paid monthly in a.** los salarios se pagan mensualmente con un mes de retraso.

ar·rest 1 *n* detención *f;* **to be under a.** estar detenido, -a. **2** *vt (criminal)* detener.

ar·ri·val llegada *f.*

ar·rive *vi* llegar **(at, in** a**).**

ar·row flecha *f.*

art arte *m; (drawing)* dibujo *m;* **arts** *(branch of knowledge)* letras *fpl.*

ar·ter·y arteria *f.*

ar·thri·tis artritis *f.*

ar·ti·cle artículo *m.*

ar·tic·u·late¹ *adj (speech)* claro, -a; *(person)* que se expresa bien.

ar·tic·u·late² *vti* articular; *(words)* pronunciar.

ar·ti·fi·cial *adj* artificial.

art·ist artista *mf; (painter)* pintor, -a *mf.*

ar·tis·tic *adj* artístico, -a.

as *adv & conj (comparison)* **as ... as ...** tan ... como ...; **as far as** hasta; **as far as I'm concerned** por lo que a mí respecta; **as many as** tantos, -as como; **as much as** tanto, -a como; **as opposed to** a diferencia de; **as little as $5** tan sólo cinco dólares; **as soon as they arrive** en cuanto lleguen; **I'll stay as long as I can** me quedaré todo el tiempo que pueda; **just as big** igual de grande; **three times as fast** tres veces más rápido; **the same as** igual que. ▪ *(manner)* como; **as you like** como quieras; **leave it as it is** déjalo tal como está; **do as I say** haz lo que yo te digo; **it serves as a table** sirve de mesa; **she was dressed as a gypsy** iba vestida de gitana; **to act as if** actuar como si **(+ subjunctive)**. ▪ *(time)* mientras; **as a child** de niño, -a; **as I**

was eating mientras comía; **as we were leaving we saw Pat** al salir vimos a Pat; **as from, as of** a partir de. ▪ *(because)* como, ya que; **as it is getting late** ya que se está haciendo tarde. ▪ *(and so)* igual que; **as I do** igual que yo; **as well** también. ▪ *(concerning)* **as for my brother** en cuanto a mi hermano.

ASAP *abbr of* **as soon as possible** lo antes posible.

as·cer·tain *vt (establish)* precisar, determinar; *(find out)* averiguar.

ash¹ *(tree)* fresno *m*.

ash² ceniza *f*.

a·shamed *adj* avergonzado, -a; **you ought to be a. of yourself!** ¿no te da vergüenza?

a·shore *adv* en tierra; **to go a.** desembarcar.

ash·tray cenicero *m*.

Ash Wednes·day miércoles *m inv* de ceniza.

A·sian *adj & n* asiático, -a *(mf)*.

a·side 1 *adv* aparte; **to stand a.** apartarse. **2** *prep* **a. from** *(apart from)* aparte de; *(as well as)* además de. **3** *n* aparte *m*.

ask 1 *vt* preguntar; *(request)* pedir; *(invite)* invitar; **to a. sb a question** preguntar algo a algn; **to a. sb how to do sth** preguntar a algn cómo se hace algo. **2** *vi (inquire)* preguntar; *(request)* pedir.

▸ **ask after** *vt* preguntar por.

▸ **ask for** *vt (help)* pedir; *(person)* preguntar por; **to a. sb for sth** pedir algo a algn.

a·sleep *adj* dormido, -a; **to fall a.** quedarse dormido, -a.

as·par·a·gus *inv* espárrago *m*.

as·pect aspecto *m*.

as·pi·rin aspirina *f*.

as·sault 1 *n* ataque *m* (**on** a); *(crime)* agresión *f*. **2** *vt* atacar; *(sexually)* violar.

as·sem·ble 1 *vt (people)* reunir; *(furniture)* montar. **2** *vi (people)* reunirse.

as·sem·bly assamblea *f*, *(of machinery etc)* montaje *m*; **morning a.** servicio *m* matinal.

as·sert *vt* afirmar; **to a. oneself** imponerse; **to a. one's rights** hacer valer sus derechos.

as·sess *vt (estimate value)* valorar; *(damages, price)* calcular; *(effect)* evaluar.

as·set ventaja *f*; **to be an a.** *(person)* ser de gran valor; **assets** activo *m*.

as·sign *vt* asignar.

as·sign·ment *(task)* tarea *f*.

as·sist *vti* ayudar.

as·sis·tance ayuda *f*.

as·sis·tant ayudante *mf*; **a. manager** subdirector, -a *mf*; **shop a.** dependiente, -a *mf*.

as·so·ci·ate¹ 1 *vt (ideas)* relacionar. **2** *vi* **to a. with** tratar con.

as·so·ci·ate² *(colleague)* colega *mf*; *(partner)* socio, -a *mf*; *(accomplice)* cómplice *mf*.

as·so·ci·a·tion asociación *f*; *(company)* sociedad *f*.

as·sort·ed *adj* surtido, -a.

as·sort·ment surtido *m*.

as·sume *vt (suppose)* suponer; *(power)* asumir; *(attitude, name)* adoptar.

as·sur·ance *(guarantee)* garantía *f*; *(confidence)* confianza *f*, *(insurance)* seguro *m*.

as·sure *vt* asegurar.

as·ter·isk asterisco *m*.

asth·ma asma *f*.

asth·mat·ic *adj & n* asmático, -a *(mf)*.

a·ston·ish *vt* asombrar.

a·ston·ish·ing *adj* asombroso, -a.

a·stray *adv* **to go a.** extraviarse; *fig* equivocarse.

as·trol·o·gy astrología *f*.

as·tro·naut astronauta *mf*.

as·tron·o·my astronomía *f*.

a·sy·lum *(protection)* asilo *m*; **to seek political a.** pedir asilo político; **mental a.** manicomio *m*.

at *prep (position)* en, a; **at school/**

work en el colegio/trabajo; **at the window** a la ventana; **at the top** en lo alto. ■ *(direction)* a; **to look at sth/sb** mirar algo/a algn; **to shout at sb** gritarle a algn. ■ *(time)* a; **at Easter/Christmas** en Semana Santa/Navidad; **at six o'clock** a las seis. ■ **at best/worst** en el mejor/peor de los casos; **not at all** en absoluto; *(don't mention it)* de nada. ■ *(rate)* a; **at 100 dollars each** a 100 dólares la unidad; **two at a time** de dos en dos.

ath·lete atleta *mf.*

ath·let·ic *adj* atlético, -a; *(sporty)* deportista.

ath·let·ics *npl* atletismo *m sing.*

At·lan·tic the A. (Ocean) el (océano) Atlántico.

at·las atlas *m.*

ATM *n* cajero *m* automático.

at·mos·phere *(air)* atmósfera *f; (ambience)* ambiente *m.*

at·om átomo *m;* **a. bomb** bomba *f* atómica.

a·tom·ic *adj* atómico, -a.

at·tach *vt (stick)* pegar; *(document)* adjuntar; **to be attached to** *(be fond of)* tener cariño a.

at·ta·ché agregado, -a *mf;* **a. case** maletín *m.*

at·tack **1** *n* ataque *m.* **2** *vt (assault)* atacar; *(problem)* abordar.

at·tack·er agresor, -a *mf.*

at·tain *vt (aim)* lograr; *(rank, age)* llegar a.

at·tempt **1** *n* intento *m;* **at the second a.** a la segunda. **2** *vt* intentar.

at·tend **1** *vt (school)* frecuentar; *(meeting)* asistir a. **2** *vi (at meeting)* asistir.

▸**attend to** *vt (business)* ocuparse de; *(in shop)* atender a.

at·ten·dance asistencia *f.*

at·ten·dant *(in museum)* guía *mf; (in parking lot)* vigilante, -a *mf.*

at·ten·tion atención *f;* **for the a. of** a la atención de.

at·ten·tive *adj (listener)* atento, -a; *(helpful)* solícito, -a.

at·tic ático *m.*

at·ti·tude actitud *f; (position of body)* postura *f.*

at·tor·ney abogado, -a *mf;* **A. General** ≃ Ministro, -a *mf* de Justicia; **district a.** fiscal *mf.*

at·tract *vt* atraer; **to a. attention** llamar la atención.

at·trac·tion *(attractive thing)* atractivo *m; (charm)* encanto *m.*

at·trac·tive *adj (person)* atractivo, -a; *(idea, proposition)* atrayente.

at·trib·ute[1] *n (quality)* atributo *m.*

at·trib·ute[2] *vt* atribuir (**to** a).

auc·tion **1** *n* subasta *f.* **2** *vt* subastar.

auc·tion·eer subastador, -a *mf.*

au·di·ble *adj* audible.

au·di·ence *(spectators)* público *m; (at concert, conference)* auditorio *m; (television)* telespectadores *mpl; (meeting)* audiencia *f.*

au·di·o *adj* de sonido.

au·di·o·vis·u·al *adj* audiovisual.

au·dit **1** *n* revisión *f* de cuentas. **2** *vt* revisar, intervenir.

Au·gust agosto *m.*

aunt *(also fam* **auntie, aunty)** tía *f.*

au pair **a. (girl)** au pair *f.*

Aus·tra·lian *adj & n* australiano, -a *(mf).*

Aus·tri·an *adj & n* austríaco, -a *(mf).*

au·then·tic *adj* auténtico, -a.

au·thor autor, -a *mf.*

au·thor·i·ty autoridad *f;* **local a.** ayuntamiento *m.*

au·thor·ize *vt* autorizar; *(payment etc)* aprobar.

au·to·bi·og·ra·phy autobiografía *f.*

au·to·graph **1** *n* autógrafo *m.* **2** *vt (book, photo)* dedicar.

au·to·mat·ic **1** *adj* automático, -a. **2** *n (car)* coche *m* automático.

au·to·mat·i·cal·ly *adv* automáticamente.

au·to·mo·bile automóvil *m, Am* carro *m.*

au·ton·o·mous *adj* autónomo, -a.

au·tumn otoño *m.*

aux·il·ia·ry *adj* auxiliar.
a·vail·a·ble *adj (thing)* disponible; *(person)* libre.
av·a·lanche avalancha *f.*
av·e·nue avenida *f, fig* vía *f.*
av·er·age 1 *n* promedio *m*; **on a.** por término medio. **2** *adj* medio, -a; *(middle)* regular.
a·vi·a·tion aviación *f.*
av·o·ca·do *(also* **avocado pear)** aguacate *m.*
a·void *vt* evitar; **to a. doing sth** evitar hacer algo.
a·void·a·ble *adj* evitable.
a·wake 1 *adj* despierto, -a. **2** *vi* despertarse.
a·ward 1 *n (prize)* premio *m*; *(medal)* condecoración *f*; *(grant)* beca *f.* **2** *vt (prize)* otorgar; *(medal)* dar; *(damages)* adjudicar.
a·ware *adj (informed)* enterado, -a; **not that I'm a. of** que yo sepa no; **to become a. of sth** darse cuenta de algo.
a·way *adv* far a. lejos; **go a.!** ¡lárgate!; **it's 3 miles a.** está a 3 millas (de distancia); **keep a. from the fire!** ¡no te acerques al fuego!; **right a.** en seguida; **to be a.** *(absent)* estar ausente; **to go a.** irse; **to play a.** *(in sport)* jugar fuera; **to turn a.** volver la cara; **to chatter/work a.** hablar/trabajar sin parar.
aw·ful *adj* espantoso, -a; *fam* **an a. lot of work** muchísimo trabajo.
aw·ful·ly *adv fam* terriblemente.
awk·ward *adj (clumsy)* torpe; *(difficult)* pesado, -a; *(moment)* inoportuno, -a.
awn·ing *(on shop)* marquesina *f.*
ax 1 *n* hacha *f.* **2** *vt (jobs)* suprimir; *(cut back)* reducir; *(plan)* cancelar.
ax·is *(pl* axes) eje *m.*
ax·le eje *m.*

B

BA *abbr of* **Bachelor of Arts.**
ba·by bebé *m*; *(young child)* niño, -a *mf.*
ba·by car·riage cochecito *m* de niño.
ba·by·sit *vi* hacer de canguro.
ba·by·sit·ter canguro *mf.*
bach·e·lor soltero *m*; **B. of Arts/ Science** licenciado, -a *mf* en Filosofía y Letras/Ciencias.
back 1 *n (of person)* espalda *f*; *(of chair)* respaldo *m*; *(of hand)* dorso *m*; *(of house, car)* parte *f* de atrás; *(of stage, cupboard)* fondo *m*; **b. to front** al revés. **2** *adj* trasero, -a; **b. door** puerta *f* de atrás; **b. seat** asiento *m* de detrás; **b. wheel** rueda *f* trasera; **b. number** número *m* atrasado. **3** *adv (at the rear)* atrás; *(towards the rear)* hacia atrás. **4** *vt (support)* apoyar; *(financially)* financiar; *(bet on)* apostar por.
▸**back out** *vi (withdraw)* volverse atrás.
▸**back up** *vt (support)* apoyar a.
back·ache dolor *m* de espalda.
back·fire *vi (car)* petardear.
back·ground fondo *m*; *(origin)* origen *m*; *(past)* pasado *m*; *(education)* formación *f*; *(circumstances)* antecedentes *mpl*; **b. music** hilo *m* musical.
back·ing *(support)* apoyo *m*; *(financial)* respaldo *m* financiero.
back·log **to have a b. of work** tener un montón de trabajo atrasado.
back·pack mochila *f.*
back·side *fam* trasero *m.*
back·stage *adv* entre bastidores.
back·up *(of disk)* copia *f* de seguridad.
back·ward 1 *adj (movement)* hacia atrás; *(child, country)* retrasado, -a. **2** *adv* (hacia) atrás.

back·wards *adv* hacia atrás; **to walk b.** andar de espaldas.

back·yard jardín *m* trasero.

ba·con tocino *m*, beicon *m*.

bac·te·ri·a *npl* bacterias *fpl*.

bad *adj* malo, -a; *(decayed)* podrido, -a; *(accident)* grave; *(headache)* fuerte; *(ill)* enfermo, -a.

badge insignia *f*, *(metal disc)* chapa *f*.

badg·er tejón *m*.

bad·ly *adv* mal; *(seriously)* gravemente; *(very much)* mucho; **we need it b.** nos hace mucha falta; **to be b. off** *(financially)* andar mal de dinero.

bad-man·nered *adj* maleducado.

bad·min·ton bádminton *m*.

bad-tem·pered *adj* **to be b.** *(temperament)* tener mal genio; *(temporarily)* estar de mal humor.

baf·fle *vt* desconcertar.

bag *(plastic, paper, shopping)* bolsa *f*, *(handbag)* bolso *m*; *fam* **bags of** montones de; **bags** *(under eyes)* ojeras *fpl*.

bag·gage equipaje *m*.

bag·gy *adj* holgado, -a; **b. trousers** pantalones *mpl* anchos.

bag·pipes *npl* gaita *f sing*.

bail fianza *f*; **on b.** bajo fianza.

bait cebo *m*.

bake *vt* cocer al horno.

baked *adj* al horno; **b. potato** patata *f* asada.

baked beans alubias *fpl* cocidas en salsa de tomate.

bak·er panadero, -a *mf*.

bak·er·y panadería *f*.

bal·ance 1 *n (equilibrium)* equilibrio *m*; *(financial)* saldo *m*; *(remainder)* resto *m*. **2** *vt* poner en equilibrio (**on** en); *(budget)* equilibrar. **3** *vi* guardar el equilibrio.

bal·ance sheet balance *m*.

bal·co·ny balcón *m*.

bald *adj* calvo, -a.

bald·ness calvicie *f*.

Bal·kans *npl* **the B.** los Balcanes.

ball¹ *(in baseball, tennis etc)* pelota *f*;

(football) balón *m*; *(in billiards, golf etc)* bola *f*, *(of wool)* ovillo *m*; **to be on the b.** *fam* ser un espabilado.

ball² *(dance)* baile *m*.

bal·le·ri·na bailarina *f*.

bal·let ballet *m*.

bal·loon globo *m*.

bal·lot votación *f*.

ball·park *n* campo *m* de béisbol; **a b. figure** una cifra aproximada.

ball·point (pen) bolígrafo *m*.

ball·room salón *m* de baile.

ban 1 *n* prohibición *f*. **2** *vt (prohibit)* prohibir; *(exclude)* excluir.

ba·nan·a plátano *m*, *Am* banana *f*.

band *(strip)* tira *f*, *(stripe)* raya *f*; *(group)* grupo *m*; *(of musicians)* banda *f*.

band·age 1 *n* venda *f*. **2** *vt* vendar.

Band-Aid® tirita® *f*.

bang *n (blow)* golpe *m*; *(noise)* ruido *m*; *(explosion)* estallido *m*; *(of gun)* estampido *m*.

▸ **bang into** *vt* golpearse contra.

bang·er *fam (firework)* petardo *m*; **old b.** *(car)* coche *m* destartalado.

ban·gle brazalete *m*.

ban·is·ter(s) pasamanos *m inv*.

bank¹ *(for money)* banco *m*.

bank² *(of river)* ribera *f*, orilla *f*.

▸ **bank on** *vt* contar con.

bank ac·count cuenta *f* bancaria.

bank card tarjeta *f* bancaria.

bank·er banquero, -a *mf*.

bank·ing banca *f*.

bank·rupt *adj* en quiebra; **to go b.** quebrar.

bank·rupt·cy bancarrota *f*.

ban·ner *(in demonstration)* pancarta *f*.

bar 1 *n (of gold)* barra *f*, *(of chocolate)* tableta *f*, *(of cage)* barrote *m*; *(pub)* bar *m*; *(counter)* barra *f*, *(of soap)* pastilla *f*. **2** *vt (door)* atrancar; *(road)* cortar; *(exclude)* excluir *(from* de); *(prohibit)* prohibir.

bar·be·cue barbacoa *f*.

barbed *adj* **b. wire** alambre *m* de espino.

bar·ber barbero, -a *mf*; **b.'s (shop)** barbería *f.*

bare *adj* desnudo, -a; *(head)* descubierto, -a; *(foot)* descalzo, -a; *(room)* sin muebles; **with his b. hands** sólo con las manos.

bare·foot *adj & adv* descalzo, -a.

bare·ly *adv* apenas.

bar·gain 1 *n (deal)* negocio *m*; *(cheap purchase)* ganga *f*; **b. price** precio *m* de oferta. **2** *vi* negociar.

▸**bargain for** *vt* esperar; **I hadn't bargained for this** no contaba con esto.

barge gabarra *f.*

▸**barge in** *vi (go in)* entrar sin permiso.

▸**barge into** *vt (room)* irrumpir en; *(person)* tropezar con.

bark¹ *vi (dog)* ladrar.

bark² *(of tree)* corteza *f.*

bark·ing ladridos *mpl.*

bar·ley cebada *f.*

barn granero *m.*

ba·rom·e·ter barómetro *m.*

bar·racks *npl* cuartel *m sing.*

bar·rage *(dam)* presa *f.*

bar·rel *(of wine)* tonel *m*; *(of beer, oil)* barril *m*; *(of firearm)* cañón *m.*

bar·ren *adj* estéril; *(land)* yermo, -a.

bar·rette pasador *m* (del pelo).

bar·ri·cade 1 *n* barricada *f.* **2** *vt* cerrar con barricadas.

bar·ri·er barrera *f.*

bar·tend·er camarero *m.*

base 1 *n* base *f*; *(foot)* pie *m*; *(of column)* base *f.* **2** *vt* basar **(on** en).

base·ball béisbol *m.*

base·ment sótano *m.*

bash 1 *n (heavy blow)* golpetazo *m*; *(dent)* bollo *m.* **2** *vt* golpear.

▸**bash up** *vt* **to b. sb up** darle a algn una paliza.

ba·sic 1 *adj* básico, -a; **b. pay** sueldo *m* base. **2** *npl* **basics** lo fundamental.

ba·si·cal·ly *adv* fundamentalmente.

ba·sin *(washbowl)* palangana *f*; *(for washing up)* barreño *m*; *(in bathroom)* lavabo *m.*

ba·sis *(pl* **bases)** base *f*; **on the b. of** en base a.

bask *vi (in sunlight)* tostarse.

bas·ket *(big)* cesta *f*; *(small)* cesto *m.*

bass 1 *n (singer)* bajo *m*; *(notes)* graves *mpl*; **b. drum** bombo *m*; **b. guitar** bajo *m.* **2** *adj* bajo, -a.

bat¹ *(in baseball)* bate *m.*

bat² *(animal)* murciélago *m.*

bat³ *vt* **without batting an eyelid** sin pestañear.

batch *(of bread)* hornada *f*; *(of goods)* lote *m.*

bath 1 *n* baño *m*; *(tub)* bañera *f*; **to have a b.** bañarse. **2** *vt* bañar.

bathe *vi* bañarse.

bath·ing baño *m.*

bath·ing suit traje *m* de baño.

bath·ing trunks *npl* bañador *m.*

bath·robe albornoz *m.*

bath·room cuarto *m* de baño.

bath·tub bañera *f.*

bat·ter 1 *n* pasta para rebozar. **2** *vt (baby)* maltratar.

▸**batter down** *vt (door)* derribar.

bat·tered *adj (car)* desvencijado, -a.

bat·ter·y *(for radio)* pila *f*; *(for car)* batería *f.*

bat·tle 1 *n* batalla *f*; *fig* lucha *f.* **2** *vi* luchar.

bat·tle·ship acorazado *m.*

baud baudio *m.*

bawl *vi* gritar.

bay bahía *f*; *(large)* golfo *m.*

BC *abbr of* **before Christ** a.C.

be* 1 *vi (permanent state)* ser; **he is very tall** es muy alto; **Washington is the capital** Washington es la capital; **sugar is sweet** el azúcar es dulce. ▪ *(temporary state, location)* estar; **how are you?** ¿cómo estás?; **this soup is cold** esta sopa está fría. ▪ *(cost)* **a return ticket is $24** un billete de ida y vuelta cuesta 24 dólares; **how much is it?** ¿cuánto es? ▪ *(weather)* **it's foggy** hay niebla; **it's cold/hot** hace frío/calor. ▪ *(time,* *date)* ser; **it's one o'clock** es la una; **it's four o'clock** son las cuatro; **it's the 11th/Tuesday today** hoy es 11/martes. ▪ **to be cold/afraid/hungry** tener frío/miedo/hambre; **she is thirty (years old)** tiene treinta años. **2** *v aux* estar; **he is writing a letter** está escribiendo una carta; **she was singing** cantaba; **they are leaving next week** se van la semana que viene; **we have been waiting for a long time** hace mucho que estamos esperando. ▪ *(passive)* ser; **he was murdered** fue asesinado. ▪ *(obligation)* **I am to see him this afternoon** debo verle esta tarde. ▪ **there is, there are** hay; **there was, there were** había; **there will be** habrá; **there would be** habría; **there have been a lot of complaints** ha habido muchas quejas; **there were ten of us** éramos diez. ▪ *(in tag questions)* ¿verdad?, ¿no?; **you're happy, aren't you?** estás contento, ¿verdad?

beach playa *f.*

bea·con baliza *f*, *(lighthouse)* faro *m.*

bead *(of necklace etc)* cuenta *f*, *(of liquid)* gota *f.*

beak *(of bird)* pico *m.*

beam *(in building)* viga *f*, *(of light)* rayo *m.*

beam·ing *adj (smiling)* radiante.

bean alubia *f*, judía *f*, *Am* frijol *m*; **broad b.** haba *f*, **coffee b.** grano *m* de café; **green** or **runner b.** judía *f* verde.

bear¹* **1** *vt (carry)* llevar; *(endure)* soportar; **to b. in mind** tener presente. **2** *vi* **to b. left** girar a la izquierda.

▸**bear out** *vt* confirmar.

bear² *(animal)* oso *m.*

bear·a·ble *adj* soportable.

beard barba *f.*

beard·ed *adj* barbudo, -a.

bear·ing *(relevance)* relación *f*, **to have a b. on** estar relacionado, -a

con; **to get one's bearings** orientarse.

beast bestia *f.*

beast·ly *adj fam* asqueroso, -a.

beat 1 *vt* *(hit)* pegar; *(drum)* tocar; *(in cooking)* batir; *(defeat)* vencer. **2** *vi** *(heart)* latir. **3** *n* *(of heart)* latido *m*; *(of policeman)* ronda *f.*

▸**beat down** *vi (sun)* caer a plomo.

▸**beat off** *vt* rechazar.

▸**beat up** *vt* dar una paliza a.

beat·ing *(thrashing)* paliza *f*, *(defeat)* derrota *f.*

beau·ti·ful *adj* hermoso, -a, bello, -a.

beau·ty belleza *f*, hermosura *f.*

beau·ty spot *(on face)* lunar *m*; *(place)* lugar *m* pintoresco.

bea·ver castor *m.*

be·cause 1 *conj* porque. **2** *prep* **b. of** a causa de.

be·come* *vi (doctor, priest)* hacerse; *(mayor, officer)* llegar a ser; *(angry, sad)* ponerse; **what has b. of him?** ¿qué ha sido de él?

bed cama *f*, **to get out of b.** levantarse de la cama; **to go to b.** acostarse; **b. and breakfast** *(service)* cama *f* y desayuno *m*; *(sign)* 'pensión'.

bed·ding ropa *f* de cama.

bed·room dormitorio *m.*

bed·side **b. table** mesilla *f* de noche.

bed·time hora *f* de acostarse.

bee abeja *f.*

beech haya *f.*

beef carne *f* de vaca, *Am* carne *f* de res.

been *pp of* **be**.

beep 1 *n* pitido *m.* **2** *vi* pitar.

beep·er busca(personas) *m inv.*

beer cerveza *f*, **a glass of b.** una caña.

beet **red b.** remolacha *f.*

bee·tle escarabajo *m.*

be·fore 1 *conj (earlier than)* antes de que (+ *subjunctive)*, antes de (+ *infinitive)*; **b. she goes** antes de que se vaya; **b.** *leaving* antes de salir. **2** *prep (place)* delante de; *(in the presence of)* ante; *(order, time)* antes de. **3** *adv (time)* antes; *(place)* (por) delante; **I have met him b.** ya lo conozco; **the night b.** la noche anterior.

be·friend *vt* trabar amistad con.

beg 1 *vt (money etc)* pedir; *(beseech)* rogar. **2** *vi (solicit)* mendigar; **to b. for money** pedir limosna.

beg·gar mendigo, -a *mf*.

be·gin* *vti* empezar, comenzar; **to b. doing** *or* **to do sth** empezar a hacer algo; **to b. with ...** para empezar ...

be·gin·ner principiante *mf*.

be·gin·ning principio *m*, comienzo *m*; **at the b. of May** a principios de mayo.

be·grudge *vt* dar de mala gana; *(envy)* envidiar; **to b. sb sth** envidiarle algo a algn.

be·half nombre *m*; **on b. of, in b. of** de parte de.

be·have *vi (person)* (com)portarse; **b. yourself!** ¡pórtate bien!

be·hav·ior comportamiento *m*, conducta *f*; *(of machine)* funcionamiento *m*.

be·hind 1 *prep* detrás de. **2** *adv (in the rear)* detrás, atrás; **I've left my umbrella b.** se me ha olvidado el paraguas; **to be b. with one's payments** estar atrasado, -a en los pagos. **3** *n fam (bottom)* trasero *m*.

beige *adj & n* beige *(m)*.

belch 1 *vi* eructar. **2** *n* eructo *m*.

Bel·gian *adj & n* belga *(mf)*.

be·lief creencia *f*; *(opinion)* opinión *f*, *(faith)* fe *f*; *(confidence)* confianza *f* *(in* en).

be·liev·a·ble *adj* creíble.

be·lieve *vti* creer; **I b. so** creo que sí; **to b. in sb/sth** creer en algn/algo.

be·liev·er *(religious)* creyente *mf*.

be·lit·tle *vt (person)* restar importancia a.

bell *(of church)* campana *f*; *(small)*

campanilla *f*; *(of school, door, bicycle)* timbre *m*; *(on animal)* cencerro *m*.

bell·boy botones *m inv*.

bel·ly *(of person)* barriga *f*, tripa *f*.

bel·ly·ache *fam* dolor *m* de barriga.

be·long *vi* pertenecer (**to** a); *(be a member)* ser socio, -a (**to** de).

be·long·ings *npl* efectos *mpl* personales.

be·low 1 *prep* debajo de. **2** *adv* abajo.

belt cinturón *m*; *(in machine)* correa *f*, *(area)* zona *f*.

▶ **belt along** *vi fam* ir a todo gas.

bench *(seat)* banco *m*.

bend 1 *vt** doblar; *(back)* encorvar; *(head)* inclinar. **2** *vi** doblarse; *(road)* torcerse; **to b. (over)** inclinarse. **3** *n (in river, road)* curva *f*, *(in pipe)* recodo *m*.

▶ **bend down** *vi* inclinarse.

be·neath 1 *prep (below)* bajo, debajo de. **2** *adv* debajo.

ben·e·fi·cial *adj (doing good)* benéfico, -a; *(advantageous)* beneficioso, -a.

ben·e·fit 1 *vt* beneficiar. **2** *vi* sacar provecho (**from** *or* **by** de). **3** *n (advantage)* beneficio *m*; *(allowance)* subsidio *m*; **I did it for your b.** lo hice por tu bien.

bent *adj (curved)* curvado, -a; **to be b. on doing sth** *(determined)* estar empeñado, -a en hacer algo.

be·reave·ment duelo *m*.

ber·ry baya *f*.

ber·serk *adj* **to go b.** volverse loco, -a.

berth *(bed)* litera *f*.

be·side *prep (next to)* al lado de, junto a; *(compared with)* comparado con; **that's b. the point** eso no viene al caso.

be·sides 1 *prep (in addition to)* además de; *(except)* excepto. **2** *adv* además.

best 1 *adj* mejor; **the b. thing would be to phone them** lo mejor sería llamarles; **the b. part of a year** casi un año. **2** adv mejor; **as b. I can** lo mejor que pueda. **3** n lo mejor; **to do one's b.** hacer todo lo posible; **to make the b. of sth** sacar el mejor partido de algo.

best man ≃ padrino m de boda.

best·sell·er best-seller m.

bet 1 n apuesta f. **2** vti* apostar (**on** a).

be·tray vt traicionar.

be·tray·al traición f.

bet·ter 1 adj mejor; **that's b.!** ¡eso es!; **to get b.** mejorar; (healthier) mejor; **b. off** (richer) más rico, -a; **the b. part of the day** la mayor parte del día. **2** adv mejor; **we had b. leave** más vale que nos vayamos. **3** vt (improve) mejorar; (surpass) superar.

bet·ting apuestas fpl.

be·tween 1 prep entre; **b. you and me** entre nosotros; **closed b. 1 and 3** cerrado de 1 a 3. **2** adv en medio; **in b.** (position) en medio; (time) mientras (tanto).

bev·er·age bebida f.

be·ware vi tener cuidado (**of** con); **b.!** ¡cuidado!

be·wil·der vt desconcertar.

be·yond 1 prep más allá de; **it is b. me why …** no comprendo por qué …; **this task is b. me** no puedo con esta tarea. **2** adv más allá.

bi·as (tendency) tendencia f (**to·wards** hacia); (prejudice) prejuicio m.

bi·as(s)ed adj parcial; **to be b. against sth/sb** tener prejuicio en contra de algo/algn.

bib (for baby) babero m.

Bi·ble Biblia f.

bi·cy·cle bicicleta f.

bid 1 vti* (at auction) pujar (**for** por). **2** n (offer) oferta f, (at auction) puja f.

big adj grande (gran before sing noun); **a b. clock** un reloj grande; **a b. surprise** una gran sorpresa; **my b. brother** mi hermano mayor; fam **b. deal!** ¿y qué?

big·head fam engreído, -a mf.

bike (bicycle) bici f, (motorcycle) moto f.

bike path carril m bici.

bi·ki·ni bikini m.

bile bilis f.

bi·lin·gual adj bilingüe.

bill (for gas etc) factura f, (in restaurant) cuenta f, (in Congress) proyecto m de ley; (currency) billete m (de banco).

bill·board cartelera f.

bill·fold billetero m.

bil·liards billar m.

bil·lion (thousand million) mil millones mpl.

bin (for storage) cajón m; (garbage) **b.** cubo m de la basura.

bind* vt (tie up) atar; (book) encuadernar.

bind·er (file) carpeta f.

bin·go bingo m.

bin·oc·u·lars npl prismáticos mpl.

bi·o·log·i·cal adj biológico, -a.

bi·ol·o·gy biología f.

bi·o·tech·nol·o·gy n biotecnología f.

birch (tree) abedul m.

bird (small) pájaro m; (large) ave f.

bird's-eye view vista f de pájaro.

birth nacimiento m; **to give b. to a child** dar a luz a un niño.

birth cer·tif·i·cate partida f de nacimiento.

birth·day cumpleaños m inv.

birth·mark antojo m.

bis·cuit bizcocho m.

bish·op obispo m; (chess) alfil m.

bit (small piece) trozo m; (small quantity) poco m; **a b. of sugar** un poco de azúcar; **b. by b.** poco a poco; **a b.** (slightly) un poco.

bitch 1 n (dog) perra f, fam (spiteful woman) bruja f. **2** vi fam **to b. (about)** (criticize) criticar.

bite 1 n (act) mordisco m; (wound) mordedura f, (mouthful, snack) bocado m; (insect) **b.** picadura f. **2** vti* morder; (insect) picar; **to b.**

one's **nails** morderse las uñas.
bit·ter adj amargo, -a; (weather) glacial; (wind) cortante; (person) amargado, -a; (struggle) enconado, -a; (hatred) implacable.
bit·ter·ness amargura f; (of weather) crudeza f; (of person) rencor m.
bi·zarre adj (odd) extraño, -a; (eccentric) estrafalario, -a.
black 1 adj (color) negro, -a; fig **b. and blue** amoratado, -a. **2** n (color) negro m; (person) negro, -a mf.
▸**black out** vi (faint) desmayarse.
black·ber·ry zarzamora f.
black·bird mirlo m.
black·board pizarra f, encerado m.
black·cur·rant grosella f negra.
black eye ojo m amoratado.
black·list lista f negra.
black·mail 1 n chantaje m. **2** vt chantajear.
black·mail·er chantajista mf.
black·out (of lights) apagón m; (fainting) pérdida f de conocimiento.
blad·der vejiga f.
blade (of grass) brizna f; (of knife etc) hoja f.
blame 1 n culpa f. **2** vt echar la culpa a; **he is to b.** él tiene la culpa.
blame·less adj (person) inocente; (conduct) intachable.
bland adj (food) soso, -a.
blank 1 adj (without writing) en blanco; **b. check** cheque m en blanco. **2** n (space) espacio m en blanco.
blan·ket manta f.
blare vi resonar.
▸**blare out** vt pregonar.
blast 1 n (of wind) ráfaga f; (of horn etc) toque m; (explosion) explosión f; (shock wave) onda f de choque. **2** vt fam **b. (it)!** ¡maldito sea!
blast·ed adj maldito, -a.
blast-off despegue m.
blaze 1 n (of burst of flame) llamarada f; (fierce fire) incendio m; (of sun) resplandor m. **2** vi (fire) arder; (sun etc) brillar.

blaz·er chaqueta f sport.
bleach (household) lejía f.
bleak adj (countryside) desolado, -a.
bleed* vti sangrar.
blem·ish (flaw) defecto m; (on fruit) maca f, fig **without b.** sin tacha.
blend 1 n mezcla f. **2** vt (mix) mezclar; (match) armonizar. **3** vi (mix) mezclarse.
blend·er (for food) licuadora f.
bless vt bendecir; **b. you!** (after sneeze) ¡Jesús!
bless·ing bendición f; (advantage) ventaja f.
blew pt of blow.
blind 1 adj ciego, -a; **a b. man** un ciego; **a b. woman** una ciega. **2** n (on window) persiana f, pl **the b.** los ciegos.
blind·fold 1 n venda f. **2** vt vendar los ojos a.
blind·ly adv a ciegas; (love) ciegamente.
blind·ness ceguera f.
blink vi (eyes) pestañear; (lights) parpadear.
bliss felicidad f.
blis·ter (on skin) ampolla f.
bliz·zard ventisca f.
blob (drop) gota f; (spot) mancha f.
block 1 n bloque m; (of wood) taco m; (group of buildings) manzana f; **a b. of apartments** un bloque de pisos. **2** vt (obstruct) obstruir.
▸**block up** vt bloquear; **to get blocked up** (pipe) obstruirse.
block·age bloqueo m.
blog 1 n blog m, bitácora f. **2** vi bloguear, tener un blog.
blog·ger n blogger mf, bloguero, -a mf, bitacorero, -a m,f.
bloke fam tío m, tipo m.
blond adj & n rubio (m).
blonde adj & n rubia (f).
blood sangre f; **b. donor** donante mf de sangre; **b. group** grupo m sanguíneo; **b. pressure** tensión f arterial; **high/low b. pressure** hipertensión f/hipotensión f.

blood·shed derramamiento *m* de sangre.

blood·shot *adj* inyectado, -a de sangre.

blood·y *adj (battle)* sangriento, -a; *(bloodstained)* manchado, -a de sangre.

bloom 1 *n (flower)* flor *f*, **in full b.** en flor. **2** *vi (blossom)* florecer.

blos·som 1 *n (flower)* flor *f*. **2** *vi* florecer.

blot *(of ink)* borrón *m*.

blotch·y *adj (skin)* enrojecido, -a; *(paint)* cubierto, -a de manchas.

blouse blusa *f*.

blow¹ golpe *m*.

blow²* **1** *vi (wind)* soplar. **2** *vt (trumpet etc)* tocar; *(smoke)* echar; *(of wind)* llevarse; **to b. one's nose** sonarse la nariz.

▸**blow away** *vt* the wind blew it away el viento se lo llevó.

▸**blow down** *vt* derribar.

▸**blow off 1** *vt (remove)* quitar. **2** *vi (hat)* salir volando.

▸**blow out 1** *vt* apagar. **2** *vi* apagarse.

▸**blow up 1** *vt (building)* volar; *(inflate)* inflar. **2** *vi (explode)* explotar.

blow dry 1 *vt* secar con secador, marcar. **2** *n* marcado *m*.

blow·torch soplete *m*.

blue 1 *adj* azul; *(sad)* triste. **2** *n* azul *m*.

blue·ber·ry arándano *m*.

blue·print proyecto *m*.

bluff 1 *n (deception)* farol *m*. **2** *vi* tirarse un farol.

blun·der 1 *n* metedura *f* de pata, *fam* patinazo *m*. **2** *vi* meter la pata.

blunt *adj (knife)* embotado, -a; *(pencil)* despuntado, -a; *(frank)* directo, -a; *(statement)* tajante.

blur 1 *n* he was just a b. apenas se le veía. **2** *vt (shape)* desdibujar; *(memory)* enturbiar.

blurred *adj* borroso, -a.

blush *vi* ruborizarse.

blus·ter·y *adj* borrascoso, -a.

board 1 *n (plank)* tabla *f*, *(meals)*

pensión *f*; **full b.** pensión completa; **room and b.** casa *f* y comida; **b. of directors** consejo *m* de administración; **on b.** a bordo. **2** *vt (ship, plane etc)* embarcar en.

board·er *(in boarding house)* huésped *mf*, *(at school)* interno, -a *mf*.

board·ing *(embarkation)* embarque *m*.

board·ing house pensión *f*.

board·ing pass tarjeta *f* de embarque.

board·ing school internado *m*.

boast *vi* jactarse **(about** de).

boat barco *m*; *(small)* barca *f*, *(large)* buque *m*.

bod·i·ly *adj* físico, -a.

bod·y cuerpo *m*; *(corpse)* cadáver *m*; *(organization)* organismo *m*.

bod·y·guard guardaespaldas *mf inv*.

bod·y·work carrocería *f*.

bo·gus *adj* falso, -a.

▸**boil¹ 1** *n* **to come to a b.** empezar a hervir. **2** *vt (water, egg)* hervir; *(food)* cocer. **3** *vi* hervir.

▸**boil over** *vi (milk)* salirse.

boil² *(on skin)* furúnculo *m*.

boiled *adj* **b. egg** huevo *m* pasado por agua.

boil·er caldera *f*.

boil·ing *adj (water)* hirviente; **it's b. hot** *(food)* quema; *(weather)* hace un calor agobiante.

bold *adj (courageous)* valiente; *(dress, proposition etc)* audaz, atrevido.

bold·ness audacia *f*, descaro *m*, osadía *f*.

Bo·liv·i·an *adj & n* boliviano, -a *(mf)*.

bolt 1 *n (on door)* cerrojo *m*; *(small)* pestillo *m*; *(with nut)* tornillo *m*. **2** *vt (lock)* cerrar con cerrojo; *(food)* engullir. **3** *vi (person)* largarse; *(horse)* desbocarse.

bomb 1 *n* bomba *f*. **2** *vt (city etc)* bombardear; *(by terrorists)* volar.

bomb·er bombardero *m*.

bomb·ing bombardeo *m*.

bond *(link)* vínculo *m*; *(financial)* bono *m*.

bone hueso *m*; *(in fish)* espina *f*.

bon·fire hoguera *f*.

bon·net *(child's)* gorro *m*.

bo·nus plus *m*; *(on wages)* prima *f*; *(on shares)* dividendo *m* extraordinario.

bon·y *adj (person)* huesudo, -a; *(fish)* lleno, -a de espinas.

boo 1 *interj* ¡bu! **2** *vt* abuchear.

boo·by trap trampa *f*; *(bomb etc)* trampa *f* explosiva.

book 1 *n* libro *m*; *(of stamps)* carpeta *f*; *(in commerce)* **books** cuentas *fpl*. **2** *vt (reserve)* reservar.

book·case estantería *f*.

booked up *adj* completo, -a.

book·ing *(reservation)* reserva *f*.

book·ing of·fice taquilla *f*.

book·keep·er contable *mf*.

book·keep·ing contabilidad *f*.

book·let *(pamphlet)* folleto *m*.

book·mak·er corredor, -a *mf* de apuestas.

book·sell·er librero, -a *mf*.

book·shelf estantería *f*.

book·store librería *f*.

boom *(noise)* estampido *m*; *(sudden prosperity)* auge *m*.

boost 1 *n* estímulo *m*. **2** *vt (increase)* aumentar; *(tourism, exports)* fomentar; **to b. sb's confidence** subirle la moral a algn.

boot *n* bota *f*; *(short)* botín *m*; *fam* **she got the b.** la echaron (del trabajo).

▸**boot out** *vt fam* echar a patadas.

booth *(in language lab etc)* cabina *f*; **telephone b.** cabina *f* telefónica.

booze *fam* **1** *n* priva *f*. **2** *vi* privar.

bor·der *n* borde *m*; *(frontier)* frontera *f*.

▸**border on** *vt (country)* lindar con.

bor·der·line 1 *adj (case etc)* dudoso, -a. **2** *n* línea *f* divisoria, frontera *f*.

bore 1 *vt* aburrir. **2** *n (person)* pesa-

do, -a *mf*; *(thing)* lata *f*; **what a b.!** ¡qué rollo!

bore·dom aburrimiento *m*.

bor·ing *adj* aburrido, -a, pesado, -a.

born *adj* nacido, -a; **to be b.** nacer; **I was b. in 1969** nací en 1969.

bor·ough municipio *m*.

bor·row *vt* pedir prestado; **can I b. your pen?** ¿me dejas tu bolígrafo?

boss *n (head)* jefe, -a *mf*; *(factory owner etc)* patrón, -ona *mf*.

▸**boss around** *vt* ser mandón, -ona con.

boss·y *adj* mandón, -ona.

botch 1 *vt* chapucear; **a botched job** una chapuza. **2** *n* chapuza *f*.

both 1 *adj* ambos, -as, los/las dos; **b. men are teachers** ambos son profesores; **hold it with b. hands** sujétalo con las dos manos. **2** *pron* **b. (of them)** ambos, -as, los/las dos; **b. of you** vosotros dos. **3** *adv* a la vez; **b. New York and Ohio are in the U.S.** tanto Nueva York como Ohio están en los Estados Unidos.

both·er 1 *vt (disturb)* molestar; *(be a nuisance to)* dar la lata a; *(worry)* preocupar; **I can't be bothered** no tengo ganas; **he didn't b. shaving** no se molestó en afeitarse. **2** *vi* **don't b.** no te molestes. **3** *n (disturbance)* molestia *f*; *(nuisance)* lata *f*; *(trouble)* problemas *mpl*. **4** *interj* ¡maldito sea!

bot·tle botella *f*; *(of perfume, ink)* frasco *m*; **baby's b.** biberón *m*.

bot·tle o·pen·er abrebotellas *m inv*.

bot·tom 1 *adj (lowest)* más bajo, -a. **2** *n* parte *f* inferior; *(of sea, garden, street, box, bottle)* fondo *m*; *(of page, hill)* pie *m*; *(buttocks)* trasero *m*; **to be at the b. of the class** ser el último/la última de la clase.

boul·der canto *m* rodado.

bounce 1 *vi (ball)* rebotar; *(check)* ser rechazado, -a (por el banco). **2** *vt (ball)* botar.

bound¹ *adj* **he's b. to know it** seguro de que lo sabe; **it's b. to happen** su-

cederá con toda seguridad; **it was b.
to fail** estaba destinado al fracaso.
bound² *adj* **to be b. for** dirigirse a.
bound·a·ry límite *m*.
bounds *npl* **the river is out of b.**
está prohibido bajar al río.
bou·quet *(of flowers)* ramillete *m*.
bou·tique boutique *f*.
bow¹ 1 *vi* hacer una reverencia. **2** *n*
(with head, body) reverencia *f*.
bow² *(for violin, arrows)* arco *m*;
(knot) lazo *m*.
bow·els *npl* entrañas *fpl*.
bowl¹ *(dish)* cuenco *m*; *(for soup)* tazón *m*; *(for washing clothes, dishes)*
barreño *m*.
bowl² *vi (in cricket)* lanzar la pelota.
bowl·er *(hat)* bombín *m*.
bowl·ing *(game)* bolos *mpl*.
bowl·ing alley bolera *f*.
bowl·ing pin bolo *m*.
bowls *npl* bolos *mpl*.
bow tie pajarita *f*.
box¹ caja *f*; *(large)* cajón *m*.
box² 1 *vi* boxear. **2** *vt (hit)* pegar.
▸ **box in** *vt (enclose)* aprisionar.
box·er boxeador *m*; *(dog)* bóxer *m*.
box·ing boxeo *m*; **b. ring** cuadrilátero *m*.
box of·fice taquilla *f*.
boy *(child)* chico *m*; *(youth)* joven
m.
boy·cott 1 *n* boicot *m*. **2** *vt* boicotear.
boy·friend novio *m*; *(live-in)* compañero *m*.
bra sostén *m*.
brace·let pulsera *f*.
brack·et *(round)* paréntesis *m*;
(square) corchete *m*.
brag *vi* jactarse **(about** de).
brag·ging fanfarronería *f*.
braid 1 *vt* trenzar. **2** *n* trenza *f*.
brain cerebro *m*; **brains** inteligencia
f; **to have brains** ser inteligente.
brain·storm *(brilliant idea)* genia-
lidad *f*.
brain·wash *vt* lavar el cerebro a.
brain·y *adj fam* inteligente.

brake 1 *n* freno *m*. **2** *vi* frenar.
brake light luz *f* de freno.
branch 1 *n (of tree)* rama *f*; *(of road)*
bifurcación *f*; **b. (office)** sucursal *f*. **2**
vi (road) bifurcarse.
▸ **branch off** *vi* desviarse.
▸ **branch out** *vi* diversificarse.
brand marca *f*; **b. name** marca *f* de
fábrica.
brand-new *adj* flamante.
bran·dy brandy *m*.
brass latón *m*.
brave *adj* valiente.
brav·er·y valentía *f*.
brawl reyerta *f*.
brawn·y *adj* fornido, -a.
Bra·zil·i·an *adj & n* brasileño, -a
(mf).
bread pan *m*; **b. and butter** pan con
mantequilla.
bread-box panera *f*.
bread·crumb miga *f* de pan;
breadcrumbs pan *m sing* rallado.
breadth *(width)* anchura *f*; *(extent)*
amplitud *f*.
bread·win·ner cabeza *mf* de familia.
break 1 *vt** romper; *(fail to keep)*
faltar a; *(destroy)* destrozar; *(financially)* arruinar; *(journey)* interrumpir; *(record)* batir; **to b. a leg**
romperse la pierna; **to b. the law**
violar la ley; **she broke the news to
him** le comunicó la noticia. **2** *vi**
romperse; *(storm)* estallar; *(story)*
divulgarse. **3** *n (fracture)* rotura *f*;
(crack) grieta *f*; *(opening)* abertura *f*;
(in a relationship) ruptura *f*; *(pause)*
pausa *f*; *(at school)* recreo *m*; *fam
(chance)* oportunidad *f*; **to take a b.**
descansar un rato; *(holiday)* tomar
unos días libres; **a lucky b.** un golpe
de suerte.
▸ **break away** *vi (become separate)*
desprenderse **(from** de).
▸ **break down 1** *vt (door)* derribar;
(resistance) acabar con. **2** *vi (in car)*
tener una avería; *(weep)* ponerse a
llorar.

▸**break in** *vi (burglar)* entrar a la fuerza.

▸**break into** *vt (house)* allanar; *(safe)* forzar.

▸**break loose** *vi* escaparse.

▸**break off 1** *vt (relations)* romper. **2** *vi (become detached)* desprenderse; *(talks)* interrumpirse; *(stop)* pararse.

▸**break out** *vi (prisoners)* escaparse; *(war etc)* estallar.

▸**break up 1** *vt (object)* romper; *(car)* desguazar; *(crowd)* disolver. **2** *vi* romperse; *(crowd)* disolverse; *(meeting)* levantarse; *(relationship)* fracasar; *(couple)* separarse; *(at end of term)* terminar.

break·down avería *f*, *(in communications)* ruptura *f*; **(nervous) b.** crisis *f* nerviosa.

break·fast desayuno *m*; **to have b.** desayunar.

break-in robo *m* (con allanamiento de morada).

break·through avance *m*.

break·up *(in marriage)* separación *f*.

breast *(chest)* pecho *m*; *(of chicken etc)* pechuga *f*.

breast·feed *vt* dar el pecho a.

breast·stroke braza *f*.

breath aliento *m*; **out of b.** sin aliento.

Breath·a·lyz·er® alcoholímetro *m*.

breathe *vti* respirar.

▸**breathe in** *vi* aspirar.

▸**breathe out** *vi* espirar.

breath·ing respiración *f*; **b. space** respiro *m*.

breath·tak·ing *adj* impresionante.

breed 1 *n (of animal)* raza *f*. **2** *vt** *(animals)* criar. **3** *vi** *(animals)* reproducirse.

breed·er *(person)* criador, -a *mf*.

breed·ing *(of animals)* cría *f*; *(of person)* educación *f*; **b. ground** caldo *m* de cultivo.

breeze brisa *f*.

breez·y *adj (weather)* ventoso, -a.

brew 1 *vt (beer)* elaborar; *(hot drink)* preparar. **2** *vi (tea)* reposar; **a storm**

is brewing se prepara una tormenta; **something's brewing** algo se está cociendo.

brew·er·y cervecería *f*.

bribe 1 *vt* sobornar. **2** *n* soborno *m*.

brick ladrillo *m*.

brick·lay·er albañil *m*.

bride novia *f*; **the b. and groom** los novios.

bride·groom novio *m*.

brides·maid dama *f* de honor.

bridge puente *m*.

brief 1 *adj (short)* breve; *(concise)* conciso, -a. **2** *n* **briefs** *(for men)* calzoncillos *mpl*; *(for women)* bragas *fpl*. **3** *vt (inform)* informar; *(instruct)* dar instrucciones a.

brief·case cartera *f*.

brief·ing *(meeting)* reunión *f* informativa.

brief·ly *adv* brevemente.

bright *adj (light, sun, eyes)* brillante; *(color)* vivo, -a; *(day)* claro, -a; *(cheerful)* alegre; *(clever)* listo, -a.

bright·en *vi (prospects)* mejorar; *(face)* iluminarse.

▸**brighten up 1** *vt (room etc)* hacer más alegre. **2** *vi (weather)* despejarse; *(person)* animarse.

bright·ly *adv* brillantemente.

bright·ness *(of sun)* resplandor *m*; *(of color)* viveza *f*.

bril·liance *(of light)* brillo *m*; *(of color)* viveza *f*; *(of person)* brillantez *f*.

bril·liant *adj* brillante; *(idea)* genial; *(very good)* estupendo, -a.

bring* *vt* traer; *(take to a different position)* llevar; *(cause)* provocar; **could you b. that book?** ¿podrías traerme el libro?

▸**bring about** *vt* provocar.

▸**bring along** *vt* traer.

▸**bring around** *vt (revive)* hacer volver en sí; *(persuade)* convencer.

▸**bring back** *vt (return)* devolver; *(reintroduce)* volver a introducir; *(make one remember)* traer a la memoria.

▸**bring down** *vt (from upstairs)* bajar

(algo); (*government*) derribar; (*reduce*) rebajar.

►**bring forward** *vt* (*meeting etc*) adelantar.

►**bring in** *vt* (*yield*) dar; (*show in*) hacer entrar; (*law etc*) introducir.

►**bring out** *vt* (*publish*) publicar; (*emphasize*) recalcar.

►**bring to** *vt* reanimar.

►**bring together** *vt* (*reconcile*) reconciliar.

►**bring up** *vt* (*educate*) educar; (*subject*) plantear; (*vomit up*) vomitar.

brink (*edge*) borde *m*.

brisk *adj* enérgico, -a; (*pace*) rápido, -a; (*trade*) activo, -a.

brisk·ly *adv* (*to walk*) rápidamente.

bris·tle cerda *f*.

Brit·ish 1 *adj* británico, -a; **the B. Isles** las Islas Británicas. **2** *npl* **the B.** los británicos.

Brit·on británico, -a *mf*.

brit·tle *adj* quebradizo, -a.

broad *adj* (*road, river*) ancho, -a; (*not detailed*) general; **in b. daylight** a plena luz del día.

broad·band *n* banda *f* ancha.

broad·cast 1 *n* emisión *f.* **2** *vt** emitir.

broad·en *vt* ensanchar.

broc·co·li brécol *m.*

bro·chure folleto *m.*

broke *adj* **to be (flat) b.** estar sin blanca.

bro·ken *adj* roto, -a; (*machinery*) averiado, -a; (*leg*) fracturado, -a; **a b. home** una familia deshecha.

bro·ken-down *adj* (*machine*) averiado, -a.

bron·chi·tis bronquitis *f.*

bronze bronce *m.*

brooch broche *m.*

brood 1 *n* (*of birds*) cría *f.* **2** *vi* (*ponder*) rumiar; **to b. over a problem** darle vueltas a un problema.

brood·y *adj* (*pensive*) pensativo, -a; (*moody*) melancólico, -a; *fam* (*woman*) con ganas de tener hijos.

brook arroyo *m.*

broom escoba *f*, (*plant*) retama *f.*

broom·stick palo *m* de escoba.

broth·er hermano *m*; **brothers and sisters** hermanos.

broth·er-in-law cuñado *m.*

brought *pt* & *pp* of **bring**.

brow (*forehead*) frente *f*, (*eyebrow*) ceja *f*, (*of hill*) cima *f.*

brown 1 *adj* marrón; (*hair*) castaño, -a; (*tanned*) moreno, -a. **2** *n* marrón *m.*

browse *vi* (*person in shop*) mirar; (*through book*) hojear.

bruise 1 *n* morado *m*, cardenal *m.* **2** *vt* contusionar.

bruised *adj* amoratado, -a.

brunch combinación *f* de desayuno y almuerzo.

bru·nette *adj* & *n* morena (*f*).

brush 1 *n* (*for hair, teeth*) cepillo *m*; (*artist's*) pincel *m*; (*for house-painting*) brocha *f.* **2** *vt* cepillar; **to b. one's hair/teeth** cepillarse el pelo/los dientes.

►**brush aside** *vt* dejar de lado.

►**brush off** *vt* ignorar.

►**brush up (on)** *vt* repasar.

bru·tal *adj* brutal, cruel.

bru·tal·i·ty brutalidad *f.*

brute (*animal*) bruto *m*; (*person*) bestia *f.*

BS *abbr of* **Bachelor of Science.**

bub·ble burbuja *f.*

►**bubble over** *vi* rebosar.

buck *fam* dólar *m.*

►**buck up 1** *vt* **b. your ideas up!** ¡espabílate! **2** *vi* (*cheer up*) animarse.

buck·et cubo *m.*

buck·le 1 *n* hebilla *f.* **2** *vt* abrochar (con hebilla). **3** *vi* (*wall, metal*) combarse.

bud 1 *n* (*shoot*) brote *m*; (*flower*) capullo *m.* **2** *vi* brotar.

Bud·dhist *adj* & *n* budista (*mf*).

bud·dy *fam Am* compadre *m*, *Esp* colega *m.*

budge *vi* (*move*) moverse.

budg·er·i·gar periquito *m.*

budg·et 1 *n* presupuesto *m*; **the B.**

(of the state) los presupuestos del Estado. **2** *vi* hacer un presupuesto (**for** para).

buf·fa·lo *(pl* **buffaloes)** búfalo *m.*

buff·er *n (device)* parachoques *m inv*; *(in computer)* memoria *f* intermedia.

buf·fet *(snack bar)* bar *m*; *(self-service meal)* bufet *m* libre.

bug 1 *n (insect)* bicho *m*; *(microbe)* microbio *m*; **I've got a b.** tengo alguna infección; *(hidden microphone)* micrófono *m* oculto; *(in computer program)* error *m.* **2** *vt fam (annoy)* fastidiar.

bug·gy *(baby's stroller)* cochecito *m* de niño.

bu·gle bugle *m.*

build 1 *vt** construir. **2** *n (physique)* físico *m.*

build·er constructor, -a *mf*; *(contractor)* contratista *mf.*

build·ing edificio *m.*

built-in *adj (cupboard)* empotrado, -a; *(incorporated)* incorporado, -a.

built-up *adj* urbanizado, -a.

bulb *(of plant)* bulbo *m*; *(lightbulb)* bombilla *f.*

Bul·gar·i·an *adj & n* búlgaro, -a *(mf).*

bulge 1 *n* protuberancia *f*, *(in pocket)* bulto *m.* **2** *vi (swell)* hincharse; *(be full)* estar repleto, -a.

bulg·ing *adj* abultado, -a; *(eye)* saltón.

bulk *(mass)* masa *f*, volumen *m*; *(greater part)* mayor parte *f.*

bulk·y *adj* voluminoso, -a.

bull toro *m.*

bull·dog buldog *m.*

bull·doz·er bulldozer *m.*

bul·let bala *f.*

bul·le·tin boletín *m.*

bul·le·tin board tablón *m* de anuncios.

bul·let·proof *adj* a prueba de balas; **b. vest** chaleco *m* antibalas.

bull·fight corrida *f* de toros.

bull·fight·er torero, -a *mf.*

bull·fight·ing los toros *mpl*; *(art)* tauromaquia *f.*

bull·ring plaza *f* de toros.

bul·ly 1 *n* matón *m.* **2** *vt* intimidar.

bum *fam (tramp)* vagabundo *m*; *(idler)* holgazán, -ana *mf.*

▸ **bum around** *vi fam* vaguear.

bum·ble·bee abejorro *m.*

bump 1 *n (swelling)* chichón *m*; *(on road)* bache *m*; *(blow)* golpe *m*; *(jolt)* sacudida *f.* **2** *vt* golpear; **to b. one's head** darse un golpe en la cabeza.

▸ **bump into** *vt (meet)* tropezar con.

bump·er *(on vehicle)* parachoques *m inv.*

bump·y *adj (road)* con muchos baches.

bun *(bread)* panecillo *m*; *(sweet)* magdalena *f.*

bunch *(of keys)* manojo *m*; *(of flowers)* ramo *m*; *(of grapes)* racimo *m*; *(of people)* grupo *m.*

bun·dle 1 *n (of clothes)* bulto *m*; *(of papers)* fajo *m.* **2** *vt (make bundle of)* liar; *(push)* empujar.

bun·ga·low bungalow *m.*

bunk *(bed)* litera *f.*

bun·ny *fam* **b. (rabbit)** conejito *m.*

buoy boya *f.*

bur·den 1 *n* carga *f.* **2** *vt* cargar (**with** con).

bu·reau *(pl* **bureaux)** *(office)* agencia *f*, oficina *f*; *(chest of drawers)* cómoda *f.*

bu·reauc·ra·cy burocracia *f.*

burg·er *fam* hamburguesa *f.*

bur·glar ladrón, -ona *mf.*

bur·glar a·larm alarma *f* antirrobo.

bur·glar·ize *vt* robar.

bur·gla·ry robo *m* en una casa.

bur·gle *vt* robar.

bur·i·al entierro *m.*

burn 1 *n* quemadura *f.* **2** *vt** quemar. **3** *vi** *(fire)* arder; *(building, food)* quemarse; *(ointment etc)* escocer.

▸ **burn down 1** *vt* incendiar. **2** *vi* incendiarse.

burn·er *(on stove)* quemador *m.*

burn·ing *adj (on fire)* ardiendo, -a en llamas.

burp 1 *n* eructo *m*. **2** *vi* eructar.

burst 1 *n (explosion)* estallido *m*; *(of tire)* reventón *m*; *(of laughter* carcajada *f*. **2** *vt* (balloon)* reventar. **3** *vi** reventarse; *(shell)* estallar.

▸**burst into** *vi* **b. into laughter/ tears** echarse a reír/llorar; **to b. into a room** irrumpir en una habitación.

▸**burst out** *vi* **to b. out laughing** echarse a reír.

burst·ing *adj* **the bar was b. with people** el bar estaba atestado de gente.

bur·y *vt* enterrar; *(hide)* ocultar; **to be buried in thought** estar absorto en pensamientos.

bus *(pl* buses *or* busses) autobús *m*; **b. shelter** marquesina *f* (de autobús); **b. station** estación *f* de autobuses.

bush *(shrub)* arbusto *m*.

bush·y *adj* espeso, -a.

busi·ness *(commerce)* negocios *mpl*; *(firm)* empresa *f*, *(matter)* asunto *m*; **on b.** de negocios; **b. hours** horas *fpl* de oficina; **b. trip** viaje *m* de negocios; **it's no b. of mine** no es asunto mío; **mind your own b.** no te metas en donde no te llaman.

busi·ness·man hombre *m* de negocios.

busi·ness·wom·an mujer *f* de negocios.

bus stop parada *f* de autobús.

bust¹ *(of woman)* pecho *m*; *(sculpture)* busto *m*.

bust² *adj fam* **to go b.** quebrar.

bus·tle *(activity, noise)* bullicio *m*.

▸**bustle about** *vi* ir y venir.

bus·tling *adj* bullicioso, -a.

bus·y *adj* ocupado, -a; *(life)* ajetreado, -a; *(street)* concurrido, -a; *(telephone)* ocupado, -a; **b. signal** señal *f* de comunicado.

bus·y·bod·y entrometido, -a *mf*, cotilla *mf*.

but 1 *conj* pero; *(after negative)* sino;

not two b. three no dos sino tres. **2** *prep* menos; **everyone b. her** todos menos ella.

butch·er carnicero, -a *mf*; **b.'s (shop)** carnicería *f*.

but·ler mayordomo *m*.

butt *(of cigarette)* colilla *f*, *fam (bottom)* culo *m*.

but·ter 1 *n* mantequilla *f*. **2** *vt* untar con mantequilla.

but·ter·cup botón *m* de oro.

but·ter·fly mariposa *f*.

but·tock nalga *f*, **buttocks** nalgas *fpl*.

but·ton 1 *n* botón *m*. **2** *vt* **to b. (up) one's jacket** abotonarse la chaqueta.

but·ton·hole ojal *m*.

buy 1 *n* **a good b.** una ganga. **2** *vt** comprar; **she bought that car from a neighbor** compró ese coche a un vecino.

buy·er comprador, -a *mf*.

buzz 1 *n (of bee)* zumbido *m*; *(of conversation)* rumor *m*. **2** *vi* zumbar.

▸**buzz off** *vi fam* largarse.

by 1 *prep (indicating agent)* por; **composed by Bach** compuesto, -a por Bach; **a film by Almodóvar** una película de Almodóvar. ▪ *(via)* por; **he left by the back door** salió por la puerta trasera. ▪ *(manner)* en, con, por; **by car/train** en coche/ tren; **by credit card** con tarjeta de crédito; **by chance** por casualidad; **by oneself** solo, -a; **you can obtain a ticket by filling in the coupon** puede conseguir una entrada rellenando el cupón. ▪ *(amount)* por; **little by little** poco a poco; **they are sold by the dozen** se venden por docenas; **to be paid by the hour** cobrar por horas; **he won by a foot** ganó por un pie. ▪ *(beside)* al lado de, junto a; **side by side** juntos. ▪ *(past)* **to walk by a building** pasar por delante de un edificio. ▪ *(time)* para; **by now** ya; **by then** para entonces; **we have to be there by**

nine tenemos que estar allí para las nueve; **by the time we arrive** (para) cuando lleguemos. ▪ *(during)* de; **by day/night** de día/noche. ▪ *(according to)* según; **is that O.K. by you?** ¿te viene bien? **2** *adv* **to go by** *(past)* pasar; **she just walked by** pasó de largo; **by and by** con el tiempo; **by and large** en conjunto.

bye(-bye) ¡adiós!, ¡hasta luego!

by·e·lec·tion elección *f* parcial.

by·pass 1 *n (road)* carretera *f* de circunvalación. **2** *vt* evitar.

by·stand·er mirón, -ona *mf*.

C

cab taxi *m*.

cab·bage col *f*.

cab·in *(hut)* choza *f*; *(on ship)* camarote *m*.

cab·i·net *(furniture)* armario *m*; *(glass-fronted)* vitrina *f*; *(in government)* gabinete *m*.

cab·i·net meet·ing consejo *m* de ministros.

ca·ble cable *m*.

ca·ble car teleférico *m*.

ca·ble TV televisión *f* por cable.

cac·tus *(pl* cacti*)* cactus *m*.

ca·fé, caf·e·te·ria cafetería *f*, bar *m*.

caf·feine cafeína *f*.

cage jaula *f*.

cake pastel *m*.

cal·cu·late *vt* calcular.

cal·cu·la·tion cálculo *m*.

cal·cu·la·tor calculadora *f*.

cal·en·dar calendario *m*.

calf *(pl* calves*)* *(of cattle)* becerro, -a *mf*, ternero, -a *mf*; *(part of leg)* pantorilla *f*.

call 1 *vt* llamar; *(meeting etc)* convocar; **what's he called?** ¿cómo se lla-

ma? **2** *vi* llamar; **to c. at sb's (house)** pasar por casa de algn. **3** *n* llamada *f*; *(visit)* visita *f*; **(phone) c.** llamada *f*.

▶**call back** *vti (phone again)* llamar otra vez.

▶**call in 1** *vt (doctor)* llamar. **2** *vi* entrar; **to call in on sb** ir a ver a algn.

▶**call on** *vt* visitar; **to c. on sb for support** recurrir a algn en busca de apoyo.

▶**call out 1** *vt (shout)* gritar; *(doctor)* hacer venir. **2** *vi* gritar.

▶**call (up)** *vt* llamar (por teléfono).

    call box cabina *f* telefónica.

    calm 1 *adj (weather, sea)* en calma; *(relaxed)* tranquilo, -a; **keep c.!** ¡tranquilo, -a! **2** *n (of weather, sea)* calma *f*. **3** *vt* calmar.

▶**calm down** *vi* calmarse.

    calm·ly *adv* con calma, tranquilamente.

    cal·o·rie caloría *f*.

    cam·cord·er videocámara *f*.

    came *pt of* **come**.

    cam·el camello, -a *mf*.

    cam·er·a cámara *f*.

    camp 1 *n* campamento *m*. **2** *vi* **to go camping** ir de camping.

    cam·paign campaña *f*.

    camp bed cama *f* plegable.

    camp·er *(person)* campista *mf*; *(vehicle)* caravana *f*.

    camp·fire fogata *f*.

    camp(·ing) site camping *m*.

    cam·pus campus *m*, ciudad *f* universitaria.

    can¹ *v aux (pt* could*)* poder; *(know how to)* saber; **I'll phone you as soon as I c.** te llamaré en cuanto pueda; **she can't do it** no puede hacerlo; **I cannot understand why** no entiendo por qué; **he could have come** podría haber venido; **c. you ski?** ¿sabes esquiar?; **she could have forgotten** puede (ser) que lo haya olvidado; **they can't be very poor** no deben ser muy pobres; **what c. it be?** ¿qué será?

    can² *(tin)* lata *f*.

Ca·na·di·an *adj & n* canadiense *(mf)*.

ca·nal canal *m*.

ca·nar·y canario *m*.

can·cel *vt (train, booking)* cancelar; *(contract)* anular; *(permission)* retirar.

can·cel·la·tion cancelación *f; (of contract)* anulación *f*.

can·cer cáncer *m*.

can·did *adj* franco, -a.

can·di·date candidato, -a *mf; (in state exam)* opositor, -a *mf*.

can·dle vela *f; (in church)* cirio *m*.

can·dle·stick palmatoria *f; (in church)* cirial *m*.

can·dy caramelo *m*.

cane **1** *n (walking stick)* bastón *m; (for punishment)* palmeta *f*. **2** *vt* castigar con la palmeta.

can·na·bis canabis *m*.

canned *adj* enlatado, -a; **c. foods** conservas *fpl*.

can·ni·bal *adj & n* caníbal *(mf)*.

ca·noe canoa *f; (for sport)* piragua *f*.

ca·noe·ing piragüismo *m*.

can o·pen·er abrelatas *m*.

can·o·py toldo *m*.

can·teen *(restaurant)* comedor *m*, cantina *f*.

can·vas lona *f; (painting)* lienzo *m*.

can·yon cañón *m*.

cap gorro *m; (soldier's)* gorra *f; (of pen)* capuchón *m; (of bottle)* chapa *f*.

ca·pa·bil·i·ty habilidad *f*.

ca·pa·ble *adj (skillful)* hábil; *(able)* capaz *(of* de).

ca·pac·i·ty capacidad *f; (position)* puesto *m;* **in her c. as manageress** en calidad de gerente.

cape *(garment)* capa *f*.

cap·i·tal *(town)* capital *f; (money)* capital *m; (letter)* mayúscula *f*.

cap·size **1** *vt* hacer zozobrar. **2** *vi* zozobrar.

cap·sule cápsula *f*.

cap·tain capitán *m*.

cap·ture *vt* capturar; *(of troops) (town)* tomar.

car coche *m*, *Am* carro *m;* **by c.** en coche.

car·a·mel azúcar *m* quemado; *(sweet)* caramelo *m*.

car·a·van *(vehicle)* caravana *f*.

car·bon carbono *m;* **c. copy** copia *f* al papel carbón.

car·bu·re·tor carburador *m*.

card tarjeta *f; (of cardboard)* cartulina *f; (in file)* ficha *f*.

card·board cartón *m*.

car·di·gan rebeca *f*.

car·di·nal **1** *n* cardenal *m*. **2** *adj* **c. numbers** números *mpl* cardinales.

care **1** *vi (be concerned)* preocuparse *(about* por); **I don't c.** no me importa; **who cares?** ¿qué más da? **2** *n (attention, protection)* cuidado *m; (worry)* preocupación *f;* **to take c. of** cuidar; *(business)* ocuparse de; **take c.** *(be careful)* ten cuidado; *(as farewell)* ¡cuídate!; **to take c. not to do sth** guardarse de hacer algo.

▸**care about** *vt (something)* preocuparse de; *(somebody)* tener cariño a.

▸**care for** *vt (look after)* cuidar; **I don't c. for that sort of thing** no me hace gracia una cosa así; **would you c. for a coffee?** ¿te apetece un café?

ca·reer carrera *f*.

care·free *adj* despreocupado, -a.

care·ful *adj* cuidadoso, -a; *(cautious)* prudente; **to be c.** tener cuidado; **be c.!** ¡ojo!

care·ful·ly *adv (painstakingly)* cuidadosamente; *(cautiously)* con cuidado.

care·less *adj* descuidado, -a; *(about clothes)* desaliñado, -a; *(driving)* negligente.

car fer·ry transbordador *m* para coches.

car·ing *adj* humanitario, -a, afectuoso, -a.

car·na·tion clavel *m*.

car·ni·val carnaval *m*.

car·ol villancico *m*.

carp *(fish)* carpa *f*.

car·pen·ter carpintero, -a *mf.*

car·pen·try carpintería *f.*

car·pet alfombra *f*; *(fitted)* moqueta *f.*

car·pet·ing (wall to wall) **c.** moqueta *f.*

car·pet sweep·er barredora *f* para alfombras.

car·riage *(horse-drawn)* carruaje *m*; *(on train)* vagón *m*, coche *m.*

car·ri·er *(company)* transportista *mf*; *(of disease)* portador, -a *mf*

car·rot zanahoria *f.*

car·ry 1 *vt* llevar; *(goods)* transportar; *(stock)* tener; *(responsibility, penalty)* conllevar; *(disease)* ser portador, -a de. **2** *vi (sound)* oírse.

▸**carry away** *vt* llevarse; **to get carried away** entusiasmarse.

▸**carry off** *vt (prize)* llevarse; **to c. it off** salir airoso, -a.

▸**carry on 1** *vt* continuar; *(conversation)* mantener. **2** *vi* continuar; **c. on!** ¡adelante!

▸**carry out** *vt (plan)* llevar a cabo; *(order)* cumplir; *(repairs)* hacer.

▸**carry through** *vt (plan)* completar.

carry·on *(baggage)* bolsa *f* de viaje.

cart 1 *n (horse-drawn)* carro *m*; *(handcart)* carretilla *f.* **2** *vt* acarrear.

▸**cart around** *vt fam* llevar y traer.

car·ton *(of cream etc)* paquete *m.*

car·toon *(strip)* tira *f* cómica; *(animated)* dibujos *mpl* animados.

car·tridge cartucho *m*; *(for pen)* recambio *m.*

carve *vt (wood)* tallar; *(stone, metal)* esculpir; *(meat)* trinchar.

car wash túnel *m or* tren *m* de lavado.

case[1] *(instance, medical)* caso *m*; *(legal)* causa *f*; **in any c.** en cualquier caso; **just in c.** por si acaso.

case[2] *(suitcase)* maleta *f*; *(small)* estuche *m*; *(soft)* funda *f.*

cash 1 *n* dinero *m* efectivo; **to pay c.** pagar al contado *or* en efectivo. **2** *vt (check)* cobrar.

cash·box caja *f.*

cash·ier cajero, -a *mf.*

cash price precio *m* al contado.

cash reg·is·ter caja *f* registradora.

ca·si·no casino *m.*

cas·se·role *(container)* cacerola *f*; *(food)* guisado *m.*

cas·sette casete *f.*

cas·sette play·er casete *m.*

cas·sette re·cord·er casete *m.*

cast 1 *vt** *(net, fishing line)* echar; *(light)* proyectar; *(glance)* lanzar; *(vote)* emitir; **to c. suspicion on sb** levantar sospechas sobre algn; *(play, film)* hacer el reparto de. **2** *n (plaster)* **c.** escayola *f*; *(of play)* reparto *m.*

cast-i·ron *adj (pan)* de hierro fundido; *(alibi)* a toda prueba.

cas·tle castillo *m*; *(in chess)* torre *f.*

cas·tor ruedecilla *f.*

ca·su·al *adj* informal; *(worker)* eventual; *(clothes)* (de) sport; *(unimportant)* casual.

ca·su·al·ty *(injured)* herido, -a *mf*; **casualties** víctimas *fpl.*

cat gato, -a *mf.*

cat·a·log catálogo *m.*

cat·a·pult tirachinas *m inv.*

ca·tas·tro·phe catástrofe *f.*

catch 1 *vt** *(thief, bus etc)* coger, *Am* agarrar; *(fish)* pescar; *(mouse etc)* atrapar; *(surprise)* sorprender; *(hear)* entender; **to c. fire** *(log)* prenderse; *(building)* incendiarse; **to c. one's breath** *(recover)* recuperar el aliento. **2** *vi** *(sleeve etc)* engancharse (**on** en); *(fire)* encenderse. **3** *n (of ball)* parada *f*, *(of fish)* presa *f*, *(on door)* pestillo *m*; *(drawback)* pega *f.*

▸**catch on** *vi (become popular)* ganar popularidad; *(understand)* caer en la cuenta.

▸**catch up** *vti* **to c. up (with) sb** *(reach)* alcanzar a algn; *(with news)* ponerse al corriente (**on** de); **to c. up with work** ponerse al día con el trabajo.

catch·ing *adj (disease)* contagioso, -a.

cat·e·go·ry categoría f.

▸**cater for, cater to** vt (need, taste) atender a.

cat·er·pil·lar oruga f.

ca·the·dral catedral f.

Cath·o·lic adj & n católico, -a (mf).

cause 1 n (of event etc) causa f; (reason) motivo m. **2** vt provocar; **to c. sb to do sth** hacer que algn haga algo.

cau·tion (care) cautela f; (warning) aviso m.

cau·tious adj cauteloso, -a.

cau·tious·ly adv con precaución.

cave cueva f.

▸**cave in** vi (roof etc) derrumbarse.

cav·i·ty (hole) cavidad f.

CCTV n closed-circuit television circuito m cerrado de televisión.

CD abbr of **compact disc** CD m.

cease 1 vt **to c. doing** or **to do sth** dejar de hacer algo. **2** vi cesar.

cease-fire alto m el fuego.

ceil·ing techo m.

cel·e·brate 1 vt celebrar. **2** vi divertirse.

cel·e·bra·tion celebración f.

ce·leb·ri·ty celebridad f.

cel·er·y apio m.

cell (in prison) celda f; (in organism) célula f.

cel·lar sótano m; (for wine) bodega f.

cel·lo·phane celofán m.

cell·phone n teléfono m móvil or Am celular. ›

ce·ment 1 n cemento m. **2** vt (fix with cement) unir con cemento.

ce·ment mix·er hormigonera f.

cem·e·ter·y cementerio m.

cent centavo m, céntimo m.

cen·ter 1 n centro m; **town c.** centro de la ciudad. **2** vt (attention, interest) centrar (**on** en).

cen·ti·grade adj centígrado, -a.

cen·ti·me·ter centímetro m.

cen·ti·pede ciempiés m inv.

cen·tral adj central.

Cen·tral A·mer·i·can adj & n centroamericano, -a (mf).

cen·tral·ize vt centralizar.

cen·tu·ry siglo m.

ce·ram·ic adj de cerámica.

ce·re·al cereal m.

cer·e·mo·ny ceremonia f.

cer·tain 1 adj (sure) seguro, -a; (true) cierto, -a; **to make c. of sth** asegurarse de algo; **to a c. extent** hasta cierto punto. **2** adv **for c.** a ciencia cierta.

cer·tain·ly adv desde luego; **c. not** de ninguna manera.

cer·tain·ty certeza f; (assurance) seguridad f.

cer·tif·i·cate certificado m; (from college) diploma m.

cer·ti·fy vt certificar.

chain 1 n cadena f; (of events) serie f; **c. of mountains** cordillera f. **2** vt **to c. (up)** encadenar.

chair silla f; (with arms) sillón m; (of meeting) presidente mf.

chair lift telesilla m.

chair·man presidente m.

cha·let chalet m, chalé m.

chalk (for writing) tiza f.

chal·lenge 1 vt desafiar; (authority etc) poner a prueba; (statement) poner en duda; **to c. sb to do sth** retar a algn a que haga algo. **2** n desafío m.

chal·leng·ing adj (idea) desafiante; (task) que presenta un desafío.

cham·ber C. of Commerce Cámara f de Comercio.

cham·pagne (French) champán m; (from Catalonia) cava m.

cham·pi·on campeón, -ona mf.

cham·pi·on·ship campeonato m.

chance 1 n (fortune) azar m; (opportunity) oportunidad f; **by c.** por casualidad; **to take a c.** arriesgarse; **(the) chances are that ...** lo más probable es que .... **2** vt arriesgar.

chan·cel·lor (head of state, in embassy) canciller m.

chan·de·lier araña f (de luces).

change 1 *vt* cambiar; **to c. gear** cambiar de marcha; **to c. one's mind/the subject** cambiar de opinión/de tema; **to c. trains** hacer trasbordo; **to get changed** cambiarse de ropa. **2** *vi* cambiar(se); **I think he's changed** lo veo cambiado. **3** *n* cambio *m*; *(money after purchase)* vuelta *f*; **for a c.** para variar; **c. of scene** cambio de aires; **small c.** suelto *m*.

▸**change over** *vi* **to c. over to sth** cambiar a algo, adoptar algo.

change·a·ble *adj (weather)* variable; *(person)* inconstante.

change·o·ver conversión *f*.

chang·ing room vestuario *m*.

chan·nel canal *m*; *(administrative)* vía *f*; **the English C.** el Canal de la Mancha.

chant 1 *n (of demonstrators)* eslogan *m*. **2** *vti (demonstrators)* corear.

cha·os caos *m*.

cha·ot·ic *adj* caótico, -a.

chap·el capilla *f*.

chapped *adj* agrietado, -a.

chap·ter capítulo *m*.

char *vt* carbonizar.

char·ac·ter carácter *m*; *(in play)* personaje *m*; *(person)* tipo *m*.

char·ac·ter·is·tic 1 *n* característica *f*. **2** *adj* característico, -a.

charge 1 *vt* cobrar; *(the enemy)* cargar contra; *(battery)* cargar; **to c. sb with a crime** acusar a algn de un crimen. **2** *vi (battery, troops)* cargar; **to c. about** andar a lo loco. **3** *n (cost)* precio *m*; *(in court)* acusación *f*; **bank charges** comisión *f*; **free of c.** gratis; **service c.** servicio *m*; **to be in c. of** estar a cargo de; **to take c. of** hacerse cargo de.

char·ger *n (for phone)* cargador *m*.

char·i·ty *(organization)* institución *f* benéfica.

charm 1 *n (quality)* encanto *m*; **lucky c.** amuleto *m*. **2** *vt* encantar.

charm·ing *adj* encantador, -a.

chart *(giving information)* tabla *f*;

(graph) gráfico *m*; *(map)* carta *f* de navegación; *(of hit records)* **the charts** la lista de éxitos.

char·ter 1 *n (of institution)* estatutos *mpl*; *(of rights)* carta *f*; **c. flight** vuelo *m* chárter. **2** *vt (plane, boat)* fletar.

chase *vt* perseguir; *(hunt)* cazar.

▸**chase after** *vt (someone)* correr detrás de; *(something)* andar tras.

▸**chase away, chase off** *vt* ahuyentar.

chasm sima *f*, *fig* abismo *m*.

chas·sis chasis *m inv*.

chat 1 *n* charla *f*. **2** *vi* charlar.

chat·ter 1 *vi (person)* parlotear; *(teeth)* castañetear. **2** *n (of person)* parloteo *m*; *(of teeth)* castañeteo *m*.

chat·ter·box parlanchín, -ina *mf*.

chat·ty *adj* hablador, -a.

chauf·feur chófer *m*.

cheap 1 *adj* barato, -a; *(fare)* económico, -a; *(contemptible)* bajo, -a. **2** *adv* barato.

cheap·ly *adv* en plan económico.

cheat 1 *vt* engañar; **to c. sb out of sth** estafar algo a algn. **2** *vi (at games)* hacer trampa; *(on an exam etc)* copiar(se). **3** *n (trickster)* tramposo, -a *mf*.

check 1 *vt* verificar; *(facts)* comprobar; *(tickets)* controlar; *(tires, oil)* revisar; *(stop)* detener; *(in chess)* dar jaque a. **2** *vi* comprobar. **3** *n (of documents etc)* revisión *f*; *(of facts)* comprobación *f*; *(in chess)* jaque *m*; *(in restaurant etc)* cuenta *f*.

▸**check in** *vi (at airport)* facturar; *(at hotel)* registrarse (**at** en).

▸**check off** *vt (names on list etc)* tachar.

▸**check on** *vt* verificar.

▸**check out 1** *vi (of hotel)* dejar el hotel. **2** *vt (facts)* verificar.

▸**check up** *vi* **to c. up on sth** comprobar algo.

check·book talonario *m* de cheques.

check·ers *(game)* damas *fpl*.

check in c. desk *(at airport)* mostrador *m* de facturación.

check·ing ac·count *n* cuenta *f* corriente.

check-mate jaque mate *m*.

check-out *(counter)* caja *f*.

check-room guardarropa *f*; *(for luggage)* consigna *f*.

check-up *(medical)* chequeo *m*.

ched·dar queso *m* cheddar.

cheek mejilla *f*; *(nerve)* cara *f*; **what c.!** ¡vaya jeta!

cheek·y *adj* fresco, -a.

cheer 1 *vi* aclamar. **2** *vt (applaud)* aclamar. **3** *n* viva *m*; **cheers** aplausos *mpl*; **cheers!** *(before drinking)* ¡salud!

▸**cheer up 1** *vi* animarse. **2** *vt* **to c. sb up** animar a algn.

cheer·ful *adj* alegre.

cheer·ing ovación *f*.

cheese queso *m*.

cheese·burg·er hamburguesa *f* de queso.

cheese·cake tarta *f* de queso.

chef chef *m*.

chem·i·cal 1 *n* sustancia *f* química. **2** *adj* químico, -a.

chem·ist farmacéutico, -a *mf*; *(scientist)* químico, -a *mf*.

chem·is·try química *f*.

cher·ry cereza *f*.

cher·ry bran·dy licor *m* de cerezas.

chess ajedrez *m*.

chess·board tablero *m* de ajedrez.

chest pecho *m*; *(for linen)* arca *f*; *(for valuables)* cofre *m*; **c. of drawers** cómoda *f*.

chest·nut *(nut)* castaña *f*.

chew *vt* masticar.

chew·ing gum chicle *m*.

chick pollito *m*.

chick·en *n* pollo *m*; *fam (coward)* gallina *f*.

▸**chicken out** *vi* rajarse (por miedo).

chick·en·pox varicela *f*.

chick·pea garbanzo *m*.

chic·o·ry achicoria *f*.

chief 1 *n* jefe *m*. **2** *adj* principal.

chief·ly *adv (above all)* sobre todo; *(mainly)* principalmente.

chil·blain sabañón *m*.

child *(pl children)* niño, -a *mf*; *(son)* hijo *m*; *(daughter)* hija *f*.

child care *(for working parents)* servicio *m* de guardería.

child·hood infancia *f*, niñez *f*.

child·ish *adj* pueril.

Chi·le·an *adj & n* chileno, -a *(mf)*.

chill 1 *n (illness)* resfriado *m*; *(coldness)* fresco *m*. **2** *vt (meat)* refrigerar; *(wine)* enfriar.

chilled *adj (wine)* frío, -a.

chil·(l)i chile *m*.

chill·y *adj* frío, -a.

chime *vi* repicar, sonar.

chim·ney chimenea *f*.

chim·ney flue cañón *m*.

chim·pan·zee chimpancé *m*.

chin barbilla *f*.

chi·na loza *f*; **bone c.** porcelana *f*.

Chi·nese 1 *adj* chino, -a. **2** *n (person)* chino, -a *mf*; *(language)* chino *m*.

chip 1 *n (in cup)* mella *f*; *(microchip)* chip *m*; *(in gambling)* ficha *f*; **chips** patatas *fpl* fritas. **2** *vt (china, glass)* mellar.

chi·ro·po·dist pedicuro, -a *mf*.

chis·el cincel *m*.

chives *npl* cebollino *m sing*.

choc-ice *(ice cream)* helado *m* cubierto de chocolate.

chock-a-block, chock-full *adj* hasta los topes.

choc·o·late 1 *n* chocolate *m*; **chocolates** bombones *mpl*. **2** *adj* de chocolate.

choice elección *f*; **a wide c.** un gran surtido; **there's no c.** no hay más remedio.

choir coro *m*.

choke 1 *vt (person)* ahogar; *(obstruct)* obstruir. **2** *vi* ahogarse.

cho·les·ter·ol colesterol *m*.

choose* 1 *vt* elegir; *(decide on)* optar por. **2** *vi* elegir.

choos·(e)y *adj* exigente.

chop 1 *vt (wood)* cortar; *(tree)* talar; *(food)* cortar a pedacitos. **2** *n (of lamb, pork etc)* chuleta *f.*

▶**chop down** *vt (tree)* talar.

▶**chop off** *vt (branch, finger etc)* cortar.

▶**chop up** *vt* cortar en pedazos.

chop·per *fam (helicopter)* helicóptero *m.*

chop·sticks *npl* palillos *mpl.*

chord *(musical)* acorde *m.*

cho·rus coro *m; (in song)* estribillo *m.*

chris·ten *vt* bautizar.

chris·ten·ing bautizo *m.*

Chris·tian *adj & n* cristiano, -a *(mf).*

Chris·tian name nombre *m* de pila.

Christ·mas Navidad *f;* Merry **C.** feliz Navidad; **C. Day** (día *m* de) Navidad *f;* **C. Eve** Nochebuena *f.*

chrome cromo *m.*

chron·ic *adj* crónico, -a.

chry·san·the·mum crisantemo *m.*

chub·by *adj* rellenito, -a.

chuck *vt fam* tirar.

chum compañero, -a *mf.*

chunk pedazo *m.*

church iglesia *f.*

chute *(for refuse)* conducto *m; (slide)* tobogán *m.*

ci·der sidra *f.*

ci·gar puro *m.*

cig·a·rette cigarrillo *m.*

cig·a·rette butt colilla *f.*

cig·a·rette light·er mechero *m.*

cin·e·ma cine *m.*

cin·na·mon canela *f.*

cir·cle 1 *n* círculo *m; (of people)* corro *m;* **in business circles** en el mundo de los negocios. **2** *vt (move round)* dar la vuelta a. **3** *vi* dar vueltas.

cir·cuit circuito *m.*

cir·cu·lar *adj & n* circular *(f).*

cir·cu·late 1 *vt (news)* hacer circular. **2** *vi* circular.

cir·cu·la·tion *(of blood)* circulación *f, (of newspaper)* tirada *f.*

cir·cum·fer·ence circunferencia *f.*

cir·cum·stance circunstancia *f,* **under no circumstances** en ningún caso.

cir·cus circo *m.*

cite *vt (quote)* citar.

cit·i·zen ciudadano, -a *mf.*

cit·y ciudad *f.*

cit·y cen·ter centro *m* urbano.

cit·y hall ayuntamiento *m.*

civ·ic *adj (authority, building)* municipal; *(duty, rights)* cívico, -a.

civ·il *adj* civil; *(polite)* educado, -a; **c. rights** derechos *mpl* civiles.

ci·vil·ian *adj & n* civil *(mf).*

civ·i·li·za·tion civilización *f.*

civ·il ser·vant funcionario, -a *mf.*

civ·il ser·vice administración *f* pública.

claim 1 *vt (benefit, rights)* reclamar; *(assert)* afirmar. **2** *n (demand)* reclamación *f, (right)* derecho *m; (assertion)* pretensión *f;* **to put in a c.** pedir una indemnización.

clam almeja *f.*

clamp wheel c. cepo *m.*

clap *vi* aplaudir.

clap·ping aplauso(s) *m(pl).*

clar·i·fy *vt* aclarar.

clar·i·net clarinete *m.*

clash 1 *vi (disagree)* estar en desacuerdo; *(colors)* desentonar; *(dates)* coincidir. **2** *n (sound)* sonido *m; (fight)* choque *m; (conflict)* conflicto *m.*

clasp 1 *n (on belt)* cierre *m; (on necklace)* broche *m.* **2** *vt (object)* agarrar.

class 1 *n* clase *f;* **second c. ticket** billete *m* de segunda (clase). **2** *vt* clasificar.

clas·sic 1 *adj* clásico, -a.

clas·si·fy *vt* clasificar.

class·mate compañero, -a *mf* de clase.

class·room aula *f.*

clause oración *f.*

claw *(of bird, lion)* garra *f*; *(of cat)* uña *f*; *(of crab)* pinza *f*.

clay arcilla *f*.

clean 1 *adj* limpio, -a; *(unmarked, pure)* sin defecto. **2** *adv* por completo; **it went c. through the middle** pasó justo por el medio. **3** *vt (room)* limpiar; **to c. one's teeth** lavarse los dientes.

clean·er limpiador, -a *mf*.

clean·ing limpieza *f*.

clean·ing wom·an señora *f* de la limpieza.

clean·ly *adv (to break, cut)* limpiamente.

cleans·ing c. lotion leche *f* limpiadora.

clear 1 *adj* claro, -a; *(road, day)* despejado, -a; *(obvious)* claro, -a; *(majority)* absoluto, -a; *(profit)* neto, -a; **to make sth c.** aclarar algo. **2** *adv* **stand c.!** ¡apártese!; **to stay c. of** evitar. **3** *vt (room)* vaciar; *(authorize)* autorizar; *(hurdle)* salvar; **to c. one's throat** aclararse la garganta; **to c. the table** quitar la mesa; **to c. sb of a charge** exculpar a algn de un delito. **4** *vi (sky)* despejar.

▸**clear away** *vt* quitar.

▸**clear off** *vi fam* largarse; **c. off!** ¡largo!

▸**clear out** *vt (room)* limpiar a fondo; *(cupboard)* vaciar.

▸**clear up 1** *vt (tidy)* recoger; *(arrange)* ordenar; *(mystery)* resolver. **2** *vi (weather)* despejarse.

clear·ance *(of area)* despeje *m*.

clear·ance sale liquidación *f* (de existencias).

clear-cut *adj* claro, -a.

clear·ing *(in wood)* claro *m*.

clear·ly *adv* claramente; *(at start of sentence)* evidentemente.

clear·way carretera *f* donde está prohibido parar.

clem·en·tine clementina *f*.

clench *vt (teeth, fist)* apretar.

cler·gy clero *m*.

cler·i·cal *adj (of an office)* de oficina.

clerk *(office worker)* oficinista *mf*; *(civil servant)* funcionario, -a *mf*; *(in shop)* dependiente, -a *mf*.

clev·er *adj (person)* inteligente; *(argument)* ingenioso, -a; **to be c. at sth** tener aptitud para algo.

click 1 *(sound)* clic *m*. **2** *vi* hacer clic (**on** en).

cli·ent cliente *mf*.

cliff acantilado *m*.

cli·mate clima *m*.

cli·max *(peak)* punto *m* culminante.

climb 1 *vt (ladder)* subir por; *(mountain)* escalar; *(tree)* subir a. **2** *vi* subir; *(plants)* trepar; *fig (socially)* ascender. **3** *n* subida *f*, ascensión *f*.

▸**climb down** *vi* bajar.

climb·er alpinista *mf*, *Am* andinista *mf*.

cling* *vi (hang on)* agarrarse (**to** a); *(clothes)* ajustarse; **to c. together** unirse.

clin·ic *(in state hospital)* ambulatorio *m*; *(specialized)* clínica *f*.

clip¹ *vt (cut)* cortar; *(ticket)* picar.

clip² *n (for hair)* pasador *m*; *(for paper)* sujetapapeles *m inv*; *(brooch)* clip *m*.

▸**clip on** *vt (brooch)* prender (**to** a); *(documents)* sujetar (**to** a).

clip·pers *npl (for hair)* maquinilla *f* para rapar; *(for nails)* cortauñas *m inv*; *(for hedge)* tijeras *fpl* de podar.

clip·ping *(newspaper)* recorte *m*.

cloak *(garment)* capa *f*.

cloak·room guardarropa *m*; *(toilets)* servicios *mpl*.

clock reloj *m*; **to be open round the c.** estar abierto las 24 horas (del día).

clock·wise *adj & adv* en el sentido de las agujas del reloj.

clone 1 *n* clon *m*. **2** *vt* clonar.

close¹ **1** *adj (in space, time)* cercano, -a; *(contact)* directo, -a; **c. to** cerca de; *(relationship)* estrecho, -a; *(friend)* íntimo, -a; *(weather)* bochornoso, -a; **c. together** juntos. **2** *adv* cerca; **they live c. by** *or* **c. at hand** viven cerca.

close² 1 *vt* cerrar; *(bring to a close)* concluir; *(meeting)* levantar. **2** *vi* *(shut)* cerrar(se). **3** *n* fin *m*, final *m*.

▸**close down** *vti* *(business)* cerrar para siempre.

▸**close in** *vi* to c. in on sb rodear a algn.

▸**close up** 1 *vt* cerrar del todo. **2** *vi* cerrarse; *(ranks)* apretarse.

closed *adj* cerrado, -a; **c.-circuit television** televisión *f* en circuito cerrado.

close·ly *adv* *(listen)* con atención; **c. contested/connected** muy reñido, -a/relacionado, -a; **to follow (events) c.** seguir de cerca (los acontecimientos).

clos·et *n* armario *m*.

clos·ing time hora *f* de cierre.

clo·sure cierre *m*.

clot 1 *n* *(of blood)* coágulo *m*. **2** *vi* coagularse.

cloth paño *m*; *(rag)* trapo *m*; *(tablecloth)* mantel *m*.

clothes *npl* ropa *f sing*.

clothes hang·er percha *f*.

clothes·line tendedero *m*.

clothes peg pinza *f*.

clothes shop tienda *f* de ropa.

cloth·ing ropa *f*.

cloud *n* nube *f*.

▸**cloud over** *vi* nublarse.

cloud·y *adj* *(sky)* nublado, -a.

clove *(of garlic)* diente *f*.

clown payaso *m*.

club *(society)* club *m*; *(for golf)* palo *m*; *(in cards)* trébol *m*.

clue *(sign)* indicio *m*; *(to mystery)* pista *f*; *(in crossword)* clave *f*; *fam* **I haven't a c.** no tengo (ni) idea.

clum·sy *adj* torpe; *(awkward)* tosco, -a.

clus·ter 1 *n* grupo *m*. **2** *vi* agruparse.

clutch 1 *vt* agarrar. **2** *n* *(in vehicle)* embrague *m*.

clut·ter *vt* **to c. (up)** llenar de cosas.

Co *abbr of* **Company** C., Cª, Cía.

coach 1 *n* autocar *m*; *(carriage)* carruaje *m*; *(of train)* coche *m*, vagón *m*.

2 *vt* *(student)* dar clases particulares a; *(team)* entrenar.

coal carbón *m*.

coal mine mina *f* de carbón.

coarse *adj* *(material)* basto, -a; *(language)* grosero, -a.

coast costa *f*.

coat 1 *n* *(overcoat)* abrigo *m*; *(short)* chaquetón *m*; *(of animal)* pelo *m*; *(of paint)* capa *f*. **2** *vt* cubrir (**with** de); *(with liquid)* bañar (**with** en).

coat hang·er percha *f*.

coat·ing capa *f*.

cob mazorca *f*.

cob·bled *adj* adoquinado, -a.

cob·web telaraña *f*.

co·caine cocaína *f*.

cock *(bird)* gallo *m*.

cock·le berberecho *m*.

cock·pit cabina *f* del piloto.

cock·roach cucaracha *f*.

cock·tail cóctel *m*.

co·coa cacao *m*.

co·co·nut coco *m*.

cod bacalao *m*.

code código *m*; *(symbol)* clave *f*; *(for telephone)* prefijo *m*.

cod-liv·er oil aceite *m* de hígado de bacalao.

co·ed 1 *adj* mixto, -a. **2** *n* colegio *m* mixto.

cof·fee café *m*.

cof·fee bar cafetería *f*.

cof·fee break pausa *f* para el café.

cof·fee·pot cafetera *f*.

cof·fee ta·ble mesita *f* de café.

cof·fin ataúd *m*.

co·gnac coñac *m*.

co·her·ent *adj* coherente.

coil 1 *vt* **to c. (up)** enrollar. **2** *n* *(loop)* vuelta *f*; *(of rope)* rollo *m*.

coin moneda *f*.

co·in·cide *vi* coincidir (**with** con).

co·in·ci·dence coincidencia *f*.

Coke® *abbr of* **Coca-Cola®** coca-cola *f*.

col·an·der colador *m*.

cold 1 *adj* frío, -a; **I'm c.** tengo frío; **it's c.** *(weather)* hace frío. **2** *n* frío *m*; *(ill-*

ness) resfriado *m;* **to catch a c.** resfriarse, acatarrarse; **to have a c.** estar resfriado, -a.

cold·ness frialdad *f.*

cole·slaw ensalada *f* de col.

col·lab·o·rate *vi* colaborar (**with** con).

col·lab·o·ra·tion colaboración *f.*

col·lapse 1 *vi (fall down)* derrumbarse; *(cave in)* hundirse. **2** *n (falling down)* derrumbamiento *m;* *(caving in)* hundimiento *m.*

col·lar *n (of garment)* cuello *m;* *(for dog)* collar *m.*

col·lar·bone clavícula *f.*

col·league colega *mf.*

col·lect 1 *vt (gather)* recoger; *(stamps etc)* coleccionar; *(taxes)* recaudar. **2** *vi (for charity)* hacer una colecta (**for** para). **3** *adv* **to call c.** llamar a cobro revertido.

col·lec·tion *(of mail)* recogida *f, (of money)* colecta *f, (of stamps)* colección *f, (of taxes)* recaudación *f.*

col·lec·tor *(of stamps)* coleccionista *mf.*

col·lege ≃ centro *m* de enseñanza superior, ≃ politécnico *m;* **to go to c.** seguir estudios superiores.

col·lide *vi* chocar.

col·li·sion choque *m.*

col·lo·qui·al *adj* coloquial.

co·logne (agua *f* de) colonia *f.*

Co·lom·bi·an *adj & n* colombiano, -a *(mf).*

co·lon *(punctuation)* dos puntos *mpl.*

colo·nel coronel *m.*

co·lo·ni·al *adj* colonial.

col·o·ny colonia *f.*

col·or 1 *n* color *m;* **c. film/television** película *f*/televisión *f* en color. **2** *vt* colorear.

col·ored *adj (pencil)* de color; *(photograph)* en color.

col·or·ful *adj (with color)* lleno, -a de color; *(person)* pintoresco, -a.

col·umn columna *f.*

co·ma coma *m;* **to go into a c.** entrar en coma.

comb 1 *n* peine *m.* **2** *vt* **to c. one's hair** peinarse.

com·bi·na·tion combinación *f.*

com·bine 1 *vt* combinar. **2** *vi* combinarse; *(companies)* asociarse.

come* *vi* venir; *(arrive)* llegar; *(happen)* suceder; **to c. apart/undone** desatarse/soltarse; **that's what comes of being too impatient** es lo que pasa por ser demasiado impaciente.

▸ **come about** *vi* ocurrir, suceder.

▸ **come across** *vt (thing)* encontrar por casualidad; **to c. across sb** tropezar con algn.

▸ **come along** *vi (arrive)* venir; *(make progress)* progresar; **c. along!** ¡venga!

▸ **come around 1** *vt (corner)* dar la vuelta a. **2** *vi (visit)* venir; *(regain consciousness)* volver en sí.

▸ **come away** *vi (leave)* salir; *(part)* desprenderse (**from** de).

▸ **come back** *vi (return)* volver.

▸ **come by 1** *vt (acquire)* adquirir. **2** *vi (visit)* **why don't you c. by?** ¿por qué no te pasas por casa?

▸ **come down** *vi* bajar; *(rain)* caer; **to c. down with the flu** pillar la gripe.

▸ **come forward** *vi (advance)* avanzar; *(volunteer)* ofrecerse.

▸ **come in** *vi (enter)* entrar; *(arrive)* *(train)* llegar; *(tide)* subir.

▸ **come into** *vt (enter)* entrar en; *(inherit)* heredar.

▸ **come off 1** *vt (fall from)* caerse de. **2** *vi (button)* caerse; *(succeed)* salir bien.

▸ **come on** *vi (make progress)* progresar; **c. on!** *(hurry)* ¡venga!

▸ **come out** *vi* salir *(of* de); *(book)* aparecer; *(stain)* quitarse; **to c. out (on strike)** declararse en huelga.

▸ **come over 1** *vi* venir. **2** *vt* **what's c. over you?** ¿qué te pasa?

▸ **come through** *vt (cross)* cruzar; *(illness)* recuperarse de; *(accident)* sobrevivir a.

▸ **come to 1** *vi (regain consciousness)*

volver en sí. **2** *vt (amount to)* ascender a; *(arrive at)* llegar a.

▸**come up** *vi (rise)* subir; *(sun)* salir; *(approach)* acercarse (**to** a); *(difficulty, question)* surgir.

▸**come up against** *vt (problems etc)* encontrarse con.

▸**come upon** *vt* = **come across**.

▸**come up to** *vt (equal)* igualar.

▸**come up with** *vt (solution etc)* encontrar.

come·back to make a c. reaparecer.

co·me·di·an cómico *m*.

com·e·dy comedia *f*.

com·fort 1 *n* comodidad *f*, *(consolation)* consuelo *m*. **2** *vt* consolar.

com·fort·a·ble *adj* cómodo, -a; *(temperature)* agradable.

com·fort·er edredón *m*.

com·ic 1 *adj* cómico, -a. **2** *n* tebeo *m*, comic *m*.

com·ic strip tira *f* cómica.

com·ing comings and goings idas y venidas *fpl*.

com·ma coma *f*.

com·mand 1 *vt* mandar. **2** *n (order)* orden *f*, *(authority)* mando *m*; *(of language)* dominio *m*.

com·mand·er comandante *mf*.

com·mem·o·rate *vt* conmemorar.

com·mence *vti* comenzar.

com·ment *n* comentario *m*.

▸**comment on** *vt (event etc)* comentar.

com·men·tar·y comentario *m*.

com·men·ta·tor comentarista *mf*.

com·merce comercio *m*.

com·mer·cial *adj* comercial.

com·mis·sion comisión *f*.

com·mit *vt (crime)* cometer; **to c. suicide** suicidarse.

com·mit·ment compromiso *m*.

com·mit·tee comisión *f*, comité *m*.

com·mod·i·ty artículo *m*.

com·mon *adj* común; *(ordinary)* corriente.

com·mon·ly *adv (generally)* en general.

com·mon·place *adj* corriente.

com·mon sense sentido *m* común.

com·mo·tion alboroto *m*.

com·mu·nal *adj (bathroom etc)* comunitario, -a.

com·mu·ni·cate 1 *vi* comunicarse (**with** con). **2** *vt* comunicar.

com·mu·ni·ca·tion comunicación *f*.

com·mun·ion comunión *f*.

com·mu·ni·ty comunidad *f*; *(people)* colectividad *f*.

com·mu·ni·ty cen·ter centro *m* social.

com·mute *vi* viajar diariamente al lugar de trabajo.

com·mut·er persona *f* que viaja diariamente al lugar de trabajo.

com·mut·ing desplazarse diariamente al lugar de trabajo.

com·pact 1 *adj* compacto, -a; *(style)* conciso, -a. **2** *n (for powder)* polvera *f*.

com·pact disc disco *m* compacto.

com·pan·ion compañero, -a *mf*.

com·pa·ny compañía *f*; *(business)* empresa *f*; **to keep sb c.** hacer compañía a algn.

com·pa·ra·ble *adj* comparable (**to**, **with** con).

com·par·a·tive 1 *adj* comparativo, -a; *(relative)* relativo, -a. **2** *n (in grammar)* comparativo *m*.

com·para·tive·ly *adv* relativamente.

com·pare 1 *vt* comparar (**to**, **with** con); **(as) compared with** en comparación con. **2** *vi* compararse.

com·par·i·son comparación *f*.

com·part·ment *(on train)* departamento *m*.

com·pass brújula *f*; **(pair of) compasses** compás *m*.

com·pat·i·ble *adj* compatible.

com·pel *vt (oblige)* obligar; **to c. sb to do sth** obligar a algn a hacer algo.

com·pen·sate *vti* compensar; **to c. sb for sth** indemnizar a algn de algo.

com·pen·sa·tion *(for loss)* indemnización *f.*

com·pete *vi* competir.

com·pe·tent *adj* competente.

com·pe·ti·tion competencia *f; (contest)* concurso *m.*

com·pet·i·tive *adj* competitivo, -a.

com·pet·i·tor competidor, -a *mf.*

com·pile *vt* compilar.

com·plain *vi* quejarse (**of**, **about** de).

com·plaint queja *f, (formal)* reclamación *f, (illness)* enfermedad *f.*

com·ple·ment 1 *n* complemento *m.* **2** *vt* complementar.

com·plete 1 *adj (entire)* completo, -a; *(absolute)* total. **2** *vt* completar; *(form)* rellenar.

com·plete·ly *adv* completamente, por completo.

com·plex 1 *adj* complejo, -a. **2** *n* complejo *m.*

com·plex·ion tez *f, fig* aspecto *m.*

com·pli·cate *vt* complicar.

com·pli·cat·ed *adj* complicado, -a.

com·pli·ca·tion complicación *f.*

com·pli·ment cumplido *m.*

com·pli·men·ta·ry *adj (praising)* elogioso, -a; *(free)* gratuito, -a.

com·ply *vi* obedecer; **to c. with** *(order)* cumplir con.

com·pose *vti* componer; **to be composed of** componerse de; **to c. oneself** calmarse.

com·posed *adj (calm)* sereno, -a.

com·pos·er compositor, -a *mf.*

com·po·si·tion *(essay)* redacción *f.*

com·pound compuesto *m.*

com·pre·hen·sive *adj* completo, -a; *(insurance)* a todo riesgo; **c. school** escuela *f* secundaria.

com·prise *vt (include)* comprender; *(consist of)* constar de; *(constitute)* constituir.

com·pro·mise acuerdo *m.*

com·pul·sive *adj* compulsivo, -a.

com·pul·so·ry *adj* obligatorio, -a.

com·put·er ordenador *m.*

com·put·er·ized *adj* informatizado, -a.

com·put·er pro·gram·mer programador, -a *mf* de ordenadores.

com·put·er sci·ence informática *f.*

com·put·ing informática *f.*

con *vt fam* estafar.

con·ceal *vt* ocultar; *(emotions)* disimular.

con·cede *vt* conceder.

con·ceit·ed *adj* presuntuoso, -a.

con·ceiv·a·ble *adj* concebible.

con·ceive *vti* concebir.

con·cen·trate 1 *vt* concentrar. **2** *vi* **to c. on sth** concentrarse en algo.

con·cen·tra·tion concentración *f.*

con·cern 1 *vt* concernir; *(worry)* preocupar. **2** *n (worry)* preocupación *f, (business)* negocio *m.*

con·cerned *adj (worried)* preocupado, -a (**about** por).

con·cern·ing *prep* con respecto a.

con·cert concierto *m.*

con·ces·sion concesión *f.*

con·cise *adj* conciso, -a.

con·clude *vti* concluir.

con·clu·sion conclusión *f.*

con·crete 1 *n* hormigón *m.* **2** *adj (made of concrete)* de hormigón; *(definite)* concreto, -a.

con·demn *vt* condenar.

con·den·sa·tion condensación *f.*

con·di·tion condición *f,* **on c. that ...** a condición de que ...

con·di·tion·er acondicionador *m.*

con·dom preservativo *m.*

con·duct 1 *n (behavior)* conducta *f.* **2** *vt (lead)* guiar; *(business, orchestra)* dirigir.

con·duct·ed tour visita *f* guiada.

con·duc·tor *(on bus)* cobrador, -a *mf* ; *(on train)* revisor, -a *mf, (of orchestra)* director, -a *mf.*

cone cono *m;* **ice-cream c.** cucurucho *m.*

con·fer 1 *vt* **to c. a title on sb** conceder un título a algn. **2** *vi (discuss)* deliberar.

con·fer·ence congreso *m*.
con·fess *vti* confesar; *(to priest)* confesarse.
con·fes·sion confesión *f*.
con·fet·ti confeti *m*.
con·fi·dence confianza *f*; **in c.** en confianza.
con·fi·dent *adj* seguro, -a.
con·fi·den·tial *adj (secret)* confidencial; *(entrusted)* de confianza.
con·fi·dent·ly *adv* con seguridad.
con·fine *vt* limitar.
con·firm *vt* confirmar.
con·fir·ma·tion confirmación *f*.
con·firmed *adj* empedernido, -a.
con·fis·cate *vt* confiscar.
con·flict 1 *n* conflicto *m*. **2** *vi* chocar (**with** con).
con·flict·ing *adj* contradictorio, -a.
con·form *vi* conformarse; **to c. to** or **with** *(customs)* amoldarse a; *(rules)* someterse a.
con·front *vt* hacer frente a.
con·fron·ta·tion confrontación *f*.
con·fuse *vt (person)* despistar; *(thing)* confundir (**with** con); **to get confused** confundirse.
con·fused *adj (person)* confundido, -a; *(mind, ideas)* confuso, -a.
con·fus·ing *adj* confuso, -a.
con·fu·sion confusión *f*.
con·gest·ed *adj (street)* repleto, -a de gente.
con·ges·tion congestión *f*.
con·grat·u·late *vt* felicitar.
con·grat·u·la·tions *npl* felicitaciones *fpl*; **c.!** ¡enhorabuena!
con·gre·gate *vi* congregarse.
con·gress congreso *m*.
con·gress·man diputado *m*, miembro *m* del Congreso.
con·gress·wom·an diputada *f*, miembro *f* del Congreso.
con·ju·gate *vt* conjugar.
con·ju·ga·tion conjugación *f*.
con·junc·tion conjunción *f*.
con·jur·er prestidigitador, -a *mf*.
con·jur·ing trick juego *m* de manos.

con man estafador *m*.
con·nect 1 *vt* unir; *(wires)* empalmar; *(install)* instalar; *(electricity)* conectar; *(on phone)* poner. **2** *vi* *(train, flight)* enlazar (**with** con).
con·nect·ed *adj* unido, -a; *(events)* relacionado, -a.
con·nec·tion conexión *f*, *(installation)* instalación *f*, *(rail, flight)* enlace *m*; *(of ideas)* relación *f*, *(person)* contacto *m*; **in c. with** *(regarding)* con respecto a.
con·quer *vt (enemy, bad habit)* vencer; *(country)* conquistar.
con·quest conquista *f*.
con·science conciencia *f*.
con·sci·en·tious *adj* concienzudo, -a.
con·scious *adj (aware)* consciente; *(choice etc)* deliberado, -a.
con·sen·sus consenso *m*.
con·sent 1 *n* consentimiento *m*. **2** *vi* consentir (**to** en).
con·se·quence consecuencia *f*.
con·se·quent·ly *adv* por consiguiente.
con·ser·va·tion conservación *f*.
con·ser·va·tive *adj* & *n* conservador, -a *(mf)*.
con·ser·va·to·ry *(greenhouse)* invernadero *m*.
con·serve 1 *vt* conservar. **2** *n* conserva *f*.
con·sid·er *vt (ponder on, regard)* considerar; *(keep in mind)* tener en cuenta; **to c. doing sth** pensar hacer algo.
con·sid·er·a·ble *adj* considerable.
con·sid·er·ate *adj* considerado, -a.
con·sid·er·a·tion consideración *f*.
con·sid·er·ing *prep* teniendo en cuenta.
con·sign·ment envío *m*.
con·sist *vi* **to c. of** consistir en.
con·sis·ten·cy *(of actions)* coherencia *f*, *(of mixture)* consistencia *f*.
con·sis·tent *adj (quality, results)* constante; *(behaviour)* coherente.

con·so·la·tion consuelo *m*; **c. prize** premio *m* de consolación.

con·sole¹ *vt* consolar.

con·sole² consola *f*.

con·so·nant consonante *f*.

con·spic·u·ous *adj* (*striking*) llamativo, -a; (*easily seen*) visible.

con·spir·a·cy conjura *f*.

con·sta·ble policía *m*.

con·stant *adj* constante; (*continuous*) incesante; (*loyal*) fiel.

con·stant·ly *adv* constantemente.

con·sti·pat·ed *adj* estreñido, -a.

con·sti·tu·tion constitución *f*.

con·straint coacción *f*.

con·struct *vt* construir.

con·struc·tion construcción *f*.

con·struc·tive *adj* constructivo, -a.

con·sul cónsul *mf*.

con·su·late consulado *m*.

con·sult *vti* consultar (**about** sobre).

con·sul·tan·cy (firm) asesoría *f*, consulting *m*.

con·sult·ant (*doctor*) especialista *mf*; (*in business*) asesor, -a *mf*.

con·sul·ta·tion consulta *f*.

con·sume *vt* consumir.

con·sum·er consumidor, -a *mf*.

con·sump·tion consumo *m*.

con·tact 1 *n* contacto *m*. **2** *vt* ponerse en contacto con.

con·tact lens·es lentes *fpl* de contacto.

con·ta·gious *adj* contagioso, -a.

con·tain *vt* contener.

con·tain·er (*box, package*) recipiente *m*; (*for shipping*) contenedor *m*.

con·tem·po·rar·y *adj & n* contemporáneo, -a (*mf*).

con·tempt desprecio *m*.

▸**con·tend with** *vt* (*problem, person*) enfrentarse a.

con·tent¹ contenido *m*; **table of contents** índice *m* de materias.

con·tent² *adj* contento, -a.

con·tent·ed *adj* satisfecho, -a.

con·test prueba *f*.

con·tes·tant concursante *mf*.

con·text contexto *m*.

con·ti·nent continente *m*; **(on) the C.** (en) Europa.

con·ti·nen·tal *adj* continental; (*European*) **C.** europeo, -a.

con·tin·u·al *adj* continuo, -a, constante.

con·tin·u·al·ly *adv* continuamente.

con·tin·ue *vt* continuar, seguir; **to c. to do sth** seguir *or* continuar haciendo algo.

con·tin·u·ous *adj* continuo, -a.

con·tin·u·ous·ly *adv* continuamente.

con·tra·cep·tion anticoncepción *f*.

con·tra·cep·tive *adj & n* anticonceptivo (*m*).

con·tract contrato *m*.

con·trac·tor contratista *mf*.

con·tra·dict *vt* contradecir.

con·tra·dic·tion contradicción *f*.

con·trar·y 1 *n* **on the c.** todo lo contrario. **2** *adv* **c. to** en contra de.

con·trast contraste *m*.

con·trast·ing *adj* opuesto, -a.

con·trib·ute 1 *vt* (*money*) contribuir; (*ideas, information*) aportar. **2** *vi* contribuir; (*in discussion*) participar; (*to publication*) colaborar (**to** en).

con·tri·bu·tion (*of money*) contribución *f*; (*to publication*) colaboración *f*.

con·trive *vi* **to c. to do sth** buscar la forma de hacer algo.

con·trived *adj* artificial.

con·trol 1 *vt* controlar; (*person, animal*) dominar; (*vehicle*) manejar; **to c. one's temper** controlarse. **2** *n* (*power*) control *m*; (*authority*) autoridad *f*; (*in car, plane*) (*device*) mando *m*; (*on TV*) botón *m* de control; **out of c.** fuera de control; **to be in c.** estar al mando; **to be under c.** (*situation*) estar bajo control; **to go out of c.** descontrolarse; **to lose c.** perder los estribos.

con·trol tow·er torre *f* de control.
con·va·lesce *vi* convalecer.
con·va·les·cence convalecencia *f.*
con·va·les·cent home clínica *f* de reposo.
con·ven·ience comodidad *f.*
con·ven·ience food comida *f* precocinada.
con·ven·ient *adj (arrangement)* conveniente; *(time)* oportuno, -a; *(place)* bien situado, -a.
con·vent convento *m.*
con·ver·sa·tion conversación *f.*
con·verse *vi* conversar.
con·ver·sion conversión *f* (**to** a; **in·to** en).
con·vert *vt* convertir (**into** en).
con·vert·i·ble 1 *adj* convertible. **2** *n (car)* descapotable *m.*
con·vey *vt (carry)* transportar; *(sound)* transmitir; *(idea)* comunicar.
con·vey·or belt cinta *f* transportadora.
con·vict *vt* declarar culpable a.
con·vic·tion *(belief)* creencia *f,* convicción *f;* *(for crime)* condena *f.*
con·vince *vt* convencer.
con·vinc·ing *adj* convincente.
con·voy convoy *m.*
cook 1 *vt* cocinar, guisar; *(dinner)* preparar. **2** *vi (person)* cocinar, guisar; *(food)* cocerse. **3** *n* cocinero, -a *mf.*
cook·book libro *m* de cocina.
cook·er cocina *f.*
cook·er·y cocina *f.*
cook·ie galleta *f.*
cook·ing cocina *f.*
cook·ing ap·ple manzana *f* ácida para cocinar.
cool 1 *adj* fresco, -a; *(calm)* tranquilo, -a; *(reserved)* frío, -a; **it's c.** *(weather)* hace fresquito. **2** *n (coolness)* fresco *m;* **to lose one's c.** perder la calma. **3** *vt (air)* refrescar; *(drink)* enfriar.
▶**cool down, cool off** *vi (something hot)* enfriarse; *fig* calmarse; *(feelings)* enfriarse.
cool·er *(for food)* nevera *f* portátil.

cool·ness *(calmness)* calma *f, (composure)* aplomo *m.*
co·op·er·ate *vi* cooperar.
co·op·er·a·tion cooperación *f.*
coop up *vt* encerrar.
co·or·di·nate 1 *vt* coordinar. **2** *n* **coordinates** *(clothes)* coordinados *mpl.*
cope *vi* arreglárselas; **to c. with** *(person, work)* poder con; *(problem)* hacer frente a.
cop·per *(metal)* cobre *m.*
cop·y 1 *n* copia *f, (of book)* ejemplar *m.* **2** *vti* copiar.
▶**copy down** *vt (letter etc)* pasar a limpio.
cord *(string)* cuerda *f, (electrical)* cordón *m.*
cor·dial *(drink)* licor *m.*
▶**cor·don off** *vt* acordonar.
cor·du·roy pana *f.*
core *(of fruit)* corazón *m; fig* centro *m.*
cork corcho *m.*
cork·screw sacacorchos *m inv.*
corn[1] *(maize)* maíz *m; (grain)* granos *mpl; (seed)* cereal *m.*
corn[2] *(on foot)* callo *m.*
corned beef carne *f* acecinada.
cor·ner 1 *n (of street)* esquina *f; (bend in road)* curva *f; (of room)* rincón *m; (in soccer)* **c. (kick)** córner *m.* **2** *vt (enemy)* arrinconar; *(market)* acaparar.
cor·net *(for ice cream)* cucurucho *m.*
corn·flakes *npl* copos *mpl* de maíz, cornflakes *mpl.*
corn·starch harina *f* de maíz.
corn·y *adj* gastado, -a.
cor·po·ral cabo *m.*
corps *(pl* **corps)** cuerpo *m.*
corpse cadáver *m.*
cor·rect 1 *vt (mistake)* corregir; *(child)* reprender. **2** *adj* correcto, -a; *(behavior)* formal.
cor·rec·tion corrección *f.*
cor·rect·ly *adv* correctamente.
cor·re·spond *vi* corresponder; *(by letter)* escribirse; **to c. to** equivaler a.

cor·re·spon·dence correspondencia f; **c. course** curso m por correspondencia.

cor·re·spond·ing adj (matching) correspondiente.

cor·ri·dor pasillo m.

cor·ru·gat·ed adj **c. iron** hierro m ondulado.

cor·rupt adj (person) corrupto, -a; (actions) deshonesto, -a.

cor·rup·tion corrupción f.

cos·met·ic cosmético m.

cos·mo·naut cosmonauta mf.

cost 1 n (price) precio m; coste m; **at all costs** a toda costa. **2** vti* costar, valer; **how much does it c.?** ¿cuánto cuesta?

Cos·ta Ri·can adj & n costarricense (mf).

cost·ly adj costoso, -a.

cos·tume traje m; **c. jewelery** bisutería f.

cot cuna f.

cot·tage casa f de campo.

cot·tage cheese requesón m.

cot·ton algodón m; (thread) hilo m.

cot·ton wool algodón m hidrófilo.

couch sofá m.

cou·chette litera f.

cough 1 vi toser. **2** n tos f.

▶ **cough up** vt fam **to c. up the money** soltar la pasta.

cough syr·up jarabe m para la tos.

could v aux pt of **can¹**.

coun·cil (body) consejo m; **town c.** consejo municipal.

coun·cil house ≃ vivienda f de protección oficial.

coun·cil·or concejal mf.

count¹ 1 vt contar. **2** vi contar; **that doesn't c.** eso no vale.

▶ **count in** vt incluir a, contar con.

▶ **count on** vt contar con.

▶ **count out** vt (banknotes) contar uno por uno.

count² (nobleman) conde m.

count·down cuenta f atrás.

coun·ter (in shop) mostrador m; (in bank) ventanilla f; (in board games) ficha f.

coun·ter- prefix contra-.

coun·ter·at·tack contraataque m.

coun·ter·clock·wise adj & adv en sentido inverso a las agujas del reloj.

coun·ter·foil (of check) matriz f.

coun·ter·part homólogo, -a mf.

coun·try (state) país m; (rural area) campo m; **native c.** patria f.

coun·try·side (area) campo m; (scenery) paisaje m.

coun·ty condado m.

coup golpe m; **c. d'état** golpe de estado.

cou·ple (of people) pareja f; (of things) par m; **a married c.** un matrimonio; **a c. of times** un par de veces.

cou·pon cupón m.

cour·age valor m.

cou·ra·geous adj valiente.

cou·ri·er (messenger) mensajero, -a mf; (guide) guía mf turístico, -a.

course (of river) curso m; (of ship, plane) rumbo m; (series) ciclo m; (for golf) campo m; (of meal) plato m; (degree) carrera f; (in single subject) curso m; (short course) cursillo m; **in the c. of construction** en vías de construcción; **a c. of treatment** un tratamiento; **of c.** claro, por supuesto; **of c. not!** ¡claro que no!

court (of law) tribunal m; (royal) corte f; (for sport) pista f, cancha f.

cour·te·ous adj cortés.

cour·te·sy cortesía f, educación f.

court·room sala f de justicia.

court·yard patio m.

cous·in primo, -a mf.

cov·er 1 vt cubrir (**with** de); (with lid) tapar; (hide) disimular; (protect) abrigar; (include) abarcar. **2** n cubierta f; (of chair etc) funda f; (of magazine) portada f; (in restaurant) cubierto m; **full c.** (in insurance) cobertura f completa; **to take c.** refugiarse.

▶ **cover over** vt (floor etc) recubrir.

▶ **cover up 1** vt cubrir; (crime) encubrir. **2** *vi* (*person*) abrigarse; **to c. up for sb** encubrir a algn.

cov·er·age cobertura *f*.

cov·er·alls *npl* mono *m sing*.

cov·er charge (*in restaurant*) precio *m* del cubierto.

cov·er·ing 1 *n* cubierta *f*. **2** *adj* (*letter*) explicatorio, -a.

cow vaca *f*.

cow·ard cobarde *mf*.

cow·ard·ice cobardía *f*.

cow·ard·ly *adj* cobarde.

cow·boy vaquero *m*.

co·zy *adj* (*atmosphere*) acogedor, -a; (*bed*) calentito, -a.

crab cangrejo *m*.

crack 1 *vt* (*cup*) partir; (*nut*) cascar; (*whip*) hacer restallar; (*joke*) contar. **2** *vi* (*glass*) partirse; (*wall*) agrietarse; *fam* **to get cracking on sth** ponerse a hacer algo. **3** *n* (*in cup*) raja *f*, (*in wall, ground*) grieta *f*, (*of whip*) restallido *m*; (*of gun*) detonación *f*; *fam* (*drug*) crack *m*.

▸**crack up** *vi* (*go insane*) desquiciarse; (*with laughter*) partirse de risa.

crack·er galleta *f* seca; (*firework*) petardo *m*.

crack·pot *fam* chiflado, -a *mf*.

cra·dle (*baby's*) cuna *f*.

craft (*occupation*) oficio *m*; (*art*) arte *m*; (*skill*) destreza *f*.

crafts·man artesano *m*.

craft·y *adj* astuto, -a.

cram 1 *vt* atiborrar; **crammed with** atestado, -a de. **2** *vi* (*for exam*) empollar.

cramp (*in leg etc*) calambre *m*.

cramped *adj* apretado, -a.

crane (*device*) grúa *f*.

crank (*handle*) manivela *f*, *fam* (*eccentric*) tipo *m* raro.

crash 1 *vt* **to c. one's car** tener un accidente con el coche. **2** *vi* (*car, plane*) estrellarse; (*collide*) chocar; **to c. into** estrellarse contra. **3** *n* (*noise*) estrépito *m*; (*collision*) choque *m*; (*of market*) quiebra *f*, **car/plane c.** accidente *m* de coche/avión.

crash course curso *m* intensivo.

crash hel·met casco *m* protector.

crash-land *vi* hacer un aterrizaje forzoso.

crate caja *f* (para embalaje).

crav·ing ansia *f*.

crawl 1 *vi* (*baby*) gatear; (*vehicle*) avanzar lentamente. **2** *n* (*swimming*) crol *m*.

cray·on cera *f*.

craze manía *f*, (*fashion*) moda *f*.

cra·zy *adj* loco, -a.

creak *vi* (*hinge*) chirriar.

cream (*of milk*) nata *f*, **c. colored** color crema.

cream cheese queso *m* crema.

cream·y *adj* cremoso, -a.

crease 1 *n* (*wrinkle*) arruga *f*, (*on trousers*) raya *f*. **2** *vt* (*clothes*) arrugar. **3** *vi* arrugarse.

cre·ate *vt* crear.

cre·a·tion creación *f*.

cre·a·tive *adj* (*person*) creativo, -a.

crea·ture (*animal*) criatura *f*.

crèche guardería *f*.

cred·i·ble *adj* creíble.

cred·it 1 *n* (*financial*) crédito *m*; (*merit*) honor *m*; **on c.** a crédito; **to be a c. to** hacer honor a. **2** *vt* **to c. sb's account** abonar en cuenta a algn.

cred·it card tarjeta *f* de crédito.

cred·it fa·cil·i·ties facilidades *fpl* de pago.

cred·it·wor·thy *adj* solvente.

creek cala *f*, riachuelo *m*.

creep* *vi* (*insect*) arrastrarse; (*cat*) deslizarse; (*person*) arrastrarse.

creep·y *adj fam* espeluznante.

cre·mate *vt* incinerar.

cre·ma·to·ri·um crematorio *m*.

crepe pa·per papel *m* crespón.

cress berro *m*.

crest (*of cock, wave*) cresta *f*, (*of hill*) cima *f*.

crew (*of plane, yacht*) tripulación *f*.

crib 1 *n* (*for baby*) cuna *f*. **2** *vt* (*copy*) copiar.

crick·et¹ (*insect*) grillo *m*.

crick·et² *(game)* cricket *m.*

crime delincuencia *f; (offence)* delito *m.*

crim·i·nal *adj & n* criminal *(mf).*

crip·ple lisiado, -a *mf.*

cri·sis *(pl crises)* crisis *f inv.*

crisp *adj* crujiente; *(lettuce)* fresco, -a.

cri·te·ri·on *(pl criteria)* criterio *m.*

crit·ic crítico, -a *mf.*

crit·i·cal *adj* crítico, -a.

crit·i·cal·ly *adv* c. ill gravemente enfermo, -a.

crit·i·cism crítica *f.*

crit·i·cize *vt* criticar.

cro·chet ganchillo *m.*

crock·er·y loza *f.*

croc·o·dile cocodrilo *m.*

cro·cus crocus *m.*

crook *fam* caco *m.*

crook·ed *adj (stick, picture)* torcido, -a; *(path)* tortuoso, -a.

crop cultivo *m; (harvest)* cosecha *f.*

▸**crop up** *vi* surgir.

cro·quet croquet *m.*

cross 1 *n* cruz *f; (of breeds)* cruce *m;* c. section sección *f* transversal. **2** *vt* cruzar. **3** *vi* cruzar; *(roads)* cruzarse. **4** *adj (angry)* enfadado, -a.

▸**cross off, cross out** *vt* tachar.

▸**cross over** *vi* cruzar.

cross·coun·try race cros *m.*

cross·eyed *adj* bizco, -a.

cross·ing pedestrian c. paso *m* de peatones; sea c. travesía *f.*

cross·ref·er·ence referencia *f* cruzada.

cross·roads cruce *m; fig* encrucijada *f.*

cross·walk paso *m* de peatones.

cross·word (puz·zle) crucigrama *m.*

crouch *vi* to c. (down) agacharse.

crow cuervo *m.*

crow·bar palanca *f.*

crowd 1 *n* muchedumbre *f; (gang)* pandilla *f;* the c. el vulgo; there was such a c. there había tantísima gente allí. **2** *vi* to c. in/out entrar/salir en tropel.

▸**crowd round** *vt* apiñarse alrededor de.

crowd·ed *adj* lleno, -a, atestado, -a.

crown corona *f.*

cru·cial *adj* decisivo, -a.

crude *adj (manners, style)* grosero, -a.

cru·el *adj* cruel (to con).

cru·el·ty crueldad *f* (to hacia).

cru·et c. set vinagreras *fpl.*

cruise 1 *vi (ship)* hacer un crucero; *(car)* viajar a velocidad constante; *(plane)* viajar a velocidad de crucero. **2** *n (on ship)* crucero *m.*

crumb miga *f.*

crum·ble 1 *vt* desmigar. **2** *vi (wall)* desmoronarse; *(bread)* desmigajarse.

crum·bly *adj* que se desmigaja.

crum·my *adj fam* chungo, -a.

crum·ple *vt (clothes)* arrugar.

crunch 1 *vt (food)* mascar. **2** *n* crujido *m.*

crunch·y *adj* crujiente.

crush 1 *vt* aplastar; *(wrinkle)* arrugar; *(grind)* moler. **2** *n (of people)* gentío *m.*

crust corteza *f.*

crutch *(for walking)* muleta *f.*

cry 1 *vi* gritar; *(weep)* llorar. **2** *n* grito *m; (weep)* llanto *m.*

▸**cry off** *vi* rajarse.

▸**cry out** *vi* gritar; to c. out for sth pedir algo a gritos.

▸**cry over** *vt* llorar por.

crys·tal cristal *m.*

cub *(young animal)* cachorro, -a *mf; (junior scout)* niño *m* explorador.

Cu·ban *adj & n* cubano, -a *(mf).*

cube cubo *m; (of sugar)* terrón *m.*

cu·bic *adj* cúbico, -a.

cuck·oo cuco *m.*

cu·cum·ber pepino *m.*

cud·dle 1 *vt* abrazar. **2** *vi* abrazarse.

▸**cuddle up to** *vt* acurrucarse contra.

cud·dly toy muñeco *m* de peluche.

cue *(in play)* pie *m;* indicación *f.*

cuff *(of sleeve)* puño *m; (of trousers)* dobladillo *m.*

cuff·links *npl* gemelos *mpl.*

cul-de-sac callejón *m* sin salida.

cul·prit culpable *mf.*

cult culto *m;* **c. film** película *f* de culto.

cul·ti·vate *vt* cultivar.

cul·ti·vat·ed *adj (person)* culto, -a.

cul·tur·al *adj* cultural.

cul·ture cultura *f.*

cul·tured *adj (person)* culto, -a.

cum·ber·some *adj (bulky)* voluminoso, -a.

cun·ning 1 *adj* astuto, -a. **2** *n* astucia *f.*

cup taza *f; (trophy)* copa *f.*

cup·board armario *m; (on wall)* alacena *f.*

cup·cake $\simeq$ magdalena *f.*

cur·a·ble *adj* curable.

curb bordillo *m.*

cure 1 *vt* curar. **2** *n (remedy)* cura *f,* remedio *m.*

cu·ri·os·i·ty curiosidad *f.*

cu·ri·ous *adj (inquisitive)* curioso, -a; *(odd)* extraño, -a.

curl 1 *vt (hair)* rizar. **2** *vi* rizarse. **3** *n (of hair)* rizo *m.*

▸**curl up** *vi (cat etc)* enroscarse; *(person)* hacerse un ovillo.

curl·y *adj* rizado, -a.

cur·rant pasa *f* (de Corinto).

cur·ren·cy moneda *f;* **foreign c.** divisas *fpl.*

cur·rent *adj* actual; *(opinion)* general; *(year)* en curso.

cur·rent ac·count cuenta *f* corriente.

cur·rent af·fairs actualidad *f sing* (política).

cur·rent·ly *adv* actualmente.

cur·ric·u·lum *(pl* curricula) plan *m* de estudios; **c. vitae** *(resume)* currículum *m* (vitae).

cur·ry curry *m.*

curse *vi* blasfemar.

cur·sor cursor *m.*

cur·tain cortina *f.*

curt·s(e)y 1 *n* reverencia *f.* **2** *vi* hacer una reverencia (**to** a).

curve 1 *n* curva *f.* **2** *vi (road, river)* describir una curva.

cush·ion cojín *m; (large)* almohadón *m.*

cus·tard natillas *fpl.*

cus·to·dy custodia *f;* **to take into c.** detener.

cus·tom *(habit)* costumbre *f.*

cus·tom·ar·y *adj* habitual.

cus·tom·er cliente *mf.*

cus·toms *n sing or pl* aduana *f.*

cus·toms du·ty derechos *mpl* de aduana.

cus·toms of·fi·cer agente *mf* de aduana.

cut 1 *vt** cortar; *(stone)* tallar; *(reduce)* reducir; *(divide up)* dividir (**into** en). **2** *vi** cortar. **3** *n* corte *m; (in skin)* cortadura *f, (wound)* herida *f, (with knife)* cuchillada *f, (of meat)* clase *f* de carne; *(reduction)* reducción *f.*

▸**cut away** *(remove)* cortar.

▸**cut back** *vt (expenses)* reducir; *(production)* disminuir.

▸**cut down** *vt (tree)* talar.

▸**cut down on** *vt* reducir.

▸**cut off** *vt (water etc)* cortar; *(place)* aislar; *(heir)* excluir.

▸**cut out 1** *vt (from newspaper)* recortar; *(delete)* suprimir; *(person)* **to be c. out for sth** estar hecho, -a para algo; *fam* **c. it out!** ¡basta ya! **2** *vi (engine)* calarse.

▸**cut up** *vt* cortar en pedazos.

cut·back reducción *f* (**in** de).

cute *adj* mono, -a, lindo, -a.

cut·ler·y cubiertos *mpl.*

cut·let chuleta *f.*

cut·ting 1 *n (from newspaper)* recorte *m; (plant)* esqueje *m.* **2** *adj (wind)* cortante; *(remark)* mordaz.

CV, cv *abbr of* curriculum vitae currículum *m* (vitae).

cy·cle 1 *n* ciclo *m; (bicycle)* bicicleta *f, (motorcycle)* moto *f.* **2** *vi* ir en bicicleta.

cy·cling ciclismo m.

cy·clist ciclista mf.

cyl·in·der cilindro m; (for gas) bombona f.

cym·bal platillo m.

cyn·i·cal adj (sceptical) descreído, -a, suspicaz; (unscrupulous) desaprensivo, -a, sin escrúpulos.

Czech 1 adj checo, -a. **2** n (person) checo, -a mf; (language) checo m.

D

dab vt (apply) aplicar; (touch lightly) tocar ligeramente.

dad, dad·dy fam papá m, papi m.

daf·fo·dil narciso m.

daft adj (idea) tonto, -a.

dai·ly 1 adj diario, -a. **2** adv diariamente. **3** n (newspaper) diario m.

dair·y lechería f; **d. farming** industria f lechera; **d. produce** productos mpl lácteos.

dai·sy margarita f.

dam (barrier) dique m; (lake) presa f.

dam·age 1 n daño m; (to health, reputation) perjuicio m. **2** vt (harm) dañar; (spoil) estropear.

dam·ag·ing adj perjudicial.

damn fam **1** interj **d. (it)!** ¡maldito, -a sea! **2** n **I don't give a d.** me importa un bledo. **3** adj maldito, -a. **4** adv (very) muy, sumamente.

damp 1 adj húmedo, -a; (wet) mojado, -a. **2** n humedad f.

damp·en vt humedecer.

damp·ness humedad f.

dance 1 n baile m; (classical, tribal) danza f. **2** vti bailar.

dance hall salón m de baile.

danc·er (by profession) bailarín, -ina mf; **she's a good d.** baila muy bien.

dan·de·li·on diente m de león.

dan·druff caspa f.

Dane danés, -esa mf.

dan·ger (peril) peligro m; (risk) riesgo m; (of war etc) amenaza f; **out of d.** fuera de peligro.

dan·ger·ous adj peligroso, -a; (risky) arriesgado, -a; (harmful) nocivo, -a; (illness) grave.

dan·ger·ous·ly adv peligrosamente.

Dan·ish 1 adj danés, -esa. **2** n (language) danés m.

dare 1 vi atreverse, osar. **2** vt (challenge) desafiar; **to d. to do sth** atreverse a hacer algo.

dar·ing adj osado, -a.

dark 1 adj (unlit, color) oscuro, -a; (hair, complexion) moreno, -a; (eyes, future) negro, -a. **2** n (darkness) oscuridad f.

dark-haired adj moreno, -a.

dark·ness oscuridad f.

dark-skinned adj de piel oscura.

dar·ling adj & n querido, -a (mf).

dart (missile) dardo m; **darts** sing (game) dardos mpl.

dart·board diana f.

dash 1 n (hyphen) guión m. **2** vi (rush) correr.

▶ **dash off** vi salir corriendo.

dash·board salpicadero m.

da·ta npl datos mpl

da·ta·base base m de datos.

data proc·ess·ing (act) proceso m de datos; (science) informática f.

date¹ n fecha f; (social event) compromiso m; (with girl, boy) cita f; (person dated) ligue m; **what's the d. today?** ¿qué día es hoy?; **out of d.** (ideas) anticuado, -a; (expression) desusado, -a; (invalid) caducado, -a; **to be up to d.** estar al día.

▶ **date back to, date from** vt datar de; (origins etc) remontarse a.

date² (fruit) dátil m.

dat·ed adj (idea) anticuado, -a; (fashion) pasado, -a de moda; (expression) desusado, -a.

daugh·ter hija f.

DATE AND TIME

Days of the week
lunes · martes · miércoles · jueves · viernes · sábado · domingo

Months of the year
enero · febrero · marzo · abril · mayo · junio · julio · agosto · septiembre · octubre · noviembre · diciembre

Days and months are written without a capital letter in Spanish. Dates are expressed in cardinal numbers (**March 3rd** *el tres de marzo*). The first of the month can be *el uno* or *el primero* (**May 1st** *el primero de mayo*)

What day is it today?
¿ Qué día es hoy?

It's Friday.
Es viernes.

What's today's date?
¿A qué fecha estamos hoy?

It's April 15th.
Estamos a quince de abril.

It's Wednesday April 12th.
Es miércoles doce de abril.

It's Thursday tomorrow.
Mañana es jueves.

I was born in 1980.
Nací en mil novecientos ochenta.

I came to Mexico a few years ago.
Vine a México hace unos años.

How long are you staying?
¿Hasta cuándo se van a quedar aquí?

We leave on Sunday/the 8th.
Nos vamos el domingo/el (día) ocho.

We got here last weekend.
Llegamos aquí el fin de semana pasado.

I waited all day.
Estuve todo el día esperando.

See you on Saturday!
¡Hasta el sábado!

See you next week!
¡Hasta la semana que viene!

Take it three times a day.
Tómeselo tres veces al día.

I see them every two weeks.
Les veo cada dos semanas.

People in Latin America sometimes use the 24-hour clock and write times with an *h* for hora(s). eg 7.30 a.m. = 7h30 (*las siete treinta*), 7.30 p.m. = 19h30 (*las diecinueve treinta*).

What's the time?
¿ Qué hora es?

It's 2 o'clock.
Son las dos.

It's nearly midday/midnight.
Son casi las doce de la mañana./
Es casi medianoche.

It's half four/four-thirty.
Son las cuatro y media/las cuatro treinta.

It's a quarter to seven.
Son las siete menos cuarto.

It's twenty after seven.
Son las siete y veinte.

I'll be there about eight.
Llegaré sobre las ocho.

I'll meet you in half an hour.
Nos vemos dentro de media hora.

My plane arrived two hours late.
Mi avión llegó con dos horas de retraso.

I got there early/late/on time.
Llegué pronto/tarde/a tiempo.

I don't have time (to...).
No tengo tiempo (de...).

It's time to go.
Es hora de irse.

daugh·ter-in-law nuera f.

daw·dle vi (walking) andar despacio; (waste time) perder el tiempo.

dawn amanecer m.

day día m; (on) the next or following d. el or al día siguiente; **the d. after tomorrow** pasado mañana; **the d. before yesterday** anteayer.

day·break amanecer m.

day·light luz f del día.

day re·turn (ticket) billete m de ida y vuelta para el mismo día.

day·time día m.

dead 1 adj muerto, -a; **he was shot d.** le mataron a tiros. **2** adv fam (tired, easy) muy.

dead-end (street) callejón m sin salida.

dead·line (date) fecha f tope; (time) hora f tope.

dead·ly 1 adj mortal; (weapon) mortífero, -a; (aim) certero, -a. **2** adv (extremely) terriblemente, sumamente.

deaf 1 adj sordo, -a; **d. mute** sordomudo, -a mf. **2** npl **the d.** los sordos.

deaf·ness sordera f.

deal (in business, politics) trato m; (amount) cantidad f, (at cards) reparto m; **business d.** contrato m; **to do a d. with sb** (transaction) cerrar un trato con algn; (agreement) pactar algo con algn; **it's a d.!** ¡trato hecho!; **a good d. (of sth)** una gran parte (de algo); **a good d. slower** mucho más despacio.

▶**deal* in** vt (goods) comerciar en; (drugs) traficar con.

▶**deal* out** vt repartir.

▶**deal* with** vt (firm, person) tratar con; (subject, problem) abordar; (in book etc) tratar de.

deal·er (in goods) comerciante mf; (in drugs) traficante mf.

deal·ings npl (relations) trato m sing; (in business) negocios mpl.

dear 1 adj (loved) querido, -a; (expensive) caro, -a; (in letter) **D. Andrew** Querido Andrew; **D. Madam** Estimada señora; **D. Sir(s)** Muy se-

ñor(es) mío(s). **2** n querido, -a mf; **my d.** mi vida. **3** interj **oh d.!, d. me!** (surprise) ¡vaya por Dios!; (disappointment) ¡qué pena!

death muerte f.

death cer·tif·i·cate certificado m de defunción.

de·bate 1 n debate m. **2** vti discutir.

deb·it 1 n débito m. **2** vt **to d. sb's account** cargar una suma en la cuenta de algn.

debt deuda f.

debt·or deudor, -a mf.

de·but debut m; **to make one's d.** debutar.

dec·ade década f, decenio m.

de·caf·fein·at·ed adj descafeinado, -a.

de·cay (of food, body) descomposición f, (of teeth) caries f inv; (of buildings) desmoronamiento m.

de·ceive vt (mislead) engañar; (lie to) mentir.

De·cem·ber diciembre m.

de·cent adj decente; (person) honrado, -a; (kind) simpático, -a.

de·cep·tion engaño m.

de·cide 1 vt decidir; **to d. to do sth** decidir hacer algo. **2** vi (reach decision) decidirse.

▶**decide on** vt (choose) optar por.

dec·i·mal 1 adj decimal; **d. point** coma f (de fracción decimal). **2** n decimal m.

de·ci·sion decisión f.

de·ci·sive adj (resolute) decidido, -a; (conclusive) decisivo, -a.

deck (of ship) cubierta f.

deck·chair tumbona f.

de·clare vt declarar; (winner, innocence) proclamar.

de·cline vi (decrease) disminuir; (amount) bajar; (business) decaer; (deteriorate) deteriorarse; (health) empeorar.

dec·o·rate vt (adorn) decorar (**with** con); (paint) pintar; (wallpaper) empapelar.

dec·o·ra·tion (decor) decoración f.

dec·or·a·tive *adj* decorativo, -a.

dec·o·ra·tor decorador, -a *mf*; *(painter)* pintor, -a *mf*; *(paper-hanger)* empapelador, -a *mf*.

de·crease 1 *n* disminución *f*; *(in speed, size, price)* reducción *f*. **2** *vi* disminuir; *(price, temperature)* bajar; *(speed, size)* reducirse. **3** *vt* disminuir; *(price, temperature)* bajar.

de·cree 1 *n* decreto *m*; *(by court)* sentencia *f*. **2** *vt* decretar.

ded·i·cate *vt* consagrar, dedicar.

ded·i·cat·ed *adj* dedicado, -a, entregado, -a.

de·duct *vt* descontar (**from** de).

de·duc·tion *(conclusion)* conclusión *f*; *(subtraction)* descuento *m*.

deed *(act)* acto *m*; *(legal document)* escritura *f*.

deep *adj* profundo, -a; *(breath, sigh)* hondo, -a; *(voice)* bajo, -a; **it's ten meters d.** tiene diez metros de profundidad.

deep-freeze 1 *n* congelador *m*. **2** *vt* congelar.

deer *n inv* ciervo *m*.

de·fault *n* **by d.** por defaut, por omisión; **to win by d.** ganar por incomparecencia del adversario.

de·feat 1 *vt* derrotar. **2** *n* *(of army, team)* derrota *f*.

de·fect defecto *m*.

de·fec·tive *adj* *(faulty)* defectuoso, -a.

de·fend *vt* defender.

de·fen·dant acusado, -a *mf*.

de·fense defensa *f*.

de·fen·sive 1 *adj* defensivo, -a. **2** *n* **to be on the d.** estar a la defensiva.

de·fi·ant *adj* *(behavior)* desafiante; *(person)* insolente.

de·fi·cien·cy falta *f*, carencia *f*.

de·fi·cient *adj* deficiente; **to be d. in sth** carecer de algo.

def·i·cit déficit *m*.

de·fine *vt* definir; *(duties, powers)* delimitar.

def·i·nite *adj* *(clear)* claro, -a; *(pro-gress)* notable; *(date, place)* determinado, -a.

def·i·nite·ly *adv* sin duda.

def·i·ni·tion definición *f*.

de·formed *adj* deforme.

de·frost *vt* *(freezer, food)* descongelar.

de·fy *vt* desafiar; *(law, order)* contravenir.

de·gen·er·ate *vi* degenerar (**into** en).

de·gree grado *m*; *(qualification)* título *m*; **to some d.** hasta cierto punto; **to have a d. in science** ser licenciado en ciencias.

de-icer anticongelante *m*.

de·ject·ed *adj* deprimido, -a.

de·lay 1 *vt* *(flight, train)* retrasar; *(person)* entretener; *(postpone)* aplazar. **2** *n* retraso *m*.

del·e·gate 1 *n* delegado, -a *mf*. **2** *vt* delegar (**to** en); **to d. sb to do sth** encargar a algn que haga algo.

del·e·ga·tion delegación *f*.

de·lete *vt* suprimir; *(cross out)* tachar.

de·lib·er·ate *adj* *(intentional)* deliberado, -a.

de·lib·er·ate·ly *adv* *(intentionally)* a propósito; *(unhurriedly)* pausadamente.

del·i·ca·cy *(food)* manjar *m* (exquisito).

del·i·cate *adj* delicado, -a; *(handwork)* fino, -a; *(instrument)* sensible; *(flavor)* fino, -a.

del·i·ca·tes·sen delicatessen *m*.

de·li·cious *adj* delicioso, -a.

de·light 1 *n* *(pleasure)* placer *m*; *(source of pleasure)* encanto *m*; **he took d. in it** le encantó. **2** *vt* encantar.

de·light·ed *adj* encantado, -a.

de·light·ful *adj* *(person)* encantador, -a; *(view)* muy agradable; *(meal, weather)* delicioso, -a.

de·lin·quent *adj & n* delincuente *(mf)*.

de·liv·er *vt* *(goods, letters)* repartir;

(parcel, manuscript etc) entregar; *(speech, verdict)* pronunciar; *(baby)* dar a luz.

de·liv·er·y *(of goods)* reparto *m*; *(of package, manuscript etc)* entrega *f*; *(of baby)* parto *m*.

de·lude *vt* engañar; **don't d. yourself** no te hagas ilusiones.

de·lu·sion *(state, act)* engaño *m*; *(false belief)* ilusión *f (vana)*; **delusions of grandeur** delirios *mpl* de grandeza.

de luxe *adj* de lujo *inv*.

de·mand 1 *n (request)* petición *f*; *(for pay rise, rights)* reclamación *f*; *(need)* necesidad *f*; *(claim)* exigencia *f*; *(economic)* demanda *f*; **to be in d.** ser solicitado, -a. **2** *vt* exigir; *(rights)* reclamar; **to d. that ...** insistir en que ... *(+ subjunctive)*.

de·mand·ing *adj (hard to please)* exigente; *(job)* agotador, -a.

dem·er·a·ra (su·gar) azúcar *m* moreno.

dem·o *fam (demonstration)* manifestación *f*; **d. tape** maqueta *f*.

de·moc·ra·cy democracia *f*.

dem·o·crat·ic *adj* democrático, -a.

de·mol·ish *vt (building)* derribar.

dem·o·li·tion demolición *f*.

de·mon demonio *m*.

dem·on·strate 1 *vt* demostrar. **2** *vi (politically)* manifestarse.

dem·on·stra·tion *(proof)* demostración *f*; *(explanation)* explicación *f*; *(political)* manifestación *f*.

de·mon·stra·tive *adj* franco, -a.

dem·on·stra·tor manifestante *mf*.

de·mor·al·ize *vt* desmoralizar.

den *(of animal)* guarida *f*; *(study)* estudio *m*.

de·ni·al *(of charge)* desmentido *m*; *(of rights)* denegación *f*.

den·im dril *m*; **denims** tejanos *mpl*, vaqueros *mpl*.

de·nounce *vt* denunciar.

dent 1 *n* abolladura *f*. **2** *vt* abollar.

den·tal *adj* dental.

den·tist dentista *mf*.

den·tures *npl* dentadura *f* postiza.

de·ny *vt (refuse)* negar; *(rumor, report)* desmentir; *(charge)* rechazar; **to d. sb sth** negarle algo a algn.

de·o·dor·ant desodorante *m*.

de·part *vi* marcharse, irse; *(from subject)* desviarse **(from** de).

de·part·ment sección *f*; *(in university)* departamento *m*; *(in government)* ministerio *m*.

de·part·ment store grandes almacenes *mpl*.

de·par·ture partida *f*; *(of plane, train)* salida *f*.

de·pend 1 *vi (rely)* fiarse **(on, upon** de). **2** *v impers (be determined by)* depender **(on** de); **it depends on the weather** según el tiempo que haga; **that depends** según.

de·pend·a·ble *adj (person)* fiable.

de·pen·dent 1 *adj* dependiente; **to be d. on sth** depender de algo. **2** *n* **his/her d.** la persona a su cargo.

de·pict *vt (in painting)* representar; *(describe)* describir.

de·plor·a·ble *adj* lamentable.

de·plore *vt* deplorar.

de·pos·it 1 *n (in bank, on rented car)* depósito *m*; *(in river, test tube)* sedimento *m*; *(in wine)* poso *m*; *(on purchase)* señal *f*; *(on house)* entrada *f*. **2** *vt* depositar; *(into account)* ingresar.

de·pot almacén *m*; *(bus garage)* cochera *f* (de autobuses).

de·press *vt (discourage)* deprimir.

de·pressed *adj (person)* deprimido, -a; **to get d.** deprimirse.

de·pres·sion depresión *f*.

de·prive *vt* privar **(of** de).

de·prived *adj* necesitado, -a.

depth profundidad *f*; *(of emotion)* intensidad *f*.

dep·u·ty *(substitute)* suplente *mf*; **d. head** subdirector, -a *mf*.

de·rail·ment descarrilamiento *m*.

der·e·lict *adj* abandonado, -a.

de·rive *vt* sacar, obtener.

de·scend 1 *vi* descender; **to d. from**

(be related to) descender de. **2** *vt (stairs)* bajar.

▶**descend upon** *vt (area)* invadir.

de·scen·dant descendiente *mf.*

de·scent descenso *m.*

de·scribe *vt* describir.

de·scrip·tion descripción *f; (type)* clase *f.*

des·ert[1] desierto *m.*

de·sert[2] *vt (place, family)* abandonar.

de·serve *vt (rest, punishment)* merecer; *(prize, praise)* ser digno, -a de.

de·sign 1 *n* diseño *m; (of building etc)* plano *m; (of room)* disposición *f; (pattern)* dibujo *m.* **2** *vt* diseñar.

des·ig·nate *vt* designar, nombrar.

de·sign·er diseñador, -a *mf.* **d. jeans** vaqueros *mpl* de marca.

de·sign·er clothes ropa *f* de marca.

de·sir·a·ble *adj* deseable; *(asset, offer)* atractivo, -a.

de·sire 1 *n* deseo *m;* **I haven't the slightest d. to go** no me apetece nada ir. **2** *vt* desear.

desk *(in school)* pupitre *m; (in office)* escritorio *m;* **(reception) d.** recepción *f.*

desk clerk recepcionista *mf.*

desk·top escritorio *m;* **d. publishing** autoedición *f.*

de·spair 1 *n* desesperación *f.* **2** *vi* desesperar(se) **(of** de).

des·patch *vt* = **dispatch.**

des·per·ate *adj (person, situation, action)* desesperado, -a; *(need)* apremiante; **to be d. for sth** necesitar algo con urgencia.

des·per·ate·ly *adv (need)* urgentemente; *(bad, busy)* terriblemente.

des·pi·ca·ble *adj* despreciable; *(behavior)* indigno, -a.

de·spise *vt* despreciar.

de·spite *prep* a pesar de.

des·sert postre *m.*

des·sert spoon cuchara *f* de postre.

des·ti·na·tion destino *m.*

des·ti·tute *adj* indigente.

de·stroy *vt* destruir; *(vehicle, old furniture)* destrozar.

de·struc·tion destrucción *f.*

de·struc·tive *adj (gale etc)* destructor, -a.

de·tach *vt (remove)* separar.

de·tach·a·ble *adj* separable **(from** de).

de·tached *adj (separated)* separado, -a.

de·tached house casa *f* independiente.

de·tail detalle *m,* pormenor *m.*

detailed *adj* detallado, -a.

de·tain *vt (police etc)* detener; *(delay)* retener.

de·tect *vt (error, movement)* advertir; *(difference)* notar; *(smell, sound)* percibir; *(discover)* descubrir.

de·tec·tive detective *mf;* **d. story** novela *f* policíaca.

de·tec·tor aparato *m* detector.

de·ten·tion *(of suspect etc)* detención *f.*

de·ter *vt (dissuade)* disuadir **(from** de); **to d. sb from doing sth** impedir a algn hacer algo.

de·ter·gent detergente *m.*

de·te·ri·o·rate *vi* deteriorarse.

de·te·ri·o·ra·tion empeoramiento *m; (of substance, friendship)* deterioro *m.*

de·ter·mi·na·tion *(resolution)* resolución *f.*

de·ter·mine *vt* determinar.

de·ter·mined *adj (person)* decidido, -a; *(effort)* enérgico, -a.

de·ter·rent fuerza *f* disuasoria.

de·tour desvío *m.*

dev·as·tat·ing *adj (news, results)* demoledor, -a.

de·vel·op 1 *vt* desarrollar; *(trade)* fomentar; *(plan)* elaborar; *(illness, habit)* contraer; *(interest)* mostrar; *(natural resources)* aprovechar; *(build on) (site)* urbanizar. **2** *vi (body, industry)* desarrollarse; *(system)* perfeccionarse; *(interest)* crecer.

▸**de·vel·op into** vt transformarse en.

de·vel·op·ment desarrollo m; (of trade) fomento m; (of skill) perfección f; (of character) formación f; (advance) avance m; (exploitation) explotación f; (of land, site) urbanización f; **there are no new developments** no hay ninguna novedad.

de·vi·ate vi desviarse (**from** de).

de·vice aparato m; (mechanism) mecanismo m.

dev·il diablo m, demonio m; fam **where the d. did you put it?** ¿dónde demonios lo pusiste?

de·vise vt idear.

de·vote vt dedicar.

de·vot·ed adj dedicado, -a (**to** a).

de·vo·tion devoción f; (to cause) dedicación f.

dew rocío m.

di·a·be·tes diabetes f.

di·a·bet·ic adj & n diabético, -a (mf).

di·ag·nose vt diagnosticar.

di·ag·no·sis (pl diagnoses) diagnóstico m.

di·ag·o·nal adj & n diagonal (f).

di·ag·o·nal·ly adv en diagonal, diagonalmente.

di·a·gram diagrama m; (of process, system) esquema m; (of workings) gráfico m.

di·al 1 n (of clock) esfera f; (on machine) botón m selector; (on radio) dial m; **d. tone** señal f de marcar. **2** vti marcar.

di·a·lect dialecto m.

di·a·log diálogo m.

di·am·e·ter diámetro m.

di·a·mond diamante m; (shape) rombo m.

di·a·per pañal m.

di·ar·rhe·a diarrea f.

di·a·ry diario m; (for appointments) agenda f.

dice 1 n dado m. **2** vt (food) cortar en cuadritos.

dic·tate 1 vt (letter, order) dictar. **2** vi (order about) dar órdenes.

dic·ta·tion dictado m.

dic·tion·ar·y diccionario m.

did pt of **do**.

die vi morir(se); **to be dying for sth / to do sth** morirse por algo / de ganas de hacer algo.

▸**die down** vi (wind) amainar; (noise, excitement) disminuir.

▸**die out** vi extinguirse.

die·sel (oil) gasoil m; **d. engine** motor m diesel.

di·et 1 n (normal food) dieta f; (selected food) régimen m. **2** vi estar a régimen.

dif·fer vi (be unlike) ser distinto, -a; (disagree) discrepar.

dif·fer·ence diferencia f; (disagreement) desacuerdo m; **it makes no d. (to me)** (me) da igual; **what d. does it make?** ¿qué más da?

dif·fer·ent adj distinto, -a.

dif·fer·ent·ly adv de otra manera.

dif·fi·cult adj difícil.

dif·fi·cul·ty dificultad f; (problem) problema m.

dig* 1 vt (earth) cavar; (tunnel) excavar; (hole) hacer. **2** vi cavar.

▸**dig out** vt fig (find) sacar; (information) descubrir.

▸**dig up** vt (weeds) arrancar; (buried object) desenterrar.

di·gest vt (food) digerir; (facts) asimilar.

di·ges·tion digestión f.

dig·ger excavadora f.

dig·it (number) dígito m.

dig·i·tal adj digital.

dig·ni·ty dignidad f.

di·lap·i·dat·ed adj en mal estado.

di·lem·ma dilema m.

di·lute vt diluir; (wine, milk) aguar.

dim 1 adj (light) tenue; (room) oscuro, -a; (outline) borroso, -a; (memory) vago, -a; fam (stupid) torpe. **2** vt (light) bajar.

dime moneda f de diez centavos.

di·men·sion dimensión f.

di·min·ish vti disminuir.

din estrépito m.

dine vi (formal use) cenar.

din·er *(person)* comensal *mf*; *(restaurant)* restaurante *m* barato.

din·ghy bote *m*; **(rubber) d.** bote *m* neumático.

din·gy *adj (street, house)* oscuro, -a; *(dirty)* sucio, -a; *(colour)* desteñido, -a.

din·ing car vagón *m* restaurante.

din·ing room comedor *m.*

din·ner *(at midday)* comida *f*; *(in evening)* cena *f.*

din·ner jack·et smoking *m.*

din·ner par·ty cena *f.*

din·ner ser·vice vajilla *f.*

di·no·saur dinosaurio *m.*

dip 1 *n (bathe)* chapuzón *m*; *(of road)* pendiente *f.* **2** *vi (road)* bajar.

▸**dip into** *vt (savings)* echar mano de.

diph·thong diptongo *m.*

di·plo·ma diploma *m.*

dip·lo·mat diplomático, -a *mf.*

dip·lo·mat·ic *adj* diplomático, -a.

di·rect 1 *adj* directo, -a. **2** *adv* directamente. **3** *vt* dirigir; **can you d. me to a bank?** ¿me puede indicar dónde hay un banco?

di·rec·tion dirección *f*; **directions** *(to place)* señas *fpl*; **directions for use** modo *m* de empleo.

di·rect·ly 1 *adv (above etc)* justo; *(speak)* directamente; *(at once)* en seguida. **2** *conj* en cuanto.

di·rec·tor director, -a *mf.*

di·rec·to·ry *(for telephone)* guía *f* telefónica.

di·rec·to·ry as·sis·tance *(service m de)* información *f.*

dirt suciedad *f.*

dirt-cheap *adv & adj fam* tirado, -a.

dirt·y 1 *adj* sucio, -a; *(joke)* verde; *(mind)* pervertido, -a; **d. word** palabrota *f*; **to get sth d.** ensuciar algo. **2** *vt* ensuciar.

dis·a·bil·i·ty discapacidad *f.*

dis·a·bled 1 *adj* minusválido, -a. **2** *npl* **the d.** los minusválidos *mpl.*

dis·ad·van·tage desventaja *f*; *(obstacle)* inconveniente *m.*

dis·a·gree *vi (differ)* no estar de acuerdo **(with** con); *(quarrel)* reñir **(about** por); **garlic disagrees with me** el ajo no me sienta bien.

dis·a·gree·a·ble *adj* desagradable.

dis·a·gree·ment desacuerdo *m*; *(argument)* riña *f.*

dis·ap·pear *vi* desaparecer.

dis·ap·pear·ance desaparición *f.*

dis·ap·point *vt* decepcionar.

dis·ap·point·ing *adj* decepcionante.

dis·ap·point·ment decepción *f.*

dis·ap·prove *vi* **to d. of** desaprobar.

dis·arm 1 *vt* desarmar. **2** *vi* desarmarse.

dis·as·ter desastre *m.*

dis·as·trous *adj* desastroso, -a.

disc disco *m.*

dis·card *vt (old things)* deshacerse de; *(plan)* descartar.

dis·charge *vt (prisoner)* soltar; *(patient)* dar de alta; *(soldier)* licenciar; *(dismiss)* despedir.

dis·con·tin·ued *adj (article)* que no se fabrica más.

dis·ci·pline 1 *n* disciplina *f.* **2** *vt (child)* castigar; *(worker)* sancionar.

disc jock·ey disc-jockey *mf*, pinchadiscos *mf inv.*

dis·close *vt* revelar.

dis·co discoteca *f.*

dis·com·fort *(pain)* malestar *m.*

dis·con·nect *vt* desconectar **(from** de); *(gas, electricity)* cortar.

dis·con·tent·ed *adj* descontento, -a.

dis·co·theque discoteca *f.*

dis·count descuento *m.*

dis·cour·age *vt (dishearten)* desanimar; *(advances)* rechazar.

dis·cov·er *vt* descubrir; *(missing person, object)* encontrar.

dis·cov·er·y descubrimiento *m.*

dis·creet *adj* discreto, -a.

dis·crim·i·nate *vi* distinguir **(between** entre); **to d. against sth/sb** discriminar algo/a algn.

dis·crim·i·na·tion *(bias)* discriminación *f.*

dis·cuss *vt* discutir; *(in writing)* tratar de.

dis·cus·sion discusión *f.*

dis·ease enfermedad *f.*

dis·em·bark *vti* desembarcar.

dis·fig·ured *adj* desfigurado, -a.

dis·grace 1 *n* desgracia *f.* **2** *vt* deshonrar.

dis·grace·ful *adj* vergonzoso, -a.

dis·guise 1 *n* disfraz *m;* **in d.** disfrazado, -a. **2** *vt (person)* disfrazar (**as** de).

dis·gust 1 *n* repugnancia *f,* asco *m.* **2** *vt (revolt)* dar asco a.

dis·gust·ed *adj* disgustado, -a, indignado, -a.

dis·gust·ing *adj* repugnante; *(behavior, state of affairs)* intolerable.

dish *(for serving)* fuente *f; (course)* plato *m;* **to wash** *or* **do the dishes** fregar los platos.

▸**dish up** *vt (meal)* servir.

dish·cloth trapo *m* de fregar.

di·shev·eled *adj (hair)* despeinado, -a; *(appearance)* fraudulento, -a.

dis·hon·est *adj (person)* poco honrado, -a.

dis·hon·es·ty *(of person)* falta *f* de honradez.

dish·tow·el paño *m* de cocina.

dish·wash·er lavaplatos *m inv.*

dis·il·lu·sioned *adj* desilusionado, -a.

dis·in·cen·tive freno *m.*

dis·in·fect *vt* desinfectar.

dis·in·fec·tant desinfectante *m.*

disk disco *m; (for computer)* disquete *m;* **d. drive** unidad *f* de disquete, disquetera *f.*

dis·like 1 *n* antipatía *f* (**for, of** a, hacia). **2** *vt* tener antipatía hacia.

dis·lo·cate *vt (joint)* dislocar.

dis·mal *adj (prospect)* sombrío, -a; *(place, weather)* deprimente; *(person)* triste.

dis·man·tle *vt* desmontar.

dis·may 1 *n* consternación *f.* **2** *vt* consternar.

dis·miss *vt (employee)* despedir.

dis·miss·al *(of employee)* despido *m.*

dis·o·be·di·ence desobediencia *f.*

dis·o·be·di·ent *adj* desobediente.

dis·o·bey *vt* desobedecer; *(law)* violar.

dis·or·der *(untidiness)* desorden *m; (riot)* disturbio *m; (illness)* trastorno *m.*

dis·or·gan·ized *adj* desorganizado, -a.

dis·patch *vt (mail)* enviar; *(goods)* expedir.

dis·pel *vt* disipar.

dis·pens·er *(device)* máquina *f* expendedora; **cash d.** cajero *m* automático.

dis·perse 1 *vt* dispersar. **2** *vi* dispersarse.

dis·play 1 *n (exhibition)* exposición *f, (on computer screen)* visualización *f.* **2** *vt* mostrar; *(goods)* exponer; *(on computer screen)* visualizar; *(feelings)* manifestar.

dis·pleased *adj* contrariado, -a.

dis·pos·a·ble *adj* desechable.

dis·pos·al at my d. a mi disposición.

dis·pose *vi* **to d. of** *(trash)* tirar; *(unwanted object)* deshacerse de.

dis·pute 1 *n (disagreement)* discusión *f, (quarrel)* disputa *f;* **industrial d.** conflicto *m* laboral. **2** *vt* refutar.

dis·qual·i·fy *vt (team)* descalificar; *(make ineligible)* incapacitar.

dis·re·gard *vt (ignore)* ignorar.

dis·re·spect·ful *adj* irrespetuoso, -a.

dis·rupt *vt (meeting, traffic)* interrumpir; *(order)* trastornar; *(schedule etc)* desbaratar.

dis·rup·tion *(of meeting, traffic)* interrupción *f; (of schedule etc)* desbaratamiento *m.*

dis·sat·is·fac·tion descontento *m.*

dis·sat·is·fied *adj* descontento, -a.

dis·sent 1 *n* disconformidad *f.* **2** *vi* disentir.

dis·solve 1 *vt* disolver. **2** *vi* disolverse.

dis·suade *vt* disuadir (**from** de).

dis·tance distancia *f*; **in the d.** a lo lejos.

dis·tant *adj (place, time)* lejano, -a; *(look)* distraído, -a; *(aloof)* distante.

dis·taste aversión *f*.

dis·taste·ful *adj* desagradable.

dis·tinct *adj (different)* diferente; *(smell, change)* marcado, -a; *(idea, intention)* claro, -a; **as d. from** a diferencia de.

dis·tinc·tion *(difference)* diferencia *f*; *(excellence)* distinción *f*; *(in exam)* sobresaliente *m*.

dis·tinc·tive *adj* distintivo, -a.

dis·tinct·ly *adv (clearly)* claramente; *(definitely)* sensiblemente.

dis·tin·guish *vt* distinguir.

dis·tin·guished *adj* distinguido, -a.

dis·tort *vt (misrepresent)* deformar.

dis·tract *vt* distraer.

dis·trac·tion *(interruption)* distracción *f*; **to drive sb to d.** volver loco a algn.

dis·tress *(mental)* angustia *f*; *(physical)* dolor *m*.

dis·tress·ing *adj* penoso, -a.

dis·trib·ute *vt* distribuir.

dis·tri·bu·tion distribución *f*.

dis·trib·u·tor distribuidor, -a *mf*; *(in car engine)* delco *m*.

dis·trict *(of country)* región *f*; *(of town)* barrio *m*; **d. attorney** fiscal *mf*.

dis·trust *vt* desconfiar de.

dis·turb *vt (inconvenience)* molestar; *(silence)* romper; *(sleep)* interrumpir; *(worry)* perturbar; *(papers)* desordenar.

dis·tur·bance *(commotion)* disturbio *m*.

dis·turb·ing *adj* inquietante.

ditch zanja *f*; *(at roadside)* cuneta *f*; *(for irrigation)* acequia *f*.

dit·to ídem.

di·van diván *m*.

dive 1 *n (into water)* zambullida *f*; *(of*

diver) buceo *m*; *(of plane)* picado *m*; *(in sport)* salto *m*. **2** *vi** zambullirse; *(diver)* bucear; *(plane)* bajar en picado; *(in sport)* saltar; **he dived for the phone** se precipitó hacia el teléfono.

div·er *(person)* buceador, -a *mf*; *(professional)* buzo *m*; *(from diving board)* saltador, -a *mf*.

di·ver·sion *(distraction)* distracción *f*.

di·vert *vt* desviar.

di·vide 1 *vt* dividir. **2** *vi (road, stream)* bifurcarse.

▶**divide off** *vt* separar.

▶**divide up** *vt (share out)* repartir.

div·i·dend dividendo *m*.

di·vine *adj* divino, -a.

div·ing submarinismo *m*; *(sport)* salto *m* de trampolín.

div·ing board trampolín *m*.

di·vi·sion división *f*; *(sharing)* reparto *m*; *(of organization)* sección *f*.

di·vorce 1 *n* divorcio *m*. **2** *vt* **she divorced him** se divorció de él.

di·vorced divorciado, -a; **to get d.** divorciarse.

diz·zi·ness vértigo *m*.

diz·zy *adj (person) (unwell)* mareado, -a.

DJ *abbr of* **disc jockey**.

do* 1 *v aux (in negatives and questions) (not translated in Spanish)* **do you drive?** ¿tienes carnet de conducir?; **don't you want to come?** ¿no quieres venir?; **he doesn't smoke** no fuma. ▪ *(emphatic) (not translated in Spanish)* **do come with us!** ¡ánimo, vente con nosotros!; **I do like your bag** me encanta tu bolso. ▪ *(substituting main verb) (not translated in Spanish)* **I don't believe him — neither do I** no le creo — yo tampoco; **I'll go if you do** si vas tú, voy yo; **I think it's dear, but he doesn't** a mí me parece caro pero a él no; **who went? — I did** ¿quién asistió? — yo. ▪ *(in question tags)*

he refused, didn't he? dijo que no, ¿verdad?; **I don't like it, do you?** a mí no me gusta, ¿y a ti? **2** vt hacer; (task) realizar; (duty) cumplir con; (distance) recorrer; **what can I do for you?** ¿en qué puedo servirle?; **what do you do (for a living)?** ¿a qué te dedicas?; **he's done it!** ¡lo ha conseguido!; **we were doing eighty** íbamos a ochenta. **3** vi (act) hacer; **do as I tell you** haz lo que te digo; **how are you doing?** ¿qué tal?; **to do well** (person) tener éxito; (business) ir bien; **five dollars will do** con cinco dólares será suficiente; **that will do!** ¡basta ya!; **this cushion will do as a pillow** este cojín servirá de almohada.

▸**do away with** vt (abolish) abolir; (discard) deshacerse de.

▸**do for** vt (destroy, ruin) arruinar; **I'm done for if I don't finish this** estoy perdido, -a si no acabo esto.

▸**do in** vt **I'm done in** (exhausted) estoy hecho, -a polvo.

▸**do out** vt (clean) limpiar a fondo.

▸**do over** vt (repeat) repetir.

▸**do up** vt (wrap) envolver; (belt etc) abrochar; (laces) atar; (dress up) arreglar; (redecorate) renovar.

▸**do with** vt **I could do with a rest** (need) un descanso no me vendría nada mal; **to have** or **be to do with** (concern) tener que ver con.

▸**do without** vt pasar sin, prescindir de.

dock 1 n **the docks** el muelle. **2** vi (ship) atracar.

dock·er estibador m.

dock·yard astillero m.

doc·tor médico, -a mf, (academic) doctor, -a mf.

doc·tor·ate doctorado m.

doc·trine doctrina f.

doc·u·ment documento m.

doc·u·men·ta·ry adj & n documental (m).

dodge vt (blow) esquivar; (pursuer) despistar; (tax) evadir.

dodg·em coche m de choque.

does 3rd person sing pres of **do**.

dog perro, -a mf.

dog·gy bag (in restaurant) bolsita f para llevarse los restos de la comida.

dog·house perrera f, fam **to be in the d.** estar en desgracia.

do·ing it was none of my d. yo no tuve nada que ver.

do-it-your·self bricolaje m.

doll (toy) muñeca f.

dol·lar dólar m.

doll·house casa f de muñecas.

dol·phin delfín m.

do·main (sphere) campo m, esfera f, (territory) dominio m; **d. name** nombre m de dominio.

dome cúpula f.

do·mes·tic adj (appliance, pet) doméstico, -a; (flight, news) nacional; (trade, policy) interior.

dom·i·nant adj dominante.

dom·i·nate vti dominar.

Do·min·i·can adj & n dominicano, -a (mf).

dom·i·no (pl **dominoes**) (piece) ficha f de dominó; **dominoes** (game) dominó m sing.

do·nate vt donar.

do·na·tion donativo m.

done 1 pp of **do**. **2** adj (finished) terminado, -a; (meat) hecho, -a; (vegetables) cocido, -a.

don·key burro, -a mf.

do·nor donante mf.

door puerta f.

door·bell timbre m (de la puerta).

door·knob pomo m.

door knock·er picaporte m.

door·man portero m.

door·mat felpudo m.

door·step peldaño m.

door·way entrada f.

dope n fam (drug) chocolate m; (idiot) tonto, -a mf.

dor·mi·to·ry (in school) dormitorio m; (in university) colegio m mayor.

dos·age (amount) dosis f inv.

dose dosis f inv.

dot punto *m*.

dot·ted line línea *f* de puntos.

dou·ble 1 *adj* doble. **2** *adv* doble; **folded d.** doblado, -a por la mitad; **it's d. the price** cuesta dos veces más. **3** *n* **to earn d.** ganar el doble.

▸**double back** *vi* to d. back on one's tracks volver sobre sus pasos.

▸**double up** *vi (bend)* doblarse.

dou·ble bed cama *f* de matrimonio.

dou·ble-breast·ed *adj* cruzado, -a.

dou·ble-cross *vt* engañar, traicionar.

dou·ble glaz·ing doble acristalamiento *m*.

doubt 1 *n* duda *f*; **no d.** sin duda; **to be in d. about sth** dudar algo. **2** *vt* dudar.

doubt·ful *adj* **I'm a bit d. about it** no me convence del todo; **it's d. whether ...** no se sabe seguro si ....

doubt·less *adv* sin duda, seguramente.

dough *(for bread)* masa *f*; *(for pastries)* pasta *f*; *fam (money)* pasta *f*.

dough·nut rosquilla *f*, dónut® *m*.

dove paloma *f*.

down 1 *adv (to or at lower level)* abajo; *(to floor)* al suelo; *(to ground)* a tierra; **to go d.** *(price, person)* bajar; **d. there** allí abajo; **to be d. with a cold** estar resfriado, -a; **to feel d.** estar deprimido, -a. **2** *prep (along)* por; **to go d. the road** bajar la calle.

down-and-out vagabundo, -a *mf*.

down·fall *(of régime)* caída *f*; *(of person)* perdición *f*.

down·hill *adv* **to go d.** ir cuesta abajo.

down·load *n* descarga *f*. *vt* bajar, descargar.

down pay·ment entrada *f*, fianza *f*.

down·pour chaparrón *m*.

down·right *adj (liar, rogue)* declarado, -a; *(lie)* manifiesto, -a. **2** *adv (totally)* completamente.

down·stairs 1 *adv* abajo; *(to first floor)* a la planta baja; **to go d.** bajar la escalera. **2** *adj (on first floor)* de la planta baja.

down-to-earth *adj* realista.

down·town *adv* en el centro (de la ciudad).

down·ward(s) *adv* hacia abajo.

doze 1 *vi* dormitar. **2** *n* cabezada *f*; **to have a d.** echar una cabezada.

▸**doze off** *vi* quedarse dormido, -a.

doz·en docena *f*; **half a d./a d. eggs** media docena/una docena de huevos.

Dr *abbr of* **Doctor** Doctor, -a *mf*, Dr., Dra.

drab *adj (dreary)* gris; *(color)* pardo, -a.

draft *(of cold air)* corriente *f* (de aire); **d. (beer)** cerveza *f* de barril.

draft·y *adj* **this room is very d.** en esta habitación hay mucha corriente.

drag 1 *vt (pull)* arrastrar. **2** *vi (trail)* arrastrarse; *(person)* rezagarse.

▸**drag along** *vt* arrastrar.

▸**drag on** *vi (war, strike)* hacerse interminable.

▸**drag out** *vt (speech etc)* alargar.

drag·on dragón *m*.

drain 1 *n (for water)* desagüe *m*; *(grating)* sumidero *m*. **2** *vt (marsh etc)* avenar; *(reservoir)* desecar. **3** *vi* **to d. (away)** *(liquid)* irse.

drain·ing board escurridero *m*.

drain·pipe tubo *m* de desagüe.

dra·ma *(play)* obra *f* de teatro; *(subject)* teatro *m*; *(tense situation)* drama *m*.

dra·mat·ic *adj (change)* impresionante; *(moment)* emocionante; *(of the theater)* dramático, -a.

dra·mat·i·cal·ly *adv (to change)* de forma espectacular.

drapes *npl* cortinas *fpl*.

dras·tic *adj (severe)* drástico, -a; *(change)* radical.

dras·ti·cal·ly *adv* radicalmente.

draw 1 *vt* (picture)* dibujar; *(line)*

trazar; *(curtains) (open)* descorrer; *(close)* correr; *(attract)* atraer; *(attention)* llamar. **2** *vi* (sketch)* dibujar; **they drew two all** empataron a dos. **3** *n (score)* empate *m*.

▸ **draw in** *vi (days)* acortarse.

▸ **draw near (to)** *vt* acercarse (a).

▸ **draw on** *vt (savings)* recurrir a; *(experience)* aprovecharse de.

▸ **draw out** *vt (withdraw)* sacar.

▸ **draw up** *vt (contract)* preparar; *(plan)* esbozar.

draw·back inconveniente *m*.

draw·er cajón *m*.

draw·ing dibujo *m*.

draw·ing pin chincheta *f*.

draw·ing room sala *f* de estar.

dread 1 *vt* temer. **2** *n* temor *m*.

dread·ful *adj (shocking)* espantoso, -a; *(awful)* fatal.

dread·ful·ly *adv (horribly)* terriblemente; *(very)* muy.

dream 1 *n* sueño *m*; *(marvel)* maravilla *f*. **2** *vti** soñar **(of, about** con).

▸ **dream up** *vt (excuse)* inventarse; *(plan)* idear.

drea·ry *adj (gloomy)* triste; *(boring)* aburrido, -a.

drench *vt* empapar.

dress 1 *n* vestido *m*; *(clothing)* ropa *f*. **2** *vt (person)* vestir; *(wound)* vendar; *(salad)* aliñar; **he was dressed in a gray suit** llevaba (puesto) un traje gris. **3** *vi* vestirse.

▸ **dress up** *vi (in disguise)* disfrazarse **(as** de); *(in best clothes)* vestirse elegante.

dress·er *(in bedroom)* tocador *m*.

dress·ing *(bandage)* vendaje *m*; **(salad) d.** aderezo *m*, aliño *m*; **d. room** *(in theater)* camerino *m*; **d. table** tocador *m*.

dress·mak·er modista *mf*.

drew *pt* of **draw**.

drib·ble 1 *vi (baby)* babear; *(liquid)* gotear. **2** *vt (ball)* regatear.

dried *adj (fruit)* seco, -a; *(milk)* en polvo.

drier = **dryer**.

drift *vi (boat)* ir a la deriva; *(person)* ir sin rumbo, vagar; **they drifted away** se marcharon poco a poco.

drill 1 *n (handtool)* taladro *m*; **dentist's d.** fresa *f*; **pneumatic d.** martillo *m* neumático. **2** *vt (wood etc)* taladrar.

drink 1 *vti** beber; **to have sth to d.** tomarse algo; **to d. to sth/sb** brindar por algo/algn. **2** *n* bebida *f*; *(alcoholic)* copa *f*.

▸ **drink up 1** *vt* beberse todo. **2** *vi* **d. up!** ¡bébelo todo!

drink·a·ble *adj* potable; *(not unpleasant)* agradable.

drink·ing wa·ter agua *f* potable.

drip 1 *n* goteo *m*; *fam (person)* necio, -a *mf*. **2** *vi* gotear; **he was dripping with sweat** el sudor le caía a gotas.

drip-dry *adj* que no necesita planchado.

drive 1 *vt* (vehicle)* conducir, *Am* manejar; *(person)* llevar; *(stake)* hincar; *(nail)* clavar; *(compel)* forzar; **to d. sb mad** volver loco, -a a algn. **2** *vi* (in car)* conducir, *Am* manejar. **3** *n* camino *m* de entrada; *(energy)* energía *f*; **to go for a d.** dar una vuelta en coche; **left-hand d.** conducción *f* por la izquierda.

▸ **drive along** *vti (in car)* conducir.

▸ **drive back 1** *vt (enemy)* rechazar; *(passenger)* llevar de vuelta a. **2** *vi* volver en coche.

▸ **drive in** *vt (nail)* clavar.

▸ **drive off** *vi* salir (en coche).

▸ **drive on** *vi (after stopping)* continuar.

▸ **drive out** *vt* expulsar.

▸ **drive up** *vi* llegar en coche.

driv·el tonterías *fpl*.

driv·er *(of car, bus)* conductor, -a *mf*; *(of train)* maquinista *mf*; *(of lorry)* camionero, -a *mf*.

driv·er's li·cense carnet *m* de conducir.

drive·way *n* camino *m* de entrada.

driv·ing les·son clase *f* de conducir.

driv·ing school autoescuela *f*.

driv·ing test examen *m* de conducir.

driz·zle 1 *n* llovizna *f*. **2** *vi* lloviznar.

droop *vi* (*flower*) marchitarse.

drop 1 *n* (*liquid*) gota *f*, (*descent*) desnivel *m*; (*in price*) bajada *f*, (*in temperature*) descenso *m*. **2** *vt* (*let fall*) dejar caer; (*lower*) bajar; (*reduce*) disminuir; (*abandon*) (*subject, charge etc*) abandonar. **3** *vi* (*of object*) caerse; (*voice, price, temperature*) bajar; (*speed*) disminuir.

▸ **drop behind** *vi* quedarse atrás.

▸ **drop in, drop round** *vi* (*visit*) pasarse (**at** por).

▸ **drop off 1** *vi* (*fall asleep*) quedarse dormido, -a. **2** *vt* (*deliver*) dejar en casa (de algn).

▸ **drop out** *vi* (*of college*) dejar los estudios; (*of society*) marginarse; (*of competition*) retirarse.

drought *n* sequía *f*.

drown 1 *vt* ahogar; (*place*) inundar. **2** *vi* ahogarse; **he drowned** murió ahogado.

drows·y *adj* soñoliento, -a; **to feel d.** tener sueño.

drug 1 *n* (*medicine*) medicamento *m*; (*narcotic*) droga *f*; **to be on drugs** drogarse. **2** *vt* (*person*) drogar; (*food, drink*) adulterar con drogas.

drug ad·dict drogadicto, -a *mf*.

drug·store establecimiento *m* donde se compran medicamentos, periódicos etc.

drum 1 *n* tambor *m*; (*container*) bidón *m*; **to play the drums** tocar la batería.

drum·mer (*in band*) tambor *mf*; (*in pop group*) batería *mf*.

drunk 1 *adj* borracho, -a; **to get d.** emborracharse. **2** *n* borracho, -a *mf*.

drunk·ard borracho, -a *mf*.

drunk·en *adj* (*driver*) borracho, -a; **d. driving** conducir en estado de embriaguez.

dry 1 *adj* seco, -a. **2** *vt* secar. **3** *vi* to **d. (off)** secarse.

▸ **dry up 1** *vt* secar. **2** *vi* secarse.

dry-clean *vt* lavar en seco.

dry-clean·er (*shop*) tintorería *f*.

dry·er secadora *f*.

du·al *adj* doble, dual.

dub *vt* (*subtitle*) doblar (**into** a).

du·bi·ous *adj* (*morals etc*) dudoso, -a; (*doubting*) indeciso, -a.

duch·ess duquesa *f*.

duck¹ pato, -a *mf*; (*as food*) pato *m*.

duck² **1** *vi* (*bow down*) agacharse. **2** *vt* (*evade*) esquivar.

due 1 *adj* (*expected*) esperado, -a; (*money*) pagadero, -a; **the train is d. (to arrive) at ten** el tren debe llegar a las diez; **in d. course** a su debido tiempo; **to be d. to** deberse a. **2** *adv* (*north etc*) derecho hacia.

du·el duelo *m*.

duf·fel coat trenca *f*.

duke duque *m*.

dull *adj* (*boring*) pesado, -a; (*place*) sin interés; (*light*) apagado, -a; (*weather*) gris; (*sound, ache*) sordo, -a.

du·ly *adv* (*properly*) debidamente; (*as expected*) como era de esperar.

dumb *adj* mudo, -a; (*stupid*) tonto, -a.

dump 1 *n* (*tip*) vertedero *m*; *fam* (*place*) lugar *m* de mala muerte; (*town*) poblacho *m*; (*dwelling*) tugurio *m*. **2** *vt* (*garbage*) verter.

dump truck volquete *m*.

dun·ga·rees *npl* mono *m sing*.

du·plex casa *f* adosada; **d. apart·ment** dúplex *m inv*.

du·pli·cate duplicado *m*; **in d.** por duplicado.

du·ra·ble *adj* duradero, -a.

du·ra·tion duración *f*.

dur·ing *prep* durante.

dusk crepúsculo *m*; **at d.** al anochecer.

dust 1 *n* polvo *m*. **2** *vt* (*furniture*) quitar el polvo a.

dust·er (*for housework*) trapo *m* (del polvo).

dust·y *adj* polvoriento, -a.

Dutch 1 *adj* holandés, -esa. **2** *n* (*language*) holandés *m*; **the D.** los holandeses *mpl*.

Dutch·man holandés *m.*

Dutch·wom·an holandesa *f.*

du·ty deber *m; (task)* función *f; (tax)* impuesto *m;* **to be on d.** estar de servicio; *(doctor, soldier)* estar de guardia; **d. chemist** farmacia *f* de guardia; **customs d.** derechos *mpl* de aduana.

du·ty-free *adj* libre de impuestos.

du·vet edredón *m.*

DVD *abbr of* **digital versatile disk, digital video disk** DVD *m;* **DVD player** reproductor *m or* lector *m* de DVD.

dwarf *(pl* **dwarves)** enano, -a *mf.*

dye 1 *n* tinte *m.* **2** *vt* teñir; **to d. one's hair black** teñirse el pelo de negro.

dy·nam·ic *adj* dinámico, -a.

dy·na·mite dinamita *f.*

dy·na·mo dínamo *f.*

dys·lex·ic *adj* disléxico, -a.

E

each 1 *adj* cada; **e. day/month** todos los días/meses. **2** *pron* cada uno, -a; **we bought one e.** nos compramos uno cada uno; **e. other** el uno al otro; **they hate e. other** se odian.

ea·ger *adj (anxious)* impaciente **(to** por); *(keen)* deseoso, -a.

ea·ger·ly *adv (anxiously)* con impaciencia; *(keenly)* con ilusión.

ea·ger·ness impaciencia *f* **(to do** por hacer); *(keenness)* afán *m.*

ea·gle águila *f.*

ear oreja *f; (inner ear)* oído *m; (of corn)* espiga *f.*

ear·ache dolor *m* de oídos.

ear·ly 1 *adj (before usual time)* temprano, -a; **to have an e. night** acostarse pronto; **you're e.!** ¡qué pronto has venido! • *(at first stage, period)*

in her e. forties a los cuarenta y pocos; **in e. July** a principios de julio. • *(in the near future)* **an e. reply** una respuesta pronta. **2** *adv (before the expected time)* temprano; **to leave e.** irse pronto; **e. on** al principio; **earlier on** antes; **five minutes e.** con cinco minutos de adelanto; **as e. as possible** tan pronto como sea posible; **to book e.** reservar con tiempo; **at the earliest** cuanto antes.

earn *vt* ganarse; *(money)* ganar; **to earn one's living** ganarse la vida.

ear·nest 1 *adj* serio, -a, formal. **2** *n* **in e.** de veras, en serio.

earn·ings *npl* ingresos *mpl.*

ear·phones *npl* auriculares *mpl,* cascos *mpl.*

ear·plug tapón *m* para los oídos.

ear·ring pendiente *m.*

earth *n* tierra *f; (electric)* toma *f* de tierra; **to be down to e.** ser práctico, -a; *fam* **where/why on e. ...?** ¿pero dónde/por qué demonios ...?

earth·quake terremoto *m.*

ease 1 *n (lack of difficulty)* facilidad *f; (affluence)* comodidad *f; (freedom from discomfort)* tranquilidad *f;* **at e.** relajado, -a. **2** *vt (pain)* aliviar; *(move gently)* deslizar con cuidado.

▸ **ease off, ease up** *vi (decrease)* disminuir; *(slow down)* ir más despacio.

ea·sel caballete *m.*

eas·i·ly *adv* fácilmente; **e. the best** con mucho el mejor.

east 1 *n* este *m.* **2** *adj* del este, oriental. **3** *adv* al este.

east·bound *adj* (con) dirección este.

Eas·ter Semana Santa *f;* **E. Sunday** Domingo *m* de Resurrección.

east·ern *adj* oriental, del este.

east·ward(s) *adv* hacia el este.

eas·y 1 *adj* fácil; *(comfortable)* cómodo, -a; *fam* **I'm e.!** me da lo mismo; **e. chair** butacón *m.* **2** *adv* **go e. on the wine** no te pases con el vino; **to take things e.** tomarse las cosas con calma; **take it e.!** ¡tranquilo!

eas·y-go·ing adj (calm) tranquilo, -a; (lax) despreocupado, -a; (undemanding) poco exigente.

eat* vt comer.

▸**eat away** vt desgastar; (metal) corroer.

▸**eat out** vi comer fuera.

▸**eat up** vt (meal) terminar; (petrol) consumir; (miles) tragar.

eau de Co·logne colonia f.

e-ban·king n banca f por Internet.

ec·cen·tric adj & n excéntrico, -a (mf).

ech·o 1 n (pl echoes) eco m. **2** vt (repeat) repetir. **3** vi resonar.

ec·o·nom·ic adj económico, -a; (profitable) rentable.

ec·o·nom·i·cal adj económico, -a.

e·con·o·mize vi economizar (on en).

e·con·o·my (national) economía f; (saving) ahorro m; **e. class** (clase f) turista f.

edge 1 n borde m; (of knife) filo m; (of water) orilla f; **on the e. of town** en las afueras de la ciudad; **to have the e. on sb** llevar ventaja a algn; **to be on e.** tener los nervios de punta. **2** vi **to e. closer** acercarse lentamente; **to e. forward** avanzar poco a poco.

ed·i·ble adj comestible.

ed·it vt editar; (proofs) corregir; (newspaper) ser redactor, -a de; (film, TV program) montar; (cut) cortar.

▸**edit out** vt suprimir.

e·di·tion edición f.

ed·i·tor (of book) editor, -a mf; (of newspaper) redactor, -a mf; (of film, TV program) montador, -a mf.

ed·i·to·ri·al 1 adj e. **staff** redacción f. **2** n editorial m.

ed·u·cate vt educar.

ed·u·cat·ed adj culto, -a.

ed·u·ca·tion (schooling) enseñanza f; (training) formación f; (studies) estudios mpl; (culture) cultura f.

ed·u·ca·tion·al adj educativo, -a.

eel anguila f.

ef·fect efecto m; (impression) impresión f; **in e.** efectivamente; **to come into e.** entrar en vigor; **to have an e. on** afectar a; **to no e.** sin resultado alguno; **effects** (possessions) efectos mpl.

ef·fec·tive adj (successful) eficaz; (impressive) impresionante.

ef·fec·tive·ly adv (successfully) eficazmente; (in fact) en efecto.

ef·fi·cien·cy (of person) eficacia f; (of machine) rendimiento m.

ef·fi·cient adj eficaz; (person) eficiente; (machine) de buen rendimiento.

ef·fi·cient·ly adv eficazmente; **to work e.** tener buen rendimiento.

ef·fort esfuerzo m; (attempt) intento m; **to make an e.** hacer un esfuerzo.

eg abbr p. ej.

egg 1 n huevo m. **2** vt **to e. sb on (to do sth)** empujar a algn (a hacer algo).

egg cup huevera f.

egg·plant berenjena f.

egg tim·er reloj m de arena.

egg white clara f de huevo.

e·go ego m; fam amor propio; fam **e. trip** autobombo m.

E·gyp·tian adj & n egipcio, -a (mf).

ei·der·down edredón m.

eight adj & n ocho (m) inv.

eight·een adj & n dieciocho (m) inv.

eighth adj & n octavo, -a (mf).

eight·y adj & n ochenta (m) inv.

ei·ther 1 pron (affirmative) cualquiera; (negative) ninguno, ninguna, ni el uno ni el otro, ni la una ni la otra; **e. of them** cualquiera de los dos; **I don't want e.** no quiero ninguno de los dos. **2** adj (both) cada, los dos, las dos; **on e. side** en ambos lados. **3** conj o; **e. ... or ...** o ...; **e. Friday or Saturday** o (bien) el viernes o el sábado. **4** adv (after negative) tampoco; **I don't want to do it e.** yo tampoco quiero hacerlo.

e·lab·o·rate 1 vt (devise) elaborar; (explain) explicar detalladamente.

2 vi explicarse; **to e. on sth** explicar algo con más detalles. **3** adj (complicated) complicado, -a; (detailed) detallado, -a; (style) esmerado, -a.

e·las·tic 1 adj elástico, -a; fig flexible; **e. band** goma elástica. **2** n elástico m.

el·bow 1 n codo m. **2** vt **to e. sb** dar un codazo a algn.

eld·er adj mayor.

eld·er·ly 1 adj anciano, -a. **2** npl **the e.** los ancianos.

eld·est 1 adj mayor. **2** n el/la mayor.

e·lect vt elegir.

e·lec·tion 1 n elección f; **general e.** elecciones fpl generales. **2** adj electoral.

e·lec·tor·ate electorado m.

e·lec·tric adj eléctrico, -a; fig electrizante.

e·lec·tri·cal adj eléctrico, -a.

e·lec·tric blan·ket manta f eléctrica.

e·lec·tric chair silla f eléctrica.

e·lec·tri·cian electricista mf.

e·lec·tric·i·ty electricidad f; **e. bill** recibo m de la luz.

e·lec·tric shock electrochoque m.

e·lec·tro·cute vt electrocutar.

e·lec·tron·ic adj electrónico, -a.

e·lec·tron·ics (science) electrónica f; (of machine) componentes mpl electrónicos.

el·e·gance elegancia f.

el·e·gant adj elegante.

el·e·gant·ly adv con elegancia.

el·e·ment elemento m; (electrical) resistencia f.

el·e·men·ta·ry adj (not developed) rudimentario, -a; (easy) fácil; **e. school** escuela f primaria.

el·e·phant elefante m.

el·e·va·tor ascensor m.

el·ev·en adj & n once (m) inv.

el·ev·enth adj & n undécimo, -a (mf).

el·i·gi·ble adj apto, -a; **he isn't e. to vote** no tiene derecho al voto.

e·lim·i·nate vt eliminar.

e·lite elite f.

else adv **anything e.?** ¿algo más?; **everything e.** todo lo demás; **no-one e.** nadie más; **someone e.** otro, -a; **something e.** otra cosa; **somewhere e.** en otra parte; **what e.?** ¿qué mas?; **where e.?** ¿en qué otro sitio?; **or e.** si no.

else·where adv en otra parte.

e·lude vt (avoid) esquivar; **his name eludes me** no consigo acordarme de su nombre.

e-mail 1 n (system) correo m electrónico, e-mail m; (message) (mensaje m por) correo m electrónico, e-mail m. **2** vt (person) enviar un correo electrónico a.

em·bark vi embarcar(se); **to e. upon sth** emprender algo.

em·bar·rass vt avergonzar.

em·bar·rass·ing adj embarazoso, -a; (situation) violento, -a.

em·bar·rass·ment vergüenza f.

em·bas·sy embajada f.

em·blem emblema m.

em·brace 1 vt abrazar; (include) abarcar. **2** vi abrazarse. **3** n abrazo m.

em·broi·der vt bordar; (story, truth) adornar.

em·broi·der·y bordado m.

em·bry·o embrión m.

em·er·ald esmeralda f.

e·merge vi salir; (problem) surgir; **it emerged that ...** resultó que ....

e·mer·gen·cy emergencia f; (medical) urgencia f; **in an e.** en caso de emergencia; **e. exit** salida f de emergencia; **e. landing** aterrizaje m forzoso; **state of e.** estado m de excepción.

em·i·grate vi emigrar.

e·mo·tion emoción f.

e·mo·tion·al adj emocional; (moving) conmovedor, -a.

em·per·or emperador m.

em·pha·sis énfasis m; **to place e. on sth** hacer hincapié en algo.

em·pha·size vt subrayar.

em·pire imperio m.

em·ploy vt emplear; (time) ocupar.

em·ploy·ee empleado, -a mf.

em·ploy·er empresario, -a mf.

em·ploy·ment empleo m.

em·ploy·ment a·gen·cy agencia f de colocaciones.

emp·ty 1 adj vacío, -a; **e. promises** promesas fpl vanas. **2** vt vaciar. **3** vi vaciarse. **4** npl **empties** envases mpl.

emp·ty-hand·ed adv con las manos vacías.

e·mul·sion e. (paint) pintura f mate.

en·a·ble vt to e. sb to do sth permitir a algn hacer algo.

e·nam·el esmalte m.

en·chant·ing adj encantador, -a.

en·close vt (surround) rodear; (fence in) cercar; (in envelope) adjuntar; **please find enclosed** le enviamos adjunto.

en·clo·sure (fenced area) cercado m; (in envelope) documento m adjunto.

en·coun·ter 1 n encuentro m. **2** vt encontrarse con; (problems) tropezar con.

en·cour·age vt (urge) animar; (help to develop) fomentar.

en·cour·age·ment estímulo m.

en·cy·clo·pe·dia enciclopedia f.

end 1 n (of stick) punta f; (of street) final m; (conclusion) fin m, final m; (aim) objetivo m; **in the e.** al final; **for hours on e.** hora tras hora; **to put an e. to** acabar con; **it makes my hair stand on e.** me pone el pelo de punta. **2** vt acabar, terminar. **3** vi acabarse, terminarse.

▸**end up** vi terminar; **to e. up doing sth** terminar por hacer algo.

en·dan·ger vt poner en peligro.

end·ing final m.

en·dive escarola f.

end·less adj interminable.

en·dorse vt (check etc) endosar; (approve) aprobar; (support) apoyar.

en·dorse·ment (on check etc) en-

doso m; (approval) aprobación f.

en·dur·ance resistencia f.

en·dure vt (bear) aguantar. **2** vi perdurar.

en·e·my adj & n enemigo, -a (mf).

en·er·get·ic adj enérgico, -a.

en·er·gy 1 n energía f. **2** adj energético, -a.

en·force vt (law) hacer cumplir.

en·gaged adj prometido, -a; (busy) ocupado, -a; **to get e.** prometerse; **it's e.** (phone) está comunicando.

en·gage·ment (to marry) noviazgo m; (appointment) cita f.

en·gage·ment ring anillo m de compromiso.

en·gine motor m; (of train) locomotora f.

en·gine driv·er maquinista mf.

en·gi·neer ingeniero, -a mf; (on train) maquinista mf.

en·gi·neer·ing ingeniería f.

Eng·lish 1 adj inglés, -esa. **2** n (language) inglés m; **the E.** los ingleses mpl.

Eng·lish·man inglés m.

Eng·lish-speak·ing adj de habla inglesa.

Eng·lish·wom·an inglesa f.

en·grave vt grabar.

en·grav·ing grabado m.

en·joy vt disfrutar; **to e. oneself** pasarlo bien; **he enjoys swimming** le gusta nadar.

en·joy·able adj agradable.

en·joy·ment disfrute m.

en·large vt ampliar.

en·light·en vt iluminar.

en·list 1 vt (recruit) reclutar; **to e. sb's help** conseguir ayuda de algn. **2** vi (in the army) alistarse.

e·nor·mous adj enorme.

e·nor·mous·ly adv enormemente; **I enjoyed myself e.** lo pasé genial.

e·nough 1 adj bastante, suficiente; **e. books** bastantes libros; **have we got e. gas?** ¿tenemos suficiente gasolina? **2** adv bastante; **sure e.** en efecto. **3** n lo suficiente; **e. to live**

on lo suficiente para vivir; **it isn't e.** no basta; **I've had e.!** ¡estoy harto!

en·quire = inquire.

en·quir·y = inquiry.

en·roll *vt* matricular. **2** *vi* matricularse.

en·roll·ment matrícula *f*.

en·sure *vt* asegurar.

en·tail *vt* suponer.

en·ter 1 *vt (go into)* entrar en; *(data into computer)* introducir; *(join)* ingresar en; **to e. one's name for a course** matricularse en un curso. **2** *vi* entrar.

▸**enter into** *vt (agreement)* firmar; *(negotiations)* iniciar.

en·ter·prise empresa *f*; **free e.** libre empresa.

en·ter·pris·ing *adj* emprendedor, -a.

en·ter·tain 1 *vt (amuse)* divertir; *(consider)* considerar. **2** *vi (have guests)* tener invitados.

en·ter·tain·er artista *mf*.

en·ter·tain·ing *adj* divertido, -a.

en·ter·tain·ment diversión *f*; *(show)* espectáculo *m*.

en·thu·si·asm entusiasmo *m*.

en·thu·si·ast entusiasta *mf*.

en·thu·si·as·tic *adj* entusiasta; *(praise)* caluroso, -a; **to be e. about sth** entusiasmarse por algo.

en·thu·si·as·ti·cal·ly *adv* con entusiasmo.

en·tire *adj* todo, -a; **the e. family** toda la familia.

en·tire·ly *adv (completely)* totalmente; *(solely)* exclusivamente.

en·ti·tle *vt (permit)* dar derecho a; **to be entitled to** tener derecho a.

en·trance entrada *f*; *(admission)* ingreso *m*; **e. examination** examen *m* de ingreso.

en·trant *(in competition)* participante *mf*.

en·try *(entrance)* entrada *f*; **no e.** dirección prohibida.

en·try form hoja *f* de inscripción.

en·ve·lope sobre *m*.

en·vi·ous *adj* envidioso, -a; **to feel e.** tener envidia.

en·vi·ron·ment entorno *m*; *(natural)* medio ambiente *m*.

en·vi·ron·men·tal *adj* medio ambiental.

en·vi·sage, en·vi·sion *vt (imagine)* imaginarse; *(foresee)* prever.

en·vy 1 *n* envidia *f*. **2** *vt* envidiar.

ep·i·dem·ic 1 *n* epidemia *f*. **2** *adj* epidémico, -a.

ep·i·sode episodio *m*.

e·qual 1 *adj* igual; **to be e. to the occasion** estar a la altura de las circunstancias. **2** *n* igual *mf*; **to treat sb as an e.** tratar a algn de igual a igual. **3** *vt* equivaler a.

e·qual·i·ty igualdad *f*.

e·qual·ize *vi (in sport)* empatar.

e·qual·ly *adv* igualmente; **e. pretty** igual de bonito; **to share sth e.** dividir algo en partes iguales.

e·qua·tion ecuación *f*.

e·qua·tor ecuador *m*.

e·quip *vt (supply)* equipar; *(person)* proveer.

e·quip·ment *(materials)* equipo *m*.

e·quiv·a·lent *adj & n* equivalente *(m)*.

e·ra era *f*.

e·rase *vt* borrar.

e·ras·er goma *f* de borrar.

e·rect 1 *adj (upright)* erguido, -a. **2** *vt (monument)* erigir.

e·ro·sion *(of land)* erosión *f*.

er·rand recado *m*.

er·rat·ic *adj (performance, behavior)* irregular; *(weather)* muy variable; *(person)* caprichoso, -a.

er·ror error *m*.

e·rupt *vi (volcano)* entrar en erupción; *(violence)* estallar.

e·rup·tion erupción *f*.

es·ca·la·tor escalera *f* mecánica.

es·cape 1 *n* fuga *f*; *(of gas)* escape *m*; **e. route** vía *f* de escape. **2** *vi* escaparse. **3** *vt (avoid)* evitar; **the name escapes me** se me escapa el nombre.

es·cort 1 n (bodyguard etc) escolta f.
2 vt (protect) escoltar.
Es·ki·mo adj & n esquimal (mf).
es·pe·cial·ly adv especialmente.
es·pres·so café m exprés.
es·say (at school) redacción f.
es·sen·tial adj esencial.
es·sen·tial·ly adv esencialmente.
es·tab·lish vt (found) establecer;
(business) montar; **to e. the truth**
demostrar la verdad.
es·tab·lished adj (person) estable-
cido, -a; (fact) conocido, -a.
es·tab·lish·ment establecimiento
m; **the E.** el sistema.
es·tate (land) finca f, (property)
bienes mpl; (inheritance) herencia f,
(housing) e. urbanización f.
es·ti·mate 1 n (calculation) cálculo
m; (likely cost of work) presupuesto
m. **2** vt calcular.
etch·ing aguafuerte m.
e·ter·nal adj eterno, -a, incesante.
ethics ética f.
e·tick·et n billete m electrónico.
et·i·quette etiqueta f.
EU abbr of **European Union** UE.
Euro- prefix Euro-.
Eu·ro·pe·an adj & n europeo, -a
(mf).
e·vac·u·ate vt evacuar.
e·vade vt evadir.
e·val·u·ate vt evaluar.
e·vap·o·rate 1 vi evaporarse. **2** vt
evaporar.
eve víspera f; **on the e. of** en víspe-
ras de.
e·ven 1 adj (smooth) liso, -a; (regular) uniforme; (equally balanced)
igual; (number) par; (in football
game etc) **to be e.** ir empatados, -as;
to get e. with sb desquitarse con
algn. **2** adv aun; **e. now** incluso ahora; **e. the children knew** hasta los
niños lo sabían; **e. as** mientras; **e. if**
incluso si; **e. though** aunque. ▪
(with negative) si siquiera; **she can't
e. write her name** ni siquiera sabe
escribir su nombre. ▪ (before com-

parative) aun, todavía; **e. worse**
aun peor.
eve·ning (early) tarde f, (late) noche
f, **in the e.** por la tarde/noche; **tomorrow e.** mañana por la tarde/
noche.
eve·ning class clase f nocturna.
e·ven·ly adv (uniformly) de modo
uniforme; (fairly) equitativamente.
e·vent (happening) suceso m; (in
sport) prueba f, **at all events** en todo
caso; **in the e. of fire** en caso de
incendio.
e·ven·tu·al adj (ultimate) final; (re-
sulting) consiguiente.
e·ven·tu·al·ly adv finalmente.
ev·er adv (always) siempre; **for e.**
para siempre; **stronger than e.** más
fuerte que nunca; **have you e. been
there?** ¿has estado allí alguna vez?;
how e. did you manage it? ¿cómo
diablos lo conseguiste?; fam **e. so
…** muy …; **thank you e. so much**
muchísimas gracias.
eve·ry adj (each) cada; (all) todos,
-as; **e. now and then** de vez en
cuando; **e. day** todos los días; **e.
other day** cada dos días; **e. one of
you** todos, -as vosotros, -as; **e. citizen** todo ciudadano.
eve·ry·bod·y pron todo el mundo,
todos, -as; **e. who …** todos los
que …
eve·ry·day adj de todos los días;
an e. occurrence un suceso
cotidiano.
eve·ry·one pron = **everybody**.
eve·ry·place adv en todos sitios.
eve·ry·thing pron todo; **he eats e.**
come de todo; **e. I have** todo lo que
tengo.
eve·ry·where adv por or en todas
partes; **e. I go** por todas partes
adonde voy.
ev·i·dence n (proof) evidencia f, (in
court case) testimonio m; (sign) indicio m; **to give e.** prestar declaración.
ev·i·dent adj evidente.
ev·i·dent·ly adv evidentemente.

e·vil 1 n *(wicked)* malvado, -a; *(harmful)* nocivo, -a. **2** n mal m.

e·voke vt evocar.

ewe oveja f.

ex her e. su ex marido; **his e.** su ex mujer.

ex- prefix ex-; **ex-minister** ex ministro m.

ex·act adj exacto, -a; **this e. spot** ese mismo lugar.

ex·act·ly adv exactamente; **e.!** ¡exacto!

ex·ag·ger·ate vti exagerar.

ex·ag·ger·a·tion exageración f.

ex·am examen m.

ex·am·i·na·tion examen m; *(medical)* reconocimiento m; **to sit an e.** hacer un examen.

ex·am·ine vt examinar; *(customs)* registrar; *(medically)* reconocer a.

ex·am·in·er examinador, -a mf.

ex·am·ple ejemplo m; **for e.** por ejemplo.

ex·ceed vt exceder.

ex·ceed·ing·ly adv extremadamente.

ex·cel vi sobresalir.

ex·cel·lent adj excelente.

ex·cept prep excepto; **e. for the little ones** excepto los pequeños; **e. that …** salvo que …

ex·cep·tion excepción f; **with the e. of** a excepción de; **to take e. to sth** ofenderse por algo.

ex·cep·tion·al adj excepcional.

ex·cep·tion·al·ly adv excepcionalmente.

ex·cerpt extracto m.

ex·cess 1 n exceso m. **2** adj excedente; **e. baggage** exceso m de equipaje; **e. fare** suplemento m.

ex·ces·sive adj excesivo, -a.

ex·ces·sive·ly adv excesivamente, en exceso.

ex·change 1 n cambio m; **(telephone) e.** central f telefónica; **in e. for** a cambio de. **2** vt intercambiar; **to e. blows** golpearse.

ex·change rate tipo m de cambio.

ex·cite vt *(enthuse)* entusiasmar; *(arouse)* provocar; **to get excited** entusiasmarse.

ex·cit·ed adj ilusionado, -a; emocionado, -a.

ex·cite·ment *(emotion)* emoción f.

ex·cit·ing adj emocionante.

ex·claim vi exclamar.

ex·cla·ma·tion exclamación f.

ex·cla·ma·tion point signo m de admiración.

ex·clude vt excluir; *(from club)* no admitir.

ex·clu·sive 1 adj exclusivo, -a; *(select)* selecto, -a. **2** n *(in newspaper)* exclusiva f.

ex·clu·sive·ly adv exclusivamente.

ex·cur·sion excursión f.

ex·cuse 1 vt disculpar; *(exempt)* dispensar; *(justify)* justificar; **e. me!** con permiso. **2** n excusa f; **to make excuses** dar excusas.

ex·e·cute vt *(order)* cumplir; *(task)* realizar; *(person)* ejecutar.

ex·e·cu·tion *(of order)* cumplimiento m; *(of task)* realización f; *(of person)* ejecución f.

ex·ec·u·tive adj & n ejecutivo, -a *(mf)*.

ex·empt 1 vt eximir *(from* de). **2** adj exento, -a; **e. from tax** libre de impuesto.

ex·emp·tion exención f.

ex·er·cise 1 n ejercicio m; **e. book** cuaderno m. **2** vt *(rights, duties)* ejercer; *(dog)* sacar de paseo. **3** vi hacer ejercicio.

ex·ert vt *(influence)* ejercer; **to e. oneself** esforzarse.

ex·er·tion esfuerzo m.

ex·haust 1 vt agotar. **2** n *(gas)* gases mpl de combustión; **e. pipe** tubo m de escape.

ex·haust·ed adj agotado, -a.

ex·haust·ing adj agotador, -a.

ex·hib·it 1 n objeto m expuesto. **2** vt exponer; *(manifest)* mostrar.

ex·hi·bi·tion exposición f.

ex·hib·i·tor expositor, -a *mf.*

ex·ile 1 *n (banishment)* exilio *m;* *(person)* exiliado, -a *mf.* **2** *vt* exiliar.

ex·ist *vi* existir; *(stay alive)* subsistir.

ex·is·tence existencia *f.*

ex·ist·ing *adj* actual.

ex·it salida *f.*

ex·or·bi·tant *adj* exorbitante.

ex·pand 1 *vt* ampliar. **2** *vi (grow)* ampliarse; *(metal)* dilatarse.

▶**expand on** *vt* ampliar.

ex·panse extensión *f.*

ex·pan·sion *(in size)* expansión *f;* *(of gas, metal)* dilatación *f.*

ex·pan·sion slot ranura *f* de expansión.

ex·pect 1 *vt (anticipate)* esperar; *(suppose)* suponer; **to e. sth from sb/sth** esperar algo de algn/algo; **to e. to do sth** contar con hacer algo; **she's expecting a baby** está esperando un niño. **2** *vi* **to be expecting** estar embarazada.

ex·pec·ta·tion esperanza *f;* **contrary to e.** contrariamente a lo que se esperaba.

ex·pe·di·tion expedición *f.*

ex·pel *vt* expulsar.

ex·pen·di·ture desembolso *m.*

ex·pense gasto *m;* **to spare no e.** no escatimar gastos; *fig* **at the e. of** a costa de.

ex·pen·sive *adj* caro, -a.

ex·pe·ri·ence 1 *n* experiencia *f.* **2** *vt (sensation)* experimentar; *(difficulty, loss)* sufrir.

ex·pe·ri·enced *adj* experimentado, -a.

ex·per·i·ment 1 *n* experimento *m.* **2** *vi* experimentar (**on, with** con).

ex·pert *adj & n* experto, -a *(mf).*

ex·per·tise pericia *f.*

ex·pi·ra·tion vencimiento *m.*

ex·pi·ra·tion date fecha *f* de caducidad.

ex·pire *vi (come to an end)* terminar; *(policy, contract)* vencer; *(ticket)* caducar.

ex·pired *adj (ticket)* caducado, -a.

ex·plain *vt* explicar; *(clarify)* aclarar; **to e. oneself** justificarse.

▶**explain away** *vt* justificar.

ex·pla·na·tion explicación *f, (clarification)* aclaración *f.*

ex·plic·it *adj* explícito, -a.

ex·plode 1 *vt* hacer explotar. **2** *vi (bomb)* explotar; **to e. with anger** montar en cólera.

ex·ploit 1 *n* hazaña *f.* **2** *vt* explotar.

ex·plo·ra·tion exploración *f.*

ex·plore *vt* explorar.

ex·plor·er explorador, -a *mf.*

ex·plo·sion explosión *f.*

ex·plo·sive 1 *adj* explosivo, -a. **2** *n* explosivo *m.*

ex·port 1 *vt* exportar. **2** *n* exportación *f.*

ex·pose *vt (uncover)* exponer; *(secret)* revelar; *(plot)* descubrir.

ex·press 1 *adj (explicit)* expreso, -a; *(letter)* urgente. **2** *n (train)* expreso *m.* **3** *vt* expresar.

ex·pres·sion expresión *f.*

ex·press·way autopista *f.*

ex·tend 1 *vt (enlarge)* ampliar; *(lengthen)* alargar; *(prolong)* prolongar; *(increase)* aumentar. **2** *vi (stretch)* extenderse; *(last)* prolongarse.

ex·ten·sion extensión *f, (of time)* prórroga *f, (of building)* anexo *m.*

ex·ten·sive *adj* extenso, -a.

ex·ten·sive·ly *adv* extensamente; *(frequently)* con frecuencia.

ex·tent *(area)* extensión *f;* **to some e.** hasta cierto punto; **to a large e.** en gran parte; **to such an e.** hasta tal punto.

ex·te·ri·or *adj & n* exterior *(m).*

ex·ter·nal *adj* externo, -a.

ex·tin·guish·er extintor *m.*

ex·tra 1 *adj* extra; *(spare)* de sobra. **2** *adv* extra; **e. fine** extra fino. **3** *n (additional charge)* suplemento *m; (in film)* extra *mf.*

ex·tract 1 *n* extracto *m.* **2** *vt (tooth, information)* extraer.

ex·tra·cur·ric·u·lar *adj* extracurricular.

ex·traor·di·nar·y *adj* extraordinario, -a; *(strange)* raro, -a.

ex·trav·a·gant *adj (wasteful)* derrochador, -a; *(excessive)* exagerado, -a.

ex·treme 1 *adj* extremo, -a; **an e. case** un caso excepcional. **2** *n* extremo *m*; **in the e.** en sumo grado.

ex·treme·ly *adv* extremadamente; **I'm e. sorry** lo siento de veras.

eye *n* ojo *m*; **I couldn't believe my eyes** no podía creerlo; **not to take one's eyes off sb/sth** no quitar la vista de encima a algn/algo; **to catch sb's e.** llamar la atención de algn; **to turn a blind e.** hacer la vista gorda (to a); **with an e.** to con miras a; **to keep an e. on sb/sth** vigilar a algn/algo.

eye·brow ceja *f*.

eye·glasses *npl* gafas *fpl*.

eye·lash pestaña *f*.

eye·lid párpado *m*.

eye·lin·er lápiz *m* de ojos.

eye·shad·ow sombra *f* de ojos.

eye·sight vista *f*.

F

fab·ric *(cloth)* tejido *m*.

fab·u·lous *adj* fabuloso, -a.

face 1 *n* cara *f*; *(surface)* superficie *f*; **f. to f.** cara a cara; **she slammed the door in my f.** me dio con la puerta en las narices; **in the f. of danger** ante el peligro; **to pull faces** hacer muecas; **f. down/up** boca abajo/ arriba; **to save f.** salvar las apariencias. **2** *vt (look onto)* dar a; *(be opposite)* estar enfrente de; *(problem)* hacer frente a; **to f. up to** hacer cara a; *(tolerate)* aguantar. **3** *vi* **to f. on to** dar a; **to f. towards** mirar hacia.

fa·cil·i·tate *vt* facilitar.

fa·cil·i·ty *(ease)* facilidad *f*; **facilities** *(means)* facilidades *fpl*; *(rooms, equipment)* instalaciones *fpl*.

fact hecho *m*; *(reality)* realidad *f*; **as a matter of f.** de hecho; **in f.** en realidad.

fac·tor factor *m*.

fac·to·ry fábrica *f*.

fac·tu·al *adj* **a f. error** un error de hecho.

fade *vi (colour)* desteñirse; *(flower)* marchitarse; *(light)* apagarse.

▶ **fade away, fade out** *vi* desvanecerse.

▶ **fade in** *vt* hacer aparecer gradualmente.

fail 1 *n (at school)* suspenso *m*; **without f.** sin falta. **2** *vt (exam)* suspender; **to f. to do sth** *(be unable)* no poder hacer algo; *(neglect)* dejar de hacer algo. **3** *vi (show, film)* fracasar; *(brakes)* fallar; *(at school)* suspender; *(health)* deteriorarse.

failed *adj (attempt, poet)* fracasado, -a.

fail·ing 1 *n (shortcoming)* defecto *m*; *(weakness)* punto *m* débil. **2** *prep* a falta de.

fail·ure fracaso *m*; *(at school)* suspenso *m*; *(person)* fracasado, -a *mf*; *(breakdown)* avería *f*; **power f.** apagón *m*; **heart f.** paro *m* cardíaco; **her f. to answer** el hecho de que no contestara.

faint 1 *adj (sound)* débil; *(color)* pálido, -a; *(outline)* borroso, -a; *(recollection)* vago, -a; *(giddy)* mareado, -a; **I haven't the faintest idea** no tengo la más mínima idea. **2** *n* desmayo *m*. **3** *vi* desmayarse.

faint·ly *adv (with little strength)* débilmente; *(unclearly)* vagamente.

fair¹ 1 *adj (impartial)* imparcial; *(just)* justo, -a; *(hair)* rubio, -a; *(weather)* bueno, -a; **it's not f.** no hay derecho; **f. enough!** ¡vale!; **a f. number** un buen número. **2** *adv* **to play f.** jugar limpio.

fair² feria f; **trade f.** feria f de muestras.

fair-haired adj rubio, -a.

fair·ly adv (justly) justamente; (moderately) bastante.

fair play juego m limpio.

fair-sized adj bastante grande.

fair·y hada f; **f. tale** cuento m de hadas.

faith fe f; (trust) confianza f.

faith·ful adj fiel.

faith·ful·ly adv yours f. (in letter) le saluda atentamente.

fake 1 adj falso, -a. **2** n (object) falsificación f; (person) impostor, -a mf. **3** vt (forge) falsificar; (feign) fingir.

fall 1 n caída f; (decrease) baja f; otoño m; **falls** (waterfall) cascada f; **Niagara Falls** las cataratas del Niágara. **2** vi* caer, caerse; (temperature, prices) bajar; **night was falling** anochecía; **to f. asleep** dormirse; **to f. ill** caer enfermo, -a; **to f. in love** enamorarse.

▸**fall apart** vi (of machine) deshacerse.

▸**fall back on** vt (as last resort) recurrir a.

▸**fall behind** vi (in race) quedarse atrás; **to f. behind with one's work** retrasarse en el trabajo.

▸**fall down** vi (picture etc) caerse; (building) derrumbarse.

▸**fall for** vt (person) enamorarse de; (trick) dejarse engañar por.

▸**fall in** vi (roof) desplomarse.

▸**fall off** vi (drop off) caer; (part) desprenderse; (diminish) disminuir.

▸**fall out** vi (hair) caerse; (quarrel) pelearse.

▸**fall over** vi caerse.

▸**fall through** vi (plan) fracasar.

false adj falso, -a; **f. teeth** dentadura f postiza; **f. alarm** falsa alarma f.

fame fama f.

fa·mil·iar adj (common) conocido, -a; **his face is f.** su cara me suena; **to be on f. terms with sb** (know well) tener confianza con algn.

fa·mil·iar·i·ty familiaridad f (with con); (intimacy) confianza f.

fa·mil·iar·ize vt (make acquainted) familiarizar (with con); **to become familiarized with sth** familiarizarse con algo.

fam·i·ly familia f; **f. doctor** médico m de cabecera; **f. planning** planificación f familiar; **f. tree** árbol m genealógico.

fa·mous adj famoso, -a (for por).

fan (held in hand) abanico m; (electric) ventilador m; (person) aficionado, -a mf; (of pop star etc) fan mf; **football f.** hincha mf.

fan·cy 1 adj de fantasía; **f. goods** artículos mpl de fantasía. **2** n (whim) capricho m; **to take a f. to sth** encapricharse con algo; **what takes your f.?** ¿qué se le antoja? **3** vt (imagine) imaginarse; (like, want) apetecer; **fam f. that!** ¡fíjate!; **do you f. a drink?** ¿te apetece una copa?

fan heat·er estufa f de aire.

fan·tas·tic adj fantástico, -a.

fan·ta·sy fantasía f.

FAQ n frequently asked questions preguntas fpl más frecuentes.

far 1 adj (distant) lejano, -a; **at the f. end** en el otro extremo. **2** adv (distant) lejos; **f. off** a lo lejos; **farther back** más atrás; **how f. is it to Chicago?** ¿cuánto hay de aquí a Chicago?; **as f. as I can** en lo que puedo; **as f. as I know** que yo sepa; **as f. as possible** en lo posible; **f. from complaining, he seemed pleased** lejos de quejarse, parecía contento; **in so f. as ...** en la medida en que ...; **to go too f.** pasarse de la raya; **f. into the night** hasta muy entrada la noche; **so f.** (in time) hasta ahora; **by f.** con mucho; **f. cleverer** mucho más listo, -a; **f. too much** demasiado.

far·a·way adj lejano, -a.

farce farsa f.

fare (ticket price) tarifa f, precio m del billete; (for boat) pasaje m; (passenger) pasajero, -a mf.

fare·well 1 *interj (old use)* ¡adiós! **2** *n* despedida *f.*

far-fetched *adj* rebuscado, -a.

farm 1 *n* granja *f*, *Am* hacienda *f.* **2** *vt* cultivar.

▶**farm out** *vt* encargar fuera.

farm·er granjero, -a *mf*, *Am* hacendado, -a *mf.*

farm·house granja *f*, *Am* hacienda *f.*

farm·ing 1 *n (agriculture)* agricultura *f*, *(of land)* cultivo *m.* **2** *adj* agrícola.

farm·yard corral *m.*

far-off *adj* lejano, -a.

far-reach·ing *adj* de gran alcance.

far·ther 1 *adj* más lejos.

far·thest 1 *adj* más lejano, -a. **2** *adv* más lejos.

fas·ci·nate *vt* fascinar.

fas·ci·nat·ing *adj* fascinante.

fas·ci·na·tion fascinación *f.*

fash·ion *(manner)* manera *f*, *(latest style)* moda *f*; **to go/be out of f.** pasar/no estar de moda; **f. parade** desfile *m* de modelos.

fash·ion show pase *m* de modelos.

fast 1 *adj (quick)* rápido, -a; *(clock)* adelantado, -a. **2** *adv* rápidamente, deprisa; **how f.?** ¿qué velocidad?; **f. asleep** profundamente dormido, -a.

fas·ten *vt (attach)* sujetar; *(fix)* fijar; *(belt)* abrochar; *(bag)* asegurar; *(shoelaces)* atar.

fas·ten·er cierre *m.*

fat 1 *adj* gordo, -a; *(thick)* grueso, -a; *(meat)* poco magro, -a. **2** *n* grasa *f*, **cooking f.** manteca *f* de cerdo.

fa·tal *adj (accident, illness)* mortal; *(ill-fated)* funesto, -a.

fa·tal·ly *adv* **f. wounded** mortalmente herido, -a.

fate destino *m.*

fa·ther padre *m*; **my f. and mother** mis padres.

Fa·ther Christ·mas Papá *m* Noel.

fa·ther-in-law suegro *m.*

fa·tigue fatiga *f.*

fat·ten·ing *adj* que engorda.

fat·ty 1 *adj (food)* graso, -a. **2** *n fam (person)* gordinflón, -ona *mf.*

fau·cet grifo *m.*

fault *(defect)* defecto *m*; *(in merchandise)* desperfecto *m*; *(blame)* culpa *f*; **to find f. with** poner reparos a; **to be at f.** tener la culpa.

fault·y *adj* defectuoso, -a.

fa·vor 1 *n* favor *m*; **in f. of** a favor de; **to ask sb a f.** pedirle un favor a algn. **2** *vt (treat favorably)* favorecer; *(approve)* estar a favor de.

fa·vor·a·ble *adj* favorable.

fa·vor·ite *adj & n* favorito, -a *(mf).*

fax 1 *n* fax *m.* **2** *vt (document)* mandar por fax; **to f. sb** mandar un fax a algn.

fear 1 *n* miedo *m*; **for f. of** por temor a. **2** *vt* temer; **I f. it's too late** me temo que ya es tarde.

fear·ful *adj (person)* temeroso, -a; *(frightening)* espantoso, -a.

fear·less *adj* intrépido, -a.

feast banquete *m.*

feat hazaña *f.*

feath·er pluma *f*, **f. duster** plumero *m.*

fea·ture 1 *n (of face)* facción *f*, *(characteristic)* característica *f*; **f. film** largometraje *m.* **2** *vi* figurar.

Feb·ru·ar·y febrero *m.*

fed·er·al *adj* federal.

fed up *adj fam* harto, -a **(with).**

fee *(of lawyer, doctor)* honorarios *mpl.*

fee·ble *adj* débil.

feed* 1 *vt (give food to)* dar de comer a; **to f. a baby** *(breastfeed)* amamantar a un bebé; *(with bottle)* dar el biberón a un bebé. **2** *vi* comer; *(cows, sheep)* pacer.

feed·back feedback *m*; *fig* reacción *f.*

feel 1 *vi* (have emotion, sensation)* sentirse; *(have opinion)* opinar; **how do you f.?** ¿qué tal te encuentras?; **I f. bad about it** me da pena; **to f. happy** sentirse feliz; **to f. cold/ sleepy** tener frío/sueño; **I feel that**

... me parece que ...; **it feels like summer** parece verano; **I f. sure that ...** estoy seguro, -a de que ...; **I f. like an ice cream** me apetece un helado; **to f. like doing sth** tener ganas de hacer algo. **2** vt* (touch) tocar; (sense) sentir; (the cold) notar; **she feels like a failure** se siente inútil. **3** n (touch, sensation) tacto m.

▸**feel for** vt (have sympathy for) compadecer.

▸**feel up to** vt tener ánimos para.

feel·ing (emotion) sentimiento m; (physical) sensación f; (opinion) opinión f; **I had the f. that ...** (impression) tuve la impresión de que ...; **to express one's feelings** expresar sus opiniones.

feet npl see **foot**.

fell pt of **fall**.

fel·low 1 n tipo m, tío m. **2 f. citizen** conciudadano, -a mf; **f. countryman/countrywoman** compatriota mf.

fel·o·ny crimen m, delito m mayor.

felt¹ pt & pp of **feel**.

felt² fieltro m.

felt-tip(ped) pen rotulador m.

fe·male 1 adj femenino, -a; (animal) hembra. **2** n (animal) hembra f, (woman) mujer f, (girl) chica f.

fem·i·nine adj femenino, -a.

fence 1 n cerca f. **2** vi (in sport) practicar la esgrima.

▸**fence in** vt meter en un cercado.

fenc·ing (sport) esgrima f.

fend vi **to f. for oneself** valerse por sí mismo.

▸**fend off** vt (blow) parar; (attack) rechazar.

fend·er (on car) parachoques m inv.

fern helecho m.

fe·ro·cious adj feroz.

fer·ry 1 n (small) barca f de pasaje; (large, for cars) ferry m. **2** vt transportar.

fer·tile adj fértil.

fer·til·iz·er abono m.

fes·ti·val festival m.

fes·tive adj festivo, -a; **the f. season** las fiestas de Navidad.

fes·tiv·i·ty the festivities las fiestas.

fetch vt (go for) ir a buscar; (bring) traer.

fete fiesta f.

feud 1 n enemistad f duradera. **2** vi pelear.

fe·ver fiebre f.

fe·ver·ish adj febril.

few 1 adj (not many) pocos, -as; **as f. as** solamente; **a f.** unos, -as, algunos, -as; **in the next f. days** dentro de unos días; **she has fewer books than I thought** tiene menos libros de lo que pensaba; **quite a f.** un buen número. **2** pron (not many) pocos, -as; **there are too f.** no hay suficientes; **a f.** (some) algunos, -as; **who has the fewest?** ¿quién tiene menos?

fi·an·cé prometido m.

fi·an·cée prometida f.

fi·ber fibra f.

fic·tion ficción f.

fid·dle fam n (musical instrument) violín m.

▸**fiddle about** vi juguetear (**with** con).

fidg·et vi moverse; **stop fidgeting!** ¡estáte quieto!; **to f. with sth** jugar con algo.

field 1 n campo m; (oil field, coal field etc) yacimiento m. **2** vt (in sport) (ball) parar y devolver; (team) presentar.

field trip viaje m de estudios.

field·work trabajo m de campo.

fierce adj (animal) feroz; (argument) acalorado, -a; (heat, competition) intenso, -a.

fif·teen adj & n quince (m) inv.

fif·teenth adj & n decimoquinto, -a (mf).

fifth adj & n quinto, -a (mf).

fif·ti·eth adj & n quincuagésimo, -a (mf).

fif·ty 1 adj cincuenta inv; **a f.-f.**

fig 72 **fingertip**

chance una probabilidad del cincuenta por ciento; **to go f.-f.** ir a medias. **2** n cincuenta m inv.

fig (fruit) higo m.

fight 1 vt* combatir; (bull) lidiar. **2** vi* pelear(se); (quarrel) reñir; fig (struggle) luchar (**for/against** por/contra). **3** n pelea f; (boxing) combate m; (quarrel) riña f; fig (struggle) lucha f.

▸**fight back 1** vt (tears) contener. **2** vi (recover ground) resistir.

▸**fight off** vt (attack) rechazar.

▸**fight out** vt arreglar discutiendo or peleando.

fight·er (person) combatiente mf; (boxing) púgil m; fig luchador, -a mf; **f. (plane)** (avión m de) caza m.

fig·ure¹ 1 n (numeral) cifra f; (form, outline) forma f; (shape, statue, character) figura f; **she has a good f.** tiene buen tipo; **f. of speech** figura retórica. **2** vt fam imaginarse. **3** vi (appear) figurar; fam **that figures** eso tiene sentido.

fig·ure² vt (guess) imaginar.

▸**figure on** vt **to f. on doing sth** esperar hacer algo.

▸**figure out** vt comprender; **I can't f. it out** no me lo explico.

file 1 n (tool) lima f; (folder) carpeta f; (archive) archivo m; (of computer) fichero m; (line) fila f; **on f.** archivado, -a; **in single f.** en fila india. **2** vt (smooth) limar; (put away) archivar. **3** vi **to f. past** desfilar.

▸**file away** vt (put away) archivar; (in card catalog) clasificar.

▸**file down** vt limar.

▸**file in/out** vi entrar/salir en fila.

fil·ing clasificación f.

fil·ing cab·i·net archivador m; (for cards) fichero m.

fill 1 vt (space, time) llenar (**with** de); (post, requirements) cubrir. **2** vi llenarse (**with** de).

▸**fill in 1** vt (space, form) rellenar; (time) pasar; (inform) fam poner al corriente (**on** de). **2** vi **to f. in for sb** sustituir a algn.

▸**fill out** vt (form) rellenar.

▸**fill up 1** vt llenar hasta arriba; **f. her up!** ¡llénelo! **2** vi llenarse.

fil·let filete m; **f. steak** filete m.

fill·ing 1 adj que llena mucho. **2** n (stuffing) relleno m; (in tooth) empaste m.

fill·ing sta·tion gasolinera f.

film 1 n película f. **2** vt filmar. **3** vi rodar.

film star estrella f de cine.

fil·ter 1 n filtro m; **f. lane** carril m de acceso. **2** vt filtrar. **3** vi (traffic) **to f. to the right** girar a la derecha.

filth (dirt) porquería f; fig porquerías fpl.

filth·y adj (dirty) asqueroso, -a; (obscene) obsceno, -a.

fin (of fish) aleta f.

fi·nal 1 adj último, -a; (definitive) definitivo, -a. **2** n (sport) final f.

fi·nal·ize vt ultimar; (date) fijar.

fi·nal·ly adv finalmente.

fi·nance 1 n finanzas fpl; **finances** fondos mpl. **2** vt financiar.

fi·nan·cial adj financiero, -a.

find 1 vt* (locate, think) encontrar; (discover) descubrir; **it has been found that ...** se ha comprobado que ...; **I found it impossible to get away** me resultó imposible irme. **2** n hallazgo m.

▸**find out 1** vt (inquire) averiguar; (discover) descubrir. **2** vi **to f. out about sth** informarse sobre algo; (discover) enterarse de algo.

fine¹ 1 n (sum of money) multa f. **2** vt multar.

fine² 1 adj (delicate etc) fino, -a; (excellent) excelente; (weather) bueno, -a; **it was f.** hacía buen tiempo. **2** adv muy bien. **3** interj ¡vale!

fin·ger dedo m (de la mano); **to keep one's fingers crossed** esperar que todo salga bien.

fin·ger·nail uña f.

fin·ger·print huella f dactilar.

fin·ger·tip punta f or yema f del dedo.

fin·ish 1 n fin m; (of race) llegada f. **2** vt (complete) acabar, terminar; (use up) agotar; **to f. doing sth** terminar de hacer algo. **3** vi acabar, terminar.

▸ **finish off** vt (complete) terminar completamente; (kill) rematar.

▸ **finish up 1** vt acabar; **to f. up doing sth** acabar haciendo algo. **2** vi **to f. up in jail** ir a parar a la cárcel.

fin·ished adj (product) acabado, -a; fam (exhausted) rendido, -a.

Finn finlandés, -esa mf.

Finn·ish 1 adj finlandés, -esa. **2** n (language) finlandés m.

fir abeto m.

fire 1 n fuego m; (accident etc) incendio m; (heater) estufa f; (gunfire) fuego m; **to open f.** abrir fuego. **2** vt (gun) disparar (**at** a); (dismiss) despedir. **3** vi (shoot) disparar (**at** sobre).

fire a·larm alarma f de incendios.

fire bri·gade (cuerpo m de) bomberos mpl.

fire·crack·er petardo m.

fire ex·it salida f de emergencia.

fire ex·tin·guish·er extintor m.

fire·man bombero m.

fire·place chimenea f, (hearth) hogar m.

fire·wood leña f.

fire·works npl fuegos mpl artificiales.

firm 1 adj firme. **2** n empresa f.

first 1 adj primero, -a; (before masculine singular noun) primer; **for the f. time** por primera vez; **in the f. place** en primer lugar. **2** adv (before anything else) primero; **f. and foremost** ante todo; **at f.** al principio. **3** n the f. el primero, la primera; **the f. of April** el uno or el primero de abril; **from the (very) f.** desde el principio.

first aid primeros auxilios.

first-class 1 adj de primera clase. **2** adv **to travel f.** viajar en primera.

first·ly adv en primer lugar.

fish 1 n (pl fish) pez m; (as food) pescado m. **2** vi pescar.

fish·er·man pescador m.

fish·ing pesca f; **to go f.** ir de pesca.

fish·ing rod caña f de pescar.

fish shop pescadería f.

fish stick palito m de pescado.

fist puño m.

fit¹ 1 vt (clothes) ir bien a; (slot) encajar; (install) colocar; **that suit doesn't f. you** ese traje no te queda bien; **a car fitted with a radio** un coche provisto de radio; **she doesn't f. the description** no responde a la descripción. **2** vi (be of right size) caber; (be suitable) encajar; (facts etc) cuadrar. **3** adj (suitable) apto, -a (**for** para); (healthy) en (plena) forma; **are you f. to drive?** ¿estás en condiciones de conducir?; **to keep f.** mantenerse en forma. **4** n **to be a good f.** encajar bien.

▸ **fit in 1** vi (tally) cuadrar (**with** con); **he didn't f. in with his colleagues** no encajó con sus compañeros de trabajo. **2** vt (find time for) encontrar un hueco para.

▸ **fit on** vt **to f. sth on(to) sth** colocar or encajar algo en algo.

▸ **fit out** vt equipar.

fit² (attack) ataque m; fig arrebato m; **by fits and starts** a trompicones.

fit·ness (health) (buen) estado m físico.

fit·ted adj empotrado, -a; **f. carpet** moqueta f.

fit·ting adj apropiado, -a.

fit·ting room probador m.

fit·tings npl accesorios mpl; **light f.** apliques mpl eléctricos.

five adj & n cinco (m) inv; **f. hundred** quinientos, -as.

fix 1 n **to be in a f.** estar en un apuro. **2** vt (fasten) fijar; (date, price) fijar; (repair) arreglar; (food, drink) preparar; **he'll f. it with the boss** (arrange) se las arreglará con el jefe.

▸ **fix on** vt (lid etc) encajar.

▸ **fix up** vt (arrange) arreglar; **to f. sb up with sth** proveer a algn de algo.

fix·ture (in sport) encuentro m; **fix-**

tures *(in building)* accesorios *mpl.*

fizzy *adj (water)* con gas.

flag **1** *n* bandera *f; (on ship)* pabellón *m.* **2** *vi (interest)* decaer; *(conversation)* languidecer.

flake **1** *n (of snow)* copo *m; (of skin, soap)* escama *f.* **2** *vi (paint)* desconcharse.

flame llama *f;* **to go up in flames** incendiarse.

flam·ma·ble *adj* inflamable.

flan tarta *f* rellena; **fruit f.** tarta *f* de fruta.

flan·nel *(material)* franela *f.*

flap **1** *vt (wings, arms)* batir. **2** *vi (wings)* aletear; *(flag)* ondear. **3** *n (of envelope, pocket)* solapa *f;* **to get into a f.** ponerse nervioso, -a.

flare **1** *n (distress signal)* bengala *f.* **2** *vi (fire)* llamear; *(trouble)* estallar.

flash **1** *n (of light)* destello *m; (of lightning)* relámpago *m; (for camera)* flash *m.* **2** *vt (torch)* dirigir; **he flashed his card** enseñó rápidamente su carnet. **3** *vi (sudden light)* destellar; *(shine)* brillar; **a car flashed past** un coche pasó como un rayo.

flash·light linterna *f.*

flask frasco *m;* **(thermos) f.** termo *m.*

flat **1** *adj (surface)* llano, -a; *(beer)* sin gas; *(battery)* descargado, -a; *(tire)* desinflado, -a; *(dull)* soso, -a; *(in music)* **B f.** si *m* bemol. **2** *adv* **to fall f. on one's face** caerse de bruces; **to go f. out** ir a todo gas. **3** *n (flat tire)* pinchazo *m.*

flat·ly *adv* rotundamente.

flat·ten *vt (make level)* allanar; *(crush)* aplastar.

flat·ter *vt* halagar; *(clothes, portrait)* favorecer.

fla·vor **1** *n* sabor *m.* **2** *vt (food)* sazonar **(with** con).

fla·vor·ing condimento *m;* **artificial f.** aroma *m* artificial.

flaw *(failing)* defecto *m; (fault)* desperfecto *m.*

flea pulga *f.*

flea mar·ket rastro *m.*

flee* **1** *vt* huir. **2** *vi* huir **(from** de).

fleet flota *f.*

Flem·ish **1** *adj* flamenco, -a. **2** *n (language)* flamenco *m.*

flesh carne *f; (of fruit)* pulpa *f;* **in the f.** en persona.

flex *vt (muscles)* flexionar.

flex·i·ble *adj* flexible.

flick **1** *n (of finger)* capirotazo *m.* **2** *vt (finger)* dar un capirotazo a.

▸**flick off** *vt (piece of fluff)* quitar con un dedo.

▸**flick through** *vt* hojear.

flick·er *vi (eyes)* parpadear; *(flame)* vacilar.

flies *npl (on trousers)* bragueta *f.*

flight vuelo *m; (escape)* huida *f; (of stairs)* tramo *m;* **to take f.** darse a la fuga.

flight at·ten·dant azafata *f.*

flim·sy *adj (cloth)* ligero, -a; *(structure)* poco sólido, -a; *(excuse)* poco convincente.

fling* *vt* arrojar.

flint *(in lighter)* piedra *f* de mechero.

flip **1** *n (flick)* capirotazo *m.* **2** *vt (toss)* tirar (al aire); **to f. a coin** echar a cara o cruz.

▸**flip through** *vt (book)* hojear.

flip-flop *(footwear)* chancleta *f.*

float **1** *n* flotador *m; (in procession)* carroza *f.* **2** *vi* flotar.

flock **1** *n* rebaño *m; (of birds)* bandada *f.* **2** *vi* acudir en masa.

flood **1** *n* inundación *f; (of river)* riada *f.* **2** *vt* inundar. **3** *vi (river)* desbordarse.

flood·light foco *m.*

floor *(of room)* suelo *m; (storey)* piso *m;* **first f.** planta *f* baja.

floor·board tabla *f* (del suelo).

flop **1** *n (failure)* fracaso *m.* **2** *vi* fracasar.

flop·py *adj* flojo, -a.

flop·py disk disquete *m,* disco *m* flexible.

flo·rist florista *mf;* **f.'s** floristería *f.*

floun·der *inv (fish)* platija *f.*

flour harina f.

flour·ish 1 n (gesture) ademán m (teatral). **2** vt (brandish) agitar. **3** vi (thrive) florecer; (plant) crecer.

flow 1 n flujo m; (of traffic) circulación f; (of people, goods) movimiento m. **2** vi (blood, river) fluir; (traffic) circular.

flow chart organigrama m.

flow·er 1 n flor f. **2** vi florecer.

flow·er bed arriate m.

flow·er shop floristería f.

flu gripe f.

flu·ent adj (eloquent) fluido, -a; he speaks f. German habla el alemán con soltura.

flu·ent·ly adv (to speak) con soltura.

fluff n pelusa f.

flu·id líquido m.

flunk vt fam catear.

flu·o·res·cent adj fluorescente.

flush 1 adj f. with (level) a ras de. **2** n (blush) rubor m. **3** vt to f. the lavatory tirar la cadena. **4** vi (blush) ruborizarse.

flute flauta f.

flut·ter vi (leaves, birds) revolotear; (flag) ondear.

fly¹* 1 vt (plane) pilotar. **2** vi (bird, plane) volar; (go by plane) ir en avión; (flag) ondear.

▸**fly over** vt (country etc) sobrevolar.

fly² (insect) mosca f; f. spray spray m matamoscas.

fly³ (on trousers) bragueta f.

fly·ing 1 adj (soaring) volante; (rapid) rápido, -a. **2** n (action) vuelo m; (aviation) aviación f.

fly·ing sau·cer platillo m volante.

fly·o·ver paso m elevado.

foam espuma f; f. rubber goma f espuma.

fo·cus 1 vt centrar (on en). **2** vi to f. on sth enfocar algo; fig centrarse en algo. **3** n foco m.

fog niebla f; (at sea) bruma f.

fog·gy adj it is f. hay niebla.

foil 1 n aluminum f. papel m de aluminio. **2** vt (plot) frustrar.

fold 1 n (crease) pliegue m. **2** vt doblar; **to f. one's arms** cruzar los brazos. **3** vi **to f. (up)** (chair etc) plegarse.

▸**fold away** vt plegar.

fold·er carpeta f.

fold·ing adj (chair etc) plegable.

folk npl (people) gente f.

folk mu·sic música f folk.

fol·low 1 vt seguir; (understand) comprender. **2** vi (come after) seguir; (result) resultar; (understand) entender; **that doesn't f.** eso no es lógico.

▸**follow around** vt **to f. sb around** seguir a algn por todas partes.

▸**follow on** vi (come after) venir detrás.

▸**follow up** vt (idea) llevar a cabo; (clue) investigar.

follower seguidor, -a mf.

fol·low·ing 1 adj siguiente. **2** n seguidores mpl.

fond adj **to be f. of sb** tenerle mucho cariño a algn; **to be f. of doing sth** ser aficionado, -a a hacer algo.

font (of characters) fuente f.

food comida f.

food poi·son·ing intoxicación f alimenticia.

fool 1 n tonto, -a mf; **to play the f.** hacer el tonto. **2** vt (deceive) engañar. **3** vi (joke) bromear.

▸**fool around** vi hacer el tonto.

fool·ish adj (silly) tonto, -a; (unwise) estúpido, -a.

fool·ish·ly adv estúpidamente.

foot 1 n (pl feet) pie m; (of animal) pata f; **on f.** a pie; **to put one's f. in it** meter la pata. **2** vt **to f. the bill** (pay) pagar la cuenta.

foot·ball fútbol americano m; (ball) balón m.

foot·bridge puente m para peatones.

foot·path sendero m.

foot·print pisada f.

foot·step paso m.

for prep (purpose) para; **what's this f.?** ¿para qué sirve esto?; **f. sale** en venta. ▪ *(because of, on behalf of)* por; **famous f. its cuisine** famoso, -a por su cocina; **will you do it f. me?** ¿lo harás por mí? ▪ *(instead of)* por; **can you go f. me?** ¿puede ir por mí? ▪ *(during)* por, durante; **I was ill f. a month** estuve enfermo durante un mes; **I've been here f. three months** hace tres meses que estoy aquí. ▪ *(distance)* por; **I walked f. ten kilometers** caminé diez kilómetros. ▪ *(at a point in time)* para; **I can do it f. next Monday** puedo hacerlo para el lunes que viene; **f. the last time** por última vez. ▪ *(in exchange for)* por; **I got the car f. five hundred dollars** conseguí el coche por quinientos dólares. ▪ *(in favor of)* a favor de; **are you f. or against?** ¿estás a favor o en contra? ▪ *(towards)* hacia, por; **affection f. sb** cariño hacia algn. ▪ **it's time f. you to go** es hora de que os marchéis.

for·bid* *vt* prohibir; **to f. sb to do sth** prohibirle a algn hacer algo.

force 1 *n* fuerza *f*; **to come into f.** entrar en vigor; **the (armed) forces** las fuerzas armadas. **2** *vt* forzar; **to f. sb to do sth** forzar a algn a hacer algo.

fore·cast 1 *n* pronóstico *m*, previsión *f*. **2** *vt** pronosticar.

fore·head frente *f*.

for·eign *adj* extranjero, -a; *(trade, policy)* exterior.

for·eign·er extranjero, -a *mf*.

fore·man capataz *m*.

fore·most *adj* principal; **first and f.** ante todo.

fore·run·ner precursor, -a *mf*.

fore·see* *vt* prever.

for·est bosque *m*.

for·ev·er *adv (constantly)* siempre; *(for good)* para siempre.

forge *vt (counterfeit)* falsificar; *(metal)* forjar.

▶**forge ahead** *vi* hacer grandes progresos.

for·ger·y falsificación *f*.

for·get* 1 *vt* olvidar; **I forgot to close the window** se me olvidó cerrar la ventana. **2** *vi* olvidarse.

▶**forget about** *vt* olvidar.

for·get·ful *adj* olvidadizo, -a.

for·give* *vt* perdonar; **to f. sb for sth** pendonarle algo a algn.

fork 1 *n (cutlery)* tenedor *m*; *(farming)* horca *f*; *(in road)* bifurcación *f*. **2** *vi (roads)* bifurcarse.

▶**fork out** *vt fam (money)* soltar.

form 1 *n* forma *f*; *(type)* clase *f*; *(document)* formulario *m*; *(at school)* clase *f*; **on/on top/off f.** en/en plena/en baja forma. **2** *vt* formar. **3** *vi* formarse.

for·mal *adj (official)* oficial; *(party, dress)* de etiqueta; *(person)* formalista.

for·mal·i·ty formalidad *f*.

for·mal·ly *adv* oficialmente.

for·mat 1 *n* formato *m*. **2** *vt (computer disk)* formatear.

for·ma·tion formación *f*.

for·mer *adj (time)* anterior; *(onetime)* antiguo, -a; *(first)* aquél/aquélla; **the f. champion** el ex-campeón.

for·mer·ly *adv* antes, antiguamente.

for·mu·la fórmula *f*.

for·mu·late *vt* formular.

fort fortaleza *f*.

forth *adv fml* and **so f.** y así sucesivamente; **to go back and f.** ir de acá para allá.

forth·com·ing *adj (event)* próximo, -a; *(communicative)* comunicativo, -a; **no money was f.** no hubo oferta de dinero.

for·ti·eth *adj & n* cuadragésimo, -a *(mf)*.

fort·night quincena *f*.

for·tress fortaleza *f*.

for·tu·nate *adj* afortunado, -a; **it was f. that he came** fue una suerte que viniera.

for·tu·nate·ly *adv* afortunadamente.

for·tune *(luck, fate)* suerte *f*; *(money)* fortuna *f*.

for·ty *adj & n* cuarenta *(m) inv*.

fo·rum foro *m*.

for·ward 1 *adv (also* **forwards**) *(direction and movement)* hacia adelante; **from this day f.** de ahora en adelante. **2** *adj (person)* fresco, -a. **3** *n (in sport)* delantero, -a *mf*. **4** *vt (send on)* remitir; *(goods)* expedir.

fos·sil fósil *m*.

fos·ter *adj* **f. child** niño(a) *mf* en régimen de acogida; **f. home** hogar *m* de acogida; **f. parents** padres *mpl* de acogida.

foul 1 *adj (smell)* fétido, -a; *(taste)* asqueroso, -a; *(language)* grosero, -a. **2** *n (in football etc)* falta *f*.

found¹ *pt & pp of* **find**.

found² *vt (establish)* fundar.

found·er fundador, -a *mf*.

foun·tain fuente *f*.

foun·tain pen pluma *f* estilográfica.

four *adj & n* cuatro *(m) inv*; **on all fours** a gatas.

four·teen *adj & n* catorce *(m) inv*.

fourth *adj & n* cuarto, -a *(mf)*.

fowl aves *fpl* de corral.

fox zorro, -a *mf*.

foy·er vestíbulo *m*.

frac·tion fracción *f*.

frac·ture 1 *n* fractura *f*. **2** *vt* fracturar.

frag·ile *adj* frágil.

frag·ment fragmento *m*.

fra·grance fragancia *f*.

frail *adj* frágil.

frame 1 *n (of window, door, picture)* marco *m*; *(of machine)* armazón *m*; **f. of mind** estado *m* de ánimo. **2** *vt (picture)* enmarcar; *(question)* formular; *(innocent person)* incriminar.

frame·work within the f. of ... dentro del marco de ....

franc franco *m*.

fran·chise *(right to vote)* derecho *m* al voto; *(right to sell product)* concesión *f*, licencia *f*.

frank *adj* franco, -a.

frank·ly *adv* francamente.

frank·ness franqueza *f*.

fran·tic *adj (anxious)* desesperado, -a; *(hectic)* frenético, -a.

fran·ti·cal·ly *adv* desesperadamente.

fraud fraude *m*; *(person)* impostor, -a *mf*.

fray *vi (cloth)* deshilacharse.

freck·le peca *f*.

freck·led *adj* pecoso, -a.

free 1 *adj* libre; **f. (of charge)** gratuito, -a; *(generous)* generoso, -a. **2** *adv* **(for) f.** gratis. **3** *vt (liberate)* poner en libertad.

free·dom libertad *f*.

free·way autopista *f*.

freeze* 1 *vt* congelar. **2** *vi (liquid)* helarse; *(food)* congelarse.

▸ **freeze up, freeze over** *vi* helarse; *(windshield)* cubrirse de hielo.

freez·er congelador *m*.

freez·ing *adj* glacial; **above/below f. point** sobre/bajo cero.

freight *(transport)* transporte *m*; *(goods, price)* flete *m*; **f. train** tren *m* de mercancías.

French 1 *adj* francés, -esa. **2** *n (language)* francés *m*; *pl* **the F.** los franceses.

French fries *npl* patatas *fpl* fritas.

French·man francés *m*.

French·wom·an francesa *f*.

fre·quent *adj* frecuente.

fre·quent·ly *adv* frecuentemente.

fresh *adj* fresco, -a; *(new)* nuevo, -a; **in the f. air** al aire libre.

fresh·en up *vi* asearse.

fret *vi* preocuparse (**about** por).

Fri·day viernes *m*.

fridge nevera *f*, frigorífico *m*.

fried *adj* frito, -a.

friend amigo, -a *mf*; **a f. of mine** un, -a amigo, -a mío, -a.

friend·ly *adj (person)* simpático, -a; *(atmosphere)* acogedor, -a.

friend·ship amistad *f*.

fright *(fear)* miedo *m*; *(shock)* susto *m*; **to get a f.** pegarse un susto.

fright·en *vt* asustar.

▸**frighten away, frighten off** *vt* ahuyentar.

fright·ened *adj* asustado, -a; **to be f. of sb** tenerle miedo a algn.

fright·en·ing *adj* espantoso, -a.

frill *(dress)* volante *m*.

fringe *(edge)* borde *m*; *fig* **on the f. of society** al margen de la sociedad.

frog rana *f*.

from *prep (time)* desde, a partir de; **f. the eighth to the seventeenth** desde el ocho hasta el diecisiete; **f. time to time** de vez en cuando. ▪ *(price, number)* desde, de; **dresses f. ten dollars** vestidos desde diez dólares. ▪ *(origin)* de; **he's f. Malaga** es de Málaga; **the train f. Bilbao** el tren procedente de Bilbao. ▪ *(distance)* de; **the town is four miles f. the coast** el pueblo está a cuatro millas de la costa. ▪ *(remove, subtract)* a; **he took the book f. the child** le quitó el libro al niño. ▪ *(according to)* según, por; **f. what the author said** según lo que dijo el autor. ▪ *(position)* desde, de; **f. here** desde aquí.

front 1 *n* parte *f* delantera; *(of building)* fachada *f*; *(military, political, of weather)* frente *m*; **in f. (of)** delante (de). **2** *adj* delantero, -a.

front door puerta *f* principal.

fron·tier frontera *f*.

frost *n (covering)* escarcha *f*; *(freezing)* helada *f*.

frost·bite congelación *f*.

frost·y *adj fig* glacial; **it will be a f. night tonight** esta noche habrá helada.

froth espuma *f*.

frown *vi* fruncir el ceño.

▸**frown upon** *vt* desaprobar.

fro·zen *adj (liquid, feet etc)* helado, -a; *(food)* congelado, -a.

fruit fruta *f*; **fruits** *(rewards)* frutos *mpl*.

fruit sal·ad macedonia *f* de frutas.

frus·trate *vt* frustrar.

frus·trat·ed *adj* frustrado, -a.

frus·trat·ing *adj* frustrante.

frus·tra·tion frustración *f*.

fry *vt* freír.

fry·ing pan sartén *f*.

fu·el combustible *m*; *(for engines)* carburante *m*.

fu·gi·tive fugitivo, -a *mf*.

ful·fill *vt (task, ambition)* realizar; *(promise)* cumplir; *(wishes)* satisfacer.

ful·fill·ing *adj* que llena.

full 1 *adj* lleno, -a *(of* de); *(complete)* completo, -a; **I'm f. (up)** no puedo más. **2** *n* **in f.** en su totalidad.

full board pensión *f* completa.

full-scale *adj (model)* de tamaño natural.

full stop punto *m*.

full-time 1 *adj* de jornada completa. **2** *adv* **to work f.** trabajar a jornada completa.

ful·ly *adv* completamente.

fumes *npl* humo *m*.

fun *(amusement)* diversión *f*; **in** or **for f.** en broma; **to have f.** pasarlo bien; **to make f. of sb** reírse de algn.

func·tion 1 *n* función *f*; *(ceremony)* acto *m*; *(party)* recepción *f*. **2** *vi* funcionar.

func·tion·al *adj* funcional.

fund 1 *n* fondo *m*; **funds** fondos *mpl*. **2** *vt (finance)* financiar.

fu·ner·al funeral *m*; **f. home** funeraria *f*.

fun·nel *(for liquids)* embudo *m*; *(of ship)* chimenea *f*.

fun·ny *adj (peculiar)* raro, -a; *(amusing)* divertido, -a; *(ill)* mal; **I found it very f.** me hizo mucha gracia.

fur *(of living animal)* pelo *m*; *(of dead animal)* piel *f*.

fu·ri·ous *adj (angry)* furioso, -a.

fur·nace horno *m*.

fur·nish *vt (house)* amueblar.

fur·ni·ture muebles *mpl*; **a piece of f.** un mueble.

fur·ther 1 *adj (new)* nuevo, -a; *(addi-*

tional) otro, -a. **2** *adv* más lejos; *(more)* más; **f. back** más atrás.

fur·ther ed·u·ca·tion estudios *mpl* superiores.

fur·ther·more *adv* además.

fur·thest *adj* más lejano, -a.

fu·ry furia *f.*

fuse 1 *n* fusible *m*; *(of bomb)* mecha *f.* **2** *vi* **the lights fused** se fundieron los plomos.

fuss 1 *n (commotion)* jaleo *m*; **to kick up a f.** armar un escándalo; **to make a f. of** *(pay attention to)* mimar a. **2** *vi* preocuparse (**about** por).

▶ **fuss over** *vt* consentir a.

fuss·y *adj (nitpicking)* quisquilloso, -a; *(thorough)* exigente.

fu·ture 1 *n* futuro *m*; **in the near f.** en un futuro próximo. **2** *adj* futuro, -a.

fuzz·y *adj (hair)* muy rizado, -a; *(blurred)* borroso, -a.

G

gadg·et aparato *m.*

Gael·ic 1 *adj* gaélico, -a. **2** *n (language)* gaélico *m.*

gag 1 *n* mordaza *f*; *(joke)* chiste *m.* **2** *vt* amordazar.

gai·e·ty regocijo *m.*

gai·ly *adv* alegremente.

gain 1 *n* ganancia *f*; *(increase)* aumento *m.* **2** *vt (obtain)* ganar; *(increase)* aumentar; **to g. weight** aumentar de peso.

▶ **gain on** *vt* ganar terreno a.

ga·la gala *f.*

ga·lax·y galaxia *f.*

gale vendaval *m.*

gal·lant *adj (chivalrous)* galante.

gal·ler·y galería *f.*

gal·li·vant *vi fam* callejear.

gal·lon galón *m.*

gal·lop 1 *n* galope *m.* **2** *vi* galopar.

gam·ble 1 *n (risk)* riesgo *m*; *(bet)* apuesta *f.* **2** *vi (bet)* jugar; *(take a risk)* arriesgarse.

▶ **gamble away** *vt (lose)* perder en el juego.

gam·bler jugador, -a *mf.*

gam·bling juego *m.*

game juego *m*; *(match)* partido *m*; *(of bridge)* partida *f.*

gang *(of criminals)* banda *f*; *(of youths)* pandilla *f.*

gang up *vi* confabularse (**on** contra).

gang·ster gángster *m.*

gang·way pasarela *f.*

gap hueco *m*; *(blank space)* blanco *m*; *(in time)* intervalo *m*; *(gulf)* diferencia *f*; *(deficiency)* laguna *f.*

gape *vi (person)* mirar boquiabierto, -a.

ga·rage garaje *m*; *(for repairs)* taller *m* mecánico; *(gas station)* gasolinera *f.*

gar·bage basura *f*; **g. can** cubo *m* de la basura.

gar·ban·zo g. (bean) garbanzo *m.*

gar·den jardín *m.*

gar·den·er jardinero, -a *mf.*

gar·den·ing jardinería *f.*

gar·gle *vi* hacer gárgaras.

gar·land guirnalda *f.*

gar·lic ajo *m.*

gar·ment prenda *f.*

gas 1 *n* gas *m*; gasolina *f*; **g. cooker** cocina *f* de gas; **g. fire** estufa *f* de gas. **2** *vt (asphyxiate)* asfixiar con gas.

gash 1 *n* herida *f* profunda. **2** *vt* **he gashed his forehead** se hizo una herida en la frente.

gas·o·line gasolina *f.*

gasp 1 *n (cry)* grito *m* sordo; *(breath)* bocanada *f.* **2** *vi (in surprise)* quedar boquiabierto, -a; *(breathe)* jadear.

gas sta·tion gasolinera *f.*

gas·sy *adj* gaseoso, -a.

gas tank depósito *m* de gasolina.

gas·works fábrica *f* de gas.

gate puerta *f*; *(at stadium)* entrada *f.*

gate·crash *vti* colarse.

gath·er *vt (collect)* juntar; *(pick up)* recoger; *(bring together)* reunir; *(understand)* suponer; **to g. speed** ir ganando velocidad; **I g. that …** tengo entendido que …. **2** *vi (come together)* reunirse.

▸ **gather around** *vi* agruparse.

gath·er·ing reunión *f.*

gaud·y *adj* chillón, -ona.

gauge 1 *n (of railway)* ancho *m* de vía; *(calibrator)* indicador *m.* **2** *vt (judge)* juzgar.

gaunt *adj (lean)* demacrado, -a; *(desolate)* lúgubre.

gauze gasa *f.*

gave *pt of* **give**.

gay *adj (homosexual)* gay; *(happy)* alegre.

gaze 1 *n* mirada *f* fija. **2** *vi* mirar fijamente.

▸ **gaze at** *vt* mirar fijamente.

GB *abbr of* **Great Britain**.

gear 1 *n (equipment)* equipo *m*; *(belongings)* bártulos *mpl*; *(clothing)* ropa *f*, *(in car etc)* marcha *f.* **2** *vt* adaptar (**to** a).

gear·box caja *f* de cambios.

geek *fam* lelo, -a *mf*, tontaina *mf.*

geese *npl see* **goose**.

gel gel *m*; *(for hair)* gomina *f.*

gem piedra *f* preciosa.

gen·der género *m.*

gen·er·al 1 *adj* general; **in g.** en general; **the g. public** el público. **2** *n (in army)* general *m.*

gen·er·al·ly *adv* generalmente.

gen·er·a·tion generación *f.*

gen·er·a·tion gap abismo *m* or conflicto *m* generacional.

gen·er·a·tor generador *m.*

gen·er·os·i·ty generosidad *f.*

gen·er·ous *adj* generoso, -a; *(plentiful)* copioso, -a.

gen·er·ous·ly *adv* generosamente.

gen·ius *(person)* genio *m*; *(gift)* don *m.*

gen·tle *adj* dulce; *(breeze)* suave.

gen·tle·man caballero *m.*

gen·tle·ness *(mildness)* ternura *f*; *(kindness)* amabilidad *f.*

gent·ly con cuidado.

gents *npl* servicio *m* de caballeros.

gen·u·ine *adj* auténtico, -a; *(sincere)* sincero, -a.

gen·u·ine·ly *adv* auténticamente.

ge·o·graph·i(·)c(al) *adj* geográfico, -a.

ge·og·ra·phy geografía *f.*

ge·o·met·ri(·)c(al) *adj* geométrico, -a.

ge·om·e·try geometría *f.*

germ microbio *m.*

Ger·man 1 *adj* alemán, -ana; **G. measles** rubeola *f.* **2** *n* alemán, -ana *mf*, *(language)* alemán *m.*

Ger·man shep·herd *(dog)* pastor *m* alemán.

ges·ture gesto *m.*

get* 1 *vt (obtain)* obtener, conseguir; *(earn)* ganar; *(fetch)* *(something)* traer; *(somebody)* ir a por; *(receive)* recibir; *(bus, train, thief etc)* coger, *Am* agarrar; *(understand)* entender; *(on phone)* **g. me Mr Brown** póngame con el Sr. Brown; **can I g. you something to eat?** ¿te traigo algo de comer?; **g. him to call me** dile que me llame; **to g. one's hair cut** cortarse el pelo; **to g. sb to do sth** *(ask)* persuadir a algn de que haga algo. **2** *vi (become)* ponerse; **to g. late** hacerse tarde; **to g. dressed** vestirse; **to g. married** casarse; **to g. to** *(come to)* llegar a; **to g. to know sb** llegar a conocer a algn.

▸ **get across** *vt (idea etc)* hacer comprender.

▸ **get along** *vi (manage)* arreglárselas; *(two people)* llevarse bien.

▸ **get around 1** *vi (person)* salir; *(news)* difundirse. **2** *vt (problem)* salvar; *(difficulty)* vencer.

▸ **get around to** *vi* **if I g. around to it** si tengo tiempo; **I'll g. around to it later** encontraré tiempo para hacerlo más tarde.

➤ **get at** *vt (reach)* alcanzar; *(criticize)* criticar.

➤ **get away** *vi* escaparse.

➤ **get back 1** *vi (return)* volver; **g. back!** *(move backwards)* ¡atrás! **2** *vt (recover)* recuperar.

➤ **get by** *vi (manage)* arreglárselas; **she can g. by in French** sabe defenderse en francés.

➤ **get down 1** *vt (depress)* deprimir. **2** *vi (descend)* bajar.

➤ **get in 1** *vi (arrive)* llegar; *(politician)* ser elegido, -a. **2** *vt (buy)* comprar; *(collect)* recoger.

➤ **get into** *vt (house, car)* entrar en; *fig* **to g. into bad habits** adquirir malas costumbres; **to g. into trouble** meterse en un lío.

➤ **get off 1** *vt (bus etc)* bajarse de; *(remove)* quitarse. **2** *vi* bajarse; *(escape)* escaparse; **to g. off lightly** salir bien librado, -a.

➤ **get on 1** *vt (board)* subir a. **2** *vi (board)* subirse; *(make progress)* hacer progresos; **how are you getting on?** ¿cómo te van las cosas?; **to g. on well (with sb)** llevarse bien (con algn); *(continue)* **to g. on with sth** seguir con algo.

➤ **get on to** *vt (find) (person)* localizar; *(find out)* descubrir; *(continue)* pasar a.

➤ **get out 1** *vt (object)* sacar. **2** *vi (of room etc)* salir (**of** de); *(of train)* bajar (**of** de); *(news)* difundirse; *(secret)* hacerse público.

➤ **get over** *vt (illness)* recuperarse de; *(difficulty)* vencer; *(convey)* hacer comprender.

➤ **get through 1** *vi (message)* llegar; *(on phone)* **to g. through to sb** conseguir comunicar con algn. **2** *vt (consume)* consumir; **to g. through a lot of work** trabajar mucho.

➤ **get together** *vi (people)* reunirse.

➤ **get up 1** *vi (rise)* levantarse. **2** *vt (wake up)* despertar.

➤ **get up to** *vt* hacer; **to g. up to mischief** hacer de las suyas.

get·to·geth·er reunión *f.*

ghast·ly *adj* espantoso, -a.

gher·kin pepinillo *m.*

ghet·to gueto *m.*

ghost fantasma *m.*

gi·ant *adj & n* gigante (*m*).

gid·dy *adj* mareado, -a; **it makes me g.** me da vértigo; **to feel g.** sentirse mareado, -a.

gift regalo *m; (talent)* don *m.*

gift·ed *adj* dotado, -a.

gig *fam (concert)* actuación *f.*

gi·ga·byte *n* gigabyte *m.*

gi·gan·tic *adj* gigantesco, -a.

gig·gle *vi* reírse tontamente.

gim·mick truco *m; (in advertising)* reclamo *m.*

gin ginebra *f,* **g. and tonic** gin tonic *m.*

gin·ger 1 *adj (hair)* pelirrojo, -a. **2** *n* jengibre *m.*

gi·raffe jirafa *f.*

girl chica *f; (child)* niña *f; (daughter)* hija *f.*

girl·friend novia *f; (female friend)* amiga *f.*

give* *vt* dar; **to g. sb sth as a present** regalar algo a algn.

➤ **give away** *vt (present)* regalar; *(disclose)* revelar.

➤ **give back** *vt* devolver.

➤ **give in 1** *vi (admit defeat)* darse por vencido, -a; *(surrender)* rendirse. **2** *vt (hand in)* entregar.

➤ **give off** *vt (smell etc)* despedir.

➤ **give out** *vt* repartir.

➤ **give up** *vt (idea)* abandonar; **to g. up smoking** dejar de fumar; **to g. oneself up** entregarse.

giv·en 1 *adj (particular)* dado, -a. **2** *conj (considering)* dado, -a.

glad *adj* contento, -a; **to be g.** alegrarse.

glad·ly *adv* con mucho gusto.

glam·or·ous *adj* atractivo, -a.

glam·our atractivo *m; (charm)* encanto *m.*

glance 1 *n* vistazo *m.* **2** *vi* echar un vistazo (**at** a).

gland glándula f.

glare 1 n (look) mirada f feroz. **2** vi (look) lanzar una mirada furiosa (**at** a).

glar·ing adj (light) deslumbrante; (obvious) evidente.

glass (material) vidrio m; (drinking vessel) vaso m; (pane of g.) cristal m. **wine g.** copa f (para vino); **glasses** (spectacles) gafas fpl.

glee gozo m.

glide vi (plane) planear.

glid·ing vuelo m sin motor.

glim·mer fig (trace) destello m.

glimpse 1 n atisbo m. **2** vt atisbar.

glit·ter·ing adj reluciente.

globe globo m.

gloom (obscurity) penumbra f, (melancholy) melancolía f.

gloom·y adj (dismal) deprimente; (despondent) pesimista; (sad) triste.

glo·ri·fied adj fam con pretensiones; **a g. boarding house** una pensión con pretensiones.

glo·ri·ous adj (momentous) glorioso, -a; (splendid) espléndido, -a.

glo·ry gloria f, (splendor) esplendor m.

gloss (sheen) brillo m; **g. (paint)** esmalte m.

gloss·y adj lustroso, -a; **g. maga·zine** revista f de lujo.

glove guante m; **g. compartment** guantera f.

glow 1 n brillo m. **2** vi brillar.

glue 1 n pegamento m. **2** vt pegar (**to** a).

glum adj alicaído, -a.

glut·ton glotón, -ona mf.

gnat mosquito m.

gnaw vti (chew) roer.

go * **1** vi ir; (depart) irse, marcharse; (bus) salir; (disappear) desaparecer; (function) funcionar; (become) quedarse, volverse; (fit) caber; (time) pasar; **how's it going?** ¿qué tal (te van las cosas)?; **to get** or **be going** marcharse; **to be going to** (in the future) ir a; (on the point of) estar a punto de;

there are only two weeks to go sólo quedan dos semanas; **to let sth go** soltar algo. **2** n (try) intento m; (turn) turno m; **to have a go at sth** probar suerte con algo; **it's your go** te toca a ti; **to have a go at sb** criticar a algn.

▸ **go about 1** vt (task) emprender; **how do you go about it?** ¿cómo hay que hacerlo? **2** vi (rumor) correr.

▸ **go after** vt (pursue) andar tras.

▸ **go against** vt (oppose) ir en contra de; (be unfavorable to) ser desfavorable a.

▸ **go ahead** vi (proceed) proceder; **we'll go on ahead** iremos adelante.

▸ **go along** vt (street) ir por.

▸ **go along with** vt (agree) estar de acuerdo con; (accompany) acompañar.

▸ **go around** vi (revolve) dar vueltas; **to go around to sb's house** pasar por casa de algn.

▸ **go away** vi marcharse.

▸ **go back** vi (return) volver.

▸ **go back on** vt **to go back on one's word** faltar a su palabra.

▸ **go back to** vt volver a; (date from) datar de.

▸ **go by** vi pasar; **as time goes by** con el tiempo.

▸ **go down** vi (descend) bajar; (sun) ponerse; (ship) hundirse; (diminish) disminuir; (temperature) bajar.

▸ **go down with** vt (disease) coger.

▸ **go for** vt (fetch) ir por; (attack) atacar, lanzarse sobre; **the same goes for you** lo mismo te digo a ti or vale para ti.

▸ **go in** vi entrar.

▸ **go in for** vt (exam) presentarse a.

▸ **go into** vt (enter) entrar en; (matter) investigar.

▸ **go off** vi (leave) irse, marcharse; (bomb) explotar; (gun) dispararse; (alarm) sonar; (food) pasarse.

▸ **go on** vi (continue) seguir, continuar; (happen) pasar; (light) encenderse; **to go on talking** seguir hablando.

▸**go out** vi (leave) salir; (fire, light) apagarse.

▸**go over** vt (cross) atravesar; (revise) repasar.

▸**go over to** vt (switch to) pasar a; **to go over to the enemy** pasarse al enemigo.

▸**go through** vt (endure) sufrir; (examine) examinar; (search) registrar; (spend) gastar.

▸**go under** vi (ship) hundirse; (business) fracasar.

▸**go up** vi subir.

▸**go with** vt (accompany) ir con; (colors) hacer juego con.

▸**go without** vt pasarse sin.

go·a·head to give sb the g. dar luz verde a algn.

goal gol m; (aim, objective) meta f.

goal·keep·er portero, -a mf.

goat (male) macho cabrío m; (female) cabra f.

god dios m.

god·daugh·ter ahijada f.

god·fa·ther padrino m.

god·moth·er madrina f.

god·send to be a g. venir como agua de mayo.

god·son ahijado m.

gog·gles npl (for diving) gafas fpl de bucear; (protective) gafas fpl protectoras.

go·ing adj (price) corriente.

go·ings-on npl tejemanejes mpl.

gold 1 n oro m. **2** adj de oro; (color) dorado, -a.

gold·en adj de oro; (color) dorado, -a.

gold·fish pez m de colores.

gold-plat·ed adj chapado, -a en oro.

golf golf m.

golf·er golfista mf.

gone pp of **go**.

good 1 adj (before noun) buen, -a; (after noun) bueno, -a; (kind) amable; (generous) generoso, -a; (morally correct) correcto, -a; **g. afternoon, g. evening** buenas tardes;

g. morning buenos días; **g. night** buenas noches; **to have a g. time** pasarlo bien; **be g.!** ¡pórtate bien!; **he's g. at languages** tiene facilidad para los idiomas; **he's in a g. mood** está de buen humor. **2** n bien m; **for your own g.** por tu propio bien; **it's no g. waiting** no sirve de nada esperar. **3** adv **she's gone for g.** se ha ido para siempre. **4** interj **g.!** ¡muy bien!

good·bye interj ¡adiós!

good-look·ing adj guapo, -a.

good·ness bondad f; **my g.!** ¡Dios mío!

goods npl (possessions) bienes mpl; (commercial) mercancías fpl.

good will buena voluntad f.

goose (pl **geese**) ganso m, oca f.

goose·ber·ry grosella f espinosa.

goose-flesh, **goose-pim·ples** npl carne f de gallina.

gorge desfiladero m.

gor·geous adj magnífico, -a; (person) atractivo, -a.

go·ril·la gorila m.

gos·pel the G. el Evangelio

gos·sip (rumor) cotilleo m; (person) chismoso, -a mf.

got pt & pp of **get**.

got·ten pp of **get**.

gour·met gourmet mf.

gov·ern vt gobernar; (determine) determinar.

gov·ern·ment gobierno m.

gov·er·nor (ruler) gobernador, -a mf; (of school) administrador, -a mf.

gown (dress) vestido m largo; (of lawyer, professor) toga f.

GP abbr of **general practitioner** médico m de cabecera.

grab vt agarrar; **to g. hold of sb** agarrarse a algn.

grace gracia f; (elegance) elegancia f.

grace·ful adj elegante; (movement) garboso, -a.

grade 1 n (rank) categoría f; (in army) rango m; (mark) nota f; (class) clase f. **2** vt clasificar.

grad·u·al *adj* gradual.

grad·u·al·ly *adv* poco a poco.

grad·u·ate 1 *n* licenciado, -a *mf*. **2** *vi (from university)* licenciarse (**in** en).

grad·u·a·tion cer·e·mo·ny ceremonia *f* de entrega de los títulos.

graf·fi·ti *npl* grafiti *mpl*.

graft 1 *n* injerto *m*. **2** *vt* injertar (**on to** en).

grain *(cereals)* cereales *mpl*; *(particle)* grano *m*.

gram gramo *m*.

gram·mar gramática *f*.

gram·mar school ≃ instituto *m* de Bachillerato.

gram·mat·i·cal *adj* gramatical.

grand *adj (splendid)* grandioso, -a; *(impressive)* impresionante.

grand·child nieto, -a *mf*.

grand·dad *fam* abuelo *m*.

grand·daugh·ter nieta *f*.

grand·fa·ther abuelo *m*.

grand·ma *fam* abuelita *f*.

grand·moth·er abuela *f*.

grand·par·ents *npl* abuelos *mpl*.

grand·son nieto *m*.

gran·ny *fam* abuelita *f*.

grant 1 *vt (give)* conceder; *(accept)* admitir; **to take for granted** dar por sentado. **2** *n (for study)* beca *f*; *(subsidy)* subvención *f*.

grape uva *f*; **g. juice** mosto *m*.

grape·fruit pomelo *m*.

graph gráfica *f*.

graph·ic *adj* gráfico, -a; **g. arts** artes *fpl* gráficas.

graph·ics (computer) g. gráficas *fpl*.

grasp 1 *vt* agarrar; *(understand)* comprender. **2** *n (grip)* agarrón *m*; *(understanding)* comprensión *f*.

grass hierba *f*; *(lawn)* césped *m*.

grass·hop·per saltamontes *m inv*.

grate 1 *vt (food)* rallar. **2** *vi* chirriar. **3** *n (fireplace)* rejilla *f*.

grate·ful *adj* agradecido, -a; **to be g. for** agradecer.

grat·er rallador *m*.

grat·i·fy·ing *adj* grato, -a.

grat·i·tude agradecimiento *m*.

grave[1] tumba *f*.

grave[2] *adj (situation)* grave.

grav·el gravilla *f*.

grave·yard cementerio *m*.

grav·i·ty gravedad *f*.

gra·vy salsa *f*.

gray *adj (color)* gris; *(hair)* cano, -a; *(sky)* nublado, -a.

graze 1 *vt (scratch)* rasguñar; *(brush against)* rozar. **2** *vi (cattle)* pacer. **3** *n* rasguño *m*.

grease 1 *n* grasa *f*. **2** *vt* engrasar.

grease·proof pa·per papel *m* apergaminado.

greas·y *adj (hair, food)* graso, -a.

great *adj* grande; *(before sing noun)* gran; *fam (excellent)* estupendo, -a; **a g. many** muchos, -as; **to have a g. time** pasarlo en grande.

great-grand·fa·ther bisabuelo *m*.

great-grand·moth·er bisabuela *f*.

great·ly *adv (with adjective)* muy; *(with verb)* mucho.

greed, gree·di·ness *(for food)* gula *f*; *(for money)* codicia *f*.

greed·y *adj (for food)* glotón, -ona; *(for money)* codicioso, -a.

Greek 1 *adj* griego, -a. **2** *n (person)* griego, -a *mf*; *(language)* griego *m*.

green 1 *n (color)* verde *m*; *(for golf)* campo *m*; **greens** verduras *fpl*. **2** *adj* verde.

green·house invernadero *m*; **g. ef·fect** efecto *m* invernadero.

greet *vt* saludar.

greet·ing saludo *m*.

gre·nade granada *f*.

grey *adj* = **gray**.

grey·hound galgo *m*.

grid *(on map)* cuadrícula *f*; *(of electricity etc)* red *f* nacional.

grief pena *f*, dolor *m*.

grieve *vi* to g. for sb llorar la muerte de algn.

grill 1 *vt (food)* asar a la parrilla. **2** *n* parrilla *f*; *(dish)* parrillada *f*.

grim adj (landscape) lúgubre; (manner) severo, -a; (unpleasant) desagradable.

grime mugre f.

grim·y adj mugriento, -a.

grin 1 vi sonreír abiertamente. **2** n sonrisa abierta.

grind* vt moler; **to g. one's teeth** hacer rechinar los dientes.

grip 1 n (hold) agarrón m; (handle) asidero m. **2** vt agarrar; **to be gripped by fear** ser presa del miedo.

grip·ping adj (film, story) apasionante.

groan 1 n gemido m. **2** vi gemir.

gro·cer tendero, -a mf.

gro·cer·y (shop) tienda f de ultramarinos; **g. store** supermercado m.

groin ingle f.

groom (bridegroom) novio m.

groove (furrow etc) ranura f; (of record) surco m.

grope vi **to g. for sth** buscar algo a tientas.

▸**grope about** vi andar a tientas; (looking for sth) buscar a tientas.

gross adj grosero, -a; (not net) bruto, -a.

gross·ly adv enormemente.

gross na·tion·al prod·uct producto m nacional bruto.

ground¹ suelo m; (terrain) terreno m; **grounds** (gardens) jardines mpl; (reason) motivo m sing.

ground² adj (coffee) molido, -a; (meat) picado, -a.

ground·work trabajo m preparatorio.

group grupo m.

grow* 1 vt (cultivate) cultivar; **to g. a beard** dejarse (crecer) la barba. **2** vi crecer; (increase) aumentar; (become) volverse.

▸**grow into** vt convertirse en.

▸**grow out of** vt (phase etc) superar; **he's grown out of his shirt** se le ha quedado pequeña la camisa.

▸**grow up** vi crecer.

growl 1 vi gruñir. **2** n gruñido m.

grown adj crecido, -a.

grown-up adj & n adulto, -a (mf); **the grown-ups** los mayores.

growth crecimiento m; (increase) aumento m; (development) desarrollo m; (diseased part) bulto m.

grub fam (food) comida f.

grub·by adj sucio, -a.

grudge 1 n rencor m; **to bear sb a g.** guardar rencor a algn. **2** vt **he grudges me my success** me envidia el éxito.

gru·el·ing adj penoso, -a.

grue·some adj espantoso, -a.

grum·ble vi refunfuñar.

grump·y adj gruñón, -ona.

grunt 1 vi gruñir. **2** n gruñido m.

guar·an·tee 1 n garantía f. **2** vt garantizar; (assure) asegurar.

guard 1 vt (protect) proteger; (keep watch over) vigilar; (control) guardar. **2** n (sentry) guardia mf; (on train) jefe m de tren; **to be on one's g.** estar en guardia; **to stand g.** montar la guardia.

guard·i·an guardián, -ana mf; (of minor) tutor, -ora mf.

Gua·te·ma·lan adj & n guatemalteco, -a (mf).

guess 1 vti adivinar; fam suponer. **2** n conjetura f; (estimate) cálculo m; **to have** or **make a g.** intentar adivinar.

guess·work conjetura f.

guest invitado, -a mf; (in hotel) cliente, -a mf, huésped, -a mf.

guest·house casa f de huéspedes.

guid·ance orientación f.

guide 1 vt guiar. **2** n (person) guía mf; (guidebook) guía f.

guide·line pauta f.

guild gremio m.

guilt culpabilidad f.

guilt·y adj culpable (of de).

guin·ea pig conejillo m de Indias.

gui·tar guitarra f.

gui·tar·ist guitarrista mf.

gulf golfo m; fig abismo m.

gull gaviota f.

gulp trago m.

gum¹ 1 n goma f. **2** vt pegar con goma.

gum² (around teeth) encía f.

gun (handgun) pistola f; (rifle) fusil m; (cannon) cañón m.

▸**gun down** vt matar a tiros.

gun·fire tiros mpl.

gun·man pistolero m.

gun·point at g. a punta de pistola.

gun·pow·der pólvora f.

gun·shot tiro m.

gush vi brotar.

gust (of wind) ráfaga f.

gut 1 n (inside body) intestino m; **guts** (entrails) tripas fpl; fam (courage) agallas fpl. **2** vt (fish) destripar; (destroy) destruir por dentro.

gut·ter (in street) cuneta f; (on roof) canalón m.

guy fam tipo m, tío m.

gym (gymnasium) gimnasio m; (gymnastics) gimnasia f.

gy·ne·col·o·gist ginecólogo, -a mf.

H

hab·it costumbre f; **to be in the h. of doing sth** soler hacer algo; **to get into the h. of doing sth** acostumbrarse a hacer algo.

hab·i·tat hábitat m.

hack 1 n (cut) corte m; (with an ax) hachazo m. **2** vt (with knife, ax) cortar.

had pt & pp of **have**.

had·dock abadejo m.

hag bruja f.

hag·gle vi regatear.

hail 1 n granizo m; **a h. of bullets** una lluvia de balas. **2** vi granizar.

hail·stone granizo m.

hair pelo m; (on arm, leg) vello m; **to have long h.** tener el pelo largo.

hair·brush cepillo m (para el pelo).

hair·cut corte m de pelo; **to have a h.** cortarse el pelo.

hair·do fam peinado m.

hair·dress·er peluquero, -a mf; **h.'s** (shop) peluquería f.

hair·dry·er, hair·dri·er secador m (de pelo).

hair·grip horquilla f.

hair·pin bend curva f muy cerrada.

hair·rais·ing adj espeluznante.

hair·spray laca f (para el pelo).

hair·style peinado m.

hair·y adj (with hair) peludo, -a; fam (frightening) espeluznante.

half 1 n (pl halves) mitad f; (period in match) tiempo m; **he's four and a h.** tiene cuatro años y medio; **to cut in h.** cortar por la mitad. **2** adj medio, -a; **h. a dozen/an hour** media docena/hora; **h. fare** media tarifa f. **3** adv a medias; **h. asleep** medio dormido, -a; **h. past one** la una y media.

half board media pensión f.

half-heart·ed adj poco entusiasta.

half-hour media hora f.

half term (holiday) vacación f a mitad de trimestre.

half-time descanso m.

half·way adv a medio camino.

hal·i·but mero m.

hall (lobby) vestíbulo m; (building) sala f; **h. of residence** colegio m mayor.

Hal·low·e(')en víspera f de Todos los Santos.

hall·stand percha f.

hall·way vestíbulo m.

halt alto m; **to call a h. to sth** poner fin a algo.

halve vt reducir a la mitad.

ham jamón m.

ham·burg·er hamburguesa f.

ham·mer 1 n martillo m. **2** vt (nail) clavar; fig **to h. home** insistir sobre. **3** vi dar golpes.

ham·mer·ing fam (defeat) paliza f.

ham·mock hamaca f.

ham·per¹ cesta f.

ham·per² vt dificultar.

ham·ster hámster *m*.

hand 1 *n* mano *f*; *(worker)* trabajador, -a *mf*; *(of clock)* aguja *f*; **by h.** a mano; **(close) at h.** a mano; **on the one/other h.** por una/otra parte; **to get out of h.** descontrolarse; **to be on h.** estar a mano; **to have a h. in** intervenir en; **to give sb a h.** echarle una mano a algn; **to give sb a big h.** *(applause)* dedicar a algn una gran ovación. **2** *vt (give)* dar.

▸ **hand back** *vt* devolver.

▸ **hand in** *vt (homework)* entregar.

▸ **hand out** *vt* repartir.

▸ **hand over** *vt* entregar.

hand·bag bolso *m*.

hand·book manual *m*.

hand·brake freno *m* de mano.

hand·cuff 1 *vt* esposar. **2** *npl* **handcuffs** esposas *fpl*.

hand·ful puñado *m*.

hand gre·nade granada *f* de mano.

hand·i·cap 1 *n (physical)* minusvalía *f*; *(in sport)* hándicap *m*. **2** *vt* impedir.

hand·i·capped *adj (physically)* minusválido, -a; *(mentally)* retrasado, -a; *fig* desfavorecido, -a.

hand·ker·chief pañuelo *m*.

han·dle 1 *n (of knife)* mango *m*; *(of cup)* asa *f*; *(of door)* pomo *m*; *(of drawer)* tirador *m*. **2** *vt* manejar; *(problem)* encargarse de; *(people)* tratar; **'h. with care'** 'frágil'.

han·dle·bars *npl* manillar *m*.

hand lug·gage equipaje *m* de mano.

hand·made *adj* hecho, -a a mano.

hand·out *(leaflet)* folleto *m*; *(charity)* limosna *f*.

hand·rail pasamanos *m inv*.

hand·shake apretón *m* de manos.

hand·some *adj (person)* guapo, -a; *(substantial)* considerable.

hand·writ·ing letra *f*.

hand·y *adj (useful)* útil; *(nearby)* a mano; *(dexterous)* diestro, -a.

hand·y·man manitas *m inv*.

hang* 1 *vt* colgar; *(head)* bajar. **2** *vi*

colgar (**from** de); *(in air)* flotar; *(criminal)* ser ahorcado, -a; **to h.** **oneself** ahorcarse.

▸ **hang around 1** *vi fam* no hacer nada; *(wait)* esperar. **2** *vt (bar etc)* frecuentar.

▸ **hang on** *vi* agarrarse; *(wait)* esperar; **to h. on to sth** *(keep)* guardar.

▸ **hang out 1** *vt (washing)* tender. **2** *vi* **his tongue was hanging out** le colgaba la lengua.

▸ **hang up** *vt (picture, telephone)* colgar.

han·gar hangar *m*.

hang·er percha *f*.

hang·glid·er alta *f* delta.

hang·o·ver resaca *f*.

hang·up *fam (complex)* complejo *m*.

hap·pen *vi* suceder, ocurrir; **if you h. to see my friend** si por casualidad ves a mi amigo.

hap·pen·ing acontecimiento *m*.

hap·pi·ly *adv (with pleasure)* felizmente; *(fortunately)* afortunadamente.

hap·pi·ness felicidad *f*.

hap·py *adj* feliz; **h. birthday!** ¡feliz cumpleaños!

ha·rass *vt* acosar.

ha·rass·ment hostigamiento *m*, acoso *m*.

har·bor 1 *n* puerto *m*. **2** *vt (criminal)* encubrir; *(doubts)* abrigar.

hard 1 *adj* duro, -a; *(solid)* sólido, -a; *(difficult)* difícil; *(harsh)* severo, -a; *(strict)* estricto, -a; **h. of hearing** duro, -a de oído; **to be h. up** estar sin blanca; **to take a h. line** tomar medidas severas; **h. drugs** droga *f* dura; **a h. worker** un trabajador concienzudo; **h. luck!** ¡mala suerte!; **h. evidence** pruebas definitivas; **h. currency** divisa *f* fuerte. **2** *adv (forcibly)* fuerte; *(with application)* mucho.

hard·ball béisbol *m*.

hard·boiled *adj* duro, -a.

hard·core *adj* irreductible.

hard disk disco *m* duro.

hard·en 1 *vt* endurecer. **2** *vi* endurecerse.

hard·ly adv apenas; **h. anyone/ever** casi nadie/nunca; **he had h. begun when …** apenas había comenzado cuando ….

hard·ness dureza f; (difficulty) dificultad f.

hard·ship privación f.

hard·ware (goods) ferretería f; (computer equipment) hardware m; **h. store** ferretería f.

hard·wear·ing adj duradero, -a.

hard·work·ing adj muy trabajador, -a.

hare liebre f.

harm 1 n daño m. 2 vt hacer daño a.

harm·ful adj perjudicial (**to** para).

harm·less adj inofensivo, -a.

har·mon·i·ca armónica f.

har·mo·ni·ous adj armonioso, -a.

har·mo·ny armonía f.

har·ness 1 n (for horse) arreos mpl. 2 vt (horse) enjaezar.

harp arpa f.

▶**harp** on vi fam hablar sin parar; **to h. on about sth** hablar sin parar sobre algo.

harsh adj severo, -a; (voice) áspero, -a; (sound) discordante.

harsh·ly adv duramente.

harsh·ness dureza f; (discordancy) discordancia f.

har·vest 1 n cosecha f; (of grapes) vendimia f. 2 vt cosechar, recoger.

has 3rd person sing pres of **have**.

has·sle fam 1 n (nuisance) rollo m; (problem) lío m; (wrangle) bronca f. 2 vt fastidiar.

haste prisa f.

has·ten vi apresurarse.

has·ti·ly adv (quickly) de prisa.

hast·y adj apresurado, -a; (rash) precipitado, -a.

hat sombrero m.

hatch[1] n escotilla f; **serving h.** ventanilla f.

hatch[2] 1 vt (egg) empollar. 2 vi (bird) salir del huevo.

hatch·back coche m de 3/5 puertas.

hate 1 n odio m. 2 vt odiar.

hate·ful adj odioso, -a.

ha·tred odio m.

haul 1 n (journey) trayecto m. 2 vt tirar; (drag) arrastrar.

haunt 1 n guarida f. 2 vt (of ghost) aparecerse en; fig atormentar; (frequent) frecuentar.

haunt·ed adj embrujado, -a.

have* 1 vt tener; (party, meeting) hacer; **h. you got a car?** ¿tienes coche?; **to h. a cigarette** fumarse un cigarrillo; **to h. breakfast/lunch/tea/dinner** desayunar/comer/merendar/cenar; **what will you h.?** ¿qué quieres tomar?; **can I h. your pen for a moment?** (borrow) ¿me dejas tu bolígrafo un momento? ■ **to h. to** (obligation) tener que, deber; **I h. to go now** tengo que irme ya. ■ (make happen) hacer; **I'll h. someone come around** haré que venga alguien. 2 v aux (compound) haber; **yes I h.!** ¡que sí!; **you haven't seen my book, h. you?** no has visto mi libro, ¿verdad?; **he's been to France, hasn't he?** ha estado en Francia, ¿verdad?

▶**have on** vt (wear) vestir; fam **to h. sb on** tomarle el pelo a algn.

▶**have out** vt **to h. it out with sb** ajustar cuentas con algn.

▶**have over** vt (invite) recibir.

hav·oc to play h. with hacer estragos en.

hawk halcón m.

hay heno m.

hay fe·ver fiebre f del heno.

hay·stack almiar m.

haz·ard 1 n peligro m, riesgo m. 2 vt arriesgar; **to h. a guess** intentar adivinar.

haze (mist) neblina f.

ha·zel·nut avellana f.

haz·y adj nebuloso, -a.

he pers pron él; **he who** el que.

head 1 n cabeza f; (mind) mente f; (of company) director, -a mf; (of coin) cara f; **to be h. over heels in love** estar locamente enamorado, -a; **to keep one's h.** mantener la calma; **to lose one's h.** perder la cabeza; **heads or tails** cara o cruz. **2** *adj* principal; **h. office** sede *f*. **3** *vt (list etc)* encabezar.

▸**head for** *vt* dirigirse hacia.

head·ache dolor *m* de cabeza; *fig* quebradero *m* de cabeza.

head·band cinta *f* para la cabeza.

head·ing título *m*; *(of letter)* membrete *m*.

head·light faro *m*.

head·line titular *m*.

head·mas·ter director *m*.

head·mis·tress directora *f*.

head·phones *npl* auriculares *mpl*.

head·quar·ters *npl* oficina *f* central; *(military)* cuartel *m* general.

head teach·er director, -a *mf*.

head·wait·er jefe *m* de comedor.

head·way **to make h.** avanzar.

heal *vi* cicatrizar. **2** *vt* curar.

health salud *f*; *fig* prosperidad *f*; **to be in good/bad h.** estar bien/mal de salud; **h. foods** alimentos *mpl* naturales; **h. service** ≃ Insalud *m*.

health·y *adj* sano, -a; *(good for health)* saludable.

heap 1 *n* montón *m*. **2** *vt* amontonar; *(praises)* colmar de; **to h. praises on sb** colmar a algn de elogios.

hear* *vt vi* oír; *(listen to)* escuchar; *(find out)* enterarse de; *(evidence)* oír; **I won't h. of it!** ¡ni hablar!; **to h. from sb** tener noticias de algn.

hear·ing oído *m*; *(legal)* audiencia *f*.

hear·ing aid audífono *m*.

hearse coche *m* fúnebre.

heart corazón *m*; **hearts** corazones *m*; **at h.** en el fondo; **to lose h.** desanimarse.

heart at·tack infarto *m* (de miocardio).

heart·beat latido *m* del corazón.

heart·break·ing *adj* desgarrador, -a.

heart·en·ing *adj* alentador, -a.

heart·y *adj (person)* francote;

(meal) abundante; **to have a h. appetite** ser de buen comer.

heat 1 *n* calor *m*; *(in sport)* eliminatoria *f*. **2** *vt* calentar.

▸**heat up** *vi (warm up)* calentarse.

heat·er calentador *m*.

heath *(land)* brezal *m*.

heath·er brezo *m*.

heat·ing calefacción *f*.

heat·wave ola *f* de calor.

heave *vt (lift)* levantar; *(haul)* tirar; *(push)* empujar; *(throw)* arrojar.

heav·en cielo *m*; **for heaven's sake!** ¡por Dios!

heav·i·ly *adv* it rained h. llovió mucho; **to sleep h.** dormir profundamente.

heav·y *adj* pesado, -a; *(rain, meal)* fuerte; *(traffic)* denso, -a; *(loss)* grande; **is it h.?** ¿pesa mucho?; **a h. drinker/smoker** un, -a bebedor, -a/ fumador, -a empedernido, -a.

heav·y·weight peso *m* pesado.

He·brew 1 *adj* hebreo, -a; **2** *n (person)* hebreo -a *mf*; *(language)* hebreo *m*.

hec·tic *adj* agitado, -a.

hedge 1 *n* seto *m*. **2** *vt* **to h. one's bets** cubrirse.

hedge·hog erizo *m*.

heel talón *m*; *(of shoe)* tacón *m*.

heft·y *adj (person)* fornido, -a; *(package)* pesado, -a.

height altura *f*; *(of person)* estatura *f*; **what h. are you?** ¿cuánto mides?

heir heredero *m*.

heir·ess heredera *f*.

held *pt & pp* of **hold**.

hel·i·cop·ter helicóptero *m*.

hell infierno *m*; **what the h. are you doing?** ¿qué diablos estás haciendo?; *fam* **go to h.!** ¡vete a hacer puñetas!; *fam* **a h. of a party** una fiesta estupenda; *fam* **she's had h. of a day** ha tenido un día fatal; *fam* **h.!** ¡demonios!

hel·lo *interj* ¡hola!; *(on phone)* ¡diga!; *(showing surprise)* ¡hala!

helm timón *m*.

hel·met casco *m*.

help 1 n ayuda f; **h.!** ¡socorro!; **(daily) h.** asistenta f. **2** vt ayudar; **can I h. you?** (in shop) ¿qué desea?; **h. yourself!** (to food etc) ¡sírvete!; **I couldn't h. laughing** no pude evitar reírme; **I can't h. it** no lo puedo remediar.

▸**help out** vt to **h. sb out** echarle una mano a algn.

help·er ayudante, -a mf.

help·ful adj (person) amable; (thing) útil.

help·ing ración f.

help·less adj (defenseless) desamparado, -a; (powerless) impotente.

hem dobladillo m.

▸**hem in** vt cercar, rodear.

hem·i·sphere hemisferio m.

hem·or·rhage hemorragia f.

hen gallina f.

hep·a·ti·tis hepatitis f.

her 1 poss adj (one thing) su; (more than one) sus; (to distinguish male from female) de ella; **are they h. books or his?** ¿los libros son de ella o de él? **2** object pron (direct object) la; **I saw h. recently** la vi hace poco. ▪ (indirect object) le; (with other third person pronouns) se; **he gave h. money** le dio dinero; **they handed it to h.** se lo entregaron. ▪ (after prep) ella; **for h.** para ella. ▪ (emphatic) ella; **look, it's h.!** ¡mira, es ella!

herb hierba f; **herb tea** infusión f.

herd (of cattle) manada f; (of goats) rebaño m.

here 1 adv aquí; **h.!** ¡presente!; **h. you are!** ¡toma! **2** interj **look h., you can't do that!** ¡oiga, no puede hacer eso!

he·red·i·tar·y adj hereditario, -a.

her·mit ermitaño, -a mf.

he·ro (pl **heroes**) héroe m; (in novel) protagonista m.

he·ro·ic adj heroico, -a.

her·o·in heroína f.

her·o·ine heroína f; (in novel) protagonista f.

her·ring arenque m.

hers poss pron (attribute) (one thing) suyo, -a; (more than one) suyos, -as; (to distinguish male from female) de ella; **they are h. not his** son de ella, no de él. ▪ (one thing) el suyo, la suya; (more than one) los suyos, las suyas.

her·self pers pron (reflexive) se; **she dressed h.** se vistió. ▪ (alone) ella misma; **she was by h.** estaba sola. ▪ (emphatic) **she told me so h.** eso me dijo ella misma.

hes·i·tant adj vacilante.

hes·i·tate vi vacilar.

hes·i·ta·tion indecisión f.

het up adj nervioso, -a.

hey interj ¡oye!, ¡oiga!

hi interj ¡hola!

hic·cup hipo m; (minor problem) problemilla m; **to have hiccups** tener hipo.

hide¹* **1** vt (conceal) esconder; (obscure) ocultar. **2** vi esconderse, ocultarse.

hide² (skin) piel f.

hide-and-seek escondite m.

hid·e·ous adj (horrific) horroroso, -a; (extremely ugly) espantoso, -a.

hide·ous·ly adv horrorosamente.

hide-out escondrijo m.

hid·ing a good h. una buena paliza.

hid·ing place escondite m.

hi·er·ar·chy jerarquía f.

hi-fi hifi m.

high 1 adj alto, -a; (price) elevado, -a; (drugged) colocado, -a; **how h. is that wall?** ¿qué altura tiene esa pared?; **it's three feet h.** tiene tres pies de alto; **h. wind** viento m fuerte; **to have a h. opinion of sb** tener muy buena opinión de algn. **2** adv alto; **to fly h.** volar a gran altura.

high-class adj de alta categoría.

high den·si·ty adj de alta densidad.

high·er adj superior; **h. education** enseñanza f superior.

high·lands npl tierras fpl altas.

high·light 1 *n (in hair)* reflejo *m*; *(of event)* atracción *f* principal. **2** *vt* hacer resaltar; *(with highlighter)* subrayar con marcador.

high·light·er marcador *m*.

high·ly *adv (very)* sumamente; **to speak h. of sb** hablar muy bien de algn.

high-pitched *adj* estridente.

high-pro·file *adj (person)* prominente, destacado(a); *(campaign)* de gran alcance.

high-rise *adj* **h. building** rascacielos *m inv*.

high school instituto *m* de enseñanza media.

high-speed *adj* **h. train** tren *m* de alta velocidad.

high street calle *f* mayor.

high-tech *adj* de alta tecnología.

high·way autopista *f*.

hi·jack 1 *vt* secuestrar. **2** *n* secuestro *m*.

hi·jack·er secuestrador, -a *mf*; *(of planes)* pirata *mf* del aire.

hi·jack·ing secuestro *m*.

hike 1 *n (walk)* excursión *f*. **2** *vi* ir de excursión.

hik·er excursionista *mf*.

hi·lar·i·ous *adj* graciosísimo, -a.

hill colina *f*; *(slope)* cuesta *f*.

hill·side ladera *f*.

hill·y *adj* accidentado, -a.

him *object pron (direct object)* lo, le; **hit h.!** ¡pégale!; **she loves h.** lo quiere. ▪ *(indirect object)* le; *(with other third person pronouns)* se; **give h. the money** dale el dinero; **give it to h.** dáselo. ▪ *(after prep)* él; **it's not like h. to say that** no es propio de él decir eso. ▪ *(emphatic)* él; **it's h.** es él.

him·self *pers pron (reflexive)* se; **he hurt h.** se hizo daño. ▪ *(alone)* por sí mismo; **by h.** solo. ▪ *(emphatic)* él mismo; **he told me so h.** me lo dijo él mismo.

hin·der *vt* dificultar.

Hin·du *adj & n* hindú *(mf)*.

hinge bisagra *f*.

▸ **hinge on** *vt* depender de.

hint 1 *n* indirecta *f*; *(clue)* pista *f*; *(advice)* consejo *m*. **2** *vi* lanzar indirectas. **3** *vt (imply)* insinuar.

▸ **hint at** *vt* aludir a.

hip cadera *f*.

hip·po·pot·a·mus hipopótamo *m*.

hire *vt (rent)* alquilar; *(employ)* contratar.

his 1 *poss adj (one thing)* su; *(more than one)* sus; *(to distinguish male from female)* de él; **he washed h. face** se lavó la cara; **is it h. dog or hers?** ¿el perro es de él o de ella? **2** *poss pron (attribute) (one thing)* suyo, -a; *(more than one)* suyos, -as; *(to distinguish male from female)* de él. ▪ *(one thing)* el suyo, la suya; *(more than one)* los suyos, las suyas.

His·pan·ic 1 *adj* hispánico, -a. **2** *n* hispano, -a *mf*.

hiss 1 *n* siseo *m*; *(in theater)* silbido *m*. **2** *vti* silbar.

his·tor·ic *adj* histórico, -a.

his·tor·i·cal *adj* histórico, -a.

his·to·ry historia *f*.

hit 1 *n (blow)* golpe *m*; *(success)* éxito *m*. **2** *vt* (strike)* pegar; *(affect)* afectar; **he was h. in the leg** le dieron en la pierna; **the car h. the kerb** el coche chocó contra el bordillo.

▸ **hit back** *vi (reply to criticism)* replicar.

▸ **hit out** *vi* **to h. out at sb** atacar a algn.

▸ **hit (up)on** *vt* dar con; **we h. on the idea of …** se nos ocurrió la idea de ….

hit-and-run driv·er conductor *m* que atropella a algn y no para.

hitch 1 *n* dificultad *f*. **2** *vi (hitchhike)* hacer autostop.

hitch·hike *vi* hacer autostop.

hitch·hik·er autostopista *mf*.

hitch·hik·ing autostop *m*.

HIV *abbr of* **human immunodeficiency virus** virus *m* de inmunodeficiencia humano, VIH *m*; **to be HIV positive/negative** ser/no ser seropositivo, -a.

hive colmena *f*.

hoard 1 *n (provisions)* reservas *fpl*; *(money etc)* tesoro *m*. **2** *vt (objects)* acumular; *(money)* atesorar.

hoard·ing *(billboard)* valla *f* publicitaria.

hoarse *adj* ronco, -a; **to be h.** tener la voz ronca.

hoax *(joke)* broma *f* pesada; *(trick)* engaño *m*.

hob·by pasatiempo *m*.

ho·bo vagabundo, -a *mf*.

hock·ey hockey *m*.

hold 1 *vt* (keep in hand)* tener (en la mano); *(grip)* agarrar; *(opinion)* sostener; *(contain)* dar cabida a; *(meeting)* celebrar; *(reserve) (ticket)* guardar; *(at police station etc)* detener; *(office)* ocupar; **to h. sb's hand** cogerle la mano a algn; **the jug holds a liter** en la jarra cabe un litro; **to h. one's breath** contener la respiración; **to h. sb hostage** retener a algn como rehén; **to h. the line** no colgar. **2** *vi* *(rope)* aguantar; *(offer)* ser válido, -a. **3** *n (in ship)* bodega *f*; *(control)* control *m*; **to get h. of** *(grip)* coger; *(get in touch with)* localizar.

▸**hold back** *vt (crowd)* contener; *(feelings)* reprimir; *(truth)* ocultar; *(suspect)* retener; *(store)* guardar.

▸**hold down** *vt (control)* dominar; *(job)* desempeñar.

▸**hold on** *vi (keep a firm grasp)* agarrarse bien; *(wait)* esperar; **h. on!** *(on phone)* ¡no cuelgue!

▸**hold on to** *vt (to stop oneself from falling)* agarrarse a; *(to stop something from falling)* agarrar; *(keep)* guardar.

▸**hold out 1** *vt (hand)* tender. **2** *vi (last) (things)* durar; *(person)* resistir.

▸**hold up** *vt (support)* apuntalar; *(rob) (train)* asaltar; *(bank)* atracar; *(delay)* retrasar; **we were held up**

for half an hour sufrimos media hora de retraso.

hold·er *(receptacle)* recipiente *m*; *(owner)* poseedor, -a *mf*; *(bearer)* portador, -a *mf*; *(of passport)* titular *mf*.

hold·up *(robbery)* atraco *m*; *(delay)* retraso *m*; *(in traffic)* atasco *m*.

hole agujero *m*; *(large, in golf)* hoyo *m*.

hol·i·day *(one day)* (día *m* de) fiesta *f*; *(several days)* vacaciones *fpl*.

hol·low 1 *adj* hueco, -a; *(cheeks, eyes)* hundido, -a. **2** *n* hueco *m*.

hol·ly acebo *m*.

ho·ly *adj* sagrado, -a; *(blessed)* bendito, -a.

Ho·ly Ghost Espíritu *m* Santo.

home 1 *n* casa *f*, hogar *m*; *(institution)* asilo *m*; *(country)* patria *f*; **at h.** en casa; **make yourself at h.!** ¡estás en tu casa!; **old people's h.** asilo *m* de ancianos; **to play at h.** jugar en casa. **2** *adj (domestic)* del hogar; *(political)* interior; *(native)* natal; **h. affairs** asuntos *mpl* interiores. **3** *adv* en casa; **to go h.** irse a casa; **to leave h.** irse de casa.

home com·put·er ordenador *m* doméstico.

home help asistenta *f*.

home·land patria *f*, *(birthplace)* tierra *f* natal.

home·less 1 *adj* sin hogar. **2** *npl* **the h.** los sin hogar.

home·made *adj* casero, -a.

home·sick *adj* **to be h.** tener morriña.

home·town ciudad *f* natal.

home·work deberes *mpl*.

ho·mo·sex·u·al *adj & n* homosexual *(mf)*.

Hon·du·ran *adj & n* hondureño, -a *(mf)*.

hon·est *adj* honrado, -a; *(sincere)* sincero, -a; *(fair)* justo, -a.

hon·est·ly *adv* honradamente; **h.?** ¿de verdad?

hon·es·ty honradez *f*.

hon·ey miel f; fam (endearment) cariño m.

hon·ey·moon luna f de miel.

honk vi (person in car) tocar la bocina.

hon·or 1 n honor m. **2** vt (respect) honrar; (obligation) cumplir.

hon·or·a·ble adj (person) honrado, -a; (actions) honroso, -a.

hood (of garment) capucha f; (of car) capota f; (bonnet) capó m.

hoof (pl **hoofs** or **hooves**) (of horse) casco m; (of cow, sheep) pezuña f.

hook gancho m; (for fishing) anzuelo m; **to take the phone off the h.** descolgar el teléfono.

▸**hook up** vti conectar (**with** con).

hooked adj (nose) aguileño, -a; (addicted) enganchado, -a (**on** a); **to get h.** engancharse.

hook·y **to play h.** hacer novillos.

hoo·li·gan gamberro, -a mf.

hoop aro m.

hoot 1 n (owl) grito m; **hoots of laughter** carcajadas fpl. **2** vi (owl) ulular; (train) silbar; (siren) pitar.

Hoo·ver® **1** n aspiradora f. **2** vt to h. pasar la aspiradora.

hop 1 vi saltar; **to h. on one leg** andar a la pata coja. **2** n (small jump) brinco m.

hope 1 n esperanza f; (false) ilusión f; **to have little h. of doing sth** tener pocas posibilidades de hacer algo. **2** vti esperar; **I h. so/not** espero que sí/no.

▸**hope for** vt esperar.

hope·ful adj (confident) optimista; (promising) prometedor, -a.

hope·ful·ly adv **h. she won't come** esperemos que no venga.

hope·less adj desesperado, -a; **to be h. at sports** ser negado, -a para los deportes.

hope·less·ly adv desesperadamente; **h. lost** completamente perdido, -a.

hops npl lúpulo m.

hop·scotch **to play h.** jugar al tejo.

ho·ri·zon horizonte m.

hor·i·zon·tal adj horizontal.

horn cuerno m; (on car) bocina f.

hor·ri·ble adj horrible.

hor·ri·bly adv horriblemente.

hor·rif·ic adj horrendo, -a.

hor·ri·fy vt horrorizar.

hor·ror horror m; **a little h.** un diablillo.

hor·ror film película f de terror.

horse caballo m.

horse·back **on h.** a caballo.

horse·pow·er caballo m (de vapor).

horse race carrera f de caballos.

horse·shoe herradura f.

hose (pipe) manguera f.

hose·pipe manguera f.

hos·pi·ta·ble adj hospitalario, -a.

hos·pi·tal hospital m.

hos·pi·tal·i·ty hospitalidad f.

hos·pi·tal·ize vt hospitalizar.

host 1 n (at home) anfitrión m; (on TV) presentador m. **2** vt (TV show etc) presentar.

hos·tage rehén m; **to take sb h.** tomar a algn como rehén.

hos·tel hostal m.

host·ess (at home etc) anfitriona f; (on TV) presentadora f.

hos·tile adj hostil.

hos·til·i·ty hostilidad f.

hot adj caliente; (weather) caluroso, -a; (spicy) picante; (temper) fuerte; **it's very h.** hace mucho calor; **to feel h.** tener calor; **it's not so h.** (not very good) no es nada del otro mundo.

hot·cake crepe f, panqueque m, Esp tortita f.

hot dog perrito m caliente.

ho·tel hotel m.

hot-wa·ter bot·tle bolsa f de agua caliente.

hound 1 n perro m de caza. **2** vt acosar.

hour hora f; **60 miles an h.** 60 millas por hora; **by the h.** por horas.

hour·ly 1 adj cada hora. **2** adv por horas.

house 1 *n* casa *f; (in theater)* sala *f;* **at my h.** en mi casa. **2** *vt* alojar; *(store)* guardar.

house·hold hogar *m;* **h. products** productos *mpl* domésticos.

house·keep·ing administración *f* doméstica.

house-warm·ing par·ty fiesta *f* que se da al estrenar casa.

house·wife ama *f* de casa.

house·work trabajo *m* doméstico.

hous·ing vivienda *f.*

hous·ing es·tate urbanización *f.*

hov·el casucha *f.*

hov·er *vi (bird)* cernerse; *(helicopter)* permanecer inmóvil (en el aire).

hov·er·craft aerodeslizador *m.*

how *adv* ¿cómo?; **h. are you?** ¿cómo estás?; **h. do you do?** mucho gusto; **h. funny!** ¡qué divertido!; **h. about …?** ¿y si …?; **h. about a stroll?** ¿qué te parece un paseo?; **h. old is she?** ¿cuántos años tiene?; **h. tall are you?** ¿cuánto mides?; **¿h. many?** ¿cuántos, -as?; **h. much?** ¿cuánto, -a?

how·ev·er *adv* no obstante, sin embargo; **h. difficult it may be** por difícil que sea; **h. much** por mucho que *(+ subjunctive).*

howl 1 *n* aullido *m.* **2** *vi* aullar.

HQ *abbr of* **headquarters.**

hub·cap tapacubos *m inv.*

hud·dle 1 *n* grupo *m.* **2** *vi* **to h. (up** *or* **together)** acurrucarse.

hug 1 *vt* abrazar. **2** *n* abrazo *m.*

huge *adj* enorme.

hull casco *m.*

hum 1 *vt (tune)* tararear. **2** *vi (bees, engine)* zumbar. **3** *n (of bees)* zumbido *m.*

hu·man 1 *adj* humano, -a; **h. race** raza *f* humana. **2** *n* ser *m* humano.

hu·man be·ing ser *m* humano.

hu·man·i·ty humanidad *f;* **the humanities** las humanidades.

hum·ble *adj* humilde.

hu·mid *adj* húmedo, -a.

hu·mid·i·ty humedad *f.*

hu·mil·i·ate *vt* humillar.

hu·mil·i·a·tion humillación *f.*

hu·mor humor *m.*

hu·mor·ous *adj (person, story)* gracioso, -a; *(writer)* humorístico, -a.

hump *(on back)* joroba *f; (small hill)* montículo *m.*

hunch *(idea)* corazonada *f.*

hun·dred 1 *n* cien *m,* ciento *m; (rough number)* centenar *m;* **a h. and twenty-five** ciento veinticinco; **five h.** quinientos, -as. **2** *adj* cien; **a h. people** cien personas; **a h. per cent** cien por cien; **two h. chairs** doscientas sillas.

hun·dredth *adj & n* centésimo, -a *(mf).*

Hun·gar·i·an *adj & n* húngaro, -a *(mf).*

hun·ger hambre *m;* **h. strike** huelga *m* de hambre.

hun·gry *adj* **to be h.** tener hambre.

hunt 1 *vt* cazar. **2** *vi (for game)* cazar; *(search)* buscar. **3** *n* caza *f; (search)* búsqueda *f.*

▶ **hunt down** *vt* perseguir.

hunt·er cazador, -a *mf.*

hunt·ing caza *f; (expedition)* cacería *f.*

hur·dle *(in sport)* valla *f; fig* obstáculo *m.*

hurl *vt* lanzar.

hur·rah, hur·ray *interj* ¡hurra!; **h. for John!** ¡viva John!

hur·ri·cane huracán *m.*

hur·ry 1 *vi* darse prisa. **2** *vt* meter prisa a. **3** *n* **to be in a h.** tener prisa.

▶ **hurry up** *vi (go faster)* darse prisa.

hurt 1 *vt** hacer daño a; *(wound)* herir; *(mentally)* ofender. **2** *vi** doler; **my arm hurts** me duele el brazo. **3** *adj (physically)* herido, -a; *(mentally)* dolido, -a.

hus·band marido *m,* esposo *m.*

hush 1 *n* silencio *m.* **2** *interj* ¡silencio!

hus·tle 1 *vt (jostle)* empujar; *(hurry along)* meter prisa a. **2** *n* **h. and bustle** ajetreo *m.*

hut cabaña *f; (shed)* cobertizo *m.*

hy·dro·gen hidrógeno *m.*

hy·giene higiene *f.*
hy·gien·ic *adj* higiénico, -a.
hymn himno *m*; **h. book** cantoral *m.*
hy·per·mar·ket hipermercado *m.*
hy·phen guión *m.*
hy·phen·at·ed *adj (word)* (escrito, -a) con guión.
hyp·no·tize *vt* hipnotizar.
hy·poc·ri·sy hipocresía *f.*
hyp·o·crite hipócrita *mf.*
hy·poth·e·sis *(pl* hypotheses*)* hipótesis *f.*
hys·ter·i·cal *adj* histérico, -a.
hys·ter·i·cal·ly *adv (to cry)* histéricamente.

I

I *pers pron* yo.
ice hielo *m.*
ice·berg iceberg *m.*
ice-cold *adj* helado, -a.
ice cream helado *m.*
ice cube cubito *m* de hielo.
ice-skat·ing patinaje *m* sobre hielo.
i·ci·cle carámbano *m.*
ic·ing alcorza *f.*
ic·ing sug·ar azúcar *m* glas.
i·con icono *m.*
ic·y *adj (road etc)* helado, -a; *(smile)* glacial.
ID ID card documento *m* nacional de identidad, DNI *m.*
i·de·a idea *f.*
i·de·al *adj & n* ideal *(m).*
i·de·al·ly *adv (if possible)* de ser posible.
i·den·ti·cal *adj* idéntico, -a.
i·den·ti·fi·ca·tion identificación *f*; *(papers)* documentación *f.*
i·den·ti·fy 1 *vt* identificar. **2** *vi* identificarse *(with* con).
i·den·ti·ty identidad *f*; **i. theft** robo *m* de identidad.

id·i·om modismo *m.*
id·i·ot idiota *mf.*
id·i·ot·ic *adj* idiota.
i·dle *adj* holgazán, -ana; *(not working) (person)* desempleado, -a.
i·dol ídolo *m.*
i·dol·ize *vt* idolatrar.
i.e. *abbr* a saber.
if *conj* si; **if I were rich** si fuera rico, -a; **if I were you** yo en tu lugar.
ig·loo iglú *m.*
ig·no·rance ignorancia *f.*
ig·no·rant *adj* ignorante *(of* de).
ig·nore *vt (warning, remark)* no hacer caso de; *(behavior, fact)* pasar por alto.
ill 1 *adj* enfermo, -a; *(bad)* malo, -a. **2** *n* mal *m.*
il·le·gal *adj* ilegal.
il·leg·i·ble *adj* ilegible.
il·lit·er·ate *adj* analfabeto, -a.
ill·ness enfermedad *f.*
il·lu·sion ilusión *f.*
il·lus·trate *vt* ilustrar.
il·lus·tra·tion ilustración *f.*
im·age imagen *f.*
i·mag·i·nar·y *adj* imaginario, -a.
i·mag·i·na·tion imaginación *f.*
i·mag·ine *vt* imaginarse; *(think)* suponer.
im·be·cile *fam* imbécil *mf.*
im·i·tate *vt* imitar.
im·i·ta·tion 1 *n* imitación *f.* **2** *adj* de imitación.
im·mac·u·late *adj* impecable.
im·ma·ture *adj* inmaduro, -a.
im·me·di·ate *adj* inmediato, -a.
im·me·di·ate·ly 1 *adv* inmediatamente. **2** *conj (as soon as)* en cuanto.
im·mense *adj* inmenso, -a.
im·mense·ly *adv* sumamente.
im·mi·grant *adj & n* inmigrante *(mf).*
im·mi·gra·tion inmigración *f.*
im·mi·nent *adj* inminente.
im·mor·tal *adj* inmortal.
im·mune *adj* inmune.
im·mu·nize *vt* inmunizar *(against* contra).

im·pact impacto *m*; *(crash)* choque *m*.

im·pa·tience impaciencia *f*.

im·pa·tient *adj* impaciente.

im·pa·tient·ly *adv* con impaciencia.

im·per·a·tive *(form of verb)* imperativo *m*.

im·per·son·ate *vt* hacerse pasar por; *(famous people)* imitar.

im·per·son·a·tor *(on TV etc)* imitador, -a *mf*.

im·per·ti·nent *adj* impertinente.

im·pe·tus ímpetu *m*; *fig* impulso *m*.

im·ple·ment 1 *n (tool)* herramienta *f*. **2** *vt (decision, plan)* llevar a cabo.

im·pli·ca·tion implicación *f*; *(consequence)* consecuencia *f*.

im·plic·it *adj (implied)* implícito, -a; *(trust)* absoluto, -a; *(faith)* incondicional.

im·ply *vt (hint)* dar a entender.

im·po·lite *adj* maleducado, -a.

im·port 1 *n* importación *f*. **2** *vt* importar.

im·por·tance importancia *f*; **of little i.** de poca importancia.

im·por·tant *adj* importante; **it's not i.** no importa.

im·port·er importador, -a *mf*.

im·pose 1 *vt* imponer *(on, upon* a). **2** *vi* **to i. on** *or* **upon** *(take advantage of)* abusar de.

im·pos·ing *adj* imponente.

im·po·si·tion would it be an i. if …? ¿le molestaría si …?

im·pos·si·bil·i·ty imposibilidad *f*.

im·pos·si·ble *adj* imposible.

im·pos·tor impostor, -a *mf*.

im·prac·ti·cal *adj* poco práctico, -a.

im·press *vt* impresionar.

im·pres·sion impresión *f*; **to be under the i. that …** tener la impresión de que …

im·pres·sive *adj* impresionante.

im·pris·on *vt* encarcelar.

im·prob·a·ble *adj* improbable.

im·prop·er *adj (indecent)* indecente.

im·prove 1 *vt* mejorar. **2** *vi* mejorarse.

▸**improve on** *vt* superar.

im·prove·ment mejora *f*.

im·pro·vise *vti* improvisar.

im·pu·dent *adj* insolente.

im·pulse impulso *m*.

im·pul·sive *adj* irreflexivo, -a.

im·pul·sive·ly *adv* de forma impulsiva.

im·pu·ri·ty impureza *f*.

in 1 *prep (place)* en; **in prison** en la cárcel; **in the distance** a lo lejos; **she arrived in New York** llegó a Nueva York. ▪ *(time) (during)* en, durante; **in May/1945** en mayo/1945; **in spring** en primavera; **in the daytime** durante el día; **in the morning** por la mañana. ▪ *(time) (within)* dentro de. ▪ *(time) (after)* al cabo de. ▪ *(manner)* en, de; **in a loud/quiet voice** en voz alta/baja; **in French** en francés; **dressed in blue** vestido, -a de azul; **in uniform de** uniforme. ▪ *(ratio, numbers)* de; **one in six** uno de cada seis; **two meters in length** dos metros de largo. ▪ *(after superlative)* de; **the smallest car in the world** el coche más pequeño del mundo. **2** *adv* **to be in** *(at home)* estar (en casa); *(in fashion)* estar de moda; **the bus is in** el autobús ha llegado.

in·a·bil·i·ty incapacidad *f*.

in·ac·ces·si·ble *adj* inaccesible.

in·ac·cu·ra·cy *(error)* inexactitud *f*.

in·ac·cu·rate *adj* incorrecto, -a.

in·ad·e·qua·cy *(lack)* insuficiencia *f*; *(inability)* incompetencia *f*.

in·ad·e·quate *adj (lacking)* insuficiente; *(unsuitable)* inadecuado, -a.

in·ap·pro·pri·ate *adj (behavior)* poco apropiado, -a.

in·au·gu·rate *vt (building)* inaugurar.

in·au·gu·ra·tion *(of building)* inauguración *f*.

in-box *n (for e-mail)* buzón *m* de entrada.

Inc, inc *abbr of* **Incorporated** ≃ S.A.

in·ca·pa·ble *adj* incapaz (**of doing sth** de hacer algo).

in·cense 1 *vt* enfurecer. **2** *n* incienso *m*.

in·cen·tive incentivo *m*.

inch pulgada *f (approx 2.54 cm)*.

in·ci·dent incidente *m*.

in·ci·den·tal·ly *adv* por cierto, a propósito.

in·cite *vt* incitar; **to i. sb to do sth** incitar a algn a hacer algo.

in·cite·ment incitación *f*.

in·cli·na·tion deseo *m*; **my i. is to stay** yo prefiero quedarme.

in·cline 1 *vt* **she's incined to be aggressive** tiende a ser agresiva. **2** *vi (slope)* inclinarse.

in·clude *vt* incluir (**in** en); *(in price)* comprender (**in** en).

in·clud·ing *prep* incluso, inclusive.

in·clu·sive *adj* inclusivo, -a; **the rent is i. of bills** el alquiler incluye las facturas.

in·come ingresos *mpl*; *(from investment)* réditos *mpl*.

in·come tax impuesto *m* sobre la renta.

in·com·pat·i·ble *adj* incompatible (**with** con).

in·com·pe·tent *adj* incompetente.

in·com·plete *adj* incompleto, -a.

in·con·ceiv·a·ble *adj* inconcebible.

in·con·sid·er·ate *adj* desconsiderado, -a.

in·con·sis·ten·cy inconsecuencia *f*.

in·con·sis·tent *adj* inconsecuente; **your evidence is i. with the facts** su testimonio no concuerda con los hechos.

in·con·spic·u·ous *adj* que pasa desapercibido, -a.

in·con·ven·ience 1 *n* molestia *f*; *(disadvantage)* inconvenientes *mpl*; **the i. of living out here** los inconvenientes de vivir aquí. **2** *vt* molestar.

in·con·ven·ient *adj* molesto, -a; *(time)* inoportuno, -a.

in·cor·po·rate *vt (include)* incluir; *(contain)* contener.

in·cor·rect *adj* incorrecto, -a.

in·crease 1 *n* aumento *m*; *(in number)* incremento; *(in price etc)* subida *f*. **2** *vt* aumentar; *(price etc)* subir. **3** *vi* aumentar.

in·creas·ing *adj* creciente.

in·creas·ing·ly *adv* cada vez más.

in·cred·i·ble *adj* increíble.

in·cred·i·bly *adv* increíblemente.

in·cu·ba·tor incubadora *f*.

in·cur *vt (blame)* incurrir en; *(debt)* contraer; *(loss)* sufrir.

in·cur·a·ble *adj* incurable.

in·de·cent *adj* indecente.

in·de·ci·sive *adj* indeciso, -a.

in·deed *adv (in fact)* efectivamente; **it's very hard i.** es verdaderamente difícil; **thank you very much i.** muchísimas gracias.

in·def·i·nite *adj* indefinido, -a.

in·def·i·nite·ly *adv* indefinidamente.

in·de·pend·ence independencia *f*.

in·de·pend·ent *adj* independiente; **to become i.** independizarse.

in·de·pend·ent·ly *adv* independientemente.

in·dex 1 *n (in book)* índice *m*; *(in library)* catálogo *m*. **2** *vt* catalogar.

in·dex card ficha *f*.

in·dex fin·ger dedo *m* índice.

in·dex-linked *adj* sujeto, -a al aumento de la inflación.

In·di·an *adj & n (of America)* indio, -a *(mf)*; *(of India)* hindú *(mf)*.

in·di·cate 1 *vt* indicar. **2** *vi (driving)* poner el intermitente.

in·di·ca·tion indicio *m*.

in·di·ca·tor indicador *m*; *(on car)* intermitente *m*.

in·dif·fer·ence indiferencia *f*.

in·dif·fer·ent *adj (uninterested)* indiferente; *(mediocre)* regular.

in·di·ges·tion indigestión *f*; **to have i.** tener un empacho.

in·dig·nant *adj* indignado, -a; **to get i. about sth** indignarse por algo.

in·di·rect *adj* indirecto, -a.

indi·rect·ly *adv* indirectamente.

in·dis·creet *adj* indiscreto, -a.

in·dis·crim·i·nate *adj* indiscriminado, -a.

in·dis·crim·i·nate·ly *adv (at random)* indistintamente, sin criterio.

in·dis·tin·guish·a·ble *adj* indistinguible.

in·di·vid·u·al 1 *adj (separate)* individual; *(for one)* particular; *(characteristic)* particular. **2** *n (person)* individuo *m*.

in·di·vid·u·al·ly *adv* individualmente.

in·door *adj (plant)* interior; **i. pool** piscina cubierta.

in·doors *adv (inside)* dentro (de casa).

in·duce *vt (persuade)* inducir; *(cause)* producir.

in·dulge 1 *vt (child)* consentir; *(person)* complacer; *(whim)* ceder a, satisfacer; **to i. oneself** darse gusto. **2** *vi* darse el gusto (**in** de).

in·dul·gent *adj* indulgente.

in·dus·tri·al *adj* industrial; *(accident)* laboral; **i. dispute** conflicto *m* laboral; **i. estate** polígono *m* industrial.

in·dus·try industria *f*.

in·ed·i·ble *adj* incomible.

in·ef·fec·tive *adj* ineficaz.

in·ef·fi·cien·cy ineficacia *f*; *(of person)* incompetencia *f*.

in·ef·fi·cient *adj* ineficaz; *(person)* inepto, -a.

in·ept *adj (person)* inepto, -a; *(remark)* estúpido, -a.

in·e·qual·i·ty desigualdad *f*.

in·ev·i·ta·ble *adj* inevitable.

in·ev·i·ta·bly *adv* inevitablemente.

in·ex·cus·a·ble *adj* inexcusable.

in·ex·pen·sive *adj* económico, -a.

in·ex·pe·ri·enced *adj* inexperto, -a.

in·ex·pli·ca·ble *adj* inexplicable.

in·fal·li·ble *adj* infalible.

in·fa·mous *adj* infame.

in·fan·cy infancia *f*.

in·fant niño, -a *mf*.

in·fan·try infantería *f*.

in·fat·u·at·ed *adj* encaprichado, -a (**with** con).

in·fat·u·a·tion encaprichamiento *m*.

in·fect *vt* infectar.

in·fec·tion infección *f*.

in·fec·tious *adj (disease)* infeccioso, -a; *fig* contagioso, -a.

in·fer *vt* inferir (**from** de).

in·fe·ri·or *adj* inferior (**to** a).

in·fe·ri·or·i·ty inferioridad *f*.

in·fest *vt* infestar (**with** de).

in·fi·nite *adj* infinito, -a.

in·fi·nite·ly *adv* infinitamente.

in·fin·i·tive infinitivo *m*.

in·fin·i·ty infinidad *f*.

in·firm *adj (ailing)* enfermizo, -a; *(weak)* débil.

in·flamed *adj* inflamado, -a; **to become i.** inflamarse.

in·flam·ma·tion inflamación *f*.

in·flate *vt* inflar.

in·fla·tion inflación *f*.

in·flex·i·ble *adj* inflexible.

in·flict *vt (damage)* causar (**on** a); *(defeat)* infligir (**on** a).

in·flu·ence 1 *n* influencia *f*; **to be under the i. (of drink)** llevar unas copas de más; *(formally)* estar en estado de embriaguez. **2** *vt* influir en.

in·flu·en·tial *adj* influyente.

in·flu·en·za gripe *f*.

in·flux afluencia *f*.

in·fo *fam* información *f*.

in·form *vt* informar (**of, about** de, sobre).

in·for·mal *adj (occasion, behavior)* informal; *(language, treatment)* familiar; *(unofficial)* no oficial.

in·for·mal·ly *adv (to speak, behave)* de manera informal.

in·for·ma·tion información *f*; **a piece of i.** un dato.

in·for·ma·tion tech·nol·o·gy informática f.

in·form·a·tive adj informativo, -a.

in·fu·ri·ate vt poner furioso, -a.

in·fu·ri·at·ing adj exasperante.

in·gen·ious adj ingenioso, -a.

in·grat·i·tude ingratitud f.

in·gre·di·ent ingrediente m.

in·hab·it vt vivir en, ocupar.

in·hab·i·tant habitante mf.

in·hale vt (gas) inhalar; (air) aspirar.

in·her·it vt heredar (from de).

in·her·i·tance herencia f.

in·hib·it vt (freedom) limitar; (person) cohibir; **to be inhibited** (person) sentirse cohibido, -a.

in·hi·bi·tion cohibición f.

in·hos·pi·ta·ble adj inhospitalario, -a.

in·hu·man adj inhumano, -a.

in·i·tial 1 adj inicial. **2** n initials (of name) iniciales fpl; (of abbreviation) siglas fpl.

in·i·tial·ly adv al principio.

in·i·ti·ate vt iniciar; (reform) promover; (lawsuit) entablar.

in·ject vt (drug etc) inyectar.

in·jec·tion inyección f.

in·jure vt herir; **to i. oneself** hacerse daño.

in·jured 1 adj herido, -a. **2** npl **the i.** los heridos.

in·ju·ry herida f.

in·jus·tice injusticia f.

ink tinta f.

ink-jet print·er impresora f de chorro de tinta.

in·kling (idea) idea f vaga, indicio m.

in·land 1 adj (del) interior. **2** adv (travel) tierra adentro.

in-laws npl familia f política.

in·mate (of prison) preso, -a mf.

inn (with lodging) posada f.

in·ner adj interior; **i. city** casco m urbano.

in·ning (in baseball) turno m para batear, Am inning m.

in·no·cence inocencia f.

in·no·cent adj & n inocente (mf).

in·oc·u·late vt inocular.

in·oc·u·la·tion inoculación f.

in·put (of data) input m, entrada f.

in·quire 1 vt preguntar. **2** vi preguntar (**about** por); (find out) informarse (**about** de).

▸**inquire into** vt investigar.

in·quir·y pregunta f, (investigation) investigación f; **'inquiries'** 'información'.

in·quis·i·tive adj curioso, -a; (questioning) preguntón, -ona.

in·sane adj loco, -a.

in·san·i·ty locura f.

in·scrip·tion (on stone, coin) inscripción f; (in book, on photo) dedicatoria f.

in·sect insecto m; **i. bite** picadura f.

in·sec·ti·cide insecticida m.

in·se·cure adj inseguro, -a.

in·sen·si·tive adj insensible.

in·sen·si·tiv·i·ty insensibilidad f.

in·sert vt introducir.

in·side 1 n interior m; **on the i.** por dentro; **to turn sth i. out** volver algo al revés. **2** adj interior; **i. lane** carril m interior. **3** adv (be) dentro, adentro; (run etc) (hacia) adentro. **4** prep (place) dentro de.

in·sid·er (of firm) empleado, -a mf de la empresa.

in·sight (quality) perspicacia f.

in·sig·nif·i·cant adj insignificante.

in·sin·cere adj poco sincero, -a.

in·sist 1 vi insistir (**on** en). **2** vt **to i. that …** insistir en que ….

in·sis·tence insistencia f.

in·sis·tent adj insistente.

in·so·lence insolencia f.

in·so·lent adj insolente.

in·som·ni·a insomnio m.

in·spect vt inspeccionar.

in·spec·tion inspección f.

in·spec·tor inspector, -a mf; (on bus, train) revisor, -a mf.

in·spi·ra·tion inspiración f.

in·spire vt inspirar; **to i. respect in sb** infundir respeto a algn.

in·stall *vt* instalar.

in·stall·ment *(of payment)* plazo *m*; *(of novel, program)* entrega *f*.

in·stance caso *m*; **for i.** por ejemplo.

in·stant 1 *n (moment)* instante *m*. **2** *adj* inmediato, -a; *(coffee, meal)* instantáneo, -a; **i. messaging** mensajería *f* instantánea.

in·stant·ly *adv* inmediatamente.

in·stant re·play repetición *f*.

in·stead 1 *adv* en cambio. **2** *prep* **i. of** en vez de.

in·stinct instinto *m*.

in·stinc·tive *adj* instintivo, -a.

in·stinc·tive·ly *adv* instintivamente.

in·sti·tu·tion institución *f*.

in·struct *vt* instruir; *(order)* mandar.

in·struc·tion instructions instrucciones *fpl*; **'instructions for use'** 'modo de empleo'.

in·struc·tive *adj* instructivo, -a.

in·struc·tor instructor, -a *mf*; *(of driving)* profesor, -a *mf*.

in·stru·ment instrumento *m*.

in·stru·men·tal *adj (music)* instrumental; **to be i. in sth** contribuir decisivamente a algo.

in·suf·fi·cient *adj* insuficiente.

in·su·late *vt* aislar (**against, from** de).

in·su·la·tion aislamiento *m*.

in·sult 1 *n* insulto *m*. **2** *vt* insultar.

in·sur·ance seguro *m*; **i. company** compañía *f* de seguros.

in·sure *vt* asegurar (**against** contra).

in·tact *adj* intacto, -a.

in·take *(of food)* consumo *m*; *(of students, recruits)* número *m* de admitidos.

in·te·grate 1 *vt* integrar. **2** *vi* integrarse.

in·teg·ri·ty integridad *f*, honradez *f*.

in·tel·lect intelecto *m*.

in·tel·lec·tu·al *adj & n* intelectual *(mf)*.

in·tel·li·gence inteligencia *f*.

in·tel·li·gent *adj* inteligente.

in·tel·li·gi·ble *adj* inteligible.

in·tend *vt (mean)* tener la intención de.

in·tense *adj* intenso, -a.

in·tense·ly *adv (extremely)* sumamente.

in·ten·si·fy *vt* intensificar.

in·ten·si·ty intensidad *f*.

in·ten·sive *adj* intensivo, -a; **i. care unit** unidad *f* de vigilancia intensiva.

in·tent *adj* **to be i. on doing sth** estar resuelto, -a a hacer algo.

in·ten·tion intención *f*.

in·ten·tion·al *adj* deliberado, -a.

in·ten·tion·al·ly *adv* a propósito.

in·ter·act *vi (people)* interrelacionarse.

in·ter·ac·tive *adj* interactivo, -a.

in·ter·cept *vt* interceptar.

in·ter·change *(on motorway)* cruce *m*.

in·ter·change·a·ble *adj* intercambiable.

in·ter·com *(at entrance)* portero *m* automático.

in·ter·con·nect·ed *adj (facts etc)* interrelacionado, -a.

in·ter·course *(sexual)* relaciones *fpl* sexuales.

in·ter·est 1 *n* interés *m*; **i. rate** tipo *m* de interés. **2** *vt* interesar; **to be interested in** interesarse en; **I'm not interested** no me interesa.

in·ter·est·ing *adj* interesante.

in·ter·fere *vi (meddle)* entrometerse (**in** en).

in·ter·fer·ence *(meddling)* intromisión *f*, *(on radio etc)* interferencia *f*.

in·ter·im 1 *n fml* **in the i.** en el ínterin. **2** *adj* interino, -a, provisional.

in·te·ri·or 1 *adj* interior. **2** *n* interior *m*.

in·ter·me·di·ar·y intermediario, -a *mf*.

in·ter·me·di·ate *adj* intermedio, -a.

in·ter·mis·sion *(at cinema, in theater)* intermedio *m*; *(in music)* interludio *m*.

in·tern (doctor) interno, -a mf; (in office) becario(a) m,f.
in·ter·nal adj interior; (dispute, injury) interno, -a.
In·ter·nal Rev·e·nue Ser·vice Hacienda f.
in·ter·na·tion·al adj internacional.
In·ter·net n the I. Internet f.
in·ter·pret vt interpretar.
in·ter·pret·er intérprete mf.
in·ter·ro·gate vt interrogar.
in·ter·ro·ga·tion interrogatorio m.
in·ter·rupt vti interrumpir.
in·ter·rup·tion interrupción f.
in·ter·sect 1 vt cruzar. **2** vi cruzarse.
in·ter·sec·tion (crossroads) cruce m.
in·ter·state 1 n autopista f interestatal. **2** adj entre estados.
in·ter·val (of time, space) intervalo m.
in·ter·vene vi (person) intervenir (in en); (event) sobrevenir.
in·ter·ven·tion intervención f.
in·ter·view 1 n entrevista f. **2** vt entrevistar.
in·ter·view·er entrevistador, -a mf.
in·ti·mate adj íntimo, -a.
in·tim·i·date vt intimidar.
in·to prep (motion) en, a; **to get i. a car** subir a un coche; **to go i. a house** entrar a una casa; **to change dollars i. pesos** cambiar dólares en or por pesos; **to translate sth i. French** traducir algo al francés; fam **to be i. sth** ser aficionado, -a a algo.
in·tol·er·a·ble adj intolerable.
in·tox·i·cate vt embriagar.
in·tox·i·cat·ed adj borracho, -a.
in·tran·si·tive adj intransitivo, -a.
in·tro·duce vt (person, program) presentar (to a); (bring in) introducir (into, to en).
in·tro·duc·tion (of person, program) presentación f; (in book, bringing in) introducción f.

in·trude vi entrometerse (**into, on** en); (disturb) molestar.
in·trud·er intruso, -a mf.
in·tru·sion intrusión f.
in·tu·i·tion intuición f.
in·un·date vt inundar (**with** de); **I was inundated with offers** me llovieron las ofertas.
in·vade vt invadir.
in·vad·er invasor, -a mf.
in·va·lid¹ (disabled person) minusválido, -a mf; (sick person) enfermo, -a mf.
in·val·id² adj nulo, -a.
in·val·u·a·ble adj inestimable.
in·vari·a·bly adv (always) invariablemente.
in·va·sion invasión f.
in·vent vt inventar.
in·ven·tion invento m.
in·ven·tor inventor, -a mf.
in·ven·to·ry inventario m.
in·vert·ed adj (in) i. **commas** (entre) comillas fpl.
in·vest vt invertir (in en).
in·ves·ti·gate vt (crime, subject) investigar; (cause, possibility) estudiar.
in·ves·ti·ga·tion (of crime) investigación f; (of cause) examen m.
in·ves·ti·ga·tor investigador, -a mf.
in·ves·tor inversor, -a mf.
in·vig·or·at·ing adj vigorizante.
in·vis·i·ble adj invisible.
in·vi·ta·tion invitación f.
in·vite vt invitar (**to** a); (comments etc) solicitar; (criticism) provocar.
in·vit·ing adj (attractive) atractivo, -a; (food) apetitoso, -a.
in·voice 1 n factura f. **2** vt facturar.
in·voke vt fml invocar.
in·volve vt (entail) suponer; (concern) implicar (in en); **to be involved in an accident** sufrir un accidente.
in·volved adj (complicated) complicado, -a; (romantically) enredado, -a.
in·volve·ment (participation) participación f; (in crime) implicación f;

emotional i. relación *f* sentimental.

in·ward 1 *adj* interior. **2** *adv* = **inwards**.

in·wards *adv* hacia dentro.

IQ *abbr of* **intelligence quotient** coeficiente *m* intelectual, CI *m*.

IRA *abbr of* **individual retirement account** cuenta *f* de retiro *or* jubilación individual.

I·ra·ni·an *adj & n* iraní *(mf)*.

I·ra·qi *adj & n* iraquí *(mf)*.

i·ris *(of eye)* iris *m inv*; *(plant)* lirio *m*.

I·rish 1 *adj* irlandés, -esa. **2** *npl* **the I.** los irlandeses.

I·rish·man irlandés *m*.

I·rish·wom·an irlandesa *f.*

i·ron 1 *n* hierro *m*; *(for clothes)* plancha *f*; **the i. and steel industry** la industria siderúrgica. **2** *vt (clothes)* planchar.

i·ron·i(·)c(al) *adj* irónico, -a.

i·ron·ing to do the i. planchar.

i·ron·ing board tabla *f* de planchar.

i·ro·ny ironía *f.*

ir·ra·tion·al *adj* irracional.

ir·reg·u·lar *adj* irregular.

ir·rel·e·vance irrelevancia *f.*

ir·rel·e·vant *adj* no pertinente.

ir·re·sist·i·ble *adj* irresistible.

ir·re·spec·tive *adj* **i. of** sin tener en cuenta.

ir·ri·gate *vt* regar.

ir·ri·ta·ble *adj* irritable.

ir·ri·tate *vt (annoy)* irritar, fastidiar.

ir·ri·tat·ing *adj* irritante.

ir·ri·ta·tion *(annoyance)* fastidio *m*; *(bad mood)* mal humor *m*.

is *3rd person sing pres of* **be**.

Is·lam·ic *adj* islámico, -a.

is·land isla *f.*

i·so·late *vt* aislar **(from** de).

i·so·lat·ed *adj* aislado, -a.

i·so·la·tion aislamiento *m*.

is·sue 1 *n (matter)* cuestión *f*, *(of journal etc)* ejemplar *m*. **2** *vt (book)* publicar; *(currency etc)* emitir; *(passport)* expedir; *(supplies)* repartir; *(order, instructions)* dar.

IT *n* **information technology** tecnologías *fpl* de la información, informática *f.*

it *pers pron (subject)* él, ella *(often omitted)*; **it's here** está aquí. ▪ *(direct object)* lo, la; **I don't believe it** no me lo creo. ▪ *(indirect object)* le; **give it a kick** dale una patada. ▪ *(after prep)* él, ella, ello; **we'll talk about it later** ya hablaremos de ello. ▪ *(impersonal)* **it's late** es tarde; **it's raining** está lloviendo; **who is it?** ¿quién es?

I·tal·ian 1 *adj* italiano, -a. **2** *n (person)* italiano, -a *mf*, *(language)* italiano *m*.

i·tal·ic *adj* **in italics** en cursiva.

itch 1 *n* picor *m*. **2** *vi (skin)* picar.

itch·y *adj* que pica.

i·tem *(in list)* artículo *m*; *(in collection)* pieza *f*; *(on agenda)* asunto *m*; **i. of clothing** prenda *f* de vestir; **news i.** noticia *f.*

its *poss adj (one thing)* su; *(more than one)* sus.

it·self *pers pron* ▪ *(reflexive)* se; **the cat scratched i.** el gato se rascó. ▪ *(emphatic)* él *or* ella mismo, -a.

i·vo·ry marfil *m*.

i·vy hiedra *f.*

J

jab 1 *n* pinchazo *m*; *(poke)* golpe *m* seco. **2** *vt* pinchar.

jack *(for car)* gato *m*; *(cards)* sota *f.*

jack·et chaqueta *f*, *(of suit)* americana *f*, **j. potatoes** patatas *fpl* al horno.

ja·cuz·zi jacuzzi *m.*

jag·ged *adj* dentado, -a.

jail 1 *n* cárcel *f*. **2** *vt* encarcelar.

jam¹ mermelada *f.*

jam² 1 *n (blockage)* atasco *m*. **2** *vt (cram)* meter a la fuerza; *(block)* atascar. **3** vi (door) atrancarse; (brakes) agarrotarse.

▸**jam into** vt (crowd) apretarse en; **to j. sth into sth** meter algo a la fuerza en algo.

jam jar pote m de mermelada.

jam-packed adj fam (with people) atestado, -a; (with things) atiborrado, -a.

jan·i·tor portero m, conserje m.

Jan·u·ar·y enero m.

Jap·a·nese 1 adj japonés, -esa. **2** n (person) japonés, -esa mf, (language) japonés m.

jar (glass) tarro m; (earthenware) tinaja f.

jaun·dice ictericia f.

jave·lin jabalina f.

jaw mandíbula f.

jay·walk·ing imprudencia f peatonal.

jazz jazz m.

jea·lous adj celoso, -a; (envious) envidioso, -a; **to be j. of** tener celos de.

jeal·ous·y celos mpl; (envy) envidia f.

jeans npl vaqueros npl, tejanos mpl.

jeep jeep m.

jeer 1 n (boo) abucheo m. **2** vi (boo) abuchear; (mock) burlarse.

jeer·ing adj burlón, -ona.

Jell-O®, jel·lo gelatina f.

jel·ly gelatina f.

jeop·ard·ize vt poner en peligro; (agreement etc) comprometer.

jerk 1 n (jolt) sacudida f, fam (idiot) imbécil mf. **2** vt (shake) sacudir.

jer·sey jersey m.

jet reactor m; **j. engine** reactor m.

jet lag desfase m horario.

Jew judío, -a mf.

jew·el joya f, (in watch) rubí m.

jew·el·er joyero, -a mf.

jew·el·ry joyas fpl, alhajas fpl.

Jew·ish adj judío, -a.

jig·saw (puzzle) rompecabezas m inv.

jin·gle vi tintinear.

jit·ters npl **to get the j.** ponerse nervioso, -a.

job trabajo m; (task) tarea f, (occupation) (puesto m de) trabajo m; **we had a j. to ...** nos costó (trabajo) ...; **it's a good j. that ...** menos mal que ...

job cen·ter oficina f de empleo.

job·less adj parado, -a.

jock·ey jinete m.

jog 1 n trote m. **2** vt empujar; (memory) refrescar. **3** vi (run) hacer footing.

john fam meódromo m.

join 1 vt juntar; (road) empalmar con; (river) desembocar en; (meet) reunirse con; (group) unirse a; (institution) entrar en; (army) alistarse a; (party) afiliarse a; (club) hacerse socio, -a de. **2** vi unirse; (roads) empalmar; (rivers) confluir; (become a member) afiliarse; (club) hacerse socio, -a. **3** n juntura f.

▸**join in 1** vi participar. **2** vt participar en.

joint 1 n articulación f, (of meat) corte m de carne para asar; (once roasted) asado m; (drugs) porro m. **2** adj colectivo, -a; **j. (bank) account** cuenta f conjunta.

joint·ly adv conjuntamente, en común.

joke 1 n chiste m; (prank) broma f. **2** vi estar de broma.

jok·er bromista mf, (in cards) comodín m.

jol·ly adj alegre.

jolt 1 n sacudida f. **2** vi moverse a sacudidas. **3** vt sacudir.

jos·tle 1 vt dar empujones a. **2** vi dar empujones.

▸**jot down** vt apuntar.

jour·nal·ist periodista mf.

jour·ney viaje m; (distance) trayecto m.

joy alegría f.

joy·ful adj alegre.

joy·stick palanca f de mando; (of video game) joystick m.

judge 1 n juez mf, jueza f. **2** vt juzgar; (estimate) considerar; (assess) valorar. **3** vi juzgar.
judg(e)·ment sentencia f, (opinion) opinión f.
ju·di·cial adj judicial.
ju·do judo m.
jug jarra f; **milk j.** jarra de leche.
jug·gle vi hacer juegos malabares (**with** con).
jug·gler malabarista mf.
juice jugo m; (of citrus fruits) zumo m.
juic·y adj jugoso, -a.
Ju·ly julio m.
jum·ble 1 n revoltijo m. **2** vt revolver.
jum·bo adj gigante.
jum·bo jet jumbo m.
jump 1 n salto m; (sudden increase) subida repentina f. **2** vi saltar; (start) sobresaltarse; (increase) aumentar de golpe. **3** vt saltar; **to j. the line** colarse.
▸**jump in, jump on 1** vt (train etc) subirse a. **2** vi subir.
jump rope comba f.
jump·y adj fam nervioso, -a.
junc·tion (of roads) cruce m.
June junio m.
jun·gle jungla f.
jun·ior 1 adj (lower in rank) subalterno, -a; (younger) menor; **j. team** equipo juvenil. **2** n (of lower rank) subalterno, -a mf; (younger person) menor mf.
jun·ior high school = instituto m de enseñanza secundaria.
junk trastos mpl; **j. mail** propaganda f (postal); (e-mail) correo m basura.
junk shop tienda f de segunda mano.
ju·ry jurado m.
just 1 adj (fair) justo, -a. **2** adv (at this very moment) ahora mismo, en este momento; (only) solamente; (barely) por poco; (exactly) exactamente; **he had j. arrived** acababa de llegar; **he was j. leaving when Rosa arrived** estaba a punto de salir cuando llegó Rosa; **j. as I came in** justo cuando entré; **I only j. caught the bus** cogí el autobús por los pelos; **j. about** casi; **j. as fast as** tan rápido como.
jus·tice justicia f.
jus·ti·fi·ca·tion justificación f.
jus·ti·fy vt justificar.
▸**jut out** vi sobresalir.

K

kan·ga·roo canguro m.
ka·ra·oke n karaoke m.
ka·ra·te kárate m.
ke·bab pincho moruno m.
keen adj (eager) entusiasta; (intense) profundo, -a; (mind, senses) agudo, -a.
keep 1 n **to earn one's k.** ganarse el pan. **2** vt* mantener; (letters, memories, silence, secret) guardar; (retain possession of) quedarse con; (hold back) entretener; (in prison) detener; (promise) cumplir; (diary, accounts) llevar; **to k. sb waiting** hacer esperar a algn; **to k. doing sth** seguir haciendo algo; **she keeps forgetting her keys** siempre se olvida las llaves; **to k. going** seguir adelante. **3** vi* (food) conservarse.
▸**keep away 1** vt mantener a distancia. **2** vi mantenerse a distancia.
▸**keep back 1** vt (information) callar; (money etc) retener. **2** vi (crowd) mantenerse atrás.
▸**keep down** vt **to k. prices down** mantener los precios bajos.
▸**keep off** vt **k. off the grass** prohibido pisar la hierba.
▸**keep on 1** vt (clothes etc) no quitarse; (continue to employ) mantener a; **it keeps on breaking** siempre se está rompiendo. **2** vi **the rain kept on** la lluvia siguió/continuó; **he just**

kept on *(talking, complaining)* siguió machacando; **k. straight on** sigue todo derecho.

▸**keep out 1** *vt* no dejar pasar. **2** *vi* no entrar; **k. out** *(sign)* prohibida la entrada.

▸**keep to** *vt (subject)* limitarse a; **to k. to one's room** quedarse en el cuarto; **k. to the point!** ¡cíñete a la cuestión!; **to k. to the left** circular por la izquierda.

▸**keep up 1** *vt* mantener. **2** *vi (in race etc)* no rezagarse.

▸**keep up with** *vt* **to k. up with the times** estar al día.

ken·nel caseta *f* para perros.

Ken·yan *adj & n* keniano, -a *(mf)*.

kept *pt & pp of* **keep**.

ker·o·sene queroseno *m*.

ketch·up ketchup *m*.

ket·tle hervidor *m*.

key 1 *n (for lock)* llave *f; (of piano, typewriter)* tecla *f*. **2** *adj* clave.

key·board teclado *m*.

key ring llavero *m*.

kick 1 *n (from person)* puntapié *m*. **2** *vi (animal)* cocear; *(person)* dar patadas. **3** *vt* dar un puntapié a.

▸**kick down, kick in** *vt (door etc)* derribar a patadas.

▸**kick off** *vi fam* empezar; *(of footballer)* sacar.

▸**kick out** *vt* echar a patadas.

kick·off saque *m* inicial.

kid¹ *fam (child)* niño, -a *mf;* **the kids** los críos.

kid² 1 *vt* tomar el pelo a. **2** *vi* tomar el pelo.

kid·nap *vt* secuestrar.

kid·nap·per secuestrador, -a *mf*.

kid·ney riñón *m*.

kill *vt* matar.

kill·er asesino, -a *mf*.

kill·ing *(of person)* asesinato *m; (of animal)* matanza *f*.

ki·lo kilo *m*.

kil·o·gram kilogramo *m*.

kil·o·me·ter kilómetro *m*.

kin familiares *mpl;* parientes *mpl*.

kind¹ 1 *n* clase *f;* **what k. of?** ¿qué tipo de? **2** *adv fam* **k. of** en cierta manera.

kind² *adj* amable.

kin·der·gar·ten jardín *m* de infancia.

kind·ly 1 *adj* (**kindlier, kindliest**) amable, bondadoso, -a. **2** *adv fml (please)* por favor; **to look k. on** aprobar.

kind·ness amabilidad *f*.

king rey *m*.

king·dom reino *m*.

ki·osk quiosco *m*.

kiss 1 *n* beso *m*. **2** *vt* besar. **3** *vi* besarse.

kit *(gear)* equipo *m; (clothing)* ropa *f; (toy model)* maqueta *f*.

kitch·en cocina *f*.

kite *(toy)* cometa *f*.

kit·ten gatito, -a *mf*.

klutz *fam (stupid person)* bobo, -a *mf, Esp* chorra *mf; (clumsy person)* torpe *mf, Esp* patoso, -a *mf*.

knack to get the k. of doing sth cogerle el truquillo a algo.

knee rodilla *f*.

kneel* *vi* **to k. (down)** arrodillarse.

knew *pt of* **know**.

knick·ers *npl* bragas *fpl*.

knife *(pl* **knives)** cuchillo *m*.

knight caballero *m; (in chess)* caballo *m*.

knit 1 *vt* tejer; *(join)* juntar. **2** *vi* hacer punto; *(bone)* soldarse.

knit·ting punto *m*.

knit·ting nee·dle aguja *f* de hacer punto.

knob *(of stick)* puño *m; (of drawer)* tirador *m; (button)* botón *m*.

knock 1 *n* golpe *m;* **there was a k. at the door** llamaron a la puerta. **2** *vt* golpear. **3** *vi* chocar (**against, into** contra); *(at door)* llamar (**at** a).

▸**knock down** *vt (demolish)* derribar; *(car)* atropellar.

▸**knock off** *vt* tirar.

▸**knock out** *vt (make unconscious)* dejar sin conocimiento; *(in boxing)* derrotar por K.O.

►**knock over** vt volcar; (car) atropellar.

knock·er (on door) aldaba f.

knot 1 n nudo m. 2 vt anudar.

know* 1 vt saber; (be acquainted with) conocer; **she knows how to ski** sabe esquiar; **we got to k. each other at the party** nos conocimos en la fiesta. 2 vi saber; **to let sb k.** avisar a algn.

know-how conocimiento m práctico.

know-it-all fam sabihondo, -a mf, sabelotodo mf.

knowl·edge conocimiento m; (learning) conocimientos mpl.

known adj conocido, -a.

knuck·le nudillo m.

Ko·ran Corán m.

Ko·re·an adj & n coreano, -a (mf).

L

lab fam laboratorio m.

la·bel 1 n etiqueta f. 2 vt poner etiqueta a.

la·bor 1 n (work) trabajo m; (workforce) mano f de obra; **to be in l.** estar de parto. 2 adj (market etc) laboral; **L. day** día m de los trabajadores. 3 vi (work) trabajar (duro).

lab·o·ra·to·ry laboratorio m.

la·bor·er peón m; **farm l.** peón m agrícola.

la·bor un·ion sindicato m.

lace n (fabric) encaje m; **laces** cordones mpl; **to do up one's laces** atarse los cordones.

lack 1 n falta f. 2 vt carecer de. 3 vi carecer (**in** de).

lad chaval m.

lad·der escalera f (de mano).

la·dle cucharón m.

la·dy señora f, **'Ladies'** (restroom) 'Señoras'.

la·dy·bug mariquita f.

la·ger cerveza f (rubia).

lake lago m.

lamb cordero m; (meat) carne f de cordero.

lame adj cojo, -a.

lamp lámpara f.

lamp·post farola f.

lamp·shade pantalla f.

land 1 n tierra f; (country) país m; (property) tierras fpl; **piece of l.** terreno m; **by l.** por tierra. 2 vt (plane) hacer aterrizar. 3 vi (plane) aterrizar; (passengers) desembarcar.

land·ing (of staircase) rellano m; (of plane) aterrizaje m.

land·la·dy (of apartment) propietaria f, casera f; (of boarding house) patrona f; (of pub) dueña f.

land·lord (of apartment) propietario m, casero m; (of pub) dueño m.

land·own·er terrateniente mf.

land·scape paisaje m.

land·slide desprendimiento m de tierras.

lane (in country) camino m; (in town) callejón m; (of highway) carril m.

lan·guage idioma m, lengua f.

lan·guage lab·o·ra·to·ry laboratorio m de idiomas.

lan·tern farol m.

lap¹ (knees) rodillas fpl.

lap² (circuit) vuelta f.

la·pel solapa f.

lap·top laptop (computer) Esp ordenador m or Am computadora f portátil.

lar·ce·ny hurto m.

lar·der despensa f.

large adj grande; (amount) importante; **by and l.** por lo general.

large·ly adv (mainly) en gran parte; (chiefly) principalmente.

large-scale adj (project, problem etc) de gran envergadura; (map) a gran escala.

lark (bird) alondra f.

la·ser láser *m*; **l. printer** impresora *f* láser.

last 1 *adj (final, most recent)* último, -a; *(past)* pasado, -a; *(previous)* anterior; **l. but one** penúltimo, -a; **l. month** el mes pasado; **l. night** anoche. **2** *adv (on final occasion)* por última vez; *(at the end)* en último lugar; *(in race etc)* último; **at (long) l.** por fin. **3** *n* el último, la última. **4** *vi (time)* durar; *(hold out)* aguantar.

last·ly *adv* por último.

latch pestillo *m*.

late 1 *adj (not on time)* tardío, -a; *(hour)* avanzado, -a; *(far on in time)* tarde; **to be five minutes l.** llegar con cinco minutos de retraso; **in the l. afternoon** a última hora de la tarde. **2** *adv* tarde; **l. at night** a altas horas de la noche.

late·com·er rezagado, -a *mf*.

late·ly *adv* últimamente.

Lat·in 1 *adj* latino, -a; **L. America** América *f* Latina, Latinoamérica *f*; **L. American** latinoamericano, -a *(mf)*. **2** *n* latino, -a *mf*; *(language)* latín *m*.

lat·ter *1 n (last)* último, -a; *(second of two)* segundo, -a. **2** *pron* éste, -a.

laugh 1 *n* risa *f*. **2** *vi* reír, reírse.

▸**laugh about** *vt* to **l. about sb/sth** reírse de algn/algo.

▸**laugh at** *vt* to **l. at sb/sth** reírse de algn/algo.

laugh·ter risa *f*.

launch 1 *n (vessel)* lancha *f*; *(of product)* lanzamiento *m*. **2** *vt (rocket, new product)* lanzar; *(ship)* botar; *(film, play)* estrenar.

Laun·dro·mat® lavandería *f* automática.

laun·dry *(place)* lavandería *f*; *(dirty clothes)* ropa *f* sucia; **to do the l.** lavar la ropa.

lav·a·to·ry retrete *m*; *(room)* baño *m*; **public l.** servicios *mpl*.

law ley *f*; *(as subject)* derecho *m*.

law court tribunal *m* de justicia.

lawn césped *m*.

lawn·mow·er cortacésped *m*.

law·suit pleito *m*.

law·yer abogado, -a *mf*.

lay* *vt (place)* poner; *(cable, trap)* tender; *(foundations)* echar; *(table, eggs)* poner; *(set down)* asentar.

▸**lay down** *vt (put down)* poner.

▸**lay off** *vt (dismiss)* despedir.

▸**lay on** *vt (provide)* proveer de; *(food)* preparar.

▸**lay out** *vt (open out)* extender; *(arrange)* disponer; *(ideas)* exponer; *(spend)* gastar.

lay·a·bout vago, -a *mf*.

lay·er capa *f*.

lay·man lego, -a *mf*.

lay·out *(arrangement)* disposición *f*; *(presentation)* presentación *f*.

la·zy vago, -a.

lead[1] *(metal)* plomo *m*; *(in pencil)* mina *f*.

lead[2] **1** *n (front position)* delantera *f*; *(advantage)* ventaja *f*; *(leash)* correa *f*; *(electric cable)* cable *m*; **to be in the l.** ir en cabeza; **to take the l.** *(in race)* tomar la delantera; *(score)* adelantarse. **2** *vt* (conduct)* conducir; *(be the leader of)* dirigir; *(life)* llevar; **to l. sb to think sth** hacer a algn pensar algo. **3** *vi* (road)* llevar (**to** a); *(in race)* llevar la delantera.

▸**lead away** *vt* llevar.

▸**lead on** *vt (deceive)* engañar, timar.

▸**lead to** *vt (result in)* dar lugar a.

lead·er jefe, -a *mf*; *(political)* líder *mf*.

lead·ing *adj (main)* principal.

leaf *(pl leaves)* hoja *f*.

leaf·let folleto *m*.

leak 1 *n (of gas, liquid)* escape *m*; *(of information)* filtración *f*. **2** *vi (gas, liquid)* escaparse. **3** *vt (information)* filtrar.

lean* 1 *vi* inclinarse; *(thing)* estar inclinado; **to l. on/against** apoyarse en/contra. **2** *vt* apoyar (**on** en).

▸**lean forward** *vi* inclinarse hacia delante.

▸**lean over** *vi* inclinarse.

leap 1 *n (jump)* salto *m*. **2** *vi** saltar.

leap year año *m* bisiesto.

learn* 1 *vt* aprender; *(find out about)* enterarse de; **to l. (how) to ski** aprender a esquiar. 2 *vi* aprender; **to l. about** *or of (find out about)* enterarse de.

learn·er *(beginner)* principiante *mf*.

learn·ing *(knowledge)* conocimientos *mpl; (erudition)* saber *m*.

lease 1 *n* contrato *m* de arrendamiento. 2 *vt* arrendar.

leash correa *f*.

least 1 *adj* menor. 2 *adv* menos. 3 *n* lo menos; **at l.** por lo menos.

leath·er 1 *n (fine)* piel *f; (heavy)* cuero *m*. 2 *adj* de piel.

leave[1]* 1 *vt* dejar; *(go away from)* abandonar; *(go out of)* salir de; **I have two cookies left** me quedan dos galletas. 2 *vi (go away)* irse, marcharse; *(go out)* salir; **the train leaves in five minutes** el tren sale dentro de cinco minutos.

▶ **leave behind** *vt* dejar atrás.

▶ **leave on** *vt (clothes)* dejar puesto, -a; *(lights, radio)* dejar encendido, -a.

▶ **leave out** *vt (omit)* omitir.

leave[2] *(time off)* vacaciones *fpl*.

lec·ture 1 *n* conferencia *f; (at university)* clase *f;* **to give a l.** dar una conferencia *(on* sobre*)*. 2 *vi (at university)* dar clases.

lec·tur·er conferenciante *mf; (at university)* profesor, -a *mf*.

leek puerro *m*.

left[1] 1 *adj* izquierdo, -a. 2 *adv* a la izquierda. 3 *n* izquierda *f;* **on the l.** a mano izquierda.

left[2] *pt & pp of* **leave**[1].

left-hand *adj* **on the l. side** a mano izquierda.

left-hand·ed *adj* zurdo, -a.

left·o·vers *npl* sobras *fpl*.

leg pierna *f; (of animal, table)* pata *f*.

le·gal *adj* legal; *(permitted by law)* lícito, -a; *(relating to the law)* jurídico, -a.

le·gal hol·i·day fiesta *f* nacional.

le·gal·ly *adv* legalmente.

leg·end leyenda *f*.

leg·i·ble *adj* legible.

leg·is·la·tion legislación *f*.

leg·is·la·tive *adj* legislativo, -a.

leg·is·la·ture asamblea *f* legislativa.

le·git·i·mate *adj* legítimo, -a.

lei·sure ocio *m; (free time)* tiempo *m* libre; **l. activities** pasatiempos *mpl*.

lem·on limón *m;* **l. juice** zumo *m* de limón; **l. tea** té *m* con limón.

lem·on·ade gaseosa *f*.

lend* *vt* prestar.

lend·er entidad *f* de crédito.

length largo *m; (duration)* duración *f; (section of string etc)* trozo *m*.

length·en 1 *vt* alargar; *(lifetime)* prolongar. 2 *vi* alargarse; *(lifetime)* prolongarse.

length·y *adj (lengthier, lengthiest)* largo, -a; *(meeting, discussion)* prolongado, -a.

le·nient *adj* indulgente.

lens *(of spectacles)* lente *f; (of camera)* objetivo *m*.

len·til lenteja *f*.

leop·ard leopardo *m*.

le·o·tard mallas *fpl*.

less menos; **l. and l.** cada vez menos; **a year l. two days** un año menos dos días.

les·son clase *f; (in book)* lección *f*.

let* 1 *vt* dejar; *(rent out)* alquilar; **to l. sb do sth** dejar a algn hacer algo; **to l. go of sth** soltar algo; **to l. sb know** avisar a algn. 2 *v aux* **l. him wait** que espere; **l.'s go!** ¡vamos!, ¡vámonos!

▶ **let down** *vt (lower)* bajar; *(fail)* defraudar.

▶ **let in** *vt (admit)* dejar entrar.

▶ **let off** *vt (bomb)* hacer explotar; *(fireworks)* hacer estallar; **to l. sb off** *(pardon)* perdonar.

▶ **let on** *vi fam* **don't l. on** *(reveal information)* no se lo digas.

▶ **let out** *vt (release)* soltar; *(news)* divulgar; *(secret)* revelar; *(cry)* soltar.

▶ **let up** *vi (cease)* cesar.

let·down decepción f.

let·ter (of alphabet) letra f; (written message) carta f.

let·ter·box buzón m.

let·tuce lechuga f.

lev·el 1 adj (flat) llano, -a; (even) nivelado, -a; **to be l. with** estar a nivel de. **2** n nivel m; **to be on a l. with** estar al mismo nivel que.

lev·el crossing paso m a nivel.

lev·er palanca f.

li·a·ble adj **the river is l. to freeze** el río tiene tendencia a helarse.

li·ar mentiroso, -a mf.

li·bel 1 n libelo m. **2** vt difamar, calumniar.

lib·er·al 1 adj liberal; (abundant) abundante; **L. Party** Partido m Liberal. **2** n **L.** liberal mf.

lib·er·ty libertad f; **to be at l. to say sth** ser libre de decir algo.

li·brar·i·an bibliotecario, -a mf.

li·brar·y biblioteca f.

Lib·y·an adj & n libio, -a (mf).

lice npl see **louse**.

li·cense (permit) permiso m; **l. plate** (of car) (placa f de la) matrícula f.

lick vt lamer.

lic·o·rice regaliz m.

lid (cover) tapa f, (of eye) párpado m.

lie¹ 1 vi mentir. **2** n mentira f.

lie²* vi (act) acostarse; (state) estar acostado, -a.

▸ **lie around** vi (person) estar tumbado, -a; (things) estar tirado, -a.

▸ **lie down** vi acostarse.

life (pl lives) vida f; **to come to l.** cobrar vida.

life belt cinturón m salvavidas.

life·boat (on ship) bote m salvavidas; (on shore) lancha f de socorro.

life·guard socorrista mf.

life in·sur·ance seguro m de vida.

life jack·et chaleco m salvavidas.

life·style estilo m de vida.

life·time vida f; **in his l.** durante su vida.

lift 1 vt levantar; (head etc) alzar; (pick up) coger. **2** n **to give sb a l.** llevar a algn en coche.

▸ **lift out** vt (take out) sacar.

▸ **lift up** vt levantar.

light¹ 1 n luz f; (lamp) lámpara f; (headlight) faro m; **to set l. to sth** prender fuego a algo; **have you got a l.?** ¿tiene fuego? **2** vt* (illuminate) iluminar; (ignite) encender. **3** adj claro, -a; (hair) rubio, -a.

▸ **light up 1** vt iluminar. **2** vi iluminarse; (light cigarette) encender un cigarrillo.

light² **1** adj ligero, -a; (rain) fino, -a. **2** adv **to travel l.** ir ligero, -a de equipaje.

light bulb bombilla f.

light·er (cigarette) **l.** mechero m.

light·house faro m.

light·ing (act) iluminación f.

light·ning (flash) relámpago m; (which hits the earth) rayo m.

like¹ 1 prep (similar to) parecido, -a a; (the same as) igual que; **l. that** así; **what's he l.?** ¿cómo es?; **to feel l.** tener ganas de. **2** adj parecido, -a; (equal) igual.

like² **1** vt **do you l. chocolate?** ¿te gusta el chocolate?; **he likes dancing** le gusta bailar; **I would l. a coffee** quisiera un café; **would you l. to go now?** ¿quieres que nos vayamos ya? **2** vi querer; **as you l.** como quieras.

like·a·ble adj simpático, -a.

like·li·hood probabilidad f.

like·ly 1 adj probable; **he's l. to cause trouble** es probable que cause problemas. **2** adv probablemente; **not l.!** ¡ni hablar!

like·wise adv (also) asimismo.

lik·ing (for thing) afición f; (for person) simpatía f; (for friend) cariño m.

lil·y lirio m.

limb miembro m.

lime (fruit) lima f; (tree) limero m.

lim·it 1 n límite m; (maximum) máximo m; (minimum) mínimo m. **2** vt (restrict) limitar (**to** a).

lim·ou·sine limusina *f.*

limp 1 *vi* cojear. **2** *n* cojera *f.*

line[1] línea *f*; *(straight)* raya *f*; *(of writing)* renglón *m*; *(of poetry)* verso *m*; *(row)* fila *f*; *(of trees)* hilera *f*; *(of people waiting)* cola *f*; *(rope)* cuerda *f*; *(telephone)* línea *f*; *(of railway)* vía *f.*

line[2] *vt (clothes)* forrar.

▶ **line up 1** *vt (arrange in rows)* poner en fila; **he has something lined up for this evening** tiene algo organizado para esta noche. **2** *vi (people)* ponerse en fila; *(in line)* hacer cola.

lin·en *(sheets etc)* ropa *f* blanca.

lin·er transatlántico *m.*

line-up *(of team)* alineación *f*; *(of band)* formación *f*; *(of police suspects)* rueda *f* de reconocimiento *or* identificación.

lin·ger *vi* tardar; *(dawdle)* rezagarse; *(smell, doubt)* persistir; *fig (memory)* perdurar.

lin·guis·tics lingüística *f.*

lin·ing forro *m.*

link 1 *n (of chain)* eslabón *m*; *(connection)* conexión *f.* **2** *vt* unir.

▶ **link up** *vi* unirse; *(meet)* encontrarse.

lino linóleo *m.*

lint brush cepillo *m* de la ropa.

li·on león *m.*

lip labio *m.*

lip·stick lápiz *m* de labios.

li·queur licor *m.*

liq·uid *adj & n* líquido, -a *(m).*

liq·ui·date *vt* liquidar.

liq·uor bebidas *fpl* alcohólicas.

list 1 *n* lista *f*; *(catalog)* catálogo *m.* **2** *vt (make a list of)* hacer una lista de; *(put on a list)* poner en una lista.

lis·ten *vi* escuchar; **to l. to sth/sb** escuchar algo/a algn.

▶ **listen out** *vi* estar atento, -a **(for** a).

lis·ten·er oyente *mf.*

li·ter litro *m.*

lit·er·al·ly *adv* literalmente.

lit·er·ar·y *adj* literario, -a.

lit·er·a·ture literatura *f*; *(documentation)* folleto *m* informativo.

lit·i·ga·tion litigio *m.*

lit·ter *(trash)* basura *f*; *(papers)* papeles *mpl*; *(offspring)* camada *f.*

lit·ter bin papelera *f.*

lit·tle 1 *adj* pequeño, -a; **a l. dog** un perrito; **a l. house** una casita. **2** *pron* poco *m*; **save me a l.** guárdame un poco; **a l. cheese** un poco de queso. **3** *adv* poco; **l. by l.** poco a poco; **as l. as possible** lo menos posible; **l. milk/money** poca leche/poco dinero.

live[1] *vti* vivir; **to l. an interesting life** llevar una vida interesante.

live[2] *adj (TV etc)* en directo; *(wire)* con corriente.

▶ **live off, live on** *vt (food, money)* vivir de.

▶ **live on** *vi (memory)* persistir.

▶ **live through** *vt* sobrevivir a, vivir.

▶ **live together** *vi* vivir juntos.

▶ **live up to** *vt (promises)* cumplir con; **to l. up to expectations** estar a la altura de lo que se esperaba.

▶ **live with** *vt* vivir con.

live·ly *adj (person)* vivo, -a; *(place)* animado, -a.

liv·er hígado *m.*

liv·ing 1 *adj* vivo, -a. **2** *n* vida *f*; **to earn** *or* **make one's l.** ganarse la vida.

living room sala *f* de estar.

liz·ard *(large)* lagarto *m*; *(small)* lagartija *f.*

load 1 *n (cargo)* carga *f*; *(weight)* peso *m*; *fam* **loads of** montones de; *fam* **that's a l. of garbage!** ¡no son más que tonterías! **2** *vt* cargar.

▶ **load up** *vti* cargar.

loaf *(pl* **loaves)** pan *m.*

loan 1 *n (to individual)* préstamo *m*; *(to company etc)* empréstito *m*; **on l.** prestado, -a. **2** *vt* prestar.

lob·by *(hall)* vestíbulo *m.*

lob·ster langosta *f.*

lo·cal *adj* local; *(person)* del pueblo.

lo·cal ar·e·a net·work red *f* local.

lo·cal·i·ty localidad *f.*

lo·cal·ly *adv* en *or* de la localidad.

lo·cate *vt (situate)* ubicar; *(find)* localizar.

lo·ca·tion ubicación *f.*

lock[1] *n (on door etc)* cerradura *f*; *(bolt)* cerrojo *m*; *(padlock)* candado *m*; *(on canal)* esclusa *f.* **2** *vt* cerrar con llave *or* cerrojo *or* candado.

lock[2] *(of hair)* mechón *m.*

▸**lock in** *vt (person)* encerrar.

▸**lock out** *vt (person)* cerrar la puerta a.

▸**lock up** *vt (house)* cerrar; *(in jail)* meter en la cárcel.

lock·er armario *m* ropero.

lock·et medallón *m.*

lodge **1** *n (gamekeeper's)* casa *f* del guarda; *(porter's)* portería *f*; *(hunter's)* refugio *m.* **2** *vt (accommodate)* alojar; *(complaint)* presentar. **3** *vi (live)* alojarse; *(get stuck)* meterse *(in* en).

lodg·er huésped, -a *mf.*

lodg·ing alojamiento *m*; **l. house** casa *f* de huéspedes.

loft desván *m.*

log *(wood)* tronco *m*; *(for fire)* leño *m.*

log·ic lógica *f.*

log·i·cal *adj* lógico, -a.

lol·li·pop chupachup® *m.*

lone *adj (solitary)* solitario, -a; *(single)* solo, -a.

lone·li·ness soledad *f.*

lone·ly *adj (person)* solo, -a; *(place)* solitario, -a.

long[1] **1** *adj (size)* largo, -a; *(time)* mucho, -a; **it's three meters l.** tiene tres metros de largo; **it's a l. way** está lejos; **at l. last** por fin; **how l. is the film?** ¿cuánto tiempo dura la película? **2** *adv* mucho tiempo; **as l. as the exhibition lasts** mientras dure la exposición; **as l. as** *or* **so l. as you don't mind** con tal de que no te importe; **before l.** dentro de poco; **how l. have you been here?** ¿cuánto tiempo llevas aquí?

long-dis·tance *adj* de larga distancia; **l. call** conferencia *f* interurbana.

long-term *adj* largo plazo.

look 1 *n (glance)* mirada *f*; *(appearance)* aspecto *m*; **to take a l. at** echar un vistazo a. **2** *vi* mirar; *(seem)* parecer; **he looks well** tiene buena cara; **she looks like her father** se parece a su padre.

▸**look after** *vt* ocuparse de, cuidar de.

▸**look around 1** *vi* mirar alrededor; *(turn head)* volver la cabeza. **2** *vt (house, shop)* ver.

▸**look at** *vt* mirar.

▸**look back** *vi* mirar hacia atrás; **to l. back on sth** *(remember)* recordar algo.

▸**look for** *vt* buscar.

▸**look forward to** *vt* esperar con ilusión; **I l. forward to hearing from you** *(in letter)* espero noticias suyas.

▸**look into** *vt* investigar.

▸**look onto** *vt* dar a.

▸**look out** *vi* **the bedroom looks out onto the garden** el dormitorio da al jardín; **l. out!** ¡cuidado!, ¡ojo!

▸**look over** *vt (examine)* revisar; *(place)* inspeccionar.

▸**look up 1** *vi (glance upwards)* alzar la vista. **2** *vt (look for)* buscar.

look·out *(person)* centinela *mf*; *(place)* mirador *m*; **to be on the l. for** estar al acecho de.

loom[1] telar *m.*

loom[2] *vi (of mountain)* alzarse; *(threaten)* amenazar.

loop lazo *m.*

loop·hole *fig* escapatoria *f.*

loose 1 *adj (not secure)* flojo, -a; *(papers, hair, clothes)* suelto, -a; *(baggy)* holgado, -a; *(not packaged)* a granel; **to set sb l.** soltar a algn; **l. change** suelto *m.* **2** *n* **to be on the l.** *(prisoner)* andar suelto.

loos·en *vt* aflojar; *(belt)* desabrochar.

lord señor *m.*

lose* *vti* perder; **to l. to sb** perder contra algn.

los·er perdedor, -a *mf*.

loss pérdida *f*.

lost *adj* perdido, -a; **to get l.** perderse; **get l.!** *fam* ¡vete a la porra!

lost and found oficina *f* de objetos perdidos.

lot a l. of (*much*) mucho, -a; (*many*) muchos, -as; **he feels a l. better** se encuentra mucho mejor; **lots of** montones de; **what a l. of bottles!** ¡qué cantidad de botellas!

lo·tion loción *f*.

lot·ter·y lotería *f*.

loud **1** *adj* (*voice*) alto, -a; (*noise*) fuerte; (*protests, party*) ruidoso, -a. **2** *adv* **to read/think out l.** leer/pensar en voz alta.

loud·ly *adv* (*to speak etc*) en voz alta.

loud·speak·er altavoz *m*.

lous·y *adj fam* fatal; **a l. trick** una cochinada.

love **1** *n* amor *m*; **to be in l. with sb** estar enamorado, -a de algn; **to make l.** hacer el amor. **2** *vt* (*person*) querer; (*sport etc*) ser muy aficionado, -a a; **he loves cooking** le encanta cocinar.

love·ly *adj* (*charming*) encantador, -a; (*beautiful*) precioso, -a; (*delicious*) riquísimo, -a.

lov·er (*enthusiast*) aficionado, -a *mf*.

lov·ing *adj* cariñoso, -a.

low **1** *adj* bajo, -a; (*poor*) pobre; (*reprehensible*) malo, -a; **to feel l.** sentirse deprimido, -a. **2** *adv* bajo.

low·er **1** *adj* inferior. **2** *vt* bajar; (*reduce*) reducir; (*price*) rebajar.

low-fat *adj* (*milk*) desnatado, -a; (*food*) light *inv*.

loy·al *adj* leal.

loy·al·ty lealtad *f*, fidelidad *f*.

loz·enge pastilla *f*.

LP LP *m*, elepé *m*.

luck suerte *f*; **bad l.!** ¡mala suerte!; **good l.!** ¡(buena) suerte!

luck·i·ly *adv* afortunadamente.

luck·y *adj* (*person*) afortunado, -a;

(*charm*) de la suerte; **that was l.** ha sido una suerte.

lu·di·crous *adj* ridículo, -a.

lug·gage equipaje *m*.

luke·warm *adj* (*water etc*) tibio, -a.

lull·a·by nana *f*.

lum·ber maderos *mpl*.

lum·ber·yard almacén *m* maderero, maderería *f*, *RP* barraca *f* maderera.

lu·mi·nous *adj* luminoso, -a.

lump (*of coal etc*) trozo *m*; (*of sugar, earth*) terrón *m*; (*swelling*) bulto *m*.

lump sum suma *f* global.

lu·na·tic *adj & n* loco, -a (*mf*).

lunch comida *f*, almuerzo *m*; **l. hour** hora *f* de comer.

lung pulmón *m*.

lux·u·ri·ous *adj* lujoso, -a.

lux·u·ry lujo *m*.

M

mac·(c)a·roni macarrones *mpl*.

ma·chine máquina *f*.

ma·chin·er·y (*machines*) maquinaria *f*; (*workings of machine*) mecanismo *m*.

mack·er·el *inv* caballa *f*.

mad *adj* loco, -a; **to be m. about sth/sb** estar loco, -a por algo/algn; **to be m. at sb** estar enfadado, -a con algn.

Mad·am señora *f*.

made *pt & pp* of **make**.

mad·man loco *m*.

mad·ness locura *f*.

mag·a·zine (*periodical*) revista *f*.

mag·got gusano *m*.

mag·ic **1** *n* magia *f*. **2** *adj* mágico, -a; **m. wand** varita *f* mágica.

mag·i·cal *adj* mágico, -a.

ma·gi·cian (*wizard*) mago, -a *mf*; (*conjuror*) prestidigitador, -a *mf*.

mag·is·trate juez, -a *mf* de paz.

mag·net imán *m*.

mag·nif·i·cent *adj* magnífico, -a.

mag·ni·fy·ing glass lupa *f*.

ma·hog·a·ny caoba *f*.

maid criada *f*.

mail 1 *n* correo *m*. **2** *vt (post)* echar (al buzón).

mail·box buzón *m*.

mail·man cartero *m*.

main *adj (problem, door etc)* principal; *(square, mast, sail)* mayor; *(office)* central; **the m. thing is to keep calm** lo esencial es mantener la calma; **m. road** carretera *f* principal. **2** *n (pipe, wire)* conducto *m* principal; **the mains** *(water or gas system)* la conducción; *(electrical)* la red (eléctrica).

main·land continente *m*.

main·ly *adv* principalmente; *(for the most part)* en su mayoría.

main·tain *vt (road, machine)* conservar en buen estado; **to m. that** sostener en que.

main·te·nance *(of vehicle, road)* mantenimiento *m*; *(divorce allowance)* pensión *f*.

maî·tre d' jefe *m* de sala.

maize maíz *m*.

maj·es·ty majestad *f*.

ma·jor 1 *adj* principal; *(contribution, operation)* importante. **2** *n (officer)* comandante *m*.

ma·jor·ette majorette *f*.

ma·jor·i·ty mayoría *f*.

make 1 *vt** hacer; *(manufacture)* fabricar; *(clothes, curtains)* confeccionar; *(meal)* preparar; *(decision)* tomar; *(earn)* ganar; **to be made of** ser de; **to m. sb do sth** obligar a algn a hacer algo; **to m. do with sth** arreglárselas con algo; **I don't know what to m. of it** no sé qué pensar de eso; **we've made it!** *(succeeded)* ¡lo hemos conseguido! **2** *n (brand)* marca *f*.

▸**make out 1** *vt (list, receipt)* hacer; *(check)* extender; *(perceive)* distinguir; *(understand)* entender; *(claim)* pretender. **2** *vi* **how did you m. out?** ¿qué tal te fue?

▸**make up 1** *vt (list)* hacer; *(assemble)* montar; *(invent)* inventar; *(apply cosmetics to)* maquillar; *(one's face)* maquillarse; *(loss)* compensar. **2** *vi* **to m. up (with sb)** hacer las paces (con algn).

▸**make up for** *vt (loss, damage)* compensar por; *(lost time, mistake)* recuperar.

mak·er fabricante *mf*.

make-up *(cosmetics)* maquillaje *m*.

ma·lar·i·a malaria *f*.

male 1 *adj (animal, plant)* macho; *(person)* varón; *(sex)* masculino. **2** *n (person)* varón *m*; *(animal, plant)* macho *m*.

mal·ice *(wickedness)* malicia *f*.

ma·li·cious *adj (wicked)* malévolo, -a.

mall *(shopping)* centro *m* comercial.

mam·mal mamífero *m*.

man *(pl* **men)** hombre *m*; **old m.** viejo *m*; **young m.** joven *m*; *(humanity)* el hombre; *(human being)* ser *m* humano.

man·age 1 *vt (company, household)* llevar; *(money, affairs, person)* manejar; *(achieve)* conseguir; **to m. to do sth** lograr hacer algo. **2** *vi (cope physically)* poder; *(financially)* arreglárselas.

man·age·ment dirección *f*.

man·ag·er *(of company, bank)* director, -a *mf*; *(of department)* jefe, -a *mf*.

man·ag·ing di·rec·tor director, -a *mf* gerente.

man·da·rin *(fruit)* mandarina *f*.

mane *(of horse)* crin *f*; *(of lion)* melena *f*.

ma·neu·ver 1 *n* maniobra *f*. **2** *vt* maniobrar; *(person)* manejar. **3** *vi* maniobrar.

ma·ni·ac maníaco, -a *mf*; *fam* loco, -a *mf*.

man·kind la humanidad.

man·made *adj (lake)* artificial; *(fibers, fabric)* sintético, -a.

man·ner *(way, method)* manera *f*, modo *m*; *(way of behaving)* forma *f* de ser; **(good) manners** buenos modales *mpl*; **bad manners** falta *f sing* de educación.

man·pow·er mano *f* de obra.

man·tel·piece *(shelf)* repisa *f* de chimenea; *(fireplace)* chimenea *f*.

man·u·al *adj & n* manual *(m)*.

man·u·fac·ture 1 *vt* fabricar. **2** *n* fabricación *f*.

man·u·fac·tur·er fabricante *mf*.

ma·nure estiércol *m*.

man·y 1 *adj* muchos, -as; **a great m.** muchísimos, -as; **as m. … as …** tantos, -as … como …; **how m. days?** ¿cuántos días?; **not m. books** pocos libros; **so m. flowers!** ¡cuántas flores!; **too m.** demasiados, -as. **2** *pron* muchos, -as.

map *(of country)* mapa *m*; *(of town, bus)* plano *m*.

mar·a·thon maratón *m or f*.

mar·ble *(stone)* mármol *m*; *(glass ball)* canica *f*.

March marzo *m*.

march 1 *n* marcha *f*. **2** *vi* marchar.

mare yegua *f*.

mar·ga·rine margarina *f*.

mar·gin margen *m*.

ma·rine 1 *adj* marino, -a. **2** *n* soldado *m* de infantería de marina; **the M. Corps** la infantería de marina.

mark 1 *n (trace)* huella *f*; *(stain)* mancha *f*; *(symbol)* signo *m*; *(sign, token)* señal *f*; *(in exam etc)* nota *f*. **2** *vt (make mark on)* marcar; *(stain)* manchar; *(exam)* corregir.

▸**mark out** *vt (area)* delimitar.

mark·er *(pen)* rotulador *m*.

mar·ket mercado *m*.

mar·ket·ing marketing *m*.

mar·ma·lade mermelada *f* (de cítricos).

mar·riage *(state)* matrimonio *m*; *(wedding)* boda *f*.

mar·ried *adj* casado, -a.

mar·row *(bone)* m. médula *f*; *(vegetable)* calabacín *m*.

mar·ry *vt* casarse con; *(priest)* casar; **to get married** casarse.

marsh pantano *m*; **salt m.** marisma *f*.

mar·shal 1 *n (in army)* mariscal *m*; *(sheriff)* policía *mf*; *(police or fire chief)* jefe, -a *mf*. **2** *vt (troops)* formar; *(facts etc)* ordenar.

Mar·tian *n & adj* marciano, -a *(mf)*.

mar·vel·ous *adj* maravilloso, -a.

mar·zi·pan mazapán *m*.

mas·car·a rímel *m*.

mas·cot mascota *f*.

mas·cu·line *adj* masculino, -a.

mash *vt* **to m. (up)** machacar; **mashed potatoes** puré *m* de patatas.

mask máscara *f*.

mass¹ *(in church)* misa *f*; **to say m.** decir misa.

mass² 1 *n* masa *f*; *(large quantity)* montón *m*; *(of people)* multitud *f*. **2** *adj* masivo, -a.

mas·sa·cre 1 *n* masacre *f*. **2** *vt* masacrar.

mas·sage 1 *n* masaje *m*. **2** *vt* dar masaje a.

mas·seur masajista *m*.

mas·seuse masajista *f*.

mas·sive *adj* enorme.

mast mástil *m*; *(radio etc)* torre *f*.

mas·ter 1 *n (of dog, servant)* amo *m*; *(of household)* señor *m*; *(teacher)* profesor *m*; **m.'s degree** ≃ máster *m*. **2** *vt (person, situation)* dominar; *(subject, skill)* llegar a dominar.

mas·ter·piece obra *f* maestra.

mat *(rug)* alfombrilla *f*; *(doormat)* felpudo *m*; *(rush mat)* estera *f*.

match¹ cerilla *f*.

match² 1 *n (sport)* partido *m*. **2** *vt (be in harmony with)* armonizar con; *(colors, clothes)* hacer juego con; **they are well matched** *(teams)* van iguales; *(couple)* hacen buena pareja. **3** *vi (harmonize)* hacer juego.

▸**match up to** *vt* estar a la altura de.

match·box caja *f* de cerillas.

match·ing *adj* a juego.
match·stick cerilla *f*.
ma·te·ri·al *(substance)* materia *f*; *(cloth)* tejido *m*; **materials** *(ingredients, equipment)* materiales *mpl*.
ma·ter·nal *adj* maternal; *(uncle etc)* materno, -a.
ma·ter·ni·ty maternidad *f*.
ma·ter·ni·ty hos·pi·tal maternidad *f*.
math matemáticas *fpl*.
math·e·mat·i·cal *adj* matemático, -a.
math·e·mat·ics matemáticas *fpl*.
mat·i·née *(cinema)* sesión *f* de tarde; *(theater)* función *f* de tarde.
mat·ter 1 *n (affair, question)* asunto *m*; *(problem)* problema *m*; *(substance)* materia *f*; **what's the m.?** ¿qué pasa? **2** *vi* importar; **it doesn't m.** no importa, da igual.
mat·tress colchón *m*.
ma·ture *adj* maduro, -a.
max·i·mum 1 *n* máximo *m*. **2** *adj* máximo, -a.
May mayo *m*.
may *v aux (pt* **might)** *(possibility, probability)* poder, ser posible; **he m. or might come** puede que venga; **you m. or might as well stay** más vale que te quedes. ▪ *(permission)* poder; **m. I?** ¿me permite?; **you m. smoke** pueden fumar. ▪ *(wish)* ojalá (+ *subjunctive*); **m. you always be happy!** ¡ojalá seas siempre feliz!
may·be *adv* quizá(s), tal vez.
may·on·naise mayonesa *f*.
may·or *(man)* alcalde *m*; *(woman)* alcaldesa *f*.
maze laberinto *m*.
MBA *abbr of* **Master of Business Administration** MBA *m*, máster *m* en administración de empresas.
me *pron (as object)* me; **he gave it to me** me lo dio; **listen to me** escúchame; **she knows me** me conoce. ▪ *(after prep)* mí; **it's for me** es para mí; **with me** conmigo. ▪ *(emphatic)*

yo; **it's me** soy yo; **what about me?** y yo, ¿qué?
mead·ow prado *m*.
meal *(food)* comida *f*.
mean¹* *vt (signify)* querer decir; *(intend)* pensar; *(wish)* querer; **what do you m. by that?** ¿qué quieres decir con eso?; **I m. it** (te) lo digo en serio; **she was meant to arrive on the 7th** tenía que *or* debía llegar el día 7; **they m. well** tienen buenas intenciones; **I didn't m. to do it** lo hice sin querer.
mean² *adj (miserly)* tacaño, -a; *(unkind)* malo, -a; *(bad-tempered)* malhumorado, -a.
mean·ing sentido *m*.
mean·ing·ful *adj* significativo, -a.
mean·ing·less *adj* sin sentido.
mean·ness *(miserliness)* tacañería *f*, *(nastiness)* maldad *f*.
means *sing or pl (method)* medio *m*; *(resources, wealth)* recursos *mpl* *(económicos)*; **by m. of** por medio de, mediante; **by all m.!** ¡por supuesto!; **by no m.** de ninguna manera.
mean·time in the m. mientras tanto.
mean·while *adv* mientras tanto.
mea·sles sarampión *m*.
meas·ure 1 *n* medida *f*; *(ruler)* regla *f*. **2** *vt (object, area)* medir.
▸**measure up** *vi* **to m. up to sth** estar a la altura de algo.
meas·ure·ment medida *f*.
meat carne *f*.
me·chan·ic mecánico *m*, *a mf*.
me·chan·i·cal *adj* mecánico, -a.
mech·a·nism mecanismo *m*.
med·al medalla *f*.
med·al·ist medalla *mf*; **to be a gold m.** ser medalla de oro.
me·di·a *npl* medios *mpl* de comunicación.
med·i·cal *adj (treatment)* médico, -a; *(book)* de medicina.
med·i·ca·tion medicación *f*.
med·i·cine *(science)* medicina *f*, *(drug etc)* medicamento *m*.

med·i·cine cab·i·net botiquín *m*.

me·di·e·val *adj* medieval.

Med·i·ter·ra·ne·an 1 *adj* mediterráneo, -a. **2** *n* **the M.** el Mediterráneo.

me·di·um *adj* mediano, -a.

me·di·um-sized *adj* de tamaño mediano.

meet* 1 *vt (by chance)* encontrar; *(by arrangement)* reunirse con; *(pass in street etc)* toparse con; *(get to know)* conocer; *(await arrival of)* esperar; *(collect)* ir a buscar; **pleased to m. you!** ¡mucho gusto! **2** *vi (by chance)* encontrarse; *(by arrangement)* reunirse; *(formal meeting)* entrevistarse; *(get to know each other)* conocerse.

▸**meet with** *vt (difficulty)* tropezar con; *(loss)* sufrir; *(success)* tener; *(person)* reunirse con.

meet·ing *(prearranged)* cita *f; (formal)* entrevista *f; (of committee etc)* reunión *f; (of assembly)* sesión *f*.

me·ga·byte *n* megabyte *m*.

mel·o·dy melodía *f*.

mel·on melón *m*.

melt 1 *vt (metal)* fundir. **2** *vi (snow)* derretirse; *(metal)* fundirse.

mem·ber miembro *mf; (of a society)* socio, -a *mf; (of party, union)* afiliado, -a *mf*.

mem·o *(official)* memorándum *m; (personal)* apunte *m*.

mem·o·ra·ble *adj* memorable.

me·mo·ri·al 1 *adj (plaque etc)* conmemorativo, -a. **2** *n* monumento conmemorativo.

mem·o·ry memoria *f; (recollection)* recuerdo *m*; **m. stick** llave *f* USB.

men *npl see* **man**.

mend *vt* reparar; *(clothes)* remendar; *(socks etc)* zurcir.

men·tal *adj* mental; **m. home, m. hospital** hospital *m* psiquiátrico; **m. illness** enfermedad *f* mental.

men·tal·ly *adv* **to be m. handicapped** ser un, -a disminuido, -a psíquico, -a.

men·tion 1 *n* mención *f*. **2** *vt* mencionar; **don't m. it!** ¡de nada!

men·u *(à la carte)* carta *f; (fixed meal)* menú *m*; **today's m.** menú del día; *(computer)* menú *m*.

mer·cy misericordia *f*; **at the m. of** a la merced de.

mere *adj* mero, -a.

mere·ly *adv* simplemente.

merge *vi* unirse; *(roads)* converger; *(companies)* fusionarse.

merg·er *(of companies)* fusión *f*.

mer·it 1 *n (of person)* mérito *m; (of plan etc)* ventaja *f*. **2** *vt* merecer.

mer·ry *adj* alegre; *(tipsy)* achispado, -a; **M. Christmas!** ¡Felices Navidades!

mer·ry-go-round tiovivo *m*.

mesh malla *f*.

mess *(confusion)* confusión *f; (disorder)* desorden *m; (mix-up)* lío *m; (dirt)* suciedad *f*.

▸**mess about, mess around 1** *vt* fastidiar. **2** *vi (act the fool)* hacer el tonto.

▸**mess around with** *vt (fiddle with)* manosear.

▸**mess up** *vt (make untidy)* desordenar; *(dirty)* ensuciar; *(spoil)* estropear.

mes·sage recado *m*.

mes·sen·ger mensajero, -a *m*.

mess·y *adj (untidy)* desordenado, -a; *(dirty)* sucio, -a.

met·al 1 *n* metal *m*. **2** *adj* metálico, -a.

met·a·phor metáfora *f*.

me·ter¹ contador *m*.

me·ter² metro *m*.

meth·od método *m*.

me·thod·i·cal *adj* metódico, -a.

met·ric *adj* métrico, -a.

mew maullido *m*.

Mex·i·can *adj & n* mejicano, -a *(mf)*, mexicano, -a *(mf)*.

mice *npl see* **mouse**.

mi·cro·chip microchip *m*.

mi·cro·phone micrófono *m*.

mi·cro·scope microscopio *m*.

mi·cro·wave (ov·en) *(horno m)* microondas *m inv*.

MEETING PEOPLE

Hello, how are you?
Hola, ¿cómo está/estás?

Hi, how's it going?
Hola, ¿qué tal?

Fine thank you, how are you?
Bien, gracias, ¿y usted/tú?

Good, and you?
Bien, ¿y usted/tú?

Good morning/afternoon.
Buenos días./Buenas tardes.

Good evening.
Buenas noches.

What's your name?
¿Cómo se llama?/¿Cómo te llamas?

My name's Eve.
Me llamo Eve.

I'm Brian and this is my wife Kim.
Me llamo Brian, y esta es Kim, mi mujer.

Nice to meet you.
Encantado(a).

How old are you?
¿Qué edad tiene/tienes?

I'm 15/25 (years old).
Tengo quince/veinticinco años.

Where are you from?
¿De dónde es/eres?

I'm from the United States./I'm American.
Soy de Estados Unidos./Soy estadounidense.

Where do you live?
¿Dónde vive/vives?

I live near San Francisco.
Vivo cerca de San Francisco.

What do you do?
¿A qué se dedica/te dedicas?

I'm a teacher/a student.
Soy profesor(ora)/estudiante.

I'm at high school.
Estoy en secundaria.

I'm a stay-at-home mom.
Soy madre y ama de casa.

I work for an insurance company.
Trabajo para una compañía de seguros.

I'm retired.
Estoy jubilado(a).

Do you have any brothers and sisters?
¿Tiene/Tienes hermanos?

I've got an older sister and two little brothers.
Tengo una hermana mayor y dos hermanos pequeños.

Do you have kids?
¿Tiene/Tienes hijos?

I have a three-year-old son named Josh.
Tengo un hijo de tres años que se llama Josh.

Are you married?
¿Está/Estás casado(a)?

I'm divorced/separated/widowed.
Estoy divorciado(a)/separado(a)/viudo(a).

What do you do in your spare time?
¿A qué se dedica/te dedicas en tu tiempo libre?

I like reading/going to the movies.
Me gusta leer/ir al cine.

I play basketball./I do yoga.
Juego al baloncesto./Hago yoga.

I'm taking Spanish classes.
Estoy haciendo un curso de español.

See you soon/later!
¡Hasta pronto/luego!

Have a good weekend/trip!
¡Buen viaje!

We should keep in touch, here's my e-mail address.
Deberíamos seguir en contacto. Este es mi e-mail.

mid adj (in) m. afternoon a media tarde; (in) m. April a mediados de abril.

mid·air adj (collision, explosion) en el aire.

mid·day mediodía m.

mid·dle 1 adj de en medio; the M. Ages la Edad Media. 2 n medio m; (waist) cintura f; in the m. of en medio de; in the m. of winter en pleno invierno.

mid·dle-aged adj de mediana edad.

mid·dle-class adj de clase media.

mid·night medianoche f.

midst in the m. of en medio de.

mid·way adv a medio camino.

mid·wife comadrona f.

might v aux see may.

might·y 1 adj (mightier, mightiest) (strong) fuerte; (powerful) poderoso, -a; (great) enorme. 2 adv fam cantidad de, muy.

mild adj (person, character) apacible; (climate) templado, -a; (punishment) leve; (tobacco, taste) suave.

mile milla f; fam miles better muchísimo mejor.

mile·age kilometraje m.

mil·i·tar·y adj militar.

milk leche f.

milk choc·o·late chocolate m con leche.

milk·man lechero m.

milk shake batido m.

mill (grinder) molino m; (for coffee) molinillo m; (factory) fábrica f.

mil·li·me·ter milímetro m.

mil·lion millón m.

mil·lion·aire millonario, -a mf.

mime vt imitar.

mim·ic vt imitar.

mince(·meat) carne f picada.

mincer picadora f de carne.

mind 1 n (intellect) mente f; (brain) cabeza f; what kind of car do you have in m.? ¿en qué clase de coche estás pensando?; to be in two minds estar indeciso, -a; to my m. a

mi parecer. 2 vt (child) cuidar; (house) vigilar; (be careful of) tener cuidado con; (object to) tener inconveniente en; m. the step! ¡ojo con el escalón!; I wouldn't m. a cup of coffee me vendría bien un café; never m. no importa. 3 vi (object) do you m. if I open the window? ¿le importa que abra la ventana?

mine¹ poss pron (el) mío, (la) mía, (los) míos, (las) mías; a friend of m. un amigo mío; these gloves are m. estos guantes son míos; which is m.? ¿cuál es el mío?

mine² (for coal etc) mina f.

min·er minero, -a mf.

min·er·al adj mineral.

min·er·al wa·ter agua f mineral.

min·i- prefix mini-.

min·i·a·ture 1 n miniatura f. 2 adj (en) miniatura.

min·i·mum adj mínimo, -a.

min·ing 1 n minería f, explotación f de minas. 2 adj minero, -a.

min·is·ter ministro, -a mf; (of church) pastor, -a mf.

min·is·try (political) ministerio m; (in church) sacerdocio m.

mi·nor adj (lesser) menor; (unimportant) sin importancia.

mi·nor·i·ty minoría f.

mint (herb) menta f; (sweet) pastilla f de menta.

mi·nus prep 5 m. 3 5 menos 3; m. 10 degrees 10 grados bajo cero.

min·ute¹ minuto m; just a m. (espera) un momento.

mi·nute² adj (tiny) diminuto, -a.

mir·a·cle milagro m.

mi·rac·u·lous adj milagroso, -a.

mir·ror espejo m; rear-view m. retrovisor m.

mis·be·have vi portarse mal.

mis·cel·la·ne·ous adj variado, -a.

mis·chief (naughtiness) travesura f; (evil) malicia f; to get up to m. hacer travesuras.

mis·chie·vous adj (naughty) travieso, -a; *(playful)* juguetón, -ona; *(wicked)* malicioso, -a.

mis·de·mean·or delito *m* menor.

mi·ser avaro, -a *mf*.

mis·er·a·ble *adj (sad)* triste; *(wretched)* miserable.

mi·ser·ly *adj* tacaño, -a.

mis·er·y *(sadness)* tristeza *f*; *(wretchedness)* desgracia *f*; *(suffering)* sufrimiento *m*; *(poverty)* miseria *f*.

mis·for·tune desgracia *f*.

mis·hap contratiempo *m*.

mis·lay* *vt* extraviar.

mis·lead* *vt* despistar; *(deliberately)* engañar.

mis·lead·ing *adj (erroneous)* erróneo, -a; *(deliberately)* engañoso, -a.

miss¹ señorita *f*.

miss² **1** *vt (train etc)* perder; *(opportunity)* dejar pasar; *(regret absence of)* echar de menos; **you have missed the point** no has captado la idea. **2** *vi (throw etc)* fallar; *(shot)* errar; **is anything missing?** ¿falta algo?

▸**miss out** **1** *vt (omit)* saltarse. **2** *vi* **don't worry, you're not missing out** no te preocupes, no te pierdes nada.

▸**miss out on** *vt* perderse.

mis·sile misil *m*; *(object thrown)* proyectil *m*.

miss·ing *adj (lost)* perdido, -a; *(disappeared)* desaparecido, -a; *(absent)* ausente; **m. person** desaparecido, -a *mf*; **three cups are m.** faltan tres tazas.

mis·sion misión *f*.

mist *(fog)* niebla *f*; *(thin)* neblina *f*; *(at sea)* bruma *f*.

mis·take **1** *n* error *m*; **by m.** por equivocación; *(unintentionally)* sin querer; **to make a m.** cometer un error. **2** *vt (meaning)* malentender; **to m. Jack for Bill** confundir a Jack con Bill.

mis·tak·en *adj* erróneo, -a; **you are m.** estás equivocado, -a.

mis·tak·en·ly *adv* por error.

mis·treat maltratar.

mis·tress *(of house)* ama *f*; *(primary school)* maestra *f*; *(secondary school)* profesora *f*; *(lover)* amante *f*.

mis·trust **1** *n* recelo *m*. **2** *vt* desconfiar de.

mist·y *adj (day)* de niebla; *(window etc)* empañado, -a.

mis·un·der·stand* *vti* malentender.

mis·un·der·stand·ing malentendido *m*; *(disagreement)* desavenencia *f*.

mit·ten manopla *f*.

mix **1** *vt* mezclar. **2** *vi (blend)* mezclarse (**with** con).

▸**mix up** *vt (ingredients)* mezclar bien; *(confuse)* confundir (**with** con); *(papers)* revolver.

mixed *adj (assorted)* surtido, -a; *(varied)* variado, -a; *(school)* mixto, -a.

mix·er *(for food)* batidora *f*.

mix·ture mezcla *f*.

mix-up confusión *f*.

moan **1** *n* gemido *m*. **2** *vi (groan)* gemir; *(complain)* quejarse *(about* de).

mob **1** *n* multitud *f*. **2** *vt* acosar.

mo·bile *adj* móvil.

mo·bile phone teléfono *m* móvil.

mod·el **1** *n* modelo *mf*; *(scale)* m. maqueta *f*. **2** *adj (railway)* en miniatura.

mo·dem módem *m*.

mod·er·ate *adj* moderado, -a; *(reasonable)* razonable; *(average)* regular; *(ability)* mediocre.

mod·er·a·tion moderación *f*.

mod·ern *adj* moderno, -a; **m. languages** lenguas *fpl* modernas.

mod·ern·ize *vt* modernizar.

mod·est *adj* modesto, -a; *(chaste)* púdico, -a; *(price)* módico, -a; *(success)* discreto, -a.

mod·es·ty *(humility)* modestia *f*; *(chastity)* pudor *m*.

mod·i·fi·ca·tion modificación *f*.

mod·i·fy *vt* modificar.

moist *adj* húmedo, -a.

mois·ture humedad f.

mold¹ (fungus) moho m.

mold² 1 n (shape) molde m. 2 vt moldear; (clay) modelar.

mold·y adj mohoso, -a; **to go m.** enmohecerse.

mole¹ (beauty spot) lunar m.

mole² (animal) topo m.

mom fam mamá f.

mo·ment momento m.

Mon·day lunes m.

mon·ey dinero m.

mon·ey or·der giro m postal.

mon·i·tor (of computer) monitor m.

monk monje m.

mon·key mono m.

mo·nop·o·lize vt (attention etc) acaparar.

mo·not·o·nous adj monótono -a.

mo·not·o·ny monotonía f.

mon·ster monstruo m.

month mes m.

month·ly 1 adj mensual. 2 adv mensualmente.

mon·u·ment monumento m.

moo vi mugir.

mood humor m; **to be in a good/bad m.** estar de buen/mal humor; **to be in the m. for (doing) sth** estar de humor para (hacer) algo.

mood·y adj (changeable) de humor variable; (bad-tempered) malhumorado, -a.

moon luna f.

moon·light luz f de la luna.

moor (heath) páramo m.

moose inv alce m.

mop (for floor) fregona f.

▸**mop up** vt (liquids) limpiar.

mo·ped ciclomotor m.

mor·al 1 adj moral. 2 n moraleja f; **morals** moral f sing, moralidad f sing.

mo·rale moral f.

more 1 adj más; **and what is m.** y lo que es más; **is there any m. tea?** ¿queda más té?; **I've no m. money** no me queda más dinero. 2 pron más; **how many m.?** ¿cuántos más?; **I need some m.** necesito

más; **many/much m.** muchos, -as/mucho más; **m. than a hundred** más de cien. 3 adv más; **I won't do it any m.** no lo volveré a hacer; **m. and m. difficult** cada vez más difícil; **m. or less** más o menos; **she doesn't live here any m.** ya no vive aquí.

more·o·ver adv además.

morn·ing mañana f, (before dawn) madrugada f, **in the m.** por la mañana; **on Monday mornings** los lunes por la mañana; **tomorrow m.** mañana por la mañana.

Mo·roc·can adj & n marroquí (mf).

mor·tal adj & n mortal (mf).

mort·gage hipoteca f.

mort·gage com·pa·ny sociedad f hipotecaria.

Mos·lem adj & n musulmán, -ana (mf).

mosque mezquita f.

mos·qui·to (pl mosquitoes) mosquito m.

moss musgo m.

most 1 adj (greatest in quantity etc) más; (the majority of) la mayor parte de; **this house suffered (the) m. damage** esta casa fue la más afectada; **who made (the) m. mistakes?** ¿quién cometió más errores?; **m. of the time** la mayor parte del tiempo; **m. people** la mayoría de la gente. 2 pron (greatest part) la mayor parte; (greatest number) lo máximo; (the majority of people) la mayoría; **at the (very) m.** como máximo. 3 adv más; **the m. intelligent student** el estudiante más inteligente; **what I like m.** lo que más me gusta; **m. of all** sobre todo.

most·ly adv (chiefly) en su mayor parte; (generally) generalmente; (usually) normalmente.

mo·tel motel m.

moth mariposa f nocturna; **clothes m.** polilla f.

moth·er madre f; **M.'s Day** Día m de la Madre.

moth·er-in-law suegra f.

mo·tion 1 *n (movement)* movimiento *m*; *(gesture)* ademán *m*. **2** *vi* **to m. (to) sb to do sth** hacer señas a algn para que haga algo.

mo·ti·vat·ed *adj* motivado, -a.

mo·tive *(reason)* motivo *m*.

mo·tor *(engine)* motor *m*.

mo·tor·boat *(lancha)* motora *f*.

mo·tor·cy·cle motocicleta *f*.

mo·tor·cy·clist motociclista *mf*.

mo·tor·ist automovilista *mf*.

mount 1 *n (horse)* montura *f*; *(for photograph)* marco *m*. **2** *vt (horse)* subirse *or* montar a; *(photograph)* enmarcar. **3** *vi (go up)* subir; *(get on horse, bike)* montar.

▸**mount up** *vi (increase)* subir; *(accumulate)* acumularse.

moun·tain montaña *f*; **m. bike** bicicleta *f* de montaña.

moun·tain·eer alpinista *mf*, *Am* andinista *mf*.

moun·tain·eer·ing alpinismo *m*, *Am* andinismo *m*.

moun·tain·ous *adj* montañoso, -a.

mourn *vti* **to m. (for) sb** llorar la muerte de algn.

mourn·ing luto *m*; **in m.** de luto.

mouse *(pl* mice*)* ratón *m*.

mousse *(dessert)* mousse *f*.

mouth *(pl* mouths*)* boca *f*; *(of river)* desembocadura *f*.

mouth·wash enjuague *m* bucal.

move 1 *n (movement)* movimiento *m*; *(in game)* jugada *f*; *(turn)* turno *m*; *(course of action)* medida *f*; *(to new home)* mudanza *f*. **2** *vt* mover; *(transfer)* trasladar; *(affect emotionally)* conmover; **to m. house** mudarse (de casa); **to m. job** cambiar de trabajo. **3** *vi (change position)* moverse; *(change house)* mudarse (de casa); *(change post)* trasladarse; *(leave)* marcharse; *(in game)* hacer una jugada.

▸**move about, move around 1** *vt* cambiar de sitio. **2** *vi (be restless)* ir y venir.

▸**move along 1** *vt (move forward)* hacer avanzar. **2** *vi (move forward)* avanzar.

▸**move away** *vi (move aside)* apartarse; *(change house)* mudarse (de casa).

▸**move back 1** *vt (to original place)* volver a. **2** *vi (withdraw)* retirarse; *(to original place)* volver.

▸**move forward** *vti* avanzar.

▸**move in** *vi (into new home)* instalarse.

▸**move on** *vi (go forward)* avanzar; *(time)* transcurrir.

▸**move out** *vi (leave house)* mudarse.

▸**move over** *vi* correrse hacia un lado.

▸**move up** *vi (go up)* subir; *(move along)* correrse hacia un lado, hacer sitio.

move·ment movimiento *m*; *(gesture)* ademán *m*; *(trend)* corriente *f*; *(of goods, capital)* circulación *f*.

mov·ie película *f*.

mov·ing *adj (that moves)* móvil; *(car etc)* en marcha; *(touching)* conmovedor, -a.

mow* *vt (lawn)* cortar.

mow·er cortacésped *m or f*.

MP3 *n* **MPEG1 Audio Layer M. player** reproductor *m* de MP3

Mr *abbr of* **mister** señor *m*, Sr.

Mrs *abbr* señora *f*, Sra.

MS *abbr of* **Master of Science** Licenciado, -a *mf* en Ciencias.

much 1 *adj* mucho, -a; **as m. … as** tanto, -a … como; **how m. chocolate?** ¿cuánto chocolate?; **so m.** tanto, -a. **2** *adv* mucho; **as m. as** tanto como; **as m. as possible** todo lo posible; **how m.?** ¿cuánto?; **how m. is it?** ¿cuánto es?; **m. better** mucho mejor; **m. more** mucho más; **too m.** demasiado. **3** *pron* mucho; **I thought as m.** lo suponía; **m. of the town was destroyed** gran parte de la ciudad quedó destruida.

Ms *abbr* señora *f*, Sra.

mud barro *m*.

mud·dle 1 *n* desorden *m*; *(mix-up)* embrollo *m*; **to get into a m.** hacerse un lío. **2** *vt* **to m. (up)** confundir.

mud·dy *adj* fangoso, -a; *(hands)* cubierto, -a de barro; *(liquid)* turbio, -a.

mug¹ *(large cup)* tazón *m*; *(beer)* jarra *f*.

mug² *vt (assault)* asaltar.

mug·ger asaltante *mf*.

mule mulo, -a *mf*.

mul·ti·cul·tur·al *adj* multicultural.

mul·ti·ple 1 *adj* múltiple. **2** *n* múltiplo *m*.

mul·ti·plex *n* cine *m* multisalas.

mul·ti·pli·ca·tion multiplicación *f*.

mul·ti·ply *vt* multiplicar (**by** por).

mum·ble 1 *vt* decir entre dientes. **2** *vi* hablar entre dientes.

mum·my *fam* mami *f*.

mumps paperas *fpl*.

mu·nic·i·pal *adj* municipal.

mur·der 1 *n* asesinato *m*. **2** *vt* asesinar.

mur·der·er asesino *m*.

mur·mur 1 *vti* murmurar. **2** *n* murmullo *m*.

mus·cle músculo *m*.

mus·cu·lar *adj (person)* musculoso, -a.

mu·se·um museo *m*.

mush·room seta *f*; *(food)* champiñón *m*.

mu·sic música *f*.

mu·si·cal 1 *adj* musical; **to be m.** estar dotado, -a para la música. **2** *n* musical *m*.

mu·si·cian músico, -a *mf*.

Mus·lim *adj & n* musulmán, -ana (*mf*).

mus·sel mejillón *m*.

must *v aux (obligation)* deber, tener que; **you m. arrive on time** tienes que *or* debes llegar a la hora. ▪ *(probability)* deber (de); **he m. be ill** debe (de) estar enfermo.

mus·tache bigote *m*.

mus·tard mostaza *f*.

must·y *adj* que huele a cerrado *or* a humedad.

mute 1 *adj* mudo, -a. **2** *n (person)* mudo, -a *mf*; *(for musical instrument)* sordina *f*.

mut·ter *vti* murmurar.

mut·ton (carne *f* de) cordero *m*.

mu·tu·al *adj* mutuo, -a; *(shared)* común.

muz·zle *(for animal)* bozal *m*.

my *poss* mi; **I washed my hair** me lavé el pelo; **my cousins** mis primos; **my father** mi padre; **one of my friends** un amigo mío.

my·self *pers pron (emphatic)* yo mismo, -a; **my husband and m.** mi marido y yo. ▪ *(reflexive)* me; **I hurt m.** me hice daño. ▪ *(after prep)* mí (mismo, -a).

mys·te·ri·ous *adj* misterioso, -a.

mys·ter·y misterio *m*.

myth mito *m*.

N

nail 1 *n (of finger, toe)* uña *f*; *(metal)* clavo *m*. **2** *vt* clavar.

▸**nail down** *vt* clavar.

nail·file lima *f* de uñas.

nail pol·ish, nail var·nish esmalte *m or* laca *f* de uñas.

na·ïve *adj* ingenuo, -a.

naked *adj* desnudo, -a.

name 1 *n* nombre *m*; *(surname)* apellido *m*; *(reputation)* reputación *f*; **what's your n.?** ¿cómo te llamas? **2** *vt* llamar; *(appoint)* nombrar.

name·ly *adv* a saber.

nan·ny niñera *f*.

nap *(sleep)* siesta *f*; **to have a n.** echar la *or* una siesta.

nap·kin (table) n. servilleta *f*.

nap·py pañal *m*.

nar·ra·tive 1 *n (genre)* narrativa *f*; *(story)* narración *f*. **2** *adj* narrativo, -a.

nar·row 1 *adj (passage, road etc)* estrecho, -a. **2** *vi* estrecharse.

▸**narrow down** *vt* reducir.

narrow·ly *adv (closely)* de cerca; *(by a small margin)* por poco.

nasti·ly *adv (to behave)* antipáticamente.

nas·ty *adj (unpleasant)* desagradable; *(unfriendly)* antipático, -a; *(malicious)* mal intencionado, -a.

na·tion nación *f.*

na·tion·al *adj* nacional.

na·tion·al·i·ty nacionalidad *f.*

na·tive 1 *adj (place)* natal; **n. language** lengua *f* materna. **2** *n* nativo, -a *mf.*

nat·u·ral *adj* natural; *(normal)* normal; *(born)* nato, -a.

nat·u·ral·ly *adv (of course)* naturalmente; *(by nature)* por naturaleza; *(in a relaxed manner)* con naturalidad.

na·ture naturaleza *f*; **n. study** historia *f* natural.

naugh·ty *adj (child)* travieso, -a.

nau·seous *adj* **to feel n.** tener ganas de vomitar.

na·val *adj* naval; **n. officer** oficial *mf* de marina.

na·vel ombligo *m.*

nav·i·gate 1 *vt (river)* navegar por; *(ship)* gobernar. **2** *vi* navegar.

nav·i·ga·tion navegación *f.*

na·vy marina *f*; **n. blue** azul *m* marino.

near 1 *adj (space)* cercano, -a; *(time)* próximo, -a; **in the n. future** en un futuro próximo; **it was a n. thing** poco faltó. **2** *adv (space)* cerca; **that's n. enough** ya vale. **3** *prep* cerca de; **n. the end of the film** hacia el final de la película.

near·by 1 *adj* cercano, -a. **2** *adv* cerca.

near·ly *adv* casi; **very n.** casi, casi; **we haven't n. enough** no alcanza ni con mucho.

neat *adj (room, habits etc)* ordenado, -a; *(appearance)* pulcro, -a.

neat·ly *adv (carefully)* cuidadosamente; *(cleverly)* hábilmente.

nec·es·sar·i·ly *adv* necesariamente.

nec·es·sar·y *adj* necesario, -a; **to do what is n.** hacer lo que haga falta; **if n.** si es preciso.

ne·ces·si·ty necesidad *f*, *(article)* requisito *m* indispensable.

neck cuello *m*; *(of animal)* pescuezo *m.*

neck·lace collar *m.*

nec·tar·ine nectarina *f.*

need 1 *n* necesidad *f*, *(poverty)* indigencia *f*; **if n. be** si fuera necesario; **there's no n. for you to do that** no hace falta que hagas eso. **2** *vt* necesitar; *(require)* requerir; **I n. to see him** tengo que verle. **3** *v aux* tener que, deber; **n. he go?** ¿tiene que ir?; **you needn't wait** no hace falta que esperes.

nee·dle aguja *f.*

need·less·ly *adv* innecesariamente.

nee·dle·work *(sewing)* costura *f*; *(embroidery)* bordado *m.*

neg·a·tive 1 *adj* negativo, -a. **2** *n (in grammar)* negación *f*, *(photo)* negativo *m.*

ne·glect *vt (not look after)* descuidar; **to n. to do sth** *(omit to do)* no hacer algo.

ne·glect·ed *adj (appearance)* desarreglado, -a; *(garden)* descuidado, -a; **to feel n.** sentirse desatendido, -a.

neg·li·gence negligencia *f.*

neg·li·gent *adj* negligente.

ne·go·ti·ate *vti* negociar.

ne·go·ti·a·tion negociación *f.*

neigh *vi* relinchar.

neigh·bor vecino, -a *mf.*

neigh·bor·hood *(district)* vecindad *f*, barrio *m*; *(people)* vecindario *m.*

neigh·bor·ing *adj* vecino, -a.

nei·ther 1 *adj & pron* ninguno de los dos, ninguna de las dos. **2** *adv & conj* ni; **n. ... nor** ni ... ni; **it's n. here nor there** no viene al caso; **she was not there and n. was her sister** ella no estaba, ni su hermana tampoco.

ne·on neón *m*; **n. light** luz *f* de neón.

neph·ew sobrino *m*.

nerve nervio *m*; *(courage)* valor *m*; *(cheek)* descaro *m*; **to get on sb's nerves** poner los nervios de punta a algn.

nerv·ous *adj (apprehensive)* nervioso, -a; *(afraid)* miedoso, -a; *(timid)* tímido, -a; **to be n.** tener miedo.

nest nido *m*.

net¹ red *f*.

net² *adj* neto, -a.

net·ting *(wire)* alambrada *f*.

net·tle ortiga *f*.

net·work red *f*.

neu·tral 1 *adj* neutro, -a. **2** *n (gear)* punto *m* muerto.

nev·er *adv* nunca, jamás; **he n. complains** no se queja nunca; **n. again** nunca (ja)más.

nev·er-end·ing *adj* interminable.

nev·er·the·less *adv* sin embargo, no obstante.

new *adj* nuevo, -a.

new-born *adj* recién nacido, -a.

new·com·er recién llegado, -a *mf*; *(to job etc)* nuevo, -a *mf*.

new·ly *adv* recién.

news noticias *fpl*; **a piece of n.** una noticia.

news bul·le·tin boletín *m* informativo.

news·flash noticia *f* de última hora.

news·let·ter hoja *f* informativa.

news·pa·per periódico *m*.

next 1 *adj (in position)* de al lado; *(in time)* próximo, -a; *(in order)* siguiente, próximo, -a; **the n. day** el día siguiente; **n. Friday** el viernes que viene. **2** *adv* después; *(next time)* la próxima vez; **what shall we do n.?** ¿qué hacemos ahora? **3** *prep* **n. to** al lado de.

next-door *adj* de al lado; **our n.**

neigh·bor el vecino *or* la vecina de al lado.

nib plumilla *f*.

nib·ble *vti* mordisquear.

nice *adj (person)* simpático, -a; *(thing)* agradable; *(nice-looking) Esp* bonito, -a, *Am* lindo, -a; **n. and cool** fresquito, -a; **to smell/taste n.** oler/saber bien.

nice·ly *adv* muy bien.

nick·el moneda *f* de cinco centavos.

nick·el-and-dime store = tienda de productos muy baratos.

nick·name apodo *m*.

niece sobrina *f*.

night noche *f*; **at twelve o'clock at n.** a las doce de la noche; **last n.** anoche; **to have a n. out** salir por la noche.

night·club sala *f* de fiestas; *(disco)* discoteca *f*.

night·gown camisón *m*.

night·in·gale ruiseñor *m*.

night·mare pesadilla *f*.

night·stand mesita *f* or mesilla *f* de noche, *RP* mesa *f* de luz, *Méx* buró *m*.

night·time noche *f*; **at n.** por la noche.

night watch·man vigilante *m* nocturno.

nil nada *f*; *(in sport)* cero *m*.

nine *adj & n* nueve (*m*) *inv*; **n. hundred** novecientos, -as.

nine·teen *adj & n* diecinueve (*m*) *inv*.

nine·ty *adj & n* noventa (*m*) *inv*.

ninth *adj & n* noveno, -a (*mf*).

nip *vt (pinch)* pellizcar; *(bite)* morder.

nip·ple *(female)* pezón *m*; *(male)* tetilla *f*.

ni·tro·gen nitrógeno *m*.

no 1 *adv* no; **no longer** ya no; **no less than** no menos de. **2** *adj* ninguno, -a; **she has no children** no tiene hijos; **I have no idea** no tengo (ni) idea; **no sensible person** ninguna persona razonable; **'no parking'** 'prohibido aparcar'; **¡no way!** ¡ni hablar!

no·ble *adj* noble.

no·bod·y *pron* nadie; **there was n. there** no había nadie; **n. else** nadie más.

nod 1 *n* (*in agreement*) señal *m* de asentimiento. **2** *vi* (*in agreement*) asentir con la cabeza. **3** *vt* **to n. one's head** inclinar la cabeza.

▶ **nod off** *vi* dormirse.

noise ruido *m*; **to make a n.** hacer ruido.

nois·i·ly *adv* ruidosamente.

nois·y *adj* ruidoso, -a.

nom·i·nate *vt* (*appoint*) nombrar.

nom·i·na·tion (*proposal*) propuesta *f*; (*appointment*) nombramiento *m*.

non- *prefix* no.

none *pron* ninguno, -a; **n. at all** nada en absoluto.

none·the·less *adv* no obstante, sin embargo.

non·ex·ist·ent *adj* inexistente.

non·fic·tion obras *fpl* de no ficción.

non·sense tonterías *fpl*; **that's n.** eso es absurdo.

non·smok·er no fumador, -a *mf*.

non·stick *adj* antiadherente.

non·stop 1 *adj* continuo, -a; (*train*) directo, -a. **2** *adv* sin parar.

noo·dles *npl* fideos *mpl*, tallarines *mpl*.

noon mediodía *m*; **at n.** a mediodía.

nor *conj* ni, ni … tampoco; **neither … n.** ni … ni; **neither you n.** I ni tú ni yo; **n. do I** (ni) yo tampoco.

norm norma *f*.

nor·mal *adj* normal.

nor·mal·ly *adv* normalmente.

north 1 *n* norte *m*. **2** *adv* hacia el norte. **3** *adj* del norte; **n. wind** viento del norte.

north·bound *adj* (con) dirección norte.

north·east nor(d)este *m*.

north·ern *adj* del norte.

north·ern·er norteño, -a *mf*.

north·ward *adj & adv* hacia el norte.

north·west noroeste *m*.

Nor·we·gian 1 *adj* noruego, -a. **2** *n* (*person*) noruego, -a *mf*; (*language*) noruego *m*.

nose nariz *f*; **her n. is bleeding** le está sangrando la nariz.

nose·bleed hemorragia *f* nasal.

nos·tril orificio *m* nasal.

nos·y *adj* entrometido, -a.

not *adv* no; **he's n. in today** hoy no está; **n. at all** en absoluto; **thank you — n. at all** gracias — no hay de qué; **n. one (of them) said thank you** nadie me dio las gracias.

no·ta·ble *adj* notable.

no·ta·bly *adv* notablemente.

note 1 *n* (*in music, written*) nota *f*; (*money*) billete *m* (de banco); **to take n. of** (*notice*) prestar atención a; **to take notes** (*at lecture*) tomar apuntes. **2** *vt* (*write down*) anotar; (*notice*) darse cuenta de.

note·book cuaderno *m*; (*computer*) ordenador *m* portátil.

note·pad bloc *m* de notas.

note·pa·per papel *m* de carta.

noth·ing 1 *n* nada; **I saw h.** no vi nada; **for h.** (*free*) gratis; **it's n. to do with you** no tiene nada que ver contigo; **n. else** nada más; **n. much** poca cosa. **2** *adv* **she looks n. like her sister** no se parece en nada a su hermana.

no·tice 1 *n* (*warning*) aviso *m*; (*attention*) atención *f*; (*in newspaper etc*) anuncio *m*; (*sign*) aviso *m*; **he gave a month's n.** presentó la dimisión con un mes de antelación; **at short n.** con poca antelación; **until further n.** hasta nuevo aviso; **to take n. of sth** prestar atención a algo. **2** *vt* darse cuenta de.

no·tice·a·ble *adj* obvio, -a, evidente.

no·ti·fi·ca·tion aviso *m*.

no·ti·fy *vt* avisar.

no·tion idea *f*.

no·to·ri·ous *adj pej* tristemente célebre.

nought cero *m*.

noun sustantivo *m*.

nour·ish·ing *adj* nutritivo, -a.

nov·el¹ novela *f*.

nov·el² *adj* original.

nov·el·ist novelista *mf*.

No·vem·ber noviembre *m*.

now 1 *adv* ahora; *(at present, these days)* actualmente; **just n., right n.** ahora mismo; **from n. on** de ahora en adelante; **n. and then, n. and again** de vez en cuando; **n. (then)** ahora bien; **n., n.!** ¡de eso nada! **2** *conj* n. (that) ahora que.

now·a·days *adv* hoy (en) día.

no·where *adv* en ninguna parte; **it's n. near ready** no está preparado, ni mucho menos.

noz·zle boquilla *f*.

nu·clear *adj* nuclear.

nude *adj* desnudo, -a; **in the n.** al desnudo.

nudge 1 *vt* dar un codazo a. **2** *n* codazo *m*.

nui·sance pesadez *f*, *(person)* pesado, -a *mf*; **what a n.!** ¡qué lata!

numb *adj (without feeling)* entumecido, -a.

num·ber 1 *n* número *m*; **have you got my (phone) n.?** ¿tienes mi (número de) teléfono?; **a n. of people** varias personas. **2** *vt (put a number on)* numerar.

nu·mer·al número *m*.

nu·mer·ous *adj* numeroso, -a.

nun monja *f*.

nurse 1 *n* enfermera *f*, *(male)* enfermero *m*. **2** *vt (look after)* cuidar.

nurs·er·y guardería *f*, *(in house)* cuarto *m* de los niños; *(garden center)* vivero *m*.

nurs·er·y rhyme canción *f* infantil.

nurs·er·y school jardín *m* de infancia.

nurs·ing n. home clínica *f*.

nut *(fruit)* fruto *m* seco; *(for bolt)* tuerca *f*.

nut·crack·er cascanueces *m inv*.

nut·shell in a n. en pocas palabras.

ny·lon 1 *n* nailon *m*; **nylons** medias *fpl* de nailon. **2** *adj* de nailon.

O

oak roble *m*.

oar remo *m*.

oats avena *f*.

o·be·di·ence obediencia *f*.

o·be·di·ent *adj* obediente.

o·bey *vt* obedecer; *(law)* cumplir.

ob·ject¹ *(thing)* objeto *m*; *(aim, purpose)* objetivo *m*; *(in grammar)* complemento *m*.

ob·ject² *vi* oponerse (**to** a); **do you o. to my smoking?** ¿le molesta que fume?

ob·jec·tion objeción *f*.

ob·jec·tive objetivo *m*.

ob·li·ga·tion obligación *f*.

o·blige *vt (compel)* obligar; *(do a favor for)* hacer un favor a; **I'm obliged to do it** me veo obligado, -a a hacerlo.

o·blig·ing *adj* solícito, -a.

o·blique *adj* oblicuo, -a inclinado, -a.

ob·scene *adj* obsceno, -a.

ob·scure 1 *adj* oscuro, -a; *(author, poet)* desconocido, -a. **2** *vt (truth)* ocultar.

ob·ser·vant *adj* observador, -a.

ob·ser·va·tion observación *f*, *(surveillance)* vigilancia *f*.

ob·serve *vt* observar; *(on surveillance)* vigilar; *(remark)* advertir.

ob·ses·sion obsesión *f*.

ob·sta·cle obstáculo *m*.

ob·sti·nate *adj (person)* obstinado, -a.

ob·struct *vt* obstruir; *(pipe etc)* atascar; *(view)* tapar; *(hinder)* estorbar; *(progress)* dificultar.

ob·tain *vt* obtener.

ob·vi·ous *adj* obvio, -a, evidente.

ob·vi·ous·ly *adv* evidentemente; **o.!** ¡claro!

oc·ca·sion ocasión *f*; *(event)* acontecimiento *m*.

oc·ca·sion·al *adj* eventual.

oc·ca·sion·al·ly *adv* de vez en cuando.

oc·cu·pant ocupante *mf*; *(tenant)* inquilino, -a *mf*.

oc·cu·pa·tion *(job, profession)* profesión *f*; *(task)* trabajo *m*.

oc·cu·py *vt (live in)* habitar en; **to o. one's time in doing sth** dedicar su tiempo a hacer algo; **to keep oneself occupied** mantenerse ocupado, -a.

oc·cur *vi (event)* suceder; *(change)* producirse; *(be found)* encontrarse; **it occurred to me that ...** se me ocurrió que ...

oc·cur·rence acontecimiento *m*.

o·cean océano *m*.

o'clock *adv* **(it's) one o'c.** (es) la una; **(it's) two o'c.** (son) las dos.

Oc·to·ber octubre *m*.

oc·to·pus pulpo *m*.

odd 1 *adj (strange)* raro, -a; *(occasional)* esporádico, -a; *(extra)* adicional; *(not even)* impar; *(unpaired)* desparejado, -a; **the o. customer** algún que otro cliente; **o. job** trabajillo *m*; **to be the o. man out** estar de más; **an o. sock** un calcetín suelto. **2** *adv* y pico; **twenty o. people** veinte y pico *or* veintitantas personas.

odd·ly *adv* extrañamente.

odds *npl (chances)* probabilidades *fpl*; *(in betting)* puntos *mpl* de ventaja; **the o. are that ...** lo más probable es que ... *(+ subjunctive)*; **at o. with sb** reñido, -a con algn; **o. and ends** *(small things)* cositas *fpl*.

o·dor olor *m*; *(fragrance)* perfume *m*.

of *prep* de; **a friend of mine** un amigo mío; **there are four of us** somos cuatro; **two of them** dos de ellos;

that's very kind of you es usted muy amable.

off 1 *prep* de; **she fell o. her horse** se cayó del caballo; **a house o. the road** una casa apartada de la carretera; **I'm o. wine** he perdido el gusto al vino. **2** *adv (absent)* fuera; **I have a day o.** tengo un día libre; **to be o. sick** estar de baja por enfermedad. • **his arrival is three days o.** faltan tres días para su llegada; **six miles o.** a seis millas. • **I'm o. to New York** me voy a Nueva York; **she ran o.** se fue corriendo. • **ten percent o.** un descuento del diez por ciento. • **with his shoes o.** descalzo. • **on and o.** de vez en cuando. **3** *adj* **to be o.** *(meat, fish)* estar pasado, -a; *(milk)* estar agrio, -a; *(gas etc)* estar apagado, -a; *(water)* estar cortado, -a; *(cancelled)* estar cancelado, -a; **on the o. chance** por si acaso; **the o. season** la temporada baja; **you're better o. like that** así estás mejor.

of·fend *vt* ofender.

of·fend·er *(criminal)* delincuente *mf*.

of·fense *(in law)* delito *m*; **to take o. at sth** ofenderse por algo.

of·fen·sive 1 *n (military)* ofensiva *f*. **2** *adj (insulting)* ofensivo, -a; *(repulsive)* repugnante.

of·fer 1 *vt* ofrecer; *(propose)* proponer; *(provide)* proporcionar; **to o. to do a job** ofrecerse para hacer un trabajo. **2** *n* oferta *f*; *(proposal)* propuesta *f*; **on o.** de oferta.

of·fer·ing ofrecimiento *m*; *(in religious ceremony)* ofrenda *f*.

off·hand 1 *adj (abrupt)* brusco, -a. **2** *adv* de improviso.

of·fice *(room)* despacho *m*; *(building)* oficina *f*; *(position)* cargo *m*.

of·fi·cer oficial *mf*; **(police) o.** agente *mf* de policía.

of·fi·cial 1 *adj* oficial. **2** *n* funcionario, -a *mf*.

of·fi·cial·ly *adv* oficialmente.

off-line adj (computer, user) desconectado, -a.

off·spring inv (child) vástago m; (children) progenitura f.

of·ten adv a menudo; **every so o.** de vez en cuando.

oh interj ¡oh!

oil 1 n aceite m; (crude) petróleo m; **oil spill** derrame m petrolero or de petróleo **2** vt engrasar.

oil·can aceitera f.

oil change cambio m de aceite.

oint·ment pomada f.

OK, o·kay 1 interj ¡vale! **2** adj bien; **is it OK if …?** ¿está bien si …?

old adj viejo, -a; (previous) antiguo, -a; **an o. man** un anciano; **o. age** vejez f, **how o. are you?** ¿cuántos años tienes?; **she's five years o.** tiene cinco años.

old-fash·ioned adj (outdated) a la antigua; (unfashionable) anticuado, -a.

ol·ive (tree) olivo m; (fruit) aceituna f, oliva f.

O·lym·pic adj olímpico, -a; **O. Games** Juegos mpl Olímpicos.

om·e·let tortilla f, **Spanish o.** tortilla española or de patatas.

o·mis·sion omisión f.

o·mit vt omitir; (accidentally) pasar por alto; (forget) olvidarse (**to** de).

on 1 prep (position) sobre, encima de, en; **it's on the table** está encima de or sobre la mesa; **on page four** en la página cuatro; **a town on the coast** un pueblo en la costa; **on the right** a la derecha; **on the way** en el camino. ▪ (time) **on April 3rd** el tres de abril; **on a sunny day** un día de sol; **on Monday** el lunes; **on the following day** al día siguiente; **on his arrival** a su llegada; **on time** a tiempo. ▪ (means) **on the radio** en la radio; **to play sth on the piano** tocar algo al piano; **on TV** en la tele; **on the phone** al teléfono; **on foot** a pie; **on the train/plane** en tren/avión. ▪ (about) sobre; **a lecture on numis-**matics una conferencia sobre numismática. **2** adj **to be on** (TV, radio, light) estar encendido, -a; (engine) estar en marcha; (tablecloth) estar puesto; **she had a coat on** llevaba un abrigo puesto; **that film was on last week** pusieron esa película la semana pasada. **3** adv **have you anything on tonight?** ¿tienes algún plan para esta noche?; **he talks on and on** habla sin parar; **to work on** seguir trabajando.

once 1 adv (one time) una vez; (formerly) en otro tiempo; **o. a week** una vez por semana; **o. in a while** de vez en cuando; **o. more** una vez más; **at o.** en seguida; **don't speak all at o.** no habléis todos a la vez. **2** conj una vez que.

one 1 adj un, una; **he'll come back o. day** un día volverá. **2** dem pron **any o.** cualquiera; **that o.** ése, ésa; (distant) aquél, aquélla; **the blue ones** los azules, las azules; **the o. on the table** el or la que está encima de la mesa; **the ones that, the ones who** los or las que; **this o.** éste, ésta. **3** indef pron uno, -a mf; **give me o.** dame uno; **o. by o.** uno tras otro; **o. never knows** nunca se sabe; **to cut o.'s finger** cortarse el dedo; **o. another** el uno al otro; **they love o. another** se quieren. **4** n (digit) uno m; **a hundred and o.** ciento uno.

one·self pron uno, -a mismo, -a mf; (reflexive) sí mismo, -a; **to talk to o.** hablar para sí; **by o.** solo, -a.

one-way adj (ticket) de ida; (street) de dirección única.

on·ion cebolla f.

on-line adj (computer, user) conectado, -a.

on·look·er espectador, -a mf.

on·ly 1 adv solamente, sólo; **he has o. just left** acaba de marcharse hace un momento; **o. yesterday** ayer mismo. **2** adj único, -a. **3** conj pero.

on·to prep see on.

on·ward(s) *adv* en adelante; **from this time o.** de ahora en adelante.

o·paque *adj* opaco, -a.

o·pen 1 *adj* abierto, -a; **wide o.** abierto de par en par; **in the o. air** al aire libre; **o. ticket** billete *m* abierto. **2** *vt* abrir; *(exhibition etc)* inaugurar; *(negotiations, conversation)* entablar. **3** *vi* abrirse. **4** *n* **in the o.** al aire libre; *fig* **to bring into the o.** hacer público.

▸**open out 1** *vt* desplegar. **2** *vi* *(flowers)* abrirse; *(view)* extenderse.

▸**open up 1** *vt* *(market etc)* abrir; *(possibilities)* crear. **2** *vi* abrirse.

o·pen·ing *(act)* apertura *f*; *(beginning)* comienzo *m*; *(aperture)* abertura *f*; *(gap)* brecha *f*; *(in market)* oportunidad *f*.

o·pen·ly *adv* abiertamente.

o·pen-mind·ed *adj* sin prejuicios.

o·pen·ness *(frankness)* franqueza *f*.

op·er·a ópera *f*.

op·er·ate 1 *vi* *(function)* funcionar; *(act)* actuar; *(surgeon)* operar. **2** *vt* *(switch on)* accionar; *(control)* manejar; *(business)* dirigir.

op·er·at·ing sys·tem sistema *m* operativo.

op·er·a·tion *(of machine)* funcionamiento *m*; *(surgical)* operación *f*.

op·er·a·tor *(of machine)* operario, -a *mf*; *(telephone)* operador, -a *mf*.

o·pin·ion opinión *f*; **in my o.** en mi opinión.

op·po·nent adversario, -a *mf*.

op·por·tu·ni·ty oportunidad *f*; *(prospect)* perspectiva *f*.

op·pose *vt* oponerse a.

op·posed *adj* opuesto, -a; **to be o. to sth** estar en contra de algo.

op·pos·ing *adj* adversario, -a.

op·po·site 1 *adj* *(facing)* de enfrente; *(page)* contiguo, -a; *(contrary)* contrario, -a; **in the o. direction** en dirección contraria. **2** *n* lo contrario *m*; **quite the o.!** ¡al contrario! **3** *prep* enfrente de. **4** *adv* enfrente.

op·po·si·tion oposición *f*; **in o. to** en contra de.

opt *vi* **to o. for** optar por; **to o. to do sth** optar por hacer algo.

op·ti·cal *adj* óptico, -a.

op·ti·cian óptico, -a *mf*.

op·ti·mist optimista *mf*.

op·ti·mis·tic *adj* optimista.

op·tion opción *f*; **I have no o.** no tengo más remedio.

op·tion·al *adj* optativo, -a.

or *conj* o; *(before a word beginning with a stressed* o *or* ho*)* u; *(with negative)* ni; **he can't read or write** no sabe leer ni escribir.

o·ral 1 *adj* oral. **2** *n* examen *m* oral.

or·ange 1 *n* naranja *f*. **2** *adj* de color naranja.

or·ange juice zumo *m* de naranja.

or·bit órbita *f*.

or·chard huerto *m*.

or·ches·tra orquesta *f*.

or·deal mala experiencia *f*.

or·der 1 *n* *(sequence, command)* orden *m*; *(commission)* pedido *m*; **to put in o.** ordenar; **is your passport in o.?** ¿tienes el pasaporte en regla?; **'out of o.'** 'averiado'; **to be on o.** estar pedido; **in o. that** para que *(+ subjunctive)*, a fin de que *(+ subjunctive)*; **in o. to** para *(+ infinitive)*, a fin de *(+ infinitive)*. **2** *vt* *(command)* ordenar; *(goods)* encargar; **to o. sb to do sth** mandar a algn hacer algo; **to o. a dish** pedir un plato.

or·di·nance *(decree)* ordenanza *f*, decreto *m*.

or·di·nar·y 1 *adj* normal; *(average)* corriente. **2** *n* **out of the o.** fuera de lo común.

ore mineral *m*.

or·gan órgano *m*.

or·gan·ic *adj* orgánico, -a.

or·gan·i·za·tion organización *f*.

or·gan·ize *vt* organizar.

or·gan·iz·er organizador, -a *mf*.

O·ri·en·tal *adj & n* oriental *(mf)*.

or·i·gin origen *m*.

EXPRESSING YOUR OPINION

What do you think?
¿Qué opina/opinas?/¿Qué le/te parece?

I really like it/liked it.
Me gusta mucho./Me gustó mucho.

It was great/amazing!
¡Estuvo muy bien!/¡Fue increíble!

It was OK.
No estuvo mal.

The tour of the castle was quite interesting.
La visita al castillo estuvo bastante interesante.

I love tequila/skiing.
Me encanta el tequila/el esquí.

I hate snow/shopping.
Odio la nieve/ir de compras.

I'd rather have coffee.
Prefiero un café.

Which do you prefer?
¿Cuál prefiere/prefieres?

I think that would be nice.
Creo que eso estaría bien.

I agree (with you).
Estoy de acuerdo (con usted/contigo).

You're absolutely right.
Tiene(s) toda la razón.

I'm sure it'll be nice tomorrow.
Seguro que hará bueno mañana.

That's true.
Es verdad.

I've changed my mind.
He cambiado de idea.

I don't know.
No lo sé.

Really?
¿De verdad?/ Ah ¿sí?

What a surprise!
¡Qué sorpresa!

Did you like the art gallery?
¿Le/Te gustó el museo?

I don't like it/didn't like it at all.
No me gusta./No me gustó nada.

It was a bit boring/too touristy.
Fue un poco aburrido/demasiado turístico.

The food's nothing special.
La comida no tiene nada de particular.

We had a great time!
¡Nos lo pasamos muy bien!

I don't like jazz/cycling.
No me gusta el jazz/ir en bici.

It's delicious/disgusting!
¡Está delicioso(a)/asqueroso(a)!

I prefer small hotels to big ones.
Prefiero los hoteles pequeños a los grandes.

I prefer the bigger/smaller one.
Prefiero el(la) más grande/el(la) más pequeño(a).

I think/I don't think it's possible.
Creo que es posible./Creo que no es posible.

I disagree (with you).
No estoy de acuerdo (con usted/contigo).

Of course (not)!
¡Claro (que no)!

Are you sure?
¿Estás/Está seguro(a)?

I don't believe you.
No le/te creo.

I'm not sure.
No estoy seguro(a).

It depends.
Depende.

That's strange!
¡Qué raro!

What a pity!
¡Qué pena!

o·rig·i·nal 1 *adj* original; *(first)* primero, -a; *(novel)* original. **2** *n* original *m*.

o·rig·i·nal·i·ty originalidad *f*.

o·rig·i·nal·ly *adv (at first)* en un principio.

o·rig·i·nate 1 *vt* originar. **2** *vi* to o. from *or* in tener su origen en.

or·na·ment adorno *m*.

or·phan huérfano, -a *mf*.

or·phan·age orfanato *m*.

or·tho·dox *adj* ortodoxo, -a.

os·trich avestruz *f*.

oth·er 1 *adj* otro, -a; **the o. one** el otro, la otra. **2** *pron* otro, -a *mf*; **many others** otros muchos; **the others** los otros, los demás; **we see each o. quite often** nos vemos con bastante frecuencia.

oth·er·wise *adv (if not)* si no; *(differently)* de otra manera; *(in other respects)* por lo demás.

ought *v aux* deber; **I thought I o. to tell you** creí que debía decírtelo; **she o. to do it** debería hacerlo; **you o. to see the exhibition** deberías ver la exposición. ▪ *(expectation)* **he o. to pass the exam** seguramente aprobará el examen; **that o. to do** con eso bastará.

ounce onza *f*.

our *poss adj* nuestro, -a.

ours *poss pron* (el) nuestro, (la) nuestra, (los) nuestros, (las) nuestras; **a friend of o.** un amigo nuestro.

our·selves *pers pron pl (reflexive)* nos; *(emphatic)* nosotros mismos, nosotras mismas; **by o.** a solas.

out 1 *adv (outside, away)* fuera; **o. there** ahí fuera; **to go o.** salir. **2** *prep* **o. of** *(place)* fuera de; *(cause, motive)* por; *(made from)* de; *(short of, without)* sin; **move o. of the way!** ¡quítate de en medio!; **he jumped o. the window** saltó por la ventana; **o. of danger** fuera de peligro; **forty o. of fifty** cuarenta de cada cincuenta. **3** *adj* **to be o.** *(unfashionable)* estar pasado, -a de moda; *(not lit)* estar apagado, -a; *(eliminated from game)* quedar eliminado, -a; **the sun is o.** ha salido el sol; **she's o.** *(not in)* ha salido.

out·break *(of war)* comienzo *m*; *(of disease)* brote *m*; *(of violence)* ola *f*.

out·burst *(of anger)* arrebato *m*.

out·come resultado *m*.

out·dat·ed *adj* anticuado, -a.

out·do* *vt* exceder; **to o. sb** superar a algn.

out·door *adj* al aire libre; *(clothes)* de calle.

out·doors *adv* al aire libre.

out·er *adj* exterior.

out·er space espacio *m* sideral.

out·fit *(kit, equipment)* equipo *m*; *(set of clothes)* conjunto *m*.

out·grow* *vt* **he's outgrowing all his clothes** toda la ropa se le está quedando pequeña; **he'll o. it** se le pasará con la edad.

out·ing excursión *f*.

out·law 1 *n* proscrito, -a *mf*. **2** *vt* prohibir.

out·let *(for goods)* mercado *m*.

out·line *(draft)* bosquejo *m*; *(outer line)* contorno *m*; *(silhouette)* perfil *m*; *(sketch)* boceto *m*.

out·look *(point of view)* punto *m* de vista; *(prospect)* perspectiva *f*.

out·num·ber *vt* exceder en número.

out·of·doors *adv* al aire libre.

out·put producción *f*; *(of machine)* rendimiento *m*.

out·rage 1 *n* ultraje *m*; **it's an o.!** ¡es un escándalo! **2** *vt* **to be outraged by sth** indignarse por algo.

out·ra·geous *adj (behavior)* escandaloso, -a; *(clothes)* extravagante.

out·right *adv (completely)* por completo; *(directly)* directamente.

out·set comienzo *m*, principio *m*.

out·side 1 *prep* fuera de; *(beyond)* más allá de; *(other than)* aparte de. **2** *adj (exterior)* exterior, externo, -a.

3 adv (a)fuera. **4** n exterior m; **on the o.** por fuera.

out·sid·er (stranger) extraño, -a mf; (in election) candidato, -a mf con pocas posibilidades de ganar.

out·skirts npl afueras fpl.

out·stand·ing adj (exceptional) destacado, -a; (unpaid, unresolved) pendiente.

out·ward adj (appearance) externo, -a; **the o. journey** el viaje de ida.

out·ward(s) adv hacia (a)fuera.

o·val 1 adj ovalado, -a. **2** n óvalo m.

ov·en horno m.

o·ver 1 prep (above) encima de; (across) al otro lado de; (during) durante; (more than) más de; **the bridge o. the river** el puente que cruza el río; **all o.** Spain por toda España; **it's all o. the carpet** está por toda la alfombra; **o. the phone** por teléfono; **men o. twenty-five** hombres mayores de veinticinco años. **2** adv (more) más; (again) otra vez; (in excess) de más; **o. there** allá; **all o.** por todas partes; **o. and o. (again)** una y otra vez; **there are still some o.** todavía quedan algunos. **3** adj (finished) acabado, -a; **it's (all) o.** se acabó; **the danger is o.** ha pasado el peligro.

o·ver·all 1 adj total. **2** adv (on the whole) en conjunto. **3** n guardapolvo m; **overalls** mono m sing.

o·ver·board adv por la borda.

o·ver·charge vt (charge too much) cobrar de más.

o·ver·coat abrigo m.

o·ver·come* vt (conquer) vencer; (overwhelm) abrumar; (surmount) superar.

o·ver·do* vt (carry too far) exagerar; (in cooking) cocer or asar demasiado.

o·ver·draft crédito m al descubierto.

o·ver·due adj (rent, train etc) atrasado, -a.

o·ver·eat vi comer en exceso.

o·ver·ex·cit·ed adj sobreexcitado, -a.

o·ver·flow vi (river) desbordarse; (cup etc) derramarse.

o·ver·head adj (por) encima de la cabeza.

o·ver·hear vt oír por casualidad.

o·ver·heat vi recalentarse.

o·ver·joyed adj rebosante de alegría.

o·ver·lap vi superponerse.

ov·er·leaf adv al dorso.

o·ver·load vt sobrecargar.

o·ver·look vt (fail to notice) pasar por alto; (ignore) no hacer caso de; (have a view of) tener vista a.

o·ver·night 1 adv por la noche; **we stayed there o.** pasamos la noche allí. **2** adj (journey) de noche.

o·ver·pass (bridge) paso m elevado.

o·ver·rat·ed adj sobrestimado, -a.

o·ver·seas 1 adv en ultramar; **to live o.** vivir en el extranjero. **2** adj de ultramar; (visitor) extranjero, -a; (trade) exterior.

o·ver·sight descuido m.

o·ver·sleep vi quedarse dormido, -a.

o·ver·spend vi gastar demasiado.

o·ver·take* vt adelantar.

o·ver·time horas fpl extra.

o·ver·turn vti volcar.

o·ver·weight adj to be o. ser gordo, -a.

o·ver·whelm vt (defeat) aplastar; (overpower) abrumar.

o·ver·whelm·ing adj (defeat) aplastante; (desire) irresistible.

o·ver·work vi trabajar demasiado.

owe vt deber.

ow·ing adj o. to debido a.

owl búho m.

own 1 adj propio, -a; **it's his o. fault** es culpa suya. **2** pron my o., your o., his o.** etc lo mío, lo tuyo, lo suyo etc; **to get one's o. back** tomarse la revancha; **on one's o.** (without help) uno, -a mismo, -a; (alone) solo, -a. **3** vt poseer.

▸**own up** vi to o. up (to) confesar.
own·er propietario, -a mf.
ox·y·gen oxígeno m.
oys·ter ostra f.
o·zone ozono m; **o. layer** capa f de ozono.

P

pace (step) paso m; (speed) ritmo m.
Pa·cif·ic the P. (Ocean) el (océano) Pacífico.
pa·ci·fi·er (of baby) chupete m.
pack 1 n paquete m; (rucksack) mochila f; (of cards) baraja f; (of hounds) jauría f. **2** vt (goods) embalar; (in suitcase) poner; (fill) atestar; (press down) (snow) apretar; **to p. one's bags** hacer las maletas; fig marcharse. **3** vi (baggage) hacer las maletas.
▸**pack away** vt (tidy away) guardar.
▸**pack up** fam **1** vt (give up) dejar. **2** vi (stop working) terminar; (machine etc) estropearse.
pack·age (parcel, software) paquete m.
pack·age tour viaje m todo incluido.
pack·ag·ing embalaje m.
packed adj (place) atestado, -a.
packed lunch almuerzo m (para tomar fuera).
pack·et paquete m.
pack·ing embalaje m.
pact pacto m.
pad 1 n almohadilla f; (of paper) bloc m. **2** vt (chair) rellenar.
pad·ded adj (cell) acolchado, -a.
pad·dle¹ (oar) pala f.
pad·dle² vi chapotear.
pad·lock candado m.
page¹ página f.
page² (at club etc) botones m inv.

pain dolor m; (grief) sufrimiento m; **to take pains over sth** esmerarse en algo.
pain·ful adj doloroso, -a.
pain·kill·er analgésico m.
paint 1 n pintura f. **2** vt pintar; **to p. sth white** pintar algo de blanco.
paint·brush pincel m; (for walls) brocha f.
paint·er pintor, -a mf.
paint·ing cuadro m; (activity) pintura f.
paint strip·per quitapinturas m inv.
pair (of gloves, shoes) par m; (of people, cards) pareja f.
pa·ja·mas npl pijama m.
Pak·i·stan·i adj & n paquistaní (mf).
pal fam amigo, -a mf.
pal·ace palacio m.
pal·ate paladar m.
pale adj (skin) pálido, -a; (color) claro, -a.
Pal·es·tin·i·an adj & n palestino, -a (mf).
pal·ette paleta f.
palm (of hand) palma f; (tree) palmera f; **p. leaf** palma f.
pam·phlet folleto m.
pan (saucepan) cazuela f.
pan·cake crepe f.
pane cristal m, vidrio m.
pan·el (of wall) panel m; (of instruments) tablero m; (jury) jurado m.
pan·ic 1 n pánico m; **to get into a p.** ponerse histérico, -a. **2** vi **he panicked** le entró pánico.
pant vi jadear.
pant·ies npl bragas fpl.
pan·to·mime (play) función f musical navideña.
pan·try despensa f.
pants npl (underpants) (ladies') bragas fpl; (men's) calzoncillos mpl; (trousers) pantalón m.
pant·y·hose panties mpl.
pa·per papel m; (newspaper) periódico m; (exam) examen m; (essay) trabajo m (escrito).

pa·per·back libro *m* en rústica.

pa·per·clip clip *m*.

pa·per knife cortapapeles *m inv.*

pap·er·work papeleo *m*.

par *(parity)* igualdad *f; (in golf)* par *m*.

par·a·chute paracaídas *m inv.*

pa·rade desfile *m*.

par·a·dise paraíso *m*.

par·af·fin parafina *f*.

par·a·graph párrafo *m*.

Par·a·guay·an *adj & n* paraguayo, -a *(mf).*

par·a·le·gal ayudante *mf* de un abogado, *RP* procurador, -a *mf*

par·al·lel *adj* paralelo, -a (**to**, **with** a).

par·a·lyze *vt* paralizar.

par·a·site parásito *m*.

par·a·sol sombrilla *f*.

par·cel paquete *m*.

par·don 1 *n* perdón *m*; **I beg your p.** (Vd.) perdone; **(I beg your) p.?** ¿cómo (dice)? 2 *vt* perdonar; **p. me!** ¡Vd. perdone!

par·ents *npl* padres *mpl.*

par·ish parroquia *f*.

park 1 *n* parque *m*. 2 *vt (car)* estacionar, *Esp* aparcar.

park·ing aparcamiento *m*; **'no p.'** 'prohibido aparcar'.

park·ing light luz *f* de estacionamiento.

park·ing lot aparcamiento *m*.

park·ing me·ter parquímetro *m*.

park·ing space aparcamiento *m*.

park·ing tick·et multa *f* de aparcamiento.

par·lia·ment parlamento *m*.

par·rot loro *m*.

pars·ley perejil *m*.

pars·nip chirivía *f*.

part 1 *n* parte *f; (piece)* trozo *m; (of machine, engine)* pieza *f; (in play etc)* papel *m*; **for the most p.** en la mayor parte; **to take p. in sth** participar en algo; **in these parts** por estos lugares. 2 *(partly)* en parte. 3 *vi* separarse; *(say goodbye)* despedirse.

▸ **part with** *vt* separarse de.

par·tial *adj* parcial; **to be p. to sth** ser aficionado, -a a algo.

par·tic·i·pant participante *mf*.

par·tic·i·pate *vi* participar (**in** en).

par·tic·i·pa·tion participación *f*.

par·ti·ci·ple participio *m*.

par·ti·cle board madera *f* aglomerada.

par·tic·u·lar 1 *adj (special)* particular; *(fussy)* exigente; **in this p. case** en este caso concreto. 2 *npl* **particulars** pormenores *mpl*; **to take down sb's particulars** tomar nota de los datos personales de algn.

par·tic·u·lar·ly *adv* particularmente.

part·ing *(in hair)* raya *f*.

par·ti·tion *(wall)* tabique *m*.

part·ly *adv* en parte.

part·ner compañero, -a *mf; (in dancing, tennis)* pareja *f; (in business)* socio, -a *mf*.

part·ner·ship *(in business)* sociedad *f*.

part·ridge perdiz *f*.

part-time 1 *adj (work etc)* de media jornada. 2 *adv* a tiempo parcial.

par·ty *(celebration)* fiesta *f; (group)* grupo *m; (political)* partido *m*.

pass 1 *n (of mountain)* desfiladero *m; (permit)* permiso *m; (in football etc)* pase *m*. 2 *vt* pasar; *(overtake)* adelantar; *(exam, law)* aprobar. 3 *vi* pasar; *(car)* adelantar; *(people)* cruzarse; *(in football etc)* hacer un pase; *(in exam)* aprobar; **we passed on the stairs** nos cruzamos en la escalera.

▸ **pass away** *vi* pasar a mejor vida.

▸ **pass by** *vt* pasar de largo. 2 *vi* pasar cerca; **if you're ever passing by** si alguna vez pasas por aquí.

▸ **pass off** 1 *vt* **to p. oneself off as sth** hacerse pasar por algo. 2 *vi (happen)* transcurrir.

▸ **pass on** *vt (hand on)* transmitir. 2 *vi (die)* pasar a mejor vida.

▸**pass out** vi (faint) desmayarse.

▸**pass over** vt (disregard) pasar por alto.

▸**pass through** vi estar de paso.

▸**pass up** vt (opportunity) renunciar a; (offer) rechazar.

pass·a·ble adj (road) transitable; (acceptable) pasable.

pas·sage (hallway) pasillo m; (in music, text) pasaje m.

pas·sage·way (interior) pasillo m; (exterior) pasaje m.

pas·sen·ger pasajero, -a mf.

pas·ser·by transeúnte mf.

pass·ing 1 n (of time) transcurso m; **in p.** de pasada. **2** adj que pasa; **p. grade** (in exam) aprobado m.

pas·sion pasión f.

pas·sion·ate adj apasionado, -a.

pas·sive adj pasivo, -a.

pass·port pasaporte m.

pass·word contraseña f.

past 1 n pasado m; **in the p.** antiguamente. **2** adj pasado, -a; (former) anterior; **in the p. weeks** en las últimas semanas. **3** adv por delante; **to run p.** pasar corriendo. **4** prep (beyond) más allá de; (more than) más de; **it's five p. ten** son las diez y cinco.

pas·ta pasta f.

paste 1 n pasta f, (glue) engrudo m. **2** vt (stick) pegar.

pas·teur·ized adj pasteurizado, -a.

pas·time pasatiempo m.

pas·try (dough) pasta f, (cake) pastel m.

pas·ture pasto m.

pat vt acariciar.

patch (of material) parche m; (of color) mancha f, **to go through a bad p.** pasar por una mala racha.

▸**patch up** vt (garment) poner un parche en; **to p. up a quarrel** hacer las paces (**with** con).

pat·ent 1 n (for product) patente f. **2** adj (obvious) patente, evidente. **3** vt (product) patentar.

path sendero m; (route) camino m.

pa·thet·ic adj patético, -a; (hopeless) malísimo, -a.

path·way sendero m.

pa·tience paciencia f, **to lose one's p. with sb** perder la paciencia con algn.

pa·tient 1 adj paciente. **2** n paciente mf.

pa·tient·ly adv con paciencia.

pat·i·o patio m.

pa·tri·ot·ic adj (person) patriota; (speech, act) patriótico, -a.

pa·trol 1 n patrulla f. **2** vt patrullar por.

pa·tron (of charity) patrocinador, -a mf, (of arts) mecenas m inv; (customer) cliente, -a mf habitual; **p. saint** (santo, -a mf) patrón, -ona mf.

pat·tern (in sewing) patrón m; (design) dibujo m.

pause 1 n pausa f, (in conversation) silencio m. **2** vi hacer una pausa.

pave vt pavimentar; (with stones) empedrar; **to p. the way for sb/ sth** preparar el terreno para algn/ algo.

paved adj pavimentado, -a.

pave·ment acera f, (road surface) calzada f.

pa·vil·ion pabellón m.

pav·ing stone losa f.

paw (foot) pata f, (of cat) garra f.

pawn (in chess) peón m.

pay 1 n (wages) paga f. **2** vt* pagar; (attention) prestar; (visit) hacer; (be profitable for) compensar; **to be** or **get paid** cobrar; **to p. sb a compliment** halagar a algn. **3** vi* pagar; (be profitable) ser rentable; **to p. for sth** pagar (por) algo.

▸**pay back** vt reembolsar.

▸**pay in** vt (money) ingresar.

▸**pay off** vt (debt) liquidar.

▸**pay out** vt (spend) gastar (**on** en).

▸**pay up 1** vt (bill) liquidar, saldar. **2** vi pagar.

pay·a·ble adj pagadero, -a.

pay·check sueldo m.

pay·ment pago m.

pay·phone teléfono *m* público.
pay slip nómina *f.*
PC *abbr of* **personal computer** PC *m*; *abbr of* **politically correct** políticamente correcto(a).
PDA *n abbr of* **personal digital assistant** PDA *m*, asistente *m* personal.
pea guisante *m.*
peace paz *f; (calm)* tranquilidad *f;* **at** *or* **in p.** en paz; **p. and quiet** tranquilidad.
peace·ful *adj (non-violent)* pacífico, -a; *(calm)* tranquilo, -a.
peach melocotón *m.*
pea·cock pavo *m* real.
peak *(of mountain)* pico *m; (summit)* cima *f;* **p. hours** horas *fpl* punta.
peaky *adj fam (ill)* pálido, -a.
pea·nut cacahuete *m.*
pear pera *f.*
pearl perla *f.*
peb·ble guijarro *m; (small)* china *f.*
pe·can *(nut)* pacana *f.*
peck *vt (bird)* picotear.
peck·ish *adj* **to feel p.** empezar a tener hambre.
pe·cu·liar *adj (odd)* extraño, -a; *(particular)* característico, -a.
pe·cu·li·ar·i·ty *(characteristic)* característica *f.*
ped·al 1 *n* pedal *m.* **2** *vi* pedalear.
pe·des·tri·an peatón, -ona *mf.*
pe·des·tri·an cross·ing paso *m* de peatones.
ped·om·e·ter *n* podómetro *m*, cuentapasos *m* inv.
peek 1 *n* ojeada *f.* **2** *vi* **to p. at sth** mirar algo a hurtadillas.
peel 1 *n* piel *f; (of orange, lemon)* cáscara *f.* **2** *vt (fruit)* pelar. **3** *vi (paint)* desconcharse; *(skin)* pelarse.
▸**peel off** *vt (skin of fruit)* pelar; *(clothes)* quitarse.
peel·er potato p. pelapatatas *m* inv.
peep 1 *n (glance)* ojeada *f, (furtive look)* mirada *f* furtiva. **2** *vi* **to p. at sth** echar una ojeada a algo.
peer *vi* mirar detenidamente.

peg clavija *f, (for coat, hat)* colgador *m.*
pen¹ pluma *f.*
pen² *(for animals)* corral *m.*
pen·al·ty *(punishment)* pena *f, (in sport)* castigo *m; (in soccer)* penalti *m.*
pen·cil lápiz *m.*
pen·cil case estuche *m* de lápices.
pen·cil sharp·en·er sacapuntas *m inv.*
pen·du·lum péndulo *m.*
pen·e·trate *vt (break through, grasp)* penetrar; *(forest, territory)* adentrarse en.
pen·guin pingüino *m.*
pen·i·cil·lin penicilina *f.*
pen·in·su·la península *f.*
pen·knife navaja *f.*
pen·ni·less *adj* sin dinero.
pen·ny *(pl* **pennies)** centavo *m.*
pen pal amigo, -a *mf* por carta.
pen·sion pensión *f,* **retirement p.** jubilación *f.*
pen·sion·er jubilado, -a *mf.*
peo·ple *npl* gente *f sing; (individuals)* personas *fpl; (nation)* pueblo *m sing;* **old p.'s home** asilo *m* de ancianos; **p. say that ...** se dice que ....
pep·per *(spice)* pimienta *f, (fruit)* pimiento *m.*
pep·per·mint hierbabuena *f, (sweet)* pastilla *f* de menta.
per *prep* por; **5 times p. week** 5 veces a la semana; **p. day/annum** al *or* por día/año; **p. capita** *or* **person** per cápita.
per·ceive *vt* percibir.
percent *adv* por ciento.
per·cent·age porcentaje *m.*
perch 1 *n (for bird)* percha *f.* **2** *vi (bird)* posarse **(on** en).
per·co·la·tor cafetera *f* de filtro.
per·fect 1 *adj* perfecto, -a; **p. tense** tiempo *m* perfecto. **2** *vt* perfeccionar.
per·fec·tion perfección *f.*
per·fect·ly *adv* perfectamente; *(absolutely)* completamente.
per·form 1 *vt (task)* realizar; *(piece*

of music) interpretar; (play) representar. **2** vi (machine) funcionar; (musician) tocar; (actor) actuar.

per·form·ance (of task) realización f, (of piece of music) interpretación f, (of play) representación f, (in sport) actuación f, (of machine etc) rendimiento m.

per·form·er (singer) intérprete mf; (actor) actor m, actriz f.

per·fume perfume m.

per·haps adv tal vez, quizá(s).

per·il (danger) peligro m.

pe·ri·od período m; (stage) etapa f; (at school) clase f; (full stop) punto m; (menstruation) regla f.

pe·ri·od·i·cal 1 n revista f. **2** adj periódico, -a.

pe·riph·er·al periférico m.

perk extra m.

▸**perk up** vi animarse.

perm 1 n permanente f. **2** vt **to have one's hair permed** hacerse la permanente.

per·ma·nent adj permanente; (address, job) fijo, -a.

per·ma·nent·ly adv permanentemente.

per·mis·sion permiso m.

per·mit 1 n permiso m. **2** vt **to p. sb to do sth** permitir a algn hacer algo.

per·pen·dic·u·lar adj perpendicular.

per·se·cute vt perseguir.

per·se·cu·tion persecución f.

per·se·ver·ance perseverancia f.

per·se·vere vi perseverar.

per·sist vi empeñarse (in en).

per·sist·ent adj (person) perseverante; (continual) constante.

per·son persona f, in p. en persona.

per·son·al adj (private) personal; (friend) íntimo, -a; pej (comment etc) indiscreto, -a; **he will make a p. appearance** estará aquí en persona.

per·son·al·i·ty personalidad f.

per·son·al·ly adv (for my part) personalmente; (in person) en persona.

per·son·nel personal m.

per·suade vt persuadir; **to p. sb to do sth** persuadir a algn para que haga algo.

per·sua·sion persuasión f.

per·ti·nent adj (relevant) pertinente; **p. to** relacionado, -a con, a propósito de.

Pe·ru·vi·an adj & n peruano, -a (mf).

pes·si·mist pesimista mf.

pes·si·mis·tic adj pesimista.

pest (animal, insect) plaga f, fam (person) pelma mf; (thing) lata f.

pes·ter vt molestar.

pet 1 n animal m doméstico. **2** adj (favorite) preferido, -a.

pet·al pétalo m.

pe·ti·tion petición f.

pe·tro·le·um petróleo m.

pet·ti·coat enaguas fpl.

pet·ty adj (trivial) insignificante; (small-minded) mezquino, -a.

pet·ty cash dinero m para gastos pequeños.

phar·ma·cist farmacéutico, -a mf.

phar·ma·cy farmacia f.

phase 1 n fase f. **2** vt **to p. sth in/out** introducir/retirar algo progresivamente.

PhD Doctor, -a mf en Filosofía.

pheas·ant faisán m.

phe·nom·e·nal adj fenomenal.

phe·nom·e·non (pl phenomena) fenómeno m.

phi·los·o·pher filósofo, -a mf.

phil·o·soph·i·cal adj filosófico, -a.

phi·los·o·phy filosofía f.

phlegm flema f.

phone 1 n teléfono m. **2** vt llamar por teléfono m.

phone book guía f telefónica.

phone booth cabina f telefónica.

phone call llamada f (telefónica).

phone card tarjeta f telefónica.

phone numb·er número m de teléfono.

pho·net·ic adj fonético, -a.

pho·to foto f.

pho·to·cop·i·er fotocopiadora f.

pho·to·cop·y 1 n fotocopia f. **2** vt fotocopiar.

pho·to·graph 1 n fotografía f. **2** vt fotografiar.

pho·tog·ra·pher fotógrafo, -a mf.

pho·tog·ra·phy fotografía f.

phrase frase f.

phrase·book libro m de frases.

phys·i·cal adj físico, -a.

phys·i·cal·ly adv físicamente; **p. handicapped** minusválido, -a.

phy·si·cian médico, -a mf.

phys·ics física f.

pi·an·ist pianista mf.

pi·an·o piano m.

pick 1 n (tool) pico m; **take your p.** (choice) elige el que quieras. **2** vt (choose) escoger; (team) seleccionar; (flowers, fruit) coger; (lock) forzar; **to p. one's nose** hurgarse la nariz.

▸**pick at** vt she picked at her food picoteó la comida con desgana.

▸**pick on** vt (persecute) meterse con.

▸**pick out** vt (choose) elegir; (identify) identificar.

▸**pick up 1** vt (object on floor) recoger; (telephone) descolgar; (collect) recoger; (shopping, person) buscar; (acquire) conseguir; (learn) aprender; **to p. up speed** ganar velocidad. **2** vi (improve) mejorarse.

pick·ax piqueta f.

pick·le vt (food) conservar en adobo or escabeche; **pickled onions** cebollas fpl en vinagre.

pick·pock·et carterista mf.

pic·nic comida f de campo, picnic m.

pic·ture 1 n (painting) cuadro m; (drawing) dibujo m; (portrait) retrato m; (photo) foto f; (on TV) imagen f; (at cinema) película f. **2** vt (imagine) imaginarse.

pic·ture frame marco m.

pic·tur·esque adj pintoresco, -a.

pie (fruit) (big) tarta f; (small) pastel m; (meat etc) empanada f; (pasty) empanadilla f.

piece pedazo m; (of paper) trozo m;

(part) pieza f; (coin) moneda f; **a p. of news** una noticia; **to break sth into pieces** hacer algo pedazos.

pier embarcadero m, muelle m.

pierce vt perforar.

pierc·ing 1 n (for body adornment) piercing m **2** adj (sound etc) penetrante.

pig cerdo m.

pi·geon paloma f.

pi·geon·hole casilla f.

pig·gy·back to give sb a p. llevar a algn a cuestas.

pig·tail trenza f.

pile 1 n montón m. **2** vt amontonar.

▸**pile up 1** vt (things) amontonar; (riches, debts) acumular. **2** vi amontonarse.

piles sing (illness) hemorroides fpl.

pile·up choque m en cadena.

pill píldora f; **to be on the p.** estar tomando la píldora (anticonceptiva).

pil·lar pilar m, columna f.

pil·lar box buzón m.

pil·low almohada f.

pil·low·case funda f de almohada.

pi·lot piloto m.

pim·ple espinilla f.

pin 1 n alfiler m. **2** vt (onto board) clavar con chinchetas.

▸**pin up** vt clavar con chinchetas.

pin·a·fore (apron) delantal m.

pin·ball flipper m.

pin·cers npl (tool) tenazas fpl.

pinch 1 n (nip) pellizco m; **a p. of salt** una pizca de sal. **2** vt pellizcar; fam (steal) birlar.

pin·cush·ion acerico m.

pine (tree) pino m.

pine·ap·ple piña f.

pink adj rosa inv.

pink·ie dedo m meñique.

pint pinta f (0,47 litro); **a p. of beer** una cerveza.

pi·o·neer 1 n (settler) pionero, -a mf; (forerunner) precursor, -a mf. **2** vt ser pionero, -a en.

pip (seed) pepita f.

pipe tubería f; (for smoking) pipa f.

pi·rate pirata *m*.

pi·rat·ed *adj (book, record, CD)* pirateado, -a.

pis·ta·chi·o pistacho *m*.

pis·tol pistola *f*.

pit hoyo *m*; *(large)* hoya *f*; *(coal mine)* mina *f* de carbón; *(of fruit)* hueso *m*.

pitch 1 *vt (throw)* lanzar; *(tent)* armar. **2** *n (for sport)* campo *m*; *(throw)* lanzamiento *m*.

pitch-black, pitch-dark *adj* negro, -a como boca de lobo.

pitch·er *(container)* cántaro *m*, jarro *m*.

pit·y 1 *n (compassion)* compasión *f*; *(shame)* lástima *f*; **what a p.!** ¡qué pena! **2** *vt* compadecerse de.

piz·za pizza *f*.

plac·ard pancarta *f*.

place 1 *n* sitio *m*, lugar *m*; *(seat)* sitio *m*; *(on bus)* asiento *m*; *(position on scale)* posición *f*; *(house)* casa *f*; *(building)* lugar *m*; **to take p.** tener lugar; **to take sb's p.** sustituir a algn; **in the first p.** en primer lugar; **we're going to his p.** vamos a su casa. **2** *vt* poner, colocar; *(face, person)* recordar.

place·mat tapete *m* individual.

place·ment *(for trainee, student)* colocación *f* en prácticas.

place set·ting cubierto *m*.

plague peste *f*.

plain 1 *adj (clear)* claro, -a; *(simple)* sencillo, -a; *(unattractive)* poco atractivo, -a; **the p. truth** la verdad lisa y llana. **2** *n (land)* llanura *f*.

plain·ly *adv* claramente; *(simply)* sencillamente; **to speak p.** hablar con franqueza.

plait 1 *n* trenza *f*. **2** *vt* trenzar.

plan 1 *n* plan *m*. **2** *vt (for future)* planear; *(economy)* planificar; *(intend)* pensar; **to p. on doing sth** tener la intención de hacer algo.

▸ **plan for** *vt (disaster)* prevenirse contra.

plane¹ avión *m*.

plane² *(tool)* cepillo *m*.

plane³ **p. (tree)** plátano *m*.

plan·et planeta *m*.

plank tabla *f*.

plant¹ 1 *n* planta *f*. **2** *vt (flowers)* plantar; *(bomb)* colocar.

plant² *(factory)* planta *f* (industrial).

plas·ter yeso *m*; *(for broken limb)* escayola *f*.

plas·ter cast *(for broken arm)* escayola *f*.

plas·tic 1 *n* plástico *m*. **2** *adj (cup, bag)* de plástico.

plas·tic sur·ger·y cirugía *f* plástica.

plate plato *m*; *(sheet)* placa *f*.

plat·form plataforma *f*; *(at meeting)* tribuna *f*; *(at station)* andén *m*.

plau·si·ble *adj* plausible.

play 1 *vt (game)* jugar a; *(team)* jugar contra; *(instrument, tune)* tocar; *(part)* hacer (el papel) de; **to p. a record** poner un disco; *fig* **to p. a part in sth** participar en algo. **2** *vi* jugar (**with** con). **3** *n* obra *f* de teatro.

▸ **play back** *vt (tape)* volver a poner.

▸ **play down** *vt* quitar importancia a.

play·er jugador, -a *mf*; *(in play)* *(man)* actor *m*; *(woman)* actriz *f*.

play·ground *(in school)* patio *m* de recreo; *(recreation ground)* parque *m* infantil.

play·group jardín *m* de infancia.

play·ing card carta *f*.

play·ing field campo *m* de deportes.

play·time recreo *m*.

plea *(request)* petición *f*, súplica *f*; *(in court)* alegato *m*.

plead 1 *vt* **to p. sb's cause** defender la causa de algn; **to p. ignorance** *(give as excuse)* alegar ignorancia. **2** *vi (beg)* rogar, suplicar; **to p. with sb to do sth** suplicar a algn que haga algo; *(in court)* **to p. guilty/not guilty** declararse culpable/inocente.

pleas·ant *adj* agradable.

pleas·ant·ly *adv* agradablemente.

please 1 *adv* por favor; **'p. do not**

smoke' 'se ruega no fumar'. **2** *vt (give pleasure to)* complacer. **3** *vi* **do as you p.** haz lo que quieras.

pleased *adj (happy)* contento, -a; *(satisfied)* satisfecho, -a; **p. to meet you!** ¡encantado, -a!

pleas·ing *adj (pleasant)* agradable.

pleas·ure placer *m*; **with p.** con mucho gusto.

pleat pliegue *m*.

pleat·ed *adj* plisado, -a.

pledge 1 *n* promesa *f*. **2** *vt* prometer.

plen·ti·ful *adj* abundante.

plen·ty p. of potatoes muchas patatas; **p. of time** tiempo de sobra.

pli·ers *npl* alicates *mpl*, tenazas *fpl*.

plot¹ 1 *n (conspiracy)* complot *m*; *(story)* argumento *m*. **2** *vi* conspirar.

plot² *(ground)* terreno *m*; *(for building)* solar *m*.

plow 1 *n* arado *m*. **2** *vt* arar.

pluck *vt (flowers)* coger; *(chicken)* desplumar.

plug 1 *n (in bath etc)* tapón *m*; *(electric)* enchufe *m*; **2/3 pin p.** clavija bipolar/tripolar. **2** *vt (hole)* tapar.
► **plug in 1** *vt* enchufar. **2** *vi* enchufarse.

plum *(fruit)* ciruela *f*.

plumb·er fontanero, -a *mf*.

plumb·ing *(system)* fontanería *f*.

plump *adj (person)* rechoncho, -a; *(baby)* rellenito, -a.

plunge 1 *vt (immerse)* sumergir; *(thrust)* arrojar. **2** *vi (dive)* zambullirse; *(fall)* caer.

plu·ral *adj & n* plural *(m)*; **in the p.** en plural.

plus *prep* más; **three p. four makes seven** tres más cuatro hacen siete.

p.m. *(from midday to early evening)* de la tarde; *(at night)* de la noche.

pneu·mat·ic *adj* neumático, -a.

pneu·mat·ic drill martillo *m* neumático.

poach *vt (egg)* escalfar.

PO Box apartado *m* (de Correos).

pock·et bolsillo *m*.

pock·et·book bolso *m*.

pock·et·ful a p. un bolsillo de.

pock·et mon·ey dinero *m* de bolsillo.

pod·cast *n* podcast *m*.

po·em poema *m*.

po·et poeta *mf*.

po·et·ic *adj* poético, -a.

po·et·ry poesía *f*.

point 1 *n (sharp end)* punta *f*; *(place)* punto *m*; *(score)* tanto *m*; *(moment)* **at that p.** en aquel momento; **to be on the p. of doing sth** estar a punto de hacer algo; **there's no p. in going** no merece la pena ir; **six p. three** seis coma tres; **up to a p.** hasta cierto punto; **power p.** toma *f* de corriente; **points** *(on railway)* agujas *fpl*. **2** *vt (way etc)* indicar; **to p. a gun at sb** apuntar a algn con una pistola. **3** *vi* **to p. at sth/sb** *(with finger)* señalar algo/a algn con el dedo.
► **point out** *vt* indicar; *(mention)* hacer resaltar.

point·ed *adj (sharp)* puntiagudo, -a.

point·less *adj* sin sentido.

poi·son 1 *n* veneno *m*. **2** *vt* envenenar.

poi·son·ous *adj (plant, snake)* venenoso, -a; *(gas)* tóxico, -a.

poke *vt (fire)* atizar; *(with finger)* dar con la punta del dedo a; *(with stick)* dar con la punta del bastón a; **to p. one's head out** asomar la cabeza.
► **poke about, poke around** *vi* fisgonear *or* hurgar en.

pok·er *(for fire)* atizador *m*.

po·lar *adj* polar.

po·lar bear oso *m* polar.

Pole *n* polaco, -a *mf*.

pole¹ palo *m*.

pole² *(north, south)* polo *m*.

po·lice *npl* policía *f sing*.

po·lice car coche *m* patrulla.

po·lice·man policía *m*.

po·lice sta·tion comisaría *f*.

po·lice·wom·an *(mujer f)* policía *f*.

pol·i·cy política *f*; *(insurance)* póliza *f* (de seguros).

po·li·o poliomielitis *f*.

Po·lish 1 *adj* polaco, -a. **2** *n (language)* polaco *m*.

pol·ish 1 *vt* pulir; *(furniture)* encerar; *(shoes)* limpiar. **2** *n (for furniture)* cera *f*; *(for shoes)* betún *m*; *(for nails)* esmalte *m*.

▸ **polish off** *vt (food)* zamparse.

▸ **polish up** *vt fig* perfeccionar.

po·lite *adj* educado, -a.

po·lite·ly *adv* educadamente.

po·lite·ness educación *f*.

po·lit·i·cal *adj* político, -a.

pol·i·ti·cian político, -a *mf*.

pol·i·tics política *f*.

poll votación *f*, *(survey)* encuesta *f*; **to go to the polls** acudir a las urnas.

pol·len polen *m*.

poll·ing sta·tion colegio *m* electoral.

pol·lute *vt* contaminar.

pol·lu·tion contaminación *f*.

po·lo n. peck sweater jersey *m* de cuello vuelto.

pol·y·es·ter poliéster *m*.

pol·y·tech·nic politécnico *m*.

pol·y·thene polietileno *m*.

pom·e·gran·ate granada *f*.

pond estanque *m*.

po·ny poney *m*.

po·ny·tail cola *f* de caballo.

poo·dle caniche *m*.

pool *(of water, oil etc)* charco *m*; **swimming p.** piscina *f*.

pooped *adj fam* hecho, -a polvo.

poor *1 adj* pobre; *(quality)* malo, -a. **2** *npl* **the p.** los pobres.

poor·ly 1 *adv (badly)* mal. **2** *adj (ill)* enfermo, -a.

pop 1 *vt (burst)* hacer reventar. **2** *vi (burst)* reventar; *fam* **I'm just popping over to Ian's** voy un momento a casa de Ian. **3** *n (drink)* gaseosa *f*; *fam (father)* papá *m*; *(music)* música *f* pop.

▸ **pop in** *vi fam* entrar un momento.

pop·corn palomitas *fpl*.

Pope the **P.** el Papa.

pop·py amapola *f*.

Pop·si·cle® polo *m*.

pop sing·er cantante *mf* pop.

pop·u·lar *adj* popular; *(fashionable)* de moda.

pop·u·lar·i·ty popularidad *f*.

pop·u·lat·ed *adj* **thinly p.** poco poblado.

pop·u·la·tion población *f*.

porch *(of house)* porche *m*; *(veranda)* terraza *f*.

pork carne *f* de cerdo.

por·ridge gachas *fpl* de avena.

port *(harbor, of computer)* puerto *m*.

por·ta·ble *adj & n* portátil *(m)*.

por·ter *(in hotel etc)* portero, -a *mf*.

port·fo·li·o *(for papers, of artist, politician)* cartera *f*.

port·hole portilla *f*.

por·tion *(part, piece)* parte *f*; *(of food)* ración *f*.

por·trait retrato *m*.

Por·tu·guese 1 *adj* portugués, -esa. **2** *n (person)* portugués, -esa *mf*; *(language)* portugués *m*.

pose 1 *vt (problem)* plantear; *(threat)* representar. **2** *vi (for painting)* posar; **to p. as** hacerse pasar por.

posh *adj* elegante; *(person)* presumido, -a; *(accent)* de clase alta.

po·si·tion posición *f*, *(location)* situación *f*, *(rank)* rango *m*; **to be in a p. to do sth** estar en condiciones de hacer algo.

pos·i·tive *adj* positivo, -a; *(sign)* favorable; *(sure)* seguro, -a.

pos·i·tive·ly *adv (constructively)* positivamente; *(to answer)* afirmativamente; *(for emphasis)* verdaderamente, realmente.

pos·sess *vt* poseer.

pos·ses·sions *npl* bienes *mpl*.

pos·ses·sive *adj* posesivo, -a.

pos·si·bil·i·ty posibilidad *f*.

pos·si·ble *adj* posible; **as much as p.** todo lo posible; **as often as p.** cuanto más mejor; **as soon as p.** cuanto antes.

pos·si·bly *adv* posiblemente; *(per-*

haps) quizás; **I can't p. come** no puedo venir de ninguna manera.

post¹ *(wooden)* poste *m.*

post² *(job)* puesto *m.*

▶ **post up** *vt (notice)* fijar.

post·age franqueo *m.*

post·age stamp sello *m* (de correos).

post·al *adj* postal.

post·al or·der giro *m* postal.

post·card *(tarjeta f)* postal *f.*

post·er póster *m; (advertising)* cartel *m.*

post·grad·u·ate posgraduado, -a *mf.*

post·man cartero *m.*

post·mark matasellos *m inv.*

post of·fice oficina *f* de correos; **where is the p.?** ¿dónde está correos?

post·pone *vt* aplazar.

post·pone·ment aplazamiento *m.*

pot *(for cooking)* olla *f, (for flowers)* maceta *f.*

po·ta·to *(pl potatoes)* patata *f, Am* papa *f.*

po·tent *adj* potente.

po·ten·tial 1 *adj* potencial. **2** *n* potencial *m.*

pot·ter alfarero, -a *mf.*

pot·ter·y *(craft, place)* alfarería *f, (objects)* cerámica *f.*

pot·ty orinal *m.*

pouch bolsa *f* pequeña; *(of animal)* bolsa *f* abdominal.

poul·try *(live)* aves *fpl* de corral; *(food)* pollos *mpl.*

pounce *vi* **to p. on** abalanzarse encima de.

pound¹ *(weight)* libra *f.*

pound² *(for dogs)* perrera *f, (for cars)* depósito *m* de coches.

pour 1 *vt* verter; **to p. sb a drink** servirle una copa a algn. **2** *vi* **it's pouring with rain** está lloviendo a cántaros.

▶ **pour away** *vt (liquid)* vaciar.

▶ **pour in** *vi (water)* entrar a raudales; *(applications)* llegar sin parar.

▶ **pour out 1** *vt* verter. **2** *vi (liquid, people)* salir a raudales.

pov·er·ty pobreza *f.*

pow·der 1 *n* polvo *m.* **2** *vt* **to p. one's nose** empolvarse la cara.

pow·dered *adj (milk)* en polvo.

pow·er fuerza *f, (energy)* energía *f, (ability, authority)* poder *m; (nation)* potencia *f;* **to be in p.** estar en el poder.

pow·er·ful *adj (influential)* poderoso, -a; *(engine, machine)* potente.

pow·er point enchufe *m.*

pow·er sta·tion central *f* eléctrica.

prac·ti·cal *adj* práctico, -a.

prac·ti·cal joke broma *f* pesada.

prac·ti·cal·ly *(almost)* casi.

prac·tice 1 *n (exercise)* práctica *f, (in sport)* entrenamiento *m; (rehearsal)* ensayo *m; (habit)* costumbre *f, (way of doing sth)* práctica *f;* **to be out of p.** no estar en forma; **in p.** en la práctica. **2** *vt* practicar; *(principle)* poner en práctica; *(profession)* ejercer. **3** *vi* practicar; *(in sport)* entrenar; *(rehearse)* ensayar; *(doctor)* practicar; *(lawyer)* ejercer.

praise 1 *n* alabanza *f.* **2** *vt* alabar.

prank travesura *f, (joke)* broma *f.*

prawn gamba *f.*

pray *vi* rezar.

prayer oración *f.*

preach *vi* predicar.

pre·cau·tion precaución *f.*

pre·cede *vt* preceder.

pre·ce·dent precedente *m.*

pre·ced·ing *adj* precedente.

pre·cinct *(administrative, police division)* distrito *m.*

pre·cious *adj* precioso, -a.

pre·cise *adj* preciso, -a; *(meticulous)* meticuloso, -a.

pre·co·cious *adj* precoz.

pred·a·tor depredador *m.*

pre·de·ces·sor antecesor, -a *mf.*

pre·dic·a·ment apuro *m,* aprieto *m.*

pre·dict *vt* predecir.

pre·dict·a·ble adj previsible.

pre·dic·tion pronóstico m.

pref·ace prefacio m.

pre·fer vt preferir; **I p. coffee to tea** prefiero el café al té.

pref·er·a·ble adj preferible (**to** a).

pre·fer·a·bly adv preferentemente.

pref·er·ence preferencia f.

pre·fix prefijo m.

preg·nan·cy embarazo m.

preg·nant adj embarazada.

pre·his·tor·i(·)c(al) adj prehistórico, -a.

prej·u·dice (bias) prejuicio m.

pre·lim·i·nar·y adj preliminar.

pre·ma·ture adj prematuro, -a.

prem·is·es npl local m; **on the p.** en el local.

pre·mi·um prima f.

prep·a·ra·tion preparación f; (plan) preparativo m.

pre·pare vt preparar; **to p. to do sth** prepararse para hacer algo. **2** vi prepararse (**for** para).

pre·pared adj (ready) preparado, -a; **to be p. to do sth** (willing) estar dispuesto, -a a hacer algo.

prep·o·si·tion preposición f.

pre·school adj preescolar.

pre·scribe vt (medicine) recetar.

pre·scrip·tion (medical) receta f.

pres·ence presencia f, (attendance) asistencia f.

pres·ent¹ **1** adj (in attendance) presente; (current) actual; **p. tense** (tiempo m) presente m. **2** n (time) presente m; **at p.** actualmente.

pre·sent² **1** vt (opportunity) ofrecer; (problems) plantear; (prize) entregar; (introduce) (person, program) presentar; **to p. sb with sth** obsequiar a algn con algo. **2** n (gift) regalo m.

pres·en·ta·tion presentación f, **p. ceremony** ceremonia f de entrega.

pre·sent·er animador, -a mf.

pres·ent·ly adv (soon) dentro de poco; (now) ahora.

pres·er·va·tion conservación f.

pre·ser·va·tive conservante m.

pre·serve 1 vt (keep) mantener. **2** n conserva f.

pre·side vi presidir; **to p. over** or **at sth** presidir algo.

pres·i·den·cy presidencia f.

pres·i·dent presidente, -a mf.

pres·i·den·tial adj presidencial.

press 1 vt apretar; (button) pulsar; (iron) planchar; (urge) presionar; **to p. sb to do sth** presionar a algn para que haga algo. **2** vi (push) apretar; **to p. (down) on sth** hacer presión sobre algo. **3** n (newspapers) prensa f.

▸ **press on** vi seguir adelante.

press con·fer·ence rueda f de prensa.

pres·sure presión f; **to bring p. (to bear) on sb** ejercer presión sobre algn.

pres·sure cook·er olla f a presión.

pres·sure gauge manómetro m.

pre·sume vt suponer.

pre·tend vt i fingir.

pre·text pretexto m; **on the p. of** so pretexto de.

pret·ty 1 adj (thing) bonito, -a; (person) guapo, -a. **2** adv bastante; **p. much the same** más o menos lo mismo.

pre·vail vi predominar; **to p. upon** or **on sb to do sth** (persuade) persuadir or convencer a algn para que haga algo.

pre·vent vt impedir; (accident) evitar; **to p. sb from doing sth** impedir a algn hacer algo.

pre·ven·tion prevención f.

pre·vi·ous adj anterior.

pre·vi·ous·ly adv previamente.

prey presa f, fig víctima f.

price precio m.

price list lista f de precios.

pric·ey adj fam carillo(a).

prick vt picar; **to p. one's finger** pincharse el dedo.

prick·ly adj espinoso, -a; (touchy) enojadizo, -a.

pride 1 n orgullo m; (arrogance) soberbia f; **to take p. in sth** enorgullecerse de algo. **2** vt **to p. oneself on** enorgullecerse de.

priest sacerdote m, cura m.

pri·mar·i·ly adv ante todo.

pri·mar·y 1 adj principal; **p. education/school** enseñanza f/escuela f primaria. **2** n (election) (elección f) primaria f.

Prime Min·is·ter primer, -a ministro, -a mf.

prime num·ber número m primo.

prim·i·tive adj primitivo, -a.

prim·rose primavera f.

prince príncipe m; **P. Charming** Príncipe Azul.

prin·cess princesa f.

prin·ci·pal 1 adj principal. **2** n (of college etc) director, -a mf.

prin·ci·ple principio m; **on p.** por principio.

print 1 vt (publish) publicar; (write) escribir con letra de imprenta. **2** n letra f, (of hand, foot) huella f, (of photo) copia f; **out of p.** agotado, -a.
▸**print out** vt imprimir.

print·ed adj impreso(a); **printed matter** impresos mpl.

print·er (person) impresor, -a mf, (machine) impresora f.

print·ing (industry) imprenta f, (process) impresión f.

print-out impresión f.

pri·or adj anterior; **without p. warning** sin previo aviso.

pri·or·i·ty prioridad f.

pris·on prisión f.

pris·on·er preso, -a mf; **to hold sb p.** detener a algn.

pri·va·cy intimidad f.

pri·vate 1 adj privado, -a; (individual) particular; (personal) personal; (letter) confidencial. **2** n (soldier) soldado m raso.

pri·vate·ly adv en privado; (personally) personalmente.

prize premio m.

prize-giv·ing distribución f de premios.

prize·win·ner premiado, -a mf.

pro¹ pro m; **the pros and cons** los pros y los contras.

pro² abbr of **professional** fam profesional mf.

pro³ prefix (in favour of) pro-.

prob·a·ble adj probable.

prob·a·bly adv probablemente.

probe 1 n (medical instrument, spacecraft) sonda f, (investigation) sondeo m. **2** vt (with medical instrument) sondar; (investigate) investigar.
▸**probe into** vt investigar.

prob·lem problema m.

prob·lem·at·i(·)c(al) adj problemático, -a.

pro·ceed vi proceder, seguir; **to p. to do sth** ponerse a hacer algo.

pro·ceeds npl ganancias fpl.

pro·cess 1 n proceso m; **in the p. of** en vías de. **2** vt procesar.

pro·cessed cheese queso m fundido.

pro·ces·sion desfile m; (religious) procesión f.

pro·ces·sor procesador m.

pro·duce 1 vt producir; (manufacture) fabricar; (give birth to) dar a luz a; (show) enseñar; (bring out) sacar. **2** n productos mpl.

pro·duc·er productor, -a mf, (manufacturer) fabricante mf.

pro·duc·tion producción f, (manufacture) fabricación f, **p. line** cadena f de montaje.

pro·duc·tive adj productivo, -a.

pro·duc·tiv·i·ty productividad f.

pro·fes·sion profesión f.

pro·fes·sion·al 1 adj profesional; (polished) de gran calidad. **2** n profesional mf.

pro·fes·sor catedrático, -a mf.

prof·it 1 n beneficio m; **to make a p. on** sacar beneficios de. **2** vi **to p. from** aprovecharse de.

prof·it·a·ble adj rentable; (worthwhile) provechoso, -a.

pro·found adj profundo, -a.

pro·gram 1 n programa m; (plan) plan m. **2** vti programar.

pro·gram·ming programación f.

prog·ress 1 n progreso m; **to make p.** hacer progresos; **in p.** en curso. **2** vi avanzar; (develop) desarrollarse; (medically) mejorar.

pro·gres·sive adj (increasing) progresivo, -a; (in politics) progresista.

pro·hib·it vt prohibir; **to p. sb from doing sth** prohibir a algn hacer algo.

proj·ect proyecto m; (at school) trabajo m.

pro·jec·tor proyector m.

pro·long vt prolongar.

prom·e·nade (at seaside) paseo m marítimo.

prom·i·nent adj (important) importante; (famous) eminente.

prom·ise 1 n promesa f; **to show p.** ser prometedor, -a. **2** vti prometer.

prom·is·ing adj prometedor, -a.

pro·mote vt ascender; (product) promocionar.

pro·mo·tion (in rank) ascenso m; (of product) promoción f.

prompt adj (quick) rápido, -a; (punctual) puntual. **2** adv **at 2 o'clock p.** a las 2 en punto.

prone adj **to be p. to do sth** ser propenso, -a a hacer algo.

pro·noun pronombre m.

pro·nounce vt pronunciar.

pro·nun·ci·a·tion pronunciación f.

proof prueba f.

prop¹ 1 n (physical support) puntal m; (psychological support) sostén m. **2** vt (lean) apoyar.

▸**prop up** vt apoyar.

prop² (in theatre) fam accesorio m.

prop·a·gan·da propaganda f.

pro·pel·ler hélice f.

prop·er adj adecuado, -a; (real) auténtico, -a; **p. noun** nombre propio.

prop·er·ly (suitably, correctly, decently) correctamente.

prop·er·ty (possession) propiedad f; **personal p.** bienes mpl.

pro·por·tion proporción f; (part, quantity) parte f.

pro·por·tion·al adj proporcional (to a).

pro·pos·al propuesta f; **p. of marriage** propuesta de matrimonio.

pro·pose 1 vt proponer; (suggest) sugerir. **2** vi (ask to marry) declararse.

prop·o·si·tion propuesta f.

props npl (in theater) accesorios mpl.

prose prosa f; (translation) traducción f inversa.

pros·e·cute vt procesar.

pros·e·cu·tion (action) proceso m, juicio m; **the p.** (in court) la acusación.

pros·pect (outlook) perspectiva f; (hope) esperanza f.

pros·per·i·ty prosperidad f.

pros·per·ous adj próspero, -a.

pro·tect vt **to p. sb from sth** proteger a algn de algo.

pro·tec·tion protección f.

pro·tec·tive adj protector, -a.

pro·test 1 n protesta f. **2** vi protestar.

Prot·es·tant adj & n protestante (mf).

pro·test·er manifestante mf.

proud adj orgulloso, -a; (arrogant) soberbio, -a.

proud·ly adv con orgullo; (arrogantly) con soberbia.

prove vt demostrar; **it proved to be disastrous** resultó desastroso, -a.

prov·erb refrán m, proverbio m.

pro·vide vt proporcionar; (supplies) suministrar.

pro·vid·ed conj **p. (that)** con tal de que.

prov·ince provincia f.

pro·vin·cial adj provincial; pej provinciano, -a.

pro·vi·sion·al adj provisional.

pro·voke vt provocar.

prowl vi merodear; **to p. about** or **around** rondar.

prowl·er merodeador *m*.

prune¹ ciruela *f* pasa.

prune² *vt* (roses etc) podar.

psy·chi·at·ric *adj* psiquiátrico, -a.

psy·chi·a·trist psiquiatra *mf*.

psy·cho·log·i·cal *adj* psicológico, -a.

psy·chol·o·gist psicólogo, -a *mf*.

psy·chol·o·gy psicología *f*.

pub bar *m*.

pub·lic 1 *adj* público, -a; **p. holiday** fiesta *f* nacional. **2** *n* **the p.** el público; **in p.** en público.

pub·li·ca·tion publicación *f*.

pub·lic·i·ty publicidad *f*.

pub·lic·ly *adv* públicamente.

pub·lish *vt* publicar, editar.

pub·lish·er editor, -a *mf*.

pub·lish·ing (business) industria *f* editorial.

pud·ding pudín *m*; (dessert) postre *m*.

pud·dle charco *m*.

puff 1 *n* (of smoke) bocanada *f*. **2** *vi* (person) jadear; **to p. on one's pipe** chupar la pipa.

pull 1 *n* **to give sth a p.** (tug) dar un tirón a algo. **2** *vt* (tug) dar un tirón a; (drag) tirar de; **to p. a muscle** sufrir un tirón en un músculo; **to p. the trigger** apretar el gatillo; **to p. sth to pieces** hacer pedazos algo.

▸**pull apart** *vt* desmontar.

▸**pull down** *vt* (building) derribar.

▸**pull in 1** *vt* (crowds) atraer. **2** *vi* **to p. in(to) (the station)** llegar a la estación.

▸**pull out 1** *vt* (withdraw) retirar. **2** *vi* (car) **to p. out to overtake** salirse para adelantar.

▸**pull over** *vi* hacerse a un lado.

▸**pull through** *vi* reponerse.

▸**pull up 1** *vt* (uproot) desarraigar; (draw close) acercar. **2** *vi* (stop) pararse.

pull·o·ver jersey *m*.

pulse (in body) pulso *m*.

pump 1 *n* bomba *f*. **2** *vt* bombear.

▸**pump up** *vt* (tire) inflar.

pump·kin calabaza *f*.

punch¹ 1 *n* (for making holes) perforadora *f*. **2** *vt* (ticket) picar.

punch² 1 *n* (blow) puñetazo *m*. **2** *vt* (with fist) dar un puñetazo a.

punc·tu·al *adj* puntual.

punc·tu·a·tion puntuación *f*.

punc·ture 1 *n* pinchazo *m*. **2** *vt* (tire) pinchar.

pun·ish *vt* castigar.

pun·ish·ment castigo *m*.

pu·pil¹ (at school) alumno, -a *mf*.

pu·pil² (in eye) pupila *f*.

pup·pet títere *m*.

pup·py cachorro, -a *mf* (de perro).

pur·chase 1 *n* compra *f*. **2** *vt* comprar.

pur·chas·er comprador, -a *mf*.

pur·chas·ing pow·er poder *m* adquisitivo.

pure *adj* puro, -a.

pure·ly *adv* simplemente.

pur·ple *adj* morado, -a.

pur·pose propósito *m*; **on p.** a propósito.

pur·pose·ly *adv* adrede.

purse (bag) bolso *m*.

pur·sue *vt* (criminal) perseguir; (person) seguir.

pur·suit (of criminal) persecución *f*; (of animal) caza *f*; (of pleasure) búsqueda *f*; (pastime) pasatiempo *m*.

push 1 *n* empujón *m*; **to give sb a p.** dar un empujón a algn. **2** *vt* empujar; (button) pulsar; **to p. one's finger into a hole** meter el dedo en un agujero. **3** *vi* empujar.

▸**push aside** *vt* (object) apartar.

▸**push in** *vi* colarse.

▸**push off** *vi* fam **p. off!** ¡lárgate!

▸**push on** *vi* (continue) seguir adelante.

▸**push through** *vt* (crowd) abrirse paso entre; (law) hacer aceptar (a la fuerza).

pushed *adj* **to be p. for time/money** estar justo, -a de tiempo/dinero.

push·y *adj* (pushier, pushiest) fam agresivo, -a.

puss, puss·y minino *m*.

put* *vt* poner; *(place)* colocar; *(insert)* meter; *(express)* expresar; *(invest)* *(money)* invertir; **to p. a stop to sth** poner término a algo; **to p. a question to sb** hacer una pregunta a algn.

▸ **put across** *vt (idea etc)* comunicar.

▸ **put aside** *vt (money)* ahorrar; *(time)* reservar.

▸ **put away** *vt (tidy up)* recoger; *(save money)* ahorrar.

▸ **put back** *vt (postpone)* aplazar.

▸ **put by** *vt (money)* ahorrar.

▸ **put down** *vt (set down)* dejar; *(criticize)* criticar; *(write down)* apuntar.

▸ **put forward** *vt (theory)* exponer; *(proposal)* hacer.

▸ **put in** *vt (install)* instalar; *(complaint, request)* presentar; *(time)* pasar.

▸ **put off** *vt (postpone)* aplazar; *(switch off) (radio, light)* apagar; **to p. sb off (doing) sth** *(dissuade)* disuadir a algn de *(hacer)* algo.

▸ **put on** *vt (clothes)* poner(se); *(switch on) (radio)* poner; *(light)* encender; **to p. on weight** engordar.

▸ **put out** *vt (switch off, extinguish)* apagar; *(place outside)* sacar; *(extend) (arm)* extender; *(hand)* tender; *(annoy)* molestar; *(inconvenience)* incordiar.

▸ **put through** *vt (on telephone)* **p. me through to Pat, please** póngame con Pat, por favor.

▸ **put together** *vt (assemble)* montar.

▸ **put up** *vt (raise)* levantar; *(picture)* colocar; *(curtains)* colgar; *(tent)* armar; *(prices)* subir; *(accommodate)* alojar; **to p. up a fight** ofrecer resistencia.

▸ **put up with** *vt* aguantar.

put·ty masilla *f*.

puz·zle 1 *n* rompecabezas *m inv*; *(mystery)* misterio *m*. **2** *vt* dejar perplejo, -a.

puz·zling *adj* extraño, -a.

py·lon torre *f* (de conducción eléctrica).

pyr·a·mid pirámide *f*.

Q

qual·i·fi·ca·tion *(diploma etc)* título *m*.

qual·i·fied *adj* capacitado, -a; **q. teacher** profesor *m* titulado.

qual·i·fy *vi (in competition)* quedar clasificado, -a; **to q. as** *(doctor etc)* sacar el título de.

qual·i·ty *(excellence)* calidad *f*, *(attribute)* cualidad *f*.

quan·ti·ty cantidad *f*.

quar·rel 1 *n (argument)* riña *f*, pelea *f*. **2** *vi (argue)* reñir.

quar·rel·ing disputas *fpl*.

quar·ry cantera *f*.

quart cuarto *m* de galón *(0,94 litros)*.

quar·ter cuarto *m*; *(coin)* cuarto *m* (de dólar); *(district)* barrio *m*; **it's a q. to three, it's a q. of three** son las tres menos cuarto.

quar·ter·back quarterback *m*, *Méx* mariscal *m* de campo.

quartz cuarzo *m*; **q. watch** reloj *m* de cuarzo.

queen reina *f*.

queer *adj (strange)* extraño, -a.

quench *vt* apagar.

que·ry *(question)* pregunta *f*.

ques·tion 1 *n* pregunta *f*, *(problem, issue)* asunto *m*; **to ask sb a q.** hacer una pregunta a algn; **out of the q.** imposible; **that's out of the q.** ¡ni hablar! **2** *vt (interrogate)* interrogar; *(query)* poner en duda.

ques·tion·a·ble *adj (doubtful)* dudoso, -a; *(debatable)* discutible.

ques·tion mark signo *m* de interrogación.

ques·tion·naire cuestionario *m*.

quib·ble vi poner pegas (**with** a).

quiche quiche f.

quick adj (fast) rápido, -a; **be q.!** ¡date prisa!

quick·ly adv deprisa.

qui·et adj (silent) silencioso, -a; (calm, not crowded) tranquilo, -a.

qui·et·ly adv (silently) silenciosamente; (calmly) tranquilamente; **he spoke q.** habló en voz baja.

quit* 1 vt (leave) dejar; **q. making that noise!** ¡deja de hacer ese ruido! **2** vi (go) irse; (resign) dimitir.

quite adv (entirely) totalmente; (rather) bastante; **q. a few** bastantes; **q. often** con bastante frecuencia; **q. (so)!** ¡exacto!

quiz n. **show** concurso m.

quo·ta (proportional share) cuota f, parte f; (prescribed amount, number) cupo m.

quo·ta·tion cita f; (commercial) cotización f.

quo·ta·tion marks npl comillas fpl.

quote 1 vt (cite) citar; **to q. a price** dar un presupuesto. **2** n cita f; (commercial) presupuesto m.

R

rab·bi rabino m.

rab·bit conejo, -a mf.

ra·bies rabia f.

race¹ 1 n (in sport) carrera f. **2** vt (car, horse) hacer correr; **I'll r. you!** ¡te echo una carrera! **3** vi (go quickly) correr.

race² (people) raza f.

race·horse caballo m de carreras.

ra·cial adj racial.

rac·ing carreras fpl.

rac·ing bike (motorbike) moto f de carreras; (bicycle) bicicleta f de carreras.

rac·ing car coche m de carreras.

rac·ing driv·er piloto mf de carreras.

rac·ism racismo m.

ra·cist adj & n racista (mf).

rack (shelf) estante m; (for clothes) percha f; **luggage r.** portaequipajes m inv; **roof r.** baca f.

rack·et¹ (din) jaleo m.

rack·et² (for tennis etc) raqueta f.

ra·dar radar m.

ra·di·a·tion radiación f.

ra·di·a·tor radiador m.

rad·i·cal adj radical.

ra·di·o radio f; **on the r.** en or por la radio; **r. station** emisora f (de radio).

ra·di·o·ac·tive adj radiactivo, -a.

rad·ish rábano m.

ra·di·us radio m.

raf·fle rifa f.

raft balsa f.

rag (torn piece) harapo m; (for cleaning) trapo m; **rags** (clothes) trapos mpl.

rage 1 n (fury) cólera f. **2** vi (person) estar furioso, -a.

rag·ged adj (clothes) hecho, -a jirones; (person) harapiento, -a.

raid 1 n (by police) redada f; (robbery etc) atraco m. **2** vt (police) hacer una redada (en); (rob) asaltar.

rail barra f; (railing) barandilla f; (on railroad) carril m; **by r.** (send sth) por ferrocarril; (travel) en tren.

rail·ings npl verja f sing.

rail·road ferrocarril m.

rail·road sta·tion estación f de ferrocarril.

rail·road track vía f férrea.

rail·way line vía f férrea.

rain 1 n lluvia f; **in the r.** bajo la lluvia. **2** vi llover; **it's raining** llueve.

rain·bow arco m iris.

rain·coat impermeable m.

rain·y adj lluvioso, -a.

raise 1 n aumento m (de sueldo). **2** vt levantar; (voice) subir; (increase) aumentar; (money, help) reunir; (issue, *question)* plantear; *(crops, children)* criar.

rai·sin pasa *f.*

rake 1 *n (garden tool)* rastrillo *m.* **2** *vt (leaves)* rastrillar.

ral·ly *(political)* mitin *m.*

▶**rally around** *vi (help out)* echar una mano.

rally around *vi (help out)* echar una mano.

ram 1 *n (sheep)* carnero *m.* **2** *vt (drive into place)* hincar; *(crash into)* chocar con.

ram·ble *(walk)* caminata *f.*

ramp rampa *f.*

ran *pt of* **run**.

ranch rancho *m.*

ran·dom 1 *n* at r. al azar. **2** *adj* fortuito, -a; **r. selection** selección *f* hecha al azar.

range 1 *n (of mountains)* cordillera *f*, *(of products)* gama *f*, *(of missile)* alcance *m*; *(stove)* cocina *f* de carbón. **2** *vi (extend)* extenderse (**to** hasta); **prices r. from five to twenty dollars** los precios oscilan entre cinco y veinte dólares.

rank *(position in army)* graduación *f*; *(in society)* rango *m*; **(taxi) r.** parada *f* de taxis.

ran·som rescate *m.*

rape 1 *n* violación *f.* **2** *vt* violar.

rap·id *adj* rápido, -a.

rap·id·ly *adv* rápidamente.

rap·ist violador, -a *mf.*

rare *adj* poco común; *(steak)* poco hecho, -a.

rare·ly *adv* raras veces.

ras·cal granuja *mf.*

rash¹ *(on skin)* sarpullido *m.*

rash² *adj (reckless)* impetuoso, -a; *(words, actions)* precipitado, -a.

rash·ly *adv* a la ligera.

rasp·ber·ry frambuesa *f.*

rat rata *f.*

rate 1 *n* tasa *f*; **at any r.** *(anyway)* en cualquier caso; *(of interest, exchange)* tipo *m*; **at the r. of** *(speed)* a la velocidad de; *(quantity)* a razón de. **2** *vt (estimate)* estimar; *(evaluate)* tasar; *(consider)* considerar.

rath·er *adv (quite)* más bien, bastante; *(more accurately)* mejor dicho; **r. than** *(instead of)* en vez de; *(more than)* más que; **she would r. stay here** prefiere quedarse aquí.

rat·ing *(score)* valoración *f.*

ra·tio razón *f.*

ra·tion 1 *n (allowance)* ración *f*; **rations** víveres *mpl.* **2** *vt* racionar.

ra·tion·al *adj* racional.

ra·tion·ing racionamiento *m.*

rat·tle 1 *n (toy)* sonajero *m*; *(instrument)* carraca *f.* **2** *vt (keys etc)* hacer sonar. **3** *vi* sonar; *(metal)* repiquetear; *(glass)* tintinear; *(window, shelves)* vibrar.

rav·en·ous *adj* **I'm r.** tengo un hambre que no veo.

raw *adj (uncooked)* crudo, -a; **r. material** materia *f* prima; **r. flesh** carne *f* viva.

ray rayo *m.*

ra·zor *(for shaving)* maquinilla *f* de afeitar.

ra·zor blade hoja *f* de afeitar.

reach 1 *vt (arrive at)* llegar a; *(contact)* localizar. **2** *vi* alcanzar. **3** *n (range)* alcance *m*; **out of r.** fuera del alcance; **within r.** al alcance.

▶**reach out** *vi (with hand)* extender la mano.

re·act *vi* reaccionar.

re·ac·tion reacción *f.*

re·ac·tor reactor *m.*

read* *vt* leer; *(decipher)* descifrar.

▶**read about** *vt* leer.

▶**read out** *vt* leer en voz alta.

▶**read up on** *vt* estudiar.

read·er lector, -a *mf*, *(book)* libro *m* de lectura.

read·i·ly *adv (easily)* fácilmente; *(willingly)* de buena gana.

read·ing lectura *f*, *fig* interpretación *f.*

read·y *adj (prepared)* listo, -a; *(willing)* dispuesto, -a; **r. to** *(about to)* a punto de; **r. cash** dinero *m* en efectivo.

read·y-cooked *adj* precocinado, -a.

read·y-made *adj* confecciona-do, -a; *(food)* preparado, -a.

re·al *adj* verdadero, -a; *(genuine)* auténtico, -a.

re·al es·tate bienes *mpl* inmuebles.

re·al es·tate a·gent agente *mf* inmobiliario, -a.

re·al·is·tic *adj* realista.

re·al·i·ty realidad *f*.

re·al·ize *vt (become aware of)* darse cuenta de; **don't you r. that …?** ¿no te das cuenta de que …?

re·al·ly *adv (truly)* verdaderamente; **r.?** ¿de veras?

re·al·tor agente *mf* inmobiliario, -a.

rear¹ 1 *n (back part)* parte *f* de atrás. **2** *adj* trasero, -a; **r. entrance** puerta *f* de atrás.

rear² 1 *vt (breed, raise)* criar. **2** *vi* **to r. up** *(horse)* encabritarse.

re·ar·range *vt (furniture)* colocar de otra manera; *(set new date)* fijar otra fecha para.

rea·son 1 *n* motivo *m*; **for no r.** sin razón. **2** *vi (argue, work out)* razonar.

rea·son·a·ble *adj (fair)* razonable; *(sensible)* sensato, -a.

rea·son·a·bly *adv (fairly, quite)* bastante.

rea·son·ing razonamiento *m*.

re·as·sure *vt (comfort)* tranquilizar; *(restore confidence in)* dar confianza a.

re·as·sur·ing *adj* consolador, -a.

re·bel 1 *adj & n* rebelde *(mf)*. **2** *vi* rebelarse **(against** contra**)**.

re·bel·lion rebelión *f*.

re·bound 1 *n (of ball)* rebote *m*. **2** *vi (ball)* rebotar.

re·build *vt* reconstruir.

re·call *vt (remember)* recordar.

re·ceipt *(paper)* recibo *m*; **receipts** *(takings)* recaudación *f sing*.

re·ceive *vt* recibir.

re·ceiv·er *(of phone)* auricular *m*; *(radio)* receptor *m*.

re·cent *adj* reciente; **in r. years** en los últimos años.

re·cent·ly *adv* recientemente.

re·cep·tion *(party, of TV pictures etc)* recepción *f*; *(welcome)* acogida *f*; **r. (desk)** recepción *f*.

re·cep·tion·ist recepcionista *mf*.

re·charge *vt (battery)* recargar.

rec·i·pe receta *f*.

re·cip·i·ent receptor, -a *mf*; *(of letter)* destinatario, -a *mf*.

re·cite *vti* recitar.

reck·less *adj (unwise)* imprudente.

reck·on *vt (calculate)* calcular; *fam (think)* creer.

▸ **reckon on** *vt* contar con.

▸ **reckon with** *vt (take into account)* contar con.

re·claim *vt (recover)* recuperar; *(demand back)* reclamar; *(marshland etc)* convertir.

rec·og·nize *vt* reconocer.

rec·ol·lect *vt* recordar.

rec·ol·lec·tion recuerdo *m*.

rec·om·mend *vt* recomendar.

rec·om·men·da·tion recomendación *f*.

re·cord 1 *n (of music etc)* disco *m*; *(in sport etc)* récord *m*; *(document)* documento *m*; *(case history)* historial *m* médico; **public records** archivos *mpl*. **2** *vt (relate)* hacer constar; *(note down)* apuntar; *(music, voice)* grabar.

re·cord·ed *adj* grabado, -a.

re·cord·er *(musical instrument)* flauta *f*; **(tape) r.** magnetófono *m*; **(video) r.** vídeo *m*.

re·cord·ing grabación *f*.

re·cord play·er tocadiscos *m inv*.

re·cov·er 1 *vt (items, time)* recuperar; *(consciousness)* recobrar. **2** *vi (from illness etc)* reponerse; *(economy)* recuperarse.

rec·re·a·tion *(entertainment)* diversión *f*; *(school playtime)* recreo *m*.

re·cruit recluta *m*.

rec·tan·gle rectángulo *m*.

rec·tan·gu·lar *adj* rectangular.

re·cy·cle *vt* reciclar.

red 1 *adj* rojo, -a; **r. light** semáforo *m* en rojo; **r. wine** vino *m* tinto; **to go r.** ponerse colorado, -a; **to have r. hair**

ser pelirrojo, -a. **2** n *(color)* rojo m; **to be in the r.** estar en números rojos.

red-hand·ed *adj* **to catch sb r.** coger a algn con las manos en la masa.

red·head pelirrojo, -a mf.

red-hot *adj* al rojo vivo.

re·di·rect vt *(forward)* remitir a la nueva dirección.

re·do* vt *(exercise, house)* rehacer.

re·duce vt reducir.

re·duc·tion *(decrease)* reducción f; *(cut in price)* descuento m.

re·dun·dan·cy despido m.

re·dun·dant *adj* **to be made r.** perder el empleo; **to make sb r.** despedir a algn.

reed *(plant)* caña f.

reef arrecife m.

reel *(spool)* bobina f, carrete m.

re·fec·to·ry refectorio m.

re·fer 1 vt **to r. a matter to a tribunal** remitir un asunto a un tribunal. **2** vi *(allude)* referirse (**to** a).

ref·e·ree 1 n árbitro, -a mf. **2** vt arbitrar.

ref·er·ence referencia f; *(character report)* informe m; **with r. to** referente a, con referencia a.

ref·er·en·dum referéndum m.

re·fill 1 n *(replacement)* recambio m; *(another drink)* otra copa f. **2** vt rellenar.

re·flect 1 vt *(light, attitude)* reflejar; **to be reflected** reflejarse. **2** vi *(think)* reflexionar.

re·flec·tion *(indication, mirror image)* reflejo m.

re·flex reflejo m.

re·form 1 n reforma f. **2** vt reformar.

re·frain vi abstenerse (**from** de).

re·fresh vt refrescar.

re·fresh·er course cursillo m de reciclaje.

re·fresh·ing *adj* refrescante.

re·fresh·ment refresco m.

re·frig·er·a·tor nevera f.

ref·uge refugio m; **to take r.** refugiarse.

ref·u·gee refugiado, -a mf.

re·fund 1 n reembolso m. **2** vt reembolsar.

re·fus·al negativa f.

re·fuse 1 vt *(reject)* rechazar; **to r. sb sth** negar algo a algn; **to r. to do sth** negarse a hacer algo. **2** vi negarse.

re·gain vt recuperar.

re·gard 1 n *(concern)* consideración f; **with r. to, as regards** (con) respecto a; **give him my regards** dale recuerdos de mi parte. **2** vt *(consider)* considerar.

re·gard·ing *prep* (con) respecto a.

re·gard·less 1 *prep* **r. of** a pesar de; **r. of the outcome** pase lo que pase. **2** *adv* a toda costa.

reg·i·ment regimiento m.

re·gion región f, zona f; **in the r. of** aproximadamente.

re·gion·al *adj* regional.

reg·is·ter 1 n registro m. **2** vt *(record)* registrar; *(letter)* certificar. **3** vi *(enter one's name)* inscribirse; *(at university)* matricularse.

reg·is·tra·tion inscripción f; *(at university)* matrícula f.

re·gret 1 n *(remorse)* remordimiento m; *(sadness)* pesar m. **2** vt arrepentirse de, lamentar.

reg·u·lar 1 *adj* regular; *(usual)* normal; *(frequent)* frecuente.

reg·u·lar·ly *adv* con regularidad.

reg·u·late vt regular.

reg·u·la·tion 1 n *(control)* regulación f; *(rule)* regla f. **2** *adj* reglamentario, -a.

re·hears·al ensayo m.

re·hearse vti ensayar.

reign 1 n reinado m. **2** vi reinar.

rein·deer reno m.

re·in·force vt *(strengthen)* reforzar.

re·in·force·ments npl refuerzos mpl.

reins *(for horse)* riendas fpl.

re·in·state vt *(to job)* reincorporar.

re·ject vt rechazar.

re·jec·tion rechazo m.

re·joice vi regocijarse (**at, over** de).

re·late 1 vt *(connect)* relacionar;

(tell) contar. **2** *vi* relacionarse (**to** con).

re·lat·ed *adj (linked)* relacionado, -a (**to** con); **to be r. to sb** ser pariente de algn.

re·la·tion *(link)* relación *f; (family)* pariente, -a *mf;* **in** *or* **with r. to** (to) respecto a.

re·la·tion·ship *(link)* relación *f; (between people)* relaciones *fpl.*

rel·a·tive 1 *n* pariente, -a *mf.* **2** *adj* relativo, -a.

rel·a·tive·ly *adv* relativamente.

re·lax 1 *vi* relajarse; **r.!** ¡cálmate! **2** *vt (calm)* relajar; *(loosen)* aflojar.

re·lax·a·tion *(rest)* relajación *f.*

re·laxed *adj* relajado, -a.

re·lease 1 *n (setting free)* liberación *f; (of product)* puesta *f* en venta; *(of film)* estreno *m; (press release)* comunicado *m.* **2** *vt (set free)* poner en libertad; *(let go)* soltar; *(product, record)* poner a la venta; *(film)* estrenar.

rel·e·vance pertinencia *f.*

rel·e·vant *adj* pertinente (**to** a); **it is not r.** no viene al caso.

re·li·a·bil·i·ty *(of person)* formalidad *f; (of thing)* fiabilidad *f.*

re·li·a·ble *adj (person)* de fiar; *(thing)* fiable.

re·lief alivio *m; (aid)* auxilio *m; (in art, geography)* relieve *m.*

re·lieve *vt* aliviar; *(substitute)* relevar.

re·li·gion religión *f.*

re·li·gious *adj* religioso, -a.

rel·ish *(seasoning)* condimento *m.*

re·load *vt (gun, camera)* recargar.

re·luc·tance desgana *f.*

re·luc·tant *adj* reacio, -a; **to be r. to do sth** estar poco dispuesto, -a a hacer algo.

re·luc·tant·ly *adv* de mala gana.

▸**re·ly on** *vt (count on)* contar con; *(be dependent on)* depender de.

re·main *vi (stay)* permanecer, quedarse; *(be left)* quedar.

re·main·ing *adj* restante.

re·mark 1 *n* comentario *m.* **2** *vt* comentar.

re·mark·a·ble *adj (extraordinary)* extraordinario, -a.

re·mark·a·bly *adv* extraordinariamente.

re·me·di·al *adj* **r. classes** clases *fpl* para niños atrasados en los estudios.

rem·e·dy 1 *n* remedio *m.* **2** *vt* remediar.

re·mem·ber 1 *vt (recall)* acordarse de. **2** *vi* acordarse.

re·mind *vt* recordar; **r. me to do it** recuérdame que lo haga.

re·mind·er aviso *m.*

re·morse remordimiento *m.*

re·mote *adj (far away)* remoto, -a; *(isolated)* aislado, -a.

re·mote con·trol mando *m* a distancia.

re·mov·al *(moving house)* mudanza *f; (getting rid of)* eliminación *f;* **r. man** hombre *m* de la mudanza; **r. van** camión *m* de mudanzas.

re·move *vt* quitar.

re·new *vt (contract etc)* renovar; *(talks etc)* reanudar.

rent 1 *n (of building, car, TV)* alquiler *m.* **2** *vt* alquilar.

▸**rent out** *vt* alquilar.

rent·al *(of house etc)* alquiler *m.*

rent·al car coche *m* de alquiler.

re·or·gan·ize *vt* reorganizar.

re·pair 1 *n* reparación *f;* **in good/ bad r.** en buen/mal estado. **2** *vt* arreglar; *(car)* reparar; *(clothes)* remendar.

re·pay *vt* devolver; *(debt)* liquidar.

re·pay·ment pago *m.*

re·peat 1 *vt* repetir. **2** *n (repetition)* repetición *f; (on TV)* reposición *f.*

re·peat·ed *adj* repetido, -a.

re·peat·ed·ly *adv* repetidas veces.

re·pel *vt (fight off)* repeler.

rep·e·ti·tion repetición *f.*

re·pet·i·tive *adj* repetitivo, -a.

re·place *vt (put back)* volver a poner en su sitio; *(substitute)* sustituir.

re·place·ment *(person)* sustituto, -a

mf; *(part)* pieza *f* de recambio.

re·play repetición *f*.

rep·li·ca réplica *f*.

re·ply 1 *n* respuesta *f*. **2** *vi* responder.

re·port 1 *n* informe *m*; *(piece of news)* noticia *f*; *(in newspaper, on TV etc)* reportaje *m*; *(rumor)* rumor *m*; **school r.** informe *m* escolar. **2** *vt (tell police, authorities about)* denunciar; *(journalist)* hacer un reportaje sobre; **it is reported that ...** se dice que ... **3** *vi (committee etc)* hacer un informe; *(journalist)* hacer un reportaje; *(to work etc)* presentarse.

re·port·ed *adj* **r. speech** estilo *m* indirecto.

re·port·ed·ly *adv* según se dice.

re·port·er periodista *mf*.

rep·re·sent *vt* representar.

rep·re·sen·ta·tive representante *mf*.

re·pro·duce 1 *vt* reproducir. **2** *vi* reproducirse.

re·pro·duc·tion reproducción *f*.

rep·tile reptil *m*.

re·pub·lic república *f*.

re·pub·li·can *adj & n* republicano, -a *(mf)*; **R. Party** Partido *m* Republicano.

rep·u·ta·ble *adj (company etc)* acreditado, -a; *(person, products)* de toda confianza.

rep·u·ta·tion reputación *f*.

re·quest 1 *n* petición *f*. **2** *vt* pedir.

re·quire *vt (need)* necesitar; *(demand)* exigir.

re·quired *adj* necesario, -a.

res·cue 1 *n* rescate *m*. **2** *vt* rescatar.

re·search 1 *n* investigación *f*. **2** *vti* investigar.

re·search·er investigador, -a *mf*.

re·sem·blance semejanza *f*.

re·sem·ble *vt* parecerse a.

re·sent *vt* ofenderse por.

re·sent·ment resentimiento *m*.

res·er·va·tion reserva *f*.

re·serve 1 *n* reserva *f*; *(in sport)* suplente *mf*; **to keep sth in r.** guardar algo de reserva. **2** *vt* reservar.

re·served *adj* reservado, -a.

res·er·voir embalse *m*, pantano *m*.

res·i·dence *(home)* residencia *f*; *(address)* domicilio *m*.

res·i·dent *adj & n* residente *(mf)*.

res·i·den·tial *adj* residencial.

re·sign 1 *vt* to **r. oneself to sth** resignarse a algo. **2** *vi* dimitir.

res·ig·na·tion *(from a job)* dimisión *f*.

re·sist *vt (not yield)* resistir; *(oppose)* oponerse a; **I couldn't r.** telling her no pude resistir a la tentación de decírselo.

re·sis·tance resistencia *f*.

re·sit *vt (exam)* volver a presentarse a.

re·sort *(recourse)* recurso *m*; *(place)* lugar *m* de vacaciones; **as a last r.** como último recurso; **tourist r.** centro *m* turístico.

▸ **resort to** *vt* recurrir a.

re·source recurso *m*.

re·spect 1 *n (reference)* respeto *m*; **in that r.** a ese respecto; **with r. to** con referencia a. **2** *vt* respetar.

re·spect·a·ble *adj* respetable; *(clothes)* decente.

re·spec·tive *adj* respectivo, -a.

re·spond *vi* responder (**to** a).

re·sponse *(reply)* respuesta *f*, *(reaction)* reacción *f*.

re·spon·si·bil·i·ty responsabilidad *f*.

re·spon·si·ble *adj* responsable (**for** de).

rest¹ 1 *n (break)* descanso *m*; *(peace)* tranquilidad *f*. **2** *vt (lean)* apoyar. **3** *vi* descansar.

rest² the r. *(remainder)* el resto; **the r. of the day** el resto del día; **the r. of the girls** las demás chicas.

res·tau·rant restaurante *m*.

rest·ful *adj* relajante.

rest·less *adj* inquieto, -a.

re·store *vt (give back)* devolver; *(repair)* restaurar.

re·strain *vt* contener; **to r. one's anger** reprimir la cólera; **to r. oneself** contenerse.

re·straint *(restriction)* restricción *f*; *(moderation)* moderación *f*.

re·strict *vt* restringir.

re·strict·ed *adj* restringido, -a; **r. area** zona *f* restringida.

re·stric·tion restricción *f*.

rest·room aseos *mpl*.

re·sult resultado *m*; **as a r. of** como consecuencia de.

re·sume *vt (journey, work, conversation)* reanudar; *(control)* reasumir. **2** *vi* recomenzar.

ré·su·mé resumen *m*.

re·tail 1 *n* **r. price** precio *m* de venta al público. **2** *vt* vender al por menor. **3** *adv* al por menor.

re·tail·er detallista *mf*.

re·tain *vt* conservar.

re·tire *vi (stop working)* jubilarse; *(withdraw)* retirarse; **to r. for the night** irse a la cama.

re·tired *adj* jubilado, -a.

re·tire·ment jubilación *f*.

re·treat 1 *n (of troops)* retirada *f*; *(shelter)* refugio *m*. **2** *vi* retirarse *(from* de).

re·trieve *vt (recover)* recuperar; *(of dog)* cobrar.

re·turn 1 *n (coming or going back)* regreso *m*; *(giving back)* devolución *f*; *(profit)* beneficio *m*; **r. ticket** billete *m* de ida y vuelta. **2** *vt (give back)* devolver. **3** *vi (come or go back)* regresar.

re·turn·a·ble *adj (bottle)* retornable.

re·veal *vt (make known)* revelar; *(show)* dejar ver.

rev·e·la·tion revelación *f*.

re·venge venganza *f*; **to take r. on sb for sth** vengarse de algo en algn.

re·verse 1 *adj* inverso, -a. **2** *n* **quite the r.** todo lo contrario; **r. (gear)** marcha *f* atrás. **3** *vt* **to r. the charges** poner una conferencia a cobro revertido. **4** *vi (in car)* dar marcha atrás; **to r. in/out** entrar/salir marcha atrás.

re·vert *vi* volver **(to** a).

re·view 1 *n (in press)* crítica *f*. **2** *vt (book etc)* hacer una crítica de.

re·vise *vt (look over)* revisar; *(at school)* repasar.

re·vi·sion revisión *f*; *(at school)* repaso *m*.

re·viv·al *(of interest, custom, country)* resurgimiento *m*; *(of play)* reposición *f*.

re·vive *vt (unconscious person)* reanimar.

re·volt rebelión *f*.

re·volt·ing *adj* repugnante.

rev·o·lu·tion revolución *f*.

rev·o·lu·tion·ar·y *adj & n* revolucionario, -a *(mf)*.

re·volve *vi* girar; *fig* **to r. around** girar en torno a.

re·volv·er revólver *m*.

re·volv·ing *adj* giratorio, -a; **r. door** puerta *f* giratoria.

re·ward 1 *n* recompensa *f*. **2** *vt* recompensar.

re·wind* 1 *vt (tape)* rebobinar. **2** *vi* rebobinarse.

rhet·o·ric retórica *f*.

rheu·ma·tism reúma *m*.

rhi·noc·er·os rinoceronte *m*.

rhu·barb ruibarbo *m*.

rhyme 1 *n* rima *f*; *(poem)* poema *m*. **2** *vi* rimar.

rhythm ritmo *m*.

rib costilla *f*.

rib·bon cinta *f*; *(in hair etc)* lazo *m*.

rice arroz *m*.

rich 1 *adj* rico, -a. **2** *npl* **the r.** los ricos.

rich·es *npl* riquezas *fpl*.

rid *vt* **to get r. of sth** deshacerse de algo.

rid·dle *(puzzle)* adivinanza *f*; *(mystery)* enigma *m*.

ride 1 *n* paseo *m*; **a short bus r.** un corto trayecto en autobús; **horse r.** paseo a caballo. **2** *vt* (bicycle, horse)* montar en; **can you r. a bike?** ¿sabes montar en bici? **3** *vi* (on horse)* montar a caballo; *(travel) (on bus, train etc)* viajar.

rid·er *(of horse) (man)* jinete *m*, *(woman)* amazona *f*; *(of bicycle)* ciclista *mf*; *(of motorbike)* motociclista *mf*.

ridge *(of mountain)* cresta *f*.

ri·dic·u·lous *adj* ridículo, -a.

rid·ing equitación *f*.

ri·fle rifle *m*.

rig (oil) r. *(onshore)* torre *f* de perforación; *(offshore)* plataforma *f* petrolífera.

right 1 *adj (not left)* derecho, -a; *(correct)* correcto, -a; *(suitable)* adecuado, -a; *(proper)* apropiado, -a; *(exact) (time)* exacto, -a; **all r.** de acuerdo; **r.?** ¿vale?; **that's r.** eso es; **isn't that r.?** ¿no es verdad?; **the r. word** la palabra justa; **to be r.** tener razón; **the r. time** *(appropriate time)* el momento oportuno; **r. angle** ángulo *m* recto. **2** *n (right side)* derecha *f*; *(right hand)* mano *f* derecha; *(in politics)* derecha *f*; **the R.** la derecha; *(lawful claim)* derecho *m*; **r. and wrong** el bien y el mal. **3** *adv (correctly)* bien; *(to the right)* a la derecha; **r. away** en seguida; **to turn r.** girar a la derecha; **go r. on** sigue recto; **r. at the top** en todo lo alto; **r. in the middle** justo en medio; **r. to the end** hasta el final.

right-hand *adj* derecho, -a.

right-hand·ed *adj (person)* que usa la mano derecha, diestro, -a.

right·ly *adv* debidamente; **and r. so** y con razón.

right-wing *adj* de derechas, derechista.

rig·id *adj* rígido, -a.

rim *(edge)* borde *m*.

rind *(of fruit, cheese)* corteza *f*.

ring¹ 1 *n (of doorbell, alarm clock)* timbre *m*; *(of phone)* llamada *f*. **2** *vt* (bell)* tocar; *(on phone)* llamar por teléfono. **3** *vi* (bell, phone etc)* sonar.

ring² 1 *n* sortija *f*; *(wedding ring)* anillo *m*; *(metal hoop)* aro *m*; *(circle)* círculo *m*; *(group of people)* corro *m*; *(in boxing)* cuadrilátero *m*; *(for bull-fights)* ruedo *m*. **2** *vt (surround)* rodear.

▸**ring out** *vi (bell etc)* resonar.

ring·lead·er cabecilla *mf*.

rinse *vt* aclarar; *(dishes)* enjuagar.

▸**rinse out** *vt* enjuagar.

ri·ot 1 *n* disturbio *m*; **r. police** policía *f* antidisturbios. **2** *vi* amotinarse.

rip 1 *n (tear)* rasgón *m*. **2** *vt* rasgar. **3** *vi* rasgarse.

▸**rip off** *vt fam* **to r. sb off** timar a algn.

▸**rip up** *vt* hacer pedacitos.

ripe *adj* maduro, -a.

rip·en *vti* madurar.

rip-off *fam* timo *m*.

rise 1 *n (of slope, hill)* cuesta *f*; *(in prices, temperature)* subida *f*; *(of wages)* aumento *m*; **to give r. to** ocasionar. **2** *vi* (prices, temperature)* subir; *(wages)* aumentar; *(from bed)* levantarse; *(stand up)* levantarse; *(city, building)* erguirse.

ris·ing 1 *adj (sun)* naciente; *(tide)* creciente; *(prices)* en aumento. **2** *n (rebellion)* levantamiento *m*.

risk 1 *n* riesgo *m*; **at r.** en peligro; **to take risks** arriesgarse. **2** *vt* arriesgar; **I'll r. it** correré el riesgo.

risk·y *adj* arriesgado, -a.

rit·u·al *adj & n* ritual *(m)*.

ri·val 1 *adj & n* rival *(mf)*. **2** *vt* rivalizar con.

riv·er río *m*.

road carretera *f*; *(street)* calle *f*; *(way)* camino *m*; **r. accident** accidente *m* de tráfico; **r. safety** seguridad *f* vial.

road·side borde *m* de la carretera.

road·way calzada *f*.

road·works *npl* obras *fpl*.

roam 1 *vt* vagar por. **2** *vi* vagar.

roar 1 *n (of lion)* rugido *m*; *(of bull, sea, wind)* bramido *m*. **2** *vi (lion, crowd)* rugir; *(bull, sea, wind)* bramar.

roast 1 *adj (meat)* asado, -a; **r. beef** rosbif *m*. **2** *n* asado *m*. **3** *vt (meat)* asar; *(coffee, nuts)* tostar. **4** *vi* asarse.

rob *vt* robar; *(bank)* atracar.

rob·ber ladrón, -a *mf*; **bank r.** atracador, -a *mf*.

rob·ber·y robo *m*.

robe *(ceremonial)* toga *f*; bata *f*.

rob·in petirrojo *m*.

ro·bot robot *m*.

rock 1 *n* roca *f*; *(stone)* piedra *f*; *(music)* música *f* rock. **2** *vt (chair)* mecer; *(baby)* acunar; *(shake)* sacudir. **3** *vi (move back and forth)* mecerse; *(shake)* vibrar.

rock·et 1 *n* cohete *m*. **2** *vi (prices)* dispararse.

rock·ing chair mecedora *f*.

rod *(of metal)* barra *f*; *(stick)* vara *f*; **fishing r.** caña *f* de pescar.

rogue granuja *m*.

role, rôle papel *m*; **to play a r.** desempeñar un papel.

roll 1 *n* rollo *m*; *(bread)* r. bollo *m*; *(of drum)* redoble *m*. **2** *vt* hacer rodar. **3** *vi (ball)* rodar; *(animal)* revolcarse.

▸**roll by** *vi (years)* pasar.

▸**roll down** *vt (blinds)* bajar; *(sleeves)* bajarse; *(hill)* bajar rodando.

▸**roll over** *vi* dar una vuelta.

▸**roll up** *vt (paper etc)* enrollar; *(blinds)* subir; **to r. up one's sleeves** (ar)remangarse.

roll·er rodillo *m*; **rollers** *(for hair)* rulos *mpl*.

roll·er skate patín *m* de ruedas.

roll·ing pin rodillo *m* (de cocina).

roll·ing stock material *m* rodante.

Ro·man *adj & n* romano, -a *(mf)*.

Ro·man Cath·o·lic *adj & n* católico, -a *(mf)* (romano, -a).

ro·mance *(love affair)* aventura *f* amorosa.

ro·man·tic *adj & n* romántico, -a *(mf)*.

roof tejado *m*; *(of car)* techo *m*.

roof rack baca *f*.

room habitación *f*; *(space)* espacio *m*; **single r.** habitación individual; **make r. for me** hazme sitio.

room·mate compañero, -a *mf* de habitación.

room·y *adj* amplio, -a.

root raíz *f*; **to take r.** echar raíces.

▸**root for** *vt* **to r. for a team** animar a un equipo.

▸**root out, root up** *vt* arrancar de raíz.

rope *(small)* cuerda *f*; *(big)* soga *f*.

▸**rope off** *vt* acordonar.

rose rosa *f*; **r. bush** rosal *m*.

rot *vi* pudrirse.

ro·ta·tion rotación *f*.

rot·ten *adj (decayed)* podrido, -a; *fam (very bad)* malísimo, -a; *(health)* enfermo, -a; **I feel r.** me encuentro fatal.

rough *adj (surface, skin)* áspero, -a; *(terrain)* accidentado, -a; *(road)* desigual; *(sea)* agitado, -a; *(rude)* grosero, -a; *(violent)* violento, -a; *(approximate)* aproximado, -a; *(plan etc)* preliminar; **r. draft** borrador *m*; **r. sketch** esbozo *m*.

rough·ly *adv (crudely)* toscamente; *(not gently)* bruscamente; *(approximately)* aproximadamente.

round 1 *adj* redondo, -a. **2** *n (of drinks)* ronda *f*; *(at golf)* partido *m*; *(at cards)* partida *f*; *(in boxing)* round *m*; *(in a competition)* eliminatoria *f*; **rounds** *(doctor's)* visita *f* sing. **3** *adv* **all year r.** durante todo el año; **to invite sb r.** invitar a algn a casa. **4** *prep (place etc)* alrededor de; **r. here** por aquí; **r. the corner** a la vuelta de la esquina.

▸**round up** *vt (cattle)* acorralar; *(people)* reunir.

round·a·bout 1 *n (merry-go-round)* tiovivo *m*; *(on road)* glorieta *f*. **2** *adj* indirecto, -a.

round trip viaje *m* de ida y vuelta.

route ruta *f*; *(of bus)* línea *f*.

rou·tine rutina *f*.

row[1] fila *f*; **three times in a r.** tres veces seguidas.

row[2] *vi (in a boat)* remar.

row[3] **1** *n (quarrel)* bronca *f*; *(noise)* jaleo *m*. **2** *vi* pelearse.

row·boat bote *m* de remos.

row house casa *f* adosada.

roy·al 1 *adj* real. **2** *npl* **the Royals** los miembros de la Familia Real.

roy·al·ty *(royal person(s))* miembro(s) *m(pl)* de la Familia Real; **royalties** derechos *mpl* de autor.

rub 1 *vt* frotar; *(hard)* restregar; *(massage)* friccionar. **2** *vi* rozar *(against* contra).

▸ **rub down** *vt* frotar; *(horse)* almohazar; *(surface)* raspar.

▸ **rub in** *vt (cream etc)* frotar con.

▸ **rub off** *vt (erase)* borrar.

▸ **rub out** *vt* borrar.

rub·ber *(substance)* caucho *m*; *(eraser)* goma *f* (de borrar).

rub·ble escombros *mpl*.

ru·by rubí *m*.

ruck·sack mochila *f*.

rud·der timón *m*.

rude *adj (impolite)* maleducado, -a; *(foul-mouthed)* grosero, -a.

rude·ness *(impoliteness)* falta *f* de educación; *(offensiveness)* grosería *f*.

rug alfombra *f*.

rug·by rugby *m*.

ru·in 1 *n* ruina *f*; **in ruins** en ruinas. **2** *vt* arruinar; *(spoil)* estropear.

rule 1 *n* regla *f*, *(of monarch)* reinado *m*; **as a r.** por regla general. **2** *vti (govern)* gobernar; *(monarch)* reinar.

▸ **rule out** *vt* descartar.

rul·er *(monarch)* soberano, -a *mf*; *(for measuring)* regla *f*.

rul·ing 1 *adj (in charge)* dirigente; **the r. party** el partido en el poder. **2** *n (of judge)* fallo *m*.

rum ron *m*.

Ru·ma·ni·an 1 *adj* rumano, -a. **2** *n (person)* rumano, -a *mf*; *(language)* rumano *m*.

rum·mage sale mercadillo *m* de caridad.

ru·mor 1 *n* rumor *m*. **2** *vt* **it is rumored that** se rumorea que.

run 1 *n (act of running, in stocking)* carrera *f*, *(trip)* vuelta *f*; **on the r.** fugado, -a; **to go for a r.** hacer footing; *(in car)* dar un paseo; **in the long r.** a largo plazo; **ski r.** pista *f* de esquí. **2** *vt** correr; *(business)* llevar; *(company)* dirigir; *(organize)* organizar; **to r. errands** hacer recados; **to r. a program** pasar un programa. **3** *vi* (person, river)* correr; *(color)* desteñirse; *(operate)* funcionar; *(film, play)* estar en cartel; **your nose is running** tienes catarro; **trains r. every two hours** hay trenes cada dos horas; **we're running low on milk** nos queda poca leche.

▸ **run across** *vt (meet)* tropezar con.

▸ **run away** *vi* fugarse.

▸ **run down** *vt (stairs)* bajar corriendo; *(knock down)* atropellar.

▸ **run in** *vi* entrar corriendo.

▸ **run into** *vt (room etc)* entrar corriendo en; *(people, problems)* tropezar con; *(crash into)* chocar contra.

▸ **run off** *vi* escaparse.

▸ **run out** *vi (exit)* salir corriendo; *(finish)* agotarse; *(contract)* vencer; **to r. out of** quedarse sin.

▸ **run over** *vt (knock down)* atropellar.

run·a·way *adj (vehicle)* incontrolado, -a; *(inflation)* galopante; *(success)* clamoroso, -a.

rung *(of ladder)* peldaño *m*.

run·ner-up subcampeón, -ona *mf*.

run·ning 1 *n* atletismo *m*; *(management)* dirección *f*. **2** *adj* **r. water** agua *f* corriente; **three weeks r.** tres semanas seguidas.

run·ny *adj (nose)* que moquea.

run·way pista *f* (de aterrizaje y despegue).

rush 1 *n (hurry)* prisa *f*, *(hustle and bustle)* ajetreo *m*; **there's no r.** no corre prisa. **2** *vt (do hastily)* hacer de prisa; **to r. sb to hospital** llevar a algn urgentemente al hospital. **3** *vi (go quickly)* precipitarse.

▸ **rush around** *vi* correr de un lado a otro.

▸ **rush off** *vi* irse corriendo.

rush hour hora *f* punta.

Rus·sian 1 *adj* ruso, -a. **2** *n (person)* ruso, -a *mf*; *(language)* ruso *m*.

rust 1 *n* herrumbre *f*. **2** *vi* oxidarse.
rust·y *adj* oxidado, -a.
RV *abbr of* **recreational vehicle** autocaravana *f*.
rye centeno *m*; **r. bread** pan *m* de centeno.

S

sack 1 *n (bag)* saco *m*. **2** *vt (employee)* despedir a.
sa·cred *adj* sagrado, -a.
sac·ri·fice 1 *n* sacrificio *m*. **2** *vt* sacrificar.
sad *adj* triste.
sad·den *vt* entristecer.
sad·dle *n (for horse)* silla *f* (de montar).
sad·ly *adv* tristemente.
sad·ness tristeza *f*.
safe 1 *adj (unharmed)* ileso, -a; *(out of danger)* a salvo; *(not dangerous)* inocuo, -a; *(secure, sure)* seguro, -a; **s. and sound** sano, -a y salvo, -a. **2** *n (for money etc)* caja *f* fuerte.
safe·guard 1 *n (protection)* salvaguarda *f*, *(guarantee)* garantía *f*. **2** *vt* proteger, salvaguardar.
safe·ly *adv* con toda seguridad; **to arrive s.** llegar sin accidentes.
safe·ty seguridad *f*.
safe·ty belt cinturón *m* de seguridad.
safe·ty pin imperdible *m*.
sag *vi (roof)* hundirse.
said 1 *pt & pp of* **say**. **2** *adj* dicho, -a.
sail 1 *n (canvas)* vela *f*; *(trip)* paseo *m* en barco; **to set s.** zarpar. **2** *vt (ship)* gobernar. **3** *vi* ir en barco; *(set sail)* zarpar.
sail·board tabla *f* de windsurf.
sail·boat barco *m* de vela.
sail·ing navegación *f*; *(yachting)* vela *f*.

sail·or marinero *m*.
saint *n* santo, -a *mf*; *(before all masculine names except those beginning* **Do** *or* **To**) San; *(before feminine names)* Santa.
sake *n* **for the s. of** por (el bien de); **for your own s.** por tu propio bien.
sal·ad ensalada *f*.
sal·ad bowl ensaladera *f*.
sal·ad dress·ing aliño *m*.
sal·a·ry salario *m*.
sale venta *f*; *(at low prices)* rebajas *fpl*; **for** *or* **on s.** en venta.
sale price *adj (article)* a precio rebajado.
sales·clerk dependiente, -a *mf*.
sales·man vendedor *m*; *(in shop)* dependiente *m*; *(commercial representative)* representante *m*.
sales tax impuesto *m* de venta.
sales·wom·an vendedora *f*, *(in shop)* dependienta *f*, *(commercial representative)* representante *f*.
sa·li·va saliva *f*.
salm·on salmón *m*.
sa·lon salón *m*.
salt 1 *n* sal *f*, **bath salts** sales de baño. **2** *vt (add salt to)* echar sal a.
salt cel·lar salero *m*.
salt·y *adj* salado, -a.
sal·va·tion salvación *f*; **S. Army** Ejército *m* de Salvación.
same 1 *adj* mismo, -a; **at the s. time** al mismo tiempo; **the two cars are the s.** los dos coches son iguales. **2** *pron* el mismo, la misma, lo mismo; **all the s., just the s.** aun así; **it's all the s. to me** (a mí) me da igual.
sam·ple 1 *n* muestra *f*. **2** *vt (wines)* catar; *(dish)* probar.
sand arena *f*.
san·dal sandalia *f*.
sand cas·tle castillo *m* de arena.
sand·pa·per papel *m* de lija.
sand·wich *(roll)* bocadillo *m*; *(sliced bread)* sandwich *m*.
sand·y *adj (earth, beach)* arenoso, -a; *(hair)* rubio, -a, rojizo, -a.
san·i·tar·y s. napkin compresa *f*.

San·ta Claus Papá Noel *m*.

sar·dine sardina *f*.

sat *pt* & *pp* of **sit**.

satch·el cartera *f* (de colegial).

sat·el·lite satélite *m*; **s. dish** antena *f* parabólica.

sat·in satén *m*.

sat·is·fac·tion satisfacción *f*.

sat·is·fac·to·ry *adj* satisfactorio, -a.

sat·is·fy *vt* satisfacer; *(fulfill)* cumplir con.

sat·is·fy·ing *adj* satisfactorio, -a.

sat·u·rate *vt* saturar (with de); **saturated fats** grasas *fpl* saturadas.

Sat·ur·day sábado *m*.

sauce salsa *f*.

sauce·pan cacerola *f*; *(large)* olla *f*.

sau·cer platillo *m*.

Sau·di A·ra·bi·an *adj* & *n* saudita *(mf)*, saudí *(m)*.

sau·na sauna *f*.

sau·sage *(frankfurter)* salchicha *f*; *(cured)* salchichón *m*; *(spicy)* chorizo *m*.

save 1 *vt (rescue)* rescatar; *(put by, computer file)* guardar; *(money)* ahorrar; *(food)* almacenar; **it saved him a lot of trouble** le evitó muchos problemas. **2** *n (in soccer)* parada *f*.

sav·ings *npl* ahorros *mpl*.

sav·ings ac·count cuenta *f* de ahorros.

sav·ings bank caja *f* de ahorros.

saw[1] *n (tool)* sierra *f*. **2** *vti* * serrar.

▸**saw off** *vt* serrar.

saw[2] *pt* of **see**.

sax·o·phone saxofón *m*.

say* *vt* decir; **it is said that …** se dice que …; **that is to s.** es decir; **what does the sign s.?** ¿qué pone en el letrero?; **shall we s. Friday then?** ¿quedamos el viernes, pues?

say·ing refrán *m*.

scab *(on cut)* costra *f*.

scaf·fold·ing andamio *m*.

scald *vt* escaldar.

scale[1] *(of fish, on skin)* escama *f*; *(in boiler)* incrustaciones *fpl*.

scale[2] escala *f*; *(extent)* alcance *m*.

scales *npl* (pair of) **s.** *(shop, kitchen)* balanza *f* sing; *(bathroom)* báscula *f* sing.

scan 1 *vt (text, graphics)* escanear; *(scrutinize)* escrutar; *(glance at)* ojear. **2** *n (by ultrasound)* exploración *f* ultrasónica; *(in gynaecology etc)* ecografía *f*.

scan·dal escándalo *m*; *(gossip)* chismes *mpl*.

Scan·di·na·vi·an *adj* & *n* escandinavo, -a *(mf)*.

scan·ner escáner *m*.

scar cicatriz *f*.

scarce *adj* escaso, -a.

scarce·ly *adv* apenas.

scar·ci·ty escasez *f*.

scare *vt* asustar.

▸**scare away, scare off** *vt* ahuyentar.

scare·crow espantapájaros *m inv*.

scarf *(pl* scarves *or* scarfs*) (long, woolen)* bufanda *f*; *(square)* pañuelo *m*.

scar·let *adj* **s. fever** escarlatina *f*.

scar·y *adj* espantoso, -a; *(film)* de terror.

scat·ter 1 *vt (papers etc)* esparcir; *(disperse)* dispersar. **2** *vi* dispersarse.

sce·nar·i·o *(of film)* guión *m*; *(situation)* situación *f* hipotética.

scene *(in theater etc)* escena *f*; *(place)* lugar *m*; **to make a s.** *(fuss)* montar un espectáculo.

scen·er·y *(landscape)* paisaje *m*; *(in theater)* decorado *m*.

scent *(smell)* olor *m*; *(perfume)* perfume *m*.

sched·ule 1 *n (plan, agenda)* programa *m*; *(timetable)* horario *m*; **on s.** a la hora (prevista); **to be behind s.** llevar retraso. **2** *vt (plan)* programar.

sched·uled *adj* previsto, -a; **s. flight** vuelo *m* regular.

scheme *(plan)* plan *m*; *(project)* proyecto *m*; *(trick)* ardid *m*.

schmuck *fam* lelo, -a *mf*.

schol·ar *(learned person)* erudito, -a *mf; (pupil)* alumno, -a *mf.*

schol·ar·ship *(grant)* beca *f.*

school *(primary)* escuela *f; (secondary)* colegio *m; (university)* universidad *f;* **s. year** año *m* escolar.

school·boy alumno *m.*

school·girl alumna *f.*

school·mate compañero, -a *mf* de clase.

school·teach·er profesor, -a *mf; (primary school)* maestro, -a *mf.*

sci·ence ciencia *f; (school subject)* ciencias *fpl.*

sci·ence fic·tion ciencia-ficción *f.*

sci·en·tif·ic *adj* científico, -a.

scis·sors *npl* tijeras *fpl.*

scold *vt* regañar, reñir.

scone bollo *m.*

scoop *(in press)* exclusiva *f.*

scoot·er *(child's)* patinete *m; (adult's)* Vespa® *f.*

scope *(range)* alcance *m; (freedom)* libertad *f.*

scorch *vt (burn)* quemar; *(singe)* chamuscar.

score **1** *n (in sport)* tanteo *m; (cards, golf)* puntuación *f; (result)* resultado *m; (twenty)* veintena *f; (music)* partitura *f.* **2** *vt (goal)* marcar; *(points)* conseguir. **3** *vi (in sport)* marcar un tanto; *(soccer)* marcar un gol; *(keep the score)* llevar el marcador.

scorn desprecio *m.*

Scot escocés, -esa *mf.*

Scotch *adj* **S. tape®** cinta *f* adhesiva, celo® *m.* **2** *n (whiskey)* whisky *m* escocés.

Scots *adj* escocés, -esa.

Scots·man escocés *m.*

Scots·wom·an escocesa *f.*

scoun·drel canalla *m.*

scout **boy s.** boy *m* scout; **(talent) s.** cazatalentos *m inv.*

scram·ble **1** *vi* trepar; **to s. up a tree** trepar a un árbol. **2** *vt* **scrambled eggs** huevos *mpl* revueltos. **3** *n (climb)* subida *f, fig* **it's going to be a s.** *(rush)* va a ser muy apresurado.

scrap¹ **1** *n (small piece)* pedazo *m;* **scraps** *(of food)* sobras *fpl.* **2** *vt (discard)* desechar; *(idea)* descartar.

scrap² **1** *n (fight)* pelea *f.* **2** *vi* pelearse **(with** con).

scrap·book álbum *m* de recortes.

scrape **1** *vt (paint, wood)* raspar; *(graze)* arañarse. **2** *vi (rub)* rozar. **3** *n (trouble)* lió *m.*

▸**scrape through** *vti (exam)* aprobar por los pelos.

scrap met·al chatarra *f.*

scrap pa·per papel *m* de borrador.

scratch **1** *n (on skin, paintwork)* arañazo *m;* **to be up to s.** dar la talla; **to start from s.** partir de cero. **2** *vt (with nail, claw)* arañar; *(paintwork)* rayar; *(to relieve itching)* rascarse.

scratch·card *n* tarjeta *f* de rasca y gana, *Arg* ≃ raspadita *f.*

scream **1** *n* chillido *m.* **2** *vt (insults etc)* gritar. **3** *vi* **to s. at sb** chillar a algn.

screen *(movable partition)* biombo *m; (cinema, TV, computer)* pantalla *f.*

screw **1** *n* tornillo *m.* **2** *vt* atornillar; **to s. sth down** *or* **in** *or* **on** fijar algo con tornillos.

screw·driv·er destornillador *m.*

scrib·ble *vt (message etc)* garabatear.

script *(of film)* guión *m; (in exam)* examen *m.*

scrub *vt* frotar.

scrub brush estregadera *f.*

scrum *(in rugby)* melée *f,* **s. half** medio *m* melée.

scu·ba div·ing submarinismo *m.*

sculp·ture escultura *f.*

scum *(on liquid)* espuma *f, fig* escoria *f.*

sea mar *m* or *f;* **by the s.** a orillas del mar; **out at s.** en alta mar; **to go by s.** ir en barco.

sea·food mariscos *mpl.*

sea·front paseo *m* marítimo.

sea·gull gaviota *f.*

seal¹ *(animal)* foca *f.*

seal² **1** *n (official stamp)* sello *m; (air-*

tight closure) cierre *m* hermético. **2** *vt (with official stamp)* sellar; *(with wax)* lacrar; *(close)* cerrar.

▸ **seal off** *vt (area)* acordonar.

seam *(in cloth)* costura *f.*

search 1 *vt (files etc)* buscar en; *(building, suitcase)* registrar; *(person)* cachear. **2** *vi* buscar; **to s. through** registrar. **3** *n* búsqueda *f; (of person)* cacheo *m;* **in s. of** en busca de.

sea·shell concha *f* marina.

sea·shore *(beach)* playa *f.*

sea·sick *adj* to get s. marearse.

sea·sick·ness mareo *m.*

sea·side playa *f.*

sea·son[1] *(of year)* estación *f; (for sport etc)* temporada *f;* **high/low s.** temporada *f* alta/baja.

sea·son[2] *vt (food)* sazonar.

sea·son·al *adj* estacional.

sea·son·ing condimento *m.*

sea·son tick·et abono *m.*

seat 1 *n* asiento *m; (place)* plaza *f; (in cinema, theater)* localidad *f; (in government)* escaño *m;* **to take a s.** sentarse. **2** *vt (guests etc)* sentar; *(accommodate)* tener cabida para.

seat·ing asientos *mpl.*

sea·weed alga *f* (marina).

sec·ond[1] **1** *adj* segundo, -a; **every s. day** cada dos días. **2** *n (in series)* segundo, -a *mf; (gear)* segunda *f;* **the s. of October** el dos de octubre. **3** *adv* **to come s.** terminar en segundo lugar.

sec·ond[2] *(time)* segundo *m.*

sec·ond·ar·y *adj* secundario, -a.

sec·ond-class 1 *adj* de segunda clase. **2** *adv* **to travel s.** viajar en segunda.

sec·ond-hand *adj & adv* de segunda mano.

sec·ond·ly *adv* en segundo lugar.

se·cret *adj* secreto, -a; **in s.** en secreto.

sec·re·tar·y secretario, -a *mf.*

se·cret·ly *adv* en secreto.

sec·tion sección *f.*

sec·u·lar *adj (music, art)* profano, -a.

se·cure 1 *adj* seguro, -a; *(window, door)* bien cerrado, -a; *(ladder etc)* firme. **2** *vt (fix)* sujetar; *(window, door)* cerrar bien; *(obtain)* obtener.

se·cure·ly *adv (firmly)* firmemente.

se·cu·ri·ty seguridad *f; (financial guarantee)* fianza *f.*

se·dan *(automobile)* turismo *m.*

se·da·tion sedación *f.*

sed·a·tive *adj & n* sedante *(m).*

see* *vti* ver; **let's s.** a ver; **s. you (later)/soon!** ¡hasta luego/pronto!; **to s. sb home** acompañar a algn a casa.

▸ **see about** *vt (deal with)* ocuparse de.

▸ **see off** *vt (say goodbye to)* despedirse de.

▸ **see out** *vt (show out)* acompañar hasta la puerta.

▸ **see through** *vt fam* **to s. through sb** ver el plumero a algn; **to s. sth through** *(carry out)* llevar algo a cabo.

▸ **see to** *vt (deal with)* ocuparse de.

seed semilla *f; (of fruit)* pepita *f.*

see·ing *conj* **s. that** dado que.

seek* **1** *vt (look for)* buscar; *(ask for)* solicitar. **2** *vi* buscar; **to s. to do sth** procurar hacer algo.

seem *vi* parecer; **I s. to remember his name was Colin** creo recordar que su nombre era Colin; **it seems to me that** me parece que; **so it seems** eso parece.

seem·ing·ly *adv* aparentemente, según parece.

see·saw balancín *m.*

seg·ment segmento *m; (of orange)* gajo *m.*

seize *vt (grab)* agarrar; **to s. an opportunity** aprovechar una ocasión; **to s. power** hacerse con el poder.

sel·dom *adv* rara vez, raramente.

se·lect *vt (thing)* escoger; *(team)* seleccionar.

se·lec·tion *(people or things chosen)* selección *f; (range)* surtido *m.*

se·lec·tive *adj* selectivo, -a.

self-as·sur·ance confianza *f* en uno mismo.

self-as·sured *adj* seguro, -a de uno mismo.

self-con·fi·dence confianza *f* en uno mismo.

self-con·fi·dent *adj* seguro, -a de uno mismo.

self-con·scious *adj* cohibido, -a.

self-con·trol autocontrol *m*.

self-de·fense autodefensa *f*.

self-em·ployed *adj (worker)* autónomo, -a.

self-ev·i·dent *adj* evidente, patente.

self·ish *adj* egoísta.

self-re·spect amor *m* propio.

self-right·teous *adj* santurrón, -ona.

self-serv·ice 1 *n (in shop etc)* autoservicio *m*. **2** *adj* de autoservicio.

sell* 1 *vt* vender. **2** *vi* venderse.

▸**sell out** *vt* we're sold out of sugar se nos ha agotado el azúcar; **sold out** *(sign at theater)* agotadas las localidades.

sell·er vendedor, -a *mf*.

se·mes·ter semestre *m*.

semi- *prefix* semi-.

sem·i·cir·cle semicírculo *m*.

sem·i·co·lon punto y coma *m*.

sem·i·con·duc·tor semiconductor *m*.

sem·i·de·tached casa *f* adosada.

sem·i·fi·nal semifinal *f*.

sem·i·nar seminario *m*.

sem·o·li·na sémola *f*.

sen·ate senado *m*.

sen·a·tor senador, -a *mf*.

send* 1 *vt* enviar; *(cause to become)* volver. **2** *vi* to s. for sb mandar llamar a algn.

▸**send away 1** *vt (dismiss)* despedir. **2** *vi* to s. away for sth escribir pidiendo algo.

▸**send back** *vt (goods etc)* devolver.

▸**send in** *vt (application etc)* mandar; *(troops)* enviar.

▸**send off** *vt (letter etc)* enviar; *(player)* expulsar.

▸**send on** *vt (luggage) (ahead)* facturar.

▸**send out** *vt (person)* echar; *(invitations)* enviar.

▸**send up** *vt* hacer subir; *(make fun of)* burlarse de.

send·er remitente *mf*.

sen·ior 1 *adj (in age)* mayor; *(in rank)* superior; *(with longer service)* más antiguo, -a; **William Armstrong S.** William Armstrong padre. **2** *n (at school)* estudiante *mf* del último curso; **she's three years my s.** *(in age)* me lleva tres años.

sen·sa·tion sensación *f*.

sen·sa·tion·al *adj (marvelous)* sensacional.

sense 1 *n (faculty)* sentido *m*; *(of word)* significado *m*; *(meaning)* sentido *m*; **s. of direction/humor** sentido *m* de la orientación/del humor; **common s.** sentido *m* común; **it doesn't make s.** no tiene sentido; **to come to one's senses** recobrar el juicio. **2** *vt* sentir.

sense·less *adj (absurd)* absurdo, -a.

sen·si·ble *adj (wise)* sensato, -a; *(choice)* acertado, -a; *(clothes, shoes)* práctico, -a.

sen·si·tive *adj* sensible; *(touchy)* susceptible; *(skin)* delicado, -a.

sen·si·tiv·i·ty sensibilidad *f*; *(touchiness)* susceptibilidad *f*.

sen·tence 1 *n* frase *f*; *(legal)* sentencia *f*; **life s.** cadena *f* perpetua. **2** *vt (judge)* condenar.

sen·ti·ment *(sentimentality)* sensiblería *f*; *(feeling)* sentimiento *m*; *(opinion)* opinión *f*.

sep·a·rate 1 *vt* separar *(from* de). **2** *vi* separarse. **3** *adj* separado, -a; *(different)* distinto, -a.

sep·a·rate·ly *adv* por separado.

sep·a·ra·tion separación *f*.

Sep·tem·ber se(p)tiembre *m*.

se·quence *(order)* orden *m*; *(series)* sucesión *f*.

ser·geant sargento m; (of police) cabo m.

se·ri·al (on TV etc) serial m; (soap opera) telenovela f.

se·ries inv serie f.

se·ri·ous adj serio, -a; (causing concern) grave; **I am s.** hablo en serio.

se·ri·ous·ly adv (in earnest) en serio; (dangerously, severely) gravemente.

ser·vant (domestic) criado, -a mf.

serve vt servir; (customer) atender; **it serves him right** bien merecido lo tiene.

▸**serve out, serve up** vt servir.

serv·er (for computers) servidor m.

serv·ice 1 n servicio m; (maintenance) mantenimiento m; **s. (charge) included** servicio incluido. **2** vt (car, machine) revisar.

serv·ice ar·e·a área f de servicio.

serv·ice sta·tion estación f de servicio.

ses·sion sesión f.

set¹ 1 vt* (put, place) poner, colocar; (time, price) fijar; (record) establecer; (mechanism etc) ajustar; **to s. one's watch** poner el reloj en hora; **to s. the table** poner la mesa; **to s. sb free** poner en libertad a algn. **2** vi* (sun, moon) ponerse; (jelly, jam) cuajar; **to s. to** (begin) ponerse a. **3** n (stage) (for film) plató m; (in theater) escenario m; (scenery) decorado m; **shampoo and s.** lavado y marcado m. **4** adj (task, idea) fijo, -a; (date, time) señalado, -a; (ready) listo, -a; **s. phrase** frase f hecha; **to be s. on doing sth** estar empeñado, -a en hacer algo.

▸**set about** vt (begin) empezar.

▸**set aside** vt (time, money) reservar.

▸**set back** vt (delay) retrasar.

▸**set down** vt (luggage etc) dejar (en el suelo).

▸**set off 1** vi (depart) salir. **2** vt (bomb) hacer estallar; (burglar alarm) hacer sonar.

▸**set out 1** vi (depart) salir; **to s. out for ...** partir hacia ...; **to s. out to do sth** proponerse hacer algo. **2** vt (arrange) disponer; (present) presentar.

▸**set up 1** vt (tent, stall) montar; (business etc) establecer. **2** vi establecerse.

set² (series) serie f; (of golf clubs, keys etc) juego m; (of tools) estuche m; (of people) grupo m; (in math) conjunto m; (tennis) set m; **TV s.** televisor m; **chess s.** juego m de ajedrez.

set·back revés m, contratiempo m.

set·tee sofá m.

set·ting (background) marco m.

set·tle 1 vt (decide on) acordar; (date, price) fijar; (debt) pagar; (account) saldar. **2** vi (bird, insect) posarse; (put down roots) afincarse; **to s. into an armchair** acomodarse en un sillón.

▸**settle down** vi (put down roots) instalarse; (marry) casarse; (child) calmarse; (situation) normalizarse.

▸**settle with** vt (pay debt to) ajustar cuentas con.

set·tle·ment (agreement) acuerdo m; (colony) asentamiento m.

set·tler colono, -a mf.

sev·en adj & n siete (m) inv.

sev·en·teen adj & n diecisiete (m) inv.

sev·enth adj & n séptimo, -a (mf).

sev·en·ti·eth adj & n septuagésimo, -a (mf).

sev·en·ty adj & n setenta (m) inv; **in the seventies** en los (años) setenta.

sev·er·al 1 adj varios, -as. **2** pron algunos, -as.

se·vere adj severo, -a; (climate, blow) duro, -a; (illness, loss) grave.

se·ver·i·ty severidad f.

sew* vti coser.

▸**sew on** vt coser.

▸**sew up** vt (mend) remendar.

sew·er alcantarilla f.

sew·ing costura f.

sew·ing ma·chine máquina f de coser.

sex sexo m; **s. education** educación f sexual; **to have s. with sb** tener relaciones sexuales con algn.

sex·u·al adj sexual.

sex·y adj sexy.

sh! interj ¡chitón!, ¡chh!

shab·by adj (garment) raído, -a; (unkempt) desaseado, -a.

shade (shadow) sombra f; (lampshade) pantalla f; (of color) matiz m; **in the s.** a la sombra.

shad·ow sombra f.

shad·y adj (place) a la sombra.

shaft (of tool) mango m; (of mine) pozo m; (of elevator) hueco m; (beam of light) rayo m.

shake* 1 vt sacudir; (bottle) agitar; **the news shook him** la noticia le conmocionó; **to s. hands with sb** estrechar la mano a algn; **to s. one's head** negar con la cabeza. **2** vi (person, building) temblar.

shall v aux (used to form future tense) (first person only) **I s.** (or **I'll**) **buy it** lo compraré; **I s. not** (or **I shan't**) **say anything** no diré nada.
• (used to form questions) (usually first person) **s. I close the door?** ¿cierro la puerta?; **s. we go?** ¿nos vamos?

shal·low adj poco profundo, -a.

shame vergüenza f; (pity) pena f; **what a s.!** ¡qué lástima!

shame·ful adj vergonzoso, -a.

sham·poo 1 n champú m. **2** vt (one's hair) lavarse.

shape forma f; **to take s.** tomar forma; **in good/bad s.** (condition) en buen/mal estado; **to be in good s.** (health) estar en forma.

share 1 n (portion) parte f; (financial) acción f. **2** vt (divide) dividir; (have in common) compartir.

▸**share in** vt participar en.

▸**share out** vt repartir.

share·hold·er accionista mf.

shark (fish) tiburón m.

sharp 1 adj (razor, pencil, knife) afilado, -a; (needle) puntiagudo, -a; (bend) cerrado, -a; (pain, cry) agudo, -a. **2** adv **at 2 o'clock s.** a las dos en punto.

sharp·en vt (knife) afilar; (pencil) sacar punta a.

sharp·en·er sacapuntas m.

sharp·ly adv (abruptly) bruscamente.

shat·ter 1 vt hacer añicos. **2** vi hacerse añicos.

shave 1 n afeitado m; **to have a s.** afeitarse. **2** vt (person) afeitar. **3** vi afeitarse.

shav·er (electric) s. máquina f de afeitar.

shav·ing brush brocha f de afeitar.

shav·ing cream crema f de afeitar.

shawl chal m.

she pers pron ella.

shed¹ (in garden) cobertizo m; (workmen's storage) barraca f.

shed² vt (blood, tears) derramar.

sheep inv oveja f.

sheep·skin piel f de carnero.

sheer adj (utter) total, puro, -a; (cliff) escarpado, -a; (drop) vertical; (stockings) fino, -a.

sheet (on bed) sábana f; (of paper) hoja f; (of tin, glass, plastic) lámina f; (of ice) capa f.

shelf (pl shelves) (on bookcase) estante m; **shelves** estantería f.

shell 1 n (of egg, nut) cáscara f; (of tortoise etc) caparazón m; (of snail etc) concha f; (from gun) obús m. **2** vt (peas) desvainar; (with guns) bombardear.

shell·fish inv marisco m; mariscos mpl.

shel·ter 1 n (protection) abrigo m; **to take s.** refugiarse (**from** de); **bus s.** marquesina f. **2** vt proteger. **3** vi refugiarse.

shelv·ing estanterías fpl.

shep·herd pastor m.

sher·iff sheriff m.

sher·ry jerez m.

shield n escudo m; (of policeman) placa f. 2 vt proteger (**from** de).

shift 1 n (change) cambio m; (period of work, group of workers) turno m; **(gear) s.** cambio m de velocidades. **2** vt (change) cambiar; (move) cambiar de sitio. **3** vi (move) mover; (change place) cambiar de sitio.

shin espinilla f.

shine 1 vi* brillar. **2** vt (lamp)* dirigir; (pt & pp **shined**) (polish) sacar brillo a; (shoes) limpiar. **3** n brillo m.

shin·y adj brillante.

ship barco m.

ship·ping barcos mpl.

ship·wreck 1 n naufragio m. **2** vt **to be shipwrecked** naufragar.

ship·yard astillero m.

shirt camisa f.

shiv·er 1 vi (with cold) tiritar; (with fear) temblar. **2** n escalofrío m.

shock 1 n (jolt) choque m; (scare) susto m; (in medical sense) shock m. **2** vt (scandalize) escandalizar.

shock ab·sorb·er amortiguador m.

shock·ing adj (causing horror) espantoso, -a; (disgraceful) escandaloso, -a.

shoe zapato m; **shoes** calzado m sing.

shoe·lace cordón m (de zapatos).

shoe pol·ish betún m.

shoot 1 n (on plant) brote m; (of vine) sarmiento m. **2** vt* (fire on) pegar un tiro a; (wound) herir (de bala); (kill) matar; (execute) fusilar; (film) rodar, filmar; (with still camera) fotografiar. **3** vi* (with gun) disparar (at **sb** sobre, a algn).

▸**shoot down** vt (aircraft) derribar.

▸**shoot off** vi (leave quickly) salir a escape.

▸**shoot up** vi (prices) dispararse.

shoot·ing 1 n (shots) tiros mpl; (murder) asesinato m; (hunting) caza f; (of film) rodaje m. **2** adj (pain) punzante.

shoot·ing star estrella f fugaz.

shop 1 n tienda f; (large store) almacén m. **2** vi hacer compras; **to go shopping** ir de compras.

shop as·sis·tant dependiente, -a mf.

shop·keep·er tendero, -a mf.

shop·ping (purchases) compras fpl.

shop·ping bag bolsa f de la compra.

shop·ping bas·ket cesta f de la compra.

shop·ping cen·ter centro m comercial.

shop win·dow escaparate m.

shore (of sea, lake) orilla f; (coast) costa f.

short 1 adj corto, -a; (not tall) bajo, -a; **in a s. while** dentro de un rato; **in the s. term** a corto plazo; **'Bob' is s. for 'Robert'** 'Bob' es el diminutivo de 'Robert'; **to be s. of food** andar escaso, -a de comida. **2** adv **to cut s.** (vacation) interrumpir; (meeting) suspender; **we're running s. of coffee** se nos está acabando el café.

short·age escasez f.

short·cut atajo m.

short·en vt (skirt, visit) acortar.

short·hand typ·ist taquimecanógrafo, -a mf.

short·ly adv (soon) dentro de poco; **s. after** poco después.

shorts npl **a pair of s.** un pantalón corto; (underpants) unos calzoncillos.

short·sight·ed adj (person) miope.

short-term adj a corto plazo.

shot¹ (act, sound) disparo m; (sport) tiro m (a puerta); (photography) foto f; (in film) toma f.

shot² pt & pp of **shoot**.

shot·gun escopeta f.

should v aux (duty) deber; **all employees s. wear helmets** todos los empleados deben llevar casco; **he s. have been an architect** debería haber sido arquitecto. ▪ *(probability)* deber de; **he s. have finished by now** ya debe de haber acabado. ▪ *(conditional use)* **if anything strange s. happen** si pasara algo raro; **I s. like to ask a question** quisiera hacer una pregunta.

shoul·der hombro *m; (beside road)* arcén *m*.

shoul·der bag bolso *m* (de bandolera).

shout 1 *n* grito *m*. **2** *vti* gritar; **to s. at sb** gritar a algn.

shout·ing gritos *mpl*.

shove 1 *n* empujón *m*. **2** *vt* empujar. **3** *vi* empujar; *(jostle)* dar empellones.

shov·el 1 *n* pala *f*. **2** *vt* mover con pala.

show 1 *vt* (ticket etc)* mostrar; *(painting etc)* exponer; *(film)* poner; *(latest plans etc)* presentar; *(teach)* enseñar; *(temperature, way etc)* indicar; **to s. sb to the door** acompañar a algn hasta la puerta. **2** *vi* (be visible)* notarse; **what's showing?** *(at cinema)* ¿qué ponen? **3** *n (entertainment)* espectáculo *m*; **on s.** expuesto, -a; **boat s.** salón *m* náutico; **motor s.** salón *m* del automóvil.

▸**show off 1** *vt (flaunt)* hacer alarde de. **2** *vi* farolear.

▸**show up 1** *vt (embarrass)* dejar en evidencia. **2** *vi (arrive)* aparecer.

show·er *(rain)* chaparrón *m; (bath)* ducha *f*; **to have a s.** ducharse.

show·ing *(cinema performance)* sesión *f*.

show-off farolero, -a *mf*.

shrimp camarón *m*.

shrink* 1 *vt* encoger. **2** *vi* encoger(se).

shrub arbusto *m*.

shrug *vt* **to s. one's shoulders** encogerse de hombros.

shud·der *vi (person)* estremecerse.

shuf·fle *vt (cards)* barajar.

shut 1 *vt** cerrar. **2** *vi** cerrarse. **3** *adj* cerrado, -a.

▸**shut down 1** *vt (factory)* cerrar. **2** *vi (factory)* cerrar.

▸**shut off** *vti (gas, water etc)* cortar.

▸**shut out** *vt (lock out)* dejar fuera a.

▸**shut up 1** *vt (close)* cerrar; *(imprison)* encerrar. **2** *vi (keep quiet)* callarse.

shut·ter *(on window)* postigo *m*.

shut·tle *(plane)* puente *m* aéreo; **(space) s.** transbordador *m* espacial.

shy *adj (timid)* tímido, -a; *(reserved)* reservado, -a.

shy·ness timidez *f*.

sick *adj (ill)* enfermo, -a; *fam (fed up)* harto, -a; **s. leave** baja *f* por enfermedad; **to feel s.** *(about to vomit)* tener ganas de devolver; **to be s.** devolver.

sick·ness *(illness)* enfermedad *f; (nausea)* náuseas *fpl*.

side *n* lado *m; (of coin etc)* cara *f, (of hill)* ladera *f, (edge)* borde *m; (of lake, river)* orilla *f, (team)* equipo *m; (in politics)* partido *m*; **by the s. of** junto a; **by my s.** a mi lado; **s. by s.** juntos; **she's on our s.** está de nuestro lado; **to take sides with sb** ponerse de parte de algn.

side·board aparador *m*.

side·burns *npl* patillas *fpl*.

side·light piloto *m*.

side·walk acera *f*.

side·ways *adv* de lado.

sid·ing *(on railroad)* apartadero *m*, vía *f* muerta.

siege sitio *m*, cerco *m*; **to lay s. to** sitiar.

sieve colador *m; (coarse)* criba *f*.

sift *vt* tamizar.

sigh 1 *vi* suspirar. **2** *n* suspiro *m*.

sight *(faculty)* vista *f, (spectacle)* espectáculo *m*; **at first s.** a primera vista; **to catch s. of** divisar; **to lose s. of sth/sb** perder algo/a algn de vista; **within s.** a la vista.

sight·see·ing **to go s.** hacer turismo.

sign 1 *n (signal)* señal *f, (trace)* rastro *m; (notice)* anuncio *m; (board)* letrero *m*. **2** *vti (letter etc)* firmar.

▸**sign on** vi (worker) firmar un contrato; (unemployed person) apuntarse al paro.

▸**sign up** vi (soldier) alistarse; (worker) firmar un contrato.

sig·nal 1 n señal f. **2** vt (direction etc) indicar.

sig·na·ture firma f.

sig·nif·i·cant adj (important) importante.

sig·nif·i·cant·ly adv (markedly) sensiblemente.

sig·ni·fy vt (mean) significar; (show, make known) indicar.

sign·post poste m indicador.

si·lence 1 n silencio m. **2** vt acallar.

si·lent adj silencioso, -a; (film) mudo, -a; **to remain s.** guardar silencio.

si·lent·ly adv silenciosamente.

silk seda f.

sill (of window) alféizar m.

sil·ly adj (stupid) tonto, -a; (ridiculous) ridículo, -a.

sil·ver 1 n (metal) plata f; (tableware) vajilla f de plata. **2** adj de plata; **s. paper** papel m de plata.

sil·ver·plat·ed adj plateado, -a.

sil·ver·ware vajilla f de plata.

sim·i·lar adj semejante (**to** a); **to be s.** parecerse.

sim·i·lar·i·ty semejanza f.

sim·ple adj sencillo, -a.

sim·pli·fy vt simplificar.

sim·ply adv (only) simplemente; (just, merely) meramente.

si·mul·ta·ne·ous adj simultáneo, -a.

si·mul·ta·ne·ous·ly adv simultáneamente.

sin pecado m.

since 1 adv (ever) **s.** desde entonces. **2** prep desde; **she has been living here s. 1975** vive aquí desde 1975. **3** conj (time) desde que; **how long is it s. you last saw him?** ¿cuánto tiempo hace (desde) que lo viste por última vez? ▪ (because, as) ya que.

sin·cere adj sincero, -a.

sin·cere·ly adv sinceramente; **Yours s.** (in letter) (le saluda) atentamente.

sin·cer·i·ty sinceridad f.

sing* vti cantar.

sing·er cantante mf.

sin·gle 1 adj solo, -a; (unmarried) soltero, -a; **s. bed/room** cama f/habitación f individual. **2** n (record) single m.

▸**single out** vt (choose) escoger.

sin·gle·mind·ed adj resuelto, -a.

sin·gu·lar 1 adj (noun form etc) singular. **2** n singular m.

sin·gu·lar·ly adv excepcionalmente.

sin·is·ter adj siniestro, -a.

sink¹ (in kitchen) fregadero m.

sink²* vi (ship) hundirse.

▸**sink in** vi (penetrate) penetrar; fig causar impresión.

sip vt beber a sorbos.

sir señor m; (title) sir.

si·ren sirena f.

sis·ter hermana f.

sis·ter-in-law cuñada f.

sit* 1 vt (child etc) sentar (**in, on** en); (exam) presentarse a. **2** vi (action) sentarse; (be seated) estar sentado, -a.

▸**sit around** vi holgazanear.

▸**sit down** vi sentarse.

▸**sit up** vi incorporarse.

site (area) lugar m; **building s.** solar m; (under construction) obra f.

sit·ting room sala f de estar.

sit·u·at·ed adj **to be s.** estar situado, -a.

sit·u·a·tion situación f.

six adj & n seis (m) inv.

six·teen adj & n dieciséis (m) inv.

sixth 1 adj sexto, -a. **2** n (in series) sexto, -a mf; (fraction) sexto m.

six·ti·eth adj & n sexagésimo, -a (mf).

six·ty adj & n sesenta (m) inv.

size tamaño m; (of garment) talla f; (of shoes) número m; (of person) estatura f.

skate 1 n patín m. **2** vi patinar.

skate·board monopatín m.

skat·er patinador, -a mf.

skat·ing patinaje m.

skat·ing rink pista f de patinaje.

skel·e·ton esqueleto m.

sketch 1 n (preliminary drawing) bosquejo m; (on TV etc) sketch m. **2** vt (preliminary drawing) bosquejar.

skew·er pincho m, broqueta f.

ski 1 n esquí m. **2** vi esquiar; **to go skiing** ir a esquiar.

skid 1 n patinazo m. **2** vi patinar.

ski·er esquiador, -a mf.

ski·ing esquí m.

skilled adj (dextrous) hábil, diestro, -a; (expert) experto, -a; (worker) cualificado, -a.

skill·ful adj hábil.

ski lift telesquí m; (with seats) telesilla f.

skill (ability) habilidad f; (technique) técnica f.

skilled adj (worker) cualificado, -a.

skim milk leche f desnatada.

skin piel f; (of face) cutis m; (complexion) tez f; (of fruit) piel f.

skin-div·ing submarinismo m.

skin·ny adj flaco, -a.

skip¹ 1 vi (jump) saltar, brincar; (with rope) saltar a la comba. **2** vt (omit) saltarse.

skip² (container) contenedor m.

skirt falda f.

skull calavera f; (cranium) cráneo m.

sky cielo m; **s. blue** azul m celeste.

sky·scrap·er rascacielos m inv.

slack adj (not taut) flojo, -a; **business is s.** hay poco negocio.

slack·en vt (rope) aflojar; (speed) reducir.

slacks npl pantalones mpl.

slam 1 n (of door) portazo m. **2** vt (bang) cerrar de golpe; **to s. the door** dar un portazo. **3** vi cerrarse de golpe.

slang jerga f popular.

slant 1 n inclinación f. **2** vi inclinarse.

slap 1 n palmada f; (in face) bofetada f. **2** vt pegar con la mano; (hit in face) dar una bofetada a; **to s. sb on the back** dar a algn una palmada en la espalda.

slate pizarra f.

slaugh·ter 1 n (of animals) matanza f; (of people) carnicería f. **2** vt (animals) matar; (people) masacrar.

slave esclavo, -a mf.

slav·er·y esclavitud f.

sleep 1 n sueño m. **2** vi* dormir; **to go to s.** dormirse.

▸**sleep in** vi (oversleep) quedarse dormido, -a.

sleep·er (on train) (coach) coche-cama m; (berth) litera f.

sleep·ing bag saco m de dormir.

sleep·ing car coche-cama m.

sleep·ing pill somnífero m.

sleep·y adj **to be** or **feel s.** tener sueño.

sleet 1 n aguanieve f. **2** vi **it's sleeting** cae aguanieve.

sleeve (of garment) manga f; (of record) funda f.

sleigh trineo m.

slen·der adj (thin) delgado, -a; fig (hope, chance) remoto, -a.

slept pt & pp of **sleep**.

slice 1 n (of bread) rebanada f; (of cake) trozo m; (of meat) loncha f. **2** vt (food) cortar en rodajas.

slide 1 n (in playground) tobogán m; (photographic) diapositiva f; **s. projector** proyector m de diapositivas. **2** vt* deslizar; (furniture) correr. **3** vi* deslizarse; (slip) resbalar.

slid·ing adj (door, window) corredizo, -a.

slight adj (small) pequeño, -a; (trivial) leve; **not in the slightest** en absoluto.

slight·ly adv (a little) ligeramente.

slim 1 adj (person) delgado, -a; (slender) esbelto, -a. **2** vi adelgazar.

slim·y adj (slimier, slimiest) (muddy) lodoso, -a; (snail) baboso, -a; fig (person) zalamero, -a.

sling 1 n (for arm) cabestrillo m. **2** vt* (throw) tirar.

slip 1 n (mistake) error m; (moral) desliz m; (under skirt) combinación f; (of paper) papelito m. **2** vi (slide) resbalar. **3** vt **to s. sth into sth** meter algo en algo; **to s. sth to sb** dar algo a algn con disimulo.

▸**slip away** vi (person) escabullirse.

▸**slip off** vt (clothes) quitarse rápidamente.

▸**slip on** vt (clothes) ponerse rápidamente.

▸**slip out** vi (leave) salir.

▸**slip up** vi (make a mistake) equivocarse.

slip·per zapatilla f.

slip·per·y adj resbaladizo, -a.

slit (opening) hendidura f; (cut) raja f.

slo·gan (e)slogan m, lema m.

slope 1 n (incline) cuesta f; (of mountain) ladera f; (of roof) vertiente f. **2** vi inclinarse.

slop·ing adj inclinado, -a.

slot (for coin) ranura f; (opening) rendija f.

slot ma·chine (for gambling) (máquina f) tragaperras f inv; (vending machine) distribuidor m automático.

slow 1 adj lento, -a; (clock) atrasado, -a; (stupid) torpe; **in s. motion** a cámara lenta; **to be s. to do sth** tardar en hacer algo. **2** adv despacio.

▸**slow down, slow up** vi ir más despacio; (in car) reducir la velocidad.

slow·ly adv despacio.

slug (animal) babosa f.

slump 1 n (drop in sales etc) bajón m; (economic depression) crisis f económica. **2** vi (sales etc) caer de repente; (prices) desplomarse; (the economy) hundirse.

slums barrios bajos mpl.

sly adj (cunning) astuto, -a.

smack 1 n (slap) bofetada f. **2** vt (slap) dar una bofetada a; (hit) golpear.

small adj pequeño, -a; (in height) bajo, -a; **s. change** cambio m.

small·pox viruela f.

smart adj (elegant) elegante; (clever) listo, -a.

smash 1 vt (break) romper; (shatter) hacer pedazos. **2** vi (break) romperse; (shatter) hacerse pedazos.

▸**smash into** vt (vehicle) estrellarse contra.

smash·ing adj fam estupendo, -a.

smell 1 n (sense) olfato m; (odor) olor m. **2** vt* oler. **3** vi* oler (of a); (stink) apestar; **it smells good/like lavender** huele bien/a lavanda.

smell·y adj (smellier, smelliest) fam maloliente, apestoso, -a.

smile 1 n sonrisa f. **2** vi sonreír.

smock (blouse) blusón m.

smoke 1 n humo m. **2** vi fumar; (chimney etc) echar humo. **3** vt (tobacco) fumar; **to s. a pipe** fumar en pipa.

smok·er (person) fumador, -a mf; (compartment) vagón m de fumadores.

smooth adj (surface) liso, -a; (skin) suave; (beer, wine) suave; (flight) tranquilo, -a.

▸**smooth out** vt (creases) alisar.

▸**smooth over** vt **to s. things over** limar asperezas.

smooth·ly adv sobre ruedas.

smug·gle vt pasar de contrabando.

smug·gler contrabandista mf.

smug·gling contrabando m.

snack bocado m.

snack bar cafetería f.

snail caracol m.

snake (big) serpiente f; (small) culebra f.

snap 1 n (photo) (foto f) instantánea f. **2** vt (branch etc) partir (en dos). **3** vi (break) romperse.

▸**snap off** vt (branch etc) arrancar.

snap·shot (foto f) instantánea f.

snatch 1 vt (grab) arrebatar. **2** vi **to s. at** intentar agarrar.

sneak·ers *npl* zapatillas *fpl* de deporte.

sneer *vi* to s. at hacer un gesto de desprecio a.

sneeze 1 *n* estornudo *m*. **2** *vi* estornudar.

sniff *vt (flower etc)* oler.

snip *vt* cortar a tijeretazos.

snook·er billar *m* ruso.

snore 1 *n* ronquido *m*. **2** *vi* roncar.

snor·ing ronquidos *mpl*.

snow 1 *n* nieve *f*. **2** *vi* nevar; **it's snowing** está nevando.

snow·ball bola *f* de nieve.

snow·drift ventisquero *m*.

snow·flake copo *m* de nieve.

snow·man hombre *m* de nieve.

snow·plow quitanieves *m inv*.

snow·storm nevada *f*.

so 1 *adv (to such an extent)* tanto; **he was so tired that …** estaba tan cansado que …; **so long!** ¡hasta luego! ▪ *(degree)* tanto; **we loved her so (much)** la queríamos tanto; **so many books** tantos libros. ▪ *(thus, in this way)* así; **and so on, and so forth** y así sucesivamente; **if so** en este caso; **I think/hope so** creo/espero que sí. ▪ *(also)* **I'm going to Spain — so am I** voy a España — yo también. **2** *conj (expresses result)* así que; **so you like England, do you?** así que te gusta Inglaterra, ¿no? ▪ *(expresses purpose)* para que; **I'll put the key here so (that) everyone can see it** pongo la llave aquí para que todos la vean.

soak 1 *vt (washing, food)* remojar. **2** *vi (washing, food)* estar en remojo.

▸**soak up** *vt* absorber.

soaked through *adj (person)* empapado, -a.

soak·ing *adj (object)* empapado, -a; *(person)* calado, -a hasta los huesos.

soap jabón *m*.

soap flakes jabón *m* en escamas.

soap pow·der jabón *m* en polvo.

soap·y *adj* jabonoso, -a.

sob 1 *n* sollozo *m*. **2** *vi* sollozar.

so·ber *adj (not drunk, moderate)* sobrio, -a.

soc·cer fútbol *m*.

soc·cer play·er futbolista *mf*.

so·cial *adj* social; **s. climber** arribista *mf*, **s. security** seguridad *f* social; **s. welfare** seguro *m* social; **s. work** asistencia *f* social; **s. worker** asistente, -a *mf* social.

so·cial·ist *adj & n* socialista *(mf)*.

so·ci·e·ty sociedad *f*.

sock calcetín *m*.

sock·et *(for electricity)* enchufe *m*.

so·da s. water soda *f*, *(fizzy drink)* gaseosa *f*.

so·fa sofá *m*; **s. bed** sofá *m* cama.

soft *adj (not hard)* blando, -a; *(skin, color, hair, light, music)* suave; *(drink)* no alcohólico, -a; **s. drinks** refrescos *mpl*.

soft·ball = juego parecido al béisbol jugado en un campo más pequeño y con una pelota más blanda.

soft·en 1 *vt (leather, heart)* ablandar; *(skin)* suavizar. **2** *vi (leather, heart)* ablandarse; *(skin)* suavizarse.

soft·ly *adv (gently)* suavemente; *(quietly)* silenciosamente.

soft·ware software *m*; **s. package** paquete *m*.

soil *(earth)* tierra *f*.

so·lar *adj* solar.

sol·dier soldado *mf*.

sole¹ *(of foot)* planta *f*, *(of shoe, sock)* suela *f*.

sole² *(fish)* lenguado *m*.

sole·ly *adv (only)* únicamente; *(entirely)* exclusivamente.

sol·emn *adj* solemne.

so·lic·i·tor abogado, -a *mf*.

sol·id 1 *adj (not liquid)* sólido, -a; *(firm)* firme; *(not hollow, pure) (metal)* macizo, -a; *(reliable)* formal. **2** *n* sólido *m*.

sol·i·dar·i·ty solidaridad *f*.

so·lo solo *m*.

so·lu·tion solución *f*.

solve *vt* resolver.

sol·vent *adj & n* solvente *(m)*.

some 1 *adj (with plural nouns)* unos, -as, algunos, -as; *(several)* varios, -as; *(a few)* unos, -as cuantos, -as; **there were s. roses** había unas rosas. ▪ *(with singular nouns)* algún, alguna; *(a little)* un poco de; **there's s. wine left** queda un poco de vino. ▪ *(certain)* cierto, -a; **to s. extent** hasta cierto punto. ▪ *(unspecified)* algún, alguna; **s. day** algún día; **s. other time** otro día. ▪ *(quite a lot of)* bastante; **it's s. distance away** queda bastante lejos. **2** *pron* algunos, -as, unos, -as. ▪ *(a few)* unos, -as cuantos, -as. ▪ *(a little)* un poco.

some·bod·y *pron* alguien; **s. else** otro, -a.

some·how *adv (in some way)* de alguna forma; *(for some reason)* por alguna razón.

some·one *pron* = **somebody**.

some·place *adv* = **somewhere**.

som·er·sault *(by acrobat etc)* voltereta *f*.

some·thing *pron & n* algo; **is s. the matter?** ¿le pasa algo?; **s. else** otra cosa; **s. of the kind** algo por el estilo.

some·time *adv* algún día.

some·times *adv* a veces.

some·what *adv* un tanto.

some·where *adv (in some place)* en alguna parte; *(to some place)* a alguna parte.

son hijo *m*.

song canción *f*; *(of bird)* canto *m*.

son-in-law yerno *m*.

soon *adv (within a short time)* dentro de poco; *(quickly)* rápidamente; *(early)* pronto; **s. afterwards** poco después; **as s. as** en cuanto; **as s. as possible** cuanto antes; **I would just as s. stay at home** prefiero quedarme en casa; **I would (just) as s. read as watch TV** tanto me da leer como ver la tele.

soot hollín *m*.

soothe *vt (calm)* tranquilizar; *(pain)* aliviar.

so·phis·ti·cat·ed *adj* sofisticado, -a.

sore 1 *adj (aching)* dolorido, -a; *(painful)* doloroso, -a; *fam (angry)* enfadado, -a; **to have a s. throat** tener dolor de garganta. **2** *n* llaga *f*.

sor·row pena *f*.

sor·ry 1 *adj* **I feel very s. for her** me da mucha pena; **to be s. (about sth)** sentir (algo); **I'm s. I'm late** siento llegar tarde. **2** *interj (apology)* ¡perdón!; *(for repetition)* ¿cómo?

sort 1 *n (kind)* clase *f*, tipo *m*; *(brand)* marca *f*; **it's a s. of teapot** es una especie de tetera. **2** *vt (classify)* clasificar.

▸**sort out** *vt (classify)* clasificar; *(put in order)* ordenar; *(problem)* solucionar.

soul alma *f*.

sound¹ 1 *n* sonido *m*; *(noise)* ruido *m*; **I don't like the s. of it** no me gusta nada la idea. **2** *vt (bell, trumpet)* tocar. **3** *vi (trumpet, bell, alarm)* sonar; *(give an impression)* parecer; **it sounds interesting** parece interesante.

sound² 1 *adj (healthy)* sano, -a; *(in good condition)* en buen estado; *(safe, dependable)* seguro, -a. **2** *adv* **to be s. asleep** estar profundamente dormido, -a.

sound·proof *adj* insonorizado, -a.

soup sopa *f*; *(thin, clear)* caldo *m*.

sour *adj (fruit, wine)* agrio, -a; *(milk)* cortado, -a.

source fuente *f*.

south 1 *n* sur *m*; **in the s. of England** en el sur de Inglaterra. **2** *adj* del sur. **3** *adv (location)* al sur; *(direction)* hacia el sur.

south·bound *adj* (con) dirección sur.

south·east *n & adj* sudeste (*m*).

south·ern *adj* del sur.

south·ern·er sureño, -a *mf*.

south·ward *adj & adv* hacia el sur.

south·west *n & adj* suroeste (*m*).

sou·ve·nir recuerdo *m*.

sov·er·eign·ty soberanía f.

sow* vt sembrar.

space 1 n espacio m; (room) sitio m. **2** vt (also **s. out**) espaciar.

space age era f espacial.

space·ship nave f espacial.

space shut·tle transbordador m espacial.

spa·cious adj espacioso, -a.

spade¹ (for digging) pala f.

spade² (in cards) (international pack) pica f, (Spanish pack) espada f.

spa·ghet·ti espaguetis mpl.

spam n (e-mail) correo m basura.

span vt (river etc) extenderse sobre, atravesar; (period of time etc) abarcar.

Span·iard español, -a mf.

Span·ish 1 adj español, -a. **2** n (language) español m, castellano m; **the S.** los españoles.

spank vt zurrar.

spank·ing cachete m.

spare 1 vt (do without) prescindir de; **can you s. me 10?** ¿me puedes dejar 10?; **I can't s. the time** no tengo tiempo; **there's none to s.** no sobra nada; **s. me the details** ahórrate los detalles. **2** adj (left over) sobrante; (surplus) de sobra; **a s. moment** un momento libre; **s. part** (pieza f de) recambio m; **s. room** cuarto m de los invitados; **s. wheel** rueda f de recambio. **3** n (for car etc) (pieza f de) recambio m.

spark chispa f.

spar·kle vi (diamond, glass) destellar; (eyes) brillar.

spar·kling adj **s. wine** vino m espumoso.

spark·plug bujía f.

spar·row gorrión m.

speak* **1** vt (utter) decir; (language) hablar. **2** vi hablar; **to s. to sb** hablar con algn; **speaking!** ¡al habla!; **who's speaking, please?** ¿de parte de quién?

▸ **speak up** vi hablar más fuerte.

speak·er (in dialog) interlocutor, -a mf; (lecturer) conferenciante mf; (of language) hablante mf; (loudspeaker) altavoz m; **(public) s.** orador, -a mf.

spear lanza f.

spe·cial adj especial.

spe·cial·ist especialista mf.

spe·ci·al·i·ty especialidad f.

spe·cial·ize vi especializarse (**in** en).

spe·cial·ly adv (specifically) especialmente; (on purpose) a propósito.

spe·ci·al·ty especialidad f.

spe·cies inv especie f.

spe·cif·ic adj específico, -a; (precise) preciso, -a; **to be s.** concretar.

spe·ci·fi·ca·tion specifications datos mpl específicos.

spe·ci·men (sample) muestra f; (example) ejemplar m.

spec·ta·cle (display) espectáculo m; **spectacles** (glasses) gafas fpl, Am lentes mpl, Am anteojos mpl.

spec·tac·u·lar adj espectacular.

spec·ta·tor espectador, -a mf.

spec·trum espectro m.

spec·u·late vi especular.

spec·u·la·tion especulación f.

speech (faculty) habla f; (address) discurso m; **to give a s.** pronunciar un discurso.

speed 1 n velocidad f; (rapidity) rapidez f. **2** vi* (exceed speed limit) conducir con exceso de velocidad.

▸ **speed up 1** vt acelerar. **2** vi (person) darse prisa.

speed·boat lancha f rápida.

speed lim·it velocidad f máxima.

speed·om·e·ter velocímetro m.

spell¹* vt (write) escribir; (letter by letter) deletrear; **how is that spelled?** ¿cómo se escribe eso?

spell² (magical) hechizo m.

spell³ (period) período m; (short period) rato m; **cold s.** ola f de frío.

spell·ing ortografía f.

spend* vt (money) gastar (**on** en); (time) pasar.

sphere esfera f.

spice 1 n especia f. **2** vt (food) sazonar.

spic·y adj sazonado, -a; (hot) picante.

spi·der araña f; **s.'s web** telaraña f.

spike (sharp point) punta f.

spill* 1 vt (liquid) derramar. **2** vi (liquid) derramarse.

▸**spill over** vi desbordarse.

spin* vt (wheel etc) hacer girar; (washing) centrifugar.

spin·ach espinacas fpl.

spine (of back) columna f vertebral.

spi·ral espiral f.

spire aguja f.

spir·its npl (alcoholic drinks) licores mpl.

spir·i·tu·al adj espiritual.

spit¹* vti escupir.

spit² (for cooking) asador m.

spite in s. of a pesar de; **in s. of the fact that** a pesar de que.

spite·ful adj (remark) malévolo, -a.

splash 1 vt (spray) salpicar. **2** vi **to s. (about)** (in water) chapotear.

splen·did adj espléndido, -a.

splin·ter (wood) astilla f.

split 1 n (crack) grieta f; (tear) desgarrón m. **2** vt* (crack) hender; (cut) partir; (tear) rajar; (divide) dividir.

▸**split up 1** vt (break up) partir; (divide up) dividir; (share out) repartir. **2** vi (couple) separarse.

spoil* vt (ruin) estropear; (child) mimar.

spoke¹ pt of **speak**.

spoke² (of wheel) radio m.

spo·ken pp of **speak**.

spokes·man portavoz mf.

sponge 1 n esponja f. **2** vt (wash) lavar con esponja.

▸**sponge down** vt lavar con esponja.

sponge cake bizcocho m.

spon·sor 1 vt patrocinar. **2** n patrocinador, -a mf.

spon·ta·ne·ous adj espontáneo, -a.

spool bobina f.

spoon cuchara f; (small) cucharita f.

spoon·ful cucharada f.

sport deporte m.

sports·man deportista m.

sports·wom·an deportista f.

spot 1 n (dot) punto m; (on fabric) lunar m; (stain) mancha f; (pimple) grano m; (place) sitio m; **to decide sth on the s.** decidir algo en el acto. **2** vt (notice) notar; (see) ver.

spot·less adj (very clean) impecable.

spot·light foco m.

spot·ted adj (speckled) moteado, -a.

spouse cónyuge mf.

spout (of jug) pico m; (of teapot) pitorro m.

sprain 1 n esguince m. **2** vt **to s. one's ankle** torcerse el tobillo.

spray 1 n (aerosol) spray m. **2** vt (insecticide, perfume) pulverizar.

spray can aerosol m.

spread 1 n (for bread) pasta f; **cheese s.** queso m para untar. **2** vt* (unfold) desplegar; (lay out) extender; (butter etc) untar; (news) difundir; (rumor) hacer correr; (panic) sembrar. **3** vi* (stretch out) extenderse; (news) difundirse; (rumor) correr; (disease, fire) propagarse.

spread·sheet hoja f de cálculo.

spring¹ (season) primavera f.

spring² 1 n (of water) fuente f; (of watch etc) resorte m. **2** vi* (jump) saltar.

spring·board trampolín m.

spring on·ion cebolleta f.

spring·time primavera f.

sprin·kle vt (with water) rociar (with de); (with sugar) espolvorear (with de).

sprin·kler (for water) aspersor m.

sprout (Brussels) sprouts coles fpl de Bruselas.

spur espuela f.

spurt vi (liquid) chorrear.

spy 1 n espía mf. **2** vi espiar (on a).

spy·ing espionaje m.

square 1 n cuadrado m; (in town) plaza f. **2** adj cuadrado, -a; **a s. meal** una buena comida.

squash¹ vt (crush) aplastar.

squash² (sport) squash m.

squat vi (crouch) agacharse.

squeak vi (hinge, wheel) chirriar; (shoes) crujir.

squeal 1 n chillido m. **2** vi (animal, person) chillar.

squeeze 1 vt apretar; (lemon etc) exprimir; (sponge) estrujar. **2** vi **to s.** in apretujarse. **3** n (pressure) estrujón m; (of hand) apretón m; (hug) abrazo m; (crush) apiñamiento m.

▸**squeeze up** vi (on bench etc) correrse.

squint 1 n bizquera f; **to have a s.** ser bizco, -a. **2** vi ser bizco, -a; **to s. at sth** (with eyes half-closed) mirar algo con los ojos entrecerrados.

squir·rel ardilla f.

squirt 1 vt lanzar a chorro. **2** vi **to s. out** salir a chorros.

St. abbr of **Saint** San, Sto., Sta; abbr of **Street** c/.

stab vt apuñalar.

sta·bil·i·ty estabilidad f.

sta·ble¹ adj estable.

sta·ble² (for horses) cuadra f.

stack 1 n (pile) montón m; fam **stacks of ...** un montón de ... **2** vt (pile up) amontonar.

sta·di·um estadio m.

staff (personnel) personal m; (of army) estado m mayor.

staff·room sala f de profesores.

stag venado m.

stage 1 n (platform) plataforma f; (in theater) escenario m; (of development, journey) etapa f; **in stages** por etapas. **2** vt (play) poner en escena.

stag·ger 1 vi tambalearse. **2** vt (hours, work) escalonar.

stain 1 n mancha f. **2** vt manchar.

stained glass win·dow vidriera f de colores.

stain·less adj (steel) inoxidable.

stair peldaño m; **stairs** escalera f sing.

stair·case escalera f.

stake (stick) estaca f.

stale adj (food) pasado, -a; (bread) duro, -a.

stalk (of plant) tallo m; (of fruit) rabo m.

stalk·er n = persona que sigue o vigila obsesivamente a otra.

stall 1 n (in market) puesto m; (in theater) **stalls** platea f sing. **2** vi (of engine) calarse.

stam·mer 1 n tartamudeo m. **2** vi tartamudear.

stamp 1 n (postage stamp) sello m, Am estampilla f; (with foot) patada f. **2** vt (with postage stamp) poner el sello a; **self-addressed stamped envelope** sobre m franqueado; **to s. one's feet** patear.

▸**stamp out** vt (racism etc) acabar con.

stamp col·lect·ing filatelia f.

stance postura f.

stand 1 n (of lamp, sculpture) pie m; (market stall) puesto m; (at exhibition) stand m; (in stadium) tribuna f; **newspaper s.** quiosco m de prensa. **2** vt* (place) poner, colocar; (tolerate) aguantar. **3** vi* (be upright) estar de pie; (get up) levantarse; (be situated) encontrarse; (remain unchanged) permanecer.

▸**stand around** vi estar sin hacer nada; (wait) esperar.

▸**stand aside** vi apartarse.

▸**stand back** vi (allow sb to pass) abrir paso.

▸**stand by 1** vi (do nothing) quedarse sin hacer nada; (be ready) estar listo, -a. **2** vt (person) apoyar.

▸**stand down** vi fig retirarse.

▸**stand for** vt (mean) significar; (tolerate) aguantar.

▸**stand in** vi sustituir (for -).

▸**stand out** vi (mountain etc, fig person) destacar(se).

▸**stand up** vi (get up) ponerse de

pie; *fig* **to s. up for sb** defender a algn; *fig* **to s. up to sb** hacer frente a algn.

stan·dard 1 *n (level)* nivel *m*; *(criterion)* criterio *m*; *(norm)* estándar *m inv*; **s. of living** nivel de vida. **2** *adj* normal.

stand·by *adj* **s. ticket** billete *m* sin reserva.

stand·ing *adj (not sitting)* de pie.

stand·point punto *m* de vista.

stand·still **at a s.** *(car, traffic)* parado, -a; *(industry)* paralizado, -a; **to come to a s.** *(car, traffic)* pararse; *(industry)* paralizarse.

stank *pt of* **stink**.

sta·ple 1 *n (fastener)* grapa *f.* **2** *vt* grapar.

sta·pler grapadora *f.*

star 1 *n* estrella *f.* **2** *vt (film)* tener como protagonista. **3** *vi (in film)* protagonizar.

stare 1 *n* mirada *f* fija. **2** *vi* mirar fijamente; **to s. at sb** mirar fijamente a algn.

start 1 *n (beginning)* principio *m*; *(of race)* salida *f*; *(advantage)* ventaja *f.* **2** *vt (begin)* empezar, comenzar; **to s. doing sth** empezar a hacer algo. **3** *vi (begin)* empezar, comenzar; *(engine)* arrancar; *(take fright)* asustarse; **starting from Monday** a partir del lunes.

▸**start off** *vi (leave)* salir.

▸**start on** *vt* empezar.

▸**start up 1** *vt (engine)* arrancar. **2** *vi (car)* arrancar.

start·er *(in car)* motor *m* de arranque; *(food)* entrada *f.*

star·tle *vt* asustar.

star·va·tion hambre *m.*

starve *vi* pasar hambre; **to s. to death** morirse de hambre.

starv·ing *adj* **I'm s.!** estoy muerto, -a de hambre.

state 1 *n* estado *m*; **The States** (los) Estados Unidos. **2** *vt* declarar.

state·ment declaración *f*; *(finan-*

cial) estado *m* de cuenta; **monthly s.** balance *m* mensual.

states·man estadista *m.*

stat·ic *adj* estático, -a.

sta·tion estación *f.*

sta·tion·ar·y *adj (not moving)* inmóvil.

sta·tion·er·y *(paper)* papel *m* de escribir; *(pens, ink etc)* artículos *mpl* de escritorio.

sta·tion·mas·ter jefe *m* de estación.

sta·tion wag·on camioneta *f.*

sta·tis·tic estadística *f.*

stat·ue estatua *f.*

stay 1 *n* estancia *f.* **2** *vi (remain)* quedarse; *(reside temporarily)* alojarse; **she's staying with us for a few days** ha venido a pasar unos días con nosotros.

▸**stay away** *vi (not attend)* no asistir; **s. away from her** no te acerques a ella.

▸**stay in** *vi* quedarse en casa.

▸**stay out** *vi* **to s. out all night** no volver a casa en toda la noche.

▸**stay out of** *vt (not interfere in)* no meterse en.

▸**stay up** *vi (not go to bed)* no acostarse; *(fence etc)* mantenerse en pie.

stead·i·ly *adv (improve)* constantemente; *(walk)* con paso seguro; *(gaze)* fijamente; *(rain, work)* sin parar.

stead·y *adj* firme; *(prices)* estable; *(demand, speed)* constante.

steak bistec *m.*

steal* *vti* robar.

steam 1 *n* vapor *m.* **2** *vt (food)* cocer al vapor.

▸**steam up** *vi (window etc)* empañarse.

steam·roll·er apisonadora *f.*

steel acero *m*; **s. industry** industria *f* siderúrgica.

steep *adj (hill etc)* empinado, -a; *(price, increase)* excesivo, -a.

stee·ple aguja *f.*

steer *vt* dirigir; *(car)* conducir; *(ship)* gobernar.

steer·ing wheel volante *m.*

stem *(of plant)* tallo *m*; *(of glass)* pie *m.*

ste·nog·ra·pher taquígrafo *m.*

step 1 *n* paso *m*; *(measure)* medida *f*; *(stair)* peldaño *m*; **s. by s.** poco a poco; **steps** *(outdoor)* escalinata *f sing*; *(indoor)* escalera *f sing.* **2** *vi* dar un paso.

▸ **step aside** *vi* apartarse.

▸ **step back** *vi* retroceder.

▸ **step down** *vi* renunciar; *(resign)* dimitir.

▸ **step forward** *vi* *(volunteer)* ofrecerse.

▸ **step in** *vi* intervenir.

▸ **step into/out of** *vt* *(car etc)* entrar en/salir de.

▸ **step up** *vt* aumentar.

step·broth·er hermanastro *m.*

step·daugh·ter hijastra *f.*

step·fa·ther padrastro *m.*

step·lad·der escalera *f* de tijera.

step·moth·er madrastra *f.*

step·sis·ter hermanastra *f.*

step·son hijastro *m.*

ster·e·o 1 *n* estéreo *m.* **2** *adj* estereo(fónico, -a).

ster·il·ize *vt* esterilizar.

ster·ling *n* libras *fpl* esterlinas.

stew estofado *m*, cocido *m.*

stew·ard *(on plane)* auxiliar *m* de vuelo.

stew·ard·ess *(on plane)* azafata *f.*

stick¹ palo *m*; *(walking stick)* bastón *m.*

stick² **1** *vt* meter; *(with glue etc)* pegar; **he stuck his head out of the window** asomó la cabeza por la ventana. **2** *vi* *(become attached)* pegarse; *(window, drawer)* atrancarse.

▸ **stick down** *vt* *(stamp)* pegar.

▸ **stick on** *vt* *(stamp)* pegar.

▸ **stick out 1** *vi* *(project)* sobresalir; *(be noticeable)* resaltar. **2** *vt* *(tongue)* sacar.

▸ **stick to** *vt* *(principles)* atenerse a.

▸ **stick up** *vt* *(poster)* fijar.

▸ **stick up for** *vt* defender.

stick·er *(label)* etiqueta *f* adhesiva; *(with slogan)* pegatina *f.*

stick·ing plas·ter tirita *f*, curita *f.*

stick·y *adj* pegajoso, -a; *(label)* engomado, -a.

stiff *adj* rígido, -a; *(joint)* entumecido, -a; **to have a s. neck** tener tortícolis.

sti·fle 1 *vt* sofocar. **2** *vi* sofocarse.

sti·fling *adj* sofocante.

still 1 *adv* *(up to this time)* todavía, aún; *(nonetheless)* no obstante; *(however)* sin embargo; *(with comparative)* *(even)* aún; **s. colder** aún más frío. **2** *adj* *(calm)* tranquilo, -a; *(motionless)* inmóvil.

stim·u·late *vt* estimular.

sting 1 *n* picadura *f.* **2** *vt** picar.

stink* *vi* apestar **(of** a).

▸ **stink out** *vt* *(room)* apestar.

stir *vt* *(liquid)* remover.

▸ **stir up** *vt* *(memories, curiosity)* despertar.

stir·rup estribo *m.*

stitch puntada *f*; *(in knitting)* punto *m*; *(for surgery etc)* punto *m* (de sutura).

stock 1 *n* *(goods)* existencias *fpl*; *(selection)* surtido *m*; *(broth)* caldo *m*; **out of s.** agotado, -a; **to have sth in s.** tener existencias de algo; **stocks and shares** acciones *fpl.* **2** *vt* *(have in stock)* tener existencias de.

▸ **stock up** *vi* abastecerse **(on, with** de).

Stock Ex·change Bolsa *f* (de valores).

stock·ing media *f*; **a pair of stockings** unas medias.

Stock Mar·ket Bolsa *f.*

stock·pile *vt* almacenar; *(accumulate)* acumular.

stock·y *adj* (**stockier, stockiest**) *(squat)* rechoncho, -a; *(heavily built)* fornido, -a.

sto·len pp of steal.

stom·ach estómago m; **s. upset** trastorno m gástrico.

stone piedra f.

stool taburete m.

stop 1 n parada f; (break) pausa f; **to come to a s.** pararse; **to put a s. to sth** poner fin a algo. **2** vt parar; (gas, water supply) cortar; (prevent) evitar; **to s. sb from doing sth** impedir a algn hacer algo; **to s. doing sth** dejar de hacer algo. **3** vi (person, moving vehicle) pararse; (cease) terminar; (stay) pararse.

▸ **stop by** vi pasarse; **I'll s. by at the office** me pasaré por la oficina.

▸ **stop off** vi pararse un rato.

▸ **stop up** vt (hole) tapar.

stop-off parada f; (flying) escala f.

stop·o·ver parada f.

stop·watch cronómetro m.

store 1 n (stock) provisión f; (warehouse) almacén m; (shop) tienda f; **department s.** gran almacén m. **2** vt (furniture, computer data) almacenar; (keep) guardar; **to s. (up)** acumular.

store·room despensa f.

stork cigüeña f.

storm tormenta f; (with wind) vendaval m.

storm·y adj (weather) tormentoso, -a.

sto·ry¹ (tale) historia f; (account) relato m; (article) artículo m; (plot) trama f; **tall s.** cuento m chino.

sto·ry² piso m.

stove (for heating) estufa f; (cooker) cocina f; (oven) horno m.

straight 1 adj (not bent) recto, -a; (hair) liso, -a; (honest) honrado, -a; (answer) sincero, -a; (drink) solo, -a. **2** adv (in a straight line) en línea recta; (directly) directamente; (frankly) francamente; **keep s. ahead** sigue todo recto; **s. away** en seguida.

straight·en vt (sth bent) enderezar, poner derecho, -a; (tie, picture) poner bien; (hair) alisar.

▸ **straighten out** vt (problem) resolver.

straight·for·ward adj (easy) sencillo, -a.

strain 1 vt (eyes, voice) forzar; (heart) cansar; (liquid) filtrar; (vegetables, tea) colar. **2** n tensión f; (effort) esfuerzo m; (exhaustion) agotamiento m.

strain·er colador f.

strand (of thread) hebra f; (of hair) pelo m.

strand·ed adj **to leave stranded** dejar plantado, -a.

strange adj (unknown) desconocido, -a; (unfamiliar) nuevo, -a; (odd) extraño, -a.

strang·er (unknown person) desconocido, -a mf; (outsider) forastero, -a mf.

stran·gle vt estrangular.

strap (on bag) correa f; (on dress) tirante m.

straw paja f; (for drinking) pajita f.

straw·ber·ry fresa f; (large) fresón m.

streak (line) raya f; (in hair) reflejo m; **s. of lightning** rayo m.

stream (brook) arroyo m; (current) corriente f; (flow) flujo m.

street calle f; **the man in the s.** el hombre de la calle.

street·car tranvía m.

street lamp farol m.

street map, street plan (plano m) callejero m.

strength fuerza f; (of rope etc) resistencia f; (of emotion, color) intensidad f.

strength·en vt reforzar; (intensify) intensificar.

stress 1 n estrés m; (emphasis) hincapié m; (on word) acento m. **2** vt (emphasize) subrayar; (word) acentuar.

stressed adj (person) estresado(a).

stress·ful adj estresante.

stretch vt (elastic) estirar; (arm, hand) alargar. **2** vi estirarse. **3** n (of *land)* extensión *f; (of time)* intervalo *m.*

▸**stretch out 1** *vt (arm, hand)* alargar; *(legs)* estirar. **2** *vi (countryside, years etc)* extenderse.

stretch·er camilla *f.*

strict *adj* estricto, -a.

strict·ly *adv (categorically)* terminantemente; *(precisely)* estrictamente; **s. speaking** en sentido estricto.

strict·ness severidad *f.*

stride 1 *n* zancada *f.* **2** *vi** **to s. (along)** andar a zancadas.

strike 1 *vt** *(hit)* golpear; *(collide with)* chocar contra; *(match)* encender; *(impress)* impresionar; **the clock struck three** el reloj dio las tres; **it strikes me ...** me parece ... **2** *vi** *(workers)* declararse en huelga. **3** *n (by workers)* huelga *f;* **on s.** en huelga; **to go (out) on s.** declararse en huelga; **to call a s.** convocar una huelga.

▸**strike out** *vi* **to s. out at sb** arremeter contra algn.

▸**strike up** *vt (friendship)* trabar; *(conversation)* entablar; *(tune)* empezar a tocar.

strik·er *(worker)* huelguista *mf.*

strik·ing *adj (eye-catching)* llamativo, -a; *(impressive)* impresionante.

string *(cord, of guitar)* cuerda *f.*

strip¹ *vi (undress)* desnudarse.

strip² tira *f; (of metal)* cinta *f,* lámina *f.*

▸**strip off** *vi (undress)* desnudarse.

stripe raya *f.*

striped *adj* a rayas.

strive* *vi* **to s. to do sth** esforzarse por hacer algo.

stroke 1 *n (blow)* golpe *m; (in swimming)* brazada *f; (illness)* apoplejía *f;* **a s. of luck** un golpe de suerte. **2** *vt* acariciar.

stroll 1 *vi* dar un paseo; **he strolled across the square** cruzó la plaza a paso lento. **2** *n* paseo *m.*

stroll·er *(for baby)* cochecito *m.*

strong *adj* fuerte; *(durable)* sólido, -a.

struc·ture estructura *f; (building)* edificio *m.*

strug·gle 1 *vi* luchar. **2** *n* lucha *f; (physical fight)* pelea *f.*

stub *(of cigarette)* colilla *f; (of check)* matriz *f.*

stub·born *adj* testarudo, -a.

stub·born·ness testarudez *f.*

stuck 1 *pt & pp of* **stick**². **2** *adj (caught, jammed)* atrancado, -a; **I'm s.** *(unable to carry on)* no puedo seguir.

stud *(on clothing)* tachón *m.*

stu·dent estudiante *mf.*

stu·di·o *(TV etc)* estudio *m; (artist's)* taller *m;* **s. apartment** estudio *m.*

stud·y 1 *vti* estudiar; **to s. to be a doctor** estudiar para médico. **2** *n* estudio *m.*

stuff 1 *vt (container)* llenar (**with** de); *(in cooking)* rellenar (**with** con or de); *(cram)* atiborrar (**with** de). **2** *n (material)* material *m; (things)* cosas *fpl,* trastos *mpl.*

stuffed up *adj (nose)* tapado, -a.

stuff·ing relleno *m.*

stuff·y *adj (room)* mal ventilado, -a; *(atmosphere)* cargado, -a.

stum·ble *vi* tropezar; *fig* **to s. across** *or* **on** tropezar *or* dar con.

stump *(of tree)* tocón *m.*

stun *vt* aturdir; *(news etc)* sorprender.

stunned *adj (amazed)* estupefacto, -a.

stun·ning *adj (blow)* duro, -a; *(news)* sorprendente; *fam (woman, outfit)* fenomenal.

stu·pid *adj* estúpido, -a.

stu·pid·i·ty estupidez *f.*

stur·dy *adj* robusto, -a.

stut·ter 1 *vi* tartamudear. **2** *n* tartamudeo *m.*

sty *(pen)* pocilga *f.*

style estilo *m; (of dress)* modelo *m; (fashion)* moda *f.*

styl·ish *adj* con estilo.

sub·ject 1 *n (citizen)* súbdito *m; (topic)* tema *m; (at school)* asignatura *f;*

(of sentence) sujeto *m*. **2** *vt* someter.

sub·junc·tive subjuntivo *m*.

sub·ma·rine 1 *n* submarino *m*. **2** *adj* submarino, -a.

sub·scribe *vi* suscribirse (**to** a).

sub·scrib·er abonado, -a *mf*.

sub·scrip·tion *(to magazine)* suscripción *f*, abono *m*.

sub·side *vi (land)* hundirse; *(floodwater)* bajar.

sub·si·dy subvención *f*.

sub·stance sustancia *f*.

sub·stan·tial *adj (sum, loss)* importante; *(meal)* abundante.

sub·sti·tute 1 *vt* sustituir. **2** *n (person)* suplente *mf*; *(thing)* sucedáneo *m*.

sub·sti·tu·tion sustitución *f*.

sub·ti·tle subtítulo *m*.

sub·tle *adj* sutil.

sub·tract *vt* restar.

sub·trac·tion resta *f*.

sub·urb barrio *m* periférico; **the suburbs** las afueras.

sub·ur·ban *adj* suburbano, -a.

sub·way *(underground railway)* metro *m*.

suc·ceed *vi (person)* tener éxito; **to s. in doing sth** conseguir hacer algo.

suc·cess éxito *m*.

suc·cess·ful *adj* de éxito; *(business)* próspero, -a; **to be s. in doing sth** lograr hacer algo.

suc·cess·ful·ly *adv* con éxito.

suc·ces·sion sucesión *f*, serie *f*; **in s.** sucesivamente.

suc·ces·sive *adj* sucesivo, -a, consecutivo, -a.

suc·ces·sor sucesor, -a *mf*.

such 1 *adj (of that sort)* tal, semejante; **artists s. as Monet** artistas como Monet. ▪ *(so much, so great)* tanto, -a; **he's always in s. a hurry** siempre anda con tanta prisa; **s. a lot of books** tantos libros. **2** *adv (so very)* tan; **it's s. a long time** hace tanto tiempo; **she's s. a clever woman** es una mujer tan inteligente.

suck 1 *vt (liquid)* sorber, chupar; *(at breast)* mamar. **2** *vi (baby)* mamar.

▸**suck up** *vt (with straw)* aspirar.

sud·den *adj (hurried)* repentino, -a; *(unexpected)* imprevisto, -a; **all of a s.** de repente.

sud·den·ly *adv* de repente.

suds *npl* espuma *f* de jabón.

sue 1 *vt* demandar. **2** *vi* presentar una demanda.

suede ante *m*; *(for gloves)* cabritilla *f*.

suf·fer *vti* sufrir; **to s. from** sufrir de.

suf·fer·er *(from disease)* enfermo, -a *mf*.

suf·fer·ing *(affliction)* sufrimiento *m*; *(pain, torment)* dolor *m*.

suf·fi·cient *adj* suficiente, bastante.

suf·fi·cient·ly *adv* suficientemente, bastante.

suf·fix sufijo *m*.

suf·fo·cate 1 *vt* asfixiar. **2** *vi* asfixiarse.

sug·ar 1 *n* azúcar *m* or *f*. **2** *vt* azucarar.

sug·ar bowl azucarero *m*.

sug·gest *vt (propose)* sugerir; *(advise)* aconsejar; *(indicate, imply)* indicar.

sug·ges·tion *(proposal)* sugerencia *f*.

su·i·cide suicidio *m*; **s. bombing** atentado *m* suicida con bomba.

suit 1 *n* traje *m* de chaqueta; *(in cards)* palo *m*. **2** *vt (be convenient for)* convenir a; *(be right, appropriate for)* ir bien a; **red really suits you** el rojo te favorece mucho; **s. yourself!** ¡como quieras!

suit·a·ble *adj (convenient)* conveniente; *(appropriate)* adecuado, -a; **the most s. woman for the job** la mujer más indicada para el puesto.

suit·case maleta *f*.

suite *(of furniture)* tresillo *m*; *(of hotel rooms, music)* suite *f*.

sulk *vi* enfurruñarse.

sul·tan·a *(raisin)* pasa *f* (de Esmirna).

SUGGESTIONS, INVITATIONS AND DESIRES

What do you want to do?
¿Qué quiere/quieres hacer?

Do you want to go to a restaurant?
¿Quiere/Quieres ir a un restaurante?

How about going for a walk?
¿Y si vamos a dar un paseo?

Let's meet at noon/outside the movie theater.
Nos vemos al mediodía/en la puerta del cine.

I don't want to go to the art gallery.
No quiero ir al museo.

I feel like an ice-cream.
Me tomaría or Me provoca un helado.

What would you rather do?
¿Qué prefiere/prefieres hacer?

I'd like to learn Spanish.
Me gustaría aprender castellano.

I don't mind.
Me da lo mismo.

I'd love to!
¡Me encantaría!

I don't feel like it.
No tengo ganas.

Are you free tomorrow night?
¿Está/Estás libre mañana por la noche?

That's very kind of you.
Muy amable.

Shall we go for a coffee?
¿Tomamos un café?

Would you like to go for a drink?
¿Quiere/Quieres o Le/Te provoca ir a tomar algo?

Let's go for a swim!
¡Vamos a darnos un baño!

I'd like to go to the beach.
Me gustaría ir a la playa.

I'd rather go shopping.
Prefiero ir de compras.

I don't feel like going to the market.
No tengo ganas de ir al mercado.

I think we should leave around 6.30.
Creo que deberíamos salir sobre las 6.30.

I wouldn't mind living here.
No me importaría vivir aquí.

It's up to you.
Usted decide/Tú decides.

That's a good idea.
Es buena idea.

I'm sorry, I can't.
Lo siento, no puedo.

I'm afraid I already have plans.
Lo siento, ya tengo planes.

Thank you for inviting me.
Gracias por invitarme.

sum *(arithmetic problem, amount)* suma *f*; *(total amount)* total *m*; *(of money)* importe *m*.

▸ **sum up** *vt* resumir.

sum·ma·rize *vt* resumir.

sum·ma·ry resumen *m*.

sum·mer 1 *n* verano *m*. **2** *adj (vacation etc)* de verano; *(resort)* de veraneo.

sum·mer·time verano *m*.

sum·mon *vt (meeting, person)* convocar; *(aid)* pedir.

▸ **summon up** *vt (resources)* reunir; **to s. up one's courage** armarse de valor.

sum·mons 1 *n (call)* llamada *f*, lla-mamiento *m*; *(to court)* citación *f* ju-dicial. **2** *vt (to court)* citar.

sun sol *m*.

sun·bathe *vi* tomar el sol.

sun·burn quemadura *f* de sol.

sun·burnt *adj (burnt)* quemado, -a por el sol; *(tanned)* bronceado, -a.

sun·dae helado *m* de fruta y nueces.

Sun·day domingo *m*.

sun·glass·es *npl* gafas *fpl* de sol.

sun·lamp lámpara *f* solar.

sun·light *(luz f del)* sol *m*.

sun·ny *adj (day)* de sol; **it is s.** hace sol.

sun·rise salida *f* del sol.

sun·roof *(on car)* techo *m* corre-dizo.

sun·set puesta *f* del sol.
sun·shade sombrilla *f*.
sun·shine (luz *f* del) sol *m*.
sun·stroke insolación *f*.
sun·tan bronceado *m*; **s. oil** (aceite *m*) bronceador *m*; **s. lotion** leche *f* bronceadora.
sun·tanned *adj* bronceado, -a.
su·per *adj fam* fenomenal.
su·perb *adj* espléndido, -a.
su·per·fi·cial *adj* superficial.
su·per·in·ten·dent *(of apartment building)* portero, -a *mf*.
su·pe·ri·or *adj* superior.
su·pe·ri·or·i·ty superioridad *f*.
su·per·mar·ket supermercado *m*.
su·per·mod·el *n* supermodelo *f*, top model *f*.
su·per·sti·tion superstición *f*.
su·per·sti·tious *adj* supersticioso, -a.
su·per·vise *vt* supervisar; *(watch over)* vigilar.
su·per·vi·sor supervisor, -a *mf*.
sup·per cena *f*; **to have s.** cenar.
sup·ple *adj* flexible.
sup·ple·ment 1 *n* suplemento *m*. **2** *vt* complementar.
sup·ply 1 *n (provision)* suministro *m*; *(delivery)* provisión *f*; **supplies** *(food)* víveres *mpl*. **2** *vt (provide)* suministrar; *(with provisions)* aprovisionar; *(information)* facilitar.
sup·port 1 *n* soporte *m*; *(moral)* apoyo *m*. **2** *vt (weight etc)* sostener; *(back)* apoyar; *(team)* ser (hincha de); *(family)* mantener.
sup·port·er *(political)* partidario, -a *mf*; *(in sport)* hincha *mf*.
sup·por·tive *adj* he was supportive (of) apoyó mucho (a), fue muy comprensivo (con).
sup·pose *vt* suponer; *(presume)* creer; **I s. not/so** supongo que no/sí; **you're not supposed to smoke in here** no está permitido fumar aquí dentro; **you're supposed to be in bed** deberías estar acostado ya.
sup·press *vt* suprimir; *(feelings,*

laugh etc) contener; *(news, truth)* callar; *(revolt)* sofocar.
sure *adj* seguro, -a; **I'm s. (that) ...** estoy seguro, -a de que ...; **make s. that it's ready** asegúrate de que esté listo.
sure·ly *adv (without a doubt)* seguramente; **s. not!** ¡no puede ser!
surf 1 *vt* to s. the Net navegar por Internet. **2** *vi (sport)* hacer surf.
sur·face superficie *f*; **s. area** área *f* de la superficie; **by s. mail** por vía terrestre *or* marítima.
surf·board tabla *f* de surf.
surf·ing surf *m*, surfing *m*.
surge 1 *n (growth)* alza *f*; *(of sea, sympathy)* oleada *f*; *(of anger, energy)* arranque *m*. **2** *vi* to s. forward *(people)* avanzar en tropel.
sur·geon cirujano, -a *mf*.
sur·ger·y *(operation)* cirujía *f*; **s. hours** horas *fpl* de consulta.
sur·gi·cal *adj* quirúrgico, -a; **s. spirit** alcohol *m* de 90°.
sur·name apellido *m*.
sur·plus 1 *n (of goods)* excedente *m*; *(of budget)* superávit *m*. **2** *adj* excedente.
sur·prise 1 *n* sorpresa *f*; **to take sb by s.** coger desprevenido, -a a algn. **2** *adj (visit)* inesperado, -a; **s. attack** ataque *m* sorpresa. **3** *vt* sorprender.
sur·prised *adj* sorprendido, -a; **I should not be s. if it rained** no me extrañaría que lloviera.
sur·pris·ing *adj* sorprendente.
sur·pris·ing·ly *adv* de modo sorprendente.
sur·ren·der *vi (give in)* rendirse.
sur·round *vt* rodear.
sur·round·ing *adj* circundante.
sur·round·ings *npl* alrededores *mpl*.
sur·veil·lance vigilancia *f*.
sur·vey *(of trends etc)* encuesta *f*.
sur·vey·or agrimensor, -a *mf*.
sur·vive 1 *vi* sobrevivir. **2** *vt* sobrevivir a.

sur·viv·or superviviente *mf*.
sus·pect 1 *n* sospechoso, -a *mf*. **2** *vt* (person) sospechar (of de); (think likely) imaginar.
sus·pend *vt* suspender; (pupil) expulsar por un tiempo.
sus·pend·ers *npl* tirantes *mpl*.
sus·pense suspense *m*.
sus·pen·sion suspensión *f*.
sus·pi·cion sospecha *f*; (mistrust) recelo *m*; (doubt) duda *f*; (trace) pizca *f*.
sus·pi·cious *adj* (arousing suspicion) sospechoso, -a; (distrustful) receloso, -a; **to be s. of sb** desconfiar de algn.
SUV *n* sport-utility vehicle todoterreno *m*.
swal·low¹ *vt* (drink, food) tragar.
swal·low² (bird) golondrina *f*.
▸ **swallow down** *vt* tragarse.
swamp ciénaga *f*.
swan cisne *m*.
swap 1 *n* intercambio *m*. **2** *vt* cambiar.
swarm enjambre *m*.
sway *vi* (swing) balancearse; (totter) tambalearse.
swear* 1 *vt* (vow) jurar. **2** *vi* (curse) decir palabrotas.
swear·word palabrota *f*.
sweat 1 *n* sudor *m*. **2** *vi* sudar.
sweat·er suéter *m*.
sweat·shirt sudadera *f*.
Swede (person) sueco, -a *mf*.
Swed·ish 1 *adj* sueco, -a. **2** *n* (language) sueco *m*.
sweep* *vti* barrer.
▸ **sweep aside** *vt* apartar bruscamente; (objections) rechazar.
▸ **sweep away** *vt* (dust) barrer; (storm) arrastrar.
▸ **sweep out** *vt* (room) barrer.
▸ **sweep up** *vi* barrer.
sweet 1 *adj* dulce; (sugary) azucarado, -a; (pleasant) agradable; (person, animal) encantador, -a. **2** *n* (candy) caramelo *m*; (chocolate) bombón *m*; (dessert) postre *m*.

sweet·corn maíz *m* dulce.
sweet·en *vt* (tea etc) azucarar.
sweet·ly *adv* dulcemente.
sweet shop confitería *f*.
swell 1 *n* (of sea) marejada *f*, oleaje *m*. **2** *adj* fam fenomenal. **3** *vi** (part of body) hincharse; (river) subir.
▸ **swell up** *vi* hincharse.
swell·ing hinchazón *f*.
swerve *vi* (car) dar un viraje brusco.
swift 1 *adj* rápido, -a, veloz. **2** *n* (bird) vencejo *m* (común).
swim 1 *vi** nadar; **to go swimming** ir a nadar. **2** *vt** (the Mississippi) pasar a nado. **3** *n* baño *m*; **to go for a s.** ir a darse un baño.
swim·mer nadador, -a *mf*.
swim·ming natación *f*.
swim·ming pool piscina *f*.
swim·ming trunks bañador *m*.
swim·suit bañador *m*.
swing 1 *n* (for playing) columpio *m*. **2** *vi** (move back and forth) balancearse; (arms, legs) menearse; (on swing) columpiarse. **3** *vt** (arms, legs) menear.
Swiss 1 *adj* suizo, -a. **2** *n inv* (person) suizo, -a *mf*; **the S. pl** los suizos.
switch 1 *n* (for light etc) interruptor *m*. **2** *vt* (jobs, direction) cambiar de.
▸ **switch off** *vt* apagar.
▸ **switch on** *vt* encender.
▸ **switch over** *vi* cambiar (to a).
swol·len *adj* (ankle, face) hinchado, -a.
swop *vt* = **swap**.
sword espada *f*.
syl·la·ble sílaba *f*.
syl·la·bus programa *m* de estudios.
sym·bol símbolo *m*.
sym·bol·ic *adj* simbólico, -a.
sym·me·try simetría *f*.
sym·pa·thet·ic *adj* (showing pity) compasivo, -a; (understanding) comprensivo, -a; (kind) amable.
sym·pa·thize *vi* (show pity) compadecerse (with de); (understand) comprender.
sym·pa·thy (pity) compasión *f*;

(condolences) pésame *m; (understanding)* comprensión *f*; **to express one's s.** dar el pésame.
sym·pho·ny sinfonía *f*.
symp·tom síntoma *m*.
syn·a·gogue sinagoga *f*.
syn·o·nym sinónimo *m*.
sy·ringe jeringuilla *f*.
syr·up jarabe *m*, almíbar *m*.
sys·tem sistema *m*.

T

ta *interj fam* gracias.
tab *(flap)* lengüeta *f*.
ta·ble mesa *f*; **to lay** *or* **set the t.** poner la mesa.
ta·ble·cloth mantel *m*.
ta·ble·mat salvamanteles *m inv*.
ta·ble·spoon cuchara *f* de servir.
ta·ble·spoon·ful cucharada *f*.
tab·let *(pill)* pastilla *f*.
tack *(small nail)* tachuela *f*.
tack·le *vt (task)* emprender; *(problem)* abordar; *(grapple with)* agarrar; *(in sport)* placar; *(in soccer)* entrar a.
tack·y *adj fam (shoddy)* cutre.
tact tacto *m*.
tact·ful *adj* diplomático, -a.
tac·tic táctica *f*; **tactics** táctica *f sing*.
taf·fy caramelo *m* duro.
tag *(label)* etiqueta *f*.
tail cola *f*.
tai·lor sastre *m*.
take* *vt* tomar; *(bus etc)* coger; *(accept)* aceptar; *(win)* ganar; *(prize)* llevarse; *(eat, drink)* tomar; *(accompany)* llevar; *(endure)* aguantar; *(consider)* considerar; *(require)* requerir; **she's taking (a degree in) law** estudia derecho; **to t. an exam (in ...)** examinarse (de ...); **it takes**

an hour to get there se tarda una hora en ir hasta allí; **it takes courage** se necesita valor.
▸**take after** *vt* parecerse a.
▸**take along** *vt* llevar (consigo).
▸**take apart** *vt (machine)* desmontar.
▸**take away** *vt (carry off)* llevarse; *(in math)* restar (**from** de); **to t. sth away from sb** quitarle algo a algn.
▸**take back** *vt (give back)* devolver; *(receive back)* recuperar; *(withdraw)* retirar.
▸**take down** *vt (lower)* bajar; *(write)* apuntar.
▸**take in** *vt (include)* abarcar; *(understand)* entender; *(deceive)* engañar.
▸**take off 1** *vt* quitar; *(lead or carry away)* llevarse; *(deduct)* descontar; **he took off his jacket** se quitó la chaqueta. **2** *vi (plane)* despegar.
▸**take on** *vt (undertake)* encargarse de; *(acquire)* tomar; *(employ)* contratar.
▸**take out** *vt* sacar; **he's taking me out to dinner** me ha invitado a cenar fuera; *(insurance)* sacarse; *(stain, tooth)* quitar.
▸**take over 1** *vt (office, post)* tomar posesión de. **2** *vi* **to t. over from sb** relevar a algn.
▸**take up** *vt (occupy)* ocupar; **I've taken up the guitar** he empezado a tocar la guitarra.
take·off *(of plane)* despegue *m*.
take·o·ver *(of company)* absorción *f*.
tak·ings *npl (of shop, business)* recaudación *f sing*.
take-out 1 *n (food)* comida *f* para llevar; *(restaurant)* restaurante *m* de comida para llevar. **2** *adj (food)* para llevar.
tale cuento *m*; **to tell tales** contar chismes.
tal·ent talento *m*.
tal·ent·ed *adj* dotado, -a.
talk 1 *vi* hablar; *(chat)* charlar; *(gossip)* chismorrear. **2** *vt* hablar; **to t. nonsense** decir tonterías. **3** *n (con-*

versation) conversación *f; (words)* palabras *fpl; (gossip)* chismes *mpl; (lecture)* charla *f;* there's t. of ... se habla de ...

▸**talk into** *vt* to t. sb into sth convencer a algn para que haga algo.

▸**talk out of** *vt* to t. sb out of sth disuadir a algn de que haga algo.

▸**talk over** *vt* discutir.

talk·a·tive *adj* hablador, -a.

tall *adj* alto, -a; a tree ten meters t. un árbol de diez metros (de alto); how t. are you? ¿cuánto mides?

tam·bou·rine pandereta *f.*

tame 1 *adj (animal)* domado, -a; *(by nature)* manso, -a. **2** *vt* domar.

tam·pon tampón *m.*

tan 1 *n (of skin)* bronceado *m.* **2** *vt (skin)* broncear. **3** *vi* ponerse moreno, -a.

tan·ger·ine clementina *f.*

tan·gled *adj* enredado, -a.

tank *(container)* depósito *m; (with gun)* tanque *m.*

tank·er *(ship)* tanque *m; (for oil)* petrolero *m.*

tap¹ *vt (knock)* golpear sauvemente; *(with hand)* dar una palmadita a. **2** *vi* to t. at the door llamar suavemente a la puerta. **3** *n* golpecito *m.*

tap² *(for water)* grifo *m.*

tape 1 *n* cinta *f;* sticky t. cinta *f* adhesiva. **2** *vt* pegar (con cinta adhesiva); *(record)* grabar (en cinta).

tape meas·ure cinta *f* métrica.

tape re·cord·er magnetófono *m,* casete *m.*

tar alquitrán *m.*

tar·get *(object aimed at)* blanco *m; (purpose)* meta *f.*

tar·iff tarifa *f,* arancel *m.*

tar·pau·lin lona *f.*

tart *(to eat)* tarta *f.*

tar·tan tartán *m.*

task tarea *f.*

taste 1 *n (sense)* gusto *m; (flavor)* sabor *m; (liking)* afición *f;* it has a burnt t. sabe a quemado; in bad t. de mal gusto; to have (good) t. te-

ner (buen) gusto. **2** *vt (sample)* probar. **3** *vi* to t. of sth saber a algo.

tast·y *adj* sabroso, -a.

tat·tered *adj* hecho, -a jirones.

tat·too 1 *vt* tatuar. **2** *n (mark)* tatuaje *m.*

tax 1 *n* impuesto *m;* t. free exento, -a de impuestos; t. collector recaudador, -a *mf* (de impuestos). **2** *vt* gravar; *(patience etc)* poner a prueba.

tax·a·ble *adj* imponible.

tax·i taxi *m.*

tax·i driv·er taxista *mf.*

tax·i rank parada *f* de taxis.

tax·pay·er contribuyente *mf.*

tea té *m; (meal)* merienda *f.*

tea·bag bolsita *f* de té.

tea break descanso *m.*

teach* 1 *vt* enseñar; *(subject)* dar clases de; to t. sb (how) to do sth enseñar a algn a hacer algo. **2** *vi* ser profesor, -a.

teach·er profesor, -a *mf.*

teach·ing enseñanza *f.*

tea·cup taza *f* de té.

team equipo *m.*

▸**team up** *vi* to t. up with sb juntarse con algn.

tea·pot tetera *f.*

tear¹ lágrima *f;* to be in tears estar llorando.

tear² 1 *vt** rasgar; to t. sth out of sb's hands arrancarle algo de las manos a algn. **2** *vi* (cloth)* rasgarse. **3** *n* desgarrón *m.*

▸**tear off** *vt* arrancar.

▸**tear out** *vt* arrancar.

▸**tear up** *vt* hacer pedazos.

tease *vt* tomar el pelo a.

tea ser·vice *or* **set** juego *m* de té.

tea·spoon cucharilla *f.*

tea·spoon·ful cucharadita *f.*

teat *(of bottle)* tetina *f.*

tea·time hora *f* del té.

tea tow·el paño *m* (de cocina).

tech·ni·cal *adj* técnico, -a.

tech·ni·cian técnico, -a *mf.*

tech·nique técnica *f.*

tech·no·log·i·cal adj tecnológico, -a.

tech·nol·o·gy tecnología f.

ted·dy bear oso m de felpa.

teen·age adj adolescente.

teen·ag·er adolescente mf.

tee-shirt camiseta f.

teeth npl see tooth.

tee·to·tal·ler abstemio, -a mf.

tel·e·com·mu·ni·ca·tions npl telecomunicaciones fpl.

tel·e·gram telegrama m.

tel·e·phone 1 n teléfono m; **to speak to sb on the t.** hablar por teléfono con algn. **2** vt telefonear a, llamar por teléfono a.

tel·e·phone booth cabina f (telefónica).

tel·e·phone call llamada f telefónica.

tel·e·phone di·rec·to·ry guía f telefónica.

tel·e·phone num·ber número m de teléfono.

tel·e·scope telescopio m.

tel·e·vise vt televisar.

tel·e·vi·sion televisión f, **t. (set)** televisor m; **on t.** en la televisión.

tell* 1 vt decir; (relate) contar; (inform) comunicar; (order) mandar; (distinguish) distinguir; **to t. sb about sth** contarle algo a algn; **to t. sb to do sth** decir a algn que haga algo. **2** vi **who can t.?** (know) ¿quién sabe?

▸**tell off** vt reñir.

tell·er (cashier) cajero, -a mf.

tell·tale chivato, -a mf.

tem·per (mood) humor m; **to keep one's t.** no perder la calma; **to lose one's t.** perder los estribos.

tem·per·a·ture temperatura f; **to have a t.** tener fiebre.

tem·ple (building) templo m.

tem·po·rar·i·ly adj temporalmente, Am temporariamente.

tem·po·rar·y adj provisional; (setback, improvement) momentáneo, -a; (teacher) sustituto, -a.

tempt vt tentar; **to t. sb to do sth** incitar a algn a hacer algo.

temp·ta·tion tentación f.

tempt·ing adj tentador, -a.

ten adj & n diez (m) inv.

ten·an·cy (of house) alquiler m; (of land) arrendamiento m.

ten·ant (of house) inquilino, -a mf.

tend vi (be inclined) tender, tener tendencia (**to** a).

ten·den·cy tendencia f.

ten·der adj (affectionate) cariñoso, -a; (meat) tierno, -a.

ten·nis tenis m.

ten·nis court pista f de tenis.

tense[1] adj tenso, -a.

tense[2] (of verb) tiempo m.

ten·sion tensión f.

tent tienda f de campaña.

tenth adj & n décimo, -a (mf).

term (period) período m; (of study) trimestre m; (word) término m; **terms** (conditions) condiciones fpl; **to be on good/bad terms with sb** tener buenas/malas relaciones con algn.

ter·mi·nal 1 terminal f, (for computer) terminal m. **2** adj (patient, illness) terminal.

ter·mi·nate 1 vt terminar; **to t. a pregnancy** abortar. **2** vi terminarse.

ter·race (of houses) hilera f de casas; (patio) terraza f.

ter·raced hous·es casas fpl (de estilo uniforme) en hilera.

ter·ri·ble adj terrible; **I feel t.** me encuentro fatal.

ter·ri·bly adv terriblemente.

ter·rif·ic adj fenomenal.

ter·ri·fy vt aterrorizar.

ter·ri·fy·ing adj aterrador, -a.

ter·ri·to·ry territorio m.

ter·ror terror m.

ter·ror·ist adj & n terrorista (mf).

ter·ror·ize vt aterrorizar.

test 1 vt probar; (analyze) analizar. **2** n (of product) prueba f, (in school) examen m; (of blood) análisis m.

tes·ta·ment testamento m; **Old/New T.** Antiguo/Nuevo Testamento.

USING THE TELEPHONE

Hello?
*¿Bueno? (Méx)/¿Hola? (RP)/¿Alo?
(Andes, Carib)*

Hello, Alan Wright speaking.
Hola, soy Alan Wright.

Hi Claire, it's Alex.
Hola Claire, soy Alex.

**Good morning/afternoon, Staff
Solutions!**
Staff Solutions, ¡buenos días!

Hello, could you put me through to Customer Services, please?
Hola, ¿me puede comunicar con el departamento de servicio al cliente, por favor?

Can I speak to Julio Rey, please? This is Steve Brown from CPS.
¿Podría hablar con Julio Rey, por favor? Soy Steve Brown de parte de CPS.

Speaking!
Soy yo.

Who's calling, please?
¿De parte de quién?

Could you repeat that/spell it?
¿Puede repetirlo/deletrearlo?

Just a moment, I'll get him/her.
Un momento, por favor. Voy a buscarlo.

Hold the line please, I'll put you through.
No cuelgue, lo comunico (Méx)/le paso.

**I'm afraid she's in a meeting/she's not
here.**
Lo siento, está en una reunión/ no está.

The line's busy, would you like to hold?
Da ocupado, ¿quiere esperar?

There's no reply.
No contestan.

Would you like to leave a message?
¿Quiere dejarle un mensaje?

Please leave a message after the tone.
*Por favor deje su mensaje después de la
señal.*

No thanks, I'll call back later.
No gracias, luego vuelvo a llamar.

Could you tell him/her I called?
¿Puede/Puedes decirle que le llamé?

Can you ask him/her to call me back as soon as possible?
¿Le puede decir que me llame lo antes posible?

My number is 42-35-59-01.
*Mi número es el cuarenta y dos, treinta
y cinco, cincuenta y nueve, cero uno.*

> In Spanish you normally read out phone
> numbers in pairs of digits.

Thank you for calling.
Gracias por llamar.

Talk to you later!
Luego te llamo.

Can I take your number?
¿Me da/das su teléfono?

You can reach me on my cell.
Me puede/puedes llamar a mi celular.

I'll text you later.
Luego te mando un mensaje/SMS.

I can't get a signal in here.
No hay señal aquí.

I don't have many minutes left.
No me quedan muchos minutos.

I need to charge my cellphone.
Necesito recargar mi celular.

You've got the wrong number.
Se equivocó de número.

Sorry, I must have the wrong number.
*Perdón, debo haber marcado el número
equivocado.*

I can barely hear you.
Casi no le/te oigo.

We got cut off.
Se cortó.

Is there a payphone around here?
¿Hay un teléfono público por aquí?

I'd like to call collect.
Quisiera hacer una llamada por cobrar.

tes·ti·mo·ny testimonio *m*, declaración *f.*

test tube probeta *f.*

text 1 *n* texto *m*; **t. (message)** mensaje *m* de texto. **2** *vt (send text message to)* enviar un mensaje de texto a.

text·book libro *m* de texto.

tex·tile 1 *n* tejido *m.* **2** *adj* textil.

tex·ture textura *f.*

Thai *adj & n* tailandés, -esa *(mf).*

than *conj* que; *(with numbers)* de; **he's older t. me** es mayor que yo; **more interesting t. we thought** más interesante de lo que creíamos; **more t. once** más de una vez; **more t. ten people** más de diez personas.

thank *vt* agradecer; **t. you** gracias.

thank·ful *adj* agradecido, -a.

thanks *npl* gracias *fpl*; **no, t.** no, gracias; **t. to** gracias a.

thanks·giv·ing **T. Day** Día *m* de Acción de Gracias.

that 1 *dem adj (pl* those*) (masculine)* ese; *(feminine)* esa; *(further away) (masculine)* aquel; *(feminine)* aquella; **at t. time** en aquella época; **t. book** ese/aquel libro; **t. one** ése/ aquél. **2** *dem pron (pl* those*)* ése *m*, ésa *f*, *(further away)* aquél *m*, aquélla *f*, *(indefinite)* eso; *(remote)* aquello; **after t.** después de eso; **like t.** así; **don't talk like t.** no hables así; **t.'s right** eso es; **t.'s where I live** allí vivo yo; **what's t.?** ¿qué es eso?; **who's t.?** ¿quién es?; **all those I saw** todos los que vi; **there are those who say that ...** hay quien dice que .... **3** *rel pron* que; **the letter t. I sent you** la carta que te envié; **the car t. they came in** el coche en el que vinieron; **the moment t. you arrived** el momento en que llegaste. **4** *conj* que; **come here so t. I can see you** ven aquí para que te vea; **he said (t.) he would come** dijo que vendría. **5** *adv* así de, tan; **that much** tanto, -a; **cut off t. much** córteme un trozo así de

grande; **t. old** tan viejo; **we haven't got t. much money** no tenemos tanto dinero.

thaw 1 *vt (snow)* derretir; *(food, freezer)* descongelar. **2** *vi* descongelarse; *(snow)* derretirse. **3** *n* deshielo *m.*

the *def art* el, la; *pl* los, las; **at** *or* **to t.** al, a la; *pl* a los, a las; **of** *or* **from t.** del, de la; *pl* de los, de las; **the voice of the people** la voz del pueblo; **George t. Sixth** Jorge Sexto.

the·a·ter teatro *m.*

theft robo *m.*

their *poss adj* su; *(pl)* sus.

theirs *poss pron* (el) suyo, (la) suya; *(pl)* (los) suyos, (las) suyas.

them *pers pron pl (direct object)* los, las; *(indirect object)* les; **I know t.** los *or* las conozco; **I shall tell t.** so se lo diré (a ellos *or* ellas); **it's t.!** ¡son ellos!; **speak to t.** hábleles. • *(with preposition)* ellos, ellas; **walk in front of t.** camine delante de ellos; **with t.** con ellos.

them·selves *pers pron pl (as subject)* ellos mismos, ellas mismas; *(as direct or indirect object)* se; *(after a preposition)* sí mismos, sí mismas; **they did it by t.** lo hicieron ellos solos.

then 1 *adv (at that time, in that case)* entonces; *(next, afterwards)* luego; **since t.** desde entonces; **till t.** hasta entonces; **go t.** pues vete. **2** *conj* entonces.

the·o·ry teoría *f.*

there *adv (indicating place)* allí, allá; *(nearer speaker)* ahí; **is Peter t.?** ¿está Peter?; **that man t.** aquel hombre; **t. is, t. are** hay; **t. were six of us** éramos seis.

there·fore *adv* por lo tanto.

ther·mom·e·ter termómetro *m.*

Ther·mos® **T. (flask)** termo *m.*

these 1 *dem adj pl* estos, -as. **2** *dem pron pl* éstos, -as; *see* **this**.

the·sis tesis *f inv.*

they *pron* ellos, ellas; **t. are dancing**

están bailando; **t. alone** ellos solos.
■ *(indefinite)* **t. say that ...** se dice que ....

thick *adj (book, slice, material)* grueso, -a; *(wood, vegetation)* espeso, -a; **a wall two meters t.** un muro de dos metros de espesor.

thick·en 1 *vt* espesar. **2** *vi* espesarse.

thick·ness *(of wall etc)* espesor *m*; *(of wire, lips)* grueso *m*; *(of liquid, forest)* espesura *f*.

thief *(pl thieves)* ladrón, -ona *mf*.

thigh muslo *m*.

thim·ble dedal *m*.

thin 1 *adj* delgado, -a; *(hair, vegetation)* ralo, -a; *(liquid)* claro, -a; **a t. slice** una loncha fina. **2** *vt* **to t. (down)** *(paint)* diluir.

thing cosa *f*; **my things** *(clothing)* mi ropa *f sing*; *(possessions)* mis cosas.

think* 1 *vt* pensar, creer; **I t. so/not** creo que sí/no; **I thought as much** ya me lo imaginaba. **2** *vi* pensar *(of, about* en); **what do you t.?** ¿a ti qué te parece?

▸**think over** *vt* reflexionar; **we'll have to t. it over** lo tendremos que pensar.

▸**think up** *vt* idear.

thin·ly *adv* ligeramente.

third 1 *adj* tercero, -a; *(before masculine singular noun)* tercer; **(on) the t. of March** el tres de marzo. **2** *n (in series)* tercero, -a *mf*; *(fraction)* tercera parte *f*.

third·ly *adv* en tercer lugar.

thirst sed *f*.

thirst·y *adj* **to be t.** tener sed.

thir·teen *adj & n* trece *(m)*.

thir·ty *adj & n* treinta *(m)*.

this 1 *dem adj (pl these) (masculine)* este; *(feminine)* esta; **t. book/these books** este libro/estos libros; **t. one** éste, ésta. **2** *dem pron (in-definite)* esto; **t. is different** esto es distinto; **it was like t.** fue así; **t. is where we met** fue aquí donde nos conocimos; **it should have come**

before t. debería haber llegado ya; *(introduction)* **t. is Mr Álvarez** le presento al Sr. Álvarez; *(on the phone)* **t. is Julia (speaking)** soy Julia. ■ *(specific person or thing)* éste *m*, ésta *f*; **I prefer these to those** me gustan más éstos que aquéllos. **3** *adv* **he got t. far** llegó hasta aquí; **t. small/big** así de pequeño/grande.

thong *n (underwear)* tanga *m*; *(sandal)* chancleta *f*, chancla *f*.

thorn espina *f*.

thor·ough *adj (careful)* minucioso, -a; *(work)* concienzudo, -a; *(knowledge)* profundo, -a; **to carry out a t. inquiry into a matter** investigar a fondo un asunto.

thor·ough·ly *adv (carefully)* a fondo; *(wholly)* completamente.

those 1 *dem* esos, -as; *(remote)* aquellos, -as. **2** *dem pron* ésos, -as; *(remote)* aquéllos, -as; *(with rel)* los, las; *see* **that 1 & 2**.

though 1 *conj* aunque; **as t.** como si; **it looks as t. he's gone** parece que se ha ido. **2** *adv* sin embargo.

thought 1 *pt & pp* of **think**. **2** *(act of thinking)* pensamiento *m*; *(reflection)* reflexión *f*.

thought·ful *adj (considerate)* atento, -a.

thought·less *adj (person)* desconsiderado, -a; *(action)* irreflexivo, -a.

thou·sand *adj & n* mil *(m) inv*; **thousands of people** miles de personas.

thread 1 *n* hilo *m*. **2** *vt (needle)* enhebrar.

threat amenaza *f*.

threat·en *vt* amenazar; **to t. to do sth** amenazar con hacer algo.

threat·en·ing *adj* amenazador, -a.

three *adj & n* tres *(m) inv*.

thresh·old umbral *m*.

threw *pt* of **throw**.

thrill *(excitement)* emoción *f*.

thrilled *adj* emocionado, -a; **I'm t. about the trip** estoy muy ilusionado, -a con el viaje.

thrill·er *(book)* novela *f* de suspense; *(film)* película *f* de suspense.

thrill·ing *adj* emocionante.

thrive* *vi (person)* rebosar de salud; *(business)* prosperar; **he thrives on it** le viene de maravilla.

thriv·ing *adj* próspero, -a.

throat garganta *f*.

throne trono *m*.

through 1 *prep (place)* a través de, por; **to look t. the window** mirar por la ventana. ▪ *(time)* a lo largo de; **all t. his life** durante toda su vida. ▪ *(by means of)* por, mediante. ▪ *(because of)* a or por causa de; **t. ignorance** por ignorancia. **2** *adj* **a t. train** un tren directo. **3** *adv (from one side to the other)* de un lado a otro; **to let sb t.** dejar pasar a algn; **to get t. to sb** comunicar con algn; **I'm t. with him** he terminado con él.

through·out 1 *prep* por todo, -a; **t. the year** durante todo el año. **2** *adv (place)* en todas partes; *(time)* todo el tiempo.

throw* *vt* tirar; *(to the ground)* derribar; *(party)* dar.

▸**throw away** *vt (trash, money)* tirar; *(money)* malgastar; *(opportunity)* perder.

▸**throw out** *vt (trash)* tirar; *(person)* echar.

▸**throw up** *vti* devolver.

thrust* 1 *vt* empujar con fuerza; **he t. a letter into my hand** me puso una carta violentamente en la mano. **2** *n (push)* empujón *m*; *(of aircraft)* empuje *m*.

thud ruido *m* sordo.

thug *(lout)* gamberro *m*; *(criminal)* criminal *m*.

thumb pulgar *m*.

thumb·tack chincheta *f*.

thun·der 1 *n* trueno *m*. **2** *vi* tronar.

thun·der·storm tormenta *f*.

Thurs·day jueves *m*.

thus *adv* así, de esta manera; **and t. ...** así que ....

tick¹ 1 *n (sound)* tic-tac *m*; *(mark)* marca *f* de visto bueno. **2** *vi* hacer tic-tac. **3** *vt* marcar.

▸**tick off** *vt (mark)* marcar.

▸**tick over** *vi (engine)* funcionar al ralentí.

tick² *(insect)* garrapata *f*.

tick·et *(for bus etc)* billete *m*; *(for theater)* entrada *f*; *(for lottery)* décimo *m*; *(receipt)* recibo *m*.

tick·et col·lec·tor revisor, -a *mf*.

tick·et of·fice taquilla *f*.

tick·le *vt* hacer cosquillas a.

tick·lish *adj* **to be t.** *(person)* tener cosquillas.

tic-tac-toe tres en raya *m*.

tide marea *f*.

ti·di·ly *adv (to put away)* ordenadamente.

ti·dy 1 *adj (room, habits)* ordenado, -a; *(appearance)* arreglado, -a. **2** *vt* arreglar. **3** *vi* **to t. (up)** ordenar las cosas.

tie 1 *vt (shoelaces etc)* atar; **to t. a knot** hacer un nudo. **2** *n (around neck)* corbata *f*; *(match)* partido *m*; *(draw)* empate *m*.

▸**tie up** *vt (parcel, dog)* atar.

ti·ger tigre *m*.

tight 1 *adj* apretado, -a; *(clothing)* ajustado, -a; *(seal)* hermético, -a; **my shoes are too t.** me aprietan los zapatos. **2** *adv (seal)* herméticamente; **hold t.** agárrate fuerte; **shut t.** bien cerrado, -a.

tight·en 1 *vt (screw)* apretar, *(rope)* tensar; *fig* **to t. (up) restrictions** intensificar las restricciones. **2** *vi* apretarse; *(cable)* tensarse.

tights *npl (thin)* panties *mpl*; *(thick)* leotardos *mpl*.

tile 1 *n (of roof)* teja *f*; *(glazed)* azulejo *m*; *(for floor)* baldosa *f*. **2** *vt (roof)* tejar; *(wall)* alicatar; *(floor)* embaldosar.

till¹ *(for cash)* caja *f*.

till² 1 *prep* hasta; **from morning t. night** de la mañana a la noche; **t. then** hasta entonces. **2** *conj* hasta que.

tilt 1 *vi* to t. over volcarse; **to t. (up)** inclinarse. **2** *vt* inclinar.

tim·ber madera *f* (de construcción).

time 1 *n* tiempo *m*; *(era)* época *f*; *(point in time)* momento *m*; *(time of day)* hora *f*; *(occasion)* vez *f*; **all the t.** todo el tiempo; **for some t. (past)** desde hace algún tiempo; **I haven't seen him for a long t.** hace mucho (tiempo) que no lo veo; **in a short t.** en poco tiempo; **in t.** a tiempo; **in three weeks' t.** dentro de tres semanas; **(at) any t. (you like)** cuando quiera; **at that t.** (en aquel) entonces; **at the same t.** al mismo tiempo; **at times** a veces; **from t. to t.** de vez en cuando; **he may turn up at any t.** puede llegar en cualquier momento; **on t.** puntualmente; **what's the t.?** ¿qué hora es?; **t. of the year** época *f* del año; **to have a good/bad t.** pasarlo bien/mal; **four at a t.** cuatro a la vez; **next t.** la próxima vez; **three times four** tres (multiplicado) por cuatro; **four times as big** cuatro veces más grande. **2** *vt (speech)* calcular la duración de; *(race)* cronometrar; *(choose the time of)* escoger el momento oportuno para.

tim·er *(device)* temporizador *m*.

time·ta·ble horario *m*.

tim·id *adj* tímido, -a.

tim·ing *(timeliness)* oportunidad *f*; *(coordination)* coordinación *f*; *(in race)* cronometraje *m*.

tin *(metal)* estaño *m*; *(container)* lata *f*.

tin·foil papel *m* de estaño.

tinned *adj* enlatado, -a; **t. food** conservas *fpl*.

tin-o·pen·er abrelatas *m inv*.

ti·ny *adj* diminuto, -a.

tip¹ *(end)* punta *f*, *(of cigarette)* colilla *f*.

tip² **1** *n (gratuity)* propina *f*; *(advice)* consejo *m*. **2** *vt* dar una propina a.

tip³ **1** *vt* inclinar. **2** *vi* to t. **(up)** ladearse; *(cart)* bascular.

▸ **tip over 1** *vt* volcar. **2** *vi* volcarse.

tipped cig·a·rette cigarrillo *m* con filtro.

tip·toe on t. de puntillas.

tire¹ *(of vehicle)* neumático *m*.

tire² **1** *vt* cansar. **2** *vi* cansarse.

▸ **tire out** *vt* agotar.

tired *adj* cansado, -a; **t. out** rendido, -a; **to be t.** estar cansado, -a; **to be t. of sth** estar harto, -a de algo.

tired·ness cansancio *m*.

tir·ing *adj* agotador, -a.

tis·sue *(handkerchief)* Kleenex® *m*.

ti·tle título *m*.

to 1 *prep (with place)* a; *(towards)* hacia; **he went to France/Japan** fue a Francia/al Japón; **I'm going to Mary's** voy a casa de Mary; **it is thirty miles to New York** Nueva York está a treinta millas; **the train to Madrid** el tren de Madrid; **to the east** hacia el este; **to the right** a la derecha. ▪ *(time)* **ten (minutes) to six** las seis menos diez. ▪ *(with indirect object)* a; **he gave it to his cousin** se lo dio a su primo. ▪ *(towards)* **he was very kind to me** se portó muy bien conmigo. ▪ *(with infinitive)* **to buy/ to come** comprar/venir; *(in order to)* para; *(with verbs of motion)* a; **he did it to help me** lo hizo para ayudarme; **he stopped to talk** se detuvo a hablar; **difficult to do** difícil de hacer; **ready to listen** dispuesto, -a a escuchar; **the first to complain** el primero en quejarse; **this is the time to do it** éste es el momento de hacerlo; **to have a great deal to do** tener mucho que hacer.

toad sapo *m*.

toad·stool hongo *m* (venenoso).

toast 1 *n* slice of t. tostada *f*. **2** *vt* tostar.

toast·er tostador *m* (de pan).

to·bac·co tabaco *m*.

to·bac·co·nist t.'s (shop) estanco *m*.

to·bog·gan tobogán *m*.

to·day *adv* hoy.

tod·dler niño, -a *mf* pequeño, -a.

toe dedo *m* del pie.

toe·nail uña *f* del dedo del pie.

tof·fee caramelo *m*.

to·geth·er *adv* junto, -a, juntos, -as; **all t.** todos juntos; **t. with** junto con.

toi·let wáter *m*; *(public)* servicios *mpl*.

toi·let pa·per or **tissue** papel *m* higiénico.

toi·let·ries *npl* artículos *mpl* de aseo.

toi·let roll rollo *m* de papel higiénico.

toi·let wa·ter *(perfume)* agua *f* de colonia.

to·ken *(for telephone)* ficha *f*; **book t.** vale *m* para comprar libros.

told *pt & pp of* **tell**.

tol·er·ance tolerancia *f*.

tol·er·ant *adj* tolerante.

tol·er·ate *vt* tolerar.

toll *(for road)* peaje *m*.

toll-free num·ber teléfono *m* gratuito.

to·ma·to *(pl* **tomatoes**) tomate *m*.

tomb tumba *f*.

to·mor·row *adv* mañana; **the day after t.** pasado mañana; **t. night** mañana por la noche.

ton tonelada *f*; *fam* **tons of** montones de.

tone tono *m*.

tongs *npl (for sugar, hair)* tenacillas *fpl*; **(fire) t.** tenazas *fpl*.

tongue lengua *f*.

ton·ic *(drink)* tónica *f*.

to·night *adv* esta noche.

tonne = **ton**.

ton·sil amígdala *f*.

ton·sil·li·tis amigdalitis *f*.

too *adv (also)* también; *(excessively)* demasiado; **t. much/many** demasiado, -a, demasiados, -as; **ten dollars t. much** diez dólares de más; **t. much money** demasiado dinero; **t. old** demasiado viejo.

took *pt of* **take**.

tool *(utensil)* herramienta *f*.

tooth *(pl* **teeth**) diente *m*.

tooth·ache dolor *m* de muelas.

tooth·brush cepillo *m* de dientes.

tooth·paste pasta *f* dentífrica.

tooth·pick mondadientes *m inv*.

top¹ 1 *n (upper part)* parte *f* de arriba; *(of hill)* cumbre *f*; *(of tree)* copa *f*; *(surface)* superficie *f*; *(of list etc)* cabeza *f*; *(of bottle etc)* tapón *m*; *(best)* lo mejor; **on t. of** encima de. **2** *adj (part)* superior, de arriba; *(best)* mejor; **the t. floor** el último piso.

▸**top up** *vt* llenar hasta el tope.

top² *(toy)* peonza *f*.

top·ic tema *m*.

torch *(burning)* antorcha *f*.

tor·ment *vt* atormentar.

tor·na·do tornado *m*.

tor·toise tortuga *f* de tierra.

tor·toise·shell 1 *adj* de carey. **2** *n* carey *m*.

tor·ture 1 *vt* torturar; *(cause anguish)* atormentar. **2** *n* tortura *f*; *(anguish)* tormento *m*.

toss 1 *vt (ball)* tirar; *(throw about)* sacudir; **to t. a coin** echar a cara o cruz. **2** *vi* **to t. about** agitarse; *(in sport)* **to t. (up)** sortear.

to·tal total *m*; *(in check)* importe *m*.

to·tal·ly *adv* totalmente.

touch 1 *vt* tocar; *(lightly)* rozar; *(emotionally)* conmover. **2** *vi* tocarse; *(lightly)* rozarse. **3** *n* toque *m*; *(light contact)* roce *m*; *(sense of touch)* tacto *m*; **in t. with sb** en contacto con algn.

▸**touch down** *vi (plane)* aterrizar.

touch·down *(of plane)* aterrizaje *m*; *(in football)* ensayo *m*.

touch·y *adj (person)* susceptible.

tough *adj (material, competitor etc)* fuerte; *(test, criminal, meat)* duro, -a; *(punishment)* severo, -a; *(problem)* difícil.

tour 1 *n (journey)* viaje *m*; *(of palace etc)* visita *f*; *(of city)* recorrido *m* turístico; *(of theatrical company, team)* gira *f*; **on t.** de gira. **2** *vt (country)* viajar por; *(building)* visitar. **3** *vi* estar de viaje.

tour·ism turismo *m.*

tour·ist turista *mf*; **t. class** clase *f* turista.

tour·ist of·fice oficina *f* de información turística.

tour·na·ment torneo *m.*

tow *vt* remolcar.

to·wards *prep* hacia; **our duty t. others** nuestro deber para con los demás.

tow·el toalla *f.*

tow·er torre *f.*

tow·er block torre *f.*

town ciudad *f*; *(small)* pueblo *m*; **to go into t.** ir al centro.

town coun·cil ayuntamiento *m.*

town hall ayuntamiento *m.*

town·house casa *f* de la ciudad.

town·ship municipio *m.*

tow truck grúa *f.*

tox·ic *adj* tóxico, -a.

toy juguete *m.*

toy·shop juguetería *f.*

trace 1 *n (sign)* indicio *m*, vestigio *m.* **2** *vt (drawing)* calcar; *(locate)* seguir la pista de.

trac·ing pa·per papel *m* de calco.

track *(mark)* huellas *fpl*; *(pathway)* camino *m*; *(for running)* pista *f*; *(of railroad)* vía *f*; *(on record)* canción *f*; **to be on the right t.** ir por buen camino; **to be on the wrong t.** haberse equivocado.

track·suit chandal *m.*

trac·tor tractor *m.*

trade 1 *n (job)* oficio *m*; *(sector)* industria *f*; *(commerce)* comercio *m.* **2** *vi* comerciar (**in** en). **3** *vt* to **t. sth for sth** trocar algo por algo.

trade·mark marca *f* (de fábrica); **registered t.** marca registrada.

trad·er comerciante *mf.*

trade un·ion sindicato *m.*

trad·ing comercio *m.*

tra·di·tion tradición *f.*

tra·di·tion·al *adj* tradicional.

traf·fic *n* tráfico *m.*

traf·fic jam atasco *m.*

traf·fic lights *npl* semáforo *m sing.*

traf·fic sign señal *f* de tráfico.

trag·e·dy tragedia *f.*

trag·ic *adj* trágico, -a.

trail 1 *vt* to **t. sth (along)** *(drag)* arrastrar algo. **2** *vi (drag)* arrastrarse; to **t. (along)** *(linger)* rezagarse. **3** *n* senda *f*; *(bigger)* pista *f*; *(of smoke)* estela *f.*

trail·er *(behind vehicle)* remolque *m*; *(caravan)* caravana *f*; **t. park** camping *m* para caravanas or roulottes.

train¹ *n* tren *m*; **to go by t.** ir en tren.

train² **1** *vt (in sport)* entrenar; *(animal)* amaestrar; *(teach)* formar. **2** *vi* entrenarse; *(be taught)* prepararse.

trained *adj (skilled)* cualificado, -a.

train·ee aprendiz, -a *mf.*

train·er *(in sport)* entrenador, -a *mf*; *(of dogs)* amaestrador, -a *mf*; *(of lions)* domador, -a *mf.*

train·ing entrenamiento *m*; *(instruction)* formación *f.*

trai·tor traidor, -a *mf.*

tram tranvía *m.*

tramp *(person)* vagabundo, -a *mf.*

tran·quil·iz·er tranquilizante *m.*

trans·fer 1 *vt* trasladar; *(funds)* transferir; **a transferred charge call** una conferencia a cobro revertido. **2** *n* traslado *m*; *(of funds)* transferencia *f*; *(picture, design)* calcomanía *f.*

trans·fu·sion transfusión *f* (de sangre).

tran·sis·tor transistor *m.*

tran·sit in **t.** de tránsito.

tran·si·tive *adj* transitivo, -a.

trans·late *vt* traducir.

trans·la·tion traducción *f.*

trans·la·tor traductor, -a *mf.*

trans·mis·sion transmisión *f.*

trans·mit *vt* transmitir.

trans·par·ent *adj* transparente.

trans·plant trasplante *m.*

trans·port 1 *vt* transportar. **2** *n* transporte *m.*

trap 1 *n* trampa *f.* **2** *vt (animal, fugi-*

tive) atrapar; **to t. sb into doing sth** lograr con ardides que algn haga algo.

trap door trampilla *f.*

trash *(inferior goods)* bazofia *f; (household waste)* basura *f; fam (worthless thing)* birria *f; fam (nonsense)* tonterías *fpl.*

trash can cubo *m* de la basura.

trash dump vertedero *m.*

trash·y *adj fam (book, film)* sin valor.

trav·el 1 *vi* viajar; *(vehicle, electric current)* ir; **to t. through** recorrer. **2** *vt* recorrer. **3** *n* viajes *mpl;* **t. agency** agencia *f* de viajes; **t. sickness** mareo *m.*

trav·el·er viajero, -a *mf;* **t.'s check** cheque *m* de viaje.

trav·el·ing 1 *adj (salesman)* ambulante. **2** *n* los viajes *mpl;* **I'm fond of t.** me gusta viajar.

tray *(for food)* bandeja *f.*

treach·er·ous *adj (dangerous)* peligroso, -a.

tread* *vi* pisar.

▶ **tread on** *vt* pisar.

treas·ure tesoro *m.*

treas·ur·er tesorero, -a *mf.*

treat 1 *n (present)* regalo *m.* **2** *vt* tratar; *(regard)* considerar; **he treated them to dinner** les invitó a cenar.

treat·ment *(of person)* trato *m; (of subject, patient)* tratamiento *m.*

treb·le 1 *vt* triplicar. **2** *vi* triplicarse.

tree árbol *m.*

trem·ble *vi* temblar.

tre·men·dous *adj (huge)* enorme; *(success)* arrollador, -a; *(shock etc)* tremendo, -a; *fam (marvellous)* estupendo, -a.

trench *(ditch)* zanja *f; (for troops)* trinchera *f.*

trend·y *adj (* **trendier, trendiest***) fam (person)* moderno, -a; *(clothes)* a la última.

tri·al *(in court)* juicio *m.*

tri·an·gle triángulo *m.*

tri·an·gu·lar *adj* triangular.

tribe tribu *f.*

trib·ute *(mark of respect)* homenaje *m;* **to pay t. to** rendir homenaje a.

trick 1 *n (ruse)* ardid *m; (dishonest)* engaño *m; (practical joke)* broma *f; (of magic, knack)* truco *m;* **to play a t. on sb** gastarle una broma a algn. **2** *vt* engañar.

trick·le 1 *vi (water)* gotear. **2** *n* hilo *m.*

trick·y *adj (situation)* delicado, -a; *(problem)* difícil.

tri·cy·cle triciclo *m.*

trig·ger *(of gun)* gatillo *m.*

trim *vt (cut)* recortar; *(expenses)* disminuir.

trip 1 *n (journey)* viaje *m; (excursion)* excursión *f.* **2** *vi* **to t. (up)** *(stumble)* tropezar (**over** con).

tri·ple 1 *vt* triplicar. **2** *vi* triplicarse.

tri·umph 1 *n* triunfo *m.* **2** *vi* triunfar.

triv·i·al *adj* trivial.

trol·ley carro *m.*

trom·bone trombón *m.*

troop·er *(soldier)* soldado *m* de caballería; *(policeman)* policía *mf.*

troops tropas *fpl.*

tro·phy trofeo *m.*

trop·i·cal *adj* tropical.

trot 1 *vi* trotar. **2** *n* trote *m.*

trou·ble 1 *n (misfortune)* desgracia *f; (problems)* problemas *mpl; (effort)* esfuerzo *m;* **to be in t.** estar en un apuro; **it's not worth the t.** no merece la pena; **to take the t. to do sth** molestarse en hacer algo; **to have liver t.** tener problemas de hígado. **2** *vt (distress)* afligir; *(worry)* preocupar; *(bother)* molestar.

trou·sers *npl* pantalón *m sing.*

trout trucha *f.*

tru·ant **to play t.** hacer novillos.

truck camión *m.*

true *adj* verdadero, -a; *(faithful)* fiel; **to come t.** cumplirse; **it's not t.** no es verdad; **it's t. that …** es verdad que ….

trump *(in card game)* triunfo *m.*

trum·pet trompeta *f.*

trunk *(of tree, body)* tronco *m; (of elephant)* trompa *f; (case)* baúl *m; (of car)* maletero *m.*

trunks *npl (swimming)* t. bañador *m sing.*

trust 1 *n* confianza *f.* **2** *vt (rely upon)* fiarse de; **to t. sb with sth** confiar algo a algn.

truth verdad *f.*

try 1 *vt (attempt)* intentar; *(test)* probar. **2** *vi* intentar; **to t. to do sth** tratar de *or* intentar hacer algo. **3** *n (attempt)* tentativa *f, (in rugby)* ensayo *m.*

▸**try on** *vt (dress)* probarse.

▸**try out** *vt* probar.

try·ing *adj (person)* molesto, -a, pesado, -a.

T-shirt camiseta *f.*

tub *(container)* tina *f, (bath)* bañera *f.*

tube tubo *m; (in body)* conducto *m.*

tuck *vt* **to t. in the bedclothes** remeter la ropa de la cama; **to t. sb in** arropar a algn; **to t. one's shirt into one's trousers** meterse la camisa por dentro (de los pantalones).

Tues·day martes *m.*

tuft *(of hair)* mechón *m; (of wool etc)* copo *m.*

tug 1 *vt (pull at)* tirar de; *(haul along)* arrastrar; *(boat)* remolcar. **2** *n (boat)* remolcador *m.*

tug·boat remolcador *m.*

tu·i·tion instrucción *f,* **private t.** clases *fpl* particulares; **t. fees** tasas *fpl.*

tu·lip tulipán *m.*

tum·ble 1 *vi (person)* caerse. **2** *n* caída *f.*

tum·ble dry·er secadora *f.*

tum·bler *(glass)* vaso *m.*

tum·my *fam* estómago *m; (belly)* barriga *f.*

tu·mor tumor *m.*

tu·na atún *m.*

tune 1 *n (melody)* melodía *f,* **in/out of t.** afinado/desafinado; **to sing out of t.** desafinar. **2** *vt (instrument)* afinar; *(engine)* poner a punto.

▸**tune in to** *vt (on radio etc)* sintonizar.

tun·ing *(of instrument)* afinación *f.*

Tu·ni·sian *adj & n* tunecino, -a *(mf).*

tun·nel túnel *m.*

tur·ban turbante *m.*

tur·key pavo *m.*

Turk turco, -a *mf.*

Turk·ish 1 *adj* turco, -a. **2** *n (language)* turco *m.*

turn 1 *vt (revolve)* girar; *(page, head, gaze)* volver; *(change)* transformar (**into** en); **he's turned forty** ha cumplido los cuarenta. **2** *vi (revolve)* girar; *(change direction)* torcer; *(turn round)* volverse; *(become)* volverse; **to t. to sb** *(for help)* acudir a algn. **3** *n (of wheel)* vuelta *f, (in road)* curva *f, (in game, line)* turno *m;* **it's your t.** te toca a ti; **to take turns (at doing sth)** turnarse (para hacer algo).

▸**turn around** *vi (of person)* volverse.

▸**turn away 1** *vt (person)* rechazar. **2** *vi* volver la cabeza; *(move away)* alejarse.

▸**turn back 1** *vt (person)* hacer retroceder. **2** *vi* volverse.

▸**turn down** *vt (gas, radio etc)* bajar; *(reject)* rechazar.

▸**turn into 1** *vt* convertir en. **2** *vi* convertirse en.

▸**turn off** *vt (light, TV, radio, engine)* apagar; *(water, gas)* cortar; *(faucet)* cerrar.

▸**turn on** *vt (light, TV, radio, engine)* encender; *(water, gas)* abrir la llave de; *(faucet)* abrir.

▸**turn out 1** *vt (extinguish)* apagar. **2** *vi* **it turns out that ...** resulta que ...; **things have turned out well** las cosas han salido bien.

▸**turn over 1** *vt (turn upside down)* poner al revés; *(page)* dar la vuelta a. **2** *vi* volverse.

▸**turn round 1** *vt* volver. **2** *vi (rotate)* girar.

▸**turn up 1** *vt (collar)* levantar; *(TV, volume)* subir; *(light)* aumentar la in-

tensidad de. **2** vi (arrive) presentarse.

turn·ing (in road) salida f.

tur·nip nabo m.

turn·pike autopista f de peaje.

turn·up (of trousers) vuelta f.

tur·tle tortuga f.

tur·tle·neck a t. sweater un jersey
de cuello alto.

tusk colmillo m.

tu·tor (at university) tutor, -a mf; **pri·vate t.** profesor, -a mf particular.

TV TV.

tweez·ers npl pinzas fpl.

twelfth adj & n duodécimo, -a (mf).

twelve adj & n doce (m) inv; **t.
o'clock** las doce.

twen·ti·eth adj & n vigésimo, -a
(mf).

twen·ty adj & n veinte (m) inv.

twice adv dos veces; **he's t. as old as
I am** tiene el doble de años que yo; **t.
as big** el doble de grande.

twig ramita f.

twi·light crepúsculo m.

twin n mellizo, -a mf; **identical
twins** gemelos mpl (idénticos); **t.
beds** camas fpl gemelas.

twine bramante m.

twirl 1 vt girar rápidamente. **2** vi
(spin) girar rápidamente; (dancer)
piruetear.

twist 1 vt torcer; **to t. one's ankle**
torcerse el tobillo. **2** n (movement)
torsión f; (in road) vuelta f.

▸**twist off** (lid) desenroscar.

two adj & n dos (m) inv.

two-way adj (street) de dos direcciones.

type 1 n (kind) tipo m; (print) caracteres mpl. **2** vti escribir a máquina.

type·writ·er máquina f de escribir.

type·writ·ten adj escrito, -a a máquina.

typ·i·cal adj típico, -a.

typ·ing mecanografía f.

typ·ist mecanógrafo, -a mf.

U

UFO abbr of **unidentified flying ob·
ject** OVNI m.

ug·li·ness fealdad f.

ug·ly adj feo, -a; (situation) desagradable.

ul·cer (sore) llaga f, (internal) úlcera
f.

ul·ti·mate adj (final) último, -a;
(aim) final; (basic) esencial.

um·brel·la paraguas m inv.

um·pire árbitro m.

ump·teen adj fam muchísimos, -as,
la tira de.

un·a·ble adj to be u. to do sth no
poder hacer algo.

un·ac·cept·a·ble adj inaceptable.

un·ac·cus·tomed adj he's u. to
this climate no está acostumbrado
a este clima.

u·nan·i·mous adj unánime.

u·nan·i·mous·ly adv unánime-
mente.

un·at·trac·tive adj (idea, appearance) poco atractivo, -a.

un·a·vail·a·ble adj no disponible;
Mr Smith is u. today Mr Smith no le
puede atender hoy.

un·a·void·a·ble adj inevitable; (accident) imprevisible.

un·a·void·a·bly adv inevitablemente.

un·a·ware 1 adj to be u. of sth
ignorar algo. **2** adv (without knowing) inconscientemente; **it caught
me u.** me cogió desprevenido.

un·bear·a·ble adj insoportable.

un·be·liev·a·ble adj increíble.

un·break·a·ble adj irrompible.

un·but·ton vt desabrochar.

un·cer·tain adj (not certain) incierto, -a; (doubtful) dudoso, -a; (hesitant) indeciso, -a.

un·cer·tain·ty incertidumbre f.

un·changed *adj* igual.

un·cle tío *m*.

un·clear *adj* poco claro, -a.

un·com·fort·a·ble *adj* incómodo, -a.

un·com·mon *adj* *(rare)* poco común.

un·con·nect·ed *adj* no relacionado, -a.

un·con·scious *adj* inconsciente *(of* de).

un·con·sti·tu·tion·al *adj* inconstitucional, anticonstitucional.

un·con·vinc·ing *adj* poco convincente.

un·co·op·er·a·tive *adj* poco cooperativo, -a.

un·cork *vt (bottle)* descorchar.

un·cov·er *vt* destapar; *(discover)* descubrir.

un·dam·aged *adj (article etc)* sin desperfectos.

un·de·cid·ed *adj (person)* indeciso, -a.

un·de·ni·a·ble *adj* innegable.

un·der 1 *prep* debajo de; *(less than)* menos de; **u. the circumstances** dadas las circunstancias; **u. there** allí debajo. **2** *adv* debajo.

un·der- *prefix (below)* sub-, infra-; *(insufficiently)* insuficientemente.

un·der·charge *vt* cobrar menos de lo debido.

un·der·clothes *npl* ropa *f sing* interior.

un·der·done *adj* poco hecho, -a.

un·der·es·ti·mate *vt* subestimar.

un·der·go* *vt (change)* sufrir; *(test etc)* pasar por.

un·der·grad·u·ate estudiante *mf* universitario, -a.

un·der·ground *adj* subterráneo, -a.

un·der·line *vt* subrayar.

un·der·mine *vt* socavar, minar.

un·der·neath 1 *prep* debajo de. **2** *adv* debajo. **3** *n* parte *f* inferior.

un·der·pants *npl* calzoncillos *mpl*.

un·der·pass paso *n* subterráneo.

un·der·shirt camiseta *f*.

un·der·stand* *vti* entender.

un·der·stand·a·ble *adj* comprensible.

un·der·stand·ing 1 *n (intellectual grasp)* comprensión *f*; *(agreement)* acuerdo *m*. **2** *adj* comprensivo, -a.

un·der·stood 1 *pt & pp of* **understand**. **2** *adj (agreed on)* convenido, -a.

un·der·take* *vt (responsibility)* asumir; *(task, job)* encargarse de; *(promise)* comprometerse a.

un·der·tak·er empresario, -a *mf* de pompas fúnebres; **undertaker's** funeraria *f*.

un·der·tak·ing *(task)* empresa *f*.

un·der·wa·ter 1 *adj* submarino, -a. **2** *adv* bajo el agua.

un·der·wear *inv* ropa *f* interior.

un·do* *vt* deshacer; *(button)* desabrochar.

un·done *adj (knot etc)* deshecho, -a; **to come u.** *(shoelace)* desatarse; *(button, blouse)* desabrocharse; *(necklace etc)* soltarse.

un·doubt·ed·ly *adv* indudablemente.

un·dress 1 *vt* desnudar. **2** *vi* desnudarse.

un·eas·y *adj (worried)* preocupado, -a; *(disturbing)* inquietante; *(uncomfortable)* incómodo, -a.

un·em·ployed 1 *adj* to be u. estar en paro. **2** *npl* **the u.** los parados.

un·em·ploy·ment paro *m*.

un·e·ven *adj (not level)* desigual; *(bumpy)* accidentado, -a; *(variable)* irregular.

un·e·vent·ful *adj* sin acontecimientos.

un·ex·pect·ed *adj (unhoped for)* inesperado, -a; *(event)* imprevisto, -a.

un·ex·pect·ed·ly *adv* inesperadamente.

un·fair *adj* injusto, -a.

un·fair·ly *adv* injustamente.

un·fair·ness injusticia *f*.

un·faith·ful adj (friend) desleal; (husband, wife) infiel.

un·fa·mil·iar adj (unknown) desconocido, -a; **to be u. with sth** no conocer bien algo.

un·fash·ion·a·ble adj pasado, -a de moda; (ideas etc) poco popular.

un·fas·ten vt (knot) desatar; (clothing, belt) desabrochar.

un·fa·vor·a·ble adj desfavorable.

un·fin·ished adj inacabado, -a.

un·fit adj (food, building) inadecuado, -a; (person) no apto, -a (**for** para); (incompetent) incompetente; (physically) incapacitado, -a; **to be u.** no estar en forma.

un·fold vt (sheet) desdoblar; (newspaper) abrir.

un·for·get·ta·ble adj inolvidable.

un·for·giv·a·ble adj imperdonable.

un·for·tu·nate adj (person, event) desgraciado, -a; **how u.!** ¡qué mala suerte!

un·for·tu·nate·ly adv desgraciadamente.

un·friend·ly adj antipático, -a.

un·fur·nished adj sin amueblar.

un·grate·ful adj (unthankful) desagradecido, -a.

un·hap·pi·ness tristeza f.

un·hap·py adj triste.

un·harmed adj ileso, -a, indemne.

un·health·y adj (ill) enfermizo, -a; (unwholesome) malsano, -a.

un·help·ful adj (advice) inútil; (person) poco servicial.

un·hook vt (from hook) descolgar; (clothing) desabrochar.

un·hurt adj ileso, -a.

un·hy·gien·ic adj antihigiénico, -a.

u·ni·form adj & n uniforme (m).

un·im·por·tant adj poco importante.

un·in·hab·it·ed adj despoblado, -a.

un·in·jured adj ileso, -a.

un·in·ten·tion·al adj involuntario, -a.

un·in·ter·est·ing adj poco interesante.

un·ion 1 n unión f; (organization) sindicato m. 2 adj sindical.

u·nique adj único, -a.

u·nit unidad f; (piece of furniture) módulo m; (team) equipo m; **kitchen u.** mueble m de cocina.

u·nite 1 vt unir. 2 vi unirse.

u·ni·ver·sal adj universal.

u·ni·verse universo m.

u·ni·ver·si·ty 1 n universidad f. 2 adj universitario, -a.

un·just adj injusto, -a.

un·kind adj (not nice) poco amable; (cruel) despiadado, -a.

un·know·ing·ly inconscientemente, inadvertidamente.

un·known adj desconocido, -a.

un·lead·ed adj (gasoline) sin plomo.

un·less conj a menos que (+ subjunctive), a no ser que (+ subjunctive).

un·like prep a diferencia de.

un·like·ly adj (improbable) poco probable.

un·lim·it·ed adj ilimitado, -a.

un·load vti descargar.

un·lock vt abrir (con llave).

un·luck·y adj (unfortunate) desgraciado, -a; **to be u.** (person) tener mala suerte; (thing) traer mala suerte.

un·made adj (bed) deshecho, -a.

un·mar·ried adj soltero, -a.

un·nec·es·sar·y adj innecesario, -a.

un·no·ticed adj desapercibido, -a; **to let sth pass u.** pasar algo por alto.

un·oc·cu·pied adj (house) desocupado, -a; (seat) libre.

un·pack 1 vt (boxes) desembalar; (suitcase) deshacer. 2 vi deshacer la(s) maleta(s).

un·paid adj (bill, debt) impagado, -a; (work) no retribuido, -a.

un·pleas·ant adj (not nice) desagradable; (unfriendly) antipático, -a (**to** con).

un·plug *vt* desenchufar.

un·pop·u·lar *adj* impopular; **to make oneself u.** ganarse la antipatía de algn.

un·pre·dict·a·ble *adj* imprevisible.

un·pre·pared *adj (speech etc)* improvisado, -a; *(person)* desprevenido, -a.

un·rea·son·a·ble *adj* poco razonable; *(demands)* desmedido, -a.

un·rec·og·niz·a·ble *adj* irreconocible.

un·re·lat·ed *adj (not connected)* no relacionado, -a.

un·re·li·a·ble *adj (person)* de poca confianza; *(information)* que no es de fiar; *(machine)* poco fiable.

un·rest *(social etc)* malestar *m.*

un·roll *vt* desenrollar.

un·safe *adj (activity, journey)* peligroso, -a; *(building, car, machine)* inseguro, -a; **to feel u.** sentirse expuesto, -a.

un·sat·is·fac·to·ry *adj* insatisfactorio, -a.

un·screw *vt* destornillar.

un·skilled *adj (worker)* no cualificado, -a.

un·sta·ble *adj* inestable.

un·stead·i·ly *adv (to walk)* con paso inseguro.

un·stead·y *adj (not firm)* inestable; *(table, chair)* cojo, -a; *(hand, voice)* tembloroso, -a.

un·suc·cess·ful *adj (person, negotiation)* fracasado, -a; *(attempt, effort)* vano, -a; *(candidate)* derrotado, -a; **to be u. at sth** no tener éxito con algo.

un·suc·cess·ful·ly *adv* sin éxito.

un·suit·a·ble *adj (person)* no apto, -a; *(thing)* inadecuado, -a.

un·suit·ed *adj (person)* no apto, -a; *(thing)* impropio, -a (**to** para).

un·sure *adj* poco seguro, -a; **to be u. of sth** no estar seguro, -a de algo.

un·tan·gle *vt* desenmarañar.

un·ti·dy *adj (room, person)* desordenado, -a; *(hair)* despeinado, -a; *(appearance)* desaseado, -a.

un·tie *vt* desatar.

un·til **1** *conj* hasta que; **u. she gets back** hasta que vuelva. **2** *prep* hasta; **u. now** hasta ahora; **not u. Monday** hasta el lunes no.

un·true *adj (false)* falso, -a.

un·used *adj (car)* sin usar; *(stamp)* sin matar.

un·u·su·al *adj (rare)* poco común; *(exceptional)* excepcional.

un·u·su·al·ly *adv* excepcionalmente.

un·veil *vt* descubrir.

un·want·ed *adj* no deseado, -a.

un·well *adj* to be u. estar malo, -a.

un·will·ing *adj* to be u. to do sth no estar dispuesto, -a a hacer algo.

un·will·ing·ly *adv* de mala gana.

un·wor·thy *adj* indigno, -a.

un·wrap *vt (gift)* desenvolver; *(package)* deshacer.

un·zip *vt* bajar la cremallera de.

up **1** *prep (movement)* **to climb up the mountain** escalar la montaña; **to walk up the street** ir calle arriba.
 ▪ *(position)* en lo alto de; **further up the street** más adelante (en la misma calle). **2** *adv (upwards)* arriba; **further up** hacia arriba; **from ten dollars up** de diez dólares para arriba; **right up (to the top)** hasta arriba (del todo); **to go** *or* **come up** subir; **to walk up and down** ir de un lado a otro. ▪ *(towards)* hacia; **to come** *or* **go up to sb** acercarse a algn. ▪ *(increased)* **bread is up** el pan ha subido. ▪ *(wrong)* **what's up (with you)?** ¿qué pasa (contigo)?; **something must be up** debe pasar algo. ▪ *(as far as, until)* hasta; **I can spend up to five dollars** puedo gastar un máximo de cinco dólares; **up to here** hasta aquí; **up to now** hasta ahora. ▪ **to be up to** *(depend on)* depender de; *(be capable of)* estar a la altura de; **he's up to something** está tramando algo. **3** *adj (out of bed)* levantado, -a; *(finished)* terminado, -a; **time's up** (ya) es la hora. **4** *vt (increase)* aumentar.

5 *n* **ups and downs** altibajos *mpl.*

up·date *vt* actualizar, poner al día.

up·grade 1 *vt* (*promote*) ascender; (*improve*) mejorar la calidad de; (*software, hardware*) actualizar. **2** *n* (*of software, hardware*) actualización *f.*

up·hill *adv* cuesta arriba.

up·hold* *vt* sostener.

up·on *prep* sobre.

up·per *adj* superior.

up·right 1 *adj* (*vertical*) vertical; (*honest*) honrado, -a. **2** *adv* derecho.

up·roar tumulto *m.*

up·scale *adj* (*newspaper, program*) dirigido, -a a un público selecto.

up·set 1 *vt** (*shock*) trastornar; (*worry*) preocupar; (*displease*) disgustar; (*spoil*) desbaratar; (*make ill*) sentar mal a. **2** *adj* (*shocked*) alterado, -a; (*displeased*) disgustado, -a; **to have an u. stomach** sentirse mal del estómago.

up·side-down al revés.

up·stairs 1 *adv* arriba. **2** *n* piso *m* de arriba.

up-to-date *adj* (*current*) al día; (*modern*) moderno, -a; **to be u. with sth** estar al tanto de algo.

up·town zona *f* residencial.

up·ward(s) *adv* hacia arriba; **from ten (years) u.** a partir de los diez años; *fam* **u. of** algo más de.

urge *vt* (*incite*) incitar; (*press*) instar; (*plead*) exhortar; (*advocate*) preconizar; **to u. that sth should be done** insistir en que se haga algo.

ur·gen·cy urgencia *f.*

ur·gent *adj* urgente; (*need, tone*) apremiante.

ur·gent·ly *adv* urgentemente.

u·rine orina *f.*

U·ru·guay·an *adj & n* uruguayo, -a (*mf*).

us *pers pron* (*as object*) nos; (*after prep, 'to be'*) nosotros, -as; **she wouldn't believe it was us** no creía que fuéramos nosotros; **let's forget it** olvidémoslo.

us·age (*habit, custom*) costumbre *f*, (*linguistic*) uso *m.*

use 1 *vt* utilizar; (*consume*) consumir; **what is it used for?** ¿para qué sirve? **2** *n* uso *m*; **'not in u.'** 'no funciona'; **to be of u.** servir; **to make (good) u. of sth** aprovechar algo; **it's no u.** es inútil; **it's no u. crying** no sirve de nada llorar.

▸ **use up** *vt* acabar; (*food*) consumir; (*gas*) agotar; (*money*) gastar.

used¹ *adj* (*second-hand*) usado, -a.

used² 1 *v aux* **where did you u. to live?** ¿dónde vivías (antes)?; **I u. to play the piano** solía tocar el piano; **I u. not to like it** antes no me gustaba. **2** *adj* **to be u. to sth** estar acostumbrado, -a a algo.

use·ful *adj* útil; (*practical*) práctico, -a; **to come in u.** venir bien.

use·ful·ness utilidad *f.*

use·less *adj* inútil.

us·er usuario, -a *mf.*

us·er-friend·ly *adj* de fácil manejo.

u·su·al *adj* corriente; **as u.** como siempre.

u·su·al·ly *adv* normalmente.

u·ten·sil utensilio *m*; **kitchen utensils** batería *f sing* de cocina.

u·til·i·ty (public) u. empresa *f* de servicio público.

ut·ter¹ *vt* (*words*) pronunciar; (*cry, threat*) lanzar.

ut·ter² *adj* total.

ut·ter·ly *adv* completamente.

U-turn cambio *m* de sentido.

V

va·can·cy (*job*) vacante *f*, (*room*) habitación *f* libre.

va·cant *adj* (*empty*) vacío, -a; (*room, seat*) libre.

va·ca·tion vacaciones *fpl*; **on v.** de vacaciones.

va·ca·tion·er summer v. veraneante *mf.*

vac·ci·nate *vt* vacunar.

vac·ci·na·tion vacuna *f.*

vac·cine vacuna *f.*

vac·uum 1 *vt* limpiar con aspiradora. **2** *n* vacío *m.*

vac·uum clean·er aspiradora *f.*

vague *adj (imprecise)* vago, -a; *(indistinct)* borroso, -a.

vague·ly *adv* vagamente.

vain *adj* in v. en vano.

val·id *adj* válido, -a.

val·ley valle *m.*

val·u·a·ble 1 *adj* valioso, -a. **2** *npl* valuables objetos *mpl* de valor.

val·ue valor *m*; to get good v. for money sacarle jugo al dinero.

valve *(of machine, heart)* válvula *f.*

van furgoneta *f.*

van·dal gamberro, -a *mf.*

van·dal·ize *vt* destrozar.

va·nil·la vainilla *f.*

van·ish *vi* desaparecer.

var·i·a·ble *adj & n* variable *(f).*

var·i·ant variante *f.*

var·ied *adj* variado, -a.

va·ri·e·ty *(diversity)* variedad *f*, *(assortment)* surtido *m*; for a v. of reasons por razones diversas.

va·ri·e·ty show espectáculo *m* de variedades.

var·i·ous *adj* diversos, -as.

var·nish 1 *n* barniz *m.* **2** *vt* barnizar.

var·y *vti* variar.

vase florero *m.*

Vas·e·line® vaselina *f.*

vast *adj* vasto, -a.

VAT *abbr of* value added tax IVA *m.*

VCR *abbr of* video cassette recorder (grabador *m* de) vídeo *m.*

veal ternera *f.*

veg·e·ta·ble verdura *f.*

veg·e·tar·i·an *adj & n* vegetariano, -a *(mf).*

veg·e·ta·tion vegetación *f.*

ve·hi·cle vehículo *m.*

veil velo *m.*

vein vena *f.*

vel·vet terciopelo *m.*

vend·ing ma·chine máquina *f* expendedora.

ven·dor vendedor, -a *mf.*

Ve·ne·tian blind persiana *f* graduable.

Ven·e·zue·lan *adj & n* venezolano, -a *(mf).*

ven·ti·la·tion ventilación *f.*

ven·ture 1 *vt* arriesgar, aventurar; he didn't v. to ask no se atrevió a preguntarlo. **2** *vi* arriesgarse; to v. out of doors atreverse a salir. **3** *n* empresa *f* arriesgada, aventura *f.*

ven·ue *(meeting place)* lugar *m* de reunión; *(for concert etc)* local *m.*

verb verbo *m.*

ver·bal *adj* verbal.

ver·dict veredicto *m*; *(opinion)* opinión *f.*

verge *(of road)* arcén *m.*

verse *(stanza)* estrofa *f*, *(poetry)* versos *mpl*; *(of song)* copla *f.*

ver·sion versión *f.*

ver·sus *prep* contra.

ver·ti·cal *adj* vertical.

ver·y *adv* muy; v. much muchísimo; at the v. latest como máximo; the v. first/last el primero/último de todos; at this v. moment en este mismo momento.

vest *(undershirt)* camiseta *f*, chaleco *m.*

vet veterinario, -a *mf.*

vet·er·an veterano, -a *mf*, *(war)* v. ex combatiente *mf.*

vi·a *prep* por.

vi·brate *vi* vibrar (with de).

vi·bra·tion vibración *f.*

vic·ar párroco *m.*

vice¹ vicio *m.*

vice² *(tool)* torno *m* de banco.

vi·cious *adj (violent)* violento, -a; *(malicious)* malintencionado, -a; *(cruel)* cruel.

vic·tim víctima *f.*

vic·to·ry victoria *f.*

vid·e·o vídeo *m*; v. (cassette) videocasete *m*; v. (cassette recorder) vídeo *m.*

vid·e·o cam·er·a videocámara f.

vid·e·o game videojuego m.

vid·e·o·tape cinta f de vídeo.

view (sight) vista f; (opinion) opinión f; **to come into v.** aparecer; **in v. of the fact that …** dado que ….

view·er (of TV) televidente mf.

view·find·er visor m.

view·point punto m de vista.

vil·la (country house) casa f de campo.

vil·lage (small) aldea f; (larger) pueblo m.

vil·lag·er aldeano, -a mf.

vil·lain villano, -a mf; (in movie, play) malo, -a mf.

vin·e·gar vinagre m.

vine·yard viñedo m.

vi·o·lence violencia f.

vi·o·lent adj violento, -a.

vi·o·lent·ly adv violentamente.

vi·o·lin violín m.

VIP abbr of **very important person** fam vip mf.

vir·gin n virgen f.

vir·tu·al adj virtual; **v. reality** realidad f virtual.

vir·tu·al·ly adv (almost) prácticamente.

vir·tue virtud f; **by v. of** en virtud de.

vi·rus virus m inv.

vi·sa visado m, Am visa f.

vis·i·ble adj visible.

vis·it **1** vt visitar. **2** n visita f; **to pay sb a v.** hacerle una visita a algn.

vis·it·ing hours npl horas fpl de visita.

vis·i·tor (guest) invitado, -a mf; (tourist) turista mf.

vi·tal adj (essential) fundamental.

vi·tal·ly adv **it's v. important** es de vital importancia.

vi·ta·min vitamina f.

viv·id adj (color) vivo, -a; (description) gráfico, -a.

vo·cab·u·lar·y vocabulario m.

vo·ca·tion·al adj profesional.

vod·ka vodka m or f.

voice voz f; **at the top of one's v. a**

voz en grito; **v. mail** buzón m de voz.

vol·ca·no (pl volcanoes) volcán m.

volt·age voltaje m.

vol·ume volumen m.

vol·un·tar·y adj voluntario, -a.

vol·un·teer **1** n voluntario, -a mf. **2** vi ofrecerse (for para).

vom·it vti vomitar.

vote **1** n voto m; (voting) votación f. **2** vti votar.

vot·er votante mf.

vouch·er vale m.

vow·el vocal f.

voy·age viaje m; (crossing) travesía f.

vul·gar adj (coarse) ordinario, -a; (in poor taste) de mal gusto.

W

wad (of paper) taco m; (of cotton wool) bolita f; (of money) fajo m.

wad·dle vi andar como los patos.

wade vi caminar por el agua.

wad·ing pool piscina f para niños.

wa·fer barquillo m.

wag **1** vt menear. **2** vi (tail) menearse.

wage earn·er asalariado, -a mf.

wages npl salario m sing.

wag·on camión m; (of train) vagón m.

waist cintura f.

wait **1** n espera f; (delay) demora f. **2** vi esperar; **to keep sb waiting** hacer esperar a algn.

▸ **wait behind** vi quedarse.

▸ **wait up** vi **to w. up for sb** esperar a algn levantado, -a.

wait·er camarero m.

wait·ing 'no w.' 'prohibido aparcar'.

wait·ing room sala f de espera.

wait·ress camarera f.

wait·staff camareros *mpl.*

wake* **1** *vt* to w. sb (up) despertar a algn. **2** *vi* to w. (up) despertar(se).

walk **1** *n* (*long*) caminata *m*; (*short*) paseo *m*; it's an hour's w. está a una hora de camino; to go for a w. dar un paseo. **2** *vt* (*dog*) pasear. **3** *vi* andar; (*to a specific place*) ir andando.

▸ **walk away** *vi* alejarse.

▸ **walk in** *vi* entrar.

▸ **walk off** *vi* marcharse; to walk off with sth (*steal, win easily*) llevarse algo.

▸ **walk out** *vi* salir.

walk·er paseante *mf*, (*in sport*) marchador, -a *mf.*

walk·ing (*hiking*) excursionismo *m.*

walk·ing stick bastón *m.*

Walk·man® (*pl* Walkmans) Walkman® *m.*

wall (*exterior*) muro *m*; (*interior*) pared *f.*

wal·let cartera *f.*

wall·pa·per **1** *n* papel *m* pintado. **2** *vt* empapelar.

wal·nut nuez *f.*

wal·rus morsa *f.*

wan·der **1** *vt* to w. the streets vagar por las calles. **2** *vi* (*aimlessly*) vagar; (*stray*) desviarse; (*mind*) divagar; his glance wandered round the room recorrió el cuarto con la mirada.

▸ **wander about** *vi* deambular.

want *vt* querer; (*desire*) desear; (*need*) necesitar; to w. to do sth querer hacer algo; you're wanted on the phone te llaman al teléfono.

WAP *n* Wireless Application Protocol WAP *m.*

war guerra *f*; to be at w. estar en guerra (with con).

ward (*of hospital*) sala *f.*

war·den (*of residence*) guardián, -ana *mf*, game w. guarda *m* de coto.

ward·robe armario *m* (ropero).

ware·house almacén *m.*

warm **1** *adj* caliente; (*water*) tibio, -a;

a w. day un día de calor; I am w. tengo calor; it is (very) w. today hoy hace (mucho) calor. **2** *vt* calentar.

▸ **warm up** **1** *vt* calentar; (*soup*) (re)calentar. **2** *vi* calentarse; (*food*) (re)calentarse; (*person*) entrar en calor.

warmth calor *m.*

warn *vt* advertir (about sobre; against contra); he warned me not to go me advirtió que no fuera; to w. sb that ... advertir a algn que ...

warn·ing (*of danger*) advertencia *f*, (*notice*) aviso *m.*

warn·ing light piloto *m.*

war·rant **1** *n* (*legal order*) orden *f* judicial. **2** *vt* (*justify*) justificar; (*guarantee*) garantizar.

war·ran·ty (*for goods*) garantía *f.*

war·ri·or guerrero, -a *mf.*

war·ship buque *m* de guerra.

wart verruga *f.*

war·time tiempos *mpl* de guerra.

war·y *adj* (warier, wariest) cauteloso, -a; to be w. of doing sth dudar en hacer algo; to be w. of sb/sth recelar de algn/algo.

was *pt of* be.

wash **1** *n* to have a w. lavarse. **2** *vt* lavar; (*dishes*) fregar; to w. one's hair lavarse el pelo. **3** *vi* (*have a wash*) lavarse.

▸ **wash away** *vt* (*of sea*) llevarse; (*traces*) borrar.

▸ **wash off** *vi* quitarse lavando.

▸ **wash out** **1** *vt* (*stain*) quitar lavando. **2** *vi* quitarse lavando.

▸ **wash up** *vi* lavarse rápidamente.

wash·a·ble *adj* lavable.

wash·ba·sin lavabo *m.*

wash·cloth manopla *f.*

wash·ing (*action*) lavado *m*; (*of clothes*) colada *f*; (*dirty*) w. ropa *f* sucia; to do the w. hacer la colada.

wash·ing ma·chine lavadora *f.*

wash·room servicios *mpl.*

wasp avispa *f.*

waste **1** *n* (*unnecessary use*) desperdicio *m*; (*of resources, effort, money*) derroche *m*; *(of time)* pérdida *f*; *(trash)* basura *f*; **radioactive w.** desechos *mpl* radiactivos. **2** *vt (squander)* desperdiciar; *(resources)* derrochar; *(time, chance)* perder.

waste·bin cubo *m* de la basura.

waste ground *(in town)* descampado *m*.

waste·pa·per papeles *mpl* usados.

waste·pa·per bas·ket papelera *f*.

watch 1 *n* reloj *m*. **2** *vt (observe)* observar; *(keep an eye on)* vigilar; *(be careful of)* tener cuidado con. **3** *vi (look)* mirar.

▸ **watch out** *vi* w. out! ¡cuidado!

▸ **watch out for** *vt* tener cuidado con; *(wait for)* esperar.

watch·strap correa *f* (de reloj).

wa·ter 1 *n* agua *f*. **2** *vt (plants)* regar.

▸ **water down** *vt (drink)* aguar.

wa·ter·col·or acuarela *f*.

wa·ter·cress berro *m*.

wa·ter·fall cascada *f*; *(very big)* catarata *f*.

wa·ter·ing can regadera *f*.

wa·ter·mel·on sandía *f*.

wa·ter·proof *adj (material)* impermeable; *(watch)* sumergible.

wa·ter·ski·ing esquí *m* acuático.

wa·ter·tight *adj* hermético, -a.

wave 1 *n (at sea)* ola *f*; *(in hair, radio)* onda *f*. **2** *vt* agitar; *(brandish)* blandir. **3** *vi* agitar el brazo; **she waved (to me)** *(greeting)* me saludó con la mano; *(goodbye)* se despidió (de mí) con la mano.

wave·length longitud *f* de onda.

wav·y *adj* ondulado, -a.

wax 1 *n* cera *m*. **2** *vt* encerar; *vt* **to have one's legs waxed** hacerse la cera en las piernas.

way *n (route, road)* camino *m*; *(distance)* distancia *f*; *(means, manner)* manera *f*; **on the w.** en el camino; **on the w. here** de camino para aquí; **which is the w. to the station?** ¿por dónde se va a la estación?; **w. in** entrada *f*; **w. out** salida *f*; **on the w. back** en el viaje de regreso; **on the**

w. up/down en la subida/bajada; **(get) out of the w.!** ¡quítate de en medio!; **you're in the w.** estás estorbando; **come this w.** venga por aquí; **which w. did he go?** ¿por dónde se fue?; **that w.** por allá; **a long w. off** lejos; **do it this w.** hazlo así; **which w. did you do it?** ¿cómo lo hiciste?; **no w.!** ¡ni hablar!

we *pers pron* nosotros, -as.

weak *adj* débil; *(team, piece of work, tea)* flojo, -a.

weak·en 1 *vt* debilitar; *(argument)* quitar fuerza a. **2** *vi* debilitarse; *(concede ground)* ceder.

weak·ness debilidad *f*; *(character flaw)* punto *m* flaco.

wealth riqueza *f*.

wealth·y *adj* rico, -a.

weap·on arma *f*.

wear 1 *vt* (clothes)* llevar (puesto, -a); *(shoes)* calzar; **he wears glasses** lleva gafas; **he was wearing a jacket** llevaba chaqueta. **2** *n (deterioration)* desgaste *m*; **normal w. and tear** desgaste *m* natural.

▸ **wear off** *vi (effect, pain)* pasar.

▸ **wear out 1** *vt* gastar; *fig (exhaust)* agotar. **2** *vi* gastarse.

wea·ry *adj (tired)* cansado, -a.

wea·sel comadreja *f*.

weath·er tiempo *m*; **the w. is fine** hace buen tiempo; **to feel under the w.** no encontrarse bien.

weath·er fore·cast parte *m* meteorológico.

weave* *vt* tejer; *(intertwine)* entretejer.

web *(of spider)* telaraña *f*; **web the Web** la Web; **w. site** sitio *m* web.

web·cam *n* cámara *f* web.

wed·ding boda *f*.

wed·ding ring alianza *f*.

wedge 1 *n* cuña *f*; *(for table leg)* calce *m*. **2** *vt* calzar.

Wednes·day miércoles *m*.

wee *adj esp Scot* pequeñito, -a.

weed mala hierba *f*.

week semana *f*; **a w. (ago) today/**

yesterday hoy hace/ayer hizo una semana; **a w. today** de aquí a ocho días.

week·day día m laborable.

week·end fin m de semana; **at** or **on the w.** el fin de semana.

week·ly 1 adj semanal. **2** adv semanalmente. **3** n (magazine) semanario m.

weep* vi llorar.

weigh vti pesar.

weight peso m; **to lose w.** adelgazar; **to put on w.** engordar.

weird adj raro, -a.

wel·come 1 adj (person) bienvenido, -a; (news) grato, -a; (change) oportuno, -a; **to make sb w.** acoger a algn calurosamente; **you're w.!** ¡no hay de qué! **2** n (greeting) bienvenida f. **3** vt acoger; (more formally) darle la bienvenida a; (news) acoger con agrado; (decision) aplaudir.

weld vt soldar.

wel·fare (social security) seguridad f social.

well¹ (for water) pozo m.

well² 1 adj (healthy) bien; **he's w.** está bien (de salud); **to get w.** reponerse; **all is w.** todo va bien. **2** adv (properly) bien; **w. done!** ¡muy bien!; **as w.** también; **as w. as** así como; **children as w. as adults** tanto niños como adultos. **3** interj (surprise) ¡vaya!; **w., as I was saying** pues (bien), como iba diciendo.

well-be·haved adj (child) formal; (dog) manso.

well-be·ing bienestar m.

well-in·formed adj bien informado, -a.

wel·ling·tons npl botas fpl de goma.

well-known adj (bien) conocido, -a.

well-man·nered adj educado, -a.

well-off adj acomodado, -a.

well-to-do adj acomodado, -a.

Welsh 1 adj galés, -esa. **2** n (language) galés m; **the W.** pl los galeses.

Welsh·man galés m.

Welsh·wom·an galesa f.

went pt of **go**.

were pt of **be**.

west 1 n oeste m; **in** or **to the w.** al oeste. **2** adj occidental. **3** adv al oeste.

west·bound adj (con) dirección oeste.

west·ern 1 adj del oeste, occidental. **2** n (film) western m.

west·ward adj hacia el oeste.

west·wards adv hacia el oeste.

wet 1 adj mojado, -a; (slightly) húmedo, -a; (rainy) lluvioso, -a; **'w. paint'** 'recién pintado'. **2** vt* mojar.

whale ballena f.

wharf (pl wharves) muelle m.

what 1 adj (in questions) qué; **ask her w. color she likes** pregúntale qué color le gusta. **2** pron (in questions) qué; **w. are you talking about?** ¿de qué estás hablando?; **he asked me w.** I thought me preguntó lo que pensaba; **I didn't know w. to say** no sabía qué decir; **w. about your father?** ¿y tu padre (qué)?; **w. about going tomorrow?** ¿qué te parece si vamos mañana?; **w. did you do that for?** ¿por qué hiciste eso?; **w. (did you say)?** ¿cómo?; **w. is it?** (definition) ¿qué es?; **what's the matter?** ¿qué pasa?; **w.'s it called?** ¿cómo se llama?; **w.'s this for?** ¿para qué sirve esto? **3** interj **w. a goal!** ¡qué golazo!

what·ev·er 1 adj **w. day you want** cualquier día que quieras; **of w. color** no importa de qué color; **nothing w.** nada en absoluto; **with no interest w.** sin interés alguno. **2** pron (anything, all that) (todo) lo que; **do w. you like** haz lo que quieras; **don't tell him w. you do** no se te ocurra decírselo; **w. (else) you find** cualquier (otra) cosa que encuentres.

wheat trigo m.

wheel 1 n rueda f. **2** vt (bicycle) empujar.

wheel·bar·row carretilla f.

wheel·chair silla *f* de ruedas.

when 1 *adv* cuando; *(in questions)* cuándo; **w. did he arrive?** ¿cuándo llegó?; **tell me w. to go** dime cuándo he de irme; **the days w. I work** los días en que trabajo. **2** *conj* cuando; **I'll tell you w. she comes** te lo diré cuando llegue.

when·ev·er *conj (when)* cuando; *(every time)* siempre que.

where *adv (in questions)* dónde; *(direction)* adónde; *(at, in which)* donde; *(direction)* adonde; **w. are you going?** ¿adónde vas?; **w. do you come from?** ¿de dónde es usted?; **tell me w. you went** dime adónde fuiste.

where·a·bouts 1 *adv* w. do you live? ¿por dónde vives? **2** *n* paradero *m*.

where·as *conj (but, while)* mientras que.

where·by *adv* por el or la or lo cual.

wher·ev·er *conj* dondequiera que; **I'll find him w. he is** le encontraré dondequiera que esté; **sit w. you like** siéntate donde quieras.

wheth·er *conj (if)* si; **I don't know w. it is true** no sé si es verdad; **I doubt w. he'll win** dudo que gane.

which 1 *adj* qué; **w. color do you prefer?** ¿qué color prefieres?; **w. one?** ¿cuál?; **w. way?** ¿por dónde?; **tell me w. dress you like** dime qué vestido te gusta. **2** *pron (in questions)* cuál, cuáles; **w. of you did it?** ¿quién de vosotros lo hizo? ▪ *(relative)* que; *(after preposition)* que, el/la que, los/las que; **here are the books (w.) I have read** aquí están los libros que he leído; **the accident (w.) I told you about** el accidente de que te hablé; **the car in w. he was traveling** el coche en (el) que viajaba; **this is the one (w.) I like** éste es el que me gusta; **I played three sets, all of w. I lost** jugué tres sets, todos los cuales perdí. ▪ *(referring to a clause)* lo cual; **he won, w.**

made me very happy ganó, lo cual me alegró mucho.

which·ev·er 1 *adj* el/la que, cualquiera que; **I'll take w. books you don't want** tomaré los libros que no quieras; **w. system you choose** cualquiera que sea el sistema que elijas. **2** *pron* el que, la que.

while 1 *conj (time)* mientras; *(although)* aunque; *(whereas)* mientras que; **he fell asleep w. driving** se durmió mientras conducía. **2** *n (length of time)* rato *m*; **in a little w.** dentro de poco.

whim capricho *m*.

whine *vi (child)* lloriquear; *(complain)* quejarse.

whip 1 *n (for punishment)* látigo *m*. **2** *vt (as punishment)* azotar; *(cream etc)* batir.

▸ **whip out** *vt* sacar rápidamente.

whirl *vi* **to w. (round)** girar con rapidez; *(leaves etc)* arremolinarse.

whisk 1 *n (for cream)* batidor *m*; *(electric)* batidora *f*. **2** *vt (cream etc)* batir.

whisk·ers *(of cat)* bigotes *mpl*.

whis·key whisky *m*.

whis·per 1 *n* susurro *m*. **2** *vt* decir en voz baja. **3** *vi* susurrar.

whis·tle 1 *n (instrument)* pito *m*; *(sound)* silbido *m*. **2** *vt (tune)* silbar. **3** *vi (person, kettle, wind)* silbar; *(train)* pitar.

white 1 *adj* blanco, -a; **to go w.** *(face)* palidecer; *(hair)* encanecer; **w. coffee** café *m* con leche. **2** *n (color, of eye)* blanco *m*; *(of egg)* clara *f*.

white·wash *vt (wall)* blanquear.

whiz(z) *vi (sound)* silbar; **to w. past** pasar volando.

who *pron (in questions) sing* quién; *pl* quiénes; **w. are they?** ¿quiénes son?; **w. is it?** ¿quién es?; **I don't know w. did it** no sé quién lo hizo. ▪ *rel (defining)* que; *(nondefining)* quien, quienes, el/la cual, los/las cuales; **those w. don't know** los que no saben; **Elena's mother, w. is**

very rich … la madre de Elena, la cual es muy rica …

who·ev·er *pron* quienquiera que; **give it to w. you like** dáselo a quien quieras; **w. you are** quienquiera que seas.

whole 1 *adj (entire)* entero, -a; *(in one piece)* intacto, -a; **a w. week** una semana entera; **he took the w. lot** se los llevó todos. **2** *n* **the w. of New York** todo Nueva York; **on the w.** en general.

whole·meal *adj* integral.

whole·sale *adv* al por mayor.

whole·sal·er mayorista *mf*.

whol·ly *adv* enteramente, completamente.

whom *pron (question)* a quién. • *(after preposition)* **of** or **from w.?** ¿de quién? • *rel* a quien, a quienes; **those w. I have seen** aquéllos a quienes he visto. • *rel (after preposition)* quien, quienes, el/la cual, los/las cuales; **my brothers, both of w. are miners** mis hermanos, que son mineros los dos.

whoop·ing cough tos *f* ferina.

whose 1 *pron* de quién, de quiénes; **w. are these gloves?** ¿de quién son estos guantes? • *rel* cuyo(s)/cuya(s); **the man w. children we saw** el hombre a cuyos hijos vimos. **2** *adj* **w. car/house is this?** ¿de quién es este coche/esta casa?

why *adv* por qué; *(for what purpose)* para qué; **w. did you do that?** ¿por qué hiciste eso?; **w. not go to bed?** ¿por qué no te acuestas?; **I don't know w. he did it** no sé por qué lo hizo; **there's no reason w. you shouldn't go** no hay motivo para que no vayas.

wick mecha *f*.

wick·ed *adj* malvado, -a; *(awful)* malísimo, -a.

wick·er 1 *n* mimbre *f*. **2** *adj* de mimbre.

wide 1 *adj (road, trousers)* ancho, -a; *(area, knowledge, support, range)* amplio, -a; **it is ten meters w.** tiene diez metros de ancho. **2** *adv* **w. awake** totalmente despierto, -a; **w. open** abierto, -a de par en par.

wide·ly *adv (to travel etc)* extensamente.

wid·en 1 *vt* ensanchar; *(interests)* ampliar. **2** *vi* ensancharse.

wide·spread *adj (unrest, belief)* general; *(damage)* extenso, -a.

wid·ow viuda *f*.

wid·ow·er viudo *m*.

width anchura *f*.

wife *(pl* **wives)** esposa *f*.

wig peluca *f*.

wild *adj (animal, tribe)* salvaje; *(plant)* silvestre; *(temperament, behavior)* alocado, -a; *(appearance)* desordenado, -a; *(passions etc)* desenfrenado, -a.

wil·der·ness desierto *m*.

wild·life fauna *f*.

wild·ly *adv (rush round etc)* como un, -a loco, -a; *(hit out)* a tontas y a locas.

will¹ 1 *n* voluntad *f*; *(testament)* testamento *m*; **good/ill w.** buena/mala voluntad; **of my own free w.** por mi propia voluntad; **to make one's w.** hacer testamento. **2** *vt* fate **willed that …** el destino quiso que …

will² *v aux* **they w. come** vendrán; **w. he be there? — yes, he w.** ¿estará allí? — sí (, estará); **you w.** or **you'll tell him, won't you?** se lo dirás, ¿verdad?; **you w. be here at eleven!** ¡debes estar aquí a las once!; **be quiet, w. you! — no, I won't** ¿quiere callarse? — no quiero; **will you have a drink? — yes, I w.** ¿quiere tomar algo? — sí, por favor.

will·ing *adj (obliging)* complaciente; **to be w. to do sth** estar dispuesto, -a a hacer algo.

will·ing·ly *adv* de buena gana.

will·ing·ness buena voluntad *f*.

wil·low **w. (tree)** sauce *m*.

win 1 *n* victoria *f*. **2** *vt* * ganar; *(prize)*

llevarse; *(victory)* conseguir. **3** *vi** ganar.

wind[1] viento *m*; *(in stomach)* gases *mpl*.

wind[2]*** **1** *vt (onto a reel)* enrollar; *(clock)* dar cuerda a. **2** *vi (road, river)* serpentear.

▶ **wind back** *vt (film, tape)* rebobinar.

▶ **wind on** *vt (film, tape)* avanzar.

wind·mill molino *m* (de viento).

win·dow ventana *f*; *(of vehicle, of ticket office etc)* ventanilla *f*; **(shop) w.** escaparate *m*.

win·dow box jardinera *f*.

win·dow clean·er limpiacristales *mf inv.*

win·dow-pane cristal *m*.

win·dow·sill alféizar *m*.

wind·shield parabrisas *m inv*; **w. wiper** limpiaparabrisas *m inv.*

wind·surf·ing windsurfing *m.*

wind·y *adj* **it is very w. today** hoy hace mucho viento.

wine vino *m*; **w. list** lista *f* de vinos.

wine·glass copa *f* (para vino).

wing ala *f.*

wink 1 *n* guiño *m*. **2** *vi (person)* guiñar el ojo.

win·ner ganador, -a *mf.*

win·ning *adj (person, team)* ganador, -a; *(number)* premiado, -a.

win·nings *npl* ganancias *fpl.*

win·ter 1 *n* invierno *m*. **2** *adj* de invierno.

wipe *vt* limpiar; **to w. one's feet / nose** limpiarse los pies/la nariz.

▶ **wipe away** *vt (tear)* enjugar.

▶ **wipe off** *vt* quitar frotando.

▶ **wipe out** *vt (erase)* borrar.

▶ **wipe up** *vi* secar los platos.

wip·er *(in vehicle)* limpiaparabrisas *m.*

wire alambre *m*; *(electric)* cable *m.*

wire·less *adj* wireless, inalámbrico(a).

wire mesh/net·ting tela *f* metálica.

wir·ing *(of house)* instalación *f* eléctrica.

wis·dom *(good sense) (of person)* cordura *f*; *(of action)* sensatez *f*; *(learning)* sabiduría *f.*

wise *adj* sabio, -a; **a w. man** un sabio; **it would be w. to keep quiet** sería prudente callarse.

wish 1 *n (desire)* deseo *m* (for de); **give your mother my best wishes** salude a su madre de mi parte; **with best wishes, Peter** *(at end of letter)* saludos de Peter. **2** *vt (want)* desear; **I w. I could stay longer** me gustaría poder quedarme más tiempo; **I w. you had told me!** ¡ojalá me lo hubieras dicho!; **to w. for sth** desear algo.

wit *(humour)* ingenio *m*; *(person)* ingenioso, -a *mf*; **wits** *(intelligence)* inteligencia *f*, *fig* **to be at one's wits' end** estar para volverse loco, -a.

witch bruja *f.*

with *prep* con; **the man w. the glasses** el hombre de las gafas; **w. no hat** sin sombrero; **he went w. me/you** fue conmigo/contigo; **he's w. Ford** trabaja para Ford; **to fill a vase w. water** llenar un jarrón de agua; **it is made w. butter** está hecho con mantequilla.

with·draw* 1 *vt* retirar; *(statement)* retractarse de; **to w. money from the bank** sacar dinero del banco. **2** *vi* retirarse; *(drop out)* renunciar.

with·draw·al retirada *f.*

with·er *vi* marchitarse.

with·hold* *vt (money)* retener; *(decision)* aplazar; *(consent)* negar; *(information)* ocultar.

with·in *prep (inside)* dentro de; **five kilometers of the town** a menos de cinco kilómetros de la ciudad; **w. the hour** dentro de una hora; **w. the next five years** durante los cinco próximos años.

with·out *prep* sin; **w. a coat** sin abrigo; **he did it w. my knowing** lo hizo sin que lo supiera yo.

wit·ness 1 *n (person)* testigo *mf*. **2** *vt (see)* presenciar.

wob·bly *adj* poco firme; *(table, chair)* cojo, -a.

wolf *(pl* **wolves)** lobo *m*.

wom·an *(pl* **women)** mujer *f*; **old w.** vieja *f*.

won·der 1 *n* no w. he hasn't come con razón no ha venido. **2** *vt (ask oneself)* preguntarse; **I w. why** ¿por qué será? **3** *vi* **it makes you w.** te da qué pensar.

won·der·ful *adj* maravilloso, -a.

won't = **will not**.

wood *(forest)* bosque *m*; *(material)* madera *f*; *(for fire)* leña *f*.

wood·en *adj* de madera.

wood·work *(craft)* carpintería *f*.

wool lana *f*.

wool·en 1 *adj* de lana. **2** *npl* woo-lens géneros *mpl* de lana.

word palabra *f*; **in other words ...** es decir ...; **I'd like a w. with you** quiero hablar contigo un momento; **words** *(of song)* letra *f*.

word·ing expresión *f*; **I changed the w. slightly** cambié algunas palabras.

word pro·cess·ing procesamiento *m* de textos.

word pro·ces·sor procesador *m* de textos.

wore *pt of* **wear**.

work 1 *n* trabajo *m*; **his w. in the field of physics** su labor en el campo de la física; **out of w.** parado, -a; **a piece of w.** un trabajo; **a w. of art** una obra de arte; **works** *(factory)* fábrica *f*. **2** *vt (drive)* hacer trabajar; *(machine)* manejar; *(mechanism)* accionar. **3** *vi* trabajar **(on, at** en) *(machine)* funcionar; *(drug)* surtir efecto; *(system)* funcionar.

▸**work out 1** *vt (plan)* idear; *(problem)* solucionar; *(solution)* encontrar; *(amount)* calcular. **2** *vi (train)* hacer ejercicio; **it works out to 5 each** sale a 5 cada uno.

worked up *adj* **to get worked up** excitarse.

work·er trabajador, -a *mf*; *(manual)* obrero, -a *mf*.

work·force mano *f* de obra.

work·ing *adj (population, capital)* activo, -a; **w. class** clase *f* obrera; **it is in w. order** funciona.

work·man *(manual)* obrero *m*.

work·out entrenamiento *m*.

work·shop taller *m*.

work·sta·tion estación *f* de trabajo.

world 1 *n* mundo *m*; **all over the w.** en todo el mundo. **2** *adj (record, war)* mundial; **w. champion** campeón, -ona *mf* mundial; **The W. Cup** el Mundial *m*.

world·wide *adj* mundial.

worm lombriz *f*.

worn *adj* gastado, -a.

worn-out *adj (thing)* gastado, -a; *(person)* agotado, -a.

wor·ry 1 *vt* preocupar. **2** *vi* preocuparse **(about** por); **don't w.** no te preocupes. **3** *n* inquietud *f*; **my main w.** mi principal preocupación.

wor·ry·ing *adj* preocupante.

worse *adj & adv* peor; **to get w.** empeorar; **w. than ever** peor que nunca.

wors·en *vti* empeorar.

wor·ship *vt* adorar.

worst 1 *adj & adv* peor; **the w. part about it is that ...** lo peor es que ... **2** *n (person)* el/la peor, los/las peores.

worth 1 *adj* **a house w. $50,000** una casa que vale 50,000 dólares; **a book w. reading** un libro que merece la pena leer; **how much is it w.?** ¿cuánto vale?; **it's w. your while, it's w. it** vale la pena. **2** *n* valor *m*; **five dollars' w. of gas** gasolina por valor de 5 dólares.

worth·while *adj* valioso, -a, que vale la pena.

wor·thy *adj (deserving)* digno, -a **(of** de).

would *v aux (conditional)* **I w. go if I had time** iría si tuviera tiempo; **he w. have won but for that** habría ganado si no hubiera sido por eso. ▪

(willingness) **w. you do me a favor?** ¿quiere hacerme un favor?; **w. you like a cigarette?** ¿quiere un cigarrillo?; **the car wouldn't start** el coche no arrancaba. ▪ *(custom)* **we w. go for walks** solíamos dar paseos.

wound 1 *n* herida *f*. 2 *vt* herir.

wrap *vt* envolver.

▸**wrap up 1** *vt* envolver. **2** *vi* **w. up well!** ¡abrígate!

wrap·per *(of sweet)* envoltorio *m*.

wrap·ping pa·per papel *m* de envolver.

wreath *(pl* wreaths*) (of flowers)* corona *f*.

wreck 1 *n (sinking)* naufragio *m*; *(ship)* barco *m* naufragado; *(of car, plane)* restos *mpl*. **2** *vt (car, machine)* destrozar; *(holiday)* estropear.

wrench *(tool)* llave *f*.

wres·tle *vi* luchar.

wres·tler luchador, -a *mf*.

wres·tling lucha *f*.

wring* *vt (clothes)* escurrir.

wrin·kle arruga *f*.

wrist muñeca *f*.

wrist·watch reloj *m* de pulsera.

write* *vti* escribir (about sobre); **to w. sb** escribir a.

▸**write back** *vi* contestar.

▸**write down** *vt* poner por escrito; *(note)* apuntar.

▸**write off** *vt sep (debt)* condonar.

▸**write off for** *vt* pedir por escrito.

▸**write out** *vt (check)* extender; *(recipe)* escribir.

write-pro·tect·ed *adj* protegido, -a contra escritura.

writ·er *(by profession)* escritor, -a *mf*; *(of book, letter)* autor, -a *mf*.

writ·ing *(script)* escritura *f*; *(handwriting)* letra *f*; **in w.** por escrito.

writ·ing pa·per papel *m* de escribir.

wrong 1 *adj (erroneous)* incorrecto, -a; *(unsuitable)* inadecuado, -a; *(time)* inoportuno, -a; *(not right) (person)* equivocado, -a; *(immoral etc)* malo, -a; **my watch is w.** mi reloj anda mal; **to go the w. way** equivo-

carse de camino; **I was w. about that boy** me equivoqué con ese chico; **to be w.** no tener razón; **what's w. with smoking?** ¿qué tiene de malo fumar?; **what's w. with you?** ¿qué te pasa? **2** *adv* mal; **to get it w.** equivocarse; **to go w.** *(plan)* salir mal. **3** *n (evil, bad action)* mal *m*; **you were w. to hit him** hiciste mal en pegarle; **to be in the w.** tener la culpa.

wrong·ly *adv (incorrectly)* incorrectamente.

X

X·mas *abbr of* **Christmas** Navidad *f*.

X-ray 1 *n (picture)* radiografía *f*; **to have an X.** hacerse una radiografía. **2** *vt* radiografiar.

Y

yacht yate *m*.

yard¹ *(measure)* yarda *f (aprox 0,914 metros)*.

yard² patio *m*; jardín *m*; *(of school)* patio *m* (de recreo).

yarn hilo *m*.

yawn 1 *vi* bostezar. **2** *n* bostezo *m*.

year año *m*; *(at school)* curso *m*; **I'm ten years old** tengo diez años.

year·ly *adj* anual.

yeast levadura *f*.

yell 1 *vi* gritar (at a). **2** *n* grito *m*.

yel·low *adj & n* amarillo, -a *(m)*.

yes *adv* sí.

yes·ter·day *adv* ayer; **the day before y.** anteayer; **y. morning** ayer por la mañana.

yet 1 *adv* **not y.** todavía no; **as y.** hasta ahora; **I haven't eaten y.** no he comido todavía. ▪ *(in questions)* ya; **has he arrived y.?** ¿ha venido ya? **2** *conj (nevertheless)* sin embargo.

yo·gurt yogur *m*.

yolk yema *f*.

you *pers pron (subject) (familiar use) (sing)* tú; *(pl)* vosotros, -as; *(polite use) (sing)* usted; *(pl)* ustedes; **how are y.?** ¿cómo estás?, ¿cómo estáis? ▪ *(object) (familiar use) (sing) (before verb)* te; *(after preposition)* ti; *(pl) (before verb)* os; *(after preposition)* vosotros, -as; **I saw y.** te vi, os vi; **with y.** contigo, con vosotros, -as. ▪ *(object) (polite use) (sing) (before verb)* le; *(after preposition)* usted; *(pl) (before verb)* les; *(after preposition)* ustedes; **I saw y.** le vi, les vi; **with y.** con usted, con ustedes. ▪ *(subject) (impers use)* **y. never know** nunca se sabe.

young 1 *adj* joven; *(brother etc)* pequeño, -a. **2** *n* **the y.** los jóvenes *mpl*; *(animals)* las crías.

young·ster muchacho, -a *mf*.

your *poss adj (familiar use) (referring to one person)* tu, tus; *(referring to more than one person)* vuestro, -a, vuestros, -as. ▪ *(polite use)* su, sus. ▪ *(impers use)* **the house is on y. right** la casa queda a la derecha; **they clean y. shoes for you** te limpian los zapatos.

yours *poss pron (familiar use) (referring to one person)* el tuyo, la tuya, los tuyos, las tuyas; *(referring to more than one person)* el vuestro, la vuestra, los vuestros, las vuestras;

the house is y. la casa es tuya. ▪ *(polite use)* el suyo, la suya; *(pl)* los suyos, las suyas; **the house is y.** la casa es suya.

your·self *(pl* **yourselves) 1** *pers pron (familiar use) sing* tú mismo, -a; *pl* vosotros, -as mismos, -as; **by y.** (tú) solo; **by yourselves** vosotros, -as solos, -as. ▪ *(polite use) sing* usted mismo, -a; *pl* ustedes mismos, -as; **by y.** (usted) solo, -a; **by yourselves** (ustedes) solos, -as. **2** *reflexive pron* **did you wash y.?** *(familiar use) sing* ¿te lavaste?; *pl* ¿os lavasteis?; *(polite use) sing* ¿se lavó?, *pl* ¿se lavaron?

youth juventud *f*, *(young man)* joven *m*.

youth club club *m* juvenil.

Yu·go·slav *adj & n* yugoslavo, -a *(mf)*.

Z

ze·bra cebra *f*.

ze·ro cero *m*.

zig·zag 1 *n* zigzag *m*. **2** *vi* zigzaguear.

zip *n* **z. (fastener)** cremallera *f*.

▸ **zip up** *vt* subir la cremallera de.

ZIP code código *m* postal.

zip·per cremallera *f*.

zit *fam (pimple)* espinilla *f*.

zone zona *f*.

zoo zoo *m*.

zuc·chi·ni calabacín *m*.